D0992591

**Also by Carole Terwilliger Meyers:**

*FamilyFun Vacation Guide: California & Hawaii*

*Bay Area Family Fun (an annotated map)*

*The Family Travel Guide: An Inspiring Collection of Family-Friendly Vacations (Editor)*

*Miles of Smiles: 101 Great Car Games & Activities*

*San Francisco Family Fun*

*How to Organize a Babysitting Cooperative and Get Some Free Time Away From the Kids*

*Eating Out With the Kids in San Francisco and the Bay Area*

*Getting in the Spirit: Annual Bay Area Christmas Events*

*Eating Out with the Kids in the East Bay*

8th Edition

# WEEKEND ADVENTURES
## in San Francisco & Northern California

Carole Terwilliger Meyers

CAROUSEL PRESS

BERKELEY, CALIFORNIA

Published by:   **CAROUSEL PRESS**
P.O. Box 6038
Berkeley, CA 94706-0038
(510) 527-5849
books@carousel-press.com
www.carousel-press.com

Distributed to the book trade by Publishers Group West

**Library of Congress Cataloging-in-Publication Data**

Meyers, Carole Terwilliger.
  Weekend adventures in San Francisco & northern California / by Carole
Terwilliger Meyers-- 8th ed.
   p. cm.
  Rev. ed. of: Weekend adventures in northern California. 7th ed. c2001.
  Includes indexes.
  ISBN 0-917120-19-1
1. Family recreation--California, Northern--Guidebooks. 2. Family
recreation--California--San Francisco--Guidebooks. 3. California,
Northern--Guidebooks. 4. San Francisco (Calif.)--Guidebooks. I. Meyers,
Carole Terwilliger. Weekend adventures in northern California. II. Title.

  F867.5.M48 2005
  917.94'60454--dc22

                          2004022741

**E-letter update:** Sign up for the free "*Weekend Adventures* E-Letter Update" at www.carousel-press.com.
**Text updates:** Changes since publication, including both businesses that have closed and new discoveries, are posted at www.carousel-press.com.
**Reader feedback:** Text errors and typos, listing changes, exciting new discoveries, praise, even complaints— we want to hear about it all.
**Special sales:** Bulk purchases of Carousel Press titles are available to corporations at special discounts. Custom editions can be produced to use as premiums and promotional items.

Manufactured in the United States of America

10 9 8 7 6 5 4 3 2 1

for Gene

# CONTENTS

# INTRODUCTION

We residents of the Bay Area are fortunate to live within easy driving distance of a wealth of exciting vacation possibilities—mountains, ocean, rivers, snow. Our biggest recreational problem is deciding, from among the many possibilities, where we should go and what we should do.

The destinations in this book radiate out from San Francisco. Most make good weekend or mid-week trips, and all can be adapted easily to longer stays.

Because it is frustrating to discover after you're home that an area where you've just vacationed has an interesting attraction you didn't know about, and because it also isn't much fun finding out too late that there is a better or cheaper (depending on what you're after) lodging you could have booked into or a restaurant you would have enjoyed trying, this book is designed so that you can determine quickly what is of special interest in the area you are planning to visit. Listings are all in some way special—bargain rates, welcoming of families, aesthetically pleasing, historically interesting, etc. Phone numbers, toll-free numbers, fax numbers, and websites are provided for obtaining further information.

Parents especially need to have this information in advance. I know because one of the worst trips I ever experienced was the first trip my husband and I took with our first baby. I hadn't planned ahead. We took off for the Gold Rush Country and went where the winds blew us—just like before we were parents. That was a mistake. We wound up in a hotel that had no compassion for a colicky baby or his parents, and we ate a series of memorably bad meals. Now my husband and I can laugh about that trip, but at the time it wasn't funny. That fateful trip turned me into a travel writer. Since then, I've never gone anywhere without exhaustively researching it beforehand. And I've never again had a bad trip since that I can blame on lack of information.

With all of this in mind, I've written this book to help make your trip-planning easier, allowing you to get the most out of your weekends away.

# CREDITS

# GUIDELINES FOR INTERPRETING LISTINGS

This book is organized by geographical area. Each chapter has the following subsections:

**A LITTLE BACKGROUND:** Historical and general background information about the area; what kinds of activities to expect.

**VISITOR INFORMATION:** Address and phone number of visitor bureau or chamber of commerce.

**GETTING THERE:** The quickest, easiest driving route from San Francisco; scenic driving routes; other transportation options.

**STOPS ALONG THE WAY:** Noteworthy places for meals or sightseeing.

**ANNUAL EVENTS:** The area's best events. When no phone number is listed, contact the visitor bureau or chamber of commerce for information.

**WHAT TO DO:** Activities and sights in the area that are of special interest, listed alphabetically and including the following information when available: Address, phone number, fax number; website. Days and hours open; months closed. Admission fee.

**WHERE TO STAY:** Lodging facilities, listed alphabetically and including the following information when available: Street address, toll-free reservations number, phone number, fax number; website (where e-mail address can usually be obtained). Number of stories if over 3; number of rooms; price range per night for two people (see price code below); months closed. Policies regarding children (if children stay free in parents' room on existing beds); if facility is unsuitable for children under a specified age). If no TVs are provided; if kitchens, gas or wood-burning fireplaces, or wood-burning stoves are provided; if any baths are shared.

What recreational facilities are available: pool; hot tub; sauna; health spa; fitness room; tennis courts; golf course. If there is a complimentary afternoon or evening snack; if there is a complimentary breakfast; if there is a restaurant; if there is room service. If smoking is not permitted; if pets are welcome. If there is an overnight parking fee.

$=under $100  $$=$100-$199  $$$=$200-$299
$$$+=more than $300

**WHERE TO EAT:** Reliable restaurants, listed alphabetically and including the following information when available: Address, phone number, fax number; website. Meals served (B, L, D, SunBr), days open; price range (see price code below). Availability of highchairs, boosters, booths, child portions/menu. If reservations are advised, accepted (but not usually needed), or not accepted. If credit cards are not accepted. When parking is difficult, whether a validated parking lot or valet parking are available.

$   =   inexpensive. Dinner for one adult might cost up to $15.

$$  =   moderate. Dinner for one adult might cost from $15 to $30.

$$$ =   expensive. Dinner for one adult might cost more than $30.

Projected cost is based on an average dinner (salad + entree + non-alcoholic drink) and is exclusive of alcoholic drinks, dessert, tax, and tip.

*Always call for current schedule and details. Remember that some restaurants and attractions close on major holidays. Also, note that some attractions and hotels post special offers on their website and offer AAA or senior citizen discounts.*

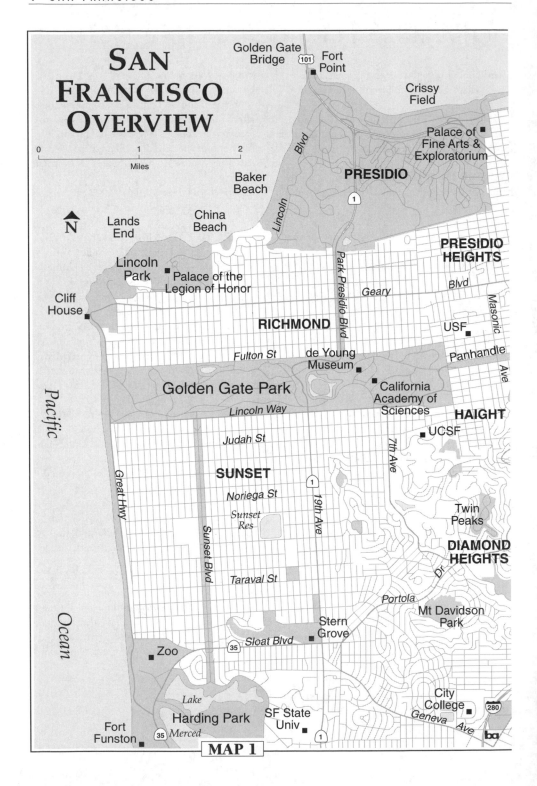

# SAN FRANCISCO OVERVIEW

Golden Gate Bridge — 101 — Fort Point

Crissy Field

Palace of Fine Arts & Exploratorium

Blvd

PRESIDIO

0          1          2

Miles

Baker Beach

N

Lands End

China Beach

Lincoln

PRESIDIO HEIGHTS

Lincoln Park — Palace of the Legion of Honor

Park Presidio Blvd

Geary          Blvd

Masonic

Cliff House

RICHMOND

USF

Fulton St     de Young Museum

Panhandle

Ave

Golden Gate Park

California Academy of Sciences

Pacific

Lincoln Way

HAIGHT

UCSF

Judah St

7th Ave

SUNSET

Noriega St

Great Hwy

Sunset Res

19th Ave

Twin Peaks

DIAMOND HEIGHTS

Sunset Blvd

Taraval St

Dr

Portola

Mt Davidson Park

Stern Grove

Ocean

Zoo

35

Sloat Blvd

City College — 280

Lake

Geneva    Ave

Harding Park

SF State Univ

1

ba

Fort Funston

35 Merced

**MAP 1**

MAP 5

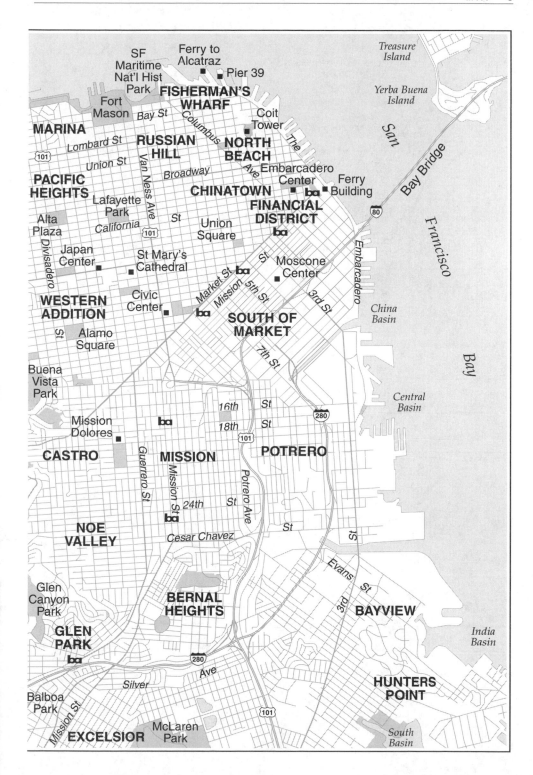

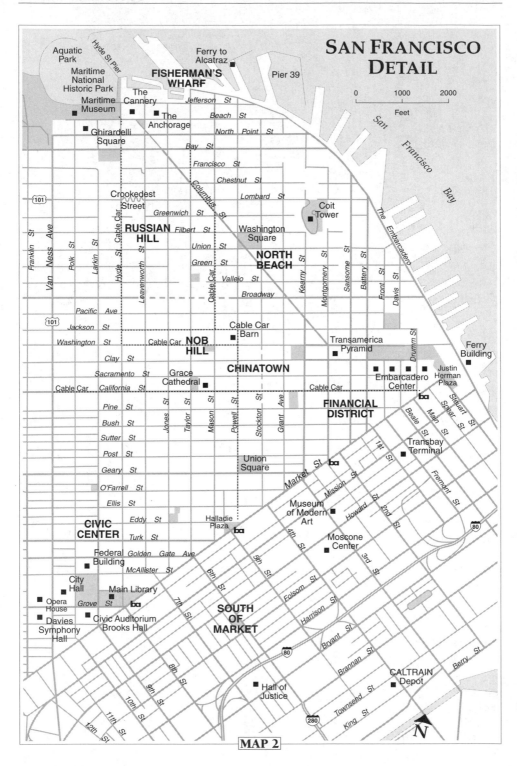

## SAN FRANCISCO DETAIL

Aquatic Park

Hyde St Pier

Maritime National Historic Park

Maritime Museum

The Cannery

Ghirardelli Square

The Anchorage

Ferry to Alcatraz

**FISHERMAN'S WHARF**

Pier 39

Jefferson St

Beach St

North Point St

Bay St

Francisco St

Chestnut St

Lombard St

Coit Tower

Crookedest Street

Greenwich St

Columbus St

**RUSSIAN HILL**

Filbert St

Union St

Washington Square

Green St

**NORTH BEACH**

Vallejo St

Broadway

Pacific Ave

Jackson St

Washington St

Cable Car Barn

Transamerica Pyramid

Ferry Building

Clay St

**NOB HILL**

**CHINATOWN**

Sacramento St

Grace Cathedral

Embarcadero Center

Justin Herman Plaza

Cable Car

California St

Cable Car

Pine St

**FINANCIAL DISTRICT**

Bush St

Sutter St

Post St

Transbay Terminal

Geary St

O'Farrell St

Ellis St

Union Square

Eddy St

Halladie Plaza

Museum of Modern Art

**CIVIC CENTER**

Turk St

Moscone Center

Federal Building

Golden Gate Ave

McAllister St

City Hall

Main Library

Opera House

Grove St

**SOUTH OF MARKET**

Davies Symphony Hall

Civic Auditorium

Brooks Hall

Market St

Mission St

Howard St

Folsom St

Harrison St

Hall of Justice

Bryant St

Brannan St

CALTRAIN Depot

Berry St

Townsend St

King St

Franklin St

Van Ness Ave

Polk St

Larkin St

Cable Car

Hyde St

Leavenworth St

Cable Car

Jones St

Taylor St

Mason St

Powell St

Stockton St

Grant Ave

Kearny St

Montgomery St

Sansome St

Battery St

Front St

Davis St

The Embarcadero

San Francisco Bay

Drumm St

Steuart St

Spear St

Main St

Beale St

1st St

2nd St

3rd St

4th St

5th St

6th St

7th St

8th St

9th St

10th St

11th St

12th St

Fremont St

101

101

80

80

280

0   1000   2000

Feet

N

**MAP 2**

# SAN FRANCISCO

*You wouldn't think such a place as San Francisco could exist. The wonderful sunlight there, the hills, the great bridges, the Pacific at your shoes. Beautiful Chinatown. Every race in the world. The sardine fleets sailing out. The little cable-cars whizzing down the city hills. The lobsters, clams, & crabs . . . Every kind of seafood there is. And all the people are open and friendly.*

> — Dylan Thomas

*San Francisco has only one drawback. 'Tis hard to leave.*

> — Rudyard Kipling

*One day if I do go to heaven, I'm going to do what every San Franciscan does who goes to heaven. I'll look around and say, 'It ain't bad, but it ain't San Francisco.'*

> — Herb Caen, June 14, 1996

*You tell people you live in California and surf, and they have a picture of a 'Gidget' movie. In San Francisco, however, it's more like some kind of German Expressionist film—all foggy, cold and dark, and nobody around. Just me and the sharks.*

> — Chris Isaak, 1999

Though the quotes above are not heard often, the saying attributed to Mark Twain, "The coldest winter I ever spent was a summer in San Francisco," is familiar to most people. Scholars dispute that the words were Twain's, but no one who has spent a summer in San Francisco will dispute the comment.

Measuring just 7 miles by 7 miles square, this relatively small big city is known for its morning and evening fog in summer. Locals coming in from the suburbs have learned always to bring along wraps. In summer it is easy to spot tourists. They are the ones wearing

7

shorts . . . or white shoes, another no-no among locals. Perhaps these visitors are confusing San Francisco with the image of Southern California's warm beaches. That is a mistake.

In general the climate is temperate, ranging between 40 and 70 degrees, with the best weather usually occurring in September and October.

## – VISITOR INFORMATION –

### San Francisco Convention & Visitors Bureau Visitor Information Center
*900 Market St./Powell St., in Halladie Plaza, (415) 391-2000, fax (415) 362-7323; www.sfvisitor.org. M-F 9-5, Sat-Sun 9-3; closed Sun Nov-May.*

Get a free copy of *The San Francisco Book*—filled with sightseeing, shopping, and dining information—and *The Lodging Guide*. Lodging reservations can be made through the bureau by calling (888) 782-9673 or (415) 391-2000.

For a recorded listing of the day's events, call (415) 391-2001. For the same information in French, call (415) 391-2003; German (415) 391-2004; Spanish (415) 391-2122; Japanese (415) 391-2101; Italian (415) 391-2002.

## – ANNUAL EVENTS –
## – JANUARY –

### Chinese New Year Festival & Parade
*Or in February or March, depending on the lunar calendar. (415) 391-9680, fax (415) 986-1933; www.chineseparade.com. Free.*

First held in 1851 and again every year since, this popular event is composed of a beauty pageant, an outdoor carnival in Chinatown, and the famous parade featuring a spectacular block-long golden dragon (this parade is one of the few illuminated night parades in the U.S.).

## – FEBRUARY –
### Pacific Orchid Exposition
*Or in March. Fort Mason Center; (415) 665-2468; www.orchidsanfrancisco.com. $11, 65+ $8, under 12 free.*

Thousands of gorgeous blooming orchid plants are on display at this stunning show of amateur and professional collections—the largest of its kind on the West Coast. In addition to the plants entered for judging and show, thousands more are available for purchase. Lectures by international orchid experts are scheduled. Sponsored by the San Francisco Orchid Society.

## – MARCH –
### St. Patrick's Day Parade
*(415) 675-9885; www.uissf.org. Free.*

This traditional parade is the city's largest and has been held annually for more than 150 years.

### San Francisco Flower & Garden Show
*At the Cow Palace; (800) 829-9751, (415) 750-5441; www.gardenshow.com. $13-$20, 4-11 $7; parking $8.*

The area's top landscapers display their talents with more than 20 full-size gardens spread across 5 acres, and an Orchid Pavilion features thousands of blooming plants for sale. Baby strollers are discouraged.

## – APRIL –
### Cherry Blossom Festival
*At Japan Center; (415) 563-2313, fax (415) 563-2307; www.nccbf.org. Free.*

Japanese cultural events at this elaborate celebration of spring include traditional dancing, martial arts demonstrations, taiko drum and koto performances, and tea ceremonies. A Japanese food bazaar operates continuously, and demonstrations of the Japanese arts of doll making, calligraphy, and flower arranging are usually scheduled. The festival culminates with a colorful 2-hour, Japanese-style parade.

## San Francisco Decorator Showcase

*(415) 447-3117; www.decoratorshowcase.org. $20-$25.*

Strict quality control gives this show house a reputation for being the best in the West—perhaps even the best in the entire country. Proceeds benefit San Francisco University High School.

## San Francisco International Film Festival

*(415) 561-5000; www.sfiff.org. $7.50+.*

Known for honoring the finest in cinematic achievement, North America's oldest film festival presents recent productions from around the world. Some children's films are usually included.

— MAY —

## Bay to Breakers

*(415) 359-2800; www.baytobreakers.com. Entry fee $30-$40, under 18 $25-$35.*

The world's largest, and perhaps zaniest, footrace is usually routed through the Financial District, up the Hayes Street hill, and on through Golden Gate Park to the Great Highway. Outrageous outfits are de rigueur and in the past have included everything from a set of crayons to Humphrey the Whale. All participants receive a commemorative t-shirt. Proceeds benefit charities.

## Carnaval San Francisco

*(415) 920-0125, fax (415) 647-6911; www.carnaval sf.com. Free.*

This spectacular Mardi Gras-like revel is a multicultural celebration of life. It includes a parade and a 2-day outdoor festival.

## Cinco de Mayo Festival

*(415) 206-0577, fax (415) 206-0499. $5, under 5 free.*

Commemorating the Battle of Puebla,

Mexico on May 5, 1862, which marked the defeat of the powerful French Napoleonic Army by a small, poorly equipped Mexican force, this is the largest such festival in the U.S. It attracts visitors and performers from throughout Latin America and includes a free parade and a festival.

## — JUNE —

### North Beach Festival
*(415) 989-2220, fax (415) 989-6427; www.sfnorthbeach.org/festival. Free.*

This granddaddy of street fairs was established by a committee of Beat generation artists in 1954 and is said to be the country's very first. It features Italian foods, sidewalk cafes, traditional Italian sword fighting demonstrations, bocce ball games, and a variety of entertainment.

### San Francisco Lesbian Gay Bisexual Transgender Pride Parade & Celebration
*(415) 864-FREE, fax (415) 864-5889; www.sfpride.org. Free.*

Though other cities now also hold annual gay pride celebrations, San Francisco's self-described "queerific" event is considered the biggest and wildest. The parade is a don't-miss. A popular highlight is the Women's Motorcycle Contingent, or "Dykes on Bikes."

### Stern Grove Festival
*Through mid-August. 19th Ave./Sloat Blvd.; (415) 252-6252, fax (415) 252-6250; www.sterngrove.org. Free.*

Featuring the finest of Bay Area performing arts, this program is the country's oldest free summer performing arts festival and has been held in the Grove's natural outdoor amphitheater each summer since 1938. It is traditional to bring a picnic lunch and the Sunday newspaper and spend the pre-performance wait indulging in food, drink, and relaxation. Bring a blanket to sit on and a jacket in case the weather turns chilly.

The city's **croquet lawns** *((415) 776-4104)* are available here year-round for play.

## — JULY —

### Fourth of July Waterfront Festival
*Pier 39, Fisherman's Wharf, San Francisco Municipal Pier; (415) 705-5500; www.pier39.com. Free.*

Continuous entertainment begins in the early afternoon. A highlight is the Sixth Army's traditional 50-cannon salute to the nation. The celebration culminates after sunset with the West Coast's largest fireworks display.

## — AUGUST —

### ACC Craft Show
*Fort Mason Center; (800) 836-3470; www.craftcouncil.org. $8, under 12 free. Valet parking.*

Produced by the American Craft Council, this is the largest juried craft fair on the West Coast. It features the latest work of more than 300 of the nation's premier craft artists.

## —SEPTEMBER—

### San Francisco Blues Festival
*Great Meadow at Fort Mason; (415) 979-5588; www.sfblues.com. $25-$30+.*

Known for its all-star lineup, this upbeat affair has been called "one of the best blues events in the world." Indeed, it is the oldest blues festival in America and features a breathtaking background view of the Golden Gate Bridge. John Lee Hooker once sang, "The blues is a healer. It healed me and it'll heal you." This show is definitely good for what ails you.

### San Francisco Fringe Festival
*Union Square; (415) 931-1094; www.sffringe.org. Free-$8.*

Independent theater companies from around the world are invited here to give eclectic, cutting-edge performances over a period of 12 days. No show lasts more than an hour, and venues are concentrated around Union Square so that patrons can easily walk from performance to performance. Tickets are available only at the performance. For entertaining audience reviews, visit the website.

## — OCTOBER —

### Cable Car Bell-Ringing Competition
*Union Square; (415) 934-3900; www.sfmuni.com/aboutmun/cablecar.htm#bellringing. Free.*

Competitions are held in both pro and amateur divisions. The previous year's champion defends his title, and amateurs (who include some well-known Bay Area personalities) ring on behalf of non-profit organizations. The

winner is then referred to as "Ding Dong Daddy." Judges are selected from among the area's musical and theatrical elite.

## Columbus Day Celebration
*(415) 434-1492; www.sfcolumbusday.org. Free.*

San Francisco's is the only Columbus Day celebration in the country that includes a re-enactment of Columbus's landing in San Salvadore. When landing at Aquatic Park, the person acting as Columbus wears a handmade Italian replica of the great navigator's clothing. The **Blessing of the Fishing Fleet** takes place the next day at Fisherman's Wharf, and the **Italian Heritage Parade** usually takes place the next weekend.

## Fleet Week
*(415) 705-5500; http://fleetweek.us/fleetweek. Free.*

To celebrate the anniversary of the Navy's birthday and honor the men and women of the U.S. Navy and Marines, the City of San Francisco throws a gigantic party each year and the public is invited. Past events have included demonstrations of high-speed boat maneuvering, parachute drops, and a fly-by of World War II vintage aircraft. **The Blue Angels**, the Navy's premier precision flying team, also perform in a breathtaking culmination. Viewing is best from Crissy Field, the Marina Green, Aquatic Park, Pier 39, and the Marin Headlands. As part of

the celebration, all Navy ships moored at the piers are usually open for public visits. Fleet Week originated in 1908 when President Teddy Roosevelt's "Great White Fleet" of battleships sailed under the Golden Gate. Mayor Dianne Feinstein established it as an annual event in 1981.

## Grand National Rodeo, Horse & Stock Show
*Cow Palace; (415) 404-4111, fax (415) 469-6111; www.grandnationalrodeo.com. $10-$35, under 13 free-$10.*

This is the largest such show held west of the Mississippi. A rodeo and horse show is scheduled each day, and ticket holders are invited to come early to enjoy a variety of related activities: dairy animal auctions; judging contests; displays of unusual livestock breeds, including literally tons of premium steers, woolly sheep, and prime swine. Kids especially enjoy the pony rides and baby animals.

## San Francisco Jazz Festival
*(800) 850-SFJF, (415) 398-5655, fax (415) 398-5569; www.sfjazz.org. Free-$55.*

The Chicago Tribune calls this "the biggest and most acclaimed jazz festival in the United States."

## — DECEMBER —

### A Christmas Carol

*Geary Theater; (415) 749-2ACT; www.act-sfbay.org. $11-$68.*

Dickens' popular seasonal ghost tale, which celebrates the rebirth of the human spirit and death of indifference, is sure to rekindle any lagging Christmas enthusiasm in grumpy holiday Scrooges. American Conservatory Theater's lively, colorful production enhances the story with a musical score of carols, songs, and dance. It is interesting to note that Dickens' story is credited with actually reviving the celebration of Christmas, which at the time his book was published in 1843 had slipped to the status of a quaint, almost obsolete custom. It is also considered responsible for some English social reform. Fortunately for all of us, his story still manages to wake up the spirit of human kindness. Performances run almost 2 hours with no intermission.

### Golden Gate Park Christmas Tree Lighting

*Golden Gate Park; (415) 831-2782; http://parks.sfgov.org. Free.*

San Francisco's official Christmas tree, a 100-foot Monterey cypress located at the east entrance to Golden Gate Park, is decorated each Christmas season with over 3,000 lights. The mayor is usually present to flip the switch. Santa also makes an appearance, and the audience is led in singing carols.

### Great Dickens Christmas Fair

*Cow Palace; (415) 897-4555; www.dickensfair.com. $15-$20, seniors $16-$17, 5-11 $6-$8; parking $7.*

See *A Christmas Carol* brought to life at this re-creation of Christmas in Victorian London. After playing unusual parlour games, purchasing some fine and unusual yuletide gifts, and feasting on authentic period food and drink such as plum pudding and hot toddies, even the grumpiest Scrooge will capture the season's spirit. Entertainment is continuous and includes parades, melodrama performances, and caroling contests—even dancing with Mr. and Mrs. Fezziwig and guests at their celebrated party. And as if this isn't enough, Her Majesty Queen Victoria and consort Prince Albert will attend. Visitors are encouraged to dress in period costume.

### Guardsmen Christmas Tree Sale

*Fort Mason Center; (415) 561-2700, fax (415) 561-2966; www.guardsmen.org. Trees $10-$200.*

Claiming to have the largest enclosed Christmas tree lot in Northern California, the Guardsmen sell more than 5,000 trees each year. This sale is famous for having the best selection of noble firs but also stocks a variety of other trees, including Douglas fir, Frazer fir, and Scotch pine. Just visiting the lot is a thrill—it resembles a small forest—and it is particularly nice on a rainy day. Trees range from tabletop size to 14 feet. Garlands, wreaths, holly, mistletoe, and ornaments are also on sale. Proceeds fund camperships and educational programs for underprivileged Bay Area children.

## Nutcracker
*War Memorial Opera House; (415) 865-2000; www.sfballet.org. $22-$135.*

The San Francisco Ballet has been presenting its delightful and festive version of the *Nutcracker* since 1942, when it blazed the path for all subsequent U.S. Nutcrackers by dancing the first full-length production. It has always been an extravagant interpretation, with hundreds of thousands of dollars worth of scenery and handmade costumes. Each performance features a cast of more than 175 dancers that includes the company's dancers plus children from the Ballet School.

**Sugar Plum Parties** follow some matinee performances. They are held in the downstairs cafe, where guests are served sugary goodies (cookies, candy, soda) and the costumed cast members are available for autographs. Purchase party tickets at the same time as purchasing *Nutcracker* tickets.

## Union Square Window Displays
Each year the biggest department stores—Macy's, Saks Fifth Avenue, Neiman Marcus—treat the public to elaborate window decorations, some with moving mechanical displays. A visit to Macy's commercial, but gorgeous, Christmas wonderland, known as Bayberry Row, is always special, and Santa is also found here. The lobby of the Westin St. Francis Hotel is always festively decorated and worth a walk-through, and street entertainers, vendors, and carolers provide further diversion.

# — WHAT TO DO —

## TOURS

### — BY BOAT —

## Blue and Gold Fleet Bay Tours
*Depart from Pier 39, Fisherman's Wharf, (415) 773-1188; (415) 705-5555, fax (415) 705-5429; www.blueandgoldfleet.com. Daily from 10am; Jan-Feb. from 11; $20, 62+ & 12-18 $16, 5-11 $12.*

This 1-hour narrated cruise of the bay goes out under the world's most beautiful bridge—the Golden Gate—and also passes close to Alcatraz Island. Other boat tours include Alcatraz, Alcatraz After Hours, Angel Island, Six Flags Marine World, the Wine Country, Sausalito, and Tiburon.

## Hornblower Cruises and The *San Francisco Spirit*
Both offer scenic dining cruises. For descriptions, see page 72.

## *Ruby* Sailing Yacht
*At foot of Mariposa St./near 3rd St., (415) 861-2165; www.rubysailing.com. Daily at 12:30 & 6, May-Nov; at other times by appt. $35, under 10 $20. Reservations required.*

Captain Joshua Pryor built the 64-foot steel sloop *Ruby* himself in 1979. He also sails her himself. The 2$^{1/2}$-hour lunch cruise circles Alcatraz, and guests can dine on deli sandwiches either on the deck or below in the salon. The evening trip sails to Sausalito and includes hors d'oeuvres. Beer and wine are available at additional charge.

## Whale-Watching Tours
*Depart from Fort Mason Center, (800) 326-7491, (415) 474-3385, fax (415) 474-3395; www.oceanicsociety.org. Sat-Sun & some F & M; Jan to mid-May. $60-$63. Must be 10 or older. Reservations required.*

Sponsored by the non-profit Oceanic Society Expeditions, these all-day trips have a professional naturalist on board to explain all about the whales and interpret their behavior. Half-day trips depart from Princeton-by-the-Sea (see page 93).

**Farallon Islands Nature Cruises** *(Sat-Sun & some F; June-Nov. $67-$70. Must be 10 or older. Reservations required.)* take participants 25 miles across the Pacific Ocean from the Golden

Gate Bridge to this National Wildlife Refuge. These islands support the largest seabird rookery in the eastern Pacific south of Alaska and are the habitat of 200,000 nesting sea birds—including tufted puffins, loons, and auklets—plus sea lions and seals.

## — BY BUS —

### Gray Line Tours
*(888) 428-6937, (415) 434-8687, fax (415) 274-5794; www.graylinesanfrancisco.com. Fares vary; under 5 free on parent's lap. Reservations required 1 day in advance.*

Day tours are available of San Francisco, Muir Woods/Sausalito, Yosemite, Monterey/Carmel, and the Wine Country. Dinner tours of San Francisco are also scheduled.

### Three Babes and a Bus
*Depart from Union Square, (800) 414-0158, (970) 884-0614; www.threebabes.com. Sat 8:30pm-1:30am. $35. Must be 21 or older. Reservations advised.*

These babes and their bus pick up guests and take them out to party in four of the city's hottest dance clubs. The fee includes cover charges and VIP entry, and participants needn't worry about parking, taxi fares, or drinking and driving.

## — BY CAR —

### Dirty Harry Tour
*www.movietours.com/harry/intro. Free.*

All the important sites seen in this 1971 classic Clint Eastwood film are described. Download this do-it-yourself tour from the website. More movie tours are also available.

### 49-Mile Drive
This planned driving route through San Francisco hits most of the high points. For a free map, contact the San Francisco Convention and Visitors Bureau (see page 8).

## — BY FIRE ENGINE —

### San Francisco Fire Engine Tours & Adventures
*Depart from The Cannery, Fisherman's Wharf. (415) 333-7077, fax (415) 333-7725; www.fireengine tours.com. W-M at 1; some additional tours. $30, 13-17 $25, under 13 $20. Reservations advised.*

This happy, exhilarating 75-minute excursion takes sightseers over the Golden Gate

Bridge in a bright-red 1955 Mack fire engine. As it can get chilly in the open-air truck, authentic insulated fire-fighter jackets are available for passengers to bundle up in. Children get a lesson in fire safety through original sing-along songs. After, the tour guides go back to their home in a vintage firehouse.

## — ON FOOT —

San Francisco is a walker's paradise. The city's naturally intriguing streets become even more interesting when walked with a knowledgeable guide. Even natives often learn something new on such as tour.

### City Guides
*(415) 557-4266, fax (415) 557-4239; www.sfcityguides.org. Free.*

Sponsored by the San Francisco Public Library, these informative tours last approximately 1½ hours and cover most of the city. Among the many options are: Alamo Square, City Hall, Coit Tower Murals, Haight-Ashbury, Historic Market Street, Japantown, Mission Murals, Nob Hill, North Beach, Pacific Heights Mansions, Presidio Walk, Union Square. For a free schedule, send a stamped, self-addressed business-size envelope to: City Guides, San Francisco Public Library, 100 Larkin St., San Francisco 94102.

### Dashiell Hammett Tour
*www.donherron.com. Schedule varies. $10, under 15 free.*

While dashing off trivia and anecdotes, guide Don Herron leads walkers to landmarks from *The Maltese Falcon* and to all Hammett's known San Francisco residences. Herron, who is always appropriately attired in trench coat and fedora, has operated this tour since 1977. Said to be the longest ongoing literary tour in the country, it lasts 4 hours and covers approximately 3 miles.

### Golden Gate Park Walking Tours
For description, see page 33.

### Mission Trail Mural Walk
*Depart from 2981 24th St./Harrison St., (415) 285-2287; www.precitaeyes.org. Sat-Sun at 1:30. $5-$12, under 18 $2.*

Sponsored by the Precita Eyes Mural Arts

Center, this 2-hour walk is led by a professional muralist and views more than 75 of the 200-plus murals found in the Mission District. The afternoon walk includes a slide show and talk by a professional muralist.

### Pacific Heights Walking Tour

For description, see page 21.

### Wok Wiz Walking Tours

*(650) 355-9657; www.wokwiz.com. Daily at 10am. $40 with lunch, $28 without lunch; under 11 $35/$23. Reservations required.*

Led by cookbook author Shirley Fong-Torres and her staff, the basic Chinatown Tour involves no hills and takes participants behind the scenes and into the heartbeat of this colorful and historic neighborhood. A dim sum lunch is optional. More theme tours are available.

For more Chinatown walks, see page 16.

### — FACTORY TOURS —

### Anchor Steam Brewery

*1705 Mariposa St./DeHaro St., Potrero Hill, (415) 863-8350, fax (415) 552-7094; www.anchorbrewing.com. Tour & tasting M-F. Free. Reservations required.*

This compact brewery was built in the 1860s, when it started producing the locally popular Anchor Steam ale. It is San Francisco's only remaining brewery. The tour concludes with a tasting. Children are welcome but, of course, may not taste.

### Basic Brown Bear Factory.

For description, see page 38.

## HISTORICAL SITES

### Alcatraz Island

*www.nps.gov/alcatraz. Depart from Pier 41 at Embarcadero/Powell St. (415) 705-5555, fax (415) 705-5429; www.blueandgoldfleet.com. Daily departures; schedule varies. $11.50, 62+ $9.75, 5-11 $8.25; audio tour + $4.50/5-11 $2.50. Reservations advised.*

Before Alcatraz opened to the public in 1973, it served as a fort in the 19th century and as a federal penitentiary from 1934 to 1963. Native Americans occupied it from 1969 to 1971. During the time it was a maximum security prison, it was home to some of the country's most hardened criminals, including Al

Capone, George "Machine Gun" Kelly, and Robert "The Birdman" Stroud. Now it is run by the National Park Service as part of the Golden Gate National Recreation Area—the largest urban park in the world. And it is as good as it's cracked up to be—the boat ride, the tour, and the 360-degree bay view. After a short, scenic ride to this infamous island, visitors follow a self-guided tour. The top-notch audio tour of the cell block, narrated in part by former inmates and guards, is highly recommended. It is interesting to note that the 84-foot-tall lighthouse still operates (when the original 214-foot-tall lighthouse was built here in 1854, it was the first on the West Coast). Picnicking is not permitted. Wear comfortable shoes, dress warmly, and expect cool, windy weather—even in summer. If the standard tour is sold out, consider the more expensive Island Hop, which makes a stop at Angel Island and then at Alcatraz, or the Alcatraz After Dark tour, which provides the opportunity to see this fascinating site without crowds. Note that the full-service restaurants at Pier 39 provide a discounted parking validation for the Pier 39 garage.

### Cable Cars

*(415) 673-MUNI; www.sfmuni.com. Daily 6am-1am. $3, under 5 free.*

Before these beloved objects were developed by Andrew Hallidie in 1873, horses had to pull cars up the city's steep hills. Now, 26 "single-enders" operate on the two Powell Street routes and 12 "double-enders" operate on

California Street. (Single-ended cable cars have controls only at one end and need to use a turntable at the end of the line to reverse direction. Double-ended cars have controls at both ends and need only a crossover track to turn back.) Catch the Powell-Hyde line at the turnaround located at the base of Powell Street (at Market Street) and ride it up and over the hills all the way to Aquatic Park. This line goes down the steepest hill and affords the most breathtaking views. The Powell-Mason line ends at Bay Street at Fisherman's Wharf. The less-used California Street line begins at Market Street and runs along California Street, passing Chinatown and then climbing over Nob Hill, ending at Van Ness Avenue. Riders can also board at designated stops along the routes.

## Chinatown

*Bounded by Broadway, Bush St., Kearny St., & Powell St.; www.sfchinatown.com & www.sanfranciscochinatown.com.*

With a population of approximately 80,000 residents and covering 24 square blocks, San Francisco's Chinatown is the largest Chinese community outside of Asia. The most memorable way to enter the area is on foot through the ornate dragon-crested archway located at Grant Avenue and Bush Street. Designed to the Taoist principles of Feng Shui, the gate features Foo dogs to scare away evil spirits, dragons for fertility and power, and fish for prosperity. A walk along pedestrian-crowded Grant Avenue, the city's oldest street, is quite an experience. For good souvenir hunting, stop in at one of the many shops. Favorite items with children include golden dragon-decorated velvet slippers, rice candy in edible wrappers, and silk coin purses.

### • Chinatown Night Market Fair

*Kearny St./Washington St., in Portsmouth Square, (415) 397-8000. Sat 6-11pm; Jun-Oct only. Free.*

Resembling a Hong Kong street fair, this weekly event is popular with locals. Merchandise is generally inexpensive and exotic. Traditional Chinese performances—lion dancing, opera, martial arts—are scheduled.

### • Chinese Culture Center of San Francisco

*750 Kearny St./Washington St., 3rd fl. in Holiday Inn, (415) 986-1822, fax (415) 986-2825; www.c-c-c.org. Tu-Sun 10-4; closed last 2 wks. in Dec. Free.*

This two-room gallery displays rotating exhibits of historical and contemporary Chinese art by both native Chinese and Chinese-Americans.

Cultural and culinary tours of Chinatown sponsored by the Chinese Culture Foundation are scheduled year-round. All require reservations and work best with children 8 and older. The **Heritage Walk** *(W at 10:30, Sat at 10:30 & 1. $17, under 12 $8.)* stresses the history and cultural achievements of the area. Stops might include a Chinese temple and historical society. The **Culinary Walk** *(By appt. $40, under 12 $20.)* introduces Chinese cuisine with stops in markets and at a fortune cookie factory, an herb shop, and a tea shop. It concludes with a dim sum lunch.

### • Dim Sum

Translated variously as meaning "touch of heart," "touch your heart," "heart's desire," and "heart's delight," dim sum items originally were served for breakfast during China's Tang Dynasty (618 to 907 A.D.) A meal of these appetizers makes an interesting change of pace for breakfast or lunch, and there is no better place to try the cuisine than here: San Francisco is said to have more dim sum parlors than any other city in the U.S.

The varieties of dim sum are seemingly endless and include steamed buns, fried dumplings, and turnovers, as well as delicacies such as steamed duck beaks and feet. It is great fun to pick and choose from items brought around to tables Hong Kong-style on carts or trays that circulate non-stop. Just flag down the servers as they pass. Be aware that in crowded restaurants it can be difficult to get a server to describe what a particular item is composed of, and sometimes they don't speak or understand English very well.

Tea arrives automatically (some restaurants charge for it). The three most common kinds are mild green, semi-fermented oolong, and strong fermented black. Chrysanthemum combines black tea with dried flowers, and jasmine combines oolong with dried flowers. To get a tea refill, do as the Chinese do and signal the waiter by turning over the lid on the teapot. Some, but not all, establishments offer other drinks.

Note that although crossed chopsticks usually are considered an omen of bad luck, in dim sum houses they signal the server that the diner is finished.

Though this quaint custom is rapidly dying, the bill in some restaurants is determined by how many serving plates are on the table at meal's end. (This concept is reminiscent of the tiny hill town of San Gimignano in Italy, which once had 70 bell towers. A family's wealth there was measured by the height of its bell tower.) To keep a running tab, just make a stack of the serving plates and steamers as they are emptied. Most teahouses charge about $2 to $4.50 per plate, and tips are usually divided by the entire staff.

- **Dim Sum restaurants**
  - **Gold Mountain** See page 70.
  - **Lichee Garden** See page 75.
  - **Meriwa** See page 78.
  - **New Asia** See page 79.
  - **Pearl City** See page 80.

- **Fortune Cookie Factories**

Always fun after a Chinatown meal is a walk through the narrow streets and alleys to find a fortune cookie factory. Though workers aren't often pleased to see tourists, it is usually possible to get at least a glimpse of the action by peeking in through a door or window. Nowadays, the traditional way of making the cookies by hand-folding is giving way to intricate machines invented in San Francisco in the 1970s by Edward Louie. Proprietors are usually glad to sell cookies, and bags of broken "misfortune" cookies can be purchased at bargain prices.

  - **Golden Gate Fortune Cookie Factory**
56 Ross Alley/Washington St., (415) 781-3956. Daily 7-8:30. Free.

Tucked away in a picturesque alley in the heart of Chinatown, this is the only fortune cookie factory in town that still makes cookies by hand. It also sells delicious mini-almond cookies.

  - **Mee Mee Bakery**
1328 Stockton St./Broadway, (415) 362-3204. Daily 8-6.

Located at the border of Chinatown and North Beach, this factory has been baking fortune cookies since 1948—longer than anyone else in town. They also sell X-rated cookies, mini-almond cookies, and both chocolate and strawberry fortune cookies.

- **Herb shop**
  - **Superior Trading Co.**

837 Washington St./Grant Ave., (415) 982-8722, fax (415) 982-7786. Daily 9:30-6.

This interesting and somewhat mysterious shop measures out aromatic herbs on scales. Unless actually planning to purchase something, it is best just to peek in the window.

- **Restaurants**

Though locals often claim good Chinese restaurants aren't found in Chinatown, in reality some are.
  - **Brandy Ho's Hunan Food** See page 59.
  - **Far East Cafe** See page 67.
  - **Lichee Garden** See page 75.
  - **Lucky Creation** See page 76.
  - **The Pot Sticker** See page 82.
  - **Sam Wo** See page 83.

- **Tea shop**
  - **Imperial Tea Court**
1411 Powell St./Broadway, (800) 567-5898, (415) 788-6080, fax (415) 788-6079; www.imperialtea.com. W-M 11-6:30; $3-$50/person. Reservations not necessary.

Decorated with a collection of bamboo birdcages, this exotic shop serves some of the world's most acclaimed, and expensive, teas. Sit down at one of the beautiful rosewood tables and relax while the selected tea is prepared. Like it? It's available for purchase, as are an assortment of tea accouterments.

- **Temple**

Though there are many temples in Chinatown, only one seems to welcome visitors.
  - **Tien Hau Temple**
125 Waverly Pl./Washington St. Daily 10-5 & 7-9pm. Donations appreciated.

Named after the goddess of the heavens and seas—who protects sailors, prostitutes, actors, and writers—this temple is located in the heart of Chinatown on a lane known for its ornate, colorfully-painted balconies. Built in 1852, it is the oldest Taoist temple in the U.S. It is easy to find—just follow the scent of incense up the narrow wooden stairs to the fourth floor. Bear in mind that the temple still is used for worship, and appropriate reverent behavior is expected.

## City Lights Books
261 Columbus Ave./Broadway, North Beach, (415) 362-8193, fax (415) 362-4921; www.citylights.com. Daily 10am-midnight.

Founded in 1953 by beatnik poet Lawrence Ferlinghetti, who still looks after the business, this multi-level independent bookstore was the first in the country to specialize in paperbacks. Many obscure titles are in its eclectic collection, providing great browsing. Don't miss stepping into the small press poetry alcove or traipsing down the creaky wooden stairs into the large cellar. Not content just to sell books, the proprietors published Allen Ginsberg's *Howl* and continue to publish unusual books. The bookstore was given landmark status in 2001.

## Coit Tower

*At top of Lombard St., North Beach, (415) 362-0808. Daily 10-6:30. $3.75, 65+ $2.50, 6-12 $1.50.*

This 210-foot-tall tower (approximately 18 stories) located atop fashionable Telegraph Hill offers a magnificent 360-degree view that includes the Golden Gate and Bay bridges and Lombard Street. Resembling the nozzle of a fire hose, it was built in 1933 as a memorial to the city's volunteer fire department. Colorful painted murals on the ground floor walls date from 1934. Depicting area activities during the Depression, they were controversial at the time because of left-wing political content. The admission fee includes an attendant-operated elevator ride to the top. Parking is extremely limited. Visitors who walk or take the 39 Coit

bus up, can then walk down the **Filbert Street Steps** and past the **Grace Marchant Garden** to Levi Plaza, located near Battery Street.

## Crookedest Street in the World

*Lombard St. betw. Hyde St. & Leavenworth St., Russian Hill.*

This famous curvy street is one way downhill. Drivers must maneuver over a bumpy brick-paved road with eight tight turns while trying not to be distracted by the magnificent view. Get here by driving up the steep incline on the west side of Lombard Street, or, for an easier time of it, drive up from the south side of Hyde Street.

The **other crookedest street** is Vermont Street, between 22nd and 23rd streets on Potrero Hill. Though it has only six turns, they are said to be tighter than Lombard's.

The **shortest crooked street** is Octavia Street between Jackson and Washington streets. It is a charming, brick-paved mini-Lombard.

The city's **steepest streets** are Filbert Street between Hyde and Leavenworth streets (with a 31.5% grade), 22nd Street between Church and Vicksburg streets (also with a 31.5% grade), and Jones Street between Union and Filbert streets (with a 29% grade).

## Ferry Building Marketplace

For description, see page 67.

## F-Line

*Runs for 5 mi. along Market St., from Castro St. to the Embarcadero, and along the waterfront to Jones St. at Fisherman's Wharf, (415) 956-0472, fax (415) 956-4790; www.streetcar.org. Daily 6am-1am. $1.25, 65+ & 5-17 35¢.*

Vintage electric trolley cars from around the world join San Francisco's own historic streetcar fleet. Even New Orleans' famous streetcar named Desire is part of the fleet.

## Fort Mason

*Laguna St./Marina Blvd., (415) 441-3400, fax (415) 441-3405; www.fortmason.org.*

In addition to housing the park headquarters for the Golden Gate National Recreation Area, this complex of buildings houses theaters, art galleries, museums, and myriad other facilities. Highlights include:

• **Book Bay Bookstore**
*Bldg. C, (415) 771-1076; www.friendsandfoundation.
org/bookbaystore.html. Daily 11-5.*

Thousands of bargain books, as well as records and tapes, are on sale here. The West's largest **Used Book Sale** is held each September. Proceeds benefit the San Francisco Public Library.

• **Greens** restaurant
For description see page 71.

• **Magic Theatre**
For description, see page 36.

• **The Mexican Museum**
For description, see page 23.

• **Museo ItaloAmericano**
For description, see page 23.

• **Museum of Craft & Folk Art**
For description, see page 23.

• **San Francisco African American Historical & Cultural Society**
For description, see page 28.

• **Young Performers Theatre**
For description, see page 37.

## Fort Point National Historic Site
*Located directly under the south anchorage of the Golden Gate Bridge, at end of Marine Dr., in the Presidio; take Lincoln Blvd. to Long Ave., turn left, at bottom follow road along water to fort; (415) 556-1693, fax (415) 561-4390; www.nps.gov/fopo. F-Sun 10-5; tour at 11 & 3. Free.*

Built in 1861, this is the only Civil War-era fort on the West Coast. Its four tiers were once home to 126 cannons; several 10,000 pound-plus originals and replicas are displayed. It is perhaps even more famous as the site in Hitchcock's *Vertigo* where Kim Novak's character jumped into the bay. Each winter **Candlelight Fort Tours** *(Nov-Feb; 6:30-8pm. Must be 15 or older. Reservations required.)* are scheduled. Participants see the fort from the viewpoint of a Civil War soldier. What was it like in the 1860s to live in drafty quarters heated by fireplaces and lighted by candles? What kind of food did the soldiers eat and how was it prepared? A walk through the 1870 gun emplacements located south of the fort concludes each tour.

## Golden Gate Bridge
Once called "the bridge that couldn't be built," this magnificent example of man's ingenuity and perseverance is one of San Francisco's most famous sights. Measuring 6,450 feet, or approximately 1.7 miles, it is the longest suspension bridge in the world, and its 746-foot-high towers are the tallest ever built. Many people are disappointed to discover that the bridge is not a golden color. Its protective dull red-orange coating is known officially as International Orange and was chosen by the bridge's architect, Irving Morrow, to make it visible in dense fog. Crossing it is a must—by car, foot, or bicycle. The round-trip is about 2 miles, and views are breathtaking. It is interesting to note that bungee-jumping is said to have originated here in 1979.

## Grace Cathedral
*1100 California St./Taylor St., (415) 749-6300, fax (415) 749-6301; www.gracecathedral.org. Daily 8-6; tour available. Free.*

Located atop Nob Hill, this majestic French Gothic cathedral stands 265 feet tall and is the largest in the western U.S. It is graced with more than 60 opulent stained-glass windows, and its gilded bronze entrance doors are

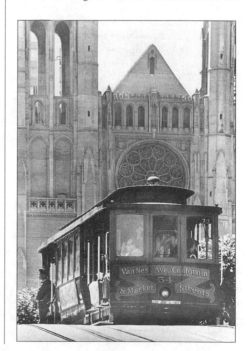

exact replicas of Lorenzo Ghiberti's "Doors of Paradise" at the Baptistry in Florence, Italy. Concerts using the cathedral's renowned 7,286-pipe organ are scheduled often, sometimes accompanied by the 44-bell carillon. The cathedral's reverberant acoustics and architecturally magnificent interior make these memorable experiences. A walking **labyrinth**—a unique tool for meditation and enlightenment and said to be a metaphor for entering one's center—is located both inside the cathedral and outside on a plaza. (A labyrinth is different from a maze, which is a puzzle and designed to confuse.) Patterned after one at Chartres cathedral, these are the first permanent labyrinths laid in the Western hemisphere in 600 years.

Annual **Cathedral Choir Christmas Concerts** feature the Grace Cathedral Choir of Men and Boys singing both traditional and new carols. They are wondrous, inspirational events. A Festival of Lessons and a Midnight Mass are traditional on Christmas Eve, and a celebratory New Year's Eve event is scheduled each year. Also, every few years the cathedral is the unusual, yet appropriate, setting for a screening of the original 1923 silent film classic *The Hunchback of Notre Dame* with live organ accompaniment.

Built of brick in 1853, **Old St. Mary's Cathedral** *(660 California St., Chinatown, (415) 288-3800; www.oldsaintmarys.org.)* was the West Coast's first Roman Catholic cathedral.

## Haight-Ashbury
*Haight St. betw. Stanyan St. & Masonic St.*

It's almost possible to step back in time here to the Summer of Love. A few locals still don bell-bottoms, tie-dyed shirts, and love beads, and these items are still for sale in some shops. Not gentrified, the area is a little rough around the edges, and Haight Street is now lined with an assortment of colorful boutiques and inexpensive restaurants and coffeehouses. Wavy Gravy describes his neighborhood as "a coexistence between the punks and the hippies, a little cutting-edge U.N. in action." See also page 39.

Visiting here also permits the chance to see some of the area's magnificent Victorian houses, including the one at 710 Ashbury, where the Grateful Dead once resided, and the mansion at 2400 Fulton, where the Jefferson Airplane lived.

Janis Joplin once lived with Country Joe McDonald in apartment 3 at 112 Page Street, Big Brother & the Holding Company formed at 1090 Page Street, and the first free medical clinic in the U.S. still operates at 558 Clayton Street. On a more somber note, the notorious Manson "family" once lived at 636 Cole Street.

## Historic houses

San Francisco is known for its abundance of beautiful turn-of-the-century Victorian houses. At last count there were over 14,000. One of the pleasures of living here is visiting people who actually reside in them. Visitors to the city interested in capturing a taste of that delight will enjoy stopping in at the two historic homes open to the public.

To see some of the city's "painted ladies," as the many colorfully painted Victorian homes sometimes are called, visit the area around Alamo Square at Hayes and Steiner streets. The 700 block of Steiner is packed with Queen Anne Victorians. Nicknamed "postcard row," it often is photographed commercially from the top of the park with the skyline in the distance. Another good area is along the Golden Gate Park Panhandle, particularly on the Fell Street side, where well-maintained mansions are plentiful. (It is interesting to note that the Panhandle was originally the carriage entrance to the park and that it is home to approximately 50 species of the park's oldest trees.)

And, of course, everyone wants to see the house used in exterior scenes for *Mrs. Doubtfire*. Check it out in Pacific Heights at 2640 Steiner Street. Seeing the house from the outside will do. Interior scenes were filmed in a studio so there is no need to peek in windows.

### • Haas-Lilienthal House
*2007 Franklin St./Jackson St., Pacific Heights, (415) 441-3004; www.sfheritage.org. House tour: W & some Sat 12-3, Sun 11-4; $8, 62+ & under 12 $5. Walking tour: Sun at 12:30; $8, 62+ & under 12 $5.*

In 1886 architect Peter R. Schmidt built this 24-room, 7½ -bath Queen Anne Victorian home of fir and redwood for Bertha and William Haas, a mercantile grocer. It cost $18,500 (average homes then cost about $2,000). The house survived the infamous 1906 earthquake relatively unscathed, with a small bulge in the plaster the only visible damage. It also escaped the fire that followed, though Mr.

Haas's downtown offices were destroyed. Family members occupied the house until 1972. Most of the furnishings are original to the house, including a lovely and extensive set of matching art nouveau pieces in the main bedroom. Children often find the doll house in the second-floor nursery especially interesting. Baby strollers are not permitted in the house.

The **Pacific Heights Walking Tour** of the surrounding neighborhood focuses on the exteriors of some of San Francisco's finest Victorian and Edwardian homes.

### • Octagon House

*2645 Gough St./Union St., Pacific Heights, (415) 441-7512. 2nd & 4th Thur & 2nd Sun of month, 12-3; closed Jan. By donation.*

Built in 1861, when this architectural style was a fad throughout the country, this eight-sided house is now one of only two left in San Francisco. The National Society of The Colonial Dames of America in California has restored and furnished it and turned it into the only museum of Colonial and Federal decorative arts on the West Coast. Items displayed date from 1700 to 1830 and are labeled with background information. Of special interest is a display featuring the signatures of 54 of the 56 signers of the Declaration of Independence. The house's

well-groomed garden and adjacent **Allyne Park** are both perfect for a stroll.

### Mission San Francisco de Asis

*3321 16th St./Dolores St., Mission district, (415) 621-8203, fax (415) 621-2294; www.mission dolores.citysearch.com. Daily 9-4, in summer to 4:30. $3, 5-12 $2.*

Known commonly as **Mission Dolores**, this relatively small mission is sixth in California's chain of 21. The mission church, completed in 1791, is the oldest intact building in the city. Its cool adobe and redwood interior offers pleasant respite from the occasional hot San Francisco day. Of special interest is the ceiling, painted in Ohlone tribal patterns and colors originally produced by vegetable dyes. A picturesque enclosed cemetery garden is landscaped to period correctness. It contains an Ohlone tule reed house, and all the plants growing here were once used in some way by resident Native Americans. The mission's cemetery is one of only two remaining in San Francisco (the other is at the Presido), and, although only 200 tombstones are visible, 10,000 people are actually buried on the mission site. A small museum completes the complex.

## Presidio of San Francisco
*Lombard St./Lyon St., (415) 561-4323; www.nps.gov/prsf. Daily 10-5. Free.*

Used as a military garrison by Spain, Mexico, and the U.S., the Presidio was established by Spain in 1776, taken over by Mexico in 1822, and then taken over by the U.S. as an Army post in 1846. It played a critical role in providing refuge for the 1906 earthquake victims. The Presidio is undergoing continuous major changes as it transforms from an Army post into a recreational area. Hiking and biking trails are available; contact the Visitor Center for information on guided walks and bicycle tours. Originally a burial plot for canine guard dogs, the post Pet Cemetery became a burial ground for pets of Army families and can be visited.

### • Crissy Field Center
*Marina Blvd./Old Mason St., at the shoreline of the Presidio, (415) 561-7690, fax (415) 561-7695; http://crissyfield.org. Visitor Center: W-Sun 9-5. Warming hut: daily 9-5. Free.*

The post's former landing strip is now a spectacular shoreline park, with several boardwalks leading through the scenic dunes and restored tidal marsh. A large grassy expanse for unstructured play and a nature center are part of the facility, and picnic tables are available. A former torpedo depot, the Visitor Center cafe is a model of sustainability. It uses recycled products, and the deli menu is prepared with mostly local organic products. The warming hut also has a small cafe and provides remarkable views of the Golden Gate Bridge.

## MUSEUMS

### — ART MUSEUMS —

## Asian Art Museum
*200 Larkin St., Civic Center, (415) 581-3500; www.asianart.org. Tu-Sun 10-5, Thur to 9. $10, 65+ $7, 13-17 $6; free on 1st Tu of month; free audio tour.*

Newly relocated in the 1917 Beaux-Arts building that was the city's main library until 1994—the redesign was done by architect Gae Aulenti, who also converted a derelict Paris train station into the celebrated Musée d'Orsay—this is the largest museum in the Western world devoted exclusively to Asian art. And with more than 15,000 objects from 40 Asian countries spanning a period of more than 6,000 years, it is the best Asian collection in the U.S. (At any one time it displays 2,500 objects in its 30 galleries representing 7 Asian cultural regions.) The museum also holds the largest collection of Indian sculpture outside India. Combining East and West, the building represents San Francisco's past and future. The main floor displays special exhibits, and the second and third floors house permanent galleries. For all visitors, a free, hands-on, drop-in program known as AsiaAlive operates in Samsung Hall at the top of the grand marble staircase on the second floor. Also, a bimonthly Saturday demonstration at the museum's teahouse includes tea and a sweet for $5. Special family programs are scheduled monthly, and Asian myth and folktale storytelling sessions are held on Sunday afternoons. Children might especially enjoy viewing the Indonesian rod puppets.

## Cartoon Art Museum
*655 Mission St./3rd St., South of Market, (415) CARTOON, fax (415) 243-8666; www.cartoonart.org. Tu-Sun 11-5. $6, 62+ $4, 6-12 $2; free 1st Tu of month.*

Presenting both a permanent collection and changing special exhibits, this museum showcases important developments in cartoon history from the early 18th century to the present. One of only two such museums in the country, its aim is "to preserve this unique art form and to enrich the public's knowledge of its cultural and aesthetic value." Cartooning workshops for ages 6 to 14 are given on Saturday afternoons.

## Fine Arts Museums of San Francisco

### • de Young Museum
*In Golden Gate Park, (415) 863-3330; www.legionofhonor.org/deyoung.*

Closed now, this museum will reopen in June 2005 in a magnificent new building designed by Pritzker Prize-winning architects Herzog & de Meuron. It holds a significant collection of American paintings, sculpture, and decorative arts from colonial times into the mid-20th century as well as the country's best collection of American trompe l'oeil paintings from the late 1800's. The permanent collection of art from Africa, Oceania, Mesoamerica, and Central and South America features outstanding works from ancient to modern times; many are not seen elsewhere.

### • Legion of Honor
*100 34th Ave./Clement St., in Lincoln Park, outer Richmond district, (415) 863-3330; www.legionofhonor.org. Tu-Sun 9:30-5. $8, 65+ $6, 12-17 $5; free on Tu.*

Situated on a scenic knoll overlooking the Golden Gate Bridge, this is the only museum in the country exhibiting primarily French art. Rodin's earliest casting of his sculpture, "The Thinker," greets visitors as they approach the entrance to this impressive neoclassical marble structure—a replica of the Hotel de Salm in Paris, where Napoleon established his new Order of the Legion of Honor in the 18th century. This museum also holds the city's collection of European and ancient art and presents free organ concerts on weekends at 4 p.m. The museum was given to the city of San Francisco on Armistice Day in 1924 and is dedicated to the memory of California men who died in World War I. A cafe offers simple food with a French flair and a dining room and terrace with a view.

For 3 days every March the museum galleries are decorated stunningly with fresh flowers. For **Bouquets to Art**, members of Bay Area flower clubs and professional florists design arrangements inspired by museum paintings. Some mimic the paintings, other pick up the colors or feeling. Overall they enliven the galleries.

The entrance to the **Holocaust Memorial** is on the north side of the parking circle. A semicircular stairway leads down to an area where cast bronze, white-painted pieces created by sculptor George Segal are displayed.

For a scenic drive, leave via Lincoln Avenue on the north side of the museum. Follow it to its conclusion at Lombard Street. This route has several vista points of the Golden Gate Bridge. It passes by Baker Beach, goes through the elegant Sea Cliff residential area, and continues into the Presidio.

### The Mexican Museum
*Fort Mason Center, Bldg. D, Laguna St./Marina Blvd., (415) 202-9700, fax (415) 441-7683; www.mexican museum.org. W-Sat 11-5. $3, seniors & 13-16 $2; free 1st W of month.*

Founded in 1975, this was the first museum in the U.S. devoted to Mexican and Mexican-American art. It has expanded to include the arts of Mexican and Latino cultures throughout the Americas. When space permits, items from the permanent pre-Columbian collection are displayed.

### Museo ItaloAmericano
*Fort Mason Center, Bldg. C, Laguna St./Marina Blvd., (415) 673-2200, fax (415) 673-2292; www.museoitaloamericano.org. W-Sun 12-5. $3, 65+ & 12-18 $2; free 1st W of month, open to 7.*

This small museum is dedicated to displaying the works of Italian and Italian-American artists.

### Museum of Craft & Folk Art
*Fort Mason Center, Bldg. A, Laguna St./Marina Blvd., (415) 775-0991, fax (415) 775-1861; www.mocfa.org. Tu-Sun 11-5, Sat 10-5, 1st W of month 11-7. $4, 62+$3, under 19 free; free 1st W of month & every Sat 10-noon.*

Serving as a showcase for high quality contemporary crafts and folk art, this museum changes exhibits every two months.

### San Francisco Museum of Modern Art
*151 3rd St./Howard St., South of Market, (415) 357-4000, fax (415) 357-4037; www.sfmoma.org. Thur-Tu 11-6, Thur to 9. $10, 62+ $7, under 12 free; half-price Thur 6-9; free 1st Tu of month; audio tours $3-$6.*

Now at home in its striking contemporary building, this museum was the first in the

West devoted entirely to 20th-century art. Its collection includes abstract art, photography, and the work of acclaimed contemporary artists. The most efficient way to see everything is to take the elevator to the fifh floor and work down. An informative audio tour is available to the permanent collection. The museum gift shop has an array of exceptional merchandise and a particularly noteworthy section for children, and casual **Caffe Museo** *((415) 357-4500, fax (415) 357-4506.)* offers a menu of scrumptious meals and light snacks.

## — FLOATING MUSEUMS —

The collection of historic ships berthed along the San Francisco waterfront is the largest (by weight) in the world.

### San Francisco Maritime National Historical Park
*Fisherman's Wharf, (415) 447-5000; www.nps.gov/safr. Visitor Center: 499 Jefferson St. Daily 9:30-5, in summer to 7. Free.*

**• Maritime Museum**
*900 Beach St./foot of Polk St., across from Ghirardelli Square. Daily 10-5. Free.*

Appropriately resembling a ship, this architecturally interesting art deco-streamline moderne building was built by the Work Project Administration (WPA) in 1939. It was originally a nightclub and aquatic activities center. The main floor displays parts of old ships, elaborately carved and painted figureheads, and exquisitely detailed ship models. The second floor is home to more models as well as to artifacts, paintings, fascinating historical photos, and maps.

**• Hyde Street Pier**
*2905 Hyde St./Jefferson St. Daily 9:30-5; in summer to 5:30. $5, under 17 free.*

The vessels moored on this scenic pier represent the period from the turn of the century through World War II—a time of rapid growth for San Francisco begun by the 1849 Gold Rush and an era during which the city was an important shipping center. Visitors can board four:

**• Balclutha.** A Cape Horn sailing ship built in Scotland in 1886, this 301-foot steel-hulled merchant ship carried whiskey, wool, and rice, but mainly coal, to San Francisco. On her return sailing to Europe she carried grain from

*Balclutha*

California. Typical of Victorian British merchant ships, she is described colorfully by the men who sailed her as a "blue water, square-rigged, lime juice windbag." She is the last of the Cape Horn fleet and ended her sailing career as an Alaskan salmon ship. Renovated by donated labor and goods, she opened to the public in 1955. A fascinating way to experience this ship is at one of the **chantey sings** *((415) 556-6435. Adult program 1st Sat of month, 8pm-12; children's program 3rd Sat at 2. Free. Reservations required.)* held in her cozy hold. Participants should dress warmly and bring a cushion to sit on, a mug for hot cider to wet the whistle, and a chantey or two to share.

**• C.A. Thayer.** A fleet of 900 ships once carried lumber from the north coast forests to California ports. Only two of these ships still exist. One is the *C.A. Thayer*—a three-mast lumber schooner built in Fairhaven (near Eureka) in 1895. She was the very last commercial sailing ship in use on the West Coast and made her last voyage in 1950 as a fishing ship. Visitors can descend into her dank wooden hold to see the crew's bunkroom and then ascend to the captain's lushly furnished, oak-paneled cabin—complete with a gilded canary cage. A 25-minute film of her last voyage is shown several times each day, and guided tours are available.

**• Eureka.** Originally named the *Ukiah*, this double-ended, wooden-hulled ferry was built in

Tiburon in 1890 to carry railroad cars and passengers across the bay. In 1922 she was rebuilt to carry automobiles and passengers and renamed the *Eureka*. Later she served as a commuter ferry (the largest in the world) between San Francisco and Sausalito, and yet later as a ferry for train passengers arriving in San Francisco from Oakland. She held 2,300 people plus 120 automobiles. Her 4-story "walking beam" steam engine is the only such engine still afloat in the U.S. A model demonstrates its operation, and a ranger-guided tour through the engine room is sometimes available. Two decks are open to the public. The lower deck houses a display of antique cars, and the main deck features original benches and a historical photo display.

• *Hercules.* This ocean-going tugboat was built in 1907.

More ships are moored at the pier but not open for boarding. The *Alma*, a scow schooner built in 1891 at Hunters Point, is a specialized cargo carrier and the last of her kind still afloat. The *Eppleton Hall*, built in England in 1914 and used in the canals there to tow coal ships, is the only vessel in the collection not directly associated with West Coast maritime history. The *Wapama*, the last surviving example of a steam schooner, is being restored at Richmond's old Kaiser Shipyard.

Non-floating displays at the pier include a turn-of-the-century ark (or houseboat), a restored donkey engine that is sometimes operated for visitors, and the reconstructed sales office of the Tubbs Cordage Company.

### S.S. *Jeremiah O'Brien*
*Pier 45, foot of Taylor St., Fisherman's Wharf, (415) 544-0100, fax (415) 544-9890; www.ssjeremiah obrien.com. Daily 10-4. $7, seniors $5, 6-14 $4.*

This massive 441-foot-long vessel is the last unaltered Liberty Ship from World War II still in operating condition. Between 1941 and 1945, in an all-out effort to replace the cargo ships being sunk in huge numbers by enemy submarines, 2,751 Liberty Ships were built to transport troops and supplies. Shipyards operated around the clock. Assembled from pre-fabricated sections, each ship took only between 6 and 8 weeks to build. Shockingly large, the *O'Brien* was built in South Portland, Maine in 1943. She was in operation for 33 years and sailed from England to Normandy during the D-Day invasion. In 1978 she was declared a national monument. Since then, dedicated volunteers—many of whom served on similar ships—have been working to restore her to her original glory. Visitors have access to

almost every part of the ship, including the sleeping and captain's quarters, wheelhouse, and guns as well as the catwalks in the eerie 3-story engine room. The triple expansion steam engine operates on the third weekend of each month. An annual fund-raising **Seamen's Memorial Cruise** occurs each May, and **Fleet Week Cruises** occur each October.

## USS Pampanito

*Pier 45, foot of Taylor St., (415) 561-6662. Sun-Thur 9-6, F-Sat 9-8; in summer, daily Thur-Tu 9-8, W 9-6. $7, 62+ $5, 6-12 $3.*

This 312-foot-long World War II submarine built in Portsmouth, New Hampshire in 1943 is credited with sinking six Japanese ships and damaging four others. She also rescued a group of British and Australian POWs from the South China Sea. The self-guided tour through her cramped belly and meticulously restored compartments is enhanced with a recorded audio tour providing narrative by former crew members, helping listeners imagine what it must have been like for men to be cooped up in this small space for months at a time.

## — SCIENCE MUSEUMS —

### California Academy of Sciences

*875 Howard St./4th St., South of Market, (415) 750-7145, fax (415) 321-8604; www.calacademy.org. Daily 10-5; in summer 9-6. $6, 65+ & 12-17 $4, 4-11 $2; free 1st W of month.*

Moved here from its home in Golden Gate Park while a new building is constructed there (to open in 2008), this oldest scientific institution in the West was founded in 1853 following the Gold Rush. An abbreviated collection of science and aquarium exhibits is displayed.

### Exploratorium

*3601 Lyon St./Marina Blvd., Marina district, (415) EXP-LORE, fax (415) 561-0307; www.exploratorium.edu. Tu-Sun 10-5. $12, 65+ & 13-17 $9.50, 4-12 $8; free 1st W of month.*

Located inside the cavernous **Palace of Fine Arts**—designed by architect Bernard Maybeck in 1915 as part of the Panama-Pacific Exposition (an early World's Fair celebrating the opening of the Panama Canal) and said to be the world's largest artificial ruin—this museum makes scientific and natural phenomena understandable through a collection of more than

650 hands-on exhibits. *Scientific American* described it as the best science museum in the world. Indeed, visitors can experience a dizzying ride on a Momentum Machine, step through a miniature tornado, and encase themselves in bubbles. To the shrieking delight of youngsters, a walk-in Shadow Box allows reverse images to remain on a wall. Teenage "Explainers" wearing easy-to-see orange vests wander the premises ready to help. The **Tactile Dome** *((415) 561-0362. $15, includes museum admission. Must be 7 or older. Reservations required.)* is a geodesic dome with 13 chambers through which visitors can walk, crawl, slide, climb, and tumble in complete darkness with only their sense of touch to guide them. Plan a pleasant picnic outside by the picturesque reflecting pond populated with ducks and even a few swans.

The **Wave Organ** is located across Marina Boulevard at the eastern tip of the breakwater forming the Marina Yacht Harbor. This unusual musical instrument—designed by Exploratorium artist Peter Richards in collaboration with stonemason George Gonzales—consists of more than 20 pipes extending down through the breakwater into the bay and provides a constant symphony of natural music. Listeners can relax in a small granite and marble amphitheater and view the San Francisco skyline. The organ plays most effectively at high tide.

## — MISCELLANEOUS MUSEUMS —

### Cable Car Barn and Museum

*1201 Mason St./Washington St., 2 blks. from Chinatown, (415) 474-1887, fax (415) 929-7546; www.cablecarmuseum.com. Daily 10-5; in summer to 6. Free.*

Located inside the lovely brick cable car barn and powerhouse dating from the 1880s, this museum lets visitors see the huge, noisy flywheels controlling the underground cables that move the cable cars along at 9$^{1}$/$_{2}$ miles per hour. Three retired cable cars—including one from the original 1873 fleet—and assorted artifacts are on display, and an informative film with vintage footage explains how the cable cars actually work. To complete the experience, catch a cable car across the street and take a ride downtown or to Fisherman's Wharf.

## California Historical Society Museum
*678 Mission St./3rd St., South of Market, (415) 357-1848, fax (415) 357-1850; www.californiahistorical society.org. W-Sat 12-4:30. $2, 62+ & students $1, under 5 free.*

Founded in 1871, this society has a collection of artifacts documenting California's history from the 16th century through the present. That adds up to over 500,000 photographs and 150,000 manuscripts, as well as thousands of books, maps, paintings, and ephemera. Among the gems are Emperor Norton's cane and a stereoscope—the precursor to today's 3-D films. This small museum is housed within the former Hundley Hardware Building.

## Lyle Tuttle's Tattoo Museum
*841 Columbus Ave./Lombard St., North Beach, (415) 775-4991; www.lyletuttle.com. Schedule varies. Free.*

Though renowned tattooist Lyle Tuttle—he tattooed Janis Joplin in the '60s—no longer works in the tatooing studios next door, he continues to oversee the world's first tattoo museum. Photos and paintings trace the history of tattooing, and artifacts displayed include everything from ancient bone tattooing needles to modern electric versions. Want a permanent souvenir? Call ahead for an appointment.

## Musée Mécanique
*Pier 45, Taylor St./The Embarcadero, at Fisherman's Wharf, (415) 346-2000; www.museemecanique.com. Daily 11-7; in summer 10-8. Free admission.*

This "mechanical museum" is filled with old arcade games—some date to the 17th century—and provides thrills small and large. It is the world's largest collection of antique coin-operated machines and is definitely one of the

world's cheeriest places. For just a quarter it is possible to operate a miniature steam shovel and collect 90 seconds worth of gumballs or to see naughty Marietta sunbathing in 3-D realism. Highlights include several player pianos, a mechanical horse ride, and jolly Laughing Sal with her original soundtrack (she was rescued from the Fun House at the now torn down Playland-at-the-Beach). But the roller coaster made out of toothpicks and the machine that makes pressed penny souvenirs are also quite special. Beeping modern video games are in the back, where they belong. Don't miss the Arm Wrestler—the strength-tester beaten by Julie Andrews in the Disney film *The Princess Diaries*.

## North Beach Museum
*1435 Stockton St./Columbus, on 2nd fl. of U.S. Bank, North Beach, (415) 566-4497. M-F 9-5, Sat 9-12. Free.*

Nostalgic photographs depicting this area's past are displayed along with an assortment of interesting artifacts.

## Randall Museum
*199 Museum Way/Roosevelt Way, near 14th St., Corona Heights, (415) 554-9600, fax (415) 554-9609; www.randallmuseum.org. Tu-Sat 10-5. Free.*

Located below Buena Vista Park, between Upper Castro and Haight-Ashbury, this small children's museum has an indoor Animal Room inhabited by uncaged but tethered hawks and owls and other small, accessible animals. Most are recovering from injuries inflicted in the wild. A highlight is the Touching Pen, where children can handle domesticated animals such as rabbits, chickens, and ducks. Exhibits are few but include a replica of a 1906 earthquake refugee shack and an operating seismograph. Nature walks and children's science and arts-and-crafts classes are scheduled regularly. The new Outdoor Learning Environment has an assortment of themed gardens kids dig exploring: the Native Plant Garden, the Hummingbird & Butterfly Garden, and the Mushroom Garden—with edible, medicinal, and just plain beautiful fungi. An outdoor Art Patio lets visitors play with clay, and picnickers can relax on a lush carpet of green known as the Great Lawn while taking in an expansive view of San Francisco below.

On Saturday afternoons, the Golden Gate Model Railroad Club shows off its **model**

**railroad** *((415) 346-3303; www.ggmrc.org. Sat 11-4. Free.)* in the museum's basement.

## Ripley's Believe It or Not! Museum

*175 Jefferson St./Taylor St., Fisherman's Wharf, (415) 771-6188, fax (415) 771-1246; www.ripleysf.com. Sun-Thur 10-10, F-Sat to midnight. $12.95, 5-12 $7.95.*

Among the 250-plus exhibits from Ripley's personal collection of oddities are a cable car made from 270,000 matchsticks and an authentic shrunken torso from Ecuador once owned by Ernest Hemingway. All this, and 2,000 more curiosities. It's unbelievable!

## San Francisco African American Historical & Cultural Society

*Fort Mason Center, Bldg. C, Laguna St./Marina Blvd., (415) 441-0640. W-Sun 12-5. $2, 62+ $1, under 12 free.*

This small museum exhibits photographs of the Civil War, artifacts from World War II, and photographs collected by a black "Buffalo Soldier" Army veteran.

## San Francisco Art Institute

*800 Chestnut St./Jones St., Russian Hill, (415) 771-7020; www.sfai.edu. Free.*

The oldest arts organization west of the Mississippi, this institution trained painter Richard Diebenkorn, photographer Annie Leibovitz, and sculptor Gutzon Borglum (he carved Mount Rushmore). The campus holds

the Diego Rivera Gallery and its famous 1931 Diego Rivera mural *(daily 8am-9pm.)*; the Walter and McBean galleries *(Tu-Sat 11-6.)*; a peaceful Spanish mission-style courtyard complete with goldfish pond; and a well-stocked art supply store. To fit in, dress in sloppy bohemian style and include plenty of black. For a bargain meal stop in at the **cafe**, where the spectacular bay view is thrown in for free.

## San Francisco Fire Museum

*655 Presidio Ave./Bush St., Presidio Heights, (415) 563-4630; www.sffiremuseum.org. Thur-Sun 1-4. Free.*

The fascinating collection of antique fire apparatus found in this small museum includes engines from the hand-drawn, horse-drawn, and motorized eras of fire fighting. Of special interest is an ornate hand-pulled engine dating from 1849 that is San Francisco's, and California's, first fire engine. In addition, historical photographs, memorabilia, and artifacts combine to tell the story of fire fighting in San Francisco, beginning in 1849 with the volunteer department and emphasizing the 1906 earthquake and fire. Visitors are welcome to stop in next door at fire station #10 to see what modern rigs are looking like.

## Wax Museum at Fisherman's Wharf

*145 Jefferson St./Taylor St., (800) 439-4305, (415) 885-4834, fax (415) 771-9248; www.waxmuseum.com.*

*M-F 10am-11pm, Sat-Sun 9-11. $12.95, 55+ $10.55, 4-11 $6.95.*

Recently completely rebuilt and expanded, this attraction displays several hundred wax celebrities situated among an assortment of backgrounds. The Chamber of Horrors intrigues older children with its "blood"-stained floors, but it can be easily by-passed if young children are in tow. The depictions of the Last Supper, the Gallery of Stars, and the Presidents are particularly interesting.

## Wells Fargo History Museum

*420 Montgomery St./California St., Financial District, (415) 396-2619; www.wellsfargohistory.com/museums. M-F 9-5. Free.*

In homage to the Old West, this 2-story museum displays an authentic stagecoach complete with strongbox, samples of various kinds of gold found in the state, a telegraph exhibit, and, of course, a re-creation of an old banking office. All this plus gold-panning equipment and historical photos, too. The oldest bank in the West—Wells Fargo—is the sponsor, and the museum rests on the site of the bank's first office.

## PARKS

### Angel Island State Park

*San Francisco departures from Pier 41 at Fisherman's Wharf; schedule varies; $12, 6-12 $6.50. East Bay departures from Jack London Square; Sat-Sun only; fares vary. Both (415) 705-8200; www.blueandgold fleet.com. Tiburon departures from 21 Main St.; (415) 435-2131, fax (415) 435-7679; www.angelisland ferry.com; schedule varies; $8, 5-11 $6, bikes $1. State Park: (415) 435-1915; www.angelisland.org; daily 8am-sunset; free; no dogs. Visitors Center: Sat-Sun 11-3:30, Apr-Oct only. Tram: schedule varies; $12.50, 62+ $10.50, 6-12 $7.50, under 5 free when seated on lap.*

Half the fun of a trip to Angel Island is the scenic ferry ride over. Visitors disembark at Ayala Cove, as did the first explorers who sailed into the bay. Picnic tables and barbecue facilities are nearby, as is a pleasant little beach for sunbathing. Packing along a picnic is highly recommended, but the island does have its own **Cove Cafe**. Approximately 12 miles of well-marked trails and paved roads allow hikers to completely circle the 740-acre island—the largest in the bay. Some lead to old military

ruins that are reminders of the island's past as a detention center for immigrants from 1910 to 1940 (the island was once called the "Ellis Island of the West"), as a prisoner-of-war processing facility, and as a Nike missile defense base from 1955 to 1962. A 3.2-mile loop trail leads from the cove to the top of 781-foot-high Mount Livermore, where a picnic area and 360-degree view await. A park map is available at the Visitors Center, and a variety of guided tours are scheduled. Except for Park Service vehicles, cars are not permitted on the island. Open-air trams circle the island via the 5-mile perimeter road, and bikes can be brought over on the ferry or rented on the island. Kayak tours can be reserved through **Sea Trek Ocean Kayaking** *((415) 488-1000; www.seatrek kayak.com.)*, and camping in primitive environmental campsites can be arranged.

### Beaches

San Francisco is *not* the place to come to go to the beach. Los Angeles is where *that* California is. Still, the city does have a few good spots to soak up some rays, weather willing. The water, however, is usually either too cold or too dangerous for swimming.

• **Aquatic Park**
*Foot of Polk St., Fisherman's Wharf, (415) 447-5000. Always open. Free.*

Located in the people-congested area across the street from Ghirardelli Square, this is a good spot for children to wade and there are great views of the bay.

• **Baker Beach**
*Off Lincoln Blvd./25th Ave., in the Presidio, (415) 561-4323; www.nps.gov/prsf/places/bakerbch.htm. Daily sunrise-sunset. Free.*

The surf here is unsafe and the temperature often chilly. Still, plenty of people are usually sunning and strolling, and the views of the Golden Gate Bridge are spectacular.

**Battery Chamberlin** is located adjacent. Rangers conduct demonstrations of the world's last remaining 50-ton "disappearing gun" on the first weekend of the month, and environmental programs are sometimes offered.

• **China Beach**
*End of Seacliff Ave./28th Ave., Richmond district, (415) 239-2366; www.nps.gov/goga/chbe. Daily dawn-dusk. Free.*

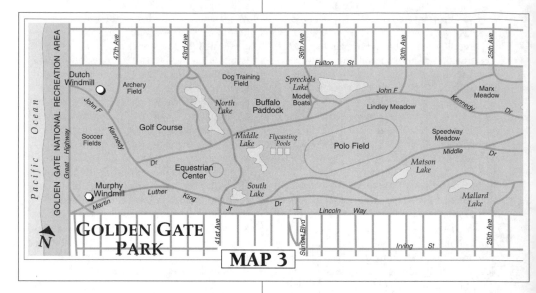

Located in an exclusive residential area, this secluded cove is surprising to come upon. Visitors park on a bluff, then walk down steep stairs to the sheltered, sandy beach. The surf is gentle, so swimming and wading are possible, and changing rooms and restrooms are available in summer.

## Fort Funston

*South end of Great Highway/Skyline Blvd., (415) 239-2366. Daily sunrise-sunset. Free.*

Acquired by the U.S. Army in 1900, these bluffs were once a link in the coastal artillery batteries lining the coast. Nike anti-aircraft missiles guarded the area from the 1950s until the fort's closure in 1963. The missile silos were located underneath what is today the main parking area. Now part of the Golden Gate National Recreation Area, this fort's former barracks houses the Ranger Station and Environmental Science Center. A short, paved loop trail offers stunning coastal views. An observation platform on a bluff above the ocean provides a bird's-eye view of the many hanggliders practicing their sport here and is a great vantage point for whale-watching in winter.

## Golden Gate National Recreation Area (GGNRA)

*(415) 561-2700; www.nps.gov/goga.*

Dedicated to deceased Congressman Phillip Burton, who contributed greatly to establishing this park, the GGNRA is the world's second-largest urban national park and is one of the most heavily visited national parks in the U.S. Located in three California counties—San Francisco, Marin, and San Mateo—its total area is more than 114 square miles, or 2½ times the size of San Francisco. These Bay Area sites are part of the GGNRA: Alcatraz, Baker Beach, China Beach, the Cliff House, Crissy Field, Fort Baker, Fort Funston, Fort Mason, Fort Point, Gerbode Valley, Lands End, Marin Headlands, Muir Woods, Ocean Beach, Olema Valley, The Presidio, Stinson Beach, Sutro Heights Park, Sweeney Ridge, Tennessee Valley, Mori Point, and Tomales Bay. Also within the boundaries but not administered by the GGNRA: Angel Island State Park, Audubon Canyon Ranch, Mount Tamalpais State Park, Samuel P. Taylor State Park, and various ranches in the Tomales Bay-Lagunitas Creek area.

## Golden Gate Park

*Bounded by Fulton St., Stanyan St., Lincoln Way, and Great Highway; (415) 831-2700, fax (415) 221-8034; http://parks.sfgov.org. Daily dawn-dusk. Free.*

One of the world's great metropolitan parks, Golden Gate Park encompasses 1,017 acres. It is nearly 200 acres larger than Manhattan's Central Park, after which it was patterned originally. Once just sand dunes, it is now one of the largest man-made parks in the world.

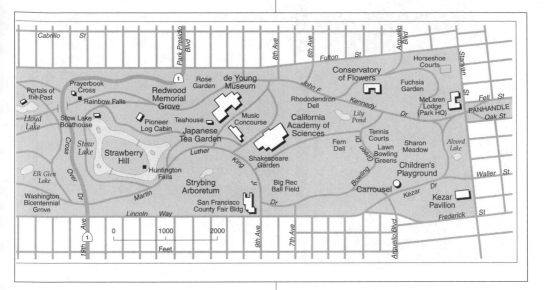

• **Annual Events**
  • **Comedy Day**
*August-October, date varies. www.comedyday.com. Free.*

Just bring a blanket, a picnic, and a smile. Laughs are provided by national headliners and local professional comedians, who in the past have ranged from upstarts—who just naturally seem to try harder—to such established luminaries as Robin Williams, Bob Goldthwait, and Father Guido Sarducci.
  • **A La Carte, A La Park**
*September; on Labor Day weekend. (415) 458-1988, fax (415) 383-0614; www.eventswestca.com. $8-$12, under 12 free; tastings $1-$5.*

Sharon Meadow (known as Hippie Hill in the '60s) overflows with food from local restaurants, wine samplings, and an eclectic line-up of live music. Proceeds benefit Free Shakespeare in the Park.
  • **Free Shakespeare in the Park**
*September. (800) 978-PLAY, (415) 422-2222, fax (415) 865-4433); www.sfshakes.org. Free.*

Performances are staged in the park and at other Bay Area locations.
  • **Opera in the Park**
*September. (415) 777-7120; www.chronicleevents.com. Free.*

Designed to make opera accessible to everyone, this event is a great way for reluctant listeners to give this art form a try.

• **Reggae in the Park**
*October. (415) 458-1988, fax (415) 383-0614; www.eventswestca.com $20-$25, 6-12 $10. No pets.*

This popular 2-day music festival aims to promote the culture of the Caribbean through reggae and world beat music.

• **Band Concourse**
*On Tea Garden Drive, across from Academy of Sciences, (415) 831-5500; www.goldengatepark band.org. Sun at 1; Apr-Oct only. Free.*

Formed in 1882, the Golden Gate Park Band is the oldest continuously operating municipal band in the U.S. Bring a picnic.

• **The Beach Chalet**
  See page 58.

• **Biking/Skating**
  On Sundays, part of John F. Kennedy Drive is closed to automobiles. Car traffic is replaced with bikers, skaters, and pedestrians. Skate and bike rentals are available at shops along Stanyan and Fulton streets.

• **Buffalo Paddock**
*At W end of Kennedy Drive, W of 36th Ave. across from Anglers Lodge.*

Foreign visitors seem particularly impressed with viewing this small herd of authentic buffalo.

• **California Academy of Sciences**
  See page 26.

### • Children's Playground
*On Bowling Green Drive, betw. King & Kennedy drives, E of California Academy of Sciences. Daily dawn-dusk.*

Constructed in 1887, this was the very first public playground in a U.S. park. Today it is equipped with creative modern play structures.

Located adjacent, an antique **Carrousel** *(415) 812-2725. F-Sun 10-4:30; daily in summer. $1.50, children 6+ 50¢.)* makes its rounds within a protective hippodrome enclosure. Built in 1914 by Herschel-Spillman, it has 62 beautifully painted hand-carved animals and its original Gebruder band organ.

### • Conservatory of Flowers
*On JFK Dr., (415) 666-7001; www.conservatoryof flowers.org. Tu-Sun 9-4:30. $5, 65+ & 12-17 $3, 5-11 $1.50; free 1st Tu of month.*

Built in Ireland in 1878 and modeled after the Palm House in London's Kew Gardens, this impressive example of Victorian architecture was shipped around Cape Horn in pieces and erected in Golden Gate Park in 1879. This tropical greenhouse consists of a central dome flanked by two wings and is the oldest remaining building in the park. It is thought to be the oldest conservatory in the U.S. as well as the only wooden conservatory in the U.S. and probably in the entire world. The conservatory's oldest and largest plant—a 35-foot-tall imperial philodendron from southeastern Brazil (Philodendron speciosum)—is located in the dome, where it has been displayed since 1901. Other noteworthy specimens include primitive

cycads (from the dinosaur era), a collection of 2,500 rare cool-growing orchids that exist almost nowhere else, and two ponds featuring giant Amazon water lilies that were displayed first in the U.S. here. Outside, giant flowerbeds are tilted at a 45-degree angle so that their floral messages can be seen from the street. Known as "carpet bedding," this old European gardening technique is costly and time-consuming and now almost extinct. Closed in 1995 due to severe storm damage, the conservatory reopened in 2003.

### • de Young Museum
See page 22.

### • Dutch Windmill
*In NW corner of park.*

Completed in 1903, this 75-foot-high windmill once pumped up well water. In February and March, the **Queen Wilhelmina Tulip Garden** bursts forth in riotous color with over 10,000 tulip bulbs.

### • Japanese Tea Garden and Teahouse
*Next to deYoung Museum, (415) 752-1171 . Daily 9-6:30, Mar-Sept; 8:30-6:30 or dusk, Oct-Feb. Garden: $3.50, 65+ & 6-12 $1.25. Tea: $2.95/person; no reservations; no cards.*

A stroll through this garden is pleasurable at any time of day, any time of year, and in almost any kind of weather. Visitors can climb up the steep arch of the "wishing bridge" (actually a drum bridge), make a wish, and drop a coin in the pond below. Steep steps lead to a miniature red pagoda, and an undulating dragon hedge is nearby. A spectacular display occurs annually during the last week of March, when the **cherry blossoms** are in bloom.

Everyone seems to enjoy stopping for refreshment at the inviting open-air teahouse, where tea and Asian cookies are served by waitresses clad in traditional Japanese kimonos. It is pleasant and relaxing to observe nature while leisurely sipping jasmine or green tea and munching on exotic cookies. An interesting note: Makoto Hagiwara, who designed the garden in 1893 for the Mid-Winter Exposition, is credited with introducing the fortune cookie to America here in 1914.

### • San Francisco Botanical Garden at Strybing Arboretum

*Entrance adjoins San Francisco County Fair Bldg., (415) 661-1316, fax (415) 661-7427; www.strybing.org. M-F 8-4:30, Sat-Sun 10-5; tour daily at 1:30, Sat-Sun also at 10:20. Free.*

Known for its magnolia and rhododendron collections, this lovely garden displays more than 7,000 plant species over its 55 acres. Many are unique to this climate, and most are labeled. Noteworthy among the 26 specialty gardens are the Japanese-style Moon-viewing Garden, the Arthur Menzies Garden of California Native Plants, the redwood forest, the small fragrance garden, the Biblical Garden, the New World Cloud Forest, and the Primitive Plant Garden.

Many garden events take place in the adjacent **San Francisco County Fair Building** ((415) 753-7090). The **Mother's Day Rose Show** allows the opportunity to see a splendid variety of climbing, miniature, and old garden roses. Cuttings perfect for presenting to Mom are for sale, with proceeds benefiting the San Francisco Rose Society. It is the largest such show in Northern California.

### • Shakespeare Garden

*Behind California Academy of Sciences.*

This formal, manicured garden is planted with the 150 flowers mentioned in William's plays. An attractive wrought-iron archway marks the entrance, where a brick pathway bordered by crabapple trees leads into the garden. Benches and grassy expanses invite lingering.

### • Stow Lake Boathouse

*(415) 752-0347. Daily 10-4; in summer to 5. Paddle & rowboats $13-$17/hr. No cards.*

A boat on Stow Lake, the largest of the park's 11 lakes, is both an unusual and memorable picnic spot. After pushing off in a rowboat, find a pleasant cove where there isn't much water movement and then get down to the business of eating a picnic meal. Be warned: When bread is tossed to the ducks and seagulls, they can fairly sink a boat with enthusiasm. Though the water is shallow and it isn't possible to get very far from shore, cushions in the boats double as life preservers. Life vests are also available upon request at no additional charge. Because boats are often wet inside, consider bringing along a blanket to sit on.

### • Walking Tours

*(415) 263-0991; www.sfparks.org. Free. Call (415) 750-5226 for a free schedule.*

All walks are led by volunteers from the San Francisco Parks Trust and require no reservations, and, except for the 45-minute Japanese Tea Garden tour, all last about 90 minutes.

• The **Japanese Garden Tour** covers the history and design of this serene landscape garden.

• The **East End Historical Walk** takes participants down the favorite paths of John McLaren and includes Conservatory Valley and the AIDS Memorial Grove.

• Participants on the **Strawberry Hill Tour** enjoy a spectacular view of the Golden Gate Bridge and San Francisco from atop the hill. They see Huntington Falls, explore the Pioneer Log Cabin, and visit the Redwood Memorial Grove and the Rose Garden.

• **Stroller Walks**, designed especially for parents of young children, cover various areas of the park.

## Mountain Lake Park

*Entrance at Lake St./Funston Ave., Richmond district.*

Well-hidden from the street, this delightful park has a lakeside path, a basketball court, tennis courts, a par course that begins at 9th Avenue, and a large, well-equipped playground off 12th Avenue. There are even ducks to feed.

It is interesting to note that spring-fed Mountain Lake supplied all of the city's water between 1852 and 1870.

## Playgrounds

### • Julius Kahn Playground
*End of Pacific St./Spruce St., Pacific Heights.*
Lots of wide-open space is found here.

### • North Beach Playground
*Columbus Ave./Greenwich St., North Beach*
This simple spot is where the late baseball legend Joe DiMaggio played in his youth. It is currently embroiled in controversy, as locals want to rename it in DiMaggio's honor while representatives of the ball player's estate deem it beneath his stature. If it is renamed, the city plans to do a $3.5 million upgrade. Either way, kids love it here.

## San Francisco Zoo
*Sloat Blvd./Great Highway, (415) 753-7080, fax (415) 681-2039; www.sfzoo.org. Daily 10-5. $10, 65+ & 12-17 $7, 3-11 $4; free 1st W of month; parking $5.*
Of special note are the ½-acre Gorilla World, which is one of the world's largest gorilla habitats; the 3-acre African Savanna habitat for giraffes, zebras, and antelope as well as a host of Africa bird species; and the Lipman Family Lemur Forest featuring species of this endangered primate. Also, the zoo's collection of extremely endangered snow leopards is one of the most successful breeding groups in the world, and the lions and tigers are particularly interesting to visit when they are fed each afternoon from 2 to 3 p.m.—except on Monday, when they fast.

A separate **Children's Zoo** *(Daily 11-4.)* has a petting area with sheep and goats. Its **Insect Zoo** is populated with the likes of 6- to 8-inch-long walking sticks and giant Madagascar hissing cockroaches, and it has a functioning honeybee hive. An adjacent butterfly garden features native plants labeled with the type of butterfly they attract. Kids also especially enjoy the large playground, a recently restored antique **carousel** *($2)* built in 1921 by the William Dentzel Carving Company, and the circa 1904 **Little Puffer** steam train *($2)*. The perfect souvenir is a plastic Storybox Key *($3)* that children can insert in boxes throughout the zoo to hear interesting information about the animals.

A popular **Valentine's Day Sex Tour**—the world's first in a zoo—is scheduled annually in February. Each year in September, members of the Zoological Society *($70/year/family)* are invited to **Night Tour**. Entertainment, demonstrations, behind-the-scenes tours, and admission are all free, and a picnic dinner is available for a small charge. Support the zoo and find out just what happens here after dark.

## Sutro Heights Park
*On 48th Ave., betw. Geary Blvd. & Anza St., outer Richmond district, (415) 556-8642.*
Formerly the estate of Adolph Sutro, this magnificent park has expansive views of the southern coastline. It is perfect for a picnic, but hold on to little kids, as drop-offs can be sudden and dangerous.

## SPECTATOR SPORTS

### Baseball

### • San Francisco Giants
*SBC Park, King St./3rd St., near China Basin, (415) 972-2000; www.sfgiants.com. Apr-Sept only. $11-$34. Tours: (415) 972-2400; www.sbcpark.com; $10, 55+ $8, under 13 $5.*
Located on the city's scenic waterfront, this new ballpark was designed to be a state-of-the-art old-fashioned ballpark. It features unobstructed views from every seat and plenty of

restrooms. A unique public promenade parallels the waterfront from right field to center field, and fans can watch the game through portholes in the fence there at no charge.

## Football

- **San Francisco 49ers**

*3Com Park, 8 mi. S of downtown, (415) 656-4900; www.49ers.com Aug-Dec only.*

## PERFORMING ARTS

Moving pictures got their start in 1878 when Leland Stanford placed a $20,000 bet. He hired photographer Eadweard Muybridge to prove that the four hooves of a running horse are all off the ground at the same time. The still photos were mounted on a carousel and spun so that the horse appeared to be moving. In 1880, Stanford won $20,000, and the first moving picture debuted at the exhibition hall of the San Francisco Art Association.

In preparation for a visit to San Francisco, or in remembrance of a trip past, the following **movies** are fun to watch. All were shot on location in San Francisco: *Birdman of Alcatraz* (1962; Burt Lancaster; NR), *The Birds* (1963; Rod Taylor, Jessica Tandy, Suzanne Pleshett; PG13), *Bullitt* (1968; Steve McQueen; NR), *The Conversation* (1974; Gene Hackman; PG), *Dark Passage* (1947; Humphrey Bogart, Lauren Bacall; NR), *Dirty Harry* (1971; Clint Eastwood; R), *D.O.A.* (1950; Edmond O'Brien; NR), *48 Hours* (1982; Nick Nolte, Eddie Murphy; R), *Foul Play* (1978; Goldie Hawn, Chevy Chase; PG), *The Graduate* (1967; Anne Bancroft, Dustin Hoffman, Katharine Ross; PG), *Greed* (1925; Erich Von Stroheim; NR), *Guess Who's Coming to Dinner?* (1967; Spencer Tracy, Sidney Poitier, Katherine Hepburn; NR), *Invasion of the Body Snatchers* (1978; Donald Sutherland, Leonard Nimoy; PG), *Jagged Edge* (1986; Glenn Close, Jeff Bridges; R), *The Maltese Falcon* (1941; Humphrey Bogart, Mary Astor; NR), *Mrs. Doubtfire* (1993; Robin Williams, Sally Field; PG13), *Pacific Heights* (1990; Melanie Griffith, Matthew Modine, Michael Keaton; R), *Pal Joey* (1957; Rita Hayworth, Frank Sinatra; NR), *Play It Again, Sam* (1972; Woody Allen; PG), *The Presidio* (1988; Sean Connery, Mark Harmon; R), *San Francisco* (1936; Clark Gable, Jeanette MacDonald; NR), *Sister Act* (1993;

Whoopi Goldberg; PG), *Star Trek IV—The Voyage Home* (1986; Leonard Nimoy, William Shatner; PG), *The Towering Inferno* (1974; Steve McQueen, Faye Dunaway, William Holden; PG), *True Believer* (1989; James Woods, Robert Downey Jr.; R), *Vertigo* (1958; James Stewart, Kim Novak; PG), *A View to a Kill* (1985; Roger Moore, Grace Jones; PG), *What's Up, Doc?* (1972; Barbra Streisand, Ryan O'Neal; G), *Woman in Red* (1984; Gene Wilder; PG-13).

## American Conservatory Theatre (A.C.T.)

*405 Geary St., in Geary Theater, Union Square, (415) 749-2ACT; www.act-sfbay.org. Schedule varies. $11-$61; the evening after openings is Pay What You Wish night.*

Nationally recognized for its groundbreaking productions of classical and contemporary works, this company's conservatory was the first U.S. training program not affiliated with a college or university. Danny Glover, Annette Bening, Denzel Washington, Benjamin Bratt, and Winona Ryder are among the distinguished former students. See also page 12.

## Beach Blanket Babylon

*678 Green St./Powell St., in Club Fugazi, North Beach, (415) 421-4222, fax (415) 421-4817; www.beachblanketbabylon.com. W-Thur at 8, F-Sat at 7 & 10, Sun at 3 & 7. $25-$75.*

Begun back in 1974 as an underground production, this fast-moving and humorous musical revue is known for its colorful, creative costumes and huge headdresses. It is the longest running musical revue in the nation. The show changes periodically, adding new surprises. Family-friendly Sunday matinees are the only performances open to minors (under age 21), and no alcohol is served then. Parents should keep in mind that there is no profanity or violence, but sexual puns are abundant. Performances sell out regularly, so reserve tickets early and arrive when the doors open to choose a table.

### Biscuits & Blues
*401 Mason St./Geary St., Union Square, (415) 292-BLUE, fax (415) 292-4701; www.biscuitandblue. citysearch.com. Shows daily. Cover $5-$17.50. Reservations advised.*

Spicy Southern cooking—including fried chicken and the famous namesake biscuits—is dished up along with hefty portions of the blues in this intimate subterranean venue. Sundays bring on a family-friendly gospel music show and a dinner special with all the fixins.

### Castro Theatre
*429 Castro St./Market St., Castro district, (415) 621-6120; www.castrotheatre.com. $5.50-$8.50.*

Considered by many to be the best place in the city to see a movie, this landmark 1922 movie palace seats 1,420 people. It presents an eclectic program of classic and new films, and a Wurlitzer organ plays "San Francisco" every night as the film is about to begin.

### Chanticleer
*(415) 252-8589, fax (415) 252-7941; www.chanticleer.org. $25-$42.*

This internationally acclaimed, locally based 12-man a cappella ensemble performs four Bay Area concert sets each year in between touring and recording. Performances in local churches during the Christmas holidays are positively ethereal.

### Cobb's Comedy Club
*915 Columbus/Lombard St., North Beach, (415) 928-4320; www.cobbscomedy.com. Sun-Thur at 8, F-Sat at 8 & 10:15. Cover $7-$30 + 2-drink min. Minors 16 & 17 welcome with parent or legal guardian. Validated*

*parking nearby.*

In this new location since 2003, this popular club features live stand-up. A full bar and dinner menu are available. Dining in guarantees best seating, but all seating is good. The pre-show dinner menu includes delicious, well-spiced entrees such as achiote-rubbed chicken or grilled halibut. A cafe menu served during the show includes popcorn shrimp and calamari, crispy Dungeness crab rolls, a focaccia burger, and an ice cream sundae topped with housemade butterscotch and fudge. It is interesting to know that this building has been a nightclub since it went up in 1923, and USO shows here wowed World War II troops with big band music.

### Donald Pippin's Pocket Opera
*At various Bay Area venues, (415) 972-8930, fax (415) 348-0931; www.pocketopera.org. $27-$32, under 18 $15.*

Bright and witty, this talented troupe skillfully performs sometimes dramatic, sometimes hilarious, but always enjoyable opera that is easy to understand. One of these performances is a great introduction to opera for anyone. Though most shows are appropriate for children, some are produced especially for them.

### Empire Plush Room
*940 Sutter St., in the York Hotel, Nob Hill, (415) 885-2800; www.plushroom.com. Schedule varies. Cover varies, + 2-drink min.*

The impressive line-up of jazz performers presented at this cabaret has included Michael Feinstein and Eartha Kitt. The room was a speakeasy in the 1920s, when it was known as the Empire Hotel, and customers would enter via a still-existing subterranean entrance in a Victorian across the street.

### Magic Theatre
*Bldg. D, in Fort Mason Center, (415) 441-8822; www.magictheatre.org.*

This is the only major Bay Area theatre company dedicated solely to producing new plays. Founded in 1967 at the legendary, long-gone Steppenwolf Bar in Berkeley, it has presented more than 200 premieres by some of the greatest writers of our time, including the 2001 world premiere of Sam Shepard's *The Late Henry Moss*—starring Sean Penn, Nick Nolte,

Woody Harrelson, and Cheech Marin—and the 2004 world premiere of David Mamet's *Dr. Faustus.*

## Post Street Theatre
See page 44.

## San Francisco Ballet
*War Memorial Opera House, 301 Van Ness Ave./Grove St., Civic Center, (415) 865-2000; wwww.sfballet.org. Feb-May. $8-$132.*

This is the country's oldest ballet company. See also page 13.

## San Francisco Mime Troupe
*At neighborhood parks throughout Bay Area, (415) 285-1717, fax (415) 285-1290; www.sfmt.org. July 4-Aug. Free.*

Since 1964, this Tony Award-winning troupe has presented sometimes caustic, always entertaining commentary on current events, political leaders, and the state of our world. The Troupe's original productions combine music, satire, and comedy. In spite of the description, children and families attend in large numbers and generally enjoy the spectacle.

## San Francisco Opera
*War Memorial Opera House, 301 Van Ness Ave./Grove St., Civic Center, (415) 864-3330; www.sfopera.org. Sept-Jan, June-July. $10-$195.*

This is the nation's second-oldest opera company (the first being the Met in NYC).

## San Francisco Symphony
*Davies Symphony Hall, 201 Van Ness Ave./Grove St., Civic Center, (415) 864-6000; www.sfsymphony.org. $15-$100.*

In addition to classic programs, the symphony presents special **Family Concerts** *(www.sfskids.com)* designed to introduce children to classical music.

## Shelton Theater
*533 Sutter St./Powell St., Union Square, (415) 522-8900; www.comedyonthesquare.com. Schedule varies. $15.*

Offbeat small productions are presented in this tiny subterranean theater.

## Teatro ZinZanni: Love, Chaos & Dinner
*At Pier 29, The Embarcadero/Battery, (415) 438-2668;* *www.teatrozinzanni.org. W-Sun. $99-$125/person + drinks & tip. Reservations essential.*

Had one too many microwaved dinners downed in front of *Seinfeld* reruns? (Not that there's anything *wrong* with that.) Then it's definitely time for a night out at this circus for adults. Sequins and feather boas are the dress of choice when entering the gorgeous antique, art nouveau-style mirrored spiegeltent from Belgium containing the wonderment that is Teatro ZinZanni. In between five preset courses —delivered to tables with great fanfare by both performers and waitstaff—the talented international cast entertains with a mixture of European cabaret, circus acts, comedy, and theatrical antics. Though not an inexpensive ticket, it is well worth the splurge for a break from the usual or to celebrate a special occasion. Everyone leaves with a smile.

## TIX Bay Area/Half-Price Tickets
*On Powell Street, betw. Geary St./Post St., Union Square, (415) 433-7827; www.theatrebayarea.org. Tu-Thur 11-6, F-Sat 11-7, Sun 11-3.*

Day-of-performance half-price tickets are available for many music, dance, and theater events. Sunday and Monday events are available on Saturday. Only cash and traveler's checks are accepted. Full-price tickets for performances are also available and can be purchased with a credit card. TIX by Mail permits purchasing half-price tickets through a quarterly catalog. For a copy, visit the website or write: TIX by Mail, 870 Market Street #375, San Francisco, CA 94102.

## Young Performers Theatre
*Fort Mason, Bldg. C, Laguna St./Marina Blvd., (415) 346-5550, fax (415) 346-4991; www.ypt.org. Sat at 1, Sun at 1 & 3:30. $9, under 13 $6.*

A combination of professional adult performers and young actors in training, this company uses imaginative stage settings and costumes. The fast-moving productions are usually short as well, making them a good introduction to theater for children ages 4 through 10. Past productions have included *Charlie and the Chocolate Factory, Wind in the Willows*, and *The Secret Garden.*

## ENTERTAINMENT COMPLEXES

### Metreon—A Sony Entertainment Center
101 4th St./Mission St., South of Market, (415) 369-6000; www.metreon.com. Daily 10-10; movies later.

Built by Sony with a futuristic-style interior, this 4-story urban entertainment complex is unique. No one has ever done anything like it before. Everything is related to entertainment and fun, including a massive play area for young children on the fourth floor based on Maurice Sendak's popular children's book *Where the Wild Things Are (Schedule varies.)*, a 15-screen movie theater, an IMAX theater that is the largest in North America and that also shows 3-D specials and screens feature films, and the Portal One gaming arcade with virtual bowling. Shops include **Sony Style**, which showcases the latest in electronics, and **PlayStation**, where every game in this line is available for play before purchase. **Jillians**—a sports bar with a 50-foot-long video wall—and an assortment of casual restaurant venues keep visitors from starving.

### Yerba Buena Gardens
Mission St./4th St., South of Market, (415) 522-9860.

Situated atop the Moscone Convention Center, this new entertainment complex holds a variety of attractions—all designed for the education and recreation of young people. It also features an outdoor stage, two cafes, a butterfly garden, a redwood grove, public sculptures, a waterfall, and a multi-language memorial to Dr. Martin Luther King, Jr. Expansive lawns, fountains, a maze and play circle, and robotic sculpture invite open-air relaxation.

• **Ice Skating and Bowling Centers**
750 Folsom St., (415) 777-3727; www.skatebowl.com. Schedules vary. Ice Skating: $7, 55+ & under 13 $5.50, skate rental $3. Bowling: $3.50-$5/game, shoe rental $3.

• **Yerba Buena Center for the Arts**
701 Mission St./3rd St., South of Market, (415) 978-ARTS, fax (415) 978-9635; www.yerbabuenaarts.org. Gallery: Tu-Sun 11-5, 1st Thur 11-8. $6, 65+ & students $3; free 1st Tu of month.

The center presents art shows and live entertainment emphasizing the diverse artists and communities of the region.

• **Zeum**
221 4th St./Howard St., (415) 777-2800, fax (415) 777-2851; www.zeum.org. W-Sun 11-5; also Tu in summer. $7, seniors $6, 4-18 $5; carousel $2.

The entire family can explore creativity and innovation through the arts and media at this high tech museum. Creating videos, viewing performances in a state-of-the-art theater, and learning about animation as art are all part of the program.

A beautifully restored, historical 1906 Looff **carousel** at the entrance formerly made rounds at the defunct Playland-at-the-Beach. It boasts 65 heavily jeweled, hand-carved animals (including camels, rams, giraffes, and a rare gray horse whose mouth is carved with closed lips) and now twirls inside a glass pavilion.

## SHOPPING

### The Cannery at Del Monte Square
Bounded by Beach St./Leavenworth St./Hyde St./Jefferson St., Fisherman's Wharf, (415) 771-3112, fax (415) 771-2424; www.thecannery.com. Shops open M-Sat at 10, Sun at 11; closing times vary.

This charming red brick shopping complex, constructed in 1907, was once the world's largest fruit and vegetable cannery. It now holds many unique shops (no chains here!), and free entertainment by street performers is scheduled daily under century-old olive trees in an inviting courtyard.

• **Basic Brown Bear Factory**
(888) 900-BEAR, (800) 554-1910, (415) 409-2806, fax (415) 409-2807; www.basicbrownbear.com. Daily 10-5; free tour on the hour.

Among the handmade bears here are everything from a basic brown to a quite elaborate cream-colored Beary Godmother with pink satin wings and a magic wand. Prices are close to wholesale, and customers can stuff their own bear using a replica of a World War II-era machine that pumped up life jackets. This is the last stuffed animal factory still manufacturing within the U.S., and the bears are not sold in any other stores.

### Chestnut Street
Betw. Fillmore St. & Scott St., Marina district.

This is a popular neighborhood shopping area.

## Clement Street

*Betw. Anza St. & 24th St., Richmond district.*

This popular neighborhood shopping street is heavily populated with Asian restaurants, produce markets, and bakeries.

## Cost Plus World Market

*2552 Taylor St./North Point St., Fisherman's Wharf, (415) 928-6200, (800) COST-PLUS; www.costplusworldmarket.com. M-Sat 9-9, Sun 10-8.*

The original store in a chain that now numbers 212, this gigantic importer has long been a favorite shopping stop for visitors. Back in the '60s, it was where everyone stocked up on "hippie" supplies: batik bedspreads, incense, candles. Current imports from around the world include inexpensive jewelry, kitchenware, furniture, baskets, and toys.

## Embarcadero Center

*Bounded by Battery St./Sacramento St./Drumm St./Clay St., (800) 733-6318, (415) 772-0700, fax (415) 489-6224; www.embarcaderocenter.com. Shops open M-F 10-7, Sat 10-6, Sun 12-5; restaurants open later. Validated parking: 4 hrs. free M-F after 5pm, Sat-Sun after 10am.*

This enormous seven-block complex of high-rise buildings holds more than 120 shops and restaurants on its lower floors, countless offices on the upper floors, and the huge Hyatt Regency hotel. A movie theater complex keeps things busy late into the night. **Justin Herman Plaza** is home to the **Vaillancourt Fountain**, nicknamed "#10 on the Richter" and described by an art critic as "something deposited by a dog with square intestines." A brochure mapping out a self-guided Sculpture Tour to the center's treasure-trove of art is available.

## Ghirardelli Square

*900 North Point St./Larkin St., Fisherman's Wharf, (415) 775-5500, fax (415) 775-0912; www.ghirardellisq.com. Shop hours vary; usually daily 10-6; to 9 in summer.*

Built in 1900 as a chocolate factory and converted into a festive marketplace in 1964, this beautiful brick complex was the nation's first quaint, upscale shopping center. Now it is a National Historic Landmark and home to an assortment of shops and restaurants. Street performers entertain on the courtyard stage each weekend (daily in summer). Don't miss

indulging at the **Ghirardelli Chocolate Manufactory** (see page 69). Each September, a **Chocolate Festival** caters to those loco for cocoa.

## Haight-Ashbury

*Haight Street betw. Stanyan St. & Fillmore St.; www.haight-ashbury.com.*

Though Bill Graham Presents has trademarked the term "Summer of Love" and not many hippy-dippy flower children are seen here any more, strolling along Haight Street is still like groovy, man. Street people, teeny boppers, and used clothing stores abound, as do unusual boutiques, galleries, restaurants, and nightclubs. It is *the* place to get pierced and buy tie-dye. What makes it clear the times have changed, though, is that now a Gap is ensconced on the famous corner. For more information, see page 20.

## Japan Center

*Three square blocks bounded by Post St., Geary St., Laguna St., & Fillmore St., (415) 922-6776; www.sfjapantown.citysearch.com. Most shops open daily 10-5, restaurants to 9. Some businesses validate for center's garages.*

This 5-acre cultural center houses shops, restaurants, art galleries, traditional Japanese baths, a Japanese-style market, a movie theater complex, and a hotel. It is designed like an indoor mall, allowing shoppers to walk from one building to another without going outside and crossing streets. A five-tiered, 100-foot-tall Peace Pagoda that was a gift from Japan is illuminated at night, and an eternal flame, brought from the Sumiyoshi Shrine in Osaka, burns above a reflecting pool. Restaurants scattered throughout the complex open exotic avenues of food exploration.

The **Nihonmachi Street Fair** *((415) 771-9861; www.nihonmachistreetfair.org. Free.)* is held on the first weekend in August. In addition to a food bazaar, it features contemporary ethnic bands and performing arts. See also page 8.

## Pier 39

*Beach St./The Embarcadero, Fisherman's Wharf, (415) 705-5500, fax (415) 981-8808; www.pier39.com. Most shops open daily 10:30-8. Parking lot across street; $6/hr., less with validation.*

This popular spot offers myriad diversions

in addition to more than 110 shops and 11 restaurants. Among the boutiques is one that specializes in puppets, another in chocolate, and another in charms, and the **California Welcome Center** *(415) 956-3493, fax (415) 956-0209; www.visitcwc.com.)* dispenses free visitor information. Most of the full-service restaurants have seafood menus, but Italian and Mediterranean cuisines are also represented. Restaurant menu boards are posted in various spots around the pier, giving visitors a chance to analyze offerings and prices. Fast food includes fish & chips, hamburgers, pizza, hot pretzels, and more.

Street performers entertain daily. The **Riptide Arcade** is packed with cutting-edge video games and located at the bay end next to a contemporary two-tiered **carousel** *(Sun-Thur 10-9, Fri-Sat 10-10. $2.)* that is hand-painted with famous San Francisco landmarks and trimmed with 1800 lights. Also here is the **Turbo Ride** *((415) 392-TURBO. $6, under 3 free.)*—a simulated thrill ride that synchronizes hydraulically powered seats to the action on a giant movie screen. **Sea lions** have taken up permanent residence on the west side of the pier and are seen there basking, barking, and belching on their floating docks. **Aquarium of the Bay** *((415) 623-5300, tickets (888) SEA-DIVE; www.aquariumofthebay.com. Daily 9-8. $12.95, 65+ & 3-11 $6.50.)* uses moving sidewalks to transport visitors through transparent acrylic tunnels for a diver's-eye view of the fishes, sharks, and other sea life residing in San Francisco Bay.

Each year in February, the **Tulipmania Festival** displays approximately 39,000 tulips throughout the pier. These harbingers of spring are a lot of work to grow here, because in this climate fresh bulbs must be planted each year. Free tours are scheduled.

## Union Square and Surrounds

World-class shopping is found on the streets surrounding this large grassy square, which was a sand dune before it opened in 1847.

### • Britex Fabrics
*At 117 Post St./Grant St. while historic 146 Geary St./Stockton St. store undergoes a seismic retrofit, (415) 392-2910, fax (415) 392-3906; www.britex fabrics.com. M-Sat 9:30-6, Thur-F to 7.*

Even people who can't thread a needle enjoy browsing the four floors of magnificent fabrics and notions in this unique San Francisco store. It is the largest fabric store in the West.

### • Crocker Galleria
*50 Post St./Kearny St., (415) 393-1505, fax (415) 392-5429; www.shopatgalleria.com. M-F 10-6, Sat 10-5.*

This "covered street" links Post and Sutter streets. Sixty stores and two restaurants on three floors are situated under its spectacular arched skylight. The design was influenced by Milan's famous Galleria Vittorio Emmanuelle.

### • Department stores include Macy's *(233 Geary St., (415) 397-3333; www.macys.com.)*, Neiman Marcus *(150 Stockton St., (415) 362-3900; www.neimanmarcus.com.)*, and Saks Fifth Avenue *(384 Post St., (415) 986-4300; www.saksfifthavenue.com.)*. All have restaurants.

### • Gump's
*135 Post St./Kearny St., (800) 766-7628, (415) 982-1616; www.gumps.com. M-Sat 10-6, Sun 12-5.*

Opened in 1861, this is the oldest store in San Francisco. Known for stocking fine oriental imports, its legendary Jade Room holds one of the finest jade collections in the world. It carries the city's largest selection of fine china and crystal and has an eye-popping collection of American crafts.

### • Maiden Lane
*Off Stockton St., between Post St. & Geary St.*

Closed to cars during business hours, this charming alley holds many interesting shops. One not to miss is the **Xanadu Gallery** at #140 *((415) 392-9999, fax (415) 984-5856; www.xanadugallery.us.)*, which specializes in art and antiquities from around the world. When this small, circular space was designed by Frank Lloyd Wright in 1948 to display fine china and silver, it was considered radical because it had no display window. A ramp spirals up to the mezzanine along curving walls, similar to the design of New York's Guggenheim Museum.

### • San Francisco Shopping Centre
*865 Market St., (415) 512-6776, fax (415) 512-6770; www.westfield.com. M-Sat 9:30-8, Sun 11-6.*

Opened in 1988, this swanky 9-story indoor shopping complex is one of the few vertical malls in the U.S. A must-see 4-story spiral escalator—the only one in the U.S.—wends its way up through a sun-lit atrium into the word's largest **Nordstrom** *((415) 243-8500;*

www.nordstrom.com.). A subterranean food court provides refreshment, and free balloons and "kiddie cruiser" strollers are available at the information center.

### • Shreve & Co.

*200 Post St./Grant St., (415) 421-2600; www.shreve.com. M-Sat 10-6, Sun 12-5.*

Opened in 1852, just 4 years after gold was discovered in California, this esteemed jewelry shop is one of San Francisco's oldest stores.

## Union Street

*Betw. Gough St. & Divisadero St., Pacific Heights, (415) 441-7055; www.unionstreet.com.*

Many of the upscale shops and restaurants that fill this trendy area are inside old Victorian and Edwardian buildings. Flower stands add a seasonal burst of color on the four blocks running between Fillmore and Octavia streets—which has the heaviest concentration of shops—but boutiques continue on in both directions and down side streets. This area is referred to as Cow Hollow, in reference to the fact that it was once the city's dairy community.

For the annual **Union Street Arts Festival** *(June. (800) 310-6563, fax (415) 456-6436; www.unionstreetfestival.com. Free.),* the street is closed off from Gough to Steiner. It begins with a Saturday morning Waiter Race in which competing servers must open a bottle of wine, pour two glasses, and carry them on their tray intact to the top of Green Street and back again. Music, food, and crafts booths round out the fun.

## Upper Fillmore Street

*Betw. Jackson St. & Ellis St., Pacific Heights, (415) 775-8366; www.fillmorestreetsf.com.*

This popular neighborhood shopping street is lined with trendy boutiques, restaurants, and coffeehouses. Don't miss the outpost for NYC's legendary **Kiel's** (#2360) for trendy lotions and potions, and **Mrs. Dewson's Hats** (#2050), where the former mayor shops. For the most mind-boggling selection of whiskeys and champagnes in town, visit **D & M Wine and Liquor Co.** (#2200).

## MISCELLANEOUS

### Diablo Grande Wine Gallery

*669 Mission St./3rd St., (415) 543-4343, fax (415)*

*543-4308; www.diablogrande.com. Tasting Tu-Sun 11-6.*

In addition to wine tasting, food-and-wine pairings and after-work wine hours are sometimes scheduled.

## — WHERE TO STAY —

According to a 2003 survey, the average hotel room in San Francisco costs $138.31 per night.

The San Francisco Convention & Visitors Bureau has a reservations service in partnership with over 220 participating hotels. For assistance, call (888) STAY-N-SF or (415) 391-2000, or visit their website at www.sfvisitor.org.

## UNION SQUARE

This is a choice area to stay in, especially if traveling *without* a car. (Hotels listed here charge between $24 and $50 per day for parking.) All of these hotels are within a few blocks of downtown, the theater district, and the cable car line. Many are quaint establishments that provide an European-style small hotel experience.

### Canterbury Hotel

*750 Sutter St./Taylor St., 3 blks. from Union Square, (800) 227-4788, (415) 474-6464, fax (415) 474-0831; www.canterbury-hotel.com. 10 stories; 255 rooms; $-$$. Children under 18 free. Fitness room. Restaurant; room service. Valet parking $28.*

Built in 1928, this well-priced hotel features comfortable, cozy guest rooms decorated in shades of persimmon, butter yellow, and sage green. A 20-foot "Canterbury Tales" mural painted for the hotel by Jo Mora in 1934 decorates the front desk, and a rooftop sundeck is among the guest amenities.

Set up in a former garden greenhouse, the wonderful glass-enclosed dining room of **Lehr's Greenhouse** features tall palms and 25-foot-high ceilings and is open daily for breakfast. The **Cigar and Cognac Lounge** is a relaxing place in the evening and features a large selection of cigars and after-dinner drinks.

### Cartwright Hotel

*524 Sutter St./Powell St., 1 blk. from Union Square, (800) 919-9779, (415) 421-2865, fax (415) 398-6345; www.cartwrighthotel.com. 8 stories; 114 rooms; $$. Afternoon & evening snack, continental breakfast. Pets ok. Self-parking $25, valet $35.*

Built in 1914 for the Panama-Pacific Exposition, this hotel is conveniently located on a fashionable shopping street. Antique-furnished rooms accented with fresh flowers and floral wallpaper add to the cozy, European ambiance. Afternoon cookies and an evening wine reception are complimentary.

## Clift Hotel

*495 Geary St./Taylor St., 2 blks. from Union Square, (800) 65-CLIFT, (415) 775-4700, fax (415) 441-4621; www.clifthotel.com. 17 stories; 329 rooms; $$$-$$$+. Fitness room. 2 restaurants; room service. Pets ok. Valet parking $40.*

Though the refined elegance of the old Clift is missed, it's hard not to embrace the ultra-cool updated redo of this historic luxury hotel dating from 1915. (It has been described as "like Helen Hayes has turned into Madonna.") It belongs high on any "must see" list, warranting at least a stop in the chic lobby for a drink and to peek under the oversized Alice-in-Wonderland-when-she-was-small chair. Hefty rates put it on the list of the world's rich and famous: Mick Jagger, Madonna, and former President Jimmy Carter have all stayed here. Service is high priority for the staff, and everyone gets the royal treatment—celebrity or not. Even kids. A family plan includes two connecting rooms, and the desk loans toys for toddlers, magazines for teens, and children's books, board games, Nintendo games, and movies. The concierge has loaner strollers and can help plan family sightseeing trips. At bedtime, snacks such as cookies and milk or popcorn and soda are available from room service. Pets placed on the VIP (Very Important Pet) list receive a basket of treats and appropriate sleeping pillows and eating bowls upon arrival.

**The Redwood Room,** a classic art deco cocktail lounge, was built from a single 2,000-year-old giant redwood tree and maintains its original 1933 redwood panels. It is a great spot to wait for seating in the hot, hot **Asia De Cuba** *((415) 929-2300, fax (415) 929-2377. B-L-D Tu-Sat; $$$. Reservations advised.).* Men all in black and women in sexy open-backed heels are right in style at this chic spot. The sumptuous dining room has a high, high ceiling and walls draped in merlot velvet. Perfect starters are a fancy cocktail—perhaps a Key Lime Tartini (though it has a nasty mid-night sting)—and either a spicy lobster shooter with crisp jicama slaw or a platter of lobster potstickers. Sesame-crusted scallops and Cuban spiced chicken are winners among the entrees. And though desserts have reached a new pricing high here, who can resist the Bay of Pigs—their version of a banana split—or the Suspiros Calientes, consisting of star anise/chocolate-covered fortune cookie ice cream with sticky buns and toffee sauce and described by the chef as "like giving your lover a kiss on the neck"?

## Donatello Hotel

*501 Post St./Mason St., 1 blk. from Union Square, (800) 227-3184, (415) 441-7100, fax (415) 885-8891; www.the-donatello.com. 15 stories; 94 rooms; $$-$$$. Children under 18 free. Hot tub; 2 saunas; fitness room. Restaurant; room service. Valet parking $28.*

Named after the Italian Renaissance sculptor, this European-style luxury hotel has the largest standard guest rooms in town. More than 300 pieces of original art decorate the hotel, and the lobby features 18th- and 19th-century antiques, imported Venetian chandeliers, and Italian marble quarried from the same site where Michelangelo selected the marble for his statue of David. The 15th-floor Penthouse Club Lounge has a wood-burning fireplace and a wraparound terrace with sweeping city views; it is stocked with snacks and reading material and is available at no charge to guests.

## Grand Hyatt San Francisco

*345 Stockton St./Post St., on Union Square, (800) 233-1234, (415) 398-1234, fax (415) 391-1780; http://grandsanfrancisco.hyatt.com. 36 stories; 685 rooms; $$$-$$$+. Children under 18 free. Fitness room. Restaurant; room service. Valet parking $39.*

In a prime location, this hotel is well known locally for its Ruth Asawa-designed bronze fountain depicting scenes of San Francisco. Room amenities include two phones and a TV in the bathroom. **Grandviews** restaurant is on the 36th floor, and the flagship **Levi Strauss Store** operates on the ground level.

## Handlery Union Square Hotel

*351 Geary St./Powell St., 1/2 blk. from Union Square, (800) 843-4343, (415) 781-7800, fax (415) 781-0269; www.handlery.com. 8 stories; 377 rooms; $$-$$$. Children under 16 free. Heated pool; sauna. Restaurant; room service. No pets. Valet parking $31.*

This family-owned and -operated hotel dates from 1908. Rooms are available in both a historical section and in a more contemporary club section, and all are equipped with comfortable modern amenities. The courtyard pool is a rare find downtown—only five hotels in the entire city have an outdoor pool—and permits sunbathing to the sounds of nearby cable cars. A plethora of packages add to the already good value.

The clubby, comfortable **Daily Grill** *(347 Geary St., (415) 616-5000, fax (415) 616-5005; www.dailygrill.com. B-L-D daily; $$. Highchairs, boosters, booths, child menu.)* is modeled after the great grills of the 1930s and '40s. It operates off the lobby and has a full bar.

## Hilton San Francisco

*333 O'Farrell St./Mason St., 2 blks. from Union Square, (800) HILTONS, (415) 771-1400, fax (415) 771-6807; www.hilton.com. 46 stories; 1,907 rooms; $$. Children under 17 free. Heated pool; hot tub; health spa; fitness room. 5 restaurants; room service. No pets. Self-parking $33, valet $38.*

Occupying a full block and incorporating three buildings, this is the largest hotel on the West Coast. It features a dramatic sunken marble lobby.

## Hotel Diva

*440 Geary St./Mason St., 2 blks. from Union Square, (800) 553-1900, (415) 885-0200, fax (415) 346-6613; www.hoteldiva.com. 7 stories; 111 rooms; $$. Children under 12 free. Fitness room. Restaurant; room service. Pets ok. Valet parking $30.*

Built in 1913, this hotel features cutting-edge contemporary design. The trip begins with the exterior window in the lobby, designed to resemble a frozen layer of glass, and with a Sidewalk of Fame out front bearing the hand imprints of famous divas, including Lily Tomlin, Angelica Huston, and Carol Channing. Movies and music videos roll continuously on four screens above the reception desk, and the elevator's cobalt blue-leather padding matches the carpeting. Updated to resemble a 1920s ocean liner, its rooms feature beds with sculptured steel headboards and sumptuous linens, buffed steel and maple wood furniture, cobalt blue carpeting, and black granite bathrooms. The two-room suites each have a wall bed in the living area (the Murphy Bed Company was founded in

San Francisco in 1900) and are especially comfortable and well priced for families.

## Hotel Monaco San Francisco

*501 Geary St./Taylor St., 2 blks. from Union Square, (866) 622-5284, (415) 292-0100, fax (415) 292-0111; www.monaco-sf.com. 7 stories; 201 rooms; $$-$$$+. Children under 18 free. Hot tub; sauna; steam room; health spa; fitness room. Afternoon & evening snack; restaurant; room service. Pets ok. Valet parking $35, self-parking less.*

Built in 1910, this landmark American beaux arts building is completely renovated. The inviting lobby has high, high ceilings with hand-painted domes, as well as an impressive 2-story French inglenook fireplace and a grand staircase with the original bronze filigree railing and marble steps—both remains from the hotel's prior incarnation as the Bellevue Hotel. Each sumptuously decorated room features a canopy bed, and guests can borrow a companion goldfish during their stay. The magnificent **Grand Cafe** (see page 70) operates within the hotel's restored turn-of-the-century ballroom.

## Hotel Nikko San Francisco

*222 Mason St./O'Farrell St., 2 blks. from Union Square, (800) NIKKO-US, (415) 394-1111, fax (415) 394-1106; www.hotelnikkosf.com. 25 stories; 554 rooms; $$$-$$$+. Children under 18 free. Indoor heated pool; hot tub; sauna; fitness room. Restaurant; room service. Valet parking $39-$43.*

Featuring clean architectural lines and a slick, marble-rich decor, this luxury hotel has San Francisco's only atrium-style, glass-enclosed rooftop lap pool. The fitness center is equipped with a traditional kamaburo dry sauna and deep Japanese soaking tub. Rooms are elegantly contemporary.

Since the hotel caters to a large Japanese business clientele, breakfast in elegant **Anzu** *(2nd fl., (415) 394-1100; www.restaurant anzu.com. B-L M-Sat, D daily, SunBr; $$-$$$. Reservations advised. Valet parking validated.)* features both American and Japanese fare. Among the wonders the chef whips up for lunch and dinner are a large variety of sushi and sashimi, a perfect petite prime filet with Maui onion-Cabernet jus, a to-die-for side dish of wild mushroom bread pudding, and a whimsical yet luscious banana-tempura split with almond brittle and honey caramel sauce—all served on exquisite Japanese-style stoneware.

## Hotel Rex

*562 Sutter St./Powell St., 2 blks. from Union Square, (800) 433-4434, (415) 433-4434, fax (415) 433-3695; www.thehotelrex.com. 7 stories; 94 rooms; $$-$$$. Evening wine; restaurant; room service. No smoking; no pets. Valet parking $30.*

Aspiring to become the Algonquin Hotel of the West Coast and designed as a focal point for the arts, this theme hotel has a clubby, writer-friendly ambiance. Sketches of Martha Graham in the '30s hang in a lobby furnished with period pieces, and literary events are scheduled regularly. Appetizers and drinks are served each evening in the wood-paneled **Lobby Bar.**

## Hotel Triton

*342 Grant Ave./Bush St., 3 blks. from Union Square, (800) 433-6611, (415) 394-0500, fax (415) 394-0555; www.hotel-tritonsf.com. 7 stories; 140 rooms; $$. Children free. Fitness room. Afternoon snack, evening wine; restaurant; room service. Pets ok. Valet parking $33.*

Situated across the street from the ornate dragon-gate entrance to Chinatown and in the heart of the "French Quarter," this playfully decorated hotel is sophisticated, casual, amusing, and chic all at the same time. Original art adorns public areas and guest room walls, much of it painted by local artist Chris Kidd, and bathrooms are positively slick. The Carlos Santana Suite sports hand-painted angels on the ceiling plus concert posters and photos of the musician on the walls, and it is stocked with meditation candles, incense, and a prayer pillow. Suites honoring Jerry Garcia and whale-artist Wyland are also available, and another very special suite has an in-room hot tub. Guests who miss their pets can borrow a goldfish, and sessions with a psychic can be arranged. A must-have souvenir rubber ducky inscribed with the hotel logo is for sale in the room honor bar. Casual **Cafe de la Presse** (see page 61) is located adjacent to the hotel.

## Hotel Union Square

*114 Powell St./Ellis St., 1 blk. from Union Square, (800) 553-1900, (415) 397-3000, fax (415) 399-1874; www.hotelunionsquare.com. 6 stories; 131 rooms; $$.*

*Children under 12 free. Valet parking $29.*

Built in 1913 for the Pan American Exposition, this comfortable hotel is decorated in a tailored contemporary style and situated just steps from the cable car turnaround. It is where Dashiell Hammett wrote *The Maltese Falcon.* Special features include a massive Egyptian mosaic mural in the lobby and a hand-carved wooden mermaid that once graced the bow of a ship on the sixth-floor landing.

## The Inn at Union Square

*440 Post St./Powell St., 1/2 blk. from Union Square, (800) 288-4346, (415) 397-3510, fax (415) 989-0529; www.unionsquare.com. 7 stories; 30 rooms; $$-$$$. Afternoon tea, evening snack, continental breakfast. No smoking. Valet parking $28-$40.*

This small, narrow, European-style hotel pampers guests with terry cloth robes, down pillows, evening turndown, complimentary overnight shoeshines, and a morning newspaper at the door. One suite is available with a private sauna.

## Kensington Park Hotel

*450 Post St./Powell St., 2 blks. from Union Square, (800) 553-1900, (415) 788-6400, (415) 399-9484; www.kensingtonparkhotel.com. 12 stories; 89 rooms; $$-$$$. Children under 12 free. Afternoon snack; restaurant. Fitness room. No pets. Valet parking $30.*

Built in a Gothic style of architecture, this circa 1924 hotel is decorated tastefully with Queen Anne-style antique mahogany furnishings and period art in its sophisticated rooms. Afternoon tea and sherry is served in the lobby, and stylish **Farallon** restaurant (see page 66) is adjacent.

The intimate **Post Street Theatre** *((415) 321-2900; www.poststreettheatre-sf.com. $35-$75.)* presents noteworthy live performances in a beautifully restored space on the hotel's second floor. It is a gem, with carved coffered ceilings and antique tiles.

## King George Hotel

*334 Mason St./Geary St., 1 blk. from Union Square, (800) 288-6005, (415) 781-5050, fax (415) 391-6976; www.kinggeorge.com. 9 stories; 153 rooms; $$. Children under 12 free. Room service. No pets. Self-parking $24, valet $28.*

Thomas Edison was an original investor in this pleasant hotel, built in 1914, and it was he who convinced management to switch from gaslight to electricity. This stylishly colorful hotel has thick walls and so is very quiet, and a large bowl of complimentary apples is always available at the desk.

A moderately priced continental breakfast and traditional afternoon tea are served in **The Windsor Tearoom** *(B daily, tea Sat-Sun 2-5; $. No reservations.)* and are open to non-guests.

Room service is provided by **Lori's Diner** *(336 Mason St./Geary St., (415) 392-8646; www.lorisdiner.com. B-L-D daily; $.)*, located next door. Featuring a '50s decor and dispensing appropriate fare—burgers, fries and onion rings, shakes—Lori's never closes.

## Pan Pacific Hotel
*500 Post St./Mason St., 1 blk. from Union Square, (800) 533-6465, (800) 327-8585, (415) 771-8600, fax (415) 398-0267; http://sanfrancisco.panpacific.com. 21 stories; 330 rooms; $$$+. Children under 18 free. Restaurant; room service. Fitness room. Pets ok. Valet parking $39.*

The luxurious rooms in this tranquil hotel feature gorgeous marble bathrooms equipped with a TV, beds topped with a cozy feather comforter, and pillows fluffed to order with a unique on-site fluffing machine. Glitzy window-walled interior elevators traverse the 17-story central atrium, and complimentary transportation via a fleet of luxury cars is provided within the city. An on-site auto detail specialist is available by appointment.

Situated off the sedate marble lobby, the acclaimed hotel restaurant, **Pacific** *((415) 929-2087. B daily, L M-F, D Tu-Sat; $$-$$$. Reservations advised.)*, sports elegant marble columns and fresh flowers on each table. Desserts are made by a pastry chef who once was the chef to Princess Grace of Monaco. **Kid's Cooking School** *((415) 929-2064)* can be scheduled in the kitchen to celebrate a birthday or other special occasion.

## Petite Auberge
*863 Bush St./Mason St., 4 blks. from Union Square, (800) 365-3004, (415) 928-6000, fax (415) 673-7214; www.petiteaubergesf.com. 5 stories; 26 rooms; $$-$$$. Some fireplaces. Afternoon snack, full breakfast. No smoking; no pets. Valet parking $30.*

Located on the lower slopes of Nob Hill, this small, ornate, baroque-style building houses charming B&B rooms furnished with French country antiques. Breakfast is served in a cheery room decorated with a wrap-around painted mural depicting a French market scene and sports a view of a tiny garden. Special features include a beveled-glass door leading to the entry, curved bay windows, and an unusual vintage elevator. A sister property, the White Swan Inn, is just a few doors away.

## The Savoy Hotel
*580 Geary St./Jones St., 3 blks. from Union Square, (800) 227-4223, (415) 441-2700, fax (415) 441-0124; www.thesavoyhotel.com. 7 stories; 83 rooms; $-$$. Afternoon snack; restaurant. No pets. Valet parking $26.*

Built in 1913, this well-priced hotel offers attractively decorated rooms with fluffy feather beds and goose down pillows. An evening wine and cheese reception is scheduled daily, and **Millennium Restaurant** (see page 79) operates off the lobby.

## Sir Francis Drake Hotel
*450 Powell St./Sutter St., 1 blk. from Union Square, (800) 227-5480, (415) 392-7755, fax (415) 391 8719; www.sirfrancisdrake.com. 21 stories; 417 rooms; $$-$$$. Fitness room. 2 restaurants; room service. Pets ok. Valet parking $35-$37.*

When built in 1928, this Gothic-Renaissance building was the tallest in town and the last word in hotels. Innovations at the time included an indoor golf course, ice water on tap, and radios in every guest room. Height is no longer its claim to fame, though it is still famous for its glamorous art deco **Harry Denton's Starlight Room** *((415) 395-8595.)* rooftop bar offering fancy cocktails, light supper, and dancing to a full orchestra as well as a panoramic view of the city. The grand two-level lobby retains its magnificent original marble walls, recessed mirrors, and murals depicting the life of explorer Sir Francis Drake, and cable cars stop at the front door. Rooms are tastefully contemporary, and afternoon tea and drinks are available in the mezzanine lobby lounge. The most famous of the hotel's doormen—who all wear a colorful bright-red Beefeater uniform—is Tom Sweeney. He is known for his terrific memory for faces.

### Villa Florence Hotel

*225 Powell St./Geary St., 1 blk. from Union Square, (800) 553-4411, (415) 397-7700, fax (415) 397-1006; www.villaflorence.com. 7 stories; 180 rooms; $$-$$$. Children under 12 free. Evening wine; restaurant. Pets ok. Parking $33-$40.*

Built in 1908, this conveniently located hotel has a colonnaded entrance with a Giotto-style wishing fountain, and its lobby is decorated with a rare 17th-century velvet tapestry and a trompe l'oeil mural depicting 16th-century Florence. A Medici-style wood-burning fireplace warms guests in the lobby, where a piano player entertains nightly. A popular Italian restaurant, **Kuleto's** (see page 74), operates off the lobby.

### The Westin St. Francis

*335 Powell St./Geary St., on Union Square, (800) WESTIN 1, (415) 397-7000, fax (415) 774-0124; www.westinstfrancis.com. 32 stories; 1,195 rooms; $$-$$$+. Children under 18 free. Fitness room; health spa. 3 restaurants; room service. Small dogs ok. Valet parking $39-$45.*

Built in 1904, this classy landmark hotel has a superb location opening right onto Union Square. Every president since William Howard Taft has walked through its lobby, as have Ernest Hemingway and Queen Elizabeth II, and Jennifer Lopez lived here during the filming of *The Wedding Planner*. The hotel consists of both a 12-story historical section and a newer 32-story tower with five outside glass elevators that go non-stop from the lobby to the 32nd floor in less than 30 seconds. All rooms are equipped with the chain's famous fluffy Heavenly Beds, which feel like sleeping in a cloud and which can be ordered for home delivery. Upon check-in, children 12 and under get a free Westin Kids Club packet filled with an assortment of age-appropriate amenities. Westin Heavenly Cribs, strollers, highchairs, bottle warmers, potty seats, and step stools can be placed in the room at no additional charge. And dogs get their own oval-shaped Heavenly Pet Bed, too. Souvenir silver and gold charms, including a cable car, are sold in a lobby boutique and make great souvenirs.

### White Swan Inn

*845 Bush St./Mason St., 4 blks. from Union Square, (800) 999-9570, (415) 775-1755, fax (415) 775-5717; www.whiteswaninnsf.com. 4 stories; 26 rooms; $$.*

*Children under 12 free. All fireplaces. Fitness room. Evening snack; full breakfast. No smoking. Valet parking $34.*

Built after the 1906 earthquake in 1915, this charming hotel resembles an English manor house with its curved bay windows, warm dark woods, and handsome antique furnishings. The cheery reception area, cozy living room, and book-lined library all have fireplaces and are inviting places to relax. Guest rooms are large, and each has a separate sitting area. They are individually decorated with English floral wallpapers and furnished with a mahogany bed fitted with a warming European-style wool mattress cover. Amenities include terry robes, evening turndown service, and a morning newspaper. Breakfast is served in a dining room just off a tiny English garden. A sister inn, Petite Auberge, is just a few doors away.

## SOUTH OF MARKET

Referred to by old-timers as "South of the Slot," signifying its location south of the street car tracks on Market Street, this colorful area was city center in the mid-1800s. Rapidly being refurbished, it is now home to several art museums and to the Moscone Convention Center.

### Argent

*50 Third St./Market St., (877) 222-6699, (415) 974-6400, fax (415) 543-8268; www.argenthotel.com. 36 stories; 667 rooms; $$-$$$+. Children under 18 free. 2 saunas; fitness room. Restaurant; room service. Valet parking $37.*

Each room in this sleek, artfully-appointed contemporary hotel is equipped with three phones. A Kid's Koncierge offers special perks and sight-seeing advice to families, as well as a kiddie kit filled with toys.

### Four Seasons Hotel San Francisco

*757 Market St./3rd St., (800) 332-3442, (415) 633-3000, fax (415) 633-3001; www.fourseasons.com/sanfrancisco. 12 floors; 277 rooms; $$$+. Fitness room; health spa. Restaurant; room service. Valet parking $39.*

Occupying the first 12 floors of a 40-story building, this sleek new property has a muted decor and displays a collection of contemporary art by mostly California artists. South-facing rooms have views over the city and bay.

Bathrooms are spacious, with a deep soaking tub and Italian marble vanities, and beds are made with down duvets and pillows. Guests have complimentary access to the ultra trendy **The Sports Club/LA** fitness center and day spa, which operates on the fourth floor. Kids get their own key to their own mini-bar stocked with familiar favorites at parent-pleasing prices, plus pint-sized bathrobes and games are available upon request. Adults simply must visit the bar for a specialty cocktail and bowl of the chef's fabulous wasabi-covered peanuts.

## Harbor Court Hotel

*165 Steuart St./Mission St., (866) 792-6283, (415) 882-1300, fax (415) 882-1313; www.harborcourthotel.com. 8 stories; 131 rooms; $$$-$$$+. Evening wine; restaurant. Pets ok. Parking $30.*

Featuring an Old World flavor, this historic 1907 landmark building has an attractive vintage brick façade and offers some rooms with spectacular views of the bay and Treasure Island. Guests get discounted use of the **YMCA** full-service fitness center next door.

## Hotel Griffon

*155 Steuart St./Mission St., (800) 321-2201, (415) 495-2100, fax (415) 495-3522; www.hotelgriffon.com. 5 stories; 62 rooms; $$-$$$+. Continental breakfast; restaurant; room service. No smoking; no pets. Self parking $27.*

Among the guest rooms in this stylish boutique hotel are eight with expansive bay views plus three penthouse suites. All feature whitewashed brick walls, tall ceilings, and window seats. Guests have discounted access to a nearby fitness center with an indoor pool and hot tub.

Just off the lobby, **Tonno Rosso** *((415) 495-6500; www.tonnorosso.com. L M-F, D daily, Sat-SunBr; $$$. Booths. Valet parking.)* serves delicious Italian seafood in a cozy setting featuring a mesmerizing bay view. Exceptional menu items include a crispy farinata Genovese (chickpea pancake topped with salad), pappardelle Portofino (wide noodles with a creamy basil-tomato sauce), flattened rosemary chicken roasted in the fireplace, and a drunken cherries-and-amaretto parfait.

## Hotel Palomar

*12 Fourth St./Market St., (877) 294-9711, (415) 348-*
*1111, fax (415) 348-0302; www.hotelpalomar.com. 198 rooms; $$$-$$$+. Fitness room. Restaurant; room service. Pets ok. Valet parking $36.*

Featuring an urbane, sophisticated interior design, with dark chocolate brown and buttery yellow colors and details like faux leopard-skin carpeting, this well-located hotel operates on the fifth through ninth floors of a completely refurbished 1907 landmark building. Original modern art is sprinkled throughout. In Spanish, its name means "where the dove comes to rest," and a quiet retreat is what is offered the weary traveler. The hotel restaurant is the very chic **Fifth Floor** (see page 67).

## Palace Hotel

*2 New Montgomery St./Market St., (800) 325-3535, (415) 512-1111, fax (415) 243-8062; www.sfpalace. com. 8 stories; 552 rooms; $$$-$$$+. Children under 18 free. Indoor pool; hot tub; sauna; fitness room; health spa. 3 restaurants; room service. Valet parking $40.*

When this grande dame hotel opened in 1875, it was the largest and most luxurious in the world. It also was the first hotel in the world with electrical lighting and the first to install an elevator, known then as a "moving room." Though that original hotel burned to the ground after the 1906 earthquake, it was rebuilt in 1909 as the present structure. A dubious claim to fame from its past is the fact that this is where President Harding, who was staying in the Presidential Suite, died in 1923. Nowadays anyone with $2,600 can stay in the Presidential Suite, and the list of those who have includes Sophia Loren and Whoopi Goldberg. **Tours** are given of the public rooms by City Guides; make reservations through the concierge.

One of the most elegant public rooms is the **Garden Court**. Filled with tall marble columns and enormous potted palms, its most glorious feature is a 25,000-pane stained-glass dome said to be worth over $7 million, and it is the only *room* on the National Register of Historic Places. **Afternoon tea** *((415) 546-5010, fax (415) 537-6299; www.gardencourt-restaurant.com. Sat 2-4; $29+; also B-L daily.)* here is an elegant affair, with fussy sandwiches, rose petal jam, and a classical harpist providing background ambiance. A special **Prince** and **Princess Tea** *($22/child; reservations required.)*

welcomes children 10 and under with a crown or scepter and includes kid-friendly hot chocolate and peanut butter & jelly finger sandwiches. The **Pied Piper Bar** and adjoining restaurant hold three noteworthy murals: Maxfield Parrish's "Pied Piper" and two Antonio Sotomayers—one depicting Mark Twain and the other madam Sally Stanford. And since Green Goddess dressing was first created here, do try it on the house salad.

## San Francisco Marriott

*55 Fourth St./Mission St., (800) 228-9290, (415) 896-1600, fax (415) 486-8101; www.marriott.com/sfodt. 39 stories; 1,500 rooms; $$$-$$$+. Indoor pool & hot tub; sauna; 2 steam rooms; fitness room. 2 restaurants; room service. No pets. Valet parking $38.*

Referred to by locals as the "Jukebox Marriott" in recognition of its distinctive architectural design, this well-positioned mega-hotel is the second-largest in San Francisco. It opened at 9 a.m. on October 17, 1989 and closed at 5:04 p.m. the same day, just after the strongest earthquake since 1906 hit this city. Fortunately, it sustained only cosmetic damage. Its spacious public areas are enhanced by the soothing sound of a variety of water fountains. Most rooms have a sweeping view of the city, and a panoramic view is available from the 39th-floor **View** lounge. Occasionally one of the hotel's restaurants will offer the Golden Gate Spectacular. An impressive, award-winning dessert designed by the hotel's pastry chef, it reconstructs the famous span in chocolate and cream.

## W

*181 Third St./Howard St., (877) W-HOTELS, (415) 777-5300, fax (415) 817-7823; www.whotels.com. 31 stories; 423 rooms; $$$-$$$+. Indoor lap pool & hot tub; fitness room. 1 restaurant; room service. Pets ok. Valet parking $40.*

Situated next door to the Museum of Modern Art, this slick and stylish hotel greets guests with a 3-story-high octagonal lobby that buzzes with activity most evenings. Rooms are decorated in attractive taupe, moss green, or rich brown fabrics, with furniture accents in blue. Each is equipped with two phones, a big 27-inch TV screen, and high-speed internet and e-mail access. Aveda amenities, stunning city views, and inviting down duvets complete the

pretty picture. Turndown brings sassy fortune cookies: "Sleep naked," "Dance more than you should."

Super sleek **XYZ** restaurant *((415) 817-7836, fax (415) 817-7885; www.xyz-sf.com. B-L M-F, D daily, Sat-SunBr; $$$. Booths. Reservations advised. Valet parking.)* features a wide open, yet cozy, dining room. Several ³/₄-circular booths provide private seating. Delicious dinner options might include as an appetizer a perfectly executed Peekytoe crab salad with fennel and sweet red grapefruit, and as an entree potato purée topped with braised Niman Ranch beef short ribs minus the bones. Desserts are special, too: a delectible spice cake with sliced poached pear, a frozen Meyer lemon parfait with wild huckleberry compote. It is not at all your usual hotel restaurant.

## NOB HILL

After its steep slopes were conquered by Andrew Hallidie's development of the cable car in 1873, Nob Hill became one of the city's most exclusive residential areas. It was known as the "Hill of Palaces" because it held so many opulent mansions. Unfortunately, all of them burned down in the fire that followed the 1906 earthquake, save the brownstone shell of what is now the private Pacific Union Club. Because of its spectacular views and steep streets, Nob Hill has been the setting for many films. Most memorable, perhaps, is *Bullitt* with Steve McQueen.

## Fairmont San Francisco

*950 Mason St./California St., (800) 527-4727, (415) 772-5000, fax (415) 772-5013; www.fairmont.com/sanfrancisco. 24 stories; 591 rooms; $$$-$$$+. Children under 17 free. Fitness room; health spa. 2 restaurants; room service. Valet parking $39.*

Situated at the top of one of San Francisco's highest hills, this elegant landmark hotel welcomes guests with a gargantuan gilded lobby appointed with marble Corinthian columns, alabaster marble floors, and a valuable art collection. The hotel has hosted many international heads of state, including former President Clinton, and numerous celebrities, and in 1973 it was the first in the U.S. to have a concierge—Tom Wolf, who is still here! It has starred in movies—*Vertigo, Shoot the Moon, Sudden Impact*—and its lobby and grand staircase were the setting for the *Hotel* TV series. Guest rooms are spacious and feature goose-down pillows, terry cloth robes, and twice-daily maid service, and the cable cars, which stop in front of the hotel, can be heard from some. The hotel's crown is the historic eight-room Penthouse Suite. The most opulent and expensive in the U.S., it rents for $10,000 per night and features a 2-story circular library, 24-karat-gold-plated bathroom fixtures, and a game room with a stained-glass skylight.

Afternoon tea is served in **The Laurel Court Restaurant** *(Daily 2:30-4:30. $25.)*. In the **Tonga Room Restaurant & Hurricane Bar** *(x5278. D daily; $$. Reservations advised.)*, simulated tropical rainstorms occur every 30 minutes in a Tiki-hut atmosphere. It is *the* place to stop in the evening for an exotic drink, and is a bargain during the happy hour buffet *(M-F 5-7; $7/person.)*. A live dance band floating aboard a boat in the room's indoor lagoon—a converted swimming pool dating from 1929—entertains beginning at 8 p.m. *(W-Sun. $5 cover.)*.

## Mark Hopkins Inter-Continental
*One Nob Hill, 999 California St./Mason St., (800) NOB-HILL , (415) 392-3434, fax (415) 421-3302; www.markhopkins.net. 18 stories; 380 rooms; $$-$$$+. Children under 14 free. Fitness room. Restaurant; room service. Valet parking $40.*

Built on the spot where once stood the mansion of Mark Hopkins, who founded the Central Pacific Railroad, this hotel opened in 1926. Combining an architectural style that is part French château, part Spanish Renaissance, it has a central tower and two wings affording spectacular city views.

The tower is crowned by the legendary **Top of the Mark** *((415) 616-6916. Cocktails M-F from 4, Sat-Sun from 5. D F-Sat, SunBr; reservations advised.)*, which has an extraordinary 360-degree view of the city and features live entertainment and dancing nightly. It is said that proposing marriage by presenting a diamond engagement ring in the bottom of a drink glass is played out more frequently here than anywhere else in the world. A plaque on the wall by the bar commemorates this as being a favorite spot for World War II Marines to have a last drink before sailing off to battle in the Pacific, believing that this was good luck and would bring them home. Wives and sweethearts gath-

ered here in the northwest corner, dubbed "The Weepers' Corner," to gaze out the windows as their men sailed out. Service men also had a tradition of buying a bottle and leaving it with the bartender so the next soldier from their squadron could enjoy a free drink.

## Nob Hill Lambourne
*725 Pine St./Stockton St., 3 blks. from Union Square, (800) 274-8466, (415) 433-2287, fax (415) 433-0975; www.nobhilllambourne.com. 20 rooms; $$. All kitchens. Afternoon snack, evening wine, continental breakfast. No smoking; no pets. Valet parking $34.*

Sitting pretty in a residential area mid-way up Nob Hill, this intimate contemporary hotel offers guests a quiet, posh retreat with easy access to downtown sights. Designed primarily for the business traveler, each room has personalized voice mail and a fax. In the interest of having guests feel healthier when they leave the hotel than when they arrived, each of the six suites here is outfitted with an instrument of torture, otherwise known as an exercise machine, and turndown brings an antioxidant supplement and inspirational quote. The honor bar is stocked with organic goodies, and music is piped from a radio in the bedroom into the bathroom. A room for spa treatments is on the main floor, and just outside the **Joice steps** up to California Street could easily qualify as Satan's StairMaster north (the more famous southern version is in Santa Monica). Carrying the theme yet further, wellness videos are available from the front desk along with a great selection of movies filmed in San Francisco.

## The Ritz-Carlton
*600 Stockton St./California St., (800) 241-3333, (415) 296-7465, fax (415) 986-1268; www.ritzcarlton.com. 9 stories; 336 rooms; $$$+. Indoor heated pool; hot tub; steam room; fitness room. 2 restaurants; room service. Valet parking $50.*

Occupying a full square block about halfway up Nob Hill, just off the California Street cable car line, this branch of the classy chain is set within a restored 1909 neoclassical landmark building. The interior features Italian marble, silk wall coverings, Bohemian crystal chandeliers, Persian carpets, and antique furnishings. A museum-quality collection of 18th- and 19th-century European and American art and antiques is displayed throughout. Room amenities include a morning newspaper, terry robes, and twice-daily maid service.

**The Terrace** offers the only outdoor hotel dining in San Francisco. In fair weather, its dressy al fresco Sunday jazz brunch *($65, 5-12 $32.)* is sublime. Diners sit outside on a red brick courtyard that is surrounded by a colorful flower garden and protected on three sides by the building's "U" shape. Inside, a battery of buffet tables offer delicacies that include caviars, smoked salmon, imported cheeses, fresh fruits, tasty cold salads, and hot entrees such as eggs Benedict, blintzes, and fish and meat courses. There is also a heavily laden pastry table and a killer dessert table. Coffee and freshly squeezed orange juice are included. Everything is carefully prepared and elegantly presented by a well-trained kitchen staff. **The Dining Room** *((415) 773-6168. D M-Sat; $$$. Reservations advised.)* serves an elegant dinner, and **The Lobby Lounge** presents a relaxing afternoon tea *((415) 773-6198. M-F 2:30-4:30, Sat-Sun 1-4:30; $29-$41. Reservations advised.).* Special teas for children include the **Easter Bunny Tea**, with service by the Easter Bunny, and bring-your-own **Teddy Bear Teas** during the weeks leading up to Christmas.

### The Stanford Court, A Renaissance Hotel
*905 California St./Powell St., (800) HOTELS-1, (415) 989-3500, fax (415) 391-0513; www.renaissance hotels.com. 8 stories; 393 rooms; $$-$$$+. Children under 18 free. Fitness room. Restaurant; room service. Pets ok. Valet parking $38.*

Built on the site where once stood Leland Stanford's house—described as "a mansion that dominated the city like the castle of a medieval hill town"—this grand old hotel is blessed with striking turn-of-the-century detail, a beaux arts fountain in the carport, and a lobby dome of Tiffany-style stained glass. Its elegant lobby is furnished with fine antiques, including Baccarat chandeliers and an 1806 grandfather clock once owned by Napoleon Bonaparte. Guest room pampering includes marble bathrooms with heated towel racks, and complimentary amenities include coffee and newspaper delivered to the room in the morning, an overnight shoeshine, and downtown limousine service.

Lobby shops include **John Small Ltd.** A small boutique indeed, it specializes in traditional British regimental items and was the hotel's first shop. Among its many treasures is an authentic Metropolitan brand bobby whistle imported from England.

The celebrated **Fournou's Ovens** *((415) 989-1910. B-L-D daily, Sat-SunBr; $$-$$$. Highchairs, boosters, child menu. Reservations advised.)* is known for its massive, beautifully tiled European-style roasting ovens and intimate, finely appointed dining rooms. Specialties are roasted meats and seafood. The wine cellar holds more than 8,000 bottles and has one of the country's largest selections of California wines. Afternoon tea *(reservations advised)* and evening cocktails are served daily in the **Lobby Lounge**.

## FINANCIAL DISTRICT

### Hyatt Regency San Francisco
*5 Embarcadero Center/Market St., (800) 233-1234, (415) 788-1234, fax (415) 398-2567; http://san franciscoregency.hyatt.com. 17 stories; 805 rooms; $$$-$$$+. Children under 18 free. 2 restaurants; room service. No pets. Valet parking $43.*

Built in 1973, this elegant hotel resembles a pyramid. Every room has a view of either the city or the bay, and nifty glass elevators run the 17-story height of what is the world's largest atrium lobby. Conveniently, one end of the California Street cable car line is just outside the front door. **Equinox** *((415) 291-6619. D W-Sun; $$$.),* Northern California's only revolving rooftop restaurant, offers a 360-degree view of the city.

### Mandarin Oriental, San Francisco
*222 Sansome St./Pine St., (800) 622-0404, (415) 276-9888, fax (415) 433-0289; www.mandarin*

oriental.com. 48 stories; 158 rooms; $$$+. Children under 12 free. Fitness room. 2 restaurants; room service. Small dogs ok. Valet parking $41.

Located in the heart of the Financial District, this luxury hotel occupies the first two floors of a skyscraper with its lobby, lounge, and two restaurants. Then it shoots up into the air and places guest rooms in twin towers on the top 11 floors of the 48-story building. This translates into quiet rooms with stupendous views. Furnishings are tasteful, contemporary, and a bit oriental, and a pot of hot jasmine tea is delivered to the room upon check-in. All bathrooms are stocked with fine English soaps and lotions, and some bathtubs feature a city view—permitting bathers to literally soak up the sights.

An afternoon Asian tea service, with snacks in a bento box and tea in a cast-iron pot, is presented in the **Mandarin Lounge** *((415) 986-2020. Daily 3-5pm; $29).* Appointed sumptuously, with silk-themed art created especially for the restaurant, **Silks** *((415) 986-2020. B daily, L M-F, D Tu-Sat; $$$. Highchairs, child menu. Reservations advised. Valet parking.)* offers an excitingly sophisticated menu of California cuisine with an Asian accent.

## Park Hyatt San Francisco

*333 Battery St./Clay St., (800) 233-1234, (415) 392-1234, fax (415) 421-2433; http://parksanfrancisco. hyatt.com. 24 stories; 360 rooms; $$-$$$+. Children under 12 free. Restaurant; room service. No pets. Parking $43.*

Built in 1989, this hotel is conveniently located across the street via a pedestrian bridge from the Embarcadero Center shopping complex. Luxurious in every way, its public areas are decorated with fine art. Each room has a bay or city view, and amenities include a goose-down duvet and terry cloth bathrobes. Guests also get complimentary shoeshines and a car is available for shuttling within a 3-mile radius. **Teddy Bear Teas** are held for children in December and include seasonal edibles as well as a teddy bear memento.

## FISHERMAN'S WHARF

The major chains are well represented in this very popular area.

## Best Western Tuscan Inn at Fisherman's Wharf

*425 North Point St./Mason St., (800) 648-4626, (415) 561-1100, fax (415) 561-1199; www.tuscan inn.com. 4 stories; 221 rooms; $$-$$$+. Children under 18 free. Evening wine; restaurant; room service. Pets ok. Valet parking $30.*

This comfortable, pleasantly appointed small hotel is reputed to be popular with filmmakers. Hot drinks and biscotti are served in the lobby each morning.

Appealing **Cafe Pescatore** *(2455 Mason St./North Point St., (415) 561-1111. B-L-D daily; $-$$. Highchairs, boosters, booths, child menu. Reservations advised.)* has windows that open to the sidewalk in warm weather and features a menu of fresh fish, pastas, and pizza baked in a wood-burning oven.

## Hilton San Francisco Fisherman's Wharf

*2620 Jones St./Bay St., (800) HILTONS, (415) 885-4700, fax (415) 771-8945; www.hilton.com. 234 rooms; $$. Children under 18 free. Fitness room. Restaurant; room service. No pets. Self-parking $28, valet $32.*

This motel claims to have the largest guest rooms at Fisherman's Wharf.

## Holiday Inn San Francisco Fisherman's Wharf

*1300 Columbus Ave./North Point St., (800) HOLIDAY, (415) 771-9000, fax (415) 771-7006; www.holiday-inn.com/sfo-fishermans. 5 stories; 585 rooms; $$-$$$. Children under 19 free. Heated pool; fitness room. 2 restaurants; room service. No pets. Self-parking $28.*

This well-located hotel comprises two buildings across the street from each other. A coin-operated laundry is available.

## Hyatt at Fisherman's Wharf

*555 North Point St./Jones St., (800) 233-1234, (415) 563-1234, fax (415) 563-2218; http://fishermans wharf.hyatt.com. 5 stories; 313 rooms; $$-$$$+. Children under 18 free. Heated lap pool; hot tub; sauna; fitness room. Restaurant; room service. Valet parking $32.*

Built on the site of an historic marble works building and incorporating that façade into its new architecture, this attractive hotel was constructed using some of the original bricks recycled into a modern interpretation of the building's inceptive design. Washers and dryers are located on each floor, and the particularly family-friendly restaurant has a children's menu and a games area with shuffleboard and a pool table.

### Radisson Hotel Fisherman's Wharf

*250 Beach St./Powell St., (877) 497-1212, (415) 392-6700, fax (415) 617-6570; www.radissonfishermans wharf.com. 4 stories; 355 rooms; $$-$$$+. Children under 18 free. Heated pool; fitness room. Restaurant. No pets. Self-parking $26.*

Covering an entire block, this lodging has many rooms with bay and city views. Family rooms are large, with two double beds and a double sofa bed. The pool is located within an enclosed, landscaped courtyard.

### San Francisco Marriott Fisherman's Wharf

*1250 Columbus Ave./Bay St., (800) 228-9290, (415) 775-7555, fax (415) 474-2099; www.marriott.com/sfofw. 5 stories; 285 rooms; $$-$$$. Children under 18 free. Fitness room; sauna. Restaurant; room service. Pets ok. Valet parking $38.*

Comfortable public spaces in this posh hotel include a lobby equipped with a TV and fireplace.

### Sheraton Fisherman's Wharf

*2500 Mason St./Beach St., (800) 325-3535, (415) 362-5500, fax (415) 956-5275; www.sheratonat thewharf.com. 4 stories; 529 rooms; $$-$$$. Children under 17 free. Heated pool; fitness room. Restaurant; room service. Valet parking $30.*

This huge, contemporary-style hotel takes up an entire city block. Sporting a maritime theme, it features mahogany furniture, hand-painted murals depicting 16th-century maps, and antique maritime artifacts. It has spacious rooms and that rarest of San Francisco amenities—a heated swimming pool.

### Suites at Fisherman's Wharf

*2655 Hyde St./North Point St., (800) 227-3608, (415) 771-0200, fax (415) 346-8058; www.shell hospitality.com. 24 suites; $$. Children under 12 free. All kitchens. No pets. Self-parking $23.*

Staying in this small building, it is possible to feel like a local rather than a visitor. In addition to offering most of the comforts of home, the lodging is located across the street from Ghirardelli Square, is right on the Hyde Street

cable car line, and is very close to the best aspects of the Fisherman's Wharf area. It also has a rooftop sundeck with a spectacular view of the Golden Gate Bridge, and a newspaper is delivered to the door each morning.

## CHINATOWN AND NORTH BEACH

### Royal Pacific Motor Inn

*661 Broadway/Columbus Ave., (800) 545-5574, (415) 781-6661, fax (415) 781-6688; www.royalpacific.city search.com. 5 stories; 74 rooms; $-$$. Sauna; fitness room. Free parking.*

Situated on the Chinatown-North Beach border, this bargain motel is right in the thick of it.

### San Remo Hotel

*2237 Mason St./Chestnut St., (800) 352-REMO, (415) 776-8688, fax (415) 776-2811; www.sanremohotel.com. 62 rooms; $-$$. All shared baths. Restaurant. No smoking. Parking nearby.*

Tucked away in a quiet residential neighborhood between Fisherman's Wharf and North Beach, this family-owned and -operated Italianate Victorian hotel was built by the founder of Bank of America just after the big earthquake in 1906. Reception and the charming, comfortable, European-style rooms are upstairs, reached via a steep and narrow staircase. With their lace-covered windows and mish-mash of antique furnishings, rooms are situated off a warren of narrow hallways made cheery by well-placed skylights. Many have views of famous city landmarks. With the exception of a rooftop penthouse featuring a great bay view, all rooms share baths; half have sinks in the room. Downstairs, the restaurant dining room features white-painted embossed tin ceilings.

### Washington Square Inn

*1660 Stockton St./Filbert St., (800) 388-0220, (415) 981-4220, fax (415) 397-7242; www.wsisf.com. 15 rooms; $$-$$$. Afternoon snack; continental breakfast. No smoking; some pets ok. Valet parking $25.*

This charming North Beach gem features a super location that permits late-evening coffeehouse hopping, and it is just a few blocks from an uncrowded cable car stop. Each room is decorated individually and furnished with English and French antiques. Several choice rooms in the front have bay windows overlooking Washington Square Park and the beautiful Sts. Peter & Paul Church, the bells from which are heard tolling the hour. Amenities include terry cloth robes, down pillows and comforters, and a morning newspaper delivered to the room. Wine and hors d'oeuvres are served in the cozy lobby, and breakfast can be delivered to the room.

## JAPANTOWN

Surprisingly, this quiet part of town is just 10 blocks from bustling Union Square. Both of these hotels have an exotic Asian flavor.

### Best Western Miyako Inn
*1800 Sutter St./Buchanan St., (888) 466-9990, (800) 528-1234, (415) 921-4000, fax (415) 923-1064; www.bestwestern.com/miyakoinn. 8 stories; 125 rooms; $$. Children under 18 free. Restaurant. No pets. Self-parking $15.*

Rooms are large, and many have dramatic views of the southwestern portion of the city. Some are equipped with steam baths.

### Radisson Miyako Hotel San Francisco
*1625 Post St./Laguna St., (800) 333-3333, (415) 922-3200, fax (415) 921-0417; www.radisson.com/san franciscoca_miyako. 13 stories; 218 rooms; $$$. Children under 18 free. Fitness room. Restaurant; room service. No pets. Valet parking $20.*

This exotic hotel has two traditional Japanese-style suites with futon feather beds on tatami mats, as well as serene western-style rooms with Japanese touches. Most rooms have deep furo bathing tubs, and some suites have a private redwood sauna. The tasteful lobby overlooks a Japanese garden where guests can stroll.

## PACIFIC HEIGHTS/PRESIDIO HEIGHTS

### Hotel Drisco
*2901 Pacific Ave./Broderick St., (800) 634-7277, (415) 346-2880, fax (415) 567-5537; www.hoteldrisco.com. 4 stories; 43 rooms; $$$-$$$+. Fitness room. Afternoon snack, evening wine, continental breakfast. No smoking; no pets. No parking.*

Built in 1903, before the '06 quake, this Edwardian-style building is in a quiet residential neighborhood. It maintains its original dark-wood interior trim and is elegantly deco-

rated and furnished. Turn-of-the-century millionaires are said to have kept their mistresses lodged here. Later in the century, President Eisenhower bunked here due to its close proximity to the Presidio. Rooms are spacious and comfortable, and the suites have good views.

### Hotel Majestic
*1500 Sutter St./Gough St., (800) 869-8966, (415) 441-1100, fax (415) 673-7331; www.thehotel majestic.com. 5 stories; 58 rooms; $$-$$$+. Some gas fireplaces. Afternoon snack, continental breakfast; room service. No smoking; no pets. Valet parking $19.*

Built originally as a private mansion in 1902 and converted to a hotel in 1904, this small Edwardian hotel survived the 1906 earthquake and fire and is the longest continuously operating hotel in San Francisco. It is restored to its original grandeur with gorgeous vintage marble, exotic woods, and rich brocades and wallpapers, and it sports bay windows and high ceilings. The hotel offers a cozy, soothing retreat from the world outside. Each sumptuously decorated room has either a canopied four-poster bed or a two-poster bed with a bonnet canopy, and fine French and English antiques are used throughout. Many rooms have clawfoot tubs. Why even rock stars have been known to head straight for their posh room immediately after a concert to cocoon. Julia Roberts, The GoGos, and numerous Nobel laureates have slept here, and the hotel was once the permanent residence of actresses Joan Fontaine and Olivia de Havilland. Limousine service to downtown is available on weekday mornings. **Avalon**, the lobby bar named for a butterfly, features a 19th-century, horseshoe-shaped French mahogany bar imported from Paris and displays a collection of rare butterflies from South America and Africa.

### Laurel Inn
*444 Presidio Ave./California St., (800) 552-8735, (415) 567-8467, fax (415) 928-1866; www.thelaurelinn.com. 4 stories; 49 rooms; $$. Children under 12 free. Some kitchens. Afternoon snack, continental breakfast. No smoking; pets ok. Free parking.*

Located far from the usual tourist haunts, in a nice residential area near Sacramento Street shopping, this motel has spacious rooms and a stylish 1950s-modern decor. East-facing rooms have good city views, and it's hard to beat the price.

## HAIGHT-ASHBURY

### Stanyan Park Hotel
*750 Stanyan St./Waller St., (415) 751-1000, fax (415) 668-5454; www.stanyanpark.com. 36 rooms; $$-$$$+. Some kitchens. Afternoon snack, continental breakfast. No smoking; no pets. No parking.*

Located at the edge of Golden Gate Park, this 1904 Victorian mansion survived the great quake of '06. It has been renovated into a pleasant hotel with attractively decorated rooms.

## BY THE SEA

### Ocean Park Motel
*2690 46th Ave./Wawona St., Sunset district, (415) 566-7020, fax (415) 665-8959; www.oceanpark motel.citysearch.com. 24 rooms; $. Some kitchens. Hot tub. Dogs ok. Free parking.*

Located near the ocean and just a block from the zoo, this landmark streamline moderne-style motel dates from the '30s, when it was San Francisco's first motel. It maintains its original nautical decor and interior cedar paneling, and some windows are shaped like portholes. Rooms are attractive and homey, and several spacious family suites are available. Amenities include a playground, barbecue area, and mature gardens with Monterey pine and cypress trees.

## MISCELLANEOUS

### American Marketing Systems
*(800) 747-7784, (415) 447-2000, fax (415) 447-2077; www.amsires.com. 1-30 stories; 400 units; $$-$$$+. All kitchens; some wood-burning & gas fireplaces. Some pools, hot tubs, saunas, fitness centers, & tennis courts. Some free parking.*

Live like a native. This service offers lodging in desirable residential areas. Among the possibilities are a penthouse with city views and a cottage with a view of the Golden Gate Bridge. According to this office, "We have it all. Just call."

### The Archbishop's Mansion
*1000 Fulton St./Steiner St., on Alamo Square, (800) 543-5820, (415) 563-7872, fax (415) 885-3193; www.sftrips.com. 15 rooms; $$$-$$$$+. Some fireplaces. Afternoon snack, continental breakfast. No smoking; no pets. Free parking.*

Located in an area rife with Victorian architecture, this fabulous French-style château dates back to the Victorian era and was once the residence for three of the town's Archbishops. Each romantic room is named after an opera and decorated uniquely, and, though all are desirable, some are even more so than others. Rooms circle a 3-story, curved mahogany grand staircase surmounted by a gorgeous stained-glass skylight dome that is truly worthy of the title "grand." A tiny elevator is available for easy access to the upper floors. All guest rooms are cozy and furnished with antiques, and many feature partial canopy beds and clawfoot tubs. The magnificent Don Giovanni Suite has two fireplaces and an extraordinary four-poster bed with a full wooden canopy (the perfect place to be in the event of an earthquake). The bed, which originally graced a French castle, has a crocheted lace and silk trim and is heavily decorated with carved feet, cherub faces, wolves, and more. The suite poses guests with the delightful dilemma of choosing between a long soak in a bubbly tub or a soothing shower that surrounds them with seven spraying heads—one to wash away each of the seven deadly sins—and a warmth as complete as that of a deep, deep tub. Public rooms feature painted frescoes and beautiful woodwork, and the lobby holds a 1904 Bechstein grand piano once owned by Noel Coward. Delightfully, breakfast is delivered to the room along with the morning paper.

### Hostels
For description, see page 445.

- **Union Square:** *312 Mason St./Geary St., (415) 788-5604, fax (415) 788-3023. 285 beds; 32 private rooms.*

This is in a prime location.

- **Civic Center:** *685 Ellis St./Larkin St., (415) 474-5721, fax (415) 776-0755. 262 beds; 10 private rooms.*

Rooms in this beautifully restored, 7-story-tall historic hotel are equipped with either two or four beds and have en suite bathrooms.

- **Fisherman's Wharf:** *Fort Mason, Bldg. 240, Bay St./Franklin St., (415) 771-7277, fax (415) 771-1468. 162 beds; 4 private rooms.*

This hostel is in a former Civil War barracks situated on a peaceful knoll with a magnificent view of the bay.

## Motel Row

A plethora of lodgings lines the 20-block corridor stretching along Lombard Street from Van Ness Avenue to the Presidio.

## — WHERE TO EAT —

There are far too many good restaurants in San Francisco to permit listing them all here. Those that are included are excellent in some way. Don't be reluctant to try places discovered while wandering. If the people dining inside look animated and happy, give it a try. It is amazing how infrequently a bad meal is served in this food-fanatical town. Even hotel restaurants (described in the "Where to Stay" section), which are often best overlooked in other places, are usually good here. They don't call San Francisco "Food City" for no reason. In fact, it is said there are more restaurants per resident in San Francisco than in any other city in the U.S.

And do try some of the local food specialties. The fortune cookie, Irish coffee, and martini were all invented here. Pisco punch, an unusual drink made with Peruvian brandy, dates back to the Gold Rush. Sourdough bread is credited to Isidore Boudin, a French immigrant who in 1849 got some sourdough from a gold prospector and mixed it in with his French bread to produce the world's first sourdough French bread. (Watch around town for **Boudin cafes** *((800) 992-1855, fax (800) 992-1877; www.boudinbakery.com.)*, where soups and stews are served in hollowed-out bread rounds.) Dry salame is made by several local companies, including Molinari and Cariani, which both date back to the 1890s. The original **Swensen's Ice Cream shop** still operates at Hyde and Union streets dishing out its Sticky Chewy Chocolate and Turkish Coffee specialties, though vanilla remains the favorite. It's It—an ice cream sandwich made with oatmeal cookies, vanilla ice cream, and a coating of chocolate— was developed in 1928 at now-gone Playland-at-the-Beach. The confection is sold now in grocery stores. Another frozen delight, the Popsicle, was created here in 1905 when 11-year-old Frank Epperson carelessly left out a mix of powdered soda and water with a stirring

stick on one very cold San Francisco night. Green Goddess salad dressing was created in 1923 at the Palace Hotel by chef Philip Roemer, who named it after a play of the same name by William Archer. Double Rainbow is the ice cream of choice, Anchor Steam the beer, Calistoga (from the Wine Country) the mineral water, Ghirardelli the chocolate, Torani the flavored syrup, and Tom's the cookie.

Note that a state law makes it illegal to smoke in any California restaurant or bar, or in any public place of business. Valet parking averages around $7 to $10.

## Acquerello

*1722 Sacramento St./Van Ness Ave., (415) 567-5432, fax (415) 567-6432; www.acquerello.com. D Tu-Sat; $$$+. Reservations advised.*

Formerly a church, the romantic, intimate dining room of this upscale Italian gem features a rustic, pitched Moorish wood ceiling. It is the kind of place where the Mayor might be seated at the next table. Menu selections include a four-course tasting menu with wines. Definitely not the usual, the delicious preparations are derived from a refined style of Italian cuisine known as cucina della nonna, or "grandmother's cooking," and feature complex reduced sauces achieved through slow, home-style cooking. Exquisite examples include a tortelloni stuffed with brandy-plumped figs and ground pork in a nut dough, and a flavorful pepper-crusted pork loin with caramelized endive and tiny Chianti-poached pears topped with gorgonzola. The kitchen sends out occasional complimentary little treats—perhaps a tiny citrus appetizer cocktail or a plump, perfect scallop sitting on mashed potatoes splashed with truffle oil. Desserts are also a pleasant surprise. Service is elegant and formal, with meals served on fine china and crystal enhanced by paper doilies.

## Alborz
*1245 Van Ness Ave./Sutter St., (415) 440-4321. L-D daily; $-$$. Highchairs, boosters. Reservations advised.*

This simple but comfortable spot offers a wall of windows looking onto the street. It has an exceptional Persian menu and starts diners off with a complimentary basket of delicious lavash flat bread and Feta cheese.  For appetizers, don't miss the kasik bodemjan (roasted eggplant baked with onion, garlic, mint, and yogurt), the mast-o-khiar (cucumber and mint mixed with delicious, rich, housemade yogurt), and salad shirazi (a mixture of diced tomatoes, cucumbers, and onions in a lemony dressing). For entrees, any of the juicy, spiced kabobs are excellent, but don't overlook the more complex house specialties—one is a richly flavored fes enjoon consisting of chicken breast cooked in a thick, delicious, and sweet walnut-pomegranate sauce. Entrees come with basmati rice splashed colorfully with saffron. The perfect ending is, of course, baklava.

## Alioto's
*#8 Fisherman's Wharf, at bottom of Taylor St./Jefferson St., (415) 673-0183, fax (415) 931-6792; www.aliotos.com. L-D daily; $$-$$$. Highchairs, booths, child portions. Validated parking.*

The view here is about as San Francisco as you can get—the fishing boats, the bay, The Bridge—and plenty of oversize booths and window-front tables provide comfortable seating. The fresh seafood is always a good choice, but the many Sicilian regional specialties are also worth trying. Spicy deviled crab served in a scallop shell, pan-fried sole picatta, and potato gnocchi with creamy tomato sauce are particularly tasty. Portions are bountiful, and both European wines and New World wines are served Old World-style in volume-marked glasses. For parties of six to ten people, the

charming little Calamari Room off the main dining room can be reserved for special events. Historical photos of the Wharf line the stairway up to the restaurant. Downstairs, the **Cafe "8"** fast-service seafood deli serves up sandwiches, seafood salads, and brick-oven pizzas. Don't miss seeing David Mizer at the crab stand out front. Sometimes referred to as "the Mozart of crab-crackers," he puts on quite a show tossing his plastic hammer in the air like a baton as he cracks shells.

## Ana Mandara
*891 Beach St./Polk St., in Ghirardelli Square, Fisherman's Wharf, (415) 771-6800, fax (415) 771-5275; www.anamandara.com. L M-F, D daily; $$$. Reservations advised. Valet parking.*

Located within a fabulous high-ceilinged, open dining room, this delightful restaurant, whose name translates as "beautiful refuge," is owned by TV's *Nash Bridges* stars Don Johnson and Cheech Marin. (It is named for a Vietnamese island owned by Johnson.) It's rumored that the elaborate decor and the theatrical ceiling lights, which mimic a star-studded evening sky, are going to do double-duty occasionally as stage sets. Full-grown potted palms and antique Vietnamese artifacts complete the effect, making this space resemble a Vietnamese village. And then there's the food. Though portions are small, the modern Vietnamese cuisine is delicious. Appetizers include crispy spring rolls filled with crab and shrimp, and superb seafood-stuffed zucchini blossoms in season. Main dishes such as marinated grilled quail and fresh fish steamed in banana leaves are excellent choices, especially with a side of spicy grilled okra. Elegant cocktails—a spicy Tapari Poison, a refreshing mint-lemongrass Ana Mandara—and beers provide the perfect accompaniment. Vietnamese coffee and green tea, grown on the chef's family plantation in Vietnam, are available with dessert. At some point, be sure to go upstairs and view the luxurious bar area.

## Ananda Fuara
*1298 Market St./9th St., Civic Center, (415) 621-1994; www.anandafuara.com. B-L-D M-Tu & Thur-Sat, B-L only on W, SunBr occassionally; $. Closed 2nd-3rd wks. in Apr & 3rd-4th wks. of Aug. No reservations. No cards.*

The translation of this cheery, all-vegetarian restaurant's name is "Fountain of Supreme Bliss." It is owned by the peace teacher and poet Sri Chinmoy and operated by his students. Female servers wear saris, and fresh flowers are on every table. The varied menu should please everyone, even vegans—who eat no dairy or eggs—and carnivores—we know what *they* eat! Menu winners include a large appetizer dish of vegan samosas filled with a potato-pea curry, a hearty soup of the day, and a house specialty "neatloaf" sandwich made with a baked mixture of grains and spices. A selection of salads, wraps, sandwiches, pizzas, baked potatoes, and entrees is also available. Drinks include a decaffeinated Indian-spiced hot Yogi Tea that is simply the best.

## Andalé

*2150 Chestnut St., Marina district, (415) 749-0506, fax (415) 749-0680.*

For description, see page 180.

## Aqua

*252 California St./Battery St., Financial district, (415) 956-9662, fax (415) 956-5229; www.aqua-sf.com. L M-F, D daily; $$$+. Reservations essential. Valet parking at D.*

With a large dining room and a tall, tall ceiling, this physically beautiful space is enhanced by gorgeous oversize flower arrangements. It is chic, bustling, and romantic all at the same time and delivers food of equal caliber. Creative, full-flavored, impeccably fresh seafood items dominate the menu, and it seems impossible to choose a wrong dish. Presentations are dazzling, with colorful flavored oils often drizzled around the perimeter of plates, and some dishes involve "table theater," with the waiter dramatically mixing and preparing items at table. Signature dishes include a savory black-mussel soufflé, a theatrical and delicious lobster casserole, and grilled tuna layered with foie gras. Non-fish entrees include duck, foie gras, and a vegetarian tasting menu. Desserts are equally good, with a daily soufflé, a variety of cheeses, and the house specialty updated root beer float enhanced with chocolate "straws" among the choices. A seven-course tasting menu with optional wine pairings is a good way to go for those who just cannot decide.

## A. Sabella's

*2766 Taylor St./Jefferson St., Fisherman's Wharf, (415) 771-6775, fax (415) 771-6777; www.asabella.com. D daily; $$$. Highchairs, boosters, child menu. Reservations accepted. Free validated parking.*

In the family since 1920, this restaurant's chef, Michael Sabella, is the great grandson of its founder. Though the restaurant changed location once in 1939—moving here from across the street—it is well settled into its third-story perch, where through large arched windows all tables enjoy a view of the wharf and the bay beyond. It is a definite exception to the rule that "locals don't eat at the Wharf because there is no fresh fish there." Fresh Dungeness crab is a specialty. (The restaurant maintains saltwater tanks filled with Dungeness crab, abalone, and Maine lobster). A delightful starter is a martini glass filled with a crab Louis cocktail prepared with avocado and housemade Louis dressing. Crab cakes with Remoulade sauce are also very good. Main courses include several crab dishes—cioppino, garlic-roasted in the shell, and whole cracked with black bean sauce—as well as mesquite-grilled salmon and swordfish and sautéed petrale sole with a delicate lemon and caper sauce. Several meats and some vegetarian pastas are also available. Desserts include the light—a poached pear with lemon-pecan bars—and the heavy—a New York-style cheesecake made from a Sabella family recipe. Note that the menu here is available in French, German, Italian, Japanese, Russian, Portuguese, Korean, and Spanish!

## Asia SF

*201 Ninth St./Howard St., (415) 255-ASIA, fax (415) 255-8887; www.asiasf.com. D daily; $$ ($20/person min.; no cover). Reservations advised.*

This place seems to have everything going for it: good food, great entertainment, central location, easy parking, reasonable prices. All the waitresses here are actually Asian men who dress as women. These "gender illusionists" also perform hourly—dancing and lip-synching atop a 40-foot-long runway at the back of the bar. This means everyone gets to see *almost* everything. The wait to get in can be long, but a dance club downstairs offers another diversion at no additional charge. And though the show is the main draw, the East-West fusion food is tasty (appetizers include several kinds of spring roll, chicken satay, and a refreshing Thai cucumber salad; an ahi burger and steamed sea bass dish are among the entrees) and the mixed drinks are fun (Trina's Pussycat made with Malibu rum and Chambord; Kiana's Kiss made with Stoli vodka, peach Schnapps, and Triple Sec) and include some sake cocktails and a few non-alcoholic specials. For desert, the tray trio of yummy miniature cones filled with Thai iced tea, kiwi sorbet, and buko ice creams is the way to go.

## B44
*44 Belden Pl./Bush St., Financial district, (415) 986-6287, fax (415) 986-6291. L M-F, D daily. Highchairs, boosters. Reservations advised.*

The best way to enjoy the Catalan menu at this engaging bistro is to pick several appetizers per person—the piquillo peppers stuffed with crab meat and the fresh white shrimp sautéed with crispy garlic and served in a little iron frying pan are both superb—and share a moist paella or entree. A sherry or Catalan wine is the perfect accompaniment. A refined chocolate banana pie or rice-and-cinnamon ice cream provide a not-too-sweet ending. Seating is in an open dining room with industrial-style decor and a full bar, or, in good weather, outside European-style in the alley closed to traffic. A visit to the restroom is enhanced by a video display depicting the annual "human tower" festival that dates back to the 14th century in owner-chef Daniel Olivella's Spanish hometown of Vilafranca del Penedes, located near Barcelona.

## Beach Chalet Brewery & Restaurant
*1000 Great Highway/Ocean Beach, in Golden Gate Park, (415) 386-VIEW, fax (415) 386-4125; www.beachchalet.com. B-L-D daily, Sat-SunBr; $-$$. Child menu. Reservations advised. Free parking lot adjoins.*

Designed in 1925 by San Francisco architect Willis Polk, this historic colonnaded Spanish stucco building with terra-cotta roof tiles is at the western end of Golden Gate Park, across the street from the Pacific Ocean. In the past it has served as a tea house and as an Army signal station, but now the upstairs is a wildly popular brewpub bistro with ocean views from every table. Target a visit for breakfast or lunch, when the menu is less pricey and the views can

be enjoyed uninterrupted by sun-shielding shades. Don't miss the sampler of house-brewed, English-style ales or the full-flavored, though essentially fizz-less, housemade root beer. Two standouts on the eclectic, bistro-style menu are a hamburger made with flavorful Niman Ranch ground chuck and an herb-crusted rotisserie-roasted chicken with garlic mashed potatoes. Sausage dishes are usually available, and the kitchen is famous for its achiote-spiced chicken wings. Children can choose from a hot dog, grilled cheese, macaroni & cheese, and chicken salad pasta. Desserts include the ultimate vertical dessert—the pastry chef's signature Chocolate Sandcastle, whimsically composed of a flourless chocolate truffle cake with bittersweet chocolate sauce and placed vertically between two chocolate castle-shaped cookies. A simple old-time hot fudge sundae and rootbeer float are also options. A nickel from each beer sold goes to charity, and live music is scheduled some nights. When the restaurant isn't too busy, informal **brewery tours** are available upon request.

Downstairs, the **Beach Chalet Visitors Center** *((415) 751-2766; www.frp.org.)* displays natural history exhibits and explains the colorful WPA wall frescoes depicting life in San Francisco during the Depression.

## Benihana
*1737 Post St., in Kintetsu Mall at Japan Center, (415) 563-4844, fax (415) 563-8022; www.benihana.com. L-D daily; $$. Highchairs. Reservations advised.*

Diners at this branch of the well-known Japanese restaurant chain sit at a community table with a large grill imbedded in the middle. Once the seats are filled with diners, the chef dramatically prepares each order as everyone watches. Though there are none, karate yells from the chefs wouldn't seem out of place. The chefs are adept performers with their knives, and the show is spectacular.

## Betelnut
*2030 Union St./Buchanan St., Pacific Heights, (415) 929-8855, fax (415) 929-8894; www.betelnut restaurant.com. L-D daily; $$. Highchairs, boosters, booths. Reservations advised. Validated parking.*

With a menu of native dishes from throughout Asia and a streamlined interior featuring lacquered walls and some very comfortable half-moon booths, this always-bustling, casual spot is modeled after the beer houses found in Asia. A favorite area to sit is in the **Dragonfly Lounge** bar, where large windows overlook the sidewalk traffic and exotic flap fans keep things cool. Last-minute seats are often available at an auspicious long red bar facing the open kitchen. Though most dishes are full-flavored and satisfying, truly exceptional items include minced chicken in lettuce cups, red-cooked pork in a spicy-sweet sauce, and tea-smoked duck. Portions are small and meant to be shared tapas-style. Beer is the perfect drink—especially with a plate of sun-dried anchovies, peanuts, and chilies to munch on— but exotic mixed drinks are also divine, and a rare Chinese tea can provide a satisfying conclusion.

## Bill's Place

*2315 Clement St./25th Ave., outer Richmond district, (415) 221-5262. L-D daily; $. Highchairs, boosters, child portions. Reservations accepted.*

A variety of hamburgers named after celebrities star on the menu here along with hot dogs and sandwiches, and breakfast is available until 1 p.m. Choice shoulder chuck is ground in the kitchen daily for the tasty burgers. Sides include perfect French fries made from fresh potatoes and made-from-scratch soups, potato salad, and coleslaw. Milkshakes are served in old-fashioned metal canisters. Seating is at tables or at a counter with swivel stools, and a collection of Presidential china decorates the walls. In mild weather, a pleasant outdoor patio landscaped with a waterfall and Japanese garden is inviting.

## Blowfish Sushi To Die For

*2170 Bryant St., South of Market, (415) 285-3848, fax (415) 285-0286; www.blowfishsushi.com.*

For description, see page 191.

## Boulevard

*1 Mission St./Stewart St., The Embarcadero, (415) 543-6084, fax (415) 495-2936; www.boulevard restaurant.com. L M-F, D daily; $$$. Highchairs, boosters, booths. Reservations advised. Valet parking.*

Co-owned by chef Nancy Oakes and acclaimed local restaurant designer Pat Kuleto, this sumptuous restaurant offers a feast for both the palate and the eyes and is perhaps the most

popular restaurant in San Francisco. Diners enter the gorgeous 1889 French-style building via a revolving door. The belle époque-style interior features stunning mosaic tiled floors as well as sensuous blown-glass light fixtures and pressed tin and ironwork accents. Some tables have three-landmark views—of the Ferry Building, Embarcadero Center, and the Bay Bridge. Large, serious forks foreshadow the exciting, full-flavored dishes to follow. One flawless meal here began with a Chinese-seasoned appetizer of two perfect prawns intertwined over a plump rock shrimp dumpling. The entree was a thick, honey-cured pork loin served with roasted potatoes and baby spinach. A pear tart with caramel sauce and vanilla bean ice cream provided the perfect finish.

## Brandy Ho's Hunan Food

*217 Columbus Ave./Pacific St., Chinatown, (415) 788-7527, fax (415) 788-7528; www.brandyhoshunan.com. L-D daily; $.*

Hot and spicy Chinese Hunan peasant cuisine is prepared to order here in an atmospheric high-ceilinged old building furnished with granite-top tables and featuring an inviting counter overlooking busy cooks in the noisy open kitchen. Medium-hot is plenty spicy, and everything is prepared without MSG. The lengthy menu offers an array of interesting choices, including tasty onion cake, deep-fried dumplings, gon-pou shrimp, and salty-dry eggplant. House-smoked meats, whole fish, and a variety of noodle and rice dishes are also available. Lunch specials are particularly well priced. A branch is at 450 Broadway ((415) 362-6268). Built into a hillside, it has a more hi-tech decor.

## Bubba Gump Shrimp Co.

*On Beach St., at Pier 39, Fisherman's Wharf, (888) 561-GUMP, (415) 781-GUMP, fax (415) 781-4864; www.bubbagump.com. L-D daily; $$. Child menu. No reservations. Validated parking in Pier 39 garage.*

The second link in the chain licensed by Paramount Pictures (the first is in Monterey), this theme restaurant is based on the shrimping scenes in the movie *Forrest Gump*. Located on the second-story level at the end of the pier, it resembles a seafood shack. Not surprisingly, the menu has many shrimp selections, most of them deep-fried, as well as fresh fish entrees and baby back ribs. The bar serves up fun drinks, including several kinds of margaritas (the Delta Sunset is particularly tasty) and some non-alcoholic, good-for-you drinks—a peanutty-chocolate Alabama Sweet Smoothie and a frothy pink Run Forrest Run. Dessert should, of course, be a box of chocolates, and that *is* an option. As a bonus, magnificent views of the bay are enjoyed from most tables. An adjacent shop sells everything Gump. (Winston Groom lived in San Francisco when he wrote *Forrest Gump*—the book. In fact, he named the main character after this city's famous department store.) For more description, see page 119.

## Buca di Beppo

*855 Howard St./Fourth St., South of Market, (415) 543-POPE, fax (415) 543-1209; www.bucadi beppo.com. L-D daily; $$. Highchairs, boosters, booths. Reservations advised.*

The party begins upon entering the door at this festive, happy, old-time southern Italian spot, whose name translates as "Joe's basement." Choose from a warren of small subterranean rooms, or pick one of the comfortable booths in the boisterous upstairs bar, where kids can wiggle and squirm until their heart's content, then study the menu posted on the wall while being entertained by favorite Italian tunes from the '50s. Another primo seating spot is the Kitchen Table; it seats up to five, and everything coming out of the kitchen parades by. Portions are huge and meant for sharing. Lord have mercy on anyone who orders a "large" of anything here, and on the poor soul who arrives without a BIG appetite. The oblong, thin-crusted, Neopolitan-style pepperoni pizza measures 2 feet long and 1 foot wide and is nothing short of great; it's served high on a footed tray so as not to crowd a tall bowl of spaghetti with one very large, fist-sized meatball and perhaps a

tasty salad, too. Or skip the pizza and order the satisfying garlic bread. More pastas and some chicken and veal dishes round out the menu. Even those who order small portions have leftovers to take home that can feed them for a night or two more. Kids have been known to grow saucer eyes when they find out soft drink orders include *unlimited* refills.

## The Buena Vista Cafe

*2765 Hyde St./Beach St., Fisherman's Wharf, (415) 474-5044, fax (415) 474-2207; www.thebuenavista.com. B-L-D daily; $. Child portions. No reservations.*

In 1952 the owner of this legendary bar challenged local travel writer Stanton Delaplane to help him re-create the Irish coffee served at Shannon Airport in Ireland. The biggest problem was getting the cream to float. Once mastered, the result is history, and this cozy bar now dispenses more Irish whiskey than any other spot in the country. A decaf version is available. (The official recipe according to its inventor, the late Joe Sheridan, is: Cream as rich as an Irish brogue; coffee as strong as a friendly hand; sugar sweet as the tongue of a rogue; and whiskey smoothe as the wit of the land.) It is de rigueur to stop at this cozy spot and find out what all the fuss is about. Delicious casual meals have been served since the 1890s and currently include hamburgers and sandwiches as well as hot entrees with fresh vegetables. A window seat provides views of the action across the street at the cable car turnaround and of the bay and Golden Gate Bridge.

## Cafe Bastille

*22 Belden Pl./Bush St., Financial district, (415) 986-5673, fax (415) 986-1013; www.cafebastille.com. L-D M-Sat; $. Reservations advised for D; no reservations for L.*

Located in the middle of a quaint alley in the "French Quarter," this Very French bistro provides a quick fix for Francophiles. Seating is at a long row of tight tables with a wall bench on one side and a chair on the other, or in the Bohemian atmosphere of the crowded cellar. In warm weather, tables are set up outside in the alley. The Americanized menu includes salads, sandwiches, a pizzetta, crêpes, and more substantial entrees such as boudin noir (black sausage) and quiche. Authentic French desserts include crème caramel, chocolate mousse, and a fabulous crêpe topped with chocolate sauce, toasted almonds, and whipped cream. Live music is scheduled upstairs Tuesday through Saturday.

## Cafe de la Presse

*352 Grant Ave., Union Square, (415) 398-2680, fax (415) 249-0916; www.cafedelapresse.com. B-L-D daily; $$. Highchairs, boosters.*

With large windows offering views of the sidewalk, this is *the* place to be for breakfast. Dine then on croissants and lattes as well as waffles, pancakes, and oatmeal. Lunch brings on salads, a good old American hamburger, a classic croque-monsieur, and some frites that rival those McDonald's is famous for. Nine beers are on tap, and 25 wines are poured by the glass. On nice days, outdoor sidewalk-side tables are an enticing option. A more formal **restaurant** *(469 Bush St./Grant Ave., (415) 249-0900.)* with a more sophisticated dinner menu is located in the back. The surrounding area is filled with French cafes and has become popular with French visitors, and international newspapers and magazines are for sale in the cafe's small gift shop.

## Cafe de Paris-L'Entrecote

*2032 Union St./Buchanan St., Pacific Heights, (415) 931-5006, fax (415) 931-5383; www.cafedeparislentre- cote.citysearch.com. L-D daily; $$-$$$. Highchairs, boosters. Reservations advised. Valet parking Sat-Sun.*

Situated within the shell of the first mansion built west of Van Ness Avenue, which was also the home of the dairy that gave the name "cow hollow" to this district, this authentic French bistro opened on Bastille Day in 1983. In a bow to history and city dictates, an unusual sort of greenhouse cafe was built around a glass-encased palm tree planted in front of the house in 1867; it is a choice room to be in during daylight, as views of the sidewalk parade are prime then. The restaurant's signature dish is a charbroiled New York steak served with their 12-ingredient secret sauce (made downstairs, out of sight even of the chef!), a flawless butter lettuce salad, and crisp pommes frites. The menu also holds seasonal surprises such as a deep-fried soft shell crab appetizer (the French would definitely love this) and house-smoked salmon. Crêpes and omelettes, a hamburger,

and several daily specials are also available. A full-flavored tarte tatin—a sort of French caramelized apple pie—is the house dessert specialty. Other endings include pêche Melba, profiteroles with chocolate sauce, and the classic crème brulee. Both the secret steak sauce and salad dressing are available bottled to take home. On weekend evenings, live music is scheduled in the bar until 2 a.m. A Cafe de Paris also exists in Geneva, and a L'Entrecote de Paris in Paris.

## Cafe Marimba

*2317 Chestnut St./Scott St., Marina district, (415) 776-1506. L W-Sun, D Tu-Sun; $. Highchairs, child menu. Reservations accepted.*

Decorated with bright colors and folk art, this popular Mexican spot has a bar with counter seating overlooking the open kitchen. Floors are concrete, and the ceiling is high. The menu concentrates on the complex cuisines of Oaxaca and Vera Cruz, with a variety of salsas, fresh seafood, several moles, chile rellenos stuffed with mushrooms, chicken tamales steamed in banana leaves, delicate empanadas, unusual soups, ceviches, and quesadillas—all made with authentic ingredients—among the choices. And, of course, margaritas reign. After, the **Marina Supermarket** just next door is the perfect place to pick up supplies.

## Café Niebaum-Coppola

*916 Kearny St./Columbus, North Beach, (415) 291-1700; www.cafecoppola.com. L-D M-Sat; $$.*

An original Francis Ford Coppola production, this flagship cafe site is located in the historical wedge-shaped Sentinel Building that houses Mr. Coppola's American Zoetrope production company. The menu includes Argentine picadas (like tapas), salads, and some pastas and sauces from the Coppola product line. For more description, see page 180.

## Caffe Sport

*574 Green St./Columbus, North Beach, (415) 981- 1251; www.caffesport.citysearch.com. L F-Sat, D Tu-Sat; $$. Reservations advised. No cards.*

The bad news is that the cramped and uncomfortable seating here of yore remains, but the good news is that the infamous slow and surly service is gone. And it is easy now to get a reservation. Celebrate by checking out the still-funky decor and still-incredible Sicilian food. Waiters seem trained to nudge diners into ordering more than they think they need, but it is unusual to be disappointed with their recommendations. Scrupulously fresh prawns in garlicky white sauce and pasta in pesto are both especially good.

## Caffe Trieste

*601 Vallejo St./Grant Ave., North Beach, (415) 392-6739, fax (415) 550-1239; www.caffetrieste.com. Daily 6:30am-11pm; $. No reservations. No cards.*

This Very Cool coffeehouse was a favorite hangout with the Beat Generation and was frequented by Jack Kerouac, Allen Ginsberg, and friends, and it is where Francis Ford Coppola wrote part of *The Godfather* script. It is also credited with having the first espresso machine on the West Coast. In traditional Italian style, the owners perform live opera every Saturday afternoon.

## California Culinary Academy

*625 Polk St./Turk St., (800) BAY-CHEF, (415) 216-4329; www.baychef.com. L-D Tu-F; SunBr occasionally; $-$$. Reservations advised.*

Founded in 1977, this training school for professional chefs operates two very different restaurants, both of which are completely student-run while overseen by chef-instructors. **The Academy Grill** offers an intimate setting and features American and Italian specialties. The more formal **Carême Room** operates in a grand room with a 40-foot-high ceiling and fine architectural details. It serves an elegant global cuisine and features fabulous Thursday and Friday buffets that showcase student work. The school's retail store sells housemade salads and pastries to go as well as logo apparel and cooking utensils.

## Calzone's

*430 Columbus Ave./Green St., North Beach, (415) 397-3600, fax (415) 397-3446; www.calzonesf.com. L-D daily; $-$$. Highchairs, boosters, booths, child menu. Reservations accepted.*

Reflecting the colors of the Italian flag, walls reaching to a high ceiling are painted dark green and decorated with colorful Italian cooking ingredients. Diners seated at marble tables downstairs enjoy superb views of sidewalk traffic, while some upstairs diners are entertained by overviews of the downstairs diners. Meals begin with a crusty hunk of Italian bread. Favorite appetizers are light and crunchy deep-fried calamari and fresh tomato bruschetta. Misshapen pizzas prepared in a wood-fired brick oven come in a choice of toppings, and delicious calzones (pizza turnovers) are also available. Housemade lasagna and gnocchi, a hamburger, and freshly made fettuccine ribbons, orzo, and angel hair pastas are also on the menu.

For dessert, **Stella Pastry and Cafe** is just next door. It is famous for its trademarked sacripantina cake, described by *Gourmet* magazine as "a San Francisco concoction of cream, air, and magic . . ."

## The Canvas Gallery

*1200 9th Ave./Lincoln Way, inner Sunset district, cafe (415) 504-0060, gallery (415) 504-0070, fax (415) 504-0010; www.thecanvasgallery.com. M-W 6am-midnight, Thur-Sat 6am-2am; $. Free parking in back.*

On a busy corner near the Hall of Flowers in Golden Gate Park, this innovative cafe operates in one large, open room with tall ceilings and a variety of seating areas. Decor is industrial chic. Diners order at the counter and then items are delivered to the table. Especially good are the individual hummus and babaganouch plates served with superb pita triangles. A large selection of sandwiches, salads, entrees, and pastries is also available. Drinks include delicious made-from-scratch cream sodas as well as thick, pudding-like traditional Spanish hot chocolate and assorted coffee drinks. The works of emerging artists hang on the walls, and evening events are scheduled regularly.

## Capp's Corner

*1600 Powell St./Green St., North Beach, (415) 989-2589; www.cappscorner.com. L-D daily; $$. Highchairs, boosters, booths, child portions. Reservations advised.*

After entering the saloon-style swinging doors, diners are in what is reputed to be the liveliest and noisiest of the few remaining North Beach family-style restaurants. When there is a wait for a table, a seat at the Victorian-era bar can make time fly. In the cozy, friendly interior dining room, where photos of prior happy diners decorate the walls, noisy family groups rub elbows with swinging singles while enjoying hearty Italian food. A bountiful three-course dinner includes minestrone soup, green salad, and entree (steak, roast duck, chicken breast picatta, osso bucco, leg of lamb, lasagna, seafood cannelloni, etc.).

## Carnelian Room

*555 California St./Montgomery St., 52nd fl. in Bank of America bldg., Financial district, (415) 433-7500, fax (415) 433-5827; www.carnelianroom.com. D daily, SunBr; $$$. Highchairs, boosters.*

In a luxurious setting atop San Francisco's tallest building, this elegant restaurant presents a fine-dining menu and has a wine cellar holding 40,000 bottles. It also provides diners a feast for their eyes, with walnut paneling and fine art on one side and breathtaking bay views on the other. A three-course, fixed-price menu offers items such as sweet pea ravioli with Meyer lemon-mint broth, peppercorn-crusted ahi tuna with ginger mashed potatoes, and a banana pecan tart. A bar lounge permits enjoying the view without dining.

## Cha-Am

*701 Folsom St./3rd St., South of Market, (415) 546-9710, fax (415) 546-0354; http://chaam.citysearch.com. L M-F, D daily; $.*

For description, see page 277.

## Chaya Brasserie

*132 The Embarcadero/Mission St., (415) 777-8688, fax (415) 247-9952; www.thechaya.com. L M-F, D daily; $$$. Reservations advised. Valet parking.*

Featuring magnificent views of the bay and Bay Bridge that are especially pretty at night, this new restaurant is a branch of a Los Angeles venue. With French-style parquet floors, Japanese-style bamboo ceilings, and dramatic contemporary art hanging on natural brick walls, this spot is a combination of a French brasserie and a Japanese teahouse, or "chaya." The Franco-Japanese menu offers up labor-intensive main dishes such as grilled salmon with fingerling potatoes and herb-Dijon mustard sauce, and grilled free-range chicken with Maine lobster tail and wild-rice risotto. A full sushi bar dining area is also an option. Desserts are a highlight: A warm Valrhona chocolate cake with raspberry sauce is to die for, and the caramelized banana tart with crushed walnut pralines is pretty good, too.

## The Cheesecake Factory

*251 Geary St./Powell St., in Macy's, 8th floor, Union Square, (415) 391-4444; www.thecheesecake factory.com. L-D daily; $-$$. Highchairs, boosters, booths. No reservations.*

Reached via a special elevator inside Macy's, this wildly popular rooftop restaurant overlooks Union Square. The eclectic menu is extensive—appetizers, pizza, specialty dishes, pastas, fish and seafood, steaks and chops, salads, sandwiches, and breakfast items are all options—and, as might be expected from the name, it features a head-spinning selection of cheesecakes. With a menu so large it is bound like a book, it is a great spot for either a snack (the avocado egg rolls are great) or a full meal. And then there are the fabulous espresso drinks and frozen, smoothie-style drinks. Though there is no children's menu, kids like the bite-size burgers on mini-buns known as "roadside sliders" and the sweet-corn tamale cakes—both on the appetizer menu. The problem here is deciding.

## Chez Papa

*1401 18th St./Missouri St., Potrero Hill, (415) 824-8210; www.chezpapasf.com. L M-Sat, D daily; $$. Highchairs. D reservations advised.*

There is usually a line out the door at this tiny, cozy French-style bistro. A comfortable banquette lines the wall, and the din of happy dinners can be positively deafening—making it a great place to go if talking is not of primary interest. The menu is broken into starters and small plates—how about a soothing bowl of puréed cauliflower soup or a plate of seared scallops and fava beans?—and larger entrees—perhaps a roasted chicken or fragrant lamb daube. It doesn't really matter. The entire menu is delectable.

## Chinatown restaurants

See page 17.

## Citizen Cake

*399 Grove St./Gough St., Hayes Valley/Civic Center, (415) 861-2228, fax (415) 861-0565; www.citizen cake.com. B-L Tu-F, D Tu-Sat, Sat-SunBr; $$-$$$. Reservations advised.*

Though the dining room is small and waits can be long, the counter usually turns over quickly. Another option is to just give up and order take-out, though it *is* nice being seated in the sleek, modern, industrial-style interior with its soothing view out tall windows. Most items are housemade, and everything is delicious. Lunch choices might include a Cuban marinated pork-Havarti cheese sandwich on scrumptious housemade bread, or a puffy Molinari pepperoni pizza. A French-style coffee bowl of hot chocolate prepared with Scharffen Berger bittersweet chocolate and topped with a fabulous housemade marshmallow makes a great dessert, but something from the celebrated pastry kitchen is not to be missed—maybe a vanilla cupcake with white chocolate frosting or a sticky toffee pudding or a blood orange cremesicle parfait. And don't forget a bag of mixed cookies to take home. When leaving, do view the glassed-in demonstration pastry kitchen and then stop in at the art gallery next door.

## Clémentine

*126 Clement St./3rd Ave., Richmond district, (415) 387-0408, fax (415) 387-0782;. D Tu-Sun; $$. Highchairs, boosters. Reservations advised.*

Daydreaming about a trip to the south of France but don't want the bother and expense of getting there? Voila! A dinner at this popular neighborhood restaurant will fulfill this fantasy, complete with servers bearing charming French accents but no attitude. It's maybe even *better* than France, and the French bread is certainly as good. A park-like entry marks the spot with pottery-bound trees threaded with tiny lights. Seating in the cozy, welcoming interior is at tables decorated with such nice touches as lush fresh flowers and salt and pepper in teensy bowls with weensy scoops. Appetizers on the mouth-watering menu include a soup of the day, perfectly dressed salads, and seasonal items like a fresh pear tart or steamed mussels. Main courses might be roasted salmon with porcini mushroom raviolis and sorrel sauce, or roasted quail plumped with foie gras mousse and baby vegetables. Classic items, such as escargots or steak and frites are also offered. Dessert brings on vanilla crème brulee, poached pears with chocolate sauce, and caramelized French toast.

## Cliff House

*1090 Point Lobos Ave., outer Richmond district, (415) 386-3330, fax (415) 387-7837; www.cliffhouse.com.*

*L M-F, D daily, Sat-SunBr; $$-$$$. Highchairs, boosters, booths. Reservations advised.*

Perched solidly on bedrock at the edge of the Pacific, this historic treasure is the only ocean-front restaurant in San Francisco. It has been around for quite some time, since 1863 to be exact, but in four different renditions, having twice burned to the ground and having gone through a major update completed in 2004. Though it has gone through many changes, the structure has always housed a restaurant and has been part of the National Park Service's Golden Gate National Recreation Area since 1977. **Sutro's** restaurant is housed in a new 2-story wing with floor-to-ceiling windows and features an American seafood menu, and the more casual **Bistro** serves a less expensive menu.

Before or after, visit the **Camera Obscura** *(www.giantcamera.com. Daily 11-sunset, weather permitting. $1, 2-12 50¢.).* Leonardo daVinci's 16th-century invention was probably a popular tourist attraction in the 1700s and 1800s. This reproduction was built here in 1946 and was once part of Playland-at-the-Beach. It uses a 10-inch mirror and two opposing plano-convex lenses to focus a live image of the shoreline outside onto a 6-foot parabolic screen inside. Rotating slowly, it presents magnified views of Ocean Beach, Seal Rocks, and crashing Pacific waves. The personalized tour is both entertaining and educational.

Nearby, barking sea lions and brown pelicans share space on historic **Seal Rocks**. They can be seen with just the naked eye or viewed through an antique telescope.

## Cordon Bleu

*1574 California St./Polk St., (415) 673-5637. L Tu-Sat, D Tu-Sun; $. No cards.*

With just nine counter seats and three tiny tables, this miniscule Vietnamese restaurant is one of the oldest in the city and has been under the same management since 1976. From the counter, diners can watch the entire cooking process while sipping a complimentary mug of hot tea. Satisfying one-plate meals consist of a large scoop of rice topped with light tomato-based meat gravy and a choice of deep-fried imperial roll, tasty barbecued beef satay (listed on the menu as shish kebab), or barbecued chicken. That's it!

**Landmark's Lumiere** movie theater *(1573 California St./Polk St., (415) 267-4893; www.landmarktheatres.com.)* is right next door, and a host of interesting shops are just around the corner.

## Delancey Street Restaurant

*600 The Embarcadero/Brannan St., (415) 512-5179, fax (415) 512-5186. L Tu-F, D Tu-Sun, Sat-SunBr; $-$$. Highchairs, boosters. Reservations advised. Valet parking.*

The comfortable open room here lets in plenty of light and even a glimpse of the bay. Though that is enough to lure in plenty of diners, this special restaurant is also a training school of the Delancey Street Foundation—the country's largest and most acclaimed self-help residential organization for former hard-core criminals. It is completely self-supporting. All tips are considered donations, and all restaurant profits go directly to caring for the residents. Interestingly, no resident who has finished the 2-year training program has ever gone on to commit a serious crime. In this win-win atmosphere, it seems impossible to leave unsatisfied. Lunch is a particular bargain, with plenty of well-priced, well-executed sandwiches—roasted ginger pork loin and chutney on sourdough bread, blackened chicken breast on a Kaiser roll. Hot dishes such as Thai red curry prawns and vegetables over rice, a hamburger, a hot dog, and an assortment of light items—including desserts such as a Chocolate Decadence that claims only 200 calories and 6 grams of fat—are also available. The menu changes daily and features international home-style dishes and also items reflecting the current residents' backgrounds.

## Eagle Cafe

*On Beach St., at Pier 39, Fisherman's Wharf, (415) 433-3689, fax (415) 434-9253. B-L-D daily; $. Boosters. No reservations.*

Situated at the pier entrance, this casual spot dates from 1920—when it was located across the street. The menu offers hearty breakfasts and a standout meatloaf sandwich at lunch, and strong drinks are always available at the antique bar.

## E&O Trading Company

*314 Sutter St./Grant Ave., 2 blks. from Union Square, (415) 693-0303, fax (415) 693-9137; www.eotrading. com. L M-Sat, D daily; $$. Highchairs, boosters. Reservations advised.*

The sleek, quiet exterior here belies the warm, roaring interior designed to resemble an Indonesian trading company warehouse. Live piano music keeps things jumping in the busy bar and is enjoyed throughout the restaurant. Well-positioned seating for meals is found both upstairs, where some diners have views of the street and others can watch the action in the bar downstairs, and adjoining the bar, where there is additionally a counter with tall stools overlooking the kitchen. Housemade English-style beers and tropical sodas prepared with housemade fruit syrups are the perfect accompaniment to the mild-mannered but complexly flavored Indonesian fare. Sharing a variety of items from the unusual southeast Asian menu is the way to go. A fabulous dinner can be composed of lamb naan (stuffed bread); Cambodian lettuce cups filled with an exotic mixture of pork, shrimp, peanuts, and coconut; Thai crab cakes with a tangy red curry sauce; papaya-avocado salad with spicy Asian greens; and delicious Hawaiian walu fish with black-and-tan sesame seed crust served atop a bed of rice atop green long beans. Noteworthy small dishes—the menu's strong point—include crispy Indonesian corn fritters and satays with spicy peanut sauce. Desserts are made in-house. For the perfect finale, select one from the bamboo dessert tray—perhaps a mango crème brulee or a tropical Napoleon—and order up some of the fragrant World Peace licorice-peppermint loose leaf tea served in a heavy metal pot. Before leaving, check out the restroom decor, the basement beer-brewing vats, and the bamboo birdcage collection hanging just off the bar area.

## Elite Cafe

*2049 Fillmore St./California St., upper Fillmore, (415) 346-8668. D daily, SunBr; $$$. Highchairs, boosters, booths. Reservations advised.*

Parties of four get the best seats here, in enclosed wooden booths left from the restaurant's prior life as an old-time Chinese restaurant. In addition to Cajun martinis and other exotic bar drinks, plus appetizers such as Cajun popcorn, the menu offers a selection of authentic spicy Cajun-Creole dishes that includes gumbo, jambalaya, blackened salmon, chicken and dumplings, and barbecue ribs.

## Ella's

*500 Presidio Ave./California St., Presidio Heights, (415) 441-5669; www.ellassanfrancisco.com. B-L-D M-F, Sat-SunBr; $. Highchairs, boosters. Reservations taken for L-D.*

This cheery spot changes its menu weekly and serves a close to perfect weekend brunch. The oh-so-simple fluffy scrambled eggs come with faultless home fries and an oversize baking soda biscuit with strawberry preserves. The waffles, pancakes, and chicken hash are also primo. And parents will be happy to know it is kid central here on weekends, with pacifiers, toys, and baby carriers everywhere. Unfortunately, reservations are not taken for weekend brunch, and even getting here early doesn't prevent a wait. Grin and bear it. The limited lunch menu includes soups, sandwiches, salads, hot entrees, and a delicious gingery punch made with fresh OJ. After, it's just a block over to Sacramento Street for some chi-chi shopping.

## El Mansour

*3119 Clement St./32nd Ave., outer Richmond district, (415) 751-2312, fax (510) 669-0444; www.elmansour.com. D daily; $$. Child portions. Reservations advised.*

Upon entering the double doors of this Moroccan restaurant, diners are encased in another world. Cloth is draped from the ceiling in the intimate dining room, giving occupants the illusion of being inside a sultan's tent. Floors covered with plush oriental carpets and hassock seating at low tables of inlaid wood add to the sensuous feeling. After diners select an entree from the fixed-price menu, a waiter in a long caftan appears to perform the ritual hand washing. Hands are gathered over a large metal pot placed in the middle of the table, then splashed with warm water. When the first course arrives—a tasty lentil soup—diners drink it right from the bowl, since no eating utensils are provided here. A bland Moroccan bread is offered to accompany it. The next course is a salad plate of spicy marinated rounds of carrots and cucumbers and a delicious mixture of tomatoes and green peppers meant to be scooped up with the bread. Then

comes bastela—a fragrant pie containing a sweet chicken and almond mixture wrapped in flaky filo pastry and sprinkled with powdered sugar. Entree choices include seafood, rabbit, couscous, and shish kabob, as well as succulent roasted chicken and tender stewed lamb topped with almonds, honey, or prunes. Tangines (stews) are another option. Dessert is fried bananas with honey and a repeat of the hand-bathing ritual. And finally the waiter pours mint tea, skillfully and beautifully, from up high. Belly dancers perform nightly.

## Enrico's Sidewalk Cafe

*504 Broadway/Kearny St., North Beach, (415) 982-6223, fax (415) 397-7244; www.enricosside walkcafe.com. L-D daily; $$. Highchairs, booths. Reservations advised. Valet parking.*

Though no longer run by Enrico Banducci—the well-known original owner, who reportedly now operates a hot dog cart in Richmond, Virginia—this landmark restaurant was the city's first coffeehouse. Coffee and snacks are still served on the informal outdoor patio, which is heated in cool weather and is one of the best spots around for people watching. More substantial meals can also be ordered there as well as in the large interior room, where paintings by local artists adorn the walls and jazz is performed nightly from 9 p.m. The dinner menu offers a large selection of tapas plus several soups, salads, pastas, and pizzas. Delicious entrees include items such as salmon coated with a fruit mustard and served with garlic mashed potatoes, and a surprisingly flavorful top sirloin served with a braised onion and perfect oven-roasted potatoes. Accomplished housemade desserts, such as malt ice cream in a chocolate cookie sandwich with toasted pecans, are hard to resist. Special events are sometimes scheduled.

## Farallon

*450 Post St./Powell St., Union Square, (415) 956-6969, fax (415) 834-1234; www.farallon restaurant. com. L Tu-Sat, D daily; $$$. Booths. Reservations advised. Valet parking at D.*

The long bar entryway of this spectacular restaurant leads under gorgeous lighting fixtures posing as jellyfish, past curving stairs slathered with "caviar," and on into a magnificent back room. An elaborate painted mosaic, successfully designed to look aged, covers the three Gothic arches of the main dining room ceiling (it was once the ceiling for the Elks Club salt-water swimming pool on the floor below) along with gargantuan belle époque sea urchin light fixtures. No table in the tiered main room is bad, and many are attached to exquisitely comfortable velvet-covered booths. The fish-centered menu of impeccably fresh seasonal "coastal cuisine" changes daily and includes innovative preparations of fish (ginger-steamed wild salmon and striped bass "pillows" with crayfish mousse and foie gras coulis), a large selection of raw items (including house-prepared caviar), and usually a lobster dish. Raw shellfish appetizers and roasted fish entrees are usually available, along with a token chicken and beef item. Luscious desserts have included Tahitian vanilla bean fritters with apricot coulis and a Bing cherry Napoleon.

## Far East Cafe

*631 Grant Ave./Sacramento St., Chinatown, (415) 982-3245, fax (415) 362-8865; www.fareastcafesf.com. L-D daily; $$. Highchairs, boosters. Reservations advised.*

Looking much as it did when it opened in 1920, this intriguing restaurant has 30 private wooden booths with curtains for a door. These wonderful, cozy enclosures provide the ultimate in privacy. The extensive a la carte menu includes sizzling rice soup, fried won tons, cashew chicken, deep-fried squab, and a variety of chow mein and chop suey dishes, and the family-style Cantonese dinner is always a good choice. Exotic shark's fin, bird's nest, and sea-weed soups are also available.

## Faz

*161 Sutter St., in Crocker Galleria, Union Square, (415) 362-0404, fax (415) 362-5865; www.fazrestaurants.com. L-D M-F; $$. Highchairs. Reservations advised.*

House specialties on the Middle Eastern menu in this quietly elegant venue include dolmas (stuffed grape leaves), hummus, and tabouleh. Soups, salads, sandwiches, pizzas, and more substantial entrees such as kabobs and seafood items are also on the menu. Desserts include baklava, a fig tart, a saffron brownie, and pistachio custard.

## Ferry Building Marketplace

*At foot of Market St./The Embarcadero, (415) 693-0996; www.ferrybuildingmarketplace.com. M-F 10-6, Sat 9-6, Sun 11-5. No dogs.*

Bay views punctuate the long (it's the length of two football fields), 2-story-high, sky-lighted interior corridor of this landmark 1898 building—a sort of indoor Main Street—filled with food-related stalls and shops. All the best, most delicious organic produce and gourmet delicacies are easy to collect and carry home: Acme baked goods, Peet's coffee, Cowgirl Creamery cheeses, Frog Hollow Farm peaches, Scharffen Berger chocolates. Shops specializing in caviar and in mushrooms are also in the mix, as are a branch of **Book Passage** (see page 215), and **Culinaire**, an antique shop specializing in food- and wine-related objects. Restaurants include **The Slanted Door** (see page 84) and a branch of the **Imperial Tea Court** (see page 17). A **farmers' market** *(www.ferryplazafarmers market.com. Tu 10:30-2:30, Thur 3-7, Sat-Sun 8-2.)* operates informally around the exterior of the building.

## Fifth Floor

*12 Fourth St./Market St., in Hotel Palomar, South of Market, (415) 348-1555, fax (415) 348-1551; www.fifth floor.citysearch.com. D M-Sat; $$$. Reservations advised. Valet parking.*

This cool, chic, very trendy restaurant features tailored furnishings, dramatic lighting, and faux zebra carpet. Described as on "the culinary wild side," suckling pig is among the entrees, and delicious desserts include butter-scotch pudding and a signature banana split.

## Fior d'Italia

*601 Union St./Stockton St., North Beach, (415) 986-1886, fax (415) 986-7031; www.fior.com. L-D daily; $$-$$$. Highchairs, boosters, booths. Reservations advised. Valet parking.*

Opened in 1886, when great sailing ships plied the bay and goats roamed Telegraph Hill, this venerable traditional northern Italian restaurant is the oldest in the U.S. The small dining area in the bar is graced with a large composite mural depicting the Church of St. Francis of Assisi in Tuscany, while the spacious main dining area in back is decorated with historic San Francisco memorabilia and outfitted with plenty of comfortable oversize booths.

Experienced servers, attired in traditional black-and-white uniforms, offer expert assistance in navigating the extensive menu. Always a good choice is the four-course, fixed-price dinner; main courses include seafood, veal, and chicken. Additionally, the regular menu offers fresh pasta, risotto, and polenta. Desserts include the classic tiramisu, fresh berries, and sometimes a delicious poached pear in caramel sauce and cream.

## The Fly Trap

*606 Folsom St./2nd St., South of Market, (415) 243-0580; www.flytraprestaurant.com. L M-F, D M-Sat; $$. 1 highchair, boosters. Reservations advised.*

Once, long ago, in a former incarnation, the restaurant in this spot solved its fly problem by putting fly paper on the tables, prompting the GIs of the 1898 Spanish-American war to refer to it as the "fly trap." The flies stuck and so did the name. When the original owner's cousin reopened the restaurant after the 1906 earthquake and fire, he irreverently named it "The Fly Trap Restaurant," and it is still called that today. A replica of Louie's Restaurant, a turn-of-the-century Market Street eatery, it has a spiffy updated interior that features high ceilings and a bank of small tables perfect for solo diners. Among the starters are several soups, including a chilled vichyssoise, and a variety of salads, including a tasty celery Victor. House specialties include an exquisite chicken coq au vin, the hard-to-find Hangtown fry, and an Old World wiener schnitzel. Steaks, seafood, pastas, and a hamburger are also available. Each entree is accompanied by thick, crispy, ridged housemade potato chips. The rich housemade desserts range from a banana split to a chocolate torte with marscapone cream, and intriguing drinks such as the Fly Trap Coffee, prepared with Godiva and Frangelica liquors, are also available.

## Fog City Diner

*1300 Battery St./The Embarcadero, (415) 982-2000, fax (415) 982-3711; www.fogcitydiner.com. B-L M-F, D daily, Sat-SunBr. Highchairs, boosters, booths, child menu. Reservations advised.*

Glitzy with chrome and glowing with neon, this inviting spot offers comfy black leather booths and good views all around. The updated, upscale diner fare includes jalapeño corn bread, tasty crab cakes, chicken breast schnitzel with homey garlic mashed potatoes, and, of course, a good old American hamburger. Opt for a side of housemade bread and butter pickles, some crispy onion rings made with Anchor Steam beer batter, and a house-invented Barbados Cosmopolitan cocktail, and you're ready to rock 'n roll (however, there's no jukebox in *this* diner). Do save room for ice cream—perhaps a fabulous sundae of the day, a milkshake or malted, or maybe a black cow (root beer float).

## Forbes Island

*At Pier 39, Fisherman's Wharf, (415) 951-4900, fax (707) 775-4578; www.forbesisland.com. D W-Sun; $$$. Reservations required. Boat shuttle $3/person; validated parking at Pier 39 garage.*

After the short 5-minute voyage over to the world's only floating island, owner/host/bartender Forbes Thor Kiddoo conducts what might be the world's shortest tour. He provides a quick glimpse of a replica 40-foot lighthouse and of some *real* sand and palm trees, then it's down the steps to the partially submerged, oriental-carpeted dining room decorated with antique nautical artifacts and paintings. The smallish menu—a selection of California cuisine with a French twist—is prepared in a tiny galley and includes an excellent Caesar salad, a divine rack of lamb with 2-inch thick chops, and a *very* French Café Liegeois coffee float. For a romantic occasion, consider requesting the single teeny table in the diminutive wine cellar. Cigars can be enjoyed outside overlooking the sea lions basking on nearby barges. And don't miss seeing the restrooms.

## Foreign Cinema

*2534 Mission St./21st St., Mission district, (415) 648-7600, fax (415) 648-7669; www.foreigncinema.com. D Tu-Sun, Sat-SunBr; $$-$$$. Highchairs, boosters, child menu. Reservations advised. Valet parking at D.*

Operating within the dramatically remodeled interior of a former department store in which everything was ripped out and left bare and trendy, this wildly popular spot attracts the hordes down its long, votive-lit corridor to party and feast. Seating is either on an open-air patio (covered by a clear plastic canopy in cool weather), where diners can watch the foreign flick of the week, or in the roaring main dining room with its 20-foot-tall ceiling. Specialties include an expansive oyster bar, baked cheese with roasted potatoes, curry-roasted chicken, and chocolate pot de crème. Several communal tables are available for walk-ins.

## The Franciscan

*At foot of Powell St./The Embarcadero, Pier 43¹/2, Fisherman's Wharf, (800) 360-7733, (415) 362-7733, fax (415) 362-0174; www.franciscanrestaurant.com. L-D daily; $$-$$$. Highchairs, boosters, booths, child menu. Reservations advised. Parking validated at adjacent lot.*

Though the outside of this restaurant is one of the ugliest bits of architecture imaginable, the inside is tasteful, with staggered tiers of seating—some in cozy half-moon booths—and every diner gets a fabulous bay view. A drink menu starts things off with some playful concoctions, including several non-alcoholic numbers, and that famous San Francisco sourdough bread keeps hunger at bay. The favorites are all here, though updated for contemporary tastes. Starters include a delicious clam chowder with bits of bacon and thyme, crab cakes, seafood cocktails, and oysters on the half shell. The crab Louis is made with Dungeness crab (according to a waiter it has "seen ice, but carefully"), mixed lettuces, and a delicious housemade dressing. The seafood combo is an attractive arrangement of grilled—not fried—fresh fish, prawns, and scallops positioned around a wild-rice cake topped with ginger-cilantro sauce. A satisfying exception to the calorie-heavy desserts is a trio of full-flavored sorbets. Fish-hating kids will love the special coloring menu offering spaghetti and a hamburger as well as grilled prawns.

## Fringale

*570 Fourth St./Brannan St., South of Market, (415) 543-0573, fax (415) 905-0317. L M-F, D M-Sat; $$. Highchairs, boosters. Reservations advised.*

Cheery yet intimate, this bright, very popular spot offers a seasonal menu of light Franco-California bistro fare that Americans can recognize. Appetizers might include a soup du jour of creamy fava bean or cauliflower purée, a house-cured salmon or foie gras medallions, and maybe a mashed potato croquette. Dinner entrees have included delicate steamed salmon topped with threads of deep-fried onions and served on a bed of tart braised leeks, a lemon-chicken breast with a side of couscous and dates, and a marinated roast rack of lamb. Among the possible desserts are a tangy lemon tart with fresh raspberries and an exceptional clafouti made with toasted almond slices and fresh raspberries. In French "fringale" means "the urge to eat," and that urge is delightfully satisfied here.

## Gary Danko

*800 North Point/Hyde St., Fisherman's Wharf, (415) 749-2060, fax (415) 775-1805; www.garydanko.com. D daily; $$$+. Reservations advised. Valet parking.*

Simply the best is found here, from buttery foie gras to smoked sturgeon on buckwheat blini to winter root vegetable soup to juniper-crusted venison to sweet Meyer lemon soufflé cake. A fixed-price dinner includes some of the owner-chef's signature dishes—glazed oysters with leeks, salmon medallions topped with horseradish mousse, seasonal flambéed fruit prepared tableside—and a cheese cart presents enticing artisanal cheeses. It is the perfect place to celebrate a special occasion. Large flower arrangements greet diners in the entryway, and two sophisticated, intimate dining rooms keep the atmosphere cozy and lively. Worthy of mention, too, is the serene, spa-like ladies room.

## Gaylord India

*900 North Point St./Larkin St., in Ghirardelli Square, Fisherman's Wharf, (415) 771-8822, fax (415) 771-4980; www.gaylords.com. L-D daily; $$$. Reservations advised.*

With its posh decor of oriental carpets, potted palms, and Chippendale-style chairs, plus its killer bay view, this restaurant wouldn't really need to have good food, too. But fortunately it does. Tandoori meats, freshly baked breads, excellent curries, and many vegetarian items are on the menu.

## Ghirardelli Chocolate Manufactory & Soda Fountain

*900 North Point, in Ghirardelli Square, Fisherman's Wharf, (415) 771-4903; www.ghirardelli.com. Sun-Thur 10am-11pm, F-Sat to 12; $. Highchairs, boosters. No reservations.*

A small working chocolate factory using original equipment from the early 1900s still operates for show in the back of this classic ice cream parlor. All of the chocolate sauces and syrups are made on site, as is the fudge sold in the shop. After reading the mouth-watering menu, which can be kept as a souvenir, each ice cream-lover takes a seat and awaits the fulfillment of their ice cream fantasy. Special concoctions include The Alcatraz Rock (rocky road and vanilla ice cream covered with a shell of chocolate, chopped almonds, whipped cream, and a whole cherry) and The Earthquake Sundae, which serves four or more people (eight flavors of ice cream with eight different toppings accented with bananas, whipped cream, chopped almonds, and cherries). Hot fudge sundaes, sodas, and milkshakes are also available. Ghirardelli chocolate goodies, including a 5-pound chocolate bar, are sold in an adjoining shop.

## Gira Polli
*659 Union St./Columbus, North Beach,*
*(415) 434-4472. Daily 4:30-9:30pm; $. Boosters.*

Solve the dilemma of circling North Beach, searching unsuccessfully for a parking place, by dashing in here and picking up a great take-home dinner while the driver circles yet again. In a flash, the "special" is ready to go—a fragrant rotisserie-roasted chicken prepared in a wood-fired oven and packed with sides of potatoes, fresh vegetables, and rolls. Soups and salads, pastas and risottos, and housemade desserts such as cannoli, lemon-flavored cheesecake, biscotti, and tiramisu are also on the menu. For those able to find a parking space, in-shop seating is available.

## Golden Turtle
*2211 Van Ness Ave./Vallejo St., (415) 441-4419, fax*
*(415) 440-7201; www.goldenturtle.net. L-D Tu-Sun; $$.*
*Highchairs, boosters. Reservations advised.*

Located within a converted Victorian with a koi pond at the entrance, this elegant, sedate Vietnamese restaurant is decorated with intricately hand-carved wood plaques and with light sconces constructed from tree branches. It serves a cuisine that is a cross between Cantonese and Szechwan Chinese. A good starter is crisp-fried imperial rolls stuffed with a pork-seafood mixture and served with thin rice noodles, lettuce, and a mild dipping sauce. Additional dramatic appetizers include barbecued quails flambé and sizzling rice soup.

Among the main dishes are a tasty grilled beef kabob, aromatic lemon grass curry prawns, steamed whole sea bass in a subtle ginger sauce, and fresh catfish in a clay pot. The Seven Jewel beef dinner consists of seven special beef dishes served in a specific order; each dish can also be ordered separately. Tea comes with the meal, and a sweet fresh-squeezed lemonade is among the drink selections. For dessert, don't miss the spectacular presentation of bananas flambé.

## Gold Mountain
*644 Broadway/Stockton St., Chinatown, (415) 296-7733. Dim sum M-F 10:30-3, Sat-Sun 8-3; $.*
*Highchairs, boosters. Reservations advised.*

In the 19th century, Chinese immigrants nicknamed San Francisco "Gold Mountain," in reference to its promise of a new life and fortune. This gigantic, bustling restaurant now promises everyone delicious dim sum, which is served on floors two and three. It is so big that the waiters use walkie-talkies to communicate. Though floor two alone seats 280 people, there still is usually a wait. Once seated, if carts don't arrive fast enough, flag down someone who looks in charge and order directly from the kitchen. Crisp taro balls and roast duck are particularly good here. See also page 16.

## Gordon Biérsch Brewery Restaurant
*2 Harrison St./The Embarcadero, (415) 243-8246, fax*
*(415) 243-9214; www.gordonbiersch.com. L-D daily; $.*
*Highchairs, boosters.*

An **Oktoberfest** is staged each October, complete with plenty of seasonal Wiesenhelles lager, platters of traditional Bavarian culinary delights, waitstaff in lederhosen, and live oompah bands. For more description, see page 195.

## Grand Cafe
*501 Geary St./Taylor St., in Hotel Monaco San Francisco, Union Square, (415) 292-0101, fax (415) 292-0150; www.grandcafe.net. B-L M-Sat, D daily, SunBr; $$-$$$. Highchairs, boosters, booths.*
*Reservations advised. Valet parking.*

Designed after La Coupole in Paris, this immense, open dining room features a 30-foot-high ceiling, ornate columns, majestic art deco-style ceiling lamps, original murals, and fanciful decorative art. Seating is in intimate booths arranged in asymmetrical formations that give all diners a good view. The menu is composed of French bistro-style fare and includes items such as salmon en croute and grilled rib eye steak with pommes frites. Desserts are prepared by a pastry chef and always include the popular banana cream pie, and herbal tea is a delightful production of individual teapot, strainer, and honey pot. The **Petite Cafe** bar area in front is a pleasant setting for a quick sandwich or pizza.

## Greens
*Laguna St./Marina Blvd., at Fort Mason Center, Bldg. A, (415) 771-6222, fax (415) 771-3472; http://greens rest.citysearch.com. L Tu-Sat, D M-Sat, SunBr; $$-$$$. Highchairs, boosters. Reservations essential. Free parking lot adjoins.*

With high ceilings, large windows framing the Golden Gate Bridge, and colorful modern art hanging on the walls, this trendy, all-vegetarian restaurant packs 'em in. Starters on the ever-changing menu might include a fragrant and flavorful black bean chili or a delicate watercress salad with pears and walnuts. Entrees include pastas and a tasty pita sandwich. Desserts are uncomplicated but delicious—perhaps a pear-almond upside down cake or a fabulous apricot tart with pistachio nuts and toasted almond ice cream. On Saturday nights, a fixed-price three-course dinner is the only menu option. Greens is run by the San Francisco Zen Center, and many of the fresh herbs and vegetables are grown at the center's West Marin farm.

**Greens To Go** *((415) 771-6330. M-Thur 8-8, F-Sat 8-5, Sun 9-4.)* dispenses many menu items as well as their delicious breads and an assortment of pastries and desserts.

## Habana
*2979 Van Ness Ave./Pacific St., Russian Hill, (415) 441-CUBA; www.habana1948.com. D daily; $$$. Valet parking.*

A low-key island decor sets the mood with wrought-iron chairs and screens, potted palms, and colorful crockery—transporting diners mentally to far-away Cuba in the far-off time of post-World War II. Do start with a delicious cocktail—perhaps the Ernest Hemingway daiquiri or a minty mojito—and a few appetizers—both the heart of palm salad and spicy pork empanadas are noteworthy. Bread and a tasty dipping sauce are complimentary. Main courses include fresh fish, marinated skirt

steak, and duck breast with a Caribbean tang. Off the entrance, a long bar resembling a diner serves up several cerviches and offers additional seating.

## Harbor Village
*Four Embarcadero Center, lobby level, Financial district, (415) 781-8833; www.harborvillage.net. Dim sum daily 11-2:30, D daily; $. Highchairs, boosters. Reservations accepted for M-F. Validated parking in center garage.*

It is worth the wait generally required to dine on the dim sum served at this upscale Hong Kong-style spot. The back room, with its large windows overlooking the treetops to the Vaillancourt Fountain and Ferry Building, is choice. Special touches include doilies and pretty blue-patterned dishes that actually match. The selection of delicacies brought around on carts changes daily. Dim sum are made with impeccably fresh ingredients, and a tasty complexity characterizes many of the refined renditions. Shrimp items, rice rolls, and tiny custard cups are particularly delicious. See also page 16.

## Hard Rock Cafe
*On Beach St., at Pier 39, Fisherman's Wharf, (415) 956-2013, fax (415) 956-7655; www.hardrock.com. L-D daily; $-$$. Highchairs, boosters, booths, child portions. Reservations accepted Sept-May. Validated parking in Pier 39 garage.*

Sitting in one of the roomy booths here allows first-rate people watching. Wall decorations include George Harrison's and Pete Townsend's guitars, Grateful Dead stuff, and a large Fillmore poster collection. And, as might be expected from the name, rock & roll blasts out at ear-splitting levels. Considering the sensory overload and the fact that many people come here to look and to be seen, it is impressive that the American-style food is quite good, the service attentive, and the prices reasonable. The house salad is crisp, cold romaine lettuce, and the housemade Thousand Island dressing is tangy with fresh onion. Hamburgers are served on whole-wheat sesame buns and are just plain good. The menu also offers an assortment of sandwiches, housemade chili, grilled fresh fish, and rich, old-fashioned desserts. A plethora of souvenir items can be ordered at the table and added to the tab.

## Henry's Hunan

*924 Sansome St./Broadway, North Beach,*
*(415) 956-7727. L-D daily; $-$$. Highchairs, boosters.*
*Reservations accepted.*

Once upon a time this was a tiny, obscure restaurant located in Chinatown. It seated 29 people. Then it was described in *The New Yorker* as "the best Chinese restaurant in the world." Lines formed, and it was no longer possible to just saunter in and sit down at one of the few tables or at the counter, where half the pleasure was in watching the cooks in action. To satisfy demand, the restaurant moved to this huge warehouse, which seats 314 and permits instant seating once again. The kitchen uses unsaturated oils, lean meats, and skinned chicken, and it uses no MSG or sugar; salt-free dishes are available. The unusual Diana's Special consists of spicy meat sauce and lettuce sandwiched between two deep-fried flour pancakes. Harvest pork (a traditional dish fed to farm workers and pallbearers to give them strength), hot and sour chicken, and bean sprout salad are all especially good, as is the cold chicken salad mixed with shredded cucumbers, shiny noodles, and peanut dressing. Specialties include excellent fresh seafood dishes and unusual house-smoked ham, chicken, and duck cured over hickory wood, tea leaves, and orange peels. The distinctive hot bean sauce—a combination of fermented black beans, powdered red peppers, garlic, oil, and vinegar—is available to go. Branches are located at 1016 Bryant Street *(at 8th St., (415) 861-5808. L-D M-Sat.),* 674 Sacramento Street *(at Kearny St., (415) 788-2234. L-D M-F.),* and 110 Natoma St. *(at 2nd St., (415) 546-4999, fax (415) 227-4999. L-D M-Sat.).*

## Hornblower Cruises

*Pier 33, Bay St./The Embarcadero, (888) HORN-BLOWER, (415) 788-8866, fax (415) 434-0425; www.hornblower.com. D daily, $75-$91; Sat-SunBr, $59; 4-12 half price, under 4 free. Reservations required.*

Diners at brunch are seated as they board, and the maitre d' announces to each table when it is their turn to visit the bounteous buffet. Magnificent views of San Francisco and the bay are enjoyed as the boat goes out under the Golden Gate Bridge, past Sausalito and Angel Island, and beside Alcatraz. Live music plays in the background, and the Captain makes the rounds to greet everyone. After dining, there is time to tour the vessel. The dinner-dance cruise is more formal, with waiters serving four-course dinners. Special events are also often scheduled. Note that though highchairs and booster seats are not available, parents are welcome to bring on board strollers with wheel locks, and children are given crayons and coloring books to keep them busy.

The *San Francisco Spirit* offers a similar Sunday Brunch cruise *(Pier 9/The Embarcadero, (800) 2-YACHTS, (415) 788-9100, fax (415) 788-5445; www.signaturesf.com. SunBr $59; 4-12 $25, under 4 free. Reservations required.).*

## House of Nanking

*919 Kearny St./Jackson St., Chinatown,*
*(415) 421-1429. L-D M-Sat; $. No reservations.*

It seems everyone knows about this exceptional restaurant, so expect lines. Seating is at small formica tables and at a counter crammed into two small rooms separated by a busy kitchen. Though the menu is not descriptive, most everything is delicious—especially the pot stickers, steamed vegetable dumplings Nanking, onion pancakes, and Nanking scallops or crispy chicken with sesame vegetables (both are deep-fried tempura-style and topped with a tasty garlic sauce). Chow meins feature large housemade noodles; rice noodles are also available. A stress-reducing option is to decide on the number of dishes desired and let the server select a balanced menu. After dining here, one restaurant critic reflected upon the idea that it must be written somewhere that the more abysmal the decor and unfriendly the service in a Chinese restaurant, the more exquisite the food.

## House of Prime Rib

*1906 Van Ness Ave./Washington St., (415) 885-4605, fax (415) 921-0854; www.houseofprimerib.citysearch. com. D daily; $$$. Highchairs, boosters, booths, child portions. Reservations advised. Valet parking.*

The specialty of the house in this posh spot has been the same since 1949—the finest aged prime rib served right from the cart and carved to order tableside. (In fact, the only other entree on the menu is grilled fresh fish.) Choose a City Cut (for small appetites), an English Cut (several thin slices), or a King Henry VIII Cut (for those with king-size appetites). The complete dinner includes a chilled green salad prepared at the table and presented with *chilled* forks, bread and butter, either mashed potatoes with gravy or a baked potato, fresh horseradish sauce, creamed fresh spinach, and Yorkshire pudding. Come here hungry.

## Il Fornaio

*1265 Battery St./Greenwich St., in Levi's Plaza, near The Embarcadero. (415) 986-0100; www.ilfornaio. com. L M-F, D daily, Sat-SunBr. Highchairs, boosters, child menu. Reservations advised. Valet parking.*

Diners have a choice of sitting inside beneath tall ceilings at tables covered elegantly with white cloths or outside on a more casual patio at marble tables sheltered by a window windbreak. Outside seating is prime in good weather and permits enjoying an adjacent park fountain that sounds like a rushing waterfall. Items on the traditional Italian menu lend themselves to sharing, and a salad, pasta, and main course making a generous meal for two. Several pizzas and risottos are also options. Breads and desserts are housemade.

## Isobune Sushi

*1737 Post St., in Kintetsu Mall at Japan Center, (415) 563-1030, fax (415) 563-3337. L-D daily; $. Boosters. No reservations.*

At this small sushi bar, items circle the counter on little floating boats. Customers remove what looks interesting.

## Jackson Fillmore

*2506 Fillmore St./Jackson St., Pacific Heights, (415) 346-5288. D daily; $$. Highchairs, boosters. Reservations advised; accepted for 3+.*

Those who show up here without reservations usually find themselves standing in a line that stretches out the door, though complimentary bruchetta and wine are sometimes provided to take off the edge. Even those *with* reservations can wind up sitting at cramped tables or on a stool at the counter. However, the exceptional antipastos and pastas make it all worthwhile. Cloud-like gnocchi, fresh fish items, and truffle dishes are options, and a hot zabaglione classico fresh from the stove makes a heavenly dessert.

## Jeanty at Jack's

*615 Sacramento St./Montgomery St., Financial district, (415) 693-0941, fax (415) 693-0947; www.jeantyatjacks.com. L M-F, D daily; $$$. Reservations advised.*

Formerly the home of a very popular vintage restaurant, this delightful multi-level space has been turned into a charming French bistro. A delicious dinner here might start with a complexly spiced tomato soup in a bowl topped with puff pasty, then move on to a delicate sole meunière atop mashed potatoes. For dessert, it's hard to go wrong with a soothing rice pudding topped with tiny brandied cherries.

## John's Grill

*63 Ellis St./Powell St., Union Square, (415) 986-DASH, (415) 982-2583; www.johnsgrill.com. L M-Sat, D daily; $-$$. Highchairs, boosters, booths. Reservations advised for D.*

This restaurant opened in 1908 and was a setting in Dashiell Hammett's *The Maltese Falcon*. Its cozy interior features original gaslight fixtures, some original period furnishings, and mahogany-paneled walls covered with photos of famous patrons and historical San Francisco scenes. The lunch menu offers a variety of salads as well as a hamburger, several pastas, and that hard-to-find Hangtown fry (an early California dish prepared with oysters and eggs). Dinner brings on extensive seafood selections. One of the most popular dishes is straight out of the book—Sam Spade's Chops (broiled rack of lamb with a baked potato and sliced tomatoes). This is one of only two national literary landmarks in California (the other is City Lights bookstore).

## Julius' Castle

*1541 Montgomery St./Union St., Telegraph Hill, (415) 392-2222, fax (415) 989-1544; www.juliuscastlerestaurant.com. D daily; $$$. Reservations advised. Valet parking.*

Magnificently situated on a narrow cul-de-sac atop Telegraph Hill—one of San Francisco's seven hills—this Historical Landmark building is deliciously cozy, and all tables get a spectacular view of the bay. It is *the* place to go for a romantic dinner, and not surprisingly many, many couples have become engaged here. Do ask the owner to tell his story about meeting

Sean Connery, who dined here behind a velvet curtain on the top floor several times while filming *The Rock*. Excellently executed entrees include classics such as roasted Muscovy duck breast with cherry sauce and pecan wild rice, and New York strip steak with roasted potatoes.

## Katia's: A Russian Tea Room
*600 5th Ave./Balboa St., Sunset district, (415) 668-9292; www.katias.com. L Tu-W, D W-Sun; $$. Boosters. Reservations taken.*

Located in the heart of San Francisco's Russian neighborhood, among side streets lined with interesting vintage houses, this intimate restaurant offers entree into a different world. By all means start with the traditional thick beet-and-cabbage borscht. Prizes among the main courses are breaded chicken cutlets Pozharski, and golubtsi—cabbage leaves stuffed with ground beef. For dessert, boiled cheese dumplings topped with exquisite fresh sour cream should not be missed. A live guitarist plays some evenings.

Across the street, teeny, tiny **Globus** (*332 Balboa St., (415) 668-4723, same fax; http:// pweb.jps.net/~globus. W-Sun 12-5.*) specializes in Slavic books.

## Khan Toke Thai House
*5937 Geary Blvd./24th Ave., outer Richmond district, (415) 668-6654. D daily; $. Boosters. Reservations advised.*

Diners remove their shoes in the entryway before entering a maze of lushly decorated small dining rooms. The richly embellished tables are low to the ground. Some have floor pillows for reclining, while others have wells in the floor beneath into which legs can dangle. Many of the unusual Thai herbs used in preparing dishes for the extensive, well-executed menu grow in a courtyard behind the restaurant. An all-inclusive dinner includes an appetizer of fried fish cakes, spicy-and-sour shrimp soup, a green salad, a choice of two entrees, either a pudding or fried banana, and hot tea or coffee. A good selection of vegetarian items is available.

## Kokkari
*200 Jackson St./Front St., Financial district, (415) 981-0983, fax (415) 982-0983; www.kokkari.com. L M-F, D M-Sat; $$$. Booths. Reservations advised. Valet parking at D.*

Named for a small fishing village on the island of Samos in the Aegean Sea, this stylish restaurant serves sophisticated versions of Greek cuisine. Starters include traditional spanakotiropita (spinach-filled filo pies) and pikilia (an array of delicious classic spreads served with grilled housemade pita and rice-filled dolmathes). Entrees include fabulous grilled lamb chops with memorably good baked potato wedges, a grilled whole striped bass, and what might be the best rendition of moussaka west of Athens. Among the delectable desserts are a creamy rice pudding with poached peaches and cherries, and an expansive array of Greek cookies and baklava. Plan to wash them down with strong Greek stone-ground coffee prepared in a giant urn over hot sand, or with a glass of ouzo selected from a choice of ten. Seating here includes comfortable booths and upholstered chairs and is a decided bonus. A sister restaurant, Evvia, is located in Palo Alto (see page 181).

## Kuleto's
*221 Powell St./Geary St., in Villa Florence Hotel, Union Square, (415) 397-7720, fax (415) 986-2304; www.kuletos.citysearch.com. B-L-D daily; $$. Highchairs, boosters, booths. Reservations advised.*

Superb northern Italian cuisine is served here in elegant surroundings. The bar features a crostini and antipasti case, and counter seating in the back is often available at the last minute and provides the additional treat of watching the skilled kitchen staff in action. Housemade pastas and grilled items are particularly good. The 100% cold-pressed extra virgin California olive oil used in the restaurant is attractively bottled and makes a good souvenir.

## La Mediterranée
*2210 Fillmore St./California St., upper Fillmore district, (415) 921-2956, fax (415) 921-4061; www.cafe lamed.com.*

For description, see page 279.

## The Last Supper Club
*1199 Valencia St./23rd St., Mission district, (415) 695-1199, fax (415) 695-1190; www.lastsupperclubsf.com. L M-F, D daily, Sat-SunBr; $$. Highchairs, boosters. Reservations advised.*

The large, usually crowded wooden bar at this stylish spot makes a wait here bearable.

Once seated in the open dining room, bread and a tasty basil-parsley-olive oil dipping sauce are brought with the home-style Italian menu. Bar drinks include a sophisticated Harry's Bar Bellini and a fragrant, minty Luna Park Mojito (named for their other roaringly popular restaurant). Soup is a must if it is the rustic, full-flavored cauliflower. A good way to go is sharing a pasta—perhaps housemade chestnut ravioli with roasted guinea fowl sugo, gnocchi with venison Bolognese, or fettuccine Alfredo made without cream but with plenty of Parmigiano-Reggiano—and an entree—fresh fish, pork osso bucco, and roasted octopus are among the choices. Save room for dessert, especially if it is either zabaglione with fresh berries (made ahead and served at room temperature) or a poached pear with rich, creamy arborio-rice pudding.

## La Taqueria
*2889 Mission St./25th St., Mission district, (415) 285-7117. L-D daily; $. Highchairs. No reservations. No cards.*

To experience fast food Mexican-style, step through one of the two arches here and head to the counter to place an order. Then pick a table, and kick back. Entertainment is provided by a colorful folk mural decorating one wall, by cooks in the open kitchen busily preparing orders, and by a jukebox with Mexican music. The menu is simple. Choose either a taco made with two steamed corn tortillas or a burrito made with a flour tortilla. Fillings are a choice of pork, beef, sausage, chicken, or vegetarian (beans and cheese). Pinto beans and fresh tomato salsa round things out; avocado and sour cream cost a bit more. Depending on the season, delicious housemade fresh fruit juice drinks include strawberry, cantaloupe, orange, banana, and pineapple.

Walk-away desserts can be picked up next door at **Dianda's Italian-American Pastry** (*2883 Mission St./25th St., (415) 647-5469, fax (415) 641-4729; http://diandas.citysearch.com. M-Sat 6:30-6:30, Sun to 5.*), where everything is made from scratch and the cannoli are particularly good.

## Le Colonial
*20 Cosmo Pl./off Taylor & Post, near Union Square, (415) 931-3600, fax (415) 931-2933;*
*www.lecolonialsf.com. D daily; $$$. Reservations advised. Valet parking.*

Operating on the site that was formerly home to legendary Trader Vic's, this is a branch in a successful upscale chain of Vietnamese restaurants. With a tropical decor evoking 1920s Vietnam—vintage black-and-white photos of turn-of-the-century Saigon adorn the walls while quiet ceiling fans gently stir the air—the outdoor verandah and elegant interior dining rooms offer sanctuary from the street bustle. Drinks are exotic and the food innovative. Appetizers include several kinds of spring rolls, and both a delicate sea bass fillet steamed in a banana leaf and a flavorful tiger prawns-mango-eggplant-basil-coconut curry are among the main courses. Fresh tropical fruit and housemade sorbets and cookies are winning desserts. An inviting upstairs lounge serves an hors d'oeuvres menu and sometimes schedules live music.

## Lichee Garden
*1416 Powell St./Vallejo St., North Beach. (415) 397-2290; www.licheegarden.citysearch.com. Dim sum daily 7-3; D daily; $. Highchairs, boosters. Reservations advised; accepted for dim sum 1 day in advance.*

This Cantonese Chinese restaurant is known for its exceptional soups, Hong Kong-style crispy noodles, and crispy Peking-style spareribs. It's a good idea to come here with a large group as seating is at big round tables, portions are generous, and sodas are served in their original large plastic containers. See also page 16.

## Liverpool Lil's
*2942 Lyon St./Lombard St., the Presidio, (415) 921-6664. L M-F, D daily, Sat-SunBr; $-$$.*

This atmospheric pub is usually packed to its authentic rafters. A limited menu—a decent hamburger, fish & chips, a few finger foods—is served in its cozy front alcoves and in a small area outside the entrance that is particularly inviting on a warm day. The on-tap brews are refreshing, and two TVs are tuned to sports. A full dinner menu is available in the popular back dining room.

## Lovejoy's Tea Room
*1351 Church St./Clipper St., Noe Valley,*

*(415) 648-5895. W-Sun 11-6, F to 7; $. 1 highchair. Reservations for 4+.*

Cozy as anything encountered in England, this tiny, absolutely charming spot provides a welcome retreat from the city streets. And diners can shop while they sip: Everything is for sale—from the tea cups to the furniture. The menu offers all things English—toasted crumpets, scones, tea sandwiches, sausage rolls, pasties. Tea service ranges from a simple cream tea to an expansive high tea, and a special Wee Tea is served to children. I say, old chap, what fun!

## Lucky Creation

*854 Washington St./Grant Ave., Chinatown, (415) 989-0818. L-D Thur-Tu; $. Boosters. Reservations accepted. No cards.*

In the sparest of atmospheres, this all vegetarian restaurant dishes up some of the most fabulous veggie dishes in town. Among the many choices are won tons, deep-fried taro shaped like goldfish, and a stunningly presented sautéed black mushrooms with baby bok choy. Clay pot dishes, noodle dishes (including delicious chow fun items), and rice plates are available, as are imitation meat dishes made with gluten.

## Luna Park

*694 Valencia St./18th St., Mission district, (415) 553-8584, fax (415) 553-8660; www.lunaparksf.com. L M-F, D daily, Sat-SunBr; $$. Booths. Reservations advised.*

A visit to this loud and lively little bistro should begin at the bar with a mojito cocktail. After enjoying the bartender's show of smashing the aromatic mint and mixing it with lots of light rum and very little seltzer, it's time to claim a table amid the merlot-colored walls and peruse the unusual menu. Winners include a fabulously flavorful, really, really good grilled artichoke with lemon aioli, a smashing breaded pork cutlet stuffed with mushrooms and Gruyère cheese, and gooey upscale s'mores made by slathering housemade graham crackers with molten marshmallow and bittersweet chocolate from little fondue pots.

## MacArthur Park

*607 Front St./Jackson St., Financial district, (415) 398-5700, fax (415) 296-7827; www.macpark.com. L M-F, D daily; $$-$$$. Highchairs, boosters, child*

*menu. Reservations advised. Valet parking at D.*

Long popular for its flavorful house-marinated and -smoked baby back ribs that are perfect with a side of garlic mashed potatoes and a glass of zingy Zinfandel, this reliable spot also serves up a huge and delicious appetizer of onion strings made with sweet Spanish onions and a killer Turtle Pie dessert consisting of a pecan crust topped with chocolate ganache and caramel sauce. A great burger and several meal-sized salads are also on the menu. Dining among two mature ficus trees, sparkling with lights in the evening, does bring to mind a park, though in reality diners are within the gorgeous exposed red-brick walls of a renovated early 1900s Barbary Coast warehouse. A cup of crayons for coloring on the butcher paper tablecloth plus a selection from the extensive menu of "big city drinks" tides diners over until their orders arrive. For more description, see page 181.

## Magic Flute

*3673 Sacramento St./Spruce St., Presidio Heights, (415) 922-1225, fax (415) 922-1257; www.magicfluteristorante.com. L M-F, Sat-SunBr, D W-Sat; $-$$. Highchairs, boosters. Reservations advised.*

Situated within a vintage Victorian on a low-key, high-quality shopping street, this pleasant spot offers comfortable indoor tables as well as outdoor garden seating. The work of local artists colorfully decorates the sponge-painted walls. Among the lunch items on the California-Italian menu are salads and pastas as well as a great cheeseburger and a portobello focaccia sandwich. A few of these items stay on the brunch menu, when egg dishes are added. The housemade desserts include a killer double fudge chocolate cake and a rich, rich tiramisu.

## Mama's on Washington Square

*1701 Stockton St./Filbert St., North Beach, (415) 362-6421. B-L Tu-Sun; $. Highchairs, boosters. No reservations. No cards.*

Diners wait in a usually long line to enter this cozy, cheery spot on a corner of Washington Square. However, once inside the hassle is over. Orders are placed at a counter from which the kitchen action is visible, and then diners are seated by their server. Breakfast choices include blueberry pancakes, thick French toast made from various breads, a variety of omelettes, and tasty Florentine eggs prepared with fresh spinach. Lunch brings on salads, sandwiches, hamburgers, hot dogs, and a zucchini and cheese frittata. Delicious desserts and fresh strawberry creations—even out of season—are a house specialty.

## Marnee Thai
*2225 Irving St./23rd Ave., Sunset district,*
*(415) 665-9500. L-D W-M; $. Reservations advised.*

Exceptional Thai cuisine is served in a tiny room completely covered with attractive, sound-absorbing woven fibers. Especially good are the mild yellow curry dishes prepared with potatoes and a complex mixture of spices softened with coconut milk, and the stir-fried chicken with cashew nuts (tossed on after the dish is cooked, allowing them to retain their crunchiness). A side order of delicious peanut sauce and a palate-refreshing cucumber salad are recommended. Allow time before or after for shopping the produce markets scattered among the mostly Asian businesses along this bustling street. A branch is at 1243 9th Ave. *(at Irving St, inner Sunset district, (415) 731-9999. L-D daily.).*

## Marrakech
*419 O'Farrell St./Taylor St., near Union Square,*
*(415) 776-6717, fax (415) 776-1538. D daily; $$.*
*Reservations accepted.*

After passing through the doors of this oasis in the urban jungle, diners enter the enveloping womb-like warmth of an exotic Middle Eastern bazaar. Resembling a posh adult playpen, the main room has comfortable padded benches and round tables circling the perimeter with low stools providing supplemental seating. Traditional Moroccan foods include a kaleidoscope plate of colorful vegetable salads, a flaky bastella pastry filled with a sweet chicken-toasted almond mixture, and couscous. Main course choices include a simple but divine chicken with lemon and olives as well as several rabbit, lamb, and shrimp dishes. Belly dancing is scheduled nightly. Families fit in fine here and are usually seated in a corner area with more space.

## Masa's
*648 Bush St./Powell St., in Executive Hotel Vintage Court, Nob Hill, (800) 258-7694, (415) 989-7154,*
*fax (415) 989-3141; www.masas.citysearch.com. D Tu-Sat; $$$+. Closed most of Jan. Reservations required. Valet parking.*

This highly acclaimed, elegant, and very expensive restaurant serves a menu of contemporary French cuisine at luxuriously set tables. A sample three-course menu might include a warm beet salad with toasted hazelnuts and Asian pears, an oyster mushroom-lobster risotto, a carved duck leg with tiny Bartlett pears and baby Brussels sprouts, and a piña colada dessert with herbal tea. Six- and nine-course tasting menus with optional wine pairings and a three- and six-course vegetarian menu are also available. Tidbits are sent out from the kitchen throughout, and a dessert cart laden with housemade lollipops, candies, and cookies provides a sweet conclusion. A dress code requests that men wear jackets. Adding intrigue, the restaurant bears the name of its founding chef, Masataka Kobayashi, who long ago was murdered off the premises in a still unsolved case.

## Max's Diner
*311 3rd St./Folsom St., South of Market, (415) 546-MAXS, fax (415) 546-9231; www.maxsworld.com. L D daily; $ $$. Boosters, booths, child menu. Reservations accepted.*

Specializing in serving large portions of '50s food, this popular diner continues the theme with lots of chrome and Formica, miniature tabletop jukeboxes filled with '50s tunes, comfortable oversize vinyl booths that offer privacy to families, and waitresses dressed in black-and-white uniforms and bobby sox. The motto is "Everything you always wanted to eat." The extensive menu offers crispy-coated chicken-fried steak, New York deli-style sandwiches, a gigantic hamburger with bacon and cheese, and a blue-plate special of well-seasoned, moist meatloaf served with tasty made-from-scratch mashed potatoes indented with a gravy-filled crater. A few appetizers and side dishes are a meal in themselves: country-style ribs, sliders (baby burgers), spicy chicken wings with blue cheese dip, giant onion rings, a salad (a wedge of iceberg lettuce topped with housemade dressing), slaw, and tasty housemade chili. Among Max's famous gargantuan desserts are a tapioca pudding layered with strawberries and topped with whipped cream, a bread pudding with vanilla sauce, a delicious seven-layer cookie topped with hot fudge and ice cream, and a large selection of ice cream concoctions. To top it all off, each diner receives a piece of Bazooka bubble gum with the check.

Across town, **Max's Opera Cafe** *(601 Van Ness Ave./Golden Gate Ave., Civic Center, (415) 771-7300, fax (415) 474-9780; www.maxs world.com. L-D daily; $-$$. Boosters, booths, child menu. No reservations.)* offers similar fare but with the added bonus of talented servers who also take turns serving stints singing at the mike in the evenings.

## McCormick & Kuleto's
*900 North Point, in Ghirardelli Square, Fisherman's Wharf, (888) 344-6861 (415) 929-1730, fax (415) 567-2919; www.mccormickandkuletos.com. L-D daily; $$-$$$. Highchairs, boosters, booths, child menu. Reservations advised. Validated parking in Ghirardelli Square garage.*

Spectacular views are available from most tables in this splendidly appointed seafood restaurant, though the half-circle booths on the second of three tiers are choice. High ceilings, floor-to-ceiling leaded glass windows, and fantastical light fixtures add to the overall elegant ambiance. Designed to please every appetite, the extensive menu changes daily. Starters include delicious crab cakes; sweet, crisp rock shrimp popcorn; and a satisfying, nicely seasoned clam chowder. Among the many seafood dishes, which are fresh whenever possible, are an excellent pan-fried petrale sole with caper-lemon butter and a delicious blackened sea bass with a side of homey mashed potatoes. Pastas, salads, sandwiches, and a variety of meats round it out. Children can choose a cheeseburger, grilled cheese, cheese quesadilla, spaghetti, chicken fingers, or fish & chips.

The restaurant's more casual **Crab Cake Lounge** offers the same incredible view with a less expensive, less extensive menu and the additional options of pizza and a hamburger.

## Mel's Drive-In
*2165 Lombard St./Fillmore St., Marina district, (415) 921-2867; www.melsdrive-in.com. B-L-D daily; $. Highchairs, boosters, booths, child menu. No reservations. Free parking lot adjoins.*

When Mel's was a *real* drive-in, carhops brought trays out to clamp on windows for in-car dining. Now the eating goes on inside the restaurant. Seating is at a long counter, in booths, or at tables with chairs, and an oldie but goodie can be played for two bits on a computerized mini-jukebox. (An interesting aside: Jukeboxes were invented in San Francisco in 1888.) Dress is just-off-the-jogging-trail casual. Menu items include the Famous Melburger with all the trimmings, a variety of veggie burgers, fries with the skins still on, and, of course, BIG onion rings. All this plus salads, soups, and sandwiches galore. For more substantial appetites, the menu offers a chicken pot pie, meat loaf served with lumpy mashed potatoes and gravy, and the day's blue-plate special. Among the drinks are flavored cokes and thick, old-fashioned milkshakes served in the mixer tin. Desserts include chocolate fudge cake, banana cream pie, and a banana split. Kids love that their meals are served in boxes that look like cars, and teens call this place "cool."

A branch at 3355 Geary Boulevard *(at Stanyan St., Presidio Heights, (415) 387-2244)* is the exact location of one of the three original Mel's. More branches are at 801 Mission St. *(at 4th St., South of Market, (415) 227-4477)* and at 1050 Van Ness Ave. *(at Geary St., (415) 292-6357).*

## Meriwa
*728 Pacific Ave./Grant Ave., Chinatown, (415) 989-8818 or (415) 989-8868. Dim sum daily 8-2, D daily; $. Highchairs, boosters. No reservations.*

Able to seat 1,000 people, this popular spot roars during dim sum. The little dishes here are among the very best and most varied currently available. See also page 16.

## Mifune
*1737 Post St., in Kintetsu Mall at Japan Center, (415) 922-0337, fax (415) 567-4211. L-D daily; $. Boosters, booths, child portions. No reservations.*

This is a branch of a well-established chain of similar restaurants in Japan that specializes in serving two types of easily digested, low-calorie fresh noodles: udon—fat, white flour noodles; and soba—thin, brown buckwheat noodles. Before walking through the noren (a slit curtain), peruse the plastic food displays in the exterior windows. Noodle toppings include chicken, beef, and shrimp tempura as well as exotic raw egg, sweet herring, and seaweed.

Sesame spice salt is on each table for pepping up the blander items. The child's Bullet Train plate consists of cold noodles with shrimp-and-vegetable tempura and is served in a ceramic replica of the famous Japanese train.

## Millennium

*580 Geary St./Jones St., in The Savoy Hotel, near Union Square, (415) 345-3900, fax (415) 345-3941; www.millenniumrestaurant.com. D daily; $$$. Booths. Reservations advised. Valet parking.*

Specializing in richly flavored vegan and vegetarian cuisine, this stylish restaurant has an exciting, eclectic menu that also interests non-vegetarians—especially those watching their fat intake. No animal products are used, most items are prepared with little or no oil, and organic ingredients are used whenever possible. House-brined olives and pickles make nice munchies. Entree selections might include a crisp sesame-shitake phyllo spring roll or a fabulous portobello mushroom prepared Moroccan-style. Delicious desserts adhere to the program, too, and usually include an irresistible chocolate item and several lighter sorbets. Beverages include an exclusively organic wine list as well as interesting cocktails and organic beers from a full bar, housemade herbal elixirs, and plenty of non-alcoholic drinks. Once a month, on the Sunday evening closest to the full moon, an Aphrodisiac Overnight Package is available that includes a dinner of aphrodisiac delights and a room for the night in the hotel.

## Moose's

*1652 Stockton St./Union St., North Beach, (800) 28-MOOSE, (415) 989-7800, fax (415) 989-7838; www.mooses.com. L Thur-Sat, D daily, SunBr; $$$. Highchairs, boosters. Reservations advised. Valet parking.*

A large, open room at this always-bustling spot makes most tables good ones, and carpeting keeps the din to a minimum. Live piano music in the evenings adds to the inviting atmosphere. The eclectic, ever-changing menu might offer asparagus soup accented with prawns or fresh oven-roasted chicken breast with housemade gnocchi and roasted artichokes, and it always has a pasta, pizza, and ground-sirloin Moose Burger. Save space for an unusual dessert, perhaps a lemon-scented vanilla rice pudding or a warm mango-and-coconut cream tart. Tea lovers will appreciate the rare varieties, including jasmine pearls and monkey-picked Tikuanyin.

## Morton's of Chicago

*400 Post St./Powell St., near Union Square, (415) 986-5830, fax (415) 986-5829; www.mortons.com. D daily; $$$. Booster seats. Reservations advised. Valet parking.*

The first Morton's steakhouse opened in Chicago in 1978. This clubby subterranean outpost, decorated with historical photographs on the wall, is the place to go when a red meat attack occurs. The minimum 14-ounce cut of tender, tasty, prime grain-fed beef served here (the filets get as big as a colossal 48 ounces, though that is meant for two) require a substantial cutting tool, and so a large Bowie-style knife is at each place setting to assist. Noteworthy side dishes include a heavenly lobster bisque, sautéed wild mushrooms, and a gigantic baked Idaho potato. Lamb chops, fresh fish, and fresh Maine lobster are also on the limited menu. Though it might be impossible, save room for one of the decadent desserts, which include an exquisite Godiva Hot Chocolate Cake and a New York cheesecake brought in from the Bronx (the only menu item not prepared on site). According to one happy diner, the reason it gets so noisy here is "so you don't hear your arteries slamming shut." Leave guilt at home.

## New Asia

*772 Pacific Ave./Stockton St., Chinatown, (415) 391-6666, fax (415) 391-6158. Dim sum daily 9-3; $. Highchairs, boosters. No reservations.*

Even with a reputed 1,000 seats, this busy spot usually requires a wait for seating in its popular ground level dining room. However, immediate seating is often available upstairs. Head servers use walkie-talkies to communicate across the vast, noisy interior. Hesitation when offered a choice of eight teas usually is translated by the server into "green," because that tea is the most popular. Delicate shrimp dumplings, deep-fried taro balls filled with sweet poi, and cloud-like pork bows are all especially good. A dim sum-to-go counter operates off the waiting area. See also page 16.

## Night Monkey

*2223 Union St./Fillmore St., Pacific Heights,*
*(415) 775-1130; www.nightmonkeyrestaurant.com.*
*D M-Sat; $$$. Reservations advised.*

Tucked into the tiniest of spaces, this intimate bistro is reminiscent of something found on an alley in London or Paris. Its red-and-black interior and multi-paned windows and doors evoke a mysterious air. On the ever-changing menu, small plates might include a superb thick tomato soup, a plate of dates and pears, or exotic tenderloin of alligator or kangaroo. Large plates have included pork loin stuffed with shallot-sage cornbread and red-eye gravy, filet mignon with chanterelles, and a caramelized acorn squash vegan plate. Luck is with those who find the delectable housemade ice cream sandwich among the dessert choices.

## North Beach Pizza

*1499 Grant Ave./Union St., North Beach, (415) 433-2444, fax (415) 433-7217; www.northbeachpizza.com.*
*L-D daily; $. Boosters, booths. No reservations.*

Lacking pretension and finesse, this restaurant serves an unfussy kind of pizza with an excellent crust in a relaxed, easy atmosphere. The pepperoni and cheese and the spicy-hot sausage versions are both particularly tasty, and a salad tossed with the creamy house Italian dressing is the perfect accompaniment. An outstanding cannelloni is among the pasta choices, and barbecued ribs and chicken plus a submarine sandwich are also on the menu. A branch is one block up the street at 1310 ((415) 433-2444). More branches are all around the town.

## One Market

*1 Market St./Steuart St., The Embarcadero, (415) 777-5577, fax (415) 777-3366; www.onemarket.com. L M-F, D M-Sat; $$$. Highchairs, boosters. Valet parking.*

Situated in a scenic corner of an attractive historic building dating from 1917, this popular restaurant has an airy, substantial interior that is a delight to be in, and it also has great bay views. Celebrity chef Bradley Ogden's all-American menu includes crab cakes and barbecued oysters as appetizers. For entrees, the changing menu might offer tender Yankee pot roast with roasted turnips and potatoes, or succulent rosemary-roasted chicken breast with wild mushrooms and three kinds of garlic mashed potatoes. For dessert, expect new takes

on old favorites—strawberry shortcake with orange ice cream, peach cobbler topped with a dab of fresh peach sorbet—plus stellar cookies and fruit sorbets.

## Palomino

*345 Spear St./Steuart St., in Hills Plaza, The Embarcadero, (415) 512-7400, fax (415) 512-0648; www.palominosf.com. L M-F, D daily, Sat-SunBr; $$-$$$. Highchairs, boosters, child menu. Reservations advised. Validated parking.*

Offering a great view of the Bay Bridge, this bustling spot has a raised seating area, unusual glass lighting fixtures, and potted palm trees that echo those lining the street outside. Kids get a color-in place mat to occupy them while their parents contemplate a more sophisticated menu. All dinners start with a crusty loaf of bread and a delicious crushed tomato-Feta cheese-kalamata olive spread. Fish and spit-roasted meat are specialties, though kids might prefer a pasta or the pizza with cracker-thin crust prepared in an apple wood-fired oven. Sixteen beers are on tap, and a large selection of wine varietals is available by the glass.

## Pearl City

*641 Jackson St./Grant Ave., Chinatown, (415) 398-8383. Dim sum daily 8-3, D daily; $. Highchairs, boosters. No reservations.*

The front room here is chilly and quiet, while the back room is warmer and noisier. Dim sum items are brought around on platters rather than carts. Excellent choices include many delicate shrimp items and very good steamed custard buns. See also page 16.

## Perry's

*1944 Union St./Laguna St., Pacific Heights, (415) 922-9022. B-L M-F, D daily, Sat-SunBr; $$. Highchairs, boosters, child menu. Reservations advised.*

Consistency is a strong point at this popular watering hole. Drinks are strong and tasty, and the cafe food is always just as remembered. A good hamburger comes on a Kaiser roll with a side of thin, greaseless fried potato rounds, and the corned beef hash is neatly chopped and topped with two poached eggs. Chops, steaks, and fresh fish flesh out the menu. For dessert, try the housemade apple brown Betty. Atmospheres vary: sidewalk tables, the boisterous bar area, the dark but quiet back room, and a sunny back porch. A branch is at 185 Sutter Street *(at Kearny St., (415) 989-6895).*

## Picnic Pick-Ups

### • A. G. Ferrari Foods
*468 Castro St., (415) 255-6590; 688 Mission St./3rd St., (415) 344-0644; 3490 California St., (415) 923-4470; www.agferrari.com.*

For description, see page 280.

### • Lucca Delicatessen
*2120 Chestnut St./Steiner St., Marina district, (415) 921-7873, fax (415) 921-2402. M-F 9-6:30, Sat-Sun 9-6. No cards.*

Owned by the same family since 1929, this deli prices its made-to-order sandwiches by weight. Housemade salads, handmade bread sticks, and a large selection of Italian wines are also available.

### • A North Beach picnic
**Molinari Delicatessen** *(373 Columbus Ave./Vallejo St., (415) 421-2337, same fax; www.molinarideli.com. M-F 8-6, Sat 7:30-5:30.)* has been on its present corner since 1912 and claims to be the oldest Italian deli in town. It can provide the makings for a great picnic. Dash into one of the Chinese markets for some fresh fruit, then into **Victoria Pastry Co.** *(1362 Stockton St./ Vallejo St., (415) 781-2015. M-Sat 7-6, Sun 8-5.)* for a dessert—perhaps a cannoli or their specialty St. Honoré cake or maybe some pignoli or brutti ma buoni cookies. And that's picnicking North Beach-style!

### • Say Cheese
*856 Cole St./Carl St., Haight-Ashbury, (415) 665-5020, fax (415) 665-2377. M-Sat 10-7, Sun 10-5.*

In addition to almost 300 kinds of cheese, a variety of made-to-order sandwiches, salads, pâtés, crackers, cheese spreads, and fresh cookies are available in this very small shop.

### • Sweet Things
*3585 California St./Spruce St., in Cal-Mart in Laurel Village, Laurel Heights, (415) 221-8583; www.sweetthings.com. M-Sat 8-7, Sun 9-6.*

For description, see page 215.

### • Vivande Porta Via
*2125 Fillmore St./California St., upper Fillmore, (415) 346-4430, fax (415) 346-2877; www.vivande.com. L-D daily; deli daily 10-7. 1 highchair, 1 booster.*

All items here are prepared in the heavenly smelling open kitchen and are, in keeping with the literal meaning of the deli's name, "food to carry away." The Italian fare varies, but main dishes might include succulent roasted chicken, mushroom or chicken turnovers in a flaky crust, or torta Milanese (a tall pie layered with ham, spinach, and cheese). Salads include cannellini beans and caviar, caponata (eggplant with raisins and pine nuts), and several fresh pastas. Sandwiches are made to order with freshly baked breads, and tempting dolci (sweets) beckon from a display case (try the hazelnut meringues labeled as "brutti ma buoni," which translates as "ugly but good"). Comfortable seating is also available for dining on the premises.

## Plouf
*40 Belden Pl./Bush St., Financial district, (415) 986-6491, fax (415) 986-6492. L M-F, D M-Sat; $$. 1 highchair. Reservations advised.*

Specializing in steamed mussels and offering eight different versions, this seafood bistro is so contemporary French that after just a few minutes diners feel like they've been beamed onto the French Riviera. One waiter witnessed here could do no wrong. Dressed in a white-and-black-striped shirt and sporting a charming, authentic French accent, he brought a huge iron pot full of mussels pastis (prepared with fennel, tomato, and onion) with a side of perfect thin, crisp pommes frites, and he regularly removed bowls of discarded shells. More seafood items are on the menu—including fish & chips with aioli sauce—along with a variety of meats and several pastas. Good wine choices straight out of France include Muscadet, Sancerre, and Burgundy. For dessert, profiteroles—little cream puff shells filled with banana ice cream and topped with warm chocolate and caramel sauces—are the way to go. Outside, tables fill the pedestrians-only alley just as they do in the south of France. However, because the weather here isn't as divine as it is there, heat lamps attempt to take off the chill. The dining room features a high, pressed-tin ceiling and has booths as well as a bank of intimate bench-and-chair tables for two. In sync with the name, which translates as "splash," stuffed sport fish decorate the walls.

## Postrio
*545 Post St./Mason St., in the Prescott Hotel, near*

Union Square, (415) 776-7825, fax (415) 776-6702; www.postrio.com. D daily; $$$. Highchairs, boosters, booths. Reservations advised. Valet parking.

Owned by Los Angeles celebrity chef Wolfgang Puck, and referred to inelegantly by some as Puck's Place, this grand spot is entered via a dramatic staircase leading down into an attractive contemporary dining room. It is a place to see, to be seen, and to enjoy a fabulous meal. The complex California-style cuisine and desserts are generally excellent, and, as would be expected in any restaurant owned by Mr. Puck, a bar menu with great wood-oven pizzas is also available.

## The Pot Sticker

150 Waverly Pl./Washington St., Chinatown, (415) 397-9985, fax (415) 397-3829. L-D daily; $. Highchairs, boosters. Reservations accepted.

Situated in a picturesque alley famous for its historic buildings sporting ornate painted balconies, this spot is known for its handmade noodles and dumplings. Dishes are lightly sauced and have lots of vegetables. Good choices include hot-and-sour soup, Mongolian beef, and princess chicken. Dramatic Hunan crispy whole fish is served with a hot sauce.

## Prego

2000 Union St./Buchanan St., Pacific Heights, (415) 563-3305, fax (415) 563-1561; www.spectrumfoods.com. L-D daily; $$-$$$. Highchairs, boosters. Reservations advised.

Said to have originally introduced to the San Francisco restaurant scene such now-standard items as tiramisu and buffalo mozzarella, this popular spot is a magnet for celebrities. A great way to start is with several antipasti—perhaps a Parma prosciutto with fruit, or deep-fried eggplant with garlic and tomato sauce. In fact, the assorted appetizer platter can make a satisfying light meal. Contorni such as polenta, pan-braised greens, and roasted Yukon Gold potatoes with rosemary and garlic are also available. Pastas are housemade and exceptional, with wonderful renditions such as fazzoletti al salmone (large green-and-white-striped raviolis filled with fresh salmon, mozzarella, and arugula and topped with a delicate tomato cream sauce) and mezzelune alle melanzane (half-moon spinach pockets filled with ricotta and topped with grilled eggplant, fresh tomato, and

fresh basil). Pizza, calzone, fresh fish, and assorted meat dishes round out the menu. The dessert plate of housemade cookies is perfect with a cappuccino.

## Ramblas

557 Valencia St./6th St., the Mission district, (415) 565-0207, fax (415) 565-0249; www.ramblastapas.com. D daily, Sat-SunBr; $$. Booths. Reservations advised.

In a deep room featuring kitchen and street views, this festive tapas bar serves a variety of the tasty Spanish tidbits and they just might be better than those found in Spain. The marinated olives, boquerones (white anchovies), piquillos (sweet red peppers filled with goat cheese), empanadillas (little turnovers filled with chorizo and spinach), and gambas (shrimp baked in garlic and olive oil) are all exquisite. Several paellas are also available. Special drinks include ThirstyBear draft beers, fruity Sangria, and a minty mojito, and desserts include both flan and cinnamony churros with warm chocolate sauce. Live flamenco guitar is scheduled on Monday and Tuesday evenings.

## Restaurant LuLu

816 Folsom St./4th St., South of Market, (415) 495-5775, fax (415) 495-7810; www.lulu.citysearch.com. L-D daily; $$. Highchairs, boosters. Reservations advised. Valet parking at D.

This casual restaurant operates in the large, open, high-ceilinged room of a converted 1910 warehouse. The house specialty is simply prepared foods of the French and Italian Riviera served family style. Almost anything from the wood-fired rotisserie or oven is tasty, but the delicate fritto misto with artichokes, the crisp rosemary-scented roast chicken, the thin-crust pizza, and the iron skillet-roasted mussels are simply fabulous. Among the nightly specials are rabbit on Tuesdays and suckling pig on Fridays. An adjoining cafe serves the same menu but takes no reservations.

## Rubicon

558 Sacramento St./Montgomery St., Financial district, (415) 434-4100, fax (415) 421-7648; www.sfrubicon.com. L W, D M-Sat; $$$. Reservations advised. Valet parking at D.

With celebrity investors including Robin Williams, Francis Ford Coppola, and Robert

DeNiro, this bustling, sophisticated spot seems to have no choice but to be a hit. The two-level dining area is tucked between attractive brick walls decorated with modern art (including Dale Chihuly glass sculptures), and beams criss-cross near windows as an earthquake safety measure. Diners can choose between two fixed-price menus and an a la carte menu. Full-flavored California-French dishes include items such as rock shrimp ravioli, pan-roasted chicken on garlic mashed potatoes, and tasty oven-roasted venison with root vegetable hash. Exceptional desserts prepared by a special pastry chef include delights such as coconut cake topped with mango ice cream, chocolate truffle cake, and cookies with housemade cherry ice cream. This restaurant is known for its impressive wine list and temperature-controlled cellar.

## Sam Wo

*813 Washington St./Grant Ave., Chinatown, (415) 982-0596. L-D daily; $. No reservations. No cards.*

People once came here for the experience of being insulted by, and to watch the reaction of others being insulted by, Edsel Ford Fong—the infamous waiter who reigned over the second floor. Unfortunately for those of us who actually became fond of him, Fong passed away in 1984. It is doubtful a replacement could ever be found. So now the main reason to come here is for the fresh housemade noodles and the unusual layout of the tiny dining rooms. Entering this "jook joint" through the cramped and busy kitchen and climbing the narrow stairs to the second and third floors is not unlike entering a submarine, only going up instead of down. Diners sit on stools at tables unexpectedly topped with real marble. Waiters shout orders down an ancient hand-operated dumbwaiter via which finished dishes are later delivered. The house specialty, noodle soup, is available in 12 varieties, and won ton soups and chow fun dishes are also on the menu. The roasted pork rice noodle roll is especially good. No soft drinks, milk, or coffee are available, and no fortune cookies arrive with the amazingly inexpensive check. It is worth knowing this place stays open until 3 a.m. every day but Sunday.

## Sanppo

*1702 Post St./Buchanan St., by Japan Center, (415) 346-3486; fax (415) 346-0927. L-D daily; $$. Highchairs, boosters. Reservations advised.*

This cozy Japanese restaurant always has a line at the door—a sure tip-off that something is worth waiting for. Appetizers include gomaae spinach (uncooked and sprinkled with sesame seeds), harusame salad (sweet potato noodles mixed with lettuce, onion, and a creamy dressing), and housemade gyoza, (similar to Chinese pot stickers). Entrees include a light tempura, deep-fried fresh oysters, and nasu hasamiyaki (grilled slices of ginger-marinated beef and eggplant). A large selection of noodle dishes is also available.

## Sanraku

*704 Sutter St./Taylor St., near Union Square, (415) 771-0803, fax (415) 771-0893; www.sanraku.com. L M-F, D daily; $-$$. Highchairs, boosters. Reservations advised.*

Service is delightfully welcoming in this tiny Japanese restaurant. Choose sushi from the small sushi bar, or better yet order it combined with a teriyaki, tempura, or donburi entree. Shrimp tempura consists of a generous portion of perfectly deep-fried shrimp and assorted vegetables. Dinners come with tea, a green salad, soup, and rice. A branch is at the Metreon *(101 4th St.).*

## Shanghai 1930

*133 Steuart St./Mission St., The Embarcadero, (415) 896-5600, fax (415) 896-5688; www.shanghai 1930.com. L M-F, D M-Sat; $$-$$$. Highchairs, booths. Reservations advised. Valet parking.*

Stepping down the curving red-carpeted staircase here that leads into the cozy womb of the spacious **Blue** bar feels like the beginning of a mysterious Chinatown adventure. The trip gets even better in the subterranean dining room ringed with comfy booths. In fact, the restaurant is modeled after the between-wars atmosphere in Shanghai, when it was known as the "Paris of the Orient." For members of the private cigar club located behind frosted glass doors in the **Guanxi Lounge**, the image is taken a step further, bringing on visions of opium dens. But back to the restaurant. Live jazz from the bar carries into the dining room, adding a delicious dreamy quality. Favorite dishes from the extensive, intriguing menu—all served artistically arranged—include minced duck in lettuce petals, sweet tangerine beef with celery hearts, hot and red firecracker chicken, and striking Jade & Ebony (succulent black mushrooms and jade-green baby bok choy). For dessert don't miss sesame seed-covered bananas, flambéed table-side and served with a trio of sorbets. Creative cocktails are the drink of choice.

## The Slanted Door

*1 Ferry Plaza/Market St., in Ferry Building, The Embarcadero, (415) 861-8032, fax (415) 861-8329; www.slanteddoor.com. L-D daily; $$. Booths. Reservations essential. Valet parking.*

Delicious Vietnamese-inspired food made from quality organic ingredients is served here in a sleek, stylish setting with a view of the bay. Best bets out of the open kitchen include the soft spring rolls, the rice noodle stir-fry, the caramelized shrimp, and the baby spinach and spicy eggplant with coconut sauce. Mick Jagger got some satisfaction from the grapefruit and jicama salad, shaking beef, and spicy green beans when he dined here. But that's just the tip of the culinary iceberg. A large selection of precious hot teas and unusual ales are also available.

## Soku's Teriyaki & Sushi

*2280 Chestnut St./Scott St., Marina district, (415) 563-0162; www.enoshimasushi.com. L-D M-Sat; $. 1 highchair, 1 booster.*

What's lacking in atmosphere here is more than made up for in delicious bargain fare and fast service. The extensive menu offers a surprisingly large choice of traditional Japanese items: teriyaki, tempura, sashimi, sukiyaki, nabe, sushi, donburi, udon noodles, and more. Dessert is either green tea or tempura ice cream.

## South Park Cafe

*108 South Park Ave./2nd St., South of Market, (415) 495-7275. D M-Sat; $$. Highchairs, boosters. Reservations advised.*

With large windows overlooking the small and popular park that fills the center oval of this unique street (designed originally to resemble London's Berkeley Square), this tiny butter-yellow French bistro is a great place to sit down

for a pleasant dinner. The regularly changing menu includes unusual dishes such as sautéed pig's ear terrine as well as more traditional items such as duck with lavender sauce. Though French-owned, it is reminiscent of a New York City cafe.

## Steps of Rome Trattoria

*362 Columbus Ave./Grant St., North Beach, (415) 986-6480, fax (415) 835-6064; http://stepsof rometrattoria.citysearch.com. D W-M; $$. Reservations accepted.*

Also reminiscent of a New York City restaurant, this charming little spot has several tables in a street-level room, plus more up narrow stairs in a second-floor dining room—all with sidewalk views. The menu is a choice of delicious housemade pastas and more substantial meat entrees, but the kitchen seems willing to produce any request. Desserts are exceptional and include a cliché tiramisu as well as a memorable creamy panna cotta with fruit sauce. Service is attentive and cheerful and the food quality surprisingly good considering a barker is used to bring people in. Just a few doors down, the related, though more informal, **Steps of Rome Cafe** *(http://stepsofrome.citysearch.com)* offers less expensive dining and a similar menu.

## St. Francis Fountain

*2801 24th St./York St., Mission district, (415) 826-4200. B-L-D daily; $. Boosters, booths, child portions. No reservations. No cards.*

Here since 1918, this informal cafe retains its old-time wooden booths and a counter with swivel stools, and it claims to be the oldest ice cream parlor in San Francisco. Specialties include a Guinness float and a hot vanilla shake. The menu features typical diner fare, including pancakes, waffles, soups, salads, sandwiches, and burgers.

## The Stinking Rose

*325 Columbus Ave./Broadway, North Beach, (415) PU-1-ROSE, fax (415) 781-2833; www.thestinking rose.com. L-D daily; $$. Highchairs, boosters. Reservations advised.*

A warren of unusual rooms awaits garlic lovers here, as does some delicious food made with as much garlic as possible. A don't-miss item is the bagna calda, consisting of tender, soft, almost sweet cloves of garlic served with bread for spreading. Among the winning dishes are wild mushroom-roasted eggplant lasagna, 40-clove garlic chicken, and delectable Silence of the Lamb Shank with Chianti glaze and fava beans. For dessert, the truly adventurous can try garlic *ice cream!* For those who still haven't had enough, a tiny shop in front sells all things garlic.

## Straits Cafe

*3300 Geary Blvd./Parker Ave., Richmond district, (415) 668-1783, fax (415) 668-3901; www.straits restaurants.com. L-D daily; $$. Highchairs, boosters. Reservations advised.*

In a nod to the tropics, supporting columns have been transformed into pseudo palm trees in this airy, casual dining room. The delicious Singaporean fare is a complex, refined, and aromatic combination of Malaysian, Indonesian, Chinese, and Indian cuisines. It seems impossible to order wrong. However, particularly tasty items include murtabak (Indian bread stuffed with spiced minced beef), gado gado (cold vegetables with spicy peanut sauce), mee goreng Indian-style noodles, spicy basil chicken, green beans sambal (long beans stir-fried with chilies), and chili crab. Meats are cooked slowly and literally fall off the bone. The mixed bar drinks are extensive and outstanding—think Raffles punch, Singapore slings, Midori margaritas—and some are available in frozen versions. Great yogurt lassis (the coco pandan version, tasting of coconut and vanilla

and flavored with fresh mint, is delightful), a housemade ginger-vanilla soda, and a variety of Singapore sodas flavored with luscious fruit syrups are also options.

## Tadich Grill

*240 California St./Battery St., Financial district, (415) 391-1849, fax (415) 391-2373. L-D M-Sat; $$. Highchairs, boosters, booths. No reservations.*

Begun in another location in 1849 as a coffee stand, this Old San Francisco institution has been here since 1967 and is California's oldest restaurant in continuous operation. With its dark wood walls, long wooden lunch counter, and private enclosed booths, it has an old-fashioned clubby feel and is a fabulously cozy place to be on a rainy day. The wait to get in can be long, but persevere. Then be wise and order simple, unsauced dishes. Pan-fried seafood is particularly good and served with tasty housemade tartar sauce. Steaks and chops are on the menu, and Hangtown fry—scrambled eggs, bacon, and oysters—is also available. Though the housemade rice pudding has been on the menu for over 100 years, desserts are weak.

## Taiwan

*445 Clement St./6th Ave., Richmond district, (415) 387-1789. L-D daily.*

For description, see page 283.

## ThirstyBear Brewing Company

*661 Howard St./3rd St., South of Market, (415) 974-0905, fax (415) 974-0955; www.thirstybear.com. L M-Sat, D daily; $-$$. Highchairs, boosters. Reservations accepted.*

This brewpub has several seating areas in a large, open room of concrete floors and aged brick walls, plus an upstairs area with pool tables. Ordering a 3-ounce taster of each of the nine different house brews, which include the popular Polar Bear pilsner and Brown Bear English-style ale, is a good idea. It will probably be impossible to pick a favorite until all are sampled, and by then most people forget which is which and have to start over—or come back again. Cocktails, single malt scotches, and housemade Sangria are also options. The menu features rustic Spanish cuisine, including tapas and paellas, and desserts are special. Flamenco is scheduled on some Sunday evenings.

## Ti Couz Crêperie

*3108 16th St./Valencia St., Mission district, (415) 25-CREPE. M-F 11am-11pm, Sat-Sun from 10am; $. Highchairs, boosters. No reservations.*

Always busy as a beehive, this Brittany-style French crêperie whips up a vast variety of the delicious pancakes. Choose either a savory buckwheat delight—perhaps a jambon and fromage (ham and cheese) or a champignon (mushroom with sauce)—or a whole-wheat sweet concoction (the orange butter version is light, while the popular chocolate with banana is more substantial). A few soups, salads, seafood items, and crêpe ice cream cones are also on the menu. Fresh citrus juices, and occasionally fresh peach juice, make refreshing accompaniments, but a full bar is also available. Seating options are as ample as the menu, but the best choice is likely the counter from which the cooks can be viewed in action.

## Tommaso's

*1042 Kearny St./Broadway, North Beach, (415) 398-9696, fax (415) 989-9415; www.tommasosnorthbeach.com. D Tu-Sun; $$. Highchairs, boosters. No reservations.*

In 1935, when this spot was known as Lupo's, it was the first restaurant to bring pizza from New York City to the West Coast. (Pizza was introduced to the U.S. at the Lombardy Pizza Restaurant in New York City in 1905.) And for quite a while it was the only restaurant in the entire U.S. to prepare all of its baked foods in a genuine oak wood-burning brick oven. (In fact, world-renowned Chez Panisse in Berkeley used this oven as a model for their own oven, which then began producing a trend-setting gourmet mini pizza.) Movie director Francis Ford Coppola has been seen dashing in from his nearby office—sometimes to chow down from the menu, other times to whip up his own creations in the kitchen. Seating in the cheery cellar consists of both a large community dining table and smaller tables in semi-private compartments separated by wooden partitions. Wall murals dating to 1935 depict scenes of Naples and the Amalfi Coast. Any of the marinated salads—broccoli, string beans, or roasted peppers—make a good starter, and the crusty bread is excellent for soaking up excess marinade. The menu offers almost 20 kinds of pizza featuring a superb thin, crisp-yet-chewy crust and several calzones (a sort of pizza turnover), plus pastas, seafood, veal, and chicken entrees. Desserts include cannoli, spumoni ice cream, and housemade tiramisu.

## Tommy Toy's

*655 Montgomery St./Washington St., in Washington and Montgomery Tower, Financial district, (415) 397-4888, fax (415) 397-0469; www.tommytoys.com. L M-F, D daily; $$$. Reservations advised. Valet parking at D.*

It's hard to imagine a more elegant, more romantic restaurant than this well-established hideaway, where men are requested to wear a coat and tie. After passing through a dark entry, diners are greeted by the striking sight of giant goldfish in a tank and then seated in a refined room displaying authentic Asian antiques. The pampering service begins immediately and doesn't stop. Chopsticks appear only by request. To begin, diners can order delicious drinks from the bar to sip while perusing the menu. Specializing in haute cuisine Chinoise, the specialty here is a blend of classic Chinese dishes with a traditional French presentation. The spectacular fixed-price, six-course Signature Dinner includes: minced squab Imperial; seafood bisque in a coconut shell crowned with puff pastry; whole fresh Maine lobster, shelled and sautéed with pine nuts and fresh mushrooms in a peppercorn sauce and served on a bed of angel hair crystal noodles; Peking duck wrapped in lotus buns; tender wok-charred medallion of beef with garlic and wine, served

with four-flavors fried rice; and peach mousse in a strawberry compote beautifully swirled with hearts. The elaborate, elegant presentations are served on oversize plates, and a fresh hot finger towel is offered after each course.

## Ton Kiang

*5821 Geary Blvd./22nd Ave., outer Richmond district, (415) 387-8273, fax (415) 387-8012; www.tonkiang.net. Dim sum daily 10-10; $. Highchairs, boosters. No reservations.*

Operating on two floors, this attractive spot specializes in Hakka-style cuisine. The exemplary dim sum items are considered the very best in San Francisco and include deep-fried taro croquettes, puffy deep-fried stuffed crab claws, ethereal chive-shrimp dumplings, exquisite steamed pea shoots, miniature egg-custard tarts, and crisp walnut cookies filled with lotus paste. See also page 16.

## Tosca Cafe

*252 Columbus Ave./Broadway, North Beach, (415) 986-9651. Tu-Sun 5pm-2am; $. No reservations. No cards.*

Opened in 1919, this popular bar is a hangout for actors and writers, and it positively roars with excitement. The jukebox is said to have great selections—if only it were possible to *hear* them—and the 60-foot-long carved mahogany bar is San Francisco's longest. More seating is at an uninspired collection of tables surrounded by comfy, wall-hugging red leather banquettes. Though the city's first cappuccino machines were introduced here in 1921, the house drink is a "coffee-less cappuccino"—a yummy brandy-laced Ghirardelli hot chocolate.

## Town Hall

*342 Howard St./Fremont St., South of Market, (415) 908-3900, fax (415) 908-3700; www.townhallsf.com. L M-F, D daily; $$$. 1 highchair, 1 booster. Reservations advised.*

Sitting in the wide-open, high-ceilinged main dining room here is the best, but when the place is jammin', a communal table near the bar is a good alternative to a long wait. The historic brick building it is within is the former Marine Electric warehouse, built just after the 1906 quake. Floors are stained the color of dark chocolate, and handmade wooden tables and chairs and original brick walls add to the invit-

ing mood. Starter specialties include seafood chowder with housemade sourdough crackers, and steamed mussels in Old Bay tomato broth. Should scrumptious wild mushroom lasagna be among the choices on the ever-changing, mostly American menu, don't hesitate. Desserts are homey and special—warm pineapple upside down cake, pear-and-sour cherry crisp, butterscotch pot de crème—and the hot chocolate made with Parisian cocoa is like velvet.

## World Wrapps

*2012 Market St./Church St., (415) 487-7300, fax (415) 487-7320; www.worldwrapps.com. L-D daily; $. Highchairs, boosters, child portions. No reservations.*

This noteworthy fast food chain opened its first restaurant in San Francisco in 1996. Tasty, wholesome, made-to-order meals include an international array of stuffed tortillas as well as some "unwrapped" rice bowls and soups. Signature mixtures include salmon and asparagus, portobello mushroom and goat cheese, and Thai chicken. They all go particularly well with an assortment of smoothies. The decor is colorful, and the seating is especially pleasant for solitary diners. Take-out orders can be placed online.

## Yank Sing

*101 Spear St./Mission St., in Rincon Ctr., South of Market, (415) 957-9300, fax (415) 957-9899; www.yanksing.com. Dim sum M-F 11-3, Sat-Sun 10-4; $$. Highchairs, boosters. Reservations advised.*

In 1957, when it opened in a previous location in Chinatown, this was the first dim sum parlor in the city to serve the cuisine as it is known in Hong Kong. Compelling reasons to forsake tradition and visit this now upscale restaurant at it location outside of Chinatown are that they take reservations and that the friendly servers willl usually answer questions. Tablecloths, fabric napkins, and fresh flowers grace each table, and etched-glass partitions break up the windowless interior. Top items include cloud-soft rice noodles stuffed with a variety of meats, succulent stuffed black mushroom caps, deep-fried crab claws, sweet taro balls, Peking duck, flaky-crusted custard tarts, and especially for kids—wedges of orange peel filled with shimmering orange Jell-O. See also page 16. A branch is located at 49 Stevenson

Street *(at 1st St., South of Market, (415) 541-4949. Daily 11-3.)*.

It is a Cantonese custom to introduce a new baby to family and friends at a Red Egg and Ginger Party. Named for some of the food items included in the luncheon menu, these parties are catered here and set menus are available.

## Yet Wah
*2140 Clement St./23rd Ave., Richmond district, (415) 387-8040; www.yetwah.com. L-D daily; $$. Highchairs, boosters. Reservations advised.*

Once just a little hole-in-the-wall at a different location on this same street, this modest establishment has blossomed into something more. The long menu lists over 200 dishes, and the quality is generally good. Favorites include hot-and-sour soup, fried won tons stuffed with Chinese sausage, pot stickers, mu shu pork, Szechwan spiced beef, and ginger-garlic lamb. Explore the menu and enjoy the adventure of trying something new. How about dragon's eye fruit for dessert? A branch is at 5238 Diamond Heights Boulevard *(at Clipper St., Twin Peaks, (415) 282-0788.)*.

## Zao Noodle Bar
*2406 California St./Fillmore St., upper Fillmore, (415) 345-8088; www.zaonoodle.com. L-D daily; $. Child items. No reservations.*

Offering quick and inexpensive meals featuring oodles of noodles with plenty of flavor, this local chain features a high energy, casual atmosphere. It features the delicious, healthy cuisine of Thailand, Vietnam, China, and Japan. Menu standouts include Middle Kingdom chicken cups (a flavorful appetizer consisting of a minced mixture of chicken, shitake mushrooms, and water chestnuts wrapped in lettuce), a low-fat chicken salad, and the surf 'n turf (a big bowl of fresh handmade fat noodles topped with a sautéed mixture of chicken, prawns, and vegetables flavored with ginger, garlic, and chilies). For fussy children, a simple chicken dish is available along with a bowl of plain noodles or a cup of rice. Drinks include myriad beers, premium whole leaf teas, sakes, and a tangy housemade sparkling ginger-orange cooler and lemonade. For dessert, try the popular deep-fried banana spring roll with chocolate sauce, or the Japanese mochi ice cream

consisting of mango, green tea, and Kona coffee ice cream balls in individual rice wrappers. For single diners and general overflow, a communal dining table runs through the center of the room. Branches are at 2031 Chestnut Street *(at Fillmore St., Marina district, (415) 928-3088)*; and at 3583 16th Street *(at Market St., Castro district, (415) 864-2888)*.

## Zarzuela
*2000 Hyde St./Union St., Russian Hill, (415) 346-0800, fax (415) 346-0880. D Tu-Sat; $$. No reservations.*

With an open, yet cozy dining room warmed by butter-yellow Mediterranean walls, this gem serves delicious Spanish tapas. Each meal starts with bread and olive oil plus a complimentary plate of exquisite olives. For a terrific tapas dinner, begin with a shared salad and small plate of salted almonds. Continue with grilled eggplant rolled around creamy goat cheese, crisp fried potatoes with garlic and sherry vinegar, and shrimps sautéed in garlic and olive oil. For a filling, well-priced meal, add a daily special such as fresh sardines, a paella, or a larger plate—traditional Catalan seafood stew, grilled lamb chops, ox-tail stew—and wash it all down with a traditional sherry. Sponge cake stuffed with fruit and soaked in liqueur is a perfect ending. After, jump on one of the cable cars passing by outside and take a refreshing ride.

## Zazie
*941 Cole St./Parnassus St., Haight-Ashbury, (415) 564-5332;. B-L-D daily; $-$$. 1 highchair, 1 booster. No reservations.*

Situated in an often sunny, always appealing neighborhood and featuring a cozy ambiance, this small spot has tall ceilings, brick walls, and a garden patio for sunny-day dining. Breakfast offers vast choices—some common, some less so: Irish oatmeal with blueberries, gingerbread pancakes with roasted pears, eggs with spicy Merguez lamb sausage, and colorful poached eggs Valence topped with roasted eggplant, goat cheese, and a spicy tomato sauce. Lunch brings on delicious sandwiches and salads. A citron presse and chocolat chaud are reminiscent of Paris, as is the restaurant in general, but the blend of cranberry juice, fresh-squeezed orange juice, and bubbly water that is the Zazie spritzer is most definitely the drink of choice. Should the wait to get in be ridiculous, many options are nearby: an Italian restaurant, a sushi bar, a crêperie, a burger shack, a coffee house, and a French bakery serving huge French café au laits.

## Zuni Cafe

*1658 Market St./Franklin St., (415) 552-2522, fax (415) 552-9149. L-D Tu-Sun, SunBr; $$-$$$. Highchairs, child portions. Reservations advised. Valet parking at D.*

It seems that all seats are good in this cheery warren of asymmetrically shaped spaces, where both the Market Street parade and chefs in the kitchen are part of the visual treat. The menu changes twice each day, and everything but the bread is housemade. A delightful brunch might consist of an antipasto plate spread with delicious Molinari salami and baked ricotta, followed by a pizza baked in the wood-burning brick oven and topped, perhaps, with artichoke hearts and capers. Other options might include eggs baked with tomato, fennel, and white beans and served in an oversize earthenware bowl, or the acclaimed house-ground hamburger on grilled rosemary focaccia bread (not available at dinner). The roasted chicken and Caesar salad are always good choices. Do leave room for dessert, especially if the divine rhubarb tart is an option.

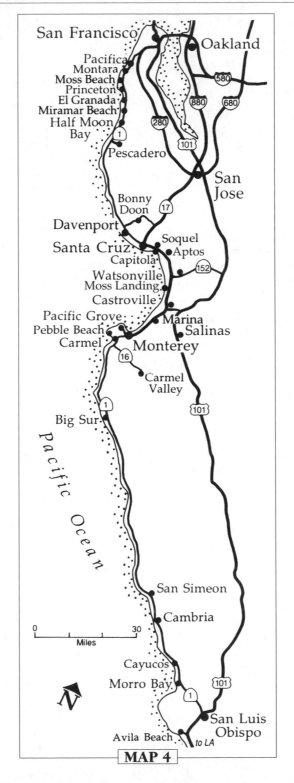

MAP 4

# COAST SOUTH

The trip down Highway 1 from San Francisco features a breathtaking, cliff-hugging ride along the Pacific Ocean.

After passing ridges of boxy houses in pastel tones (referred to as being made of "ticky-tacky" by folk singer Malvina Reynolds in her famous '60s song "Little Boxes") and the beach town of Pacifica, Highway 1 winds to the ocean through a eucalyptus-lined path in the coastal foothills. A stretch of this road known as Devil's Slide hugs cliffs dropping steeply into the sea. In fact, part of the road itself occasionally drops off, causing traffic congestion due to detours. Though many people make informal stops in the Devil's Slide area to take pictures, it is unsafe. Restraint is in order until an official parking area is found. Once the road passes this hilly area, it moves inland and becomes more flat and straight.

When the Bay Area is blazing with sunshine, this area can be disappointingly socked in with fog. And vice versa. In fact, on many late summer and early fall days when San Francisco is covered with fog, this area is at its most beautiful. The area's spectacular unspoiled beaches are a popular destination anytime, but they are especially so then, when the weather is usually warm and clear.

Be careful, though, about going in the water as tides can be dangerous. Always check with a ranger station or lifeguard before swimming.

---

## Pacifica

### — VISITOR INFORMATION —

**Pacifica Chamber of Commerce and Visitor Center**
*225 Rockaway Beach Ave. #1, (650) 355-4122, fax (650) 355-6949; www.pacificachamber.com.*

### — ANNUAL EVENTS —

**Pacific Coast Fog Fest**
*September. (650) 355-8200; www.pacificcoast fogfest.com. Free.*

This family-friendly event celebrates the cold fog that wraps up this area in a cotton candy-like mist each fall.

### — WHAT TO DO —

**Sanchez Adobe Historic Site**
*1000 Linda Mar Blvd., (650) 359-1462; www.san mateocountyhistory.com. Tu-Thur 10-4, Sat-Sun 1-5. Free.*

Actively used since prehistoric times, this site was an Ohlone Indian village and then in

1786 became a support farm for Mission Dolores. The adobe house was built for a family of settlers in 1846 and later became a hotel, speakeasy, and artichoke storage shed. A video and a docent-led tour explain more details. An Indian refuse dump, known as a "shell midden," can be viewed in the yard.

### — WHERE TO STAY —

**Seabreeze Motel**
*100 Rockaway Beach Ave., (650) 359-3903, fax (650) 359-5624. 20 rooms; $. Continental breakfast; restaurant.*

This is the place for a quick, inexpensive escape. Rooms are simple, but the beach and roaring sea are only a few steps away.

**Nicks Seashore Restaurant** (*(650) 359-3900; www.nicksrestaurant.net. B-L-D daily; $$-$$$. Highchairs, boosters, booths, child portion. Reservations advised.*), a merry steak and seafood house under the same ownership, is just next door offering comfy booths and a view of surfers frolicking on the waves outside.

### — WHERE TO EAT —

**Taco Bell**
*5200 Hwy. 1, (650) 355-0591. L-D daily; $. Highchairs, child portions. No reservations. No cards.*

Located inside an attractive redwood building, this fast-food restaurant's exceptional beachfront location on **Pacifica State Beach** (*(650) 738-7381; www.parks.ca.gov.*) makes it worthy of a stop-in. The restaurant operates a special walk-up window for surfers, who provide diners free entertainment in the ocean just outside.

## Montara

### — WHERE TO STAY —

**Point Montara Lighthouse Hostel**
*On 16th St./Hwy. 1, (650) 728-7177, same fax; www.norcalhostels.org. 45 beds; private rooms.*

This restored 1875 lighthouse still operates from its cliff-side perch. Lodging is in a modern duplex that was formerly the light-keeper's quarters. Facilities include two kitchens, a laundry, a private beach, and bicycle rentals. The lighthouse is not open for tours. See also page 445.

## Moss Beach

### — WHAT TO DO —

**Fitzgerald Marine Reserve**
*At the end of California Ave., (650) 728-3584; www.eparks.net. Daily sunrise-sunset. Free. No dogs.*

Tidepooling is excellent here. Usually some pools are accessible, with the occasional sea star or hermit crab caught by the tide. And because visitors are not permitted to remove anything, the sand is rich with shells and interesting natural debris. Visiting when the tide is out assures seeing a large variety of specimens, and naturalist-led walks are usually scheduled then on weekends. Although the parking area can be deceptively warm and calm, the area by the ocean is usually windy and cold. Take wraps. Picnic tables are provided near the parking lot.

### — WHERE TO STAY —

**Seal Cove Inn**
*221 Cypress Ave., (800) 995-9987, (650) 728-4114, fax (650) 728-4116; www.sealcoveinn.com. 10 rooms; $$$. All wood-burning fireplaces. Evening snack; full breakfast. No smoking; no pets.*

The owner of this coastal inn is well known for traveling through Europe evaluating other people's inns. She is Karen Brown, author and publisher of the popular *Karen Brown's Country Inns* series of guidebooks. Set way back from the road, her inn fronts a bank of mature cypress and offers access to secluded beaches and tidepools. Antiques and original watercolors cozy up the interior of the newly constructed lodge, and comfortable public areas include a sitting room with a wood-burning fireplace and a patio with views of the distant ocean. All rooms feature a private terrace or balcony, complimentary wine and soft drinks, a towel warmer, fresh flowers, and turndown service. Breakfast can be taken privately in-room or with other guests in the dining room.

### — WHERE TO EAT —

**Moss Beach Distillery**
*140 Beach Way/Ocean Blvd., (800) 675-MOSS, (650) 728-5595; www.mossbeachdistillery.com. D daily, SunBr; $$$. Reservations advised for D.*

Magnificently situated on a scenic bluff overlooking the unspoiled Fitzgerald Marine

Reserve, this out-of-the-way surf-and-turf dinner house dates from the Prohibition era of the 1920s, when it was a notorious speakeasy. Reputed to be haunted (it once was featured on TV's *Unsolved Mysteries*), it is now an official California State Historic Site and well worth seeking out for a romantic repast. Plan to arrive before sundown to take in the incredible cliff-top view and to snuggle under one of the blankets thoughtfully provided on the ocean-side cocktail deck. A few lucky folks can snag a wooden bench swing, too. Tables in the cozy interior also offer spectacular views.

# Princeton-by-the-Sea

## — A LITTLE BACKGROUND —

This scenic fishing village makes an inviting stop. A hotbed for bootlegging during Prohibition, it is known now for its surfers and seafood restaurants.

## — GETTING THERE —

Located about 25 miles south of San Francisco.

## — WHAT TO DO —

### Surfer-watching

• **Maverick's**
*www.maverickssurf.com.*
    Named for a surfer's dog, this legendary surfing Mecca is located just north of Pillar Point Harbor. Sporting killer waves—literally—in the winter, it was here on December 23, 1994 that world-famous big wave surfer Mark Foo died while surfing the world-class monster waves that break in this treacherous area. He had flown in from Honolulu that day especially to surf the unusually large waves, which have been know to reach up to 30 feet. Maverick's is rated one of the world's three best surfing spots (the others are Todos Santos Island off Ensenada in Baja California, Mexico, and Waimea Bay on the North Shore of Oahu in Hawaii).

### Whale-watching

• **Oceanic Society Expeditions**
(800) 326-7491, (415) 474-3385, fax (415) 474-3395; www.oceanic-society.org. Sat-Sun & some F; Dec-May.

$35, 60+ $33, 7-15 $18. Must be 10 or older. Reservations required.
    Each boat trip has a professional naturalist on board to educate participants about the whales and interpret their behavior. See also page 13.

## — WHERE TO STAY —

### Pillar Point Inn
380 Capistrano Rd., (800) 400-8281, (650) 728-7377, fax (650) 728-8345; www.pillarpointinn.com. 11 rooms; $$$-$$$+. All gas fireplaces. Afternoon snack; full breakfast. No smoking; no pets.
    Facing a picturesque small boat harbor, this contemporary inn features a Cape Cod-style of architecture. All of the rooms are spacious and sport cloud-like feather beds and harbor views. A complimentary video library is also available. Several good seafood restaurants and the busy harbor itself are just across the street.

## — WHERE TO EAT —

### Barbara's Fishtrap
281 Capistrano Rd., (650) 728-7049, fax (650) 728-2519. L-D daily; $-$$. Highchairs, boosters, child portions. No reservations. No cards.
    Perched on stilts over rocks and sea, this tiny roadside diner has a harbor view and casual atmosphere. It is a pleasant spot for a quick meal. In addition to a rustic interior room with fishnets hanging from the ceiling, it has an enclosed patio kept warm with heat lamps. Though usually there is a short wait for seating, fast service encourages a quick turnover. Lunch is served until 5 p.m. and includes an award-winning New England-style clam chowder, bouillabaisse, fish & chips, a killer crab sandwich, and deep-fried calamari as well as a hamburger. The dinner menu additionally offers scallops, prawns, and steak served with sides of soup or salad, French bread, French fries or baked potato, and a vegetable. The house specialty—rockfish fresh off the harbor fishing boats—is available either broiled or dipped in batter and deep-fried tempura-style.

### Half Moon Bay Brewing Company
390 Capistrano Rd., (650) 728-BREW, fax (650) 728-7563; www.hmbbrewingco.com. L-D daily; $-$$. Highchairs, boosters, child menu.

Featuring a dining room of cozy niches and a rustic decor of unfinished sandblasted wood, this brewpub has great harbor views and is ideal for a relaxing meal. Carpeting subdues the noise level, and children fit in well. The menu is the same all day, with a well priced "pub grub" section of sandwiches and the de rigueur fish & chips. Soups, salads, and heartier entrees—fresh fish, ribs, steak—are also available. Kids can choose macaroni and cheese, a peanut butter & jelly sandwich, or a grilled cheese sandwich from a coloring menu. Desserts are rich and gooey: brownie a la mode, a root beer float, chocolate mousse cake. The full menu is also available in the bar (videos of surfing at nearby Maverick's are always running here, and live music is often scheduled) and out on a patio equipped with heaters and fire pits (well-behaved pets are welcome there); both areas have an ocean view. Beers—including Mavericks Amber Ale and Sandy Beach Blonde (a hefeweizen)—are brewed on the premises. A short tour of the brewing facility is available.

# Miramar Beach

## — A LITTLE BACKGROUND —

A few miles north of Half Moon Bay, a turn toward the sea on Magellan Avenue leads to peaceful Miramar Beach. Off the beaten path, it provides a chance to view the area in the way some of the luckier local residents do. Brown pelicans and scurrying sandpipers are easily observed from the beach, which is reached by climbing down a breakfront constructed of large boulders.

## — WHAT TO DO —

### Bach Dancing and Dynamite Society
307 Mirada Rd., (650) 726-4143, fax (650) 712-0506; www.bachddsoc.org. F-Sat eve., Sun aft. $25, under 21 $20.

Live jazz and classical music are performed at this beach house. Arrive early, as there are no advance reservations. A buffet with a wine and juice bar is available, and minors are welcome.

### Dunn Mehler Art Gallery
337 Mirada Rd./Medio Ave., (650) 726-7667, fax (650) 726-5977; www.dunnmehler.com. W-M 10-6.

Situated in a contemporary redwood building just across the street from the ocean, this sophisticated gallery showcases an array of mostly three-dimensional art from American artisans.

## — WHERE TO STAY —

### Cypress Inn on Miramar Beach
407 Mirada Rd./Medio Ave., (800) 83-BEACH, (650) 726-6002, fax (650) 712-0380; www.cypressinn.com. 18 rooms; $$$-$$$$+. Children free. All fireplaces. Afternoon snack; full breakfast. No smoking.

Located on a quiet frontage road across the street from the ocean, this impressive inn is decorated with bright accents of Mexican folk art. Each room in the main building has a private balcony and faces the ocean, allowing guests always to hear the soothing sound of the ocean in the background and just to sit in their room watching the brown pelicans dive for fish. To experience a bit of heaven, reserve the third-floor Las Nubes room. Its name meaning literally "the clouds," this penthouse room has a luxurious tiled bathroom with an oversize whirlpool tub, plus a bank of windows overlooking the ocean. Occupants want to stay forever. Four rooms are located in a newly added beach house behind the main inn. The afternoon snack includes tea and exquisite hors d'oeuvres.

## — WHERE TO EAT —

### Miramar Beach Restaurant & Bar
131 Mirada Rd., (650) 726-9053, fax (650) 726-5060; www.beachfrontdining.com. L M-Sat, D daily, SunBr; $$-$$$. Highchairs, boosters, booths, child menu. Reservations advised.

Situated off the beaten path and across the street from the ocean, this casual spot offers expansive views and is especially nice at lunch and Sunday brunch. The lunch menu has salads, hot sandwiches, hamburgers, omelettes, and housemade chowder with garlic bread. Pricier dinners include seafood, steak, and pasta and come with salad, fresh vegetables, and rice pilaf. After dining, visit the beach behind the rocky breakfront across from the restaurant to take a walk, build a sand castle, or maybe observe a flock of brown pelicans bobbing on the surf and diving for food.

# Half Moon Bay

## — A LITTLE BACKGROUND —

First called San Benito, then Spanishtown after an influx of Spaniards in 1860, Half Moon Bay was finally named for the crescent-shaped bay north of town. The oldest of the coastal towns in this area, it has an old-fashioned Main Street. Uncutesied, it looks much as it always has, and boasts the state's first steel-reinforced concrete bridge—circa 1900 and spanning Pilarcitos Creek at the north end of town. The area is known for its fresh flowers and produce, and a colorful **flower market** is held downtown on the third Saturday of each month (except October).

## — VISITOR INFORMATION —

**Half Moon Bay Coastside Chamber of Commerce & Visitors Bureau**
*520 Kelly Ave., (650) 726-8380, fax (650) 726-8389; www.halfmoonbaychamber.org.*
This information source is located in the historic 1908 Alves House. Originally known as the Ben Cunha House, it is an elegant Eastlake Victorian with scalloped shingles and a polygonal tower.

**Harvest Trails**
*765 Main St., Half Moon Bay 94019, (650) 726-4485, fax (650) 726-4495.*
For a free map to the area's farms, send a self-addressed, stamped, legal-size envelope.

## — GETTING THERE —

Located approximately 25 miles south of San Francisco.

## — ANNUAL EVENTS —

**Chamarita**
*May or June. (650) 726-2729.*
Held here for over 100 years, this Portuguese festival takes place seven weekends after Easter and includes a barbecue, parade, and carnival.

**Half Moon Bay Art & Pumpkin Festival**
*October. (650) 726-9652; www.miramarevents.com. Free.*
Children are invited to wear costumes and participate in the Great Pumpkin Parade celebrating the year's biggest pumpkin. Pumpkin-carving and pie-eating contests, a variety of pumpkin foods, and assorted on-going entertainment are part of the fun. Farmer Mike, known as the "Picasso of pumpkin carvers," is usually busy making creative faces on gargantuan gourds, and craft booths run for blocks. A pumpkin weigh-off—which in 2003 squashed the world record with a 1,180-pounder from Oregon—is held earlier in the week. The Half Moon Bay Beautification Committee, which sponsors the festival, pays the winning farmer $5 per pound. Pumpkin patches, brightly colored with their seasonal loot, are open nearby for picking.

## — WHAT TO DO —

**Half Moon Bay Nursery**
*11691 San Mateo Rd. (Hwy. 92), 3 mi. E of town, (650) 726-5392. Daily 9-5.*
In business for almost a half-century, this nursery provides a fabulous plant browse and is the perfect place to select blooming seasonal plants to spiff up a home garden. When Pavarotti is playing in the background, some people think they've died and gone to heaven.

**Obester Winery**
*12341 San Mateo Rd. (Hwy. 92), 2 mi. E of town, (650) 726-WINE, fax (650) 726-7074; www.obester winery.com. Tasting daily 10-5.*
Though the tasting room inside this rustic building is tiny, a spacious picnic area with tables is available out back. A non-alcoholic grape juice varietal, such as Gewurztraminer or

Pinot Noir, is usually served to kids while their parents taste the real thing. On Bottle Your Own days, customers can bring in bottles to fill directly from the barrel.

## Picnic

Put one together by visiting the **Half Moon Bay Bakery** *(514 Main St., (650) 726-4841.)*, which is still using its original brick ovens. It is known for its Portuguese sweet and French breads and its great donuts. Sandwiches are available to go.

While picking up supplies, allow some time for poking around in some of the shops on Main Street. Don't miss **Half Moon Bay Feed & Fuel** *(331 Main St., (650) 726-4814; www.halfmoonbayfeedandfuel.com. M-F 8-6, Sat 9-5, Sun 10-4.)*, an old-time farm supply store established in 1911. It sells farm, pet, and garden supplies to locals and has plenty of chicks, ducklings, bunnies, and other small farm animals to pet and purchase.

The area's spectacular beaches are popular picnic destinations summer through fall, when the weather tends to be warm and clear. **Dunes Beach** *(At end of Young Ave.)*, which is part of **Half Moon Bay State Beach** *(At end of Kelley Ave., (650) 726-8819, fax (650) 726-8816; www.parks.ca.gov. $2/vehicle.)*, is prime.

### — WHERE TO STAY —

## Beach House at Half Moon Bay

*4100 Hwy. 1, (800) 315-9366, (650) 712-0220, fax (650) 712-0693; www.beach-house.com. 54 rooms; $$-$$$+. All mini-kitchens & wood-burning fireplaces. Heated pool; hot tub; fitness room. Evening wine, continental breakfast.*

Those who are particularly lucky arrive here at dusk on a night when the fog clings above the water on a fluffy cloud, setting off a continuous bleat from a nearby foghorn. Contemporary-style rooms have private balconies and views of the ocean beyond the harbor, permitting the occasional sighting of an egret or brown pelican. Beds, made with comfortable cotton blankets and feather duvets, face the peaceful fishing harbor. A 6-mile coastal trail runs adjacent, leading into nearby Princeton-by-the-Sea—the perfect destination for dinner. Breakfast includes fresh-squeezed orange juice, great coffee, and an assortment of scones, muffins, and croissants; all can be gathered and taken to the room to enjoy at leisure. Plan ahead and order a scrumptious box lunch to enjoy the next day on the beach.

## Half Moon Bay Lodge

*2400 S. Cabrillo Hwy. (Hwy. 1), (800) 368-2468, (650) 726-9000, fax (650) 726-7951; www.halfmoonbaylodge.com. 81 rooms; $$-$$$. Children under 17 free. Some wood-burning fireplaces. Heated pool; hot tub; fitness room. No smoking.*

Located at the quiet southern end of town, this modern hacienda-style lodge motel overlooks the fourth fairway of the **Half Moon Bay Golf Links**—designed by Arnold Palmer and rated first in the Bay Area. An oversize hot tub is within a semi-enclosed room. Special amenities for children include beach and pool toys that they can keep and kid-sized robes for use during their stay.

## Mill Rose Inn

*615 Mill St., (800) 900-ROSE, (650) 726-8750, fax (415) 726-3031; www.millroseinn.com. 6 rooms; $$-$$$+. Some fireplaces. Hot tub. Afternoon snack, full breakfast. No smoking; no pets.*

Just 2 easy blocks from Main Street, this was San Mateo County's first B&B. Guests are greeted by a magnificent English country-style garden filled with hundreds of varieties of roses and other blooms. All rooms in the 1902 house have European antiques, fluffy comforters, and private entrances. Some have brass beds and clawfoot tubs. Breakfast and a newspaper are brought to the room. Advance reservations are wise for the secluded hot tub inside a locked garden gazebo.

## The Ritz-Carlton

*One Miramontes Point Rd., (800) 241-3333, (650) 712-7000, fax (650) 712-7070; www.ritzcarlton.com. 6 stories; 261 rooms; $$$-$$$+. Most gas fireplaces. Hot tub; health spa; fitness room; 6 lighted tennis courts; 2 18-hole golf courses. 2 restaurants; room service. Valet parking $25.*

Located on a treeless bluff overlooking the sea that is reminiscent of sites found in Scotland, this classy resort is designed to resemble a 19th-century grand seaside lodge. But never fear, this is not your parents' Ritz-Carlton: there is no dress code. Most rooms have a view of the ocean that can cause a maid to lean out a window mid-clean for a wistful gaze. All rooms feature white marble bathrooms with deep soaking tubs, silky Frette linens, goosedown pillows, and featherbeds and duvets. The Club Level offers the added amenity of snacks all day long. "It is my pleasure" rolls off the lips of employees who seem genuinely to enjoy attending to details. Facilities include a coastal walking path leading to a secluded beach and to picnic spots at scenic overlooks, an outdoor fire circle where guests can enjoy a s'mores basket from the bar, and a bluff-top hot tub. A bagpiper often plays ocean-side at sunset. The full-service spa has a central co-ed Roman mineral bath plus a sauna and steam room. Treatments include a pumpkin body peel and both a four-hands and a maternity massage, and there is a massage room just for couples. The Ritz Kids program operates during busy times.

The gourmet **Navio** restaurant *((650) 712-7040. Valet parking.)*, whose name means "ship" in Portuguese, is a nod to the area's nautical heritage. It features a barrel ceiling resembling the lower deck of a vintage wooden sailing ship. On one side floor-to-ceiling windows provide ocean views, and on the other an open display kitchen provides further diversion. The kitchen creates a captivating menu of coastal cuisine using fresh local ingredients. A multi-course tasting menu with matched wines is sometimes available.

## San Benito House
*356 Main St., (650) 726-3425; www.sanbenito house.com. 12 rooms; $-$$. Unsuitable for children under 10. No TVs; some shared baths. Sauna. Continental breakfast; restaurant. No smoking.*

From its beginning in 1905, this lodging has offered well-priced rooms. Upstairs, guest rooms feature vividly colored solid walls, high ceilings, and bathrooms with old-fashioned clawfoot tubs. Rooms are decorated with European antiques, contemporary paintings, and historical photographs. Guests can stroll in the formal English garden and, perhaps, indulge in some competition on the croquet lawn. Breakfast can be served in-room or even in bed.

Downstairs, the cozy **restaurant** *(D Thur-Sun; $$-$$$. Highchairs, boosters, child menu. Reservations advised.)* invites romantic dining. The Mediterranean-style cuisine makes use of fresh local produce and seafood, and the soups and French pastries are particularly delicious.

Make reservations when booking a room, as this cozy dining room is very popular with locals. (Overnight guests get a 10% discount in the restaurant.) A **deli** *(Daily 11-3; $.)* dispenses inexpensive salads and sandwiches made with house-baked bread, and a lively Western-style **saloon** *(Daily from 4pm.)* is the perfect spot for a nightcap.

### — WHERE TO EAT —

## Cameron's Pub
*1410 S. Cabrillo Hwy. (Hwy. 1), (650) 726-5705, fax (650) 726-9613; www.cameronsinn.com. L Tu-Sun, D daily; $. Highchairs, boosters, child menu.*

Home to the world's only double-decker smoking bus and maybe to the world's only double-decker video game bus, this neighborhood pub fills a warren of rooms. Its extensive menu includes baked potatoes, homemade soups, sandwiches, pizza, and burgers, plus homemade pies, a full soda fountain with sundaes and shakes, and 26 beers on tap. Pub-style games include shuffleboard, darts, pinball, chess, and pool, and authentic English telephone booths are positioned both inside and out. Live entertainment is scheduled regularly. Celebrities staying at the nearby Ritz-Carlton sometimes stop in (Pierce Brosnan and family have been patrons), but everyone is welcome— even babies and great-grandmums. A replica English village shop sells imported English food staples and goods. Don't forget to pick up a copy of the humorous, free *Cameron's Gazette.*

Want to stay the night? Three **guest rooms** are just upstairs. Two rooms share a bath but surprisingly, since this is billed as a B&B, breakfast is *not* included.

## Pasta Moon
*315 Main St., (650) 726-5125, fax (650) 726-7631; www.pastamoon.com. L M-Sat, D daily, SunBr; $$. Reservations advised.*

A favorite with locals ever since it opened, this is a simple but elegant space with large windows and white tablecloths. Breads are exceptional, and the housemade pasta is a must—perhaps a fabulous dish of wide pappardelle noodles mixed with house-cured pancetta, garlic, pinenuts, wild mushrooms, and a tomato cream sauce. Fresh fish and pizza are also among the choices on the lengthy menu. The affogato—white chocolate gelato with

espresso and candied orange peel—is sublime
for dessert.

## Sushi Main Street

*696 Mill St./Main St., (650) 726-6336; www.sushi
mainst.com. L M-Sat, D daily; $$. Highchairs, boost-
ers. Reservations advised.*

Serving everything Japanese and some
things not, this cave-like spot is decorated with
Asian artifacts that include Balinese carvings
and ancient temple bells. Seating is at rough-
hewn stone tables or at a sushi bar. Hot and
cold sake, plum wine, edamame (green soy
beans), kelp salad, gyoza (Japanese pot stickers),
mochi-wrapped ice cream, and banana tempura
are on the menu along with traditional tem-
puras, teriyakis, noodles, clay pot dishes, and
sushi (the Half Moon Bay roll has artichoke
hearts, avocado, and radish sprouts). At lunch,
the bento box special is hard to beat.

## 2 Fools Cafe & Market

*408 Main St., (650) 712-1222. L-D daily; $. Child
menu. No reservations.*

This popular, informal cafe offers a good
selection of tasty housemade items, including
soups, salads, sandwiches, fish & chips, and
both a sirloin burger and veggie burger. Fresh
local salmon is used in both a salad and sand-
wich. The Foolish Kids Coloring Menu gives
children a choice of a peanut butter & jelly or a
grilled cheese sandwich, a cheeseburger, and fish
& chips, plus a picture to color. Seating is either
in a cheery interior room or out on a tiny, quiet
patio in back. If the wait is too long, consider
ordering take-out.

# Pescadero

## — A LITTLE BACKGROUND —

Named for the town creek that once was filled
with trout ("pescadero" means literally "fishing
place"), this tiny burg was settled by Portuguese
farmers. Now this peaceful place is known best
for its agricultural products—straw flowers and
artichokes—and Duarte's Tavern.

Do take a walk. Of special note are the col-
orful fields of straw flowers, the old-fashioned
general store, and a picturesque 130-year-old
church.

For a lovely ride through the backcountry,

follow the quiet, winding road that begins in
front of the restaurant (State Road) 7 miles
north to San Gregorio. Here, the **San Gregorio
General Store** *((650) 726-0565; www.sangre
goriostore.com. Daily 9-6.)*, an old-fashioned
country emporium that has been serving area
residents since 1889, makes an interesting stop
for picnic supplies or a snack. Live music is
scheduled every Saturday and Sunday.

After stocking up, for a picturesque picnic
spot head to nearby **San Gregorio State Beach**
*((650) 879-2170; www.parks.ca.gov. Daily 8am-
sunset.)*, which often has sun when none is to
be found elsewhere along this stretch of coast.
Note that about a mile north of here is a popu-
lar clothing-optional beach.

## — GETTING THERE —

Located 50 miles south of San Francisco, and
about 15 miles south of Half Moon Bay. The
town is located about 1 mile inland from
Highway 1.

## — WHAT TO DO —

### Año Nuevo State Reserve

*(650) 879-0227, reservations (800) 444-4445;
www.parks.ca.gov. Dec-March: reservations required &
can be made up to 8 wks. in advance; $4/person.
Apr-Nov 8:30-3, wildlife protection area open by free
permit. Park open daily 8-sunset; $4/vehicle. Closed
Dec 1-14. No pets.*

Huge elephant seals return to this beach
each year to mate and bear their young. It is the
largest elephant seal rookery on the U.S. main-
land (two others are at Pierdras Blancas by San
Simeon and at Point Reyes). Docent-guided

tours, lasting 2½ hours and covering 3 miles, take visitors close enough to observe the seals basking in the sun or sleeping. Usually that is the extent of the activity seen, but occasionally one of the weighty bulls (some weigh almost 8,000 pounds!) roars into battle with a challenging male. When picking a tour date note that the adults arrive in December—when most of the battles occur—and the babies are born in January. Mating usually happens in February, when the population is at its peak. Then the adult seals begin to leave, and the weaned pups are left alone until April, when the adult females return to molt. Note that no food service is available at the reserve, and no drinking water is available along the tour trail.

Depending on the season, pick-your-own olallieberries (June), pumpkins (October), kiwi fruit (November), or Christmas trees are waiting across the street at 476-acre, usually sunny **Coastways Ranch** *(640 Cabrillo Hwy. (Hwy. 1), (650) 879-0414; www.well.com/user/dmsml/ coastways. June-July daily 9-5, Oct-Dec 10-4; closed Jan-May & Aug-Sept.).* This little piece of paradise has been farmed by the Hudson family since 1917. It has twisting dirt trails, picnic tables, and a snack bar. Call ahead for current information on crops, and bring along throwaway surgical gloves to protect hands.

## Pescadero State Beach
*New Year's Creek Rd., (650) 879-2170; www.parks. ca.gov. 8am-sunset.*

Sand dunes at the north end invite sliding, a creek invites wading, and tidepools invite exploring. The adjoining 210-acre **Pescadero Marsh Natural Preserve** is a refuge for waterfowl and wildlife; it teems with migrating birds and native plants. Marked trails are available for hiking, and docent-led nature walks occur on weekends. Tidepool explorations are scheduled when the tides are right.

## Phipps Country Store and Farm
*2700 Pescadero Rd./Hwy. 1, ½ mi. E of town, (650) 879-0787, fax (650) 879-1622; www.phipps country.com. Store: daily 10-5; Apr-Oct 10-6. Farm: Apr-Sept, $3, 60+ & under 4 free; Oct-Mar, free.*

Plants, fresh produce, herbs and spices, and 60 varieties of dried heirloom beans are for sale at the country store. Fresh goose eggs are often available from January through July (geese

do not lay eggs year round). A small fee is charged to visit the 50-acre organic farm, which offers pick-your-own strawberries and blackberries in season. The fee includes viewing domestic farm animals—pigs, goats, and chickens—as well as exotic birds and a songbird aviary. Picnic facilities are available.

### – WHERE TO STAY –
## Costanoa Coastal Lodge & Camp
*2001 Rossi Rd., (877) 262-7848, (650) 879-1100, fax (650) 879-2275; www.costanoa.com. 40 rooms, 12 cabins, 135 tent cabins; $-$$$. Children under 18 free. No TVs. Hot tub; sauna; steam room. Continental breakfast included with some lodging. No smoking; no pets.*

Situated on a bluff on the up side of Highway 1, this "boutique campground" offers an upscale camping experience. Guests can stay in tents and bring their own sleeping bags, stay in canvas cabins equipped with bedding that includes heated mattress pads and down comforters, or stay in comfortable conventional cabins with fireplaces, an expansive pastoral view, and private decks with porch swings. Any of these choices bring with them the adventure of trekking through the chilly local air to communal "comfort stations." The upscale part means that the restrooms look attractive, smell nice, and have heated floors. (Regulations governing use of this prime coastal land limit the number of toilets and prohibit building a full service restaurant.) Alternatively, lodge rooms with bathrooms en suite are also available, as are traditional campsites for tents and RVs. Prices reflect the various levels of pampering. Simple deli meals are available in the **General Store**, and the property abuts four state parks and offers easy access to their hiking trails. Amenities include mountain bike rentals, year-round horseback riding, a children's mega-sandbox, and massage rooms. Costanoa Kids Camp for ages 5 through 12 is offered in summer and by request.

## Pigeon Point Lighthouse Hostel
*210 Pigeon Point Rd., (650) 879-0633, fax (650) 879-9120; www.norcalhostels.org. 52 beds; private rooms; hot tub $7/person.*

Named after the first big ship that crashed on the rocks here—the *Carrier Pigeon*—this scenic lighthouse was built in 1872 and is the second-tallest freestanding lighthouse in the U.S. Guest beds are in adjacent bungalows, and a cliff-top hot tub is open in the evenings by reservation. See also page 445.

Due to damage, lighthouse tours at **Pigeon Point Light Station State Historic Park** *((650) 879-2120; www.parks.ca.gov.)* are no longer available. However, the grounds remain open, and excellent tidepools are located just to the north.

### — WHERE TO EAT —

### Duarte's Tavern
*202 Stage Rd., (650) 879-0464, fax (650) 879-9460; www.duartestavern.com. B-L-D daily; $-$$. Highchairs, boosters, booths. Reservations advised for D.*

Diners have been coming here (the name is pronounced "Do-arts") since 1894 to enjoy drinks in the old-time bar, and since 1936 for a home-style meal in the cozy, casual coffee shop. Breakfast is served until 1 p.m. on weekdays and features giant buttermilk pancakes and outstanding omelettes—especially the sautéed garlic-and-artichoke and the linguica (a spicy Portuguese sausage) versions—as well as more common items. At lunch or dinner try the delicious creamy artichoke heart or green chili soups, giant boiled artichokes with garlic mayo

dip, fried oysters, homemade pie, and fresh applesauce. Grilled fresh fish is available at dinner, and a popular fixed-price cioppino feed occurs each Friday, Saturday, and Sunday night by reservation. (Artichoke items are made with 'chokes picked fresh in nearby fields.)

### Norm's Market
*287 Stage Rd., (650) 879-0147; www.arcangeli grocery.com. M-Sat 10-7, Sun 10-6.*

This is the best spot in the area for picnic supplies. A deli in the back makes sandwiches to go. Do try the delicious local goat cheese and the artichoke salsa, and be sure to pick up extra of the super artichoke-garlic and artichoke-pesto breads to finish baking at home—*and* don't forget some garlic-herb croutons and olallieberry muffins!

---

# Davenport

### — A LITTLE BACKGROUND —

Once a well-known whaling town, this tiny village was wiped out by a fire in 1915. All that remains from those days is the town jail.

### — GETTING THERE —

Located 70 miles south of San Francisco, and 9 miles north of Santa Cruz.

### — WHAT TO DO —

### Bonny Doon Tasting Room
*2 Pine Flat Rd., in Bonny Doon (1 mi. S of town, then 5 mi. up the hill), (866) 666-3396, (831) 425-4518, fax (831) 425-3528; www.bonnydoonvineyard.com. Tasting daily 11-5.*

The pleasant side trip taken to reach this winery follows a meandering country road to the tiny mountain town of Bonny Doon. (Not actually a town or city, but instead a community of landowners, this area once grew more grapes than Napa or Sonoma.) Picnic tables are provided in a redwood grove complete with a gurgling creek. Winery specialties include exotic French and Italian varietals and a Muscat Canelli. A rich, raspberry-flavored framboise dessert wine makes delicious sipping. Do try one of the unusual, brandy-like fruit eaux de vie.

## Davenport Jail Museum
*2 Davenport Ave./Ocean Ave., (831) 429-1964. Sat-Sun 10-2. Free.*

Due to the generally peaceful nature of the area's residents, this two-cell jail built in 1914 was used only twice. In 1987, it was transformed into a small museum with exhibits on the history of Santa Cruz county's north coast.

## Rancho del Oso Nature and History Center
*3600 Hwy. 1, 7 mi. N of town, (831) 427-2288; www.parks.ca.gov. Park: daily sunrise-sunset; guided nature walk on Sun at 1. History center: Sat-Sun 12-4. Free.*

Located on Waddell Creek and part of **Big Basin Redwoods State Park** (see page 370), this bucolic spot has a marked nature trail leading through one of the few remaining native Monterey pine forests. Former president Herbert Hoover's brother, Theodore, settled this valley in 1914, and his family home is now the museum. After viewing vintage photos and checking out the old logging artifacts and wildlife exhibit, consider a picnic either in the sheltered courtyard or on the deck overlooking the preserve.

Just across the street, where fresh water Waddell Creek enters the ocean, **Waddell Beach** is a popular spot for windsurfing and hang-gliding.

### — WHERE TO STAY/EAT —
## Davenport Bed & Breakfast Inn
*31 Davenport Ave./Hwy. 1, (800) 870-1817, (831) 425-1818, fax (831) 423-1160; www.davenportinn.com. 12 rooms; $-$$. Credit toward breakfast in restaurant; restaurant. No smoking; no pets.*

Some of the eclectically decorated, colorful rooms here have skylights and ocean views.

The **Davenport Cash Store Restaurant** (*B-L-D daily. Highchairs, boosters.*) is rebuilt on the site of an old-time cash store that was destroyed by fire in the 1950s. Fresh seafood and house-made bread and pastries are hallmarks of the menu served in a comfortable, large open space. An adjoining **store** features an eclectic array of exotic merchandise from around the world that includes everything from local handmade soap to African crafts.

# Santa Cruz

### —A LITTLE BACKGROUND—
Close enough to San Francisco to visit just for the day, Santa Cruz has long been a popular summer destination. Weather is reliably clear and sunny, and the beach features fine sand and a gentle surf. In fact, it is a Very Southern California-style beach town. The beach people add to the simile with zinc on their noses, surfboards hanging out of their cars, and the Beach Boys blaring from their tape decks. Why, even the police officers wear shorts!

The 1989 Loma Prieta earthquake wreaked havoc here. The damage was severe along popular Pacific Avenue, which is now rebuilt and better than ever.

Beware! Don't drive here without a good map. The street layout is not always logical.

### — VISITOR INFORMATION —
## Santa Cruz County Conference & Visitors Council
*1211 Ocean St., (800) 833-3494, (831) 425-1234, fax (831) 425-1260; www.santacruzca.org.*

### — GETTING THERE —
Located approximately 65 miles south of San Francisco. Take either Highway 101 or the more scenic Highway 280 to Highway 17; or take magnificently scenic Highway 1 all the way.

### — ANNUAL EVENTS —
## Cabrillo Festival of Contemporary Music
*August. (831) 426-6966, fax (831) 426-6968; www.cabrillomusic.org. Free-$35.*

This is said to be one of the country's best small music festivals. The program includes a variety of contemporary orchestral works, including world premieres, and some events occur at Mission San Juan Bautista.

### — WHAT TO DO —
## Antonelli Brothers Begonia Gardens
*2545 Capitola Rd., (888) 423-4664, (831) 475-5222, fax (831) 475-7066; http://antnelli.infopoint.com. Daily 9-5. Free.*

Acres of indoor plants, ferns, and beautiful begonia baskets are available for purchase at this covered garden store. Peak of bloom is August and September, but a good show can also be enjoyed April through October. Picnic tables are available outside.

### Beach & Boardwalk
*400 Beach St., (831) 423-5590; www.beachboard walk.com. From 11am daily, June-Sept; Sat-Sun, Oct-May; closing time varies. Admission to Boardwalk free; rides $1.95-$3.90, all-day ticket $25.95.*

Fortunately, this is one beach boardwalk that has not degenerated over the years. Built in 1907, it was spiffed up a few years ago with a cheerful painting. Now the only boardwalk left on the West Coast and the oldest amusement park in California, it offers a variety of arcade games, fast-food stands, and souvenir shops—plus 23 major rides and 11 kiddie rides. Don't miss the salt water taffy—pulled and wrapped with antique machines—and the caramel apples at **Marini's** *((831) 423-7258; www.marinis candies.com.)*, where four generations of the family have been making candy since 1915. The half-mile-long concrete walkway parallels a clean, gorgeous beach (a city ordinance permits no alcohol on beaches). Thrill rides include the **Giant Dipper**, a rickety wooden roller coaster built in 1924 and rated by *The New York Times* as one of the ten best in the country, and Logger's Revenge, a refreshing water flume ride.

An old-fashioned **carousel**, built in New Jersey by Charles Looff in 1911 and the largest of the four remaining classic merry-go-rounds in Northern California, features 70 hand-carved horses (all with authentic horsehair tails) and 2 chariots as well as its rare, original 1894 342-pipe Ruth Und Sohn band organ and a ring toss—one of the few left in the world. Both the roller coaster and the carousel are now National Historic Landmarks, and the Boardwalk itself is a California Historic Landmark. All this plus free band concerts on Friday nights in summer and indoor miniature golf, too!

### Museum of Art & History
*705 Front St./Cooper St., downtown, (831) 429-1964, fax (831) 429-1954; www.santacruzmah.org. Tu-Sun 11-5, Thur to 7. $4, 62+ $2, under 18 free; free 1st Fri of month.*

The permanent collection exhibited here focuses on the social history of Santa Cruz County. Contemporary works by local artists are also displayed.

### The Mystery Spot
*465 Mystery Spot Rd., 3 mi. N of town (call for directions; finding it can be a bit of a mystery, too), (831) 423-8897, fax (831) 429-6653; www.mysteryspot.com. Daily 9-4:30; in summer to 7. $5, under 3 free.*

Located in a grove of redwoods, this small, quiet, cool spot measures only about 150 feet in diameter. Visitors get a guided tour during which gravitational forces appear to be defied, and everyone leaves with a souvenir bumper sticker.

### Natural Bridges State Beach
*2531 West Cliff Dr., at N end, (831) 423-4609; www.parks.ca.gov. Daily 8am-sunset. $5/vehicle.*

Enjoy a picnic in the sun on the sandy beach, or in the shade at sturdy tables. All but one of the mudstone arches, after which the beach is named, have collapsed, but there are still plenty of tidepools to explore. Swimming in the ocean is recommended only when a lifeguard is on duty, but sometimes a lagoon forms where small children can wade safely. From October through February, large numbers of **monarch butterflies** make their winter home here. A short nature trail leads to good viewing points where they are seen hanging in clusters on mature eucalyptus trees, and guided walks are scheduled on weekends then. During monarch season, the Visitor Center *(Daily 10-4.)* displays informative exhibits.

## Pacific Avenue/Downtown Santa Cruz
*Pacific Ave. betw. Water St. & Cathcart St., (831) 429-8433, fax (831) 429-1512; www.downtown santacruz.com.*

These five landscaped blocks comprise downtown Santa Cruz. Once the park-like setting was home to a variety of boutiques, art galleries, and restaurants operating from within restored historic buildings. But the 1989 Loma Prieta earthquake turned the area into a disaster zone of destruction. Now things are hopping again, especially in the evening.

Don't miss browsing impressive **Bookshop Santa Cruz** *(1520 Pacific Ave., (831) 423-0900; www.bookshopsantacruz.com. Daily 9-11.)*, which is now in a grand new building.

## Santa Cruz City Museum of Natural History
*1305 East Cliff Dr., (831) 420-6115, fax (831) 420-6451; www.santacruzmuseums.org. Tu-Sun 10-5. By donation: $1, under 12 50¢.*

Located across the street from wonderful Seabright Beach, this museum displays the county's natural treasures. Exhibits include Native American relics, fossils, local wildlife specimens, an operating beehive, and a "touch tank" of live sea animals. Kids love the large grassy area surrounding the vintage 1913 Carnegie building housing the museum, not to mention the sandbox and the life-size, 50-foot-long female grey whale sculpture that begs to be climbed on. Parking can be difficult.

## Santa Cruz Mission State Historic Park
*144 School St., (831) 429-2850, fax (831) 429-2870; www.parks.ca.gov. Thur-Sun 10-4. $2, 6-18 $1, family $5.*

A restored adobe building here is all that remains of the original mission complex and is now the only remaining example of mission Indian housing in California. Exhibits include a furnished living quarters for Native American families. A large Victorian garden gone wild, with several tall redwoods and a giant avocado tree that is one of the oldest in the state, invites leisurely picnicking. Living History Day, when docents in period dress oversee a variety of

crafts activities, occurs each month. Tours are also available.

**Mission Santa Cruz** *( 126 High St./Emmet St., (831) 426-5686, fax (831) 423-1043; www.geocities.com/missionbell. Tu-Sat 10-4, Sun 10-2; call to verify schedule. By donation.)* is a block away. It is 12th in the chain of missions. Built in 1794 and destroyed in an earthquake in 1857, the mission was rebuilt in 1931 as this half-size replica. It now houses a small museum displaying original statues, candlesticks, and paintings, as well as ornate vestments and a baptismal font.

## Santa Cruz Surfing Museum
*On West Cliff Dr., at Lighthouse Point, (831) 420-6289, fax (831) 420-6451; www.santacruzmuseums.org. Thur-M 12-4; also W in summer. Free.*

The first place ever surfed outside of Hawaii, Santa Cruz is an appropriate spot for an homage to surfing. This tiny one-room museum displays vintage surfboards (don't miss the 10-foot redwood long board from the 1930s or the contemporary polyurethane board sporting shark bites) and the world's first wetsuit (made in Santa Cruz). It is housed within the small brick **Mark Abbott Memorial Lighthouse,** which was funded by Chuck and Esther Abbott in memory of their 18-year-old son who drowned in a 1965 surfing accident near Pleasure Point. A scenic 3-mile bike and pedestrian pathway begins here.

**Seal Rock,** home to a herd of sea lions, and **Steamer Lane,** where surfers do their thing, are visible off shore.

## Santa Cruz Wharf
*Near the Boardwalk, (831) 420-5270; www.ci.santa-cruz.ca.us/pr/wharf. Daily 5am-2am.*

It is possible to either walk or drive to the end of this ½ mile-long pier. Anglers fish from the side, and seafood restaurants, snack stands, and picnic tables are scattered along its length. Seals can be fed through fishing holes at the end of the pier, and deep-sea fishing trips originate at concessions located here.

## Seymour Marine Discovery Center
*W end of Delaware Ave., (831) 459-3800, fax (831) 459-1221; http://seymourcenter.ucsc.edu. Tu-Sat 10-5, Sun 12-5; tours 1-3. $5, 60+ & 6-16 $3; free 1st Tu of month.*

Part of a marine research station for U.C. Santa Cruz, this center provides impressive views of the Monterey Bay National Marine Sanctuary. It features exhibit galleries, aquariums stocked with local sea life, and a touching pool with hermit crabs, sea stars, and sea anemones. Research is conducted on marine mammal behavior, fish diseases, and coral genetics. Guided tours include viewing the sea lion tanks and the skeleton of an 86-foot-long blue whale that washed ashore up the coast on Pescadero Beach in 1979.

## Surfing schools

Surfers have been riding the waves in Santa Cruz since the early 1920s. Part of *Endless Summer* was shot here, and *Surfer Magazine* named Santa Cruz one of the top ten surf towns in the country. Why even The Beach Boys sing about surfing here!

• **Richard Schmidt Surf School**
*236 San Jose Ave., (831) 423-0928; www.richard schmidt.com. Lessons year-round; camp June-Aug. Group lesson $80/hr.; camp $900/wk.*

This sage instructor gives a "stand-up guarantee" that promises a free ride (refund) to anyone who doesn't stand up in their first class. Camp attendees bring their own sleeping bags and share tents. Amenities include a pool, hot tub, and hammocks plus inspirational surfing videos and a midweek massage. Educational excursions take participants to a surf museum and a surfboard factory.

• **Club Ed Surf School**
*2350 Paul Minnie Ave., (800) 287-SURF, (831) 464-0177, fax (831) 464-0107; www.club-ed.com. Group lesson $60/2 hrs.; camp $1,050/wk.*

## Tea House Spa

*112 Elm St./Pacific Ave., downtown, (831) 426-9700; www.teahousespa.com. Daily 11am-midnight. Tubs: $10-$15/person/hr.*

Private rooms with whirlpool hot tubs overlook a mature bamboo garden planted in the late 1940s. Two of the four rooms have cedar-lined saunas. Tea is prepared and left to be enjoyed at leisure, and fragrant Bonny Doon Farms lavender soap and shampoo are provided and can be purchased to go. Massage is available.

## University of California, Santa Cruz Campus

*1156 High St., (831) 459-0111; www.ucsc.edu. Parking: $5 M-F, free Sat-Sun.*

Located high in the hills above town, the buildings of this spectacularly beautiful campus are hidden among a forest of old-growth redwoods. Gorgeous views of the Monterey Bay are seen from many locations. Pick up a map at the Public Information Office *((831) 459-2495)* and take a self-guided walking tour. **Guided tours** *((831) 459-4008. M-F at 10, 1, 3. Free. Reservations required.)* are also available, and free shuttle buses loop the campus daily. The **Arboretum** *((831) 427-2998, fax (831) 427-1524; www2.ucsc.edu/arboretum. Daily 9-5. Free.)* has an extensive collection of plants from Australia and New Zealand and of South African proteas. **Bay Tree Bookstore** *((831) 459-4544; http://slugstore.ucsc.edu. M-F 8:30-5:30, Sat 10-4.)* dispenses student books and supplies as well as the now-famous "U C Santa Cruz Banana Slugs" t-shirt worn by John Travolta in *Pulp Fiction.*

## Wilder Ranch State Historic Park

*1401 Old Coast Rd., off Hwy. 1, 2 mi. N of town; www.parks.ca.gov. Park: (831) 423-9703; sunrise-sunset. Visitor Center: (831) 426-0505; F-Sun 11-4, tour Sat-Sun at 1. $5/vehicle.*

The perfect spot to spend a lazy day in the country, this 4,505-acre turn-of-the-century ranch complex invites visitors to bring along a picnic. Formerly a dairy, it is built in an arroyo, or valley, that protects it from whipping coastal winds and is reached via a short walk down from the parking lot. When the Visitor Center is open, docents dressed in old-fashioned garb bring life to the old buildings, and visitors can inspect a large Queen Anne Victorian home, an even older adobe, a bunk house, several barns, a chicken coop, and miscellaneous other structures. Domesticated animals—horses, cows, goats, chickens, and guinea hens—also add atmosphere. At other times, the Old Cove Landing Trail provides a 4-mile nature walk on which pond turtles, cormorants, and harbor seals are often sighted; a fern grotto is also seen. A self-guiding brochure is available at the trailhead.

## —WHERE TO STAY—

### Babbling Brook Inn

*1025 Laurel St., (800) 866-1131, (831) 427-2437, fax (831) 427-2457; www.babblingbrookinn.com. 13 rooms; $$-$$$. Unsuitable for children under 13. Some wood-burning & gas fireplaces. Afternoon & evening snack, full breakfast. No smoking; no pets.*

Shaded by tall redwoods, this secluded hillside inn was built as a log cabin in 1909. Rooms have been added through the years. Now it is the oldest and largest B&B in the area and is on the National Register of Historic Places. Most guest rooms are named after impressionist painters and decorated in the artist's favorite themes and colors. And the inn delivers what its name promises: a babbling brook runs through the property, plus there are even a few cascading waterfalls. The acre of beautifully landscaped grounds surrounding the inn has paths, a covered footbridge, an 18th-century water wheel, and a lacy wrought-iron gazebo.

### Casa Blanca Inn

*101 Main St., (800) 644-1570, (831) 423-1570, fax (831) 423-0235; www.casablanca-santacruz.com. 39 rooms; $$-$$$+. Some kitchens; some wood-burning & gas fireplaces. Restaurant; limited room service. No pets.*

Located across the street from the beach and Boardwalk, this converted 1918 mansion features spacious, pleasantly decorated rooms. Additional rooms with terraces and a country-style decor are available in a newer 1950s annex.

The **Casablanca** restaurant (*(831) 426-9063. D daily, SunBr; $$-$$$. Highchairs, boosters, child portions. Reservations advised.*) has the largest wine cellar in the county and features a sophisticated menu of seafood, pastas, and meats.

### Chateau Victorian

*118 First St., (831) 458-9458; www.chateau victorian.com. 7 rooms; $$. Unsuitable for children under 18. No TVs; all wood-burning fireplaces. Afternoon snack, continental breakfast. No smoking.*

Built around the turn of the century, this B&B is only a block from the beach and Boardwalk. Attention to detail is apparent throughout. The L-shaped Lighthouse Room on the second floor is a favorite. The inn's largest room, it is furnished with an armoire, a queen-size brass bed, and comfortable chairs by the fireplace.

### Coast Santa Cruz Hotel

*175 West Cliff Dr., (800) 663-1144, (831) 426-4330, fax (831) 427-2025; www.coasthotels.com. 10 stories; 163 rooms; $$-$$$+. Children under 12 free. Heated pool; child wading pool; hot tub. Restaurant; room service.*

Formerly known as the Dream Inn, this hotel is located right on the beach within easy walking distance of the Boardwalk. Each room has a private balcony or patio overlooking Cowell's Beach and Monterey Bay. The pool and hot tub are one story up from the sand and enjoy the same view.

The **Mainsail** restaurant has a fantastic beach and ocean view, and its windows are usually open to the sounds of waves breaking on the shore.

### Ocean Echo Inn & Beach Cottages

*401 Johans Beach Dr., (831) 462-4192, fax (831) 462-0658; www.oceanecho.com. 15 units; $-$$$. Some kitchens. Pets ok in winter.*

Tucked in a quiet beach cove just a few miles south of the Boardwalk, these attractive rooms and cottages are on a private beach within sound of the surf. Many have ocean views and sundecks.

### Pleasure Point Inn

*2-3665 East Cliff Dr./37th Ave., (877) 557-2567, (831) 469-6161, fax (831) 479-1347; www.pleasure pointinn.com. 4 rooms; $$-$$$. All gas fireplaces. Hot tub. Continental breakfast.*

Situated ocean front, on a scenic corner amid an eclectic mix of grand homes and modest surfer shacks in Santa Cruz's Pleasure Point area, this small inn blends in so well that it can be difficult to find. It was remodeled from a '70s beach house into a streamlined retro '30s inn with a curved exterior reminiscent of a cruising ship. Rooms are spacious and have a relaxing seaside decor accented with smooth blue marble and knotty pine. Each is equipped with a comforter-topped bed, gas fireplace, heated bathroom floor, and Jacuzzi bathtub. An expansive buffet breakfast is served in an ocean-view dining room. A hot tub gurgles continuously on a rooftop sundeck overlooking a popular surfing site, and a bluff-top trail in front of the inn is primo for walking, biking, and running. For those who want to take up the area's premier sport, the "Room and Board" package includes a 2-night stay and lessons at the Club Ed Surf School.

## Santa Cruz Hostel

*321 Main St., (831) 423-8304, fax (831) 429-8541; www.hi-santacruz.org. 40 beds; private rooms.*

Located on Beach Hill within the restored 1870s Carmelita Cottages, this hostel is just 2 blocks from the Boardwalk action.

## Sea & Sand Inn

*201 West Cliff Dr., (831) 427-3400, same fax; www.santacruzmotels.com/sea_and_sand.html. 20 rooms; $-$$$+. Children under 12 free. Afternoon snack, continental breakfast.*

Perched on a cliff high above the beach, all rooms here have views of the ocean and Boardwalk, and some suites have private patio hot tubs. The soothing sound of the surf breaking on the shore below is continuous, and an extensive grassy area between the rooms and the ocean is bordered with colorful plants and flowers and furnished with tables and chairs, inviting repose. Though there is no direct beach access, it is just a short walk to the beach and Boardwalk.

## Motel Row

Many motels are located in the area surrounding the Boardwalk, including some inexpensive ones dating from the 1930s. Rooms are usually available at the last minute.

## — WHERE TO EAT —

## Crow's Nest

*2218 East Cliff Dr., (831) 476-4560, fax (831) 476-6085; www.crowsnest-santacruz.com. L-D daily, SunBr; $$. Highchairs, boosters, child menu. Reservations advised in summer.*

Fresh local seafood at reasonable prices is the specialty here, but steaks, pastas, and salads are also on the menu. Children get a color-in menu and a goodie from the treasure chest. Protected by a glass windbreaker, diners can enjoy ocean views outdoors and watch yachts come and go from the Santa Cruz Yacht Harbor. The less formal **Upstairs Bar & Grill** is open throughout the day and regularly schedules live entertainment and dancing.

## Donnelly Fine Chocolates

*1509 Mission St., (888) 685-1871, (831) 458-4214, fax (831) 425-0678; www.donnellychocolates.com. M-F 10:30-6, Sat 12-5; call to confirm.*

This former caramel apple shop located in the middle of a muddle of unimpressive storefronts resembles not in the least a trendy European chocolate *shoppe*. Yet, stuffed in the back of a teeny, tiny shop, surfer-chef Richard Donnelly and his troupe make ultra-fine, European-style chocolates the old-fashioned way—by hand. And every visitor gets a sample. Though Donnelly chocolates are known for their unusual spice and herb fillings—including ginseng and lavender—the classics continue to sell best. They can *almost* be considered diet chocolates . . . because they cost $65 per pound—enough to make anyone think twice before popping more than one in their mouth. Made with the best ingredients, they rate four yums on the yum scale. Yum, yum, yum, and yum! Chocolates are dispensed in sophisticated boxes wrapped in gorgeous handmade Japanese papers and tied up with smooth fabric ribbons. The package is almost as delicious as its contents. A selection of these award-winning chocolates makes a very special gift. Not in the mood for chocolate? Donnelly sells ice cream, too.

## El Palomar

*1336 Pacific Ave., downtown, (831) 425-7575, fax (831) 423-3037; www.elpalomarrestaurant.com. B-L-D daily, SunBr; $-$$. Highchairs, boosters, booths, child menu. No reservations.*

Housed in the cool, attractively remodeled back room of a 1930s hotel, with ornately decorated high ceilings and colorful mural-adorned walls, this restaurant serves well-prepared, authentic Michoacan-style Mexican dishes and seafood. Tortillas are made by hand each day, and there is a large selection of Mexican beers. In addition to the expected staples, the menu includes the more unusual: pozole (pork and hominy stew), sopes (puffy tortillas with fillings), and occasionally menudo (tripe soup). A bar in the back has a retractable ceiling that is opened in good weather, and the restaurant's inexpensive taco bar adjoins.

## Gabriella Cafe

*910 Cedar St., downtown, (831) 457-1677, fax (831)*

423-3919; www.gabriellacafe.com. L-D daily, SunBr; $$. Highchairs. Reservations advised.

In an intimate cottage space, with fresh flowers and candles adorning the tables and with angel images throughout, this romantic, European-style hideaway produces accomplished seasonal fare. Exceptional dinner choices have included delectable silver dollar-size sweet pea pancakes topped with crème frâiche and smoked salmon for a starter; grilled wild salmon with mission fig beurre blanc, fingerling potatoes, and grilled romaine as an entree; and apricot bread pudding for dessert. Indeed, the entire menu is composed of such lip-smacking descriptions. Perhaps the interesting fare is to be expected, coming as it does from a fascinating chef. When he isn't busy in the kitchen, Santa Cruz native Jim Denevan might be found at the beach drawing giant fish or spirals in the sand. (What are sand spirals you might wonder? They're sort of like the English crop circles reputedly made by aliens in the deep of night, only he makes them himself in broad daylight in sand.)

Jim also hosts unusual **Outstanding in the Field dinners** ((877) 886-7400, www.outstanding inthefield.com. May-Nov.) at which participants are seated at long, long tables set with white linens amid the organic fields of a local farm—a sort of restaurant without walls. He creates elaborate feasts on-site using the farm's produce and local meats.

## Capitola

### — A LITTLE BACKGROUND —

Dating back to 1861, when it was a tent village, this artsy-craftsy beach town was the state's first seaside resort. In those days, ladies would wear heavy wool swim suits and walk out into the surf holding on to a steadying rope to "sea bathe." The lovely mile-long beach is sheltered between two bluffs and offers both swimming in calm ocean waters and wading in the fresh water of Soquel Creek. Be cautious, however, as sometimes that creek water isn't so pristine.

Fronting the beach, The Esplanade is lined with coffeehouses and restaurants serving everything from hamburgers to lobster. Many have outdoor patios overlooking the beach.

In summer, free shuttle buses take visitors from parking lots on Bay Avenue to the beach. Some shuttle bikes are also available for loan.

### — VISITOR INFORMATION —
**Capitola Chamber of Commerce**
716-G Capitola Ave., (800) 474-6522, (831) 475-6522, fax (831) 475-6530; www.capitolachamber.com.

### — GETTING THERE —
Located approximately 5 miles south of Santa Cruz.

### — ANNUAL EVENTS —
**Begonia Festival**
September; on Labor Day weekend. (800) 919-8155, (831) 476-3566; www.begoniafestival.com. Free.

Begun years ago as a way to make use of the beautiful blooms discarded by local begonia growers interested only in the bulbs, this popular festival includes a sand sculpture contest, fishing derby, and nautical parade of flower-covered floats down Soquel Creek. Throughout the festival, the town's merchants and homeowners put on their own shows with begonia displays and decorations. (The only other begonia festival in the world is held in Ballarat, Australia.)

### — WHAT TO DO —
**Bargetto Winery**
3535 N. Main St., in Soquel, (800) 4BARGETTO, (831) 475-2258, fax (831) 475-2664; www.bargetto.com. Tasting M-Sat 11-5, Sun 12-5; tour by appt.

One of the largest wineries in the area, this family-run wine producer is known both for its premium dessert fruit wines made from hand-picked fruit—including olallieberry and raspberry—and its excellent homemade wine vinegars. It also produces a popular Pinot Grigio and an authentic Mead made from honey. Bring a picnic to enjoy on the outdoor patio overlooking gurgling Soquel Creek. A tasting bar is open on weekends on the patio. Sparkling grape juice is poured for kids and non-drinkers.

**Capitola Historical Museum**
410 Capitola Ave., (831) 464-0322; www.capitola museum.org. F-Sun 12-4. Free.

Situated near the town railroad trestle, this tiny museum is situated within a historical little red house. Historical walking tours are sched-

*Capitola Venetian Hotel*

uled regularly. Where else can visitors learn that many of the streets are named for places the residents came from and that the Jewel Box area is where streets are named after jewels?

## — WHERE TO STAY —

### Capitola Venetian Hotel

*1500 Wharf Rd., (800) 332-2780, (831) 476-6471, fax (831) 475-3897; www.capitolavenetian.com. 20 units; $-$$$. All kitchens; some fireplaces. No pets.*

Built in the 1920s, this mini-village of charming stucco apartments in ice cream colors is located right on the beach. It was California's first condominium complex. Some units have balconies and ocean views, and one spectacular unit has both a panoramic ocean view and a fireplace in the bedroom.

### Harbor Lights Motel

*5000 Cliff Dr., (831) 476-0505. 10 rooms; $$. Children under 5 free. Some kitchens; 1 fireplace. No pets.*

This ordinary motel boasts an extraordinary location just across from the beach. Some rooms have views of Monterey Bay, the village, and the beach.

## — WHERE TO EAT —

### The Country Court Tea Room

*911-B Capitola Ave./Hill St., (831) 462-2498. L & tea Tu-F, Sat-SunBr; $. Reservations advised. No cards.*

Operating within a vintage mansion's converted carriage house, this cozy spot is filled with nooks and crannies in which to enjoy a traditional high tea. Though the artistically presented delicacies vary, round one might consist of a golden raisin-and-apricot scone topped with fresh fruit; round two, a tray of delicate finger sandwiches; round three, angel food cake with fresh raspberries and cream. Call ahead for the menu, or don't and be surprised. Tea is served in tiny individual pots topped with cozies. Most of the decorative items in the rooms are for sale.

### Dharma's Natural Foods

*4250 Capitola Rd./42nd Ave., (831) 462-1717, fax (831) 464-TOFU; http://dharmaland.com. B-L-D daily; $. Highchairs, boosters. No reservations.*

Legend has it that this vegetarian and vegan haven—it is the oldest completely vegetarian restaurant in the U.S.—once suffered a "Big Mac attack" by McDonald's, who sued over its original name of McDharma's. Formerly just a food stand by the beach in Santa Cruz, it has settled into a pleasant, spacious spot in a suburban shopping center. Items on the extensive menu include several vegetarian burgers, a variety of Mexican dishes, sautés, salads, pastas, and soups; at breakfast it's tofu scrambles. Ingredients are organic when available.

## Gayle's Bakery & Rosticceria

*504 Bay Ave./Capitola Ave., (831) 462-1200;*
*www.gaylesbakery.com. Daily 6:30am-8:30pm; $. No*
*reservations.*

The talent behind it all here is Gayle, who once was a pastry chef at Berkeley's Chez Panisse, and her husband Joe, who once was a house painter and musician. Their story is of the little bakery that grew and grew, expanding from a tiny storefront operation to occupying the entire building. It is an unpretentious bakery extraordinaire, featuring cases laden with a plethora of soul-satisfying, made-from-scratch choices that sometimes make a person dissolve into an abyss of indecision. What to put on the lunch tray? The German red potato salad, in which the potatoes are actually cooked thoroughly? Yes. Christie's coleslaw made with fresh ginger, cilantro, and peanuts? But of course. The albacore sandwich prepared with housemade mayo and cheese focaccia? Most definitely. But leave room for a dessert—perhaps the divine, moist German chocolate cake, or maybe an éclair or Napoleon or crocodile bar or some other decadent delight. Sidle up to the coffee bar for a drink, and then settle down indoors at one of the "earthquake tables" made from crockery broken in that infamous 1980s quake, or outdoors at one of the cheery tables on the heated brick patio. A take-home order can be prepared for pick-up after dining; don't forget to include a loaf or two of European-style bread, a bag of the melt-in-your mouth crostini, and maybe one of the dome-shaped lavender marzipan-frosted princess cakes, too. Oh, and then there are the soups, not to mention the pizzas and spit-roasted meats prepared in a brick roasting oven imported from Italy . . .

## Shadowbrook

*1750 Wharf Rd., (800) 975-1511, (831) 475-1511,*
*fax (831) 475-7664; www.shadowbrook-capitola.com.*
*D W-M, SunBr; L in summer; $$-$$$. Highchairs,*
*boosters, child menu. Reservations advised.*

Located on the banks of Soquel Creek, the heart of this popular restaurant is a log cabin originally built as a summer home in the 1920s. Diners descend to the restaurant either by riding a bright red, self-operated funicular cable car down a flower-laden hill from the street above, or by strolling down an adjacent serpentine step-path through manicured gardens with fountains and koi-stocked ponds. Most tables offer a view of the creek, often with the added entertainment of ducks and geese cavorting on the water. The menu features prime rib and fresh fish as well as a generous assortment of other entrees and a variety of daily specials. Scampi prepared with succulent giant prawns is a house specialty, as is a custard-filled dessert crêpe topped with caramel sauce. Choice appetizers include Caesar salad and delicious creamy artichoke soup. Each evening a jukebox provides music for dancing in the bar, where live entertainment is scheduled on weekends. Though children are truly welcome, this restaurant exudes a romantic atmosphere.

# Aptos

## — A LITTLE BACKGROUND —

Located just a few miles south of the well-known coastal towns of Capitola and Santa Cruz, this tiny, less frenetic burg often gets lost in the shuffle. But that's all the more reason to head here for a restorative getaway.

First inhabited by the Ohlone Indians, the town was then settled by Rafael Castro when he received it in 1833 as a 6,000-acre land grant for raising cattle. The property started breaking up in 1872 when sugar millionaire Claus Spreckles bought 2,400 acres from Castro. He built a summer home and deer park, which he stocked with deer, elk, and other game. Most of the village was constructed between 1850 and 1900, when it was a busy logging town, and at one time it bustled with 13 saloons and 2 railroad stations.

Because Aptos is a very confusing town to navigate, it's smart to carry a good map (the chamber of commerce will send one free). Otherwise, it is possible to just go round and round in scenic circles. The town has three basic areas: Aptos Village, Seacliff State Beach, and Rio Del Mar. Tiny Aptos Village is sprinkled for 2 blocks along Soquel Drive just northeast of Highway 1, and is home to several restaurants, an assortment of shops, and an historic inn.

Be particularly careful in late afternoon at the poorly marked intersection of Spreckles and Soquel drives, which seems designed especially to snag out-of-towners. Making a left-hand turn here can leave even a careful driver with an unwanted souvenir ticket.

— **VISITOR INFORMATION** —

### Aptos Chamber of Commerce
*7605-A Old Dominion Ct., (831) 688-1467; www.aptoschamber.com.*

— **ANNUAL EVENTS** —

### Watsonville Fly-In & Air Show
*May; Memorial Day weekend. In Watsonville; (831) 763-5600, fax (831) 763-4083; www.watsonville flyin.org.$4-$10; F-Sun parking $5.*

This is one of the largest antique fly-in and air shows on the West Coast. It features an assortment of vintage and classic planes, including some war birds from World Wars I and II and some home-built models.

### Roses of Yesterday and Today
*May & June. In Watsonville, 803 Brown's Valley Rd. (call for directions); (831) 728-1901, fax (831) 724-1408; www.rosesofyesterday.com. Daily 9-4. Free; catalog $5.*

Tucked into a redwood canyon, this demonstration garden for a mail-order nursery is an extraordinary sight when its approximately 450 varieties of old-fashioned roses bloom in unison. Picnic tables are available.

### Fourth of July Parade
*July. (831) 688-1467; www.aptoschamber.com.*

This is billed as "the world's shortest parade."

— **WHAT TO DO** —

### The Forest of Nisene Marks State Park
*On Aptos Creek Rd., behind Aptos Village, (831) 763-7062; www.parks.ca.gov. Sunrise-sunset. $2/vehicle.*

Aptos Creek Road meanders back among tall, dense redwood groves and into this scenic 10,000-acre park. An easy trail leads to the epicenter of the devastating 1989 Loma Prieta earthquake, which flattened buildings as far away as 80 miles north in San Francisco.

### Seacliff State Beach
*201 State Park Dr., (831) 429-2850; www.parks.ca.gov. Sunrise-sunset. $5/vehicle.*

Aimlessly following the area's winding roads often eventually leads to this locally popular beach. From the parking area, it is a short, scenic walk to view the *Palo Alto*. This former tanker was converted into a nightclub in 1930 and cracked up in a storm soon after. Its current incarnation is as an unusual fishing pier. Campsites are available.

— **WHERE TO STAY** —

### KOA Kampground
*1186 San Andreas Rd., in Watsonville, (800) KOA-7701, (831) 722-0551, fax (831) 722-0989; www.koa.com.*

Located 1 mile from the beach, this particularly posh campground has a heated pool, hot tub, sauna, and playground, plus mini golf (fee) and bike rentals. See also page 443.

### Rio Sands Motel
*116 Aptos Beach Dr., (800) 826-2077, (831) 688-3207, fax (831) 688-6107; www.riosands.com. 50 rooms; $-$$. Children under 5 free. Some kitchens. Heated pool; hot tub. Continental breakfast. No pets.*

Located just 1 block from the beach, this 1950s-era traditional motel offers the bonus of a nice garden-pool area with barbecue facilities.

### Seascape Resort
*One Seascape Resort Dr., Rio Del Mar area, (800) 929-7727, (831) 688-6800, fax (831) 685-0615; www.seascaperesort.com. 285 rooms; $$$-$$$$+. All kitchens & fireplaces. 2 pools; hot tub; sauna. Restaurant; room service. No smoking; no pets.*

This cliff-top resort offers spacious contemporary condominium units with expansive ocean views. Guests have access to both an adjacent 18-hole golf course and a sports club with 9 tennis courts and a fully equipped fitness center. Special facilities for families include a playground and an inexpensive summer children's program for ages 5 through 10. A small shopping center and full-service day spa are just across the street.

Want to have a marshmallow roast on the beach? A bellman is available to take guests down to the beach in a golf cart, build a fire, and leave them with the makings for s'mores. For those in search of a more refined menu, **Sanderlings** *((831) 662-7120. B-L M-Sat, D daily, SunBr; $$-$$$.)* offers a creative menu in an elegant, yet relaxed, setting.

## — WHERE TO EAT —

### Bittersweet Bistro

*787 Rio Del Mar Blvd., in Deer Park Shopping Center, Rio Del Mar area, (831) 662-9799, fax (831) 662-9779; www.bittersweetbistro.com. D daily; $$-$$$. Child menu. Reservations advised.*

Though situated at the edge of a shopping center, this restaurant does not disappoint. Operating inside a beautifully remodeled historical building that once sat right smack in the middle of Highway 1, it has original art decorating the walls and manages to be both simple and elegant—just like the food. The chef uses high quality local ingredients whenever possible. One dinner here started with a shared pear-and-blood orange salad accented with Roquefort cheese and arranged on a plate splashed with a colorful balsamic glaze. Entrees were a delicious Mediterranean angel hair pasta with tomatoes, pine nuts, and Feta cheese, and a delicate grilled fresh mahi-mahi served atop garlic mashed potatoes and sautéed fresh spinach. Portions are large, but some people manage to save room for Death by Chocolate— a giant platter showcasing some of the made-from-scratch chocolate desserts the restaurant is justly famous for. Enough for three or four people, it holds a variety of outrageous concoctions, including a heavenly chocolate mousse and a devilishly refined chocolate bread pudding.

### Britannia Arms

*8017 Soquel Dr., in Aptos Village, (831) 688-1233; www.britanniaarms.com. B-L-D daily; $.*

This informal spot serves up 16 imported draft beers, authentic pub fare like bangers and mash, and American favorites like baby back ribs. It has an authentic pub atmosphere and features satellite TV, darts, and pool. For those staying nearby, an authentic black English taxi is available at no charge for pick up and return.

### Palapas Restaurant y Cantina

*21 Seascape Village, Rio Del Mar area, (831) 662-9000; www.palapasrestaurant.com. L-D daily; $$. Highchairs, boosters, booths, child menu. Reservations advised.*

Featuring a Mexican-style thatched roof and boasting both comfortable half-moon booths and expansive ocean views, this popular restaurant specializes in fresh seafood. Among the temptations are sand dabs grilled in white wine and served with a light tomatillo sauce, a spicy version of scampi, and crabmeat enchiladas. Vegetarian selections include a delicious enchilada filled with marinated tofu and topped with guacamole. All this and fabulously crisp complimentary tortilla chips with just-right dipping salsa, too, not to overlook handmade tortillas, fresh sauces, mango margaritas made with fresh Mexican fruit, and 35 different tequilas.

# Moss Landing and Area

## — A LITTLE BACKGROUND —

There is enough to see and do in this commercial fishing port to fill a weekend itinerary. This small town is home to over 25 antique shops, most on quiet Moss Landing Road. Among the most interesting are the artistically arranged **Hamlin's Antiques,** and **Martin & Company Antiques,** with its eclectic collection displayed in a warren of cozy rooms. Another shop operates out of a recycled train caboose. Hours are casual, but most are open Wednesday through Sunday from 11 a.m. to 4 p.m. A tiny post office acts as the town's unofficial museum and is also on Moss Landing Road. It displays historical photos of Moss Landing's past as a shipping port, a whaling station and cannery, and then a fishing village.

Fishing boats are often seen unloading their catch by the docks. **Tom's Sportfishing** *((831) 633-2564; www.tomssportfishing.com. $45-$60/person. Departs daily at 6am.)* takes visitors out deep-sea fishing on the *Kahuna.*

This area also is prime for bird-watching. Pelicans, cormorants, gulls, terns, herons, and egrets are all drawn here to feast on the rich

marine life. Rarer birds often show up during migrations.

— VISITOR INFORMATION —

**Moss Landing Chamber of Commerce**
*8071 Moss Landing Rd., (831) 633-4501; www.monterey-bay.net/ml.*

**Marina Chamber of Commerce**
*211 Hillcrest, in Marina, (831) 384-9155; www.marinachamber.com.*

— GETTING THERE —

Located 8 miles north of the Monterey Peninsula, and 8 miles west of Salinas. Turn off Highway 1 just before reaching the two land-mark smokestacks on the east side of the high-way, and before Little Baja and its Mexican pottery on the west side.

— ANNUAL EVENTS —

**Castroville Artichoke Festival**
*May. In Castroville; (831) 633-CHOK; www.artichoke-festival.org. $6, under 12 $3.*
    This is one of the state's oldest agricultural festivals. It was at this festival in 1947 that then-starlet Marilyn Monroe became the very first California Artichoke Queen.

Starlet Named Artichoke Queen

— WHAT TO DO —

**Elkhorn Slough Safari**
*(831) 633-5555; www.elkhornslough.com. Schedule varies. $26, 65+ $24, 3-14 $19; unsuitable for children under 3. Reservations required.*

The best way to see great numbers of birds up close in their natural habitat is to take this tour in an open-air, flat-bottom aluminum pontoon boat. Tours last 2 hours and travel through Elkhorn Slough. (Wondering what a "slough" (pronounced "slew") is? Simply "a wet, muddy place.") One of the state's largest wet-lands, it winds inland for 7 miles and provides an important feeding and resting place for a variety of wildlife. A naturalist is aboard to point out unusual specimens, and participants are encouraged to help count various kinds of birds for an on-going research project. Lots of cute sea otters are also usually spotted, and sometimes a "raft" of them is seen holding onto each other while floating. Don't forget binoculars and a camera.

### Fort Ord
*In Marina.*
    A few miles south of Moss Landing, the expansive sand dune area that was formerly the Fort Ord military base is now operated by the Bureau of Land Management. It is slowly meta-morphosing into recreational use. Hiking and mountain bike trails snake through its 8,000 acres.
    A skydiving facility is based here. (Afraid of skydiving? Here's some food for thought: At **Skydive Monterey Bay** *((888) BAY-JUMP, (831) 384-3483, fax (831) 384-7522; www.skydive montereybay.com. $138+/person. Reservations advised.)* it is claimed that "skydivers aren't afraid of dying, they're afraid of not living.")
    For those who prefer to check out the skies from the ground, the new **Monterey Institute for Research in Astronomy (MIRA)** *(200 Eighth St., (831) 883-1000, fax (831) 883-1031; www.mira.org.)* schedules Star Parties regularly at its **Weaver Student Observatory**, giving participants the chance to look through a 14-inch telescope.
    The largest art foundry on the West Coast, the **Monterey Sculpture Center** *(711 Neeson Rd., (831) 384-2100, (831) 384-1700, fax (831) 834-0575; www.firebirdfoundry.com. Free tour. Reservations advised.)* conducts informal tours that permit seeing sculptures manufactured from beginning to end. Participants view clay being carved for molds, molten metal being poured into the molds, and patina colors being applied to the finished product. Discounts are

available in an impressive gallery shop stocked with finished projects. Just down the street, original sculptures by local artists are displayed on 2 acres of scenic dunes.

## Monterey Bay Kayaks
*2390 Hwy. 1, (800) 649-5357; www.monterey kayaks.com.*

For description, see page 116.

### — WHERE TO STAY —

## Best Western Beach Dunes Inn
*3290 Dunes Dr., in Marina, (800) 528-1234, (831) 883-0300, fax (831) 384-8137; www.pacificplaza hotels.com. 84 rooms; $. Hot tub.*

This bargain lodging is situated amid the dunes just a short walk from Marina State Beach.

## Monterey Dunes Co.
*(800) 55-DUNES, (831) 633-4883, fax (831) 633-3722; www.montereydunes.com. 120 units; $$-$$$+. All kitchens & wood-burning fireplaces. Pool; hot tub; saunas; 6 tennis courts.*

These fabulous beachfront vacation homes are nestled on 125 acres of sand dunes and are available to rent. All have spectacular views, some have private hot tubs, and facilities include a sand volleyball court and a basketball court.

## Pajaro Dunes
*2661 Beach Rd., in Watsonville, (800) 675-8808, (831) 722-4671, fax (831) 728-7444; www.pajarodunes.com. 120 units; $$$+. All kitchens & wood-burning fireplaces. 19 tennis courts. No pets.*

Situated in the shoreline dunes, this private compound consists of condominiums, townhouses, and homes. Hiking and biking trails, jogging paths, and volleyball and basketball courts round out the recreational facilities. Bike rentals are also available.

### — WHERE TO EAT —

## Giant Artichoke
*11261 Merritt St., off Hwy. 1, in Castroville, (831) 633-3501. B-L-D daily; $. Highchairs, boosters. No reservations.*

Located in "the artichoke capital of the world," where three-quarters of the nation's artichokes are grown, this novelty restaurant makes a good rest stop. To find it, just look for the giant artichoke. Artichoke specialties include French-fried artichokes with mayonnaise dip, artichoke soup, artichoke salad, artichoke quiche, artichoke cake, and even an artichoke milkshake. Other more standard short-order items are also on the menu.

## Phil's Fish Market & Eatery
*7600 Sandholtd Rd., (831) 633-2152, fax (831) 633-8611; www.philsfishmarket.com. Daily 10-9; $. Child menu.*

Begun as a fish market in 1982, when Phil was a commercial fisherman, this humble spot has evolved into a wildly popular restaurant. That's because owner Phil, a warm and kind man, takes his Italian grandmother's peasant recipes and marries them to great effect with the freshest seafood and rock-bottom prices. Diners pig out on steamed Sicilian stuffed artichokes (with a bread crumb-garlic-mozzarella filling), hearty fresh Manhattan chowder, and blackened salmon with sun-dried tomato sauce. Monterey Bay spot prawns (sautéed in white wine, capers, and roma tomatoes with a lemon-caper butter sauce), a seafood quesadilla, seafood salad, fish & chips, and even a burger are also on the extensive menu. California's First Family, the Schwarzeneggers—Arnold, Maria, and the kids—has eaten here.

## The Whole Enchilada
*Hwy. 1/Moss Landing Rd., (831) 633-3038; www.wenchilada.com. L-D daily; $-$$. Highchairs, boosters. Reservations advised.*

This roadside cantina serves a slew of margaritas, including cucumber and prickly pear flavors, and also lines up some unusual suspects on its menu: seafood flautas, oyster shooters, an Oaxacan tamale wrapped in banana leaves. And because Castroville, the "artichoke capital of the world," is just a few miles east of town, it also offers a big artichoke appetizer.

# Monterey Peninsula

### — A LITTLE BACKGROUND —

Popular for years because of its proximity to San Francisco, this area (Monterey, Pacific Grove, Pebble Beach, Carmel, and Carmel

Valley) is a well-established vacation destination. A vast variety of overnight accommodations and restaurants is available. Due to the area's immense popularity, there is no off-season and reservations are essential for both lodging and the more popular restaurants.

The **Monterey Bay National Marine Sanctuary** is the nation's 11th and largest protected marine area. It covers more than 300 miles—from the Farallon Islands near San Francisco in the north to Cambria in the south. Protected resources include the nation's most expansive kelp forests, one of North America's largest underwater canyons, and a deep ocean environment that is the closest to shore in the continental U.S. The Monterey Bay Aquarium acts as the sanctuary's interpretive center.

## — GETTING THERE —

Located approximately 115 miles south of San Francisco, and 40 miles south of Santa Cruz.

# Monterey

## — VISITOR INFORMATION —

### Monterey County Convention & Visitors Bureau
*150 Olivier St., (888) 221-1010, (831) 657-6400, fax (831) 648-5373; www.montereyinfo.org. M-F 8:30-5.*

### Monterey Visitors Center
*Franklin St./Camino El Estero, by Lake El Estero. No phone. Schedule varies.*

## — ANNUAL EVENTS —

### Monterey Scottish Games & Celtic Festival
*August. In Toro County Park; (831) 647-6311; www.montereyscotgames.com. $12-$15, 65+ & 13-18 $10-$12, 5-12 $5-$6.*

Celebrating everything Scottish, this event is described as being like a Celtic three-ring circus. One ring features piping (as in bagpipes) and drumming contests, with massive pipe bands competing against each other. Another ring features unusual athletic events such as the Caber Toss (in which a huge pole is tossed end-over-end for accuracy) and Putting the Stone (in which a heavy stone is tossed). And another presents the Highland Dancing Championships,

which in current times is participated in predominantly by females. Events, including several sheepdog demonstrations, run continuously.

### Monterey Historic Automobile Races
*August; www.montereyhistoric.com.*
### Grand Prix
*September.*
*Both at Mazda Raceway Laguna Seca, in Salinas; (800) 327-SECA, (831) 648-5111; www.laguna-seca.com.*

Originally held in Pebble Beach, the Historic Automobile Races demonstrate the abilities of a broad range of vintage sports and racing cars. At the Grand Prix, Indy cars take the stage for 3 days featuring the world's best drivers.

### Monterey Jazz Festival
*September. At Monterey Fairgrounds; (831) 373-3366, tickets (925) 275-9255, fax (831) 373-0244; www.montereyjazzfestival.org. $30+.*

The oldest continuously presented jazz festival in the country, this well-known event offers 3 days of nonstop entertainment.

### Christmas in the Adobes
*December. (831) 649-7118. $15, 6-17 $2.*

Each year a group of historic adobes are festively decked with period decorations and illuminated only by candlelight. Docents dress in era costumes, and luminarias guide visitors along walkways into the cozy, warm interiors, where they can shed the chill of the night with musical entertainment and fragrant refreshments such as Mexican hot chocolate and wassail. At the Stevenson House, former resident Robert Louis Stevenson is portrayed by an actor and Scottish music and bagpipes provide enchanting entertainment. Visitors gain entry to a few adobes that are usually closed to the public, including the Casa Amesti, which is now a private men's club. Purchase tickets early as this event often sells out.

## — WHAT TO DO —

### Cannery Row
*(831) 649-6690; www.canneryrow.org.*

Once booming with sardine canneries, Cannery Row became a ghost town in 1945 when the sardines mysteriously disappeared from the area's ocean. In *Cannery Row*, John

Steinbeck described it as "a poem, a stink, a grating noise, a quality of light, a tone, a habit, a nostalgia, a dream." Now this mile-long road houses restaurants, art galleries, shops, a **Bargetto Winery Tasting Room** *(#700, (831) 373-4053, same fax; www.bargetto.com. Tasting daily 10:30-6.)*, **Steinbeck's Spirit of Monterey Wax Museum** *(#700, (831) 375-3770, fax (831) 646-5309; www.wax-museum.com. Open daily, schedule varies. $5.95, 6-18 $3.95.)*, and the **Monterey Bay Aquarium** *(see page 116).* **A Taste of Monterey** *(#700, (888) 646-5446, (831) 646-5446, fax (831) 375-0835; www.taste monterey.com. Tasting daily 11-6.)* provides samplings from local wineries along with a 180-degree view of the bay and a theater presenting wine-related videos.

Reading John Steinbeck's *Cannery Row* provides background for visiting this historic street. Lee Chong's Heavenly Flower Grocery, mentioned in Steinbeck's novel, is now **Wing Chong Market**—a souvenir shop *(#835)*, and La Ida's Cafe is now **Kalisa's** sandwich shop *(#851)*. Doc's lab *(#800)* is currently owned by the city. Just a block north of the aquarium, the **American Tin Cannery Premium Outlet** *(125 Ocean View Blvd., in Pacific Grove, (831) 372-1442. M-Sat 10-7, Sun 10-6.)* and its attractive industrial interior is worth a detour. Also here, health-conscious **First Awakenings** *(#105, (831) 372-1125. B-L daily; $. Highchairs, boosters, booths, child menu. No reservations.)* has a pleasant outdoor patio and soothing live guitar music. At breakfast it's fresh fruit crêpes and a variety of omelettes, and at lunch look for salads and sandwiches.

## Edgewater Family Fun Center
*640 Wave St., (831) 649-1899, fax (831) 649-2387. Sun-Thur 11-9, F-Sat 11-10. Free admission.*

This family entertainment center has the latest video games and a candy shop stocked with cotton candy, caramel apples, and popcorn. It also is home to what might be the world's fastest **carousel**. Built by Herschell-Spillman in 1905, it has 36 horses and 2 chariots.

**Bay Bikes** *(585 Cannery Row, (831) 646-9090, fax (831) 655-3497; www.baybikes.com. Daily 9-5, in summer 9-7. $6+/1 hr., $20+/day.)* rents both 21-speed mountain bikes and multi-passenger Italian surrey bikes to ride on the spectacular waterfront bike trail that hugs the bay from Fisherman's Wharf to Lover's Point. Children's bikes, child seats and trailers, and jogging strollers are also available. Safety equipment is included with rentals.

## El Estero Park
*Del Monte Ave./Camino El Estero/Fremont Blvd., (831) 646-3866. Daily 10-dusk. Free.*

Hiking and bike trails and a lake filled with hungry ducks await here. Paddleboats and canoes can be rented, and children may fish from boats. Located by the lake on Pearl Street, **Dennis the Menace Playground** features colorful play equipment designed by former area resident and the creator of the *Dennis the Menace* comic strip, Hank Ketchum. Notable are a hedge maze with a corkscrew slide in its center, a long suspension bridge, and an authentic Southern Pacific steam train engine to climb on. Picnic tables and a snack concession are available.

## Fisherman's Wharf
*(831) 649-6544, fax (831) 649-4124; www.montereywharf.com.*

Lined with restaurants and shops, the wharf also offers inexpensive entertainment. Sometimes an organ grinder greets visitors at the entrance, his friendly monkey anxious to take coins from children's hands. Sea lions hang out around the wharf pilings and often put on a free show. Several businesses offer whale watching, sailing, and deep-sea fishing expeditions.

## Jacks Peak County Park
*25020 Jacks Peak Park Rd., off Hwy. 68 to Salinas, (888) 588-2267, (831) 372-8551; www.co.monterey. ca.us/parks. Schedule varies. $2-$3/vehicle.*

This 525-acre park is in a Monterey pine forest with 8 miles of trails and a variety of picnic areas. Follow the .3-mile Jacks Peak Trail to the summit for a great view of Monterey Bay, Carmel Bay, and the valley.

## Maritime Museum of Monterey
*5 Custom House Plaza, (831) 372-2608, fax (831) 655-3054; www.montereyhistory.org. Tu-Sun 11-5. $5, 60+ & 13-18 $2.50.*

Beginning with the history of Spanish ships that anchored in the area 4 centuries ago, this museum celebrates California's seafaring heritage. See ship models, bells, compasses, and related items, and learn about the area's naval history. Most impressive is the 2-story-tall, 10,000-pound 1889 Fresnel lens once used at the Point Sur Lighthouse.

## Monterey Bay Aquarium

*886 Cannery Row, (831) 648-4888; www.montereybay aquarium.org. Daily 10-6; in summer 9:30-6. $19.95, 66+ $17.95, 13-17 $15.95, 3-12 $8.95. Reservations: (800) 756-3737; $3/order.*

Built on the site of what was once the row's largest sardine cannery, this spectacular $112 million facility is one of the nation's largest seawater aquariums. It is operated by a non-profit organization whose mission is to inspire conservation of the oceans. Well-arranged and architecturally interesting, the aquarium provides a close-up view of the underwater habitats and creatures of Monterey Bay—an area known for its spectacular and varied marine life. Among the nearly 200 galleries and exhibits is a tank that displays a 3-story-high kelp forest and another that is home to some of the area's playful sea otters. More than 30,000 fish, mammal, bird, invertebrate, and plant specimens are on display, and almost all are native to Monterey Bay. Don't miss the walk-through aviary of shorebirds or the bat ray petting pool. Children especially enjoy the Touch Pool, where they can handle a variety of sea stars and other tidepool life, and the fabulous Splash Zone, where kids under age 10 can

view a wall of comical moray eels and see a magnificent leafy sea dragon. The Outer Bay, which features one of the world's largest acrylic windows, permits peeking into a simulated ocean, with sharks, ocean sunfish, green sea turtles, and schools of yellowfin and giant bluefin tuna (the Maseratis of the ocean) swimming in more than a million gallons of water. This area also has a fascinating display of sea jellies, including the largest jelly tank anywhere—a don't-miss psychedelic tank filled with orange sea nettles shown against a vibrant blue background. Both a fast-food cafeteria and a pricier restaurant are available inside; picnic tables are available outside. Or get a hand-stamp for re-entry, and dine somewhere nearby.

## Monterey Bay Kayaks

*693 Del Monte Ave., (800) 649-5357, (831) 373-KELP, fax (831) 373-0119; www.montereykayaks.com. Daily 9-6, in summer 9-8. $65/3-hr. class.*

Observe sea lions and otters up close near Fisherman's Wharf and along Cannery Row. Classes led by marine biologists include a half-hour of safety instruction, and no experience is necessary. Tour kayaks hold two people. Children must be at least 4½ feet tall; smaller children can be accommodated in a triple kayak with two adults.

## Monterey Museum of Art

*559 Pacific St., (831) 372-5477, fax (831) 372-5680; www.montereyart.org. W-Sat 11-5, Sun 1-4, 3rd Thurs to 7. $5, under 12 free; free 1st Sun of month.*

Located downtown, this museum is dubbed "the best small town museum in the United States." Indeed, it provides the delight of a well-displayed small collection of regional art and photography. Important artists of the Monterey Peninsula, including Ansel Adams and Edward Weston, are represented. A strong graphics collection includes works by Rembrandt, Manet, and Picasso.

An extension of the museum, the historic **La Mirada adobe** *(720 Via Mirada, (831) 372-3689, (831) 372-6043.)* is located several miles away. (It is open the same hours, and a ticket bought in either location permits admission to the other on that day or a different day.) One of the first adobes built during the Mexican occupation of Monterey, it displays antique furnishings and early California art. Works by contemporary regional artists are displayed in a dramatic modern addition. Spectacular gardens are planted with more than 75 varieties of rose and 300 varieties of rhododendron.

## Monterey State Historic Park
*20 Custom Plaza, (831) 649-7118, fax (831) 647-6236; www.parks.ca.gov. Daily 10-4, in summer 10-5; walking tour daily, schedule varies. Free.*

Downtown Monterey holds the largest collection of historic buildings west of Williamsburg. This facility consists of both historical sites and preserved adobes. Guided tours are scheduled for the very special **Stevenson House,** said to be haunted by a forlorn woman dressed in black; the **Cooper-Molera Adobe** *(Polk St./Alvarado St./Munras St. Tours M, W, F-Sat at 1.),* a 2-acre complex with chickens, sheep, old-time carriages, and a visitor center; the **Larkin House** *(Pacific St./Jefferson St. Tours M, W, F at 2, Sat-Sun at 3.);* and the **Casa Soberanes** *(Del Monte Ave./Pacific St.. Tours M, W, F at 11:30, Sun. at 1.).* Historic Garden Tours are given May through September *(Tu, Sat at 12. $5 donation.).*

**The Path of History,** a self-guided walking tour following gold-colored tiles embedded in the sidewalk, leads past 44 historic buildings, sites, and gardens.

## Rent-A-Roadster
*229 Cannery Row, (831) 647-1929, fax (831) 647-1928; www.rent-a-roadster.com. Daily 10-5. $30-$40/hr.*

Easy-to-drive, authentic reproductions of 1929 Model A Ford Roadsters can be rented for a drive down the coast or a tour of the 17-Mile Drive. Roadsters seat four—two in the front and two in the rumble seat; a red 1930 deluxe Phaeton model seats five. It is worth the rental price just to honk the old-fashioned horn and watch reactions.

## Ventana Vineyards Tasting Room
*2999 Monterey-Salinas Hwy. (Hwy. 68), 3 mi. from downtown, (800) BEST-VIN, (831) 372-7415, fax (831) 375-0797; www.ventanavineyards.com. Tasting daily 11-5; no tours.*

The tasting room here is in the historic, atmospheric Old Stone House. Don't miss sampling the white wines, particularly the Chardonnays and Rieslings the winery is known for. A flower-beladen deck surrounded by tall pines is available for picnicking. It is interesting to note that the only existing French oak trees in the U.S. grow on a nearby bluff. Planted in 1978, they will be harvested eventually and turned into wine barrels.

## — WHERE TO STAY —

## Casa Munras Garden Hotel
*700 Munras Ave, (800) 222-2446, (831) 375-2411, fax (831) 375-1365; www.casamunras-hotel.com. 166 rooms; $$-$$$. Children under 12 free. Some gas fireplaces. Heated pool. Restaurant.*

One of the first residences built outside the walls of the old Presidio in 1824, the original Casa is built of individual adobe bricks made by hand from native materials. Parts of the dining room and porch of the original house remain. Converted into a hotel in 1941, its grounds are spacious, attractive, and peaceful, and all rooms have brass beds.

## Clarion Hotel
*1046 Munras Ave., (800) 821-0805, (831) 373-1337, fax (831) 372-2451; http://clarionhotelmonterey.com. 52 rooms; $-$$$. Children under 12 free. Some kitchens & gas fireplaces. Indoor heated pool & hot tub. Continental breakfast. No pets.*

Though the architecture of this motel is simple, its facilities are noteworthy.

## Hotel Pacific
*300 Pacific St., (800) 554-5542, (831) 373-5700, fax (831) 373-6921; www.hotelpacific.com. 105 rooms; $$$-$$$+. Children under 12 free. All gas fireplaces. 2 hot tubs. Afternoon snack, continental breakfast.*

Situated near the Wharf, this lodging melds the amenities of a B&B with the convenience of a motel. It features adobe-style architecture and attractive gardens with fountains. All rooms are spacious suites equipped with down comforters and featherbeds, and nightly turndown service is included.

## Hyatt Regency Monterey
*1 Old Golf Course Rd., (800) 228-9000, (831) 372-1234, fax (831) 375-3960; www.hyatt.com. 575 rooms; $$-$$$. Children under 18 free. 2 heated pools; 2 hot tubs; fitness room; 6 tennis courts (some night lights). 2 restaurants; room service.*

Located on the outskirts of town, this quiet, luxurious resort is adjacent to the scenic Old Del Monte Golf Course the oldest golf course west of the Mississippi. **Knuckles Historical Sports Bar** has 14 big-screen TVs tuned to the action in a casual, peanut shells-on-the-floor atmosphere.

## Monterey Bay Inn

*242 Cannery Row, (800) 424-6242, (831) 373-6242, fax (831) 373-7603; www.montereybayinn.com. 4 stories; 47 rooms; $$-$$$. Children under 12 free. 2 hot tubs; sauna. Afternoon snack, continental breakfast; room service.*

Located a short walk from the aquarium, all rooms in this waterfront lodging have private balconies, sleeper sofas, and plush robes. Most rooms also have spectacular bay views, and all guests have access to the rooftop hot tub and its breathtaking view of the bay. Breakfast is brought to the room.

## Monterey Marriott

*350 Calle Principal, (800) 228-9290, (831) 649-4234, fax (831) 372-2968; www.marriott.com. 10 stories; 363 rooms; $$$-$$$+. Children under 18 free. Heated pool; hot tub; health spa. 2 restaurants; room service. No pets. Valet parking $15.*

Located near the Wharf, this attractive hotel is built on the former site of the grand old Hotel San Carlos. It is the tallest building in town and offers spectacular views. Rooms are quiet and tastefully appointed, and a sports bar presents live music in the evening.

## Monterey Plaza Hotel & Spa

*400 Cannery Row, (800) 368-2468, (831) 646-1700, fax (831) 646-0285; www.montereyplazahotel.com. 285 rooms; $$-$$$+. Children under 18 free. Health spa. Restaurant; room service. No smoking; valet parking $16.*

Built partially over the bay, with rooms on both sides of the street, this well-situated luxury hotel features comfortably appointed, attractively decorated rooms with marble bathrooms. Some have private balconies and expansive bay views. A penthouse-level health spa is equipped with two hot tubs on a sundeck, two saunas, and a fitness center—all available free to guests who book a treatment and for a daily fee otherwise.

Dinner at a bayside window table in the **Duck Club** *(B-L-D daily; $$-$$$. Highchairs. Valet parking.)* is a delight. For starters, try the crab cakes or delicious traditional Caesar salad.

Entrees include several housemade pastas, a selection of fresh seafood, and, of course, duck: crisp-roasted with Valencia orange sauce or wood-roasted with green peppercorn mustard sauce. Dessert choices include a chocolate layer cake, a large selection of housemade ice creams, and a plate of housemade cookies.

## Old Monterey Inn

*500 Martin St., (800) 350-2344, (831) 375-8284, fax (831) 375-6730; www.oldmontereyinn.com. 10 rooms; $$$-$$$+. Unsuitable for children. No TVs; some fireplaces. Evening snack, full breakfast. No smoking.*

Built in 1929, this aesthetically magnificent half-timbered, Tudor-style inn resembles an elegant English country house. It is on an acre of tended flower gardens surrounded by massive Monterey pines, in a quiet neighborhood near enough to downtown to permit walking. Though any room here should please, a few are quite special: The private Garden Cottage has a cozy fireplace and two-person whirlpool tub; the Library has book-lined walls and a large stone fireplace; and the Serengeti Room sports antique travel mementos for decorations and a bed covered by genuine jungle mosquito netting. All rooms have a unique and tasteful decor, and the fluffy beds are made with soft featherbeds over the mattress and topped with down comforters. Thoughtful touches such as small chocolates in antique silver dishes, candles by the bathtub, terry-lined silk robes, a CD player equipped with a soothing classical disc, an enjoyable collection of books, and stamped postcards make guests feel well cared for. Some sort of snack is always available in the communal area. In the morning, coffee is delivered to the room. Breakfast is served later at an enormous, beautifully set table in a dining room graced by plank floors, a huge copper fireplace, and a hand-plastered ceiling. Alternatively, breakfast can be served in bed.

## Spindrift Inn

*652 Cannery Row, (800) 841-1879, (831) 646-8900, fax (831) 646-5342; www.spindriftinn.com. 4 stories; 42 rooms; $$$-$$$+. Children under 10 free. All wood-burning fireplaces. Afternoon snack, continental breakfast; room service. Valet parking $16.*

Located right in the heart of Cannery Row, just 2 blocks from the aquarium, this tasteful lodging offers some rooms with faux canopy beds. All are equipped with gas-started fireplaces that accept wood, and many have bay views that permit occupants to greet a foggy morning as Steinbeck described in *The Grapes of Wrath* journal, "I remember how grey and doleful Monday morning was. I could lie and look at it from my bed . . ." Breakfast is brought to the room on a silver tray, along with a newspaper. The inn provides all guests a good view from its rooftop garden, and its backyard is tiny McAbee Beach, where ruins of concrete sardine holding tanks await exploration.

## Motel Row

Modern motel accommodations abound along Munras Avenue.

## — WHERE TO EAT —

## Abalonetti Seafood Trattoria

*57 Fisherman's Wharf, (831) 373-1851, fax (831) 373-2058; www.pisto.com. L-D daily; $-$$. Highchairs, boosters, child menu. Reservations advised.*

This small, unpretentious restaurant is named for a famous dish in which calamari (squid) is pounded until tender, breaded, and then sautéed in butter. Over half the menu is devoted to squid dishes—the house specialty. Other seafood and Italian items, as well as pizza, are also available, and the dining room provides a good view of Monterey Bay.

## Britannia Arms

*444 Alvarado Street, (831) 656-9543; www.britannia arms.com*

For description, see page 111.

## Bubba Gump Shrimp Co.

*720 Cannery Row, (888) SAY-GUMP, (831) 373-1884, fax (831) 373-0354; www.bubbagump.com. L-D daily; $. Highchairs, child menu. No reservations.*

Based on the movie *Forrest Gump*, which won six Oscars, this is the first in a chain of seafood restaurants revolving around memorabilia from the movie—script pages, storyboards, costumes, photos, scrawled Gumpisms on tabletops. The movie plays continuously on video monitors. By the way, the men's room is Bubba's, the women's room Jenny's. For more description, see page 59.

## The Chart House

*444 Cannery Row, (831) 372-3362, fax (831) 372-1277; www.chart-house.com. D daily.*

Offering spectacular views, this restaurant operates inside a former cannery. For more description, see page 368.

## Fresh Cream

*99 Pacific St., 100-C Heritage Harbor, (831) 375-9798, fax (831) 375-2283; www.freshcream.com. D daily; $$$. Reservations advised.*

Situated on the second story of a building across from the Wharf, this classy, serene restaurant offers a great harbor view along with excellent classical French cuisine. Appetizers include housemade lobster raviolis with a rich lobster butter sauce and a sprinkling of both black and gold caviars. Entrees include fresh local fish and veal, a flawless rack of lamb Dijonnaise, and a succulent roast duck with black currant sauce. Desserts are spectacular: a Grand Marnier soufflé and an incredible edible chocolate box holding a mocha milkshake.

## Ghirardelli Soda Fountain & Chocolate Shop

*660 Cannery Row, (831) 373-0997; www.ghirar delli.com.*

This is a much smaller version of the flagship fountain in San Francisco. For more description, see page 69.

## Mike's Seafood

*25 Fisherman's Wharf, (831) 372-6153. L-D daily; $-$$. Highchairs, boosters, child portions. Reservations advised at D.*

Arrive before sundown to take advantage of the excellent bay views afforded from tables in this busy and popular seafood restaurant. Steaks, hamburgers, and chicken are also on the menu.

## Montrio

*414 Calle Principal/Franklin St., (831) 648-8880; www.montrio.com. L-D daily; $-$$. Child menu. Reservations advised.*

Operating within a dramatically remodeled 1910 firehouse, with tall ceilings and contemporary lighting, this popular spot is always buzzing. If full, opt for a seat in the bar and order there. Small plates and salads are on the innovative menu: Basmati rice cakes; a roasted beet salad with apples and Feta cheese. Menu favorites include crispy crab cakes, risotto, and juicy rotisserie chicken with mashed potatoes.

### The Sardine Factory
*701 Wave St., (831) 373-3775, fax (831) 646-8900; www.sardinefactory.com. D daily; $$$. Highchairs, boosters, child menu. Reservations advised. Valet parking.*

This building, which once housed a canteen patronized by cannery workers, now is home to an elegant, award-winning restaurant with five very different dining rooms and over 30,000 bottles of wine in its cellar. The kitchen is known for its fresh seafood and aged beef. Special items include fresh abalone, fresh Australian lobster tail, and aged beef. Appetizers include a highly acclaimed abalone cream bisque created for President Reagan's inaugural, as well as fresh clams, mussels, oysters, and Dungeness crab in season. But no sardines. A knock-out dessert features a spectacular foot-high lighted ice swan bearing a scoop of sorbet.

### Stokes Restaurant & Bar
*500 Hartnell St., (831) 373-1110, fax (831) 373-1202; www.stokesrestaurant.com. L M-Sat, D daily; $$-$$$. Reservations advised.*

Dating from 1833 and one of the oldest buildings in Monterey, the historic 2-story Stokes Adobe has been updated with a comfortable, airy, rustic-modern interior. Owner-chef Brandon Miller showcases local ingredients, and his always evolving menu usually includes an acclaimed lavender-infused grilled pork chop and sometimes a really good cassoulet. The refined soups are particularly delicious. Small tapas plates make nice starters or, for smaller appetites, a few can compose a satisfying meal.

### Whaling Station Inn
*763 Wave St., (831) 373-3778, fax (831) 373-2460; www.pisto.com. D daily; $$$+. Highchairs, boosters, child portions. Reservations advised. Valet parking.*

Situated inside a building that dates from 1929 and once housed a Chinese grocery store, this restaurant produces creative and delicious dishes. On one visit, seafood selections included barbecued Monterey Bay prawns—the fresh, sweet, firm-fleshed kind that are so hard to find—and blackened fresh salmon. Entrees came with a house salad consisting of Cajun-

spiced walnuts on a bed of Belgian endive, spinach, and baby lettuce dressed with a sweet dressing fragrant with sesame oil. Steamed baby carrots and asparagus on a bed of purple cabbage accompanied the entrees, and a diamond of spicy polenta completed the plate. Grilled quail, rack of lamb, and prime steaks are among the non-seafood entrees. Desserts are made fresh in the kitchen each day, and an irresistible tray of them is presented at the end of each memorable repast.

### Wharfside
*60 Fisherman's Wharf, (831) 375-3956, fax (831) 375-296. L-D daily; $$. Highchairs, boosters, child menu. No reservations.*

Through the window downstairs, it is sometimes possible to watch the various varieties of ravioli—meat and spinach, cheese, squid, salmon, shrimp, crab, lobster—being laboriously prepared. Dining takes place upstairs, where great views of the bay are enjoyed. Pastas and seafood round out the menu.

# Pacific Grove

## — A LITTLE BACKGROUND —

Originally settled as a Chinese fishing village, Pacific Grove was established in 1875 as a Methodist Episcopal Church summer camp. Some modest summer cottages and distinctive Victorian-style homes remain today. Due to some ordinances put into effect in those early days, it wasn't until 1969 that a liquor store opened within the town limits. In fact, Pacific Grove was the last dry city in California. Still old-fashioned, the low-key main shopping street still has free diagonal parking as well as an additional row of parking in the street's center.

## — VISITOR INFORMATION —

### Pacific Grove Chamber of Commerce
*584 Central Ave., (800) 656-6650, (831) 373-3304, fax (831) 373-3317; www.pacificgrove.org.*

## — ANNUAL EVENTS —

### Historic Home Tour
*October; (831) 373-3304. $15. Must be 12 or older.*

## Monarch Butterflies

*October. Free.*

Each year hundreds of thousands of stunning orange-and-black monarch butterflies return to Pacific Grove to winter on the needles of favored local pine trees. They migrate all the way from western Canada and Alaska and stay until March, when they again fly north.

Somewhat of a mystery is how they find their way here each year since, with a lifespan of less than a year, no butterfly makes the trip twice. It is, in fact, the great-grandchildren of the prior year's butterfly visitors that return. Somehow the monarchs program a genetic message into their progeny, which then return to these same trees the following fall and repeat the cycle.

Reacting to the weather somewhat as does a golden poppy, monarchs prefer to flutter about on sunny days between the hours of 10 a.m. and 4 p.m. In fact, they can't fly when temperatures drop below 55 degrees. So on cold and foggy days, which are quite common in this area, they huddle together with closed wings and are often overlooked as dull pieces of bark or dead leaves. On cold days observers must be careful where they step: Monarchs that have dropped to the ground to sip dew off the grass might be resting there, having found it too cold to fly back to their perch.

During early March the butterflies can be observed mating. Watch for females chasing males in a spiral flight. (Males are recognized by a characteristic black dot on their wings.) When a female finds a male she likes, they drop to the ground to mate. Literally standing on his head at one point, the male, while still mating, then lifts the female back to a perch in a tree, where they continue mating for almost an entire day!

Butterfly nets should be left at home. To discourage visitors from bothering these fragile creatures, Pacific Grove has made molesting a butterfly a misdemeanor crime carrying a $1,000 fine.

To celebrate the annual return of the butterflies, the town of Pacific Grove, also known as Butterfly Town U.S.A., has hosted a **Butterfly Parade** every October since 1938. Completely non-commercial, this delightful parade provides the low-key pleasure of viewing local grade school children marching down the street dressed as butterflies. Traditional bands and majorette corps from local schools also participate. Weather always cooperates: This parade has *never* been rained on.

For more information on the monarchs, contact non-profit Friends of the Monarchs *(P.O. Box 51683, Pacific Grove 93950; (888) PGMONARCHS; www.pgmonarchs.org.)*. To receive a child's packet of information on the monarch (stories, a coloring page, etc.), send a request and $1 for postage and handling.

### — WHAT TO DO —

## Antique Clock Shop
*489 Lighthouse Ave., (831) 372-6435. Tu-Sat 12-5.*

This charming converted cottage holds a constantly changing inventory of clocks. Be there on the hour for a chiming treat.

## Lover's Point
*626 Ocean View Blvd.*

Located at the southern tip of Monterey Bay, this park holds a chunky granite statue honoring the monarch butterfly. It offers a pleasant beach for sunbathing and wading, and a grassy picnic area with barbecue pits.

## Monarch Grove Sanctuary
*1073 Lighthouse Ave./Ridge Rd., (888) PG-MONARCH, (831) 375-0982. Daily dawn-dusk, Oct-Mar. Free.*

The densest clusters of monarchs congregate in this pine and eucalyptus grove located behind the Butterfly Grove Inn. Guided tours are available from mid-October through mid-February; call to reserve space.

## Pacific Grove Museum of Natural History

*165 Forest Ave./Central Ave., (831) 648-5716, fax (831) 372-3256; www.pgmuseum.org. Tu-Sat 10-5. Free.*

Opened in 1882, this museum is dedicated to telling the natural history of Monterey County through exhibits of marine and bird life, native plants, shells, and Native American artifacts. Notable exhibits include a large jade-stone that visitors rub upon entering, a display of mollusks, a large display of stuffed seabirds, and an enclosed space featuring fluorescent minerals. An informative 10-minute video tells about the monarch butterfly, and the butterfly's life history is portrayed in drawings. In summer larvae are often on view, and milkweed—the only plant on which the female monarch will lay her eggs—attracts butterflies to a native plant garden outside the museum. Also outside, a full-size Sandy the Gray Whale invites kids to climb on board.

Each year during the third weekend in April, this tiny museum sponsors a **Wildflower Show**. As many as 600 varieties are displayed.

## Point Piños Lighthouse

*On Asilomar Blvd., about 2 blks. N of end of Lighthouse Ave., (831) 648-5716, fax (831) 372-3256; www.pgmuseum.org. Thur-M 1-4. By donation: $2, youths $1.*

Docents dressed in period costume give informal tours of this oldest continuously operating Pacific Coast lighthouse, built in 1855 out of granite quarried nearby. The area surrounding the lighthouse is a good spot to walk, picnic, and observe sea otters; note that this is the site of Doc's Great Tide Pool in Steinbeck's *Cannery Row*.

## Poor Man's 17-Mile Drive

It costs nothing to take this scenic 4.2-mile drive past rugged seascapes and impressive homes. Begin at Ocean View Boulevard and 3rd Street. At Point Piños, turn left on Sunset Drive. Tidepooling is good in several spots, and from April to August beautiful lavender ice plant cascades in full bloom over the rocky beach front.

## — WHERE TO STAY —

## Andril Cottages

*569 Asilomar Blvd., (831) 375-0994, fax (831) 655-2693; www.andrilcottages.com. 16 units; $$-$$$+; 1-wk. min. in summer. Children under 5 free. All*

*kitchens & fireplaces. Hot tub. Pets ok.*

These woodsy, pine-paneled cottages are especially comfortable for longer stays. Situated around a tree-shaded courtyard furnished with picnic tables, they are just a block from the ocean.

## Asilomar Conference Grounds

*800 Asilomar Blvd., (888) 733-9005, (831) 372-8016, fax (831) 372-7227; www.asilomarcenter.com. 314 units; $$. Children under 2 free. No TVs; some kitchens, & wood-burning fireplaces. Heated pool. Full breakfast; dining room. No smoking; no pets.*

Founded as a YWCA camp in 1913 and boasting eight buildings designed by architect Julia Morgan, this 107-acre facility is used now mainly as a conference grounds. It is part of the California State Parks system. Rooms are divided among 28 lodge buildings, including four historic ones, and are equipped with neither phones nor TVs. When underbooked, rooms are made available to the general public. Reservations can be made up to 90 days in advance, and last-minute accommodations are often available. It is the perfect place to try during holidays, when everything else in the area is booked and conferences generally are not in session, and it is choice for a family reunion. In Spanish the word "asilomar" means "retreat by the sea," and, indeed, the grounds are located in a quiet, scenic dunes area just a short walk from the ocean. Black-tailed deer and red foxes often are spotted on the grounds.

Both guests and non-guests are welcome to dine on set-menu **conference meals** that are served family-style *(B 7:30-9, L 12-1, D 6-7; $). Highchairs, boosters. Reservations not necessary.).* A sample breakfast consists of cream of wheat, orange juice, coffeecake, scrambled eggs, potato fries, sausage, and dry cereal; a sample lunch includes a mango lassi, barley soup, chicken curry salad, cabbage slaw, and fresh papaya.

## Beachcomber Inn

*1996 Sunset Dr., (800) 634-4769, (831) 373-4769, fax (831) 373-0899. 26 rooms; $-$$. Heated pool; sauna. Continental breakfast; restaurant. No smoking; no pets.*

Factors rendering this typical motel special include its ocean-side location, a 90-degree pool, and free bikes and safety helmets for the use of guests.

The **Fishwife Restaurant** (1996¹/₂ Sunset Dr., (831) 375-7107. L-D daily; $-$$. Child portions.) is located adjacent and justly popular with locals. A large variety of fresh seafood and pastas is featured, not to mention soups and flautas.

## Butterfly Grove Inn

1073 Lighthouse Ave., (800) 337-9244, (831) 373-4921, fax (831) 373-4921; www.butterflygroveinn.com. 29 rooms; $-$$$. Children under 18 free. Some kitchens & fireplaces. Heated pool; hot tub. Small dogs ok.

This attractive complex offers a choice of either two-bedroom family suites in a Victorian house or spacious rooms in a newly built motel. Located on a quiet side street, it is adjacent to the Monarch Grove Sanctuary.

## Centrella Bed & Breakfast Inn

612 Central Ave., (800) 233-3372, (831) 372-3372, fax (831) 372-2036; www.centrellainn.com. 26 rooms; $$-$$$. Children under 5 free. Some TVs & wood-burning & gas fireplaces. Afternoon snack, full breakfast. No smoking; no pets.

This restored turn-of-the-century Victorian has won awards for its interior decor. Rooms are furnished with antiques and feature floral wallpapers and fabrics, and some bathrooms have clawfoot tubs. Suites on the third floor are particularly nice. Families with children under 12 are accommodated only in the cottage suites, each of which has a fireplace and private garden.

## The Gosby House Inn

643 Lighthouse Ave., (800) 527-8828, (831) 375-1287, fax (831) 655-9621; www.foursisters.com. 22 rooms; $-$$. Children under 5 free. No TVs; some fireplaces & shared baths. Afternoon snack, full breakfast. No smoking; no pets.

Located in the heart of the town's shopping area, this Queen Anne Victorian features a charming rounded corner tower and many bay windows. Built in 1887 by a cobbler from Nova Scotia, it is now an historic landmark. Noteworthy features include attractive wallpapers, a well-tended garden, and an assortment of stuffed bears and bunnies that welcome guests throughout the inn (all are available for purchase).

For a hopelessly romantic getaway, make dinner reservations at **Gernot's Victoria House**

Restaurant (649 Lighthouse Ave., (831) 646-1477. D Tu-Sun; $$-$$$. Boosters, child portions. Reservations advised.). Located just next door in another restored Victorian, this lovely dining room offers a continental menu with selections such as Austrian wiener schnitzel and wild boar Bourguignon.

## Seven Gables Inn

555 Ocean View Blvd., (831) 372-4341; www.pginns.com. 14 rooms; $$-$$$+. Unsuitable for children under 12. No TVs. Afternoon tea, full breakfast. No smoking; no pets.

Located across the street from the ocean, this elegant yellow Victorian mansion was built in 1886. Rooms and cottages all have ocean views and are furnished with fine European and American antiques.

## Motel Row

Numerous motels are located at the west end of Lighthouse Avenue and along Asilomar Boulevard.

## — WHERE TO EAT —

## Bay Cafe

589 Lighthouse Ave., (831) 375-4237. B-L daily; $. Highchairs, boosters, child portions.

The all-American menu here includes plate-size pancakes, house-baked meats, and made-from-scratch mashed potatoes and gravy.

## Fandango

223 17th St./Lighthouse Ave., (831) 372-3456, fax (831) 372-2673; www.fandangorestaurant.com. L M-Sat, D daily, SunBr; $$-$$$. Reservations advised.

In a warren of small rooms, this chic, casual spot serves an eclectic menu of delicious continental-style cuisine: crisp duck a l'orange, mesquite-grilled seafood and meats, Mediterranean couscous, paella, and pastas. Decadent housemade desserts include a frozen Grand Marnier soufflé big enough for two. Patio seating is available.

## Lighthouse Cafe

602 Lighthouse Ave., (831) 372-7006. B-L daily; $. Highchairs, boosters.

This comfortable little cafe specializes in fluffy omelettes, char-broiled chicken and hamburgers, housemade soups, salads, and sandwiches.

## Old Bath House

*620 Ocean View Blvd./17th St., (831) 375-5195, fax (831) 375-5379; www.oldbathhouse.com. D daily; $$$. Highchairs, boosters, child menu. Reservations advised.*

Every table in this elegant Victorian has a splendid view of Monterey Bay. Entrees include imaginative preparations of meats and fish. Divine desserts are made in the restaurant's own pastry kitchen. A Grand Marnier soufflé is made to order and well worth the wait for preparation.

## Red House Cafe

*662 Lighthouse Ave., (831) 643-1060, fax (831) 372-1738; www.redhousecafe.com. B-L Tu-Sun, D Thur-Sat; $. Child items. No reservations. No cards.*

Sandwiches and salads are attractive and tasty, and soups sublime, in this cute little cottage converted into a charming cafe. Drinks include made-from-scratch lemonade and unfiltered apple juice, and desserts are devastatingly delicious.

Hidden around back is **Miss Trawick's Garden Shop** *(664 Lighthouse Ave., (831) 375-4605, fax (831) 656-0960. M-Sat 10-5, Sun 11-5.)*, and what a find it is. Do stop in for a browse through the myriad garden-related delights tucked here and there throughout the warren of spaces.

## Tinnery at the Beach

*631 Ocean View Blvd., (831) 646-1040, fax (831) 646-5913; www.thetinnery.com. B-L-D daily; $$. Highchairs, boosters, booths, child portions. No reservations.*

Located at Lover's Point, this comfortable, casual restaurant offers outstanding views of the bay. Breakfast is particularly pleasant, with omelettes, egg dishes, and strawberry pancakes on the menu. The extensive, eclectic international dinner menu includes entrees such as tempura prawns, pasta primavera, and prime rib.

# Carmel-by-the-Sea

## — A LITTLE BACKGROUND —

*They had take the direct country road across the hills from Monterey, instead of the Seventeen Mile Drive around by the coast so that Carmel Bay came upon them without any fore-glimmering of its beauty. Dropping down throgent pines, they passed woods-embowered cottages, quaint and rustic, of artists and writers, and went on across wind-blown rolling sand hills held to place by sturdy lupines and nodding with pale California poppies. Saxon screamed in sudden wonder of delight, then caught her breath and gazed at the amazing peacock-blue of a breaker, shot through with golden sunlight, over-falling in a mile-long sweep and thundering into white ruin of foam on a crescent beach of scarcely less white.*

— Jack London,
from *Valley of the Moon*, 1913

A well-established getaway destination, Carmel is best known for its abundant shops, cozy lodgings, and picturesque white sand beach.

It is also known for the things that it doesn't have. No street signs, streetlights, electric or neon signs, jukeboxes, parking meters, or buildings over 2 stories high are allowed in town. No sidewalks, curbs, or house numbers are found in the residential sections. These absent items help Carmel keep its village ambiance.

Do be careful. Eccentric laws in the town make it illegal to wear high heels on the sidewalks, throw a ball in the park, play a musical instrument in a bar, or dig in the sand at the beach other than when making a sand castle.

It seems that almost every weekend some special event is scheduled in the area, making available lodging perpetually scarce. Book accommodations far in advance, especially for the quainter venues, and consider taking advantage of the special rates often available for midweek stays.

## — VISITOR INFORMATION —

## Carmel California Visitor & Information Center

*San Carlos/5th, (800) 550-4333, (831) 624-2522, fax (831) 624-1329; www.carmelcalifornia.org.*

## — GETTING THERE —

Located 120 miles south of San Francisco, and 70 miles south of San Jose.

## — ANNUAL EVENTS —

### AT&T Pebble Beach National Pro-Am
*January & February. In Pebble Beach; (800) 541-9091, (831) 644-0333, fax (831) 649-1763; www.attpb golf.com. $40, under 13 free.*

This high profile event was formerly known as the Bing Crosby Golf Tournament.

### Carmel Art Festival
*May. (831) 642-2503; www.carmelartfestival.com. Free.*

Among the events are special exhibits, art demonstrations in the galleries, and the kick-off to the town's annual **Art Walk**—when galleries stay open late on Friday nights and host special events.

### Carmel Bach Festival
*July & August. (831) 624-2046, fax (831) 624-2788; www.bachfestival.org. $15-$55.*

Held annually since 1935 (except for two years off during World War II), this baroque music festival varies its highlights from year to year. Candlelight concerts are usually presented in the town's picturesque mission, and a children's concert is always scheduled.

### Pebble Beach Concours d'Elegance™
*August. In Pebble Beach; (877) 693-0009, (831) 622-1700, fax (831) 622-9100; www.pebblebeachconcours.net. $100.*

Car buffs don their dressiest summer attire for a stroll on the spacious lawn at the Lodge at Pebble Beach, where this elegant affair is held. Classic vintage and antique automobiles are displayed. This is considered America's premiere event of its kind.

## — WHAT TO DO —

### Art galleries
• **New Masters Gallery**
*Dolores St./Ocean Ave., (800) 336-4014, (831) 625-1511, fax (831) 625-5137; www.newmastersgallery.com. Daily 10-5.*

The work of accomplished contemporary artists is shown here.

• **Rodrigue Studio**
*6th Ave./Lincoln St., (831) 626-4444, fax (831) 626-4488; www.georgerodrigue.com. Daily 10-6.*

This gallery is devoted entirely to Cajun artist George Rodrigue's pop art blue dog.

## Beaches
• **Carmel Beach**
*At the foot of Ocean Ave., (831) 626-2522; www.carmelcalifornia.com.*

Known for its white powdery sand and spectacular sunsets, this world-famous beach is a choice spot for a refreshing walk, a picnic, or flying a kite. Swimming is unsafe.

The **Great Sand Castle Contest** *((800) 550-4333; www.carmelcalifornia.com. Free.)* is held here each September or October, depending on the tides. Contestants are encouraged to bribe judges with food and drink.

• **Carmel River State Beach**
*At the end of Scenic Rd./Carmelo St., (831) 649-2836; www.parks.ca.gov. Daily 9-dusk. Free.*

Very popular with families and divers, this beach has a fresh-water lagoon that is safe for wading plus an adjoining bird sanctuary. It is located behind the Carmel Mission, where the Carmel River flows into Carmel Bay, and offers beautiful views of Point Lobos. Locals refer to it as Oliver's Cove; the southern end is known as Monastery Beach. Swimming is dangerous. Picnic facilities are available.

## Mission San Carlos Borromeo del Rio Carmelo
*3080 Rio Rd., 1 mi. S of town off Hwy. 1, (831) 624-3600, fax (831) 624-0658; www.carmelmission.org. M-F 9:30-4:30, Sat-Sun 10:30-4:30; services on Sun. $4, 5-17 $1.*

Father Junipero Serra, who established this mission in 1770 and used it as his headquarters for managing the entire chain of missions, is buried here at the foot of the altar. It is also known as the Carmel Mission. An intriguing star window graces the rough sandstone walls and Moorish bell tower of the façade, and a museum displays Native American artifacts, mission tools, and re-creations of both the original mission kitchen and California's first library. Near a cemetery where over 3,000 mission Indians are buried, the quadrangle courtyard garden features a restful fountain stocked with colorful koi. A **fiesta** is held each year on the last Sunday in September.

Across the street, 37-acre **Mission Trail Park** *((831) 624-3543; www.carmelcalifornia. com. Daily dawn-dusk. Free.)* has several hiking trails. The broad Serra Trail is an easy uphill hike. Doolittle Trail goes farther on for great views of the bay and a visit to the 1929 Tudor **Flanders Mansion**, where it is possible to tour the grounds and stroll through the **Lester Rowntree Arboretum**.

## Pacific Repertory Theatre

*Monte Verde St./8th Ave., in Golden Bough Playhouse, (831) 622-0700, fax (831) 622-0703; www.pacrep.org. Performances Feb-Oct. $7-$20. Must be 7 or older.*

In a building reconstructed on the site of a playhouse that has burned to the ground twice (each time after performances of *By Candlelight!*), this ambitious company presents varied fare in an intimate venue.

## Pebble Beach Equestrian Center

*Portola Rd./Alva Ln., in Pebble Beach, (831) 624-2756, fax (831) 624-3999; www.ridepebblebeach.com. Group rides daily at 10, 12, 2, 3:30. $47/person. Must be 12 or older. Reservations required.*

Escorted rides follow the extensive bridle trails that wind through scenic Del Monte Forest, around the legendary Spyglass Hill Golf Course, down to the beach, and over the sand dunes. Family rides for ages 7 and older and pony rides for ages 3 through 6 are also available. Riders have a choice of English or Western saddles, and English riding lessons are available.

## Point Lobos State Reserve

*3 mi. S of town off Hwy. 1, (831) 624-4909; www.parks.ca.gov. Daily 9-4:30, in summer 9-6:30; museum 11-3. $5/vehicle.*

Described as "the greatest meeting of land and water in the world," Point Lobos provides the opportunity to see the rustic, undeveloped beauty of the Monterey Peninsula. Flat-topped, gnarled-limbed Monterey cypress trees are native to just the 4-mile stretch between here and Pebble Beach, and sea otters are often spotted in the 1,250-acre reserve's protected waters. Self-guiding trails are available, and guided ranger walks are scheduled daily in summer. A restored whaler's cabin, built in 1851 by a Chinese fisherman, now serves as an interpretive center. Artifacts and photographs tell about the area's history and one display highlights the location's various incarnations in movies. Dress warmly, and bring along binoculars, a camera, and maybe a picnic, too.

## 17-Mile Drive

*At Pebble Beach exit off Hwy. 1, betw. Carmel & Monterey, (800) 654-9300, (831) 647-7500; www.pebblebeach.com/17miledrive.html. Daily sunrise-sunset. $8.25/vehicle.*

A toll has been collected for this world-famous drive since 1901, when it was 25 cents, and the scenery—a combination of showplace homes, prestigious golf courses, and raw seascapes—is well worth the price of admission. Sights include the Restless Sea, where several ocean crosscurrents meet; Seal and Bird Rock, where herds of sea lions and flocks of shoreline birds congregate; the Pebble Beach Golf Links, one of three used during the annual AT&T Pebble Beach National Pro-Am tournament; and the landmark Lone Cypress, which clings to a jagged, barren rock base. Picnic facilities and short trails are found in several spots.

Consider splurging on lunch or dinner at one of the ocean-view restaurants at the elegant Inn at Spanish Bay (see page 128) or Lodge at Pebble Beach (see page 129). The gate fee will be reimbursed when the tab is paid.

## Shopping complexes

### • The Barnyard

*Hwy. 1/Carmel Valley Rd., (831) 624-8886; www.the barnyard.com. Daily 10-5:30, restaurants 8am-10pm.*

This collection of shops is worthy of a

browse. Don't miss **Succulent Gardens** *((831) 624-0426; www.succulentgardens.com.)* with its rare and unusual varieties of flowering cacti and succulents. **Thunderbird Bookshop Cafe** *((831) 624-1803, fax (831) 624-0549; www.thunder birdbooks.com. L daily, D Thur-F; $-$$. Highchairs, boosters, child portions.)*, a combination bookstore/restaurant, features dining among world-famous authors. Sandwiches and hamburgers are available at lunch, full meals at dinner, and coffee-and during the off hours.

### • Carmel Plaza
*Ocean Ave./Junipero St., (831) 624-0138, fax (831) 624-5286; www.carmelplaza.com. M-Sat 10-6, Sun 12-5.*

This upscale collection of noteworthy shops surrounds a courtyard filled with flowers.

## Tor House
*26304 Ocean View Ave., (831) 624-1813, fax (831) 624-3696; www.torhouse.org. Tours F-Sat 10-3, on the hr. $7; students $2-$4. Must be 12 or older. Reservations required.*

Poet Robinson Jeffers built this medieval-style house and tower retreat out of huge granite rocks hauled up from the beach below. He did much of the work himself. He was of the opinion that the manual labor cleared his mind and that, as he put it, his "fingers had the art to make stone love stone." All of his major works and most of his poetry were written while he lived with his wife and twin sons on this craggy knoll overlooking Carmel Bay.

### — WHERE TO STAY —

## Carmel River Inn
*Hwy. 1 at bridge, (800) 882-8142, (831) 624-1575, fax (831) 624-0290; www.carmelriverinn.com. 43 units; $-$$. Some kitchens & wood-burning fireplaces. Heated pool. Pets ok.*

Located on the outskirts of town on the banks of the Carmel River, this lodging complex stretches over 10 acres of gardens, forest, and meadow. Guests have a choice of motel rooms or individual one- or two-bedroom cottages, many of which have balconies or patios overlooking the river.

## Cobblestone Inn
*Junipero St./8th Ave., (800) 833-8836, (831) 625-5222, fax (831) 625-0478; www.foursisters.com/ inns/cobblestoneinn.html. 24 rooms; $$-$$$. Children*

under 2 free. All gas fireplaces. Afternoon snack, full breakfast. No smoking; no pets.

Located only 2 blocks from the main shopping street, this charming inn is filled with teddy bears awaiting guests in fanciful poses. Should one capture a heart, all are available for adoption by purchase. Spacious guest rooms are furnished with country-style pine pieces and iron-frame beds. Shutters provide privacy, and fireplaces constructed with large river rocks provide atmosphere and warmth. Refrigerators are stocked with complimentary cold drinks. In the morning all guests are greeted with a newspaper at the door, and breakfast can be enjoyed either outside on a sunny slate-and-brick-paved courtyard filled with flowers blooming in stone containers, or inside with the bears. Two bicycles are available for guests to borrow.

## Cypress Inn
*Lincoln St./7th Ave., (800) 443-7443, (831) 624-3871, fax (831) 624-8216; www.cypress-inn.com. 33 rooms; $$-$$$+. Some gas fireplaces. Evening snack, continental breakfast. Pets ok.*

Featuring a Moorish Mediterranean style of architecture, this inn dates from 1929 and is located right in town. Owned now by actress Doris Day along with several partners, its rooms are distinctively decorated and comfortable and a few have ocean views. All guest rooms have fresh flowers and are stocked with a decanter of cream sherry, a fruit basket, and bottled drinking water. A full **afternoon tea** *(Daily 2-3:45; $15. Reservations required.)* is served—with sandwiches, scones, and cookies—and is open to non-guests.

## Green Lantern Inn Bed & Breakfast
*7th Ave./Casanova St., (888) 414-4392, (831) 624-4392, fax (831) 624-9591; www.greenlanterninn.com. 19 rooms; $-$$$. Children under 10 free. Some fireplaces. Continental breakfast. No smoking.*

Operating as an inn since 1926, this pleasant group of rustic multi-unit cottages is located on a quiet side street just a few blocks from the village and 2 blocks from the beach.

## Highlands Inn, Park Hyatt Carmel
*120 Highlands Dr., off Hwy. 1, 4 mi. S of town, (800) 682-4811, (831) 620-1234, fax (831) 626-1574; www.highlandsinn.hyatt.com. 142 rooms; $$$-$$$+. Children under 18 free. Some kitchens & wood-burn-*

*ing fireplaces. Heated pool; 3 hot tubs; fitness room. 2 restaurants; room service. Small dogs ok.*

Located in a fragrant pine forest in the scenic Carmel Highlands, up a hill just past the town gas station with its old-time pump and two authentic red English phone booths, this inn was built on its spectacular cliff-side setting in 1916. Through the years it has been host to many famous guests, including the Beatles and two presidents—Kennedy and Ford. Luxurious contemporary-style guest rooms are designed for privacy, making it possible to just hole up and listen to the birds tweeting and the sounds of the not-too-distant surf. All have ocean views and are equipped with robes and even binoculars. Complimentary bikes are available to guests, and upon check-in children are given a special amenities bag filled with goodies.

At breakfast it's an expansive buffet and at lunch it's hamburgers and specials in the casual **California Market** *(B-L-D daily; $-$$. Highchairs, boosters, child menu.)*, where diners can enjoy a view of the rugged coastline from either the inside dining room or the outside balcony. The celebrated **Pacific's Edge** restaurant *((831) 622-5445. D daily; $$$. Highchairs, boosters. Reservations advised. Valet parking.)* also features a stunning view (plan to dine during daylight hours). One dinner enjoyed here included a perfectly prepared boiled artichoke appetizer served with sesame mayonnaise; ginger-carrot soup; a colorfully presented entree of grilled swordfish on grilled Maui onions topped with a chunky sauce of kalamata olives, oven-dried tomatoes, and parsley; and a classic crème brulee chosen from an array of elegant desserts.

## The Inn at Spanish Bay

*2700 17-Mile Drive, in Pebble Beach, (800) 654-9300, (831) 647-7500, fax (831) 644-7955; www.pebble beach.com. 270 rooms; $$$+. All gas fireplaces. Heated pool; hot tub; sauna; fitness room; health spa; 8 tennis courts (2 with night lights); 18-hole golf course. 3 restaurants; room service. No smoking; no pets.*

Nestled oceanfront beside a protected marine sanctuary, this luxury resort is designed to complement its spectacular surroundings. The decor blends in with the misty wash of natural colors seen outside, and most rooms have a patio or balcony. Bicycle rentals, a shuttle to Carmel and Monterey destinations, and milk

and cookies at bedtime can all be arranged. A full-time Nature Concierge is on the staff, as is a talented floral arranger, and the **Ansel Adams Gallery** *(M-F 10-6.)* operates as one of the resort's shops. The Scottish-style **Links at Spanish Bay** golf course—which Jack Nicklaus considers "possibly the best in the world" and about which Tom Watson enthuses, "Spanish Bay is so much like Scotland, you can almost hear the bagpipes"—surrounds the resort.

**Roys' at Pebble Beach** *((831) 647-7423, fax (831) 644-7957. B-L-D daily; $$. Highchairs, boosters, child menu.)* offers spectacular ocean views across the dunes along with the celebrated, strikingly colorful Euro-Asian cuisine of Hawaii-based chef Roy Yamaguchi. Noteworthy on the lunch menu are tasty spring rolls in a chili-plum sauce and a well-seasoned Thai chicken salad with minty dressing. Fresh local seafood and designer pizzas are also options, as are gorgeous, killer desserts.

## Lamp Lighter Inn

*Ocean Ave./Camino Real, (831) 624-7372; www.carmellamplighter.com. 9 units; $$-$$$. Children under 1 free. Some kitchens; 1 wood-burning fireplace. Continental breakfast. No smoking.*

Conveniently located between the village and the ocean, this enclave has both charming rooms and gingerbread-style cottages. It very well might fulfill guest's fairy tale fantasies. Several of the cozy, comfortable cottages accommodate families; the Hansel and Gretel has a special sleeping loft for kids. The Blue Bird Room has a cathedral ceiling of age-patinaed redwood and a picture window looking into a large oak tree. Children especially enjoy finding all 17 elves in the Elves Garden. Accommodations in an annex, located 1 block closer to the beach, are a little less expensive and a lot less interesting; however, several have ocean views.

## La Playa Hotel & Cottages-by-the-Sea

*Camino Real/8th Ave., (800) 582-8900, (831) 624-6476, fax (831) 624-7966; www.laplayahotel.com. 80 units; $$-$$$+. Children under 12 free. Some kitchens & fireplaces. Heated pool. Restaurant; room service. No pets.*

This luxury Mediterranean-style hotel is conveniently located just 2 blocks from the beach and 4 blocks from town. Taking up an entire square block, it is the largest and the only full-service resort hotel in Carmel. Guest room beds have rustic carved headboards sporting the hotel's mermaid motif, and the beautifully maintained gardens are abloom with colorful flowers year-round. A group of charming, spacious cottages situated a block closer to the ocean are also available.

The casual **Terrace Grill** (B-L-D daily; $$-$$$.) features an elaborate Sunday brunch with a buffet of fresh fruits and pastries, Belgian waffles, and made-to-order omelettes. Diners can also order from a menu, and a perfect spicy Bloody Mary is made at the bar. The restaurant's namesake terrace has both ocean and garden views and is covered overhead and heated, so al fresco dining can be enjoyed regardless of the weather.

## Lincoln Green Inn
Carmelo St./15th Ave., (800) 262-1262, (831) 624-7738, fax (831) 626-1243; www.vagabondshouseinn.com/cottages.html. 4 units; $$. Some kitchens; all gas fireplaces. Pets ok.

Located on the outskirts of town, just a few blocks from where the Carmel River flows into the ocean, this cluster of comfortable English housekeeping cottages features living rooms with cathedral-beamed ceilings and stone fireplaces.

## The Lodge at Pebble Beach
On 17-Mile Drive, in Pebble Beach, (800) 654-9300, (831) 647-7500, fax (831) 626-3725; www.pebblebeach.com. 161 rooms; $$$+. All fireplaces. Heated pool; child wading pool; sauna; 14 tennis courts. 3 restaurants; room service. Pets ok.

Complete luxury and the best sporting facilities await guests here. Golfers can enjoy playing some of the best courses in the country, and horse rentals and equestrian trails, jogging and hiking trails, and a par course are nearby.

Non-guests are welcome to stop in and enjoy the spectacular ocean view here over a drink or meal. Try the **Club XIX** ((831) 625-8519. L-D daily; $$-$$$. Reservations advised.) at lunch, when diners can sit on a terrace overlooking both the 18th hole and the ocean while enjoying fare as casual as their dress—a Cobb salad, a club sandwich. Dinner is more elegant, with diners seated in the plushly appointed dining room and feasting on refined dishes such as

cassoulet of lobster and duck confit or boneless quail stuffed with sweetbreads and morels.

## Mission Ranch
26270 Dolores St./Rio Rd., (800) 538-8221, (831) 624-6436, fax (831) 626-4163; www.missionranch carmel.com. 31 rooms; $$-$$$. Some gas fireplaces. Fitness room; 6 clay tennis courts. Continental breakfast; restaurant. No smoking; no pets.

Owned by actor Clint Eastwood, who has invested a fistful of dollars in furnishings, this former dairy farm is located near the Carmel Mission. It has operated as a lodging facility since 1937. Special accommodation choices include roomy cottages that work well for families, the 1857 Victorian-style Martin Family Farmhouse with B&B-style rooms, and the 1852 Bunkhouse cottage; simpler rooms are also available. Eastwood fans take note: The 19th-century pot-belly stove that appeared in *Unforgiven* is found in the inn's restaurant, which is situated in the ranch's former creamery.

## Normandy Inn
Ocean Ave./Monte Verde St., (800) 343-3825, (831) 624-3825, fax (831) 624-4614; www.normandyinn carmel.com. 48 units; $-$$$+. Children free. Some kitchens & wood-burning fireplaces. Heated pool (unavail. Jan-Mar). Afternoon sherry, continental breakfast. No smoking; no pets.

Conveniently located on the town's main shopping street and just 4 blocks from the ocean, this inn features an attractive half-beamed, Normandy-style architecture and has several large cottages. The comfortably appointed rooms are decorated in French country style and have featherbeds, and the pool is invitingly secluded.

## Pine Inn
Ocean Ave./Monte Verde St., (800) 228-3851, (831) 624-3851, fax (831) 624-3030; www.pine-inn.com. 49 rooms; $$-$$$. Children under 18 free. 1 gas fireplace. Restaurant; room service. No smoking; no pets.

This inn, which opened in 1889, is the oldest in town. It is decorated in elegant Victorian style and conveniently located in the center of town.

## San Antonio House
San Antonio St./7th Ave., (800) 313-7770, (831) 624-4334, fax (831) 624-4935; www.carmelgardencourt inn.com. 5 rooms; $$-$$$. Unsuitable for children under 12. All gas fireplaces. Continental breakfast. No smoking; no pets.

This attractive guesthouse offers large rooms, a lovely garden, and a location in a quiet residential area just 1 block from the beach. One room has a private patio, another its own dollhouse, and a breakfast tray is brought to each room in the morning.

## Sea View Inn
Camino Real/12th Ave., (831) 624-8778, fax (831) 625-5901; www.seaviewinncarmel.com. 8 rooms; $-$$. Unsuitable for children under 12. No TVs; some shared baths. Afternoon & evening snack, continental breakfast. No smoking.

Located 3 blocks from the beach, this converted Victorian home offers pleasantly appointed rooms. The most requested guest room features a cozy canopy bed.

## The Stonehouse Inn
8th Ave./Monte Verde St., (877) 748-6618, (831) 624-4569; www.carmelstonehouse.com. 6 rooms; $$-$$$. Unsuitable for children under 12. Some shared baths. Afternoon snack, full breakfast. No smoking.

Built by local Indians in 1906, this rustic stone country house is close to the village. The original owner often entertained well-known artists and writers, and the antique-furnished rooms are now named in honor of some of those guests.

## Vagabond's House Inn Bed and Breakfast
4th Ave./Dolores St., (800) 262-1262, (831) 624-7738, fax (831) 626-1243; www.vagabondshouseinn.com. 11 rooms; $$-$$$. Unsuitable for children under 12. Some kitchens & wood-burning & gas fireplaces. Continental breakfast. Pets ok.

This rustic English Tudor-style building features cozily furnished rooms that open off a quiet, flower-bedecked courtyard.

— WHERE TO EAT —

## Carmel Bakery
Ocean Ave./Lincoln St., (831) 626-8885. Sun-Thur 6:30am-7pm, F-Sat to 9.

Apricot log pastries, wild blueberry scones, and focaccia with spicy pepper topping are just a few of the delicacies available at this popular bakery. Caramel apples are also on the menu. Pastries and drinks can be enjoyed on site or while walking the boutique-laden streets.

## Cottage of Sweets
Ocean Ave./Lincoln St., (831) 624-5170, fax (831) 620-0106; www.cottageofsweets.com. M-Thur 10-7, F-Sun 10-8.

Among the sweet surprises in this charming candy cottage are imported chocolates, diet candy, gourmet jelly beans, taffy, and 45 kinds of licorice

## Em Le's
Dolores St./5th Ave., (831) 625-6780, fax (831) 625-0563; www.emles.com. B-L-D daily; $. 1 highchair, boosters.

Football broadcaster John Madden is part owner of this cozy, casual spot touted as the town's only vintage soda fountain. Among the large variety of breakfast items are buttermilk waffles, in a choice of light or dark bake, and wild blueberry pancakes. The basic all-American cuisine includes fried chicken, meatloaf, mashed potatoes, and apple pie. Pleasant views of sidewalk traffic and counter seating add to the low-key Carmel charm.

## The Forge in the Forest
5th Ave./Junipero St., (831) 624-2233, fax (831) 624-1102; www.forgeintheforest.com. L M-Sat, D daily, SunBr; $-$$. Highchairs, child menu. Reservations advised.

This popular employee-owned spot operates in a warren of spaces that include a heated outdoor patio. Its name is that of the blacksmith shop that once was in this same space, and an old general store from the same era has been converted into a dining room. The menu is eclectic—fresh seafood, pasta, pizza, salads, sandwiches—and the hours are late, making it popular with night owls.

## Jack London's Bar & Grill
Dolores St./5th Ave., (831) 624-2336, fax (831) 626-0941; www.jacklondonsgrill.com. L-D daily, SunBr; $-$$. Highchairs, boosters.

Even locals come here to enjoy the excellent bar drinks and cozy bistro atmosphere. Kids are welcome and can order fancy non-alcoholic drinks. American and Mexican menu items include pizzas, hamburgers, fajitas, salads, soups, and steaks.

### La Boheme
*Dolores St./7th Ave., (831) 624-7500, fax (831) 624-6539; www.laboheme.com. D daily; $$. Closed part of Dec or Jan. 1 booster, child portions. No reservations.*

Cozy and colorfully decorated, and featuring an overhanging indoor roof built by a retired French race car driver, this charming petite cafe is outrageously romantic. Just one three-course fixed-price dinner is served each evening, plus one vegetarian entree option. With no menu choices to fret over, diners are free to concentrate on each other. The French and Italian country-style dishes are served informal family-style. One dinner enjoyed here began with a large, crisp salad accented with olives and substantial slices of ham, salami, and cheese. Then came a perfectly seasoned cream of broccoli soup, followed by a main course of pork loin in a cream sauce flavored with juniper berries. At additional cost, strawberries Romanoff made a refreshing, light dessert. The soup and entree change each evening, so it is a good idea to call ahead for the night's menu.

### Patisserie Boissiere Cafe & Restaurant
*Mission St./Ocean Ave., (831) 624-5008. L daily, D W-Sun; $$. Reservations advised at D.*

The menu at this elegant little gem offers housemade soups as well as more substantial entrees. Though it would be hard to do so, don't overlook the pastries and desserts—lemon cheesecake, chocolate whiskey cake, zabaglione, and plenty more.

### Piatti
*6th Ave./Junipero St., (831) 625-1766, fax (831) 625-1833; www.piatti.com. L-D daily.*

For description, see page 386.

### Rocky Point Restaurant
*On Hwy. 1, 12 mi. S of town, (831) 624-2933, fax (831) 624-4091; www.rocky-point.com. B-L-D daily; $$-$$$. Highchairs, boosters, child portions. Reservations advised.*

Take a scenic drive down the coast toward Big Sur, stopping here to enjoy the spectacular view along with a multi-course charcoal-broiled steak or fresh seafood dinner. Sandwiches and hamburgers are on the lunch menu, making it a relative bargain.

### The Tuck Box
*Dolores St./Ocean Ave., (831) 624-6365, fax (831) 624-5079; www.tuckbox.com. B-L-afternoon tea daily; $. Boosters. No reservations. No cards.*

Featuring fairy-tale architecture and verily reeking of quaintness, this tiny English-style tearoom can be quite difficult to get seated in. If ever it is without a long line in front, go! Additional seating is available on a tiny outdoor patio. A limited breakfast menu offers simple egg items served with delightful fresh scones and a choice of either homemade olallieberry preserves or orange marmalade. At lunch, sandwiches, salads, and omelettes are available along with Welsh rarebit. Afternoon tea features scones, pies, and, of course, plenty of hot English tea.

Across the street, tiny **Picadilly Park** invites relaxing contemplation with its benches, flower garden, and goldfish pond.

### Village Corner
*Dolores St./6th Ave., (831) 624-3588, fax (831) 622-8855; www.carmelsbest.com. B-L-D daily; $-$$. Highchairs, boosters, booths, child menu. Reservations advised.*

The large patio here is heated year-round and provides the chance to relax and watch the rest of the town stroll by. The Mediterranean bistro menu offers bruschetta and deep-fried local calamari for appetizers. Entrees include several pastas as well as a delicious Cajun-style blackened salmon and a dramatic paella for two. Local wines pair perfectly.

# Carmel Valley

### – A LITTLE BACKGROUND –

Reliably sunny and peaceful, Carmel Valley is often overlooked by visitors to the Monterey Peninsula. That's a shame, because it is a wonderful place to relax and is only a few miles inland from Carmel. Before World War II, this area was popular with the rich and famous, who came here to hunt boar and play polo. Now lodgings, restaurants, and shops dot Highway 16/Carmel Valley Road along its 15-mile stretch east into the hub of town.

### – VISITOR INFORMATION –

## Carmel Valley Chamber of Commerce
*13 W. Carmel Valley Rd., (831) 659-4000, fax (831) 659-8415; www.carmelvalleychamber.com.*

### – WHAT TO DO –

## Bernardus Winery
*5 W. Carmel Valley Rd., 13 mi. from Hwy. 1, (800) 223-2533, (831) 659-1900, fax (831) 659-1676; www.bernardus.com. Tasting daily 11-5.*

The father of owner Ben (Bernardus) Pon is the designer of the Volkswagen bus and was the person who first exported the Beetle to the U.S. Ben himself has been a professional race car driver for Porsche and represented Holland in skeet shooting at the 1972 Olympics. With such an accomplished background, it isn't surprising that he would make a success of his upstart winery, which makes wines in the old French Bordeaux and Burgundian styles and is known for its Chardonnay and Sauvignon Blanc.

The luxurious **Bernardus Lodge** *(415 Carmel Valley Rd., (831) 658-3400. $$$+. Unsuitable for young children. Restaurant. No smoking.)* adjoins. Fine dining and a full service spa are among the amenities.

## Château Julien Wine Estate
*8940 Carmel Valley Rd., 5 mi. from Hwy. 1, (831) 624-2600, fax (831) 624-6138; www.chateaujulien.com. Tasting M-F 8-5, Sat-Sun 11-5; tours by appt.: M-F at 10:30 & 2:30, Sat-Sun at 12:30 & 2:30.*

Styled after an actual château located on the French-Swiss border, this castle-like structure has no formal tasting bar. Tasters gather informally around a large table in the middle of a high-ceilinged room. While their parents are enjoying an informal tasting of Chardonnays and Merlots—the two varietals this winery is noted for—children can partake of juice and crackers. A garden patio invites picnicking.

## Garland Ranch Regional Park
*On Carmel Valley Rd., 8.6 mi. from Hwy. 1, (831) 659-4488, fax (831) 659-5902; www.mprpd.org/parks/garland.html. Daily sunrise-sunset. Free.*

Running along the banks of the Carmel River, this park boasts more than 5,000 acres. The 1.4-mile Lupine Loop Trail provides an easy nature walk; more self-guided hiking trails lead up into the mountains. This park is home to the very spot in the Carmel River where the boys caught frogs in Steinbeck's *Cannery Row.* Though frog collecting is not permitted, listening to them is. A Visitors Center provides orientation and maps.

### – WHERE TO STAY –

## Carmel Valley Ranch
*One Old Ranch Rd., 6 mi. from Hwy. 1, (800) 4-CARMEL, (831) 625-9500, fax (831) 624-2858; www.wyndham.com. 144 rooms; $$-$$$+. Children under 17 free. All wood-burning fireplaces. 2 heated pools; hot tub; sauna; fitness room; 12 tennis courts (2 clay); 18-hole golf course. 3 restaurants; room service.*

Built in an elegant ranch-style architecture featuring local stone and oak, this luxurious all-suite resort is situated on 1,700 scenic acres surrounded by rolling hills. It is the only resort on the Monterey Peninsula with a guarded gate. Each suite features cathedral ceilings and has a large private deck, two TVs, and three two-line phones; some have decks with private outdoor hot tubs.

**The Oaks** restaurant *(B-L-D daily, SunBr. Highchairs. Reservations advised.)* has a stunning view of the valley.

## Quail Lodge Resort & Golf Club
*8205 Valley Greens Dr., 3 mi. from Hwy. 1, (888) 828-8787, (831) 624-2888, fax (831) 624-3726; www.quail lodge.com. 100 units; $$$-$$$+. Children under 18 free. Some gas fireplaces. 2 pools (1 heated); hot tub; health spa; 4 tennis courts; 18-hole golf course. Continental breakfast; 3 restaurants; room service. No smoking; pets ok.*

These lakeside cottages are situated on 850 acres of golf fairways, meadows, and lakes that were once the site of the Carmel Valley Dairy. Guests can use hiking trails and visit 11 lakes that are also wildlife sanctuaries. Attracting a classy crowd, the resort's parking lot has been seen holding a DeLorean and several Ferraris at the same time.

The dressy **Covey Restaurant** *(D daily; $$$. Highchairs, boosters, booths. Reservations advised.)* overlooks a lake and offers refined European cuisine with a California touch.

The **Carmel TomatoFest** *((888) 989-8171, (831) 625-6041, fax (831) 625-2818; www.tom ato fest.com. $75-$85, under 12 free.),* featuring a tasting of hundreds of varieties and a buffet of tomato dishes, occurs here each September.

## Tassajara Zen Mountain Center

*39171 Tassajara Rd., 40 mi. from Hwy. 1. Reservations: (415) 865-1899 (M-F 9-12:30 & 1:30-4); www.sfzc.org/ zmcindex.htm. 29 units; $$-$$$; rate includes 3 veg- etarian meals. Closed Sept-Apr. Child rates; number of children permitted is controlled. No TVs; some fire- places; some shared baths. Hot springs pool; steam rooms. No smoking. Day use: (831) 659-2229; $25, children $12; reservations essential.*

Owned by the San Francisco Zen Center, this traditional Zen Buddhist monastery is America's oldest. Located deep in the Ventana Wilderness in the Los Padres National Forest, it is home to 50 male and female monks. Getting there requires a 14-mile drive down a steep dirt road (a four-wheel-drive or stick shift is strongly advised), but overnight guests have the option of arranging a ride in on a four-wheel- drive "stage." The famous hot mineral springs are semi-enclosed in a Japanese-style bathhouse. Men's and women's baths and steam rooms are separate, and swimsuits are optional; mixed bathing is permitted after dinner. More activi- ties include hiking, river wading, and picnick- ing. Guests stay in simple wood or stone cabins with no electricity. Kerosene lamps provide lighting, and everyone shares one phone. This is *not* a place to sleep in—bells go off at 5:30 a.m. to announce meditation time for any guests who want to participate. Getting a reservation can be difficult; call early. Reservations open on April 3 for overnight stays and on April 25 for day visits. Day guests must bring their own towels and food.

## — WHERE TO EAT —

### Katy 'n Harry's Wagon Wheel Coffee Shop

*Hwy. 16/Valley Greens Dr., in Valley Hills Shopping Center, 3 mi. from Hwy. 1, (831) 624-8878. B-L daily; $. No reservations. No cards.*

Extremely popular with locals, this place is usually packed. Tables are tiny, but portions are generous. Breakfast is the busiest meal and is served until the 2 p.m. closing time. The menu includes omelettes, eggs Benedict, oatmeal, assorted styles of pancakes (don't miss the owner's favorite—raspberry), and fresh- squeezed orange juice. A late breakfast permits chowing-down more than enough grub to satisfy a tummy until dinner. The hamburgers, French fries, and homemade beans are also reputed to be very good.

# Big Sur

## — A LITTLE BACKGROUND —

*Whoever settles here hopes that he will be the last invader.*

— Henry Miller, *Big Sur and the Oranges of Hieronymus Bosch*

Big Sur is such a special place that many people who have been here don't feel generous about sharing it. However, facilities are so limited that it's hard to imagine the area getting overrun with tourists. Except, perhaps, in the thick of summer.

The town of Big Sur seems to have no cen- ter. At the southern end of the coast redwoods range, it stretches along Highway 1 for 6 miles offering a string of amenities. Then, as one con- tinues driving south, the highway begins a 90- mile stretch of some of the most spectacular scenery in the U.S.

Note that the river's bottom here is rocky. Bring along waterproof shoes for wading.

## — VISITOR INFORMATION —

### Big Sur Chamber of Commerce

*P.O. Box 87, Big Sur 93920, (831) 667-2100; www.bigsurcalifornia.org.*

### Monterey County Convention & Visitors Bureau

See page 114.

— GETTING THERE —

Located approximately 25 miles south of the Monterey Peninsula.

## — WHAT TO DO —

Big Sur is so non-commercial that there is little to list in this section. Visitors can look forward to relaxing, swimming in the river, picnicking on the beach, or taking a hike through the woods. Look out for poison oak, and bring along a good book.

### Andrew Molera State Park
*On Hwy. 1, (831) 667-2315; www.parks.ca.gov. Daily sunrise-sunset. $7/vehicle.*

Located near the photogenic Bixby Bridge, this beach park has plenty of hiking trails. Several are short and easy: The flat, 2-mile-round-trip Bluffs Trail follows the ocean to a promontory, and the more challenging 5-mile-round-trip Bobcat Trail follows the Big Sur River through dense redwoods. Walk-in campsites are available.

Operating within the park, **Molera Horseback Tours** *((800) 942-5486, (831) 625-5486, fax (831) 624-4789; www.molerahorse backtours.com. Schedule varies; closed Dec-Mar. $25+. Must be 6 or older. Reservations advised.)* takes riders to the beach.

### Henry Miller Library
*On Hwy. 1, just S of Nepenthe restaurant, (831) 667-2574, same fax; www.henrymiller.org. Thur-Sun 11-6; also F in summer. Free*

Henry Miller lived in Big Sur for 18 years. The former home of his good friend, Emil White, has been turned into a shrine honoring the late artist and author. It is filled with memorabilia, photos, and letters, and the bathroom features erotic tiles by Ephraim Doner. The library also serves as a community art center and bookstore, and picnicking on the redwood-sheltered lawn is encouraged. Special events often occur on weekends.

### Pfeiffer Beach
*At end of Sycamore Canyon Rd., (831) 667-2315. $5/vehicle.*

Watch for unmarked Sycamore Canyon Road on the west side of Highway 1. This narrow road begins about 1.7 miles south of Fernwood Resort and winds for 2 lovely miles to a beach parking lot. The only easily accessible public beach in the area, it features striking rock formations and arches carved out by the rough surf. Visitors can wade in a stream that meanders through the sandy beach but should stay out of the turbulent ocean. If it all looks vaguely familiar, it might be because this is where Elizabeth Taylor and Richard Burton acted out some love scenes in *The Sandpiper*.

### Pfeiffer Big Sur State Park
*On Hwy. 1, (831) 667-2315; www.parks.ca.gov. Daily sunrise-sunset. $5/vehicle.*

Activities at this 821-acre park include hiking (among the many trails is a half-mile nature trail), river swimming, and ranger-led nature walks and campfires, and an open meadow is perfect for playing baseball or throwing a Frisbee. Facilities include picnic tables, a restaurant, and a store. Campsites are available.

### Point Sur State Historic Park
*Off Hwy. 1, 19 mi. S of Carmel, (831) 625-4419; www.parks.ca.gov. Schedule varies. $5, 13-18 $3, 5-12 $2.*

Built in 1889, the **Point Sur Lightstation** is the center of this park. It is open for strenuous 3-hour guided tours that include a ¹/₂-mile hike and a 300-foot climb. Tours are not recommended for small children. Because parking is limited, only the first 40 people to arrive can be accommodated. No pets, strollers, or picnicking permitted.

## — WHERE TO STAY —

### Big Sur Lodge
*Off Hwy. 1, (800) 4-BIG-SUR, (831) 667-3100, same fax; www.bigsurlodge.com. 61 rooms; $-$$$. Children stay free. No TVs; some kitchens & fireplaces. Heated pool. Restaurant. No pets.*

Situated within Pfeiffer-Big Sur State Park (guests have complimentary access), this complex has many spacious two-bedroom motel units. Each has a private deck or porch. They are distributed throughout the spacious, grassy grounds, where deer are often seen grazing; those close to the pleasant pool area seem most desirable. In season, a casual, moderately priced restaurant serves meals all day.

## Esalen Institute

*55000 Hwy. 1, (831) 667-3000, fax (831) 667-2724; www.esalen.org. $$-$$$+. Heated pool; 7 hot tubs. No smoking; no pets.*

Located on a breathtaking crest above the ocean, this legendary educational facility offers lodging and dining in conjunction with its workshops. Accommodations range from rustic loft rooms to dorm-style rooms. Space is open to the general public when the facility is under-booked. (Then a bed space runs $90 to $150 per person per day and includes three meals; family rates are available. Call for reservations no earlier than 5 days before date of desired visit.) Some will want to be forewarned, others informed, that nude bathing is de rigueur in the swimming pool and mineral spring-fed hot tubs in the 2-story cliff-top bathhouse. Non-guests can access the **pools** only from 1 to 3 a.m. *($20/person. Reservations required.)*—unless a massage is booked, in which case use of the baths is included. Self-exploration workshops include meditation, yoga, vision improvement, massage, and more. Call for a copy of the workshop catalogue.

## New Camaldoli Hermitage

*62475 Hwy. 1, 25 mi. S of town, in Lucia, 2 mi. off Hwy. 1, (831) 667-2456, fax (831) 667-0209; www.con templation.com. 9 rooms; $60-70 donation/person. Includes 3 simple vegetarian meals.*

Founded in 1958 by three Benedictine monks from Camaldoli, Italy, this quiet 800-acre wildlife and wilderness preserve allows guests to meditate, read, rest, and pray. Solitary, silent, non-directed retreats in the Catholic tradition of the Benedictine order are open to people of all faiths. Chapel services are available for those who wish to participate, and each of the modest single-occupancy rooms has a private garden overlooking the ocean. Five remote trailers are also an option.

A **gift shop** *((800) 826-3740, fax (831) 667-0813. Daily 8:30-11 & 1:15-5.)* sells pottery and religious items as well as brandy-dipped fruitcake and date-nut cake made by the 22 resident Camaldolese monks.

## Ripplewood Resort

*On Hwy. 1, (831) 667-2242; www.ripplewood resort.com. 16 cabins; $-$$. Children under 12 free. No TVs; some kitchens & wood-burning fireplaces.*

*Restaurant. No smoking; no pets.*

Rustic, pleasantly decorated redwood cabins are located both above and below the highway. The ones below are in a dense, dark grove of redwoods just a stone's throw from the Big Sur River. A cafe serves breakfast and lunch.

## Ventana Inn & Spa

*On Hwy. 1, (800) 628-6500, (831) 667-2331, fax (831) 667-0573; www.ventanainn.com. 59 rooms; $$$+. Unsuitable for children under 18. Most wood-burning fireplaces. 2 heated pools; hot tub; sauna; health spa; fitness room. Afternoon snack, continental breakfast; restaurant.*

The striking, clean-lined, award-winning architecture of this serene resort seems to fit in perfectly with its spectacular, secluded location in the hills 1,200 feet above the ocean. It is a choice spot for a restive, revitalizing, and hedonistic retreat. Rooms lined in unfinished redwood are distributed among 12 buildings. All have either a private balcony or patio and either an ocean or mountain view, and some have private hot tubs. Clothing is optional in the Japanese hot baths and on the sun decks.

Known for its accomplished California-style cuisine, **Cielo** *(L-D daily. Highchairs, boosters.)* has seating both in a cedar-paneled dining room with mountain and ocean views and out on a large terrace with a panoramic ocean view.

## Deetjen's Big Sur Inn

*48865 Hwy. 1, (831) 667-2378; www.deetjens.com.*
*B-D daily; $-$$$. Highchairs, boosters, child portions.*
*Reservations advised for D.*

For aesthetic pleasure it's hard to beat lingering over a hearty breakfast in this Norwegian-style inn, especially when it's raining outside and the table is positioned in front of the fireplace. The mellow, rustic, and informal setting provides a complementary background to the fresh, simple, and wholesome foods produced by its kitchen. Dinner by candlelight is more expensive and sedate, and children don't fit in as well then.

Rustic, casual **lodging** *((831) 667-2377, fax (831) 667-0466. 20 units; $-$$. No TVs; some wood-burning fireplaces & stoves; some shared baths. No smoking; no pets.)* is available in rooms and cabins built of local redwood and situated comfortably amid a forest of redwoods and firs. They usually book up far in advance.

## Nepenthe

*On Hwy. 1, (831) 667-2345, fax (831) 667-2394;*
*www.nepenthebigsur.com. L-D daily; $$. Highchairs.*
*No reservations.*

Located at the top of a cliff 808 feet above the ocean and offering a breathtaking view of the coastline, this famous restaurant was designed by a student of Frank Lloyd Wright. It is an elaboration of a cabin that Orson Welles originally built as a retreat for Rita Hayworth and himself. When the weather is mild, dine outside on a casual terrace. The menu features simple foods such as steak, fresh seafood, roasted chicken, housemade soup, and a very good hamburger. Or stop in at the bar for a drink. Overall, this restaurant seems to be living up to the promise of its name, which refers to a mythical Egyptian drug that induced forgetfulness and the surcease of sorrow.

**Café Kevah** *((831) 667-2345. Closed Jan-Feb.)*, located downstairs, serves moderately-priced brunch and lunch items on a patio with the same striking view. On a warm afternoon it is a choice spot to enjoy a refreshing cold drink and tasty pastry.

The classy **Phoenix** gift shop *((831) 667-2347, fax (831) 667-2826. Daily 10:30-7.)* provides pleasant browsing before or after dining.

# San Simeon

## San Simeon Chamber of Commerce

*250 San Simeon Dr. #3A, (800) 342-5613, (805) 927-3500, fax (805) 927-6453; www.sansimeonsbest.com.*

Located approximately 75 miles south of Big Sur.

For a more leisurely trip, try the train package offered by **Key Holidays** *((800) 783-0783, (925) 945-8938), fax (925) 256-7597; www.keyholidays.com.)*. Via rail is the way guests traveled to the castle in its heyday. Invitations then always included train tickets. Today travelers can still relax and enjoy the scenery while Amtrak's Coast Starlight transports them to San Luis Obispo. From there, after seeing the local sights, they take a bus tour of the coast and overnight in Morro Bay. The next day participants are bused to the famed castle for a guided tour, then down scenic Highway 1 for a stop in the village of Cambria, and then back to San Luis Obispo for the return train ride. The package does not include meals. Rates vary, and discounts are available for children.

## Hearst Castle™

*(805) 927-2020; www.hearstcastle.org. $20-24, 6-17 $10-$12; night tour $30/$15. Reservations advised, (800) 444-4445; tickets can also be purchased at the Visitor Center after 8 a.m. on day of tour.*

Located in the small town of San Simeon on the wind-blown coast south of Big Sur, this spectacular mansion is perched atop La Cuesta Encantada (The Enchanted Hill™). It was designed by architect Julia Morgan and is filled with art treasures and antiques gathered by newspaper czar William Randolph Hearst from all over the world in the early part of the century. The castle took 28 years to build. Though unfinished, the estate contains 56 bedrooms, 102 bathrooms, 19 sitting rooms, a kitchen, a movie theater, 2 libraries, a billiard room, a dining hall, and an assembly hall! Colorful vines and plants grace the lovely gardens, and wild zebras, tahr goats, and sambar deer graze the

hillsides—remnants of the private zoo that once included lions, monkeys, and a polar bear.

Before 1958, visitors could get no closer than was permitted by a coin-operated telescope located on the road below. Now maintained by the State of California Department of Parks and Recreation as an Historical Monument, the castle is open to the public. Five tours are available; all include a scenic bus ride up to the castle.

• **Tour 1** is suggested for a first visit and includes gardens, pools, a guesthouse, and the ground floor of the main house—Casa Grande.

• **Tour 2** covers the upper floors of the main house, including Mr. Hearst's private suite, the libraries, a guest duplex, the kitchen, and the pools.

• **Tour 3** covers the 36-room guest wing and includes the pools and a guesthouse.

• **Tour 4** stresses the gardens. It includes the elegant 19-room Casa del Mar guesthouse, the wine cellar, and the pools. This tour is given only April through October.

• **Tour 5** is the Evening Tour. It combines high-lights of the daytime tours and additionally features volunteers in period dress, bringing the magnificent surroundings to life. This tour is given only on Friday and Saturday evenings in spring and fall.

During the entire month of December, the castle and guesthouses are lighted and deco-rated in splendid fashion for the Christmas holidays—just as they were when Mr. Hearst lived here.

Children under 6 are free only if they sit on their parent's lap during the bus ride. Tours require walking about ½ mile and climbing approximately 150 to 400 steps; comfortable shoes are advised. Baby strollers are not permit-ted. Tours take approximately 2 hours. Picnic tables and a snack bar are available near the Visitor Center.

### William Randolph Hearst Memorial State Beach

*(805) 927-2020; www.parks.ca.gov. Daily dawn-dusk. $3/vehicle.*

In addition to providing a very nice swim-ming beach, this park has picnic tables, barbe-cue grills, and a 640-foot-long fishing pier. No license is required to fish from the pier, and equipment rentals are available.

— **WHERE TO STAY** —

### Best Western Cavalier Oceanfront Resort

*9415 Hearst Dr., (800) 826-8168, (805) 927-4688, fax (805) 927-6472; www.cavalierresort.com. 90 rooms; $-$$$. Children free. Some wood-burning fireplaces. 2 heated pools; hot tub; fitness room. Restaurant; room service. Pets ok.*

The only ocean-front resort in San Simeon, this contemporary-style resort motel has over 900 feet of ocean frontage. Many rooms have expansive ocean views, and some also have private patios. Each night at sunset firepits are lit on the beach, and chairs are pro-vided for guests to relax in.

— **WHERE TO EAT** —

### Sebastian's General Store/Patio Cafe

*422 San Simeon Rd., (805) 927-4217. Store: daily 8:30-5:30. Cafe: B-L daily; $; closed Nov-Mar; no reservations; no cards.*

Built in 1852 and moved to its present location in 1878, this store is now a State

Historical Landmark. Inexpensive short-order items are served in the outdoor cafe. In winter, watch for monarch butterflies congregating in the adjacent eucalyptus and cypress trees.

# Cambria

## — A LITTLE BACKGROUND —

In this town filled with rose-covered cottages and Victorian storefronts, many residents are Brits. This is reflected in street names like Cornwall, Canterbury, and Cambridge. Note that the preferred pronunciation of Cambria is with a short "a," as in "Camelot.")

## — VISITOR INFORMATION —

### Cambria Chamber of Commerce
*767 Main St., Cambria, (805) 927-3624, fax (805) 927-9426; www.cambriachamber.org.*

## — GETTING THERE —

Located 5 miles south of San Simeon.

## — WHAT TO DO —

### The Pewter Plough Playhouse
*824 Main St., (805) 927-3877, fax (805) 927-1023; www.pewterploughplayhouse.com. Performances F-Sat at 8, some Sun at 3. $15, 60+ $13. Reservations advised.*

Stage plays are presented year-round in this intimate theater. Free dramatic readings occur on the first Wednesday evening of each month at 7, and jazz is sometimes presented in the lounge on Sunday evening from 7 to 11 p.m.

### The Soldier Gallery
*789 Main St., (805) 927-3804, fax (805) 927-0164; www.soldiergallery.com. Daily 10-5.*

An ideal souvenir stop, this shop offers everything from an inexpensive unpainted pewter animal to a dearly priced and elaborately painted Alice in Wonderland chess set. Assorted sizes and styles of pewter soldiers from various wars and nations are also for sale.

## — WHERE TO STAY —

### Bluebird Inn
*1880 Main St., (800) 552-5434, (805) 927-4634, fax (805) 927-5215; www.bluebirdmotel.com. 37 rooms; $-$$. Children under 6 free. Some gas fireplaces. No pets.*

Situated by Santa Rosa Creek and within easy walking range of the village, this attractive motel surrounds a landmark mansion dating from 1880. Many rooms are creek-side, with private balconies or patios, and one spacious two-bedroom family suite is available.

### The Blue Whale Inn
*6736 Moonstone Beach Dr., (800) 753-9000, (805) 927-4647; www.bluewhaleinn.com. 6 rooms; $$$. All gas fireplaces. Afternoon snack, full breakfast. No smoking; no pets.*

Situated across the street from the ocean, this luxurious inn boasts ocean-view mini-suites with canopy beds and private outdoor entrances. Guests have access to a communal sitting area with a panoramic ocean view, and breakfast is served in an adjacent room with a similar view.

### Cambria Pines Lodge
*2905 Burton Dr., (800) 445-6868, (805) 927-4200, fax (805) 927-4016; www.cambriapineslodge.com.*

125 units; $-$$. Children under 5 free. Some wood-burning fireplaces. Indoor heated pool & hot tub; sauna. Full breakfast; restaurant. Dogs ok.

Located on a pine-covered hill above town, this is a spacious 25-acre facility with rustic cabins. The lodge was originally built in 1927 by an eccentric European baroness who wanted to live in opulent style near the Hearst Castle. Recently updated, the Main Lodge now houses a moderately priced restaurant and the woodsy, casual Fireside Lounge, where live entertainment is scheduled every night in front of its large stone fireplace. Colorful peacocks run loose on the property, and a volleyball area is available to guests. A nature trail leads down into the village.

## FogCatcher Inn

6400 Moonstone Beach Dr., (800) 425-4121, (805) 927-1400, fax (805) 927-0204; www.fogcatcher inn.com. 67 rooms; $$$. Children under 12 free. All mini-kitchens & gas fireplaces. Heated pool; hot tub. Continental breakfast. No smoking; pets ok.

Situated across the street from the ocean, this pseudo English Tudor-style inn has a big two-bedroom suite for families and another ocean-view suite for honeymooners. Many rooms have ocean views.

## The J. Patrick House

2990 Burton Dr., (800) 341-5258, (805) 927-3812, fax (805) 927-6759; www.jpatrickhouse.com. 8 rooms; $$-$$$. Unsuitable for children under 13. No TVs; all wood-burning fireplaces or stove. Evening snack, full breakfast. No smoking; no pets.

Situated in the woods above the East Village, this authentic log cabin holds one guest room; seven more are in an adjacent Carriage House. All beds are topped with duvets and handmade quilts. Evening wine and hors d'oeuvres and bedtime chocolate chip cookies and milk are included. An all-vegetarian breakfast is served in the sunroom.

## The Pickford House Bed & Breakfast

2555 MacLeod Way, (888) 270-8470, (805) 927-8619, fax (805) 927-8016; www.thepickfordhouse.com. 8 rooms; $$. Some gas fireplaces. Evening snack, full breakfast. No smoking; no pets.

Though this inn was built in 1983, it is far from modern in feeling. All rooms bear the names and personalities of silent film stars and

have fresh roses and clawfoot bathtubs. Notable among them is the Valentino Room, which is furnished with dark-wood antiques and has a great view. Evening hors d'oeuvres are served at a massive inlaid mahogany bar dating from 1860, and everyone gets a bedtime cocktail or sweet. Breakfast features the traditional Danish pancake fritters known as aebleskivers.

## White Water Inn

6790 Moonstone Beach Dr., (800) 995-1715, (805) 927-1066, fax (805) 927-0921; www.whitewater inn.com. 17 rooms; $$-$$$. All gas fireplaces. Continental breakfast. No smoking; no pets.

Situated across the street from the ocean, this contemporary motel court has two mini-suites with a private patio and ocean-view hot tub, plus six rooms with oversize whirlpool bathtubs. Breakfast is delivered to the room, and movies can be borrowed from the desk.

## Motel Row

Numerous motels are located along scenic Moonstone Beach Drive in Cambria.

— **WHERE TO EAT** —

## Brambles Dinner House

4005 Burton Dr., (805) 927-4716, fax (805) 927-3761; www.bramblesdinnerhouse.com. D daily, SunBr; $$-$$$. Highchairs, boosters, booths, child portions. Reservations advised.

Located inside a rambling 1874 English-style cottage with Victorian decor, this cozy restaurant has some very private booths and a special room for families. Known for its prime rib, traditional Yorkshire pudding, and fresh salmon barbecued over an oak-wood pit, the kitchen also prepares an extensive selection of steaks, chicken items, and fresh seafood. Hinting at the owner's heritage, several Greek dishes appear on the menu: a tasty salad with Feta cheese, dolmathes (stuffed grape leaves), and saganaki (fried cheese). A hamburger is also available, and a rich English trifle is among the desserts. Interesting paintings and china plates decorate the walls, and the entrance is crowded with a collection of clocks that are for sale.

## Linn's Main Bin

2277 Main St., (805) 927-0371; www.linnsfruitbin.com. B-L-D daily, SunBr; $. Highchairs, child menu.

For description, see Linn's Downtown SLO Bin on page 205.

### Robin's Restaurant
*4095 Burton Dr., (805) 927-5007, fax (805) 927-1320; www.robinsrestaurant.com. L-D daily; $-$$. Highchairs, boosters, child menu. Reservations advised.*

Operating within a converted house surrounded by a manicured garden, this pleasant spot uses homegrown herbs in delicious ethnic and vegetarian dishes. The seafood bisque is a must, as are tasty curries prepared to order. Salads, sandwiches, pastas, seafood, and tofu dishes are also on the menu. Housemade desserts round out the offerings. Patio seating is available.

### The Tea Cozy
*4286 Bridge St., (805) 927-8765, same fax; www.teacozy.com. Tea W-Sun 10-5. No reservations.*

In England it is customary to conclude a visit to one of the stately homes with a stop at a local tearoom, and the English proprietors here are attempting to interest Americans in this tradition. Situated within a modest 1890s schoolteacher's house, this cozy tearoom offers light meals and pastries along with a nice cup of tea (or coffee). The extensive Royal Tea and smaller Cream Tea are served all day. Imported English foods and an appealing collection of antique china are also available for purchase.

# Morro Bay

## — A LITTLE BACKGROUND —

Named "El Morro" in 1542 by explorer Juan Rodriguez Cabrillo because it reminded him of a turbaned Moor, the name of the huge volcanic rock here—visible from just about everywhere in town—evolved over time into "Morro," which means "knoll" in Spanish. The area is also referred to as the "Gibraltar of the Pacific." The rock stands 576 feet high and is now a State Monument.

Peregrine falcons—said to be the fastest moving animal in the world and an endangered species—nest at the top. Because the area's wide variety of landscapes offer myriad nesting sites for some of California's most interesting birds, bird-watching is particularly good here.

Commercial fishing is this small, picturesque town's main industry. Albacore and abalone are the local specialties, and they frequently show up on restaurant menus.

Lodgings often fill up on weekends, so reservations should be made well in advance.

## — VISITOR INFORMATION —

### Morro Bay Visitors Center & Chamber of Commerce
*845 Embarcadero Rd., (800) 231-0592, (805) 772-4467, fax (805) 772-6038; www.morrobay.org.*

— GETTING THERE —

Located approximately 30 miles south of San Simeon.

— ANNUAL EVENTS —

## Morro Bay Harbor Festival

*October. (800) 366-6043, (805) 772-1155, fax (805) 772-2107; www.mbhf.com. $7, under 12 free.*

General merriment includes a sand sculpture spectacular, a Hawaiian shirt contest, and ship tours, plus live entertainment and plenty of seafood and wine tasting. Proceeds benefit community nonprofit organizations, which volunteer their time to the festival.

— WHAT TO DO —

## Coleman Beach Park

*Embarcadero Rd./Coleman Dr., E of Morro Rock.*

Children are sure to enjoy this idyllic playground in the sand.

## Fishing

The pier is a prime spot for fishing. Chartered fishing boats are also available.

## Giant Chess Board

*Embarcadero/Front, in Centennial Park, (805) 772-6278, fax (805) 772-2693. By reservation M-F 8-5.*

At the base of a 44-step stairway is one of the two largest chessboards in the U.S. (The other is in New York City's Central Park.) The redwood chess pieces stand 2- and 3-feet high and weigh from 18 to 40 pounds, making a game here physical as well as mental exercise. From noon to 5 p.m. each Saturday, the Morro Bay Chess Club sponsors games on the giant 16- by 16-foot concrete board, and the general public is welcome to challenge.

## Morro Bay Aquarium & Marine Rehabilitation

*595 Embarcadero, (805) 772-7647. M-F 9:30-5, Sat-Sun closing time varies. $2, 5-11 $1.*

This teeny, tiny aquarium is a draw for the gift shop located in front. However, the price is right, and over 300 live marine specimens can be observed. All are said to be injured and distressed animals that can't be returned to the wild. Some preserved specimens are also displayed, and very noisy seals beg to be fed.

## Morro Bay State Park

*On State Park Rd., at S end of town, (805) 772-2560; www.parks.ca.gov. Campsites available.*

### • Bird Sanctuary

This is the third largest bird sanctuary in the world. Following a trail through the marsh and hills allows the possibility of catching a glimpse of over 250 bird species.

### • Heron and Cormorant Rookery

*At Fairbank Point, off State Park Rd.*

No one is allowed inside the rookery, which is one of the last where the Great Blue Heron can be found, but the herons can be viewed from an observation area.

### • Museum of Natural History

*At White Point, (805) 772-2694, fax (805) 772-7129; www.morrobaymuseum.org. Daily 10-5. $2, under 17 free.*

Situated on a scenic perch over the bay, this small museum presents lectures, slide shows, and movies about the wildlife and Native American history of the area. Large windows provide excellent views of the estuary, and a telescope permits up-close viewing of wildlife. Guided tours are sometimes available. In winter, guided walks visit the monarch butterflies that congregate at Pismo State Beach, home to the largest overwintering colony of monarchs in the United States.

## The Shell Shop

*590 Embarcadero, (805) 772-8014, fax (805) 772-4137; www.theshellshop.net. Daily 9:30-7, in winter 9:30-5.*

The perfect souvenir stop, this shop has the largest selection of seashells on the Central Coast and offers them at bargain prices.

## Tiger's Folly II Harbor Cruises

*1205 Embarcadero Blvd., (805) 772-2257, fax (805) 772-1034. Daily June-Sept; Sat-Sun Oct-May; schedule varies. $10, 4-12 $5.*

The 1-hour harbor cruise aboard this sternwheeler requires no reservation, but the special Sunday champagne brunch and dinner cruises do.

— WHAT TO DO NEARBY —

## Avila Beach

*20 mi. S of town off Hwy. 101.*

This tiny, old-fashioned beach community

is a great place for watching surfers and for swimming in a usually mild surf.

## Cayucos
*6 mi. N of town on Hwy. 1, (800) 563-1878; www.cayucoschamber.com.*

This quiet little beach town has a string of inexpensive motels. It also boasts both a fine beach with a gentle surf and a 400-foot-long fishing pier where equipment rentals are available.

### – WHERE TO STAY –

## Blue Sail Inn
*851 Market Ave., (888) 337-0707, (805) 772-7132, fax (805) 772-8406; www.bluesailinn.com. 48 rooms; $-$$. Some gas fireplaces. Hot tub. No pets.*

This streamline moderne motel is centrally located, allowing guests to walk to restaurants. The hot tub area has a view of Morro Rock, as do most of the rooms.

## Embarcadero Inn
*456 Embarcadero, (800) 292-ROCK, (805) 772-2700, same fax; www.embarcaderoinn.com. 32 rooms; $$-$$$+. Children under 12 free. Some gas fireplaces. 2 indoor hot tubs. Continental breakfast. No pets.*

Situated in a quiet spot at the south end of the busy Embarcadero strip, this attractive modern motel has a weathered-wood exterior. All rooms have bay views, and most have balconies. A library of videos is available at no charge to guests, and local calls are free.

## The Inn at Morro Bay
*60 State Park Rd., (800) 321-9566, (805) 772-5651, fax (805) 772-4779; www.innatmorrobay.com. 98 rooms; $$-$$$+. Children under 12 free. Some fireplaces. Heated pool; health spa. Restaurant; room service. No pets.*

Located at the southern end of town in Morro Bay State Park, this small resort is sheltered by a strand of old eucalyptus and provides a quiet, restful spot to spend the night. Choice rooms have gorgeous views of the estuary, and some have private decks and hot tubs. Guests have complimentary use of mountain bikes. An 18-hole public golf course is just across the street, and a heron rookery located in an adjacent grove of eucalyptus often treats guests to the raucous ranting of its occupants.

The **Orchid** restaurant *(B M-Sat, D daily, SunBr.)* offers diners a mesmerizing panoramic view of the estuary and sand spit, and wildlife-watching from here is very good. Depending on the time of year, diners see herons carrying nesting materials or sea otters basking on their backs. Kayaks and sailboats come and go as well. A different theme menu is served each night. A three-course Sunday brunch includes both a perfect eggs Benedict served with a side of scalloped potatoes topped with wispy deep-fried potatoes, and a savory paella prepared with fresh local catch. Each entree includes a glass of champagne, fresh-squeezed orange juice, coffee, and access to a dessert bar laden with items such as giant chocolate-dipped strawberries and housemade ice cream with a variety of toppings.

### – WHERE TO EAT –

## Abba's Pacific Cafe
*571 Embarcadero, (805) 772-8827. L-D W-M; $-$$. Highchairs, boosters. Reservations advised.*

Moved from its former extremely tight quarters, this very popular spot now offers a great view along with its great food. At dinner, the perfect starter is the house special of scampi fra Diavala, which consists of perfect prawns in a tasty red sauce suitable for dunking with bread. Entrees are listed on a chalk board and sometimes include a salmon Lilliano—poached, wrapped around spinach, and topped with a light red sauce—and snapper Griglia—grilled and topped with a light white-wine sauce. All meals end with a complimentary liqueur, but don't miss dessert when it happens to be marinated fresh strawberries, fresh peach cobbler, or housemade vanilla ice cream. Lunch is a less expensive selection of salads, sandwiches, and hamburgers.

## Dorn's Original Breakers Cafe
*801 Market St., (805) 772-4415, fax (805) 772-4695; www.dornscafe.com. B-L-D daily; $-$$. Highchairs, boosters, child menu. Reservations advised.*

This casual restaurant features a great bay view and is especially pleasant at breakfast. The menu then offers a choice of hearty breakfasts, plus novelty items such as chocolate chip pancakes with chocolate syrup. The extensive dinner menu features fresh local fish and an award-winning Boston clam chowder.

## The Great American Fish Company

*1185 Embarcadero, (805) 772-4407. L-D daily; $$.*
*Highchairs, boosters, child portions. No reservations.*

Located a short, scenic stroll from the cen-
ter of town, this restaurant provides a comfort-
able, casual atmosphere and good views of the
rock. The extensive menu includes mesquite-
grilled fresh fish and shark, as well as deep-fried
fresh local prawns and Monterey squid. A steak
and hamburger are also available.

## Hofbrau der Albatross

*901 Embarcadero, (805) 772-2411, fax (805) 772-*
*5001. L-D daily; $. Highchairs, boosters, child por-*
*tions. No reservations.*

Popular with locals and visitors alike, this
casual spot features cafeteria-style service. The
fish & chips are superb, and a very good French
dip sandwich and hamburger are also available.

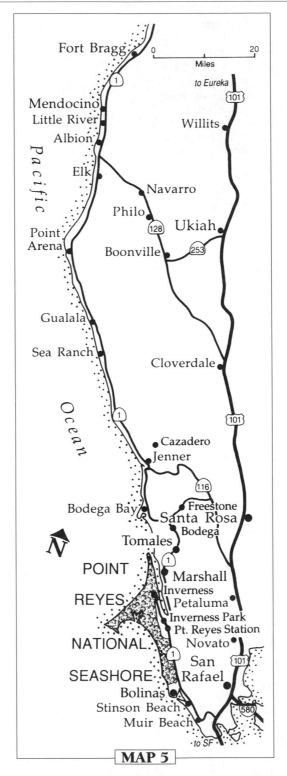

MAP 5

# COAST NORTH

## — A LITTLE BACKGROUND —

Highway 1 north from San Francisco allows an escape into a quieter, less-populated area. The two-lane road leading to Stinson Beach winds through fragrant eucalyptus groves, then rustic countryside that is rife with wildflowers in spring. It hugs ocean-side cliffs for long stretches, riding like a roller coaster and providing breathtaking views. The inland route known as Panoramic Highway is steep, with many blind curves. One of its nicknames is Kamikaze Alley, bestowed because of accidents occurring regularly in the fog. On sunny summer days, both roads become congested when everyone heads to the beach to soak up some of the famous California sunshine that is so elusive in the northern part of the state.

A word of warning: The rocky cliffs and beaches along the coast are scenic and beautiful, and people sometimes forget that they are also dangerous. Though it is tempting to stand at the edge, where the surf is pounding, people have been washed out to sea doing just that. Don't be one of them. Be careful. Stay on trails. Obey posted signs. And take special care not to let children run loose.

## — VISITOR INFORMATION —

### Redwood Empire Association
*At Pier 39, in San Francisco. (800) 200-8334, (415) 956-3491, fax (415) 956-0209; www.redwood empire.com.*

Information on the coastal counties north of San Francisco is available here.

### West Marin Chamber of Commerce
*P.O. Box 1045, Point Reyes Station 94956, (415) 663-9232, fax (415) 663-8818; www.pointreyes.org.*

## — GETTING THERE —

From San Francisco, take Highway 101 to Highway 1 north.

# Muir Beach

It was in this area (the exact spot is still in dispute) more than 400 years ago that Sir Francis Drake beached the *Golden Hinde,* formerly known as the *Pelican,* and claimed California for Queen Elizabeth I.

## Green Gulch Farm
*1601 Shoreline Hwy., just before town, (415) 383-3134, fax (415) 383-3128; www.sfzc.org.*

Reached via a sharp downhill turnoff, this retreat is operated by the San Francisco Zen Center. Public meditation programs are scheduled daily, and a longer program on Sundays includes a dharma talk. Retreats, workshops, and children's programs are also scheduled. Visitors are welcome to take informal afternoon walks in the organic garden, which supplies the herbs and vegetables for Greens restaurant in San Francisco; plants are available for purchase from the nursery.

Overnight lodging is available in the peaceful, Japanese-style **Lindisfarne Guest House** *(12 rooms, 1 cottage; $$. No TVs; all shared baths. Vegetarian meals included. No smoking.),* which is constructed without nails. A separate apartment is available for families with children, and guests may take their meals at communal tables with the permanent residents.

## Mount Tamalpais State Park
*801 Panoramic Hwy., (415) 388-2070; www.parks. ca.gov. Daily 7am-sunset; Summit visitor schedule varies; free guided hikes Sat-Sun at 9:30am. $5/vehicle.*

From some locations, Mt.Tam, as the mountain is affectionately nicknamed, resembles the resting figure the local Native Americans called "The Sleeping Maiden," who they believed safeguarded the area. This 6,300-acre park offers 50 miles of hiking trails, and the view from its 2,571-foot peak is spectacular (the Verna Dunshee Trail at East Peak is an easy 3/4 -mile loop near the summit). It is interesting to note that the mountain bike was first developed here for use on this park's hills, and it is said to be "the best spot on Earth to shoot a car

commercial." Campsites are available.

Since 1904, the 7.1-mile **Dipsea Race** has been run on the first Sunday of each June. Hordes of runners tromp the trail then from the center of Mill Valley to Stinson Beach. The **Mountain Play** *(May-June. (415) 383-1100, fax (415) 383-4848; www.mountainplay.org. $28-$30, 65+ & 4-17 $20-$22.)* has been presented in the natural outdoor amphitheater atop the mountain annually since 1913. Productions have run the gamut from the obscure to Shakespeare to well-known Broadway musicals. In the old days people came on burros, by stagecoach, or on the old Mount Tamalpais Scenic Railway, also known as the "Crookedest Railroad in the World" because it had 281 curves—including a five-fold switchback known as the Double Bow Knot—along its 8 1/4-mile route. Now many audience members ride the free shuttle buses up the mountain and, after the performance, hike 4 miles down to board a shuttle bus for the rest of the journey back to the parking area.

## Muir Beach
Reached by turning onto a leafy, blackberry-lined lane located just south of the Pelican Inn, this popular beach is unsafe for swimming. However, it is excellent for sunbathing and people-watching, and picnic tables are available.

## Muir Beach Overlook

Panoramic coastline views make this a great picnic spot. In winter, it is a good perch from which to watch the whale migration.

## Muir Woods National Monument

*Off Hwy. 1, on Panoramic Hwy., (415) 388-2595, fax (415) 389-6957; www.nps.gov/muwo. Daily 8-sunset. $3, under 17 free.*

Located just off Highway 1 and enveloping 560 acres, this magnificent, fragrant old-growth redwood forest has 2 miles of walking trails. The easy paved Main Trail has interpretive exhibits, while seven more-challenging, unpaved trails lead away from the crowds. Naturalist John Muir, for whom the forest was named, said of it, "This is the best tree lover's monument that could be found in all the forests of the world." The largest tree here measures 240 feet high by 16 feet wide. Because nearly 2 million people come here each year, only a visit early or late in the day (before 10 or after 4) provides the hope of some solitude; rainy days are also quiet. And no matter what time of year it is, visitors are advised to bring along warm wraps. The dense forest lets in very little sunlight, and the weather is usually damp, foggy, and cold. Children ages 6 through 12 can sign up for the free Junior Ranger program (see also page 445) at the Visitors Center when they arrive. They'll get a sticker badge and workbook that helps them explore nature. Picnicking is not permitted, but a snack bar dispenses simple foods.

## Slide Ranch

*2025 Shoreline Hwy., (415) 381-6155, fax (415) 381-5762; www.slideranch.org. $15, under 3 free. Reservations advised.*

Perched dramatically on the ocean side of Highway 1 near Muir Beach, this ranch offers the city slicker a chance to get back to the land . . . a chance to learn about a self-sustaining rural lifestyle through exposure to frontier arts . . . a chance to slow the pace. During Farm Day programs, adults and children learn together about things such as cheese making, composting, and papermaking. Though the program varies according to the season and the ages of participants, a typical day begins with smiling staff members greeting visitors in a fragrant grove of eucalyptus. A visit to the sheep and goat pen usually follows, giving children the chance to "pet a four-legged sweater" and milk a goat. More activities include collecting eggs, feeding chickens, carding and spinning sheep wool, making bread and cheese, helping in the garden, and hiking along one of the coastal wildland trails.

## — WHERE TO STAY AND EAT —

## The Pelican Inn

*10 Pacific Way, (866) 383-6005, (415) 383-6000, fax (415) 383-3424; www.pelicaninn.com. 7 rooms; $$$. No TVs. Full breakfast; restaurant. No smoking; no pets.*

Sheltered by towering pines and alders, this authentic reconstruction of an actual 16th-century English Tudor inn was built in 1979. It offers snug rooms furnished with English antiques, oriental carpets, and canopied beds, and each room has a private water closet.

The lunch menu in the **pub restaurant** *(L-D daily; $-$$. Highchairs, boosters, child portions. Reservations accepted.)* features housemade traditional English pub fare such as bangers and mash, shepard's pie, and the ever-popular ploughman's plate. Dinner brings on prime rib, beef Wellington, and lamb chops, and British ales and beers that complement the food are on tap. Diners can be seated outside on an enclosed patio or inside in a rustic candle-lit dining room furnished with several long communal tables plus a few private tables for couples. On cold, foggy days, a fireplace warms the interior. High tea is served by reservation from 4 to 5 p.m. on Sunday afternoons.

# Stinson Beach

## — A LITTLE BACKGROUND —

This town has no gas station. According to a local resident, "It disappeared one night and didn't come back." For more information, see www.stinsonbeachonline.com.

## — WHAT TO DO —

## Audubon Canyon Ranch/Bolinas Lagoon Preserve

*4900 Hwy. 1, 3.5 mi. N of town, (415) 868-9244; www.egret.org. Sat-Sun-holidays 10-4; mid-March-mid-July. By donation. No smoking; no pets.*

Situated on picturesque Bolinas Lagoon just north of town, this 1,000-acre nature preserve is a non-profit project sponsored by the four Bay Area Audubon Societies. It is open only during the breeding season, when pairs of Great Blue Herons (measuring 4 to 5 feet tall and with a wingspan of nearly 6 feet), Snowy Egrets, and Great Egrets nest noisily in the tall redwood trees located in the ranch's Schwarz Grove. Approximately 60 other bird species also make their home here, making this a bird-watcher's paradise. Nests contain an average of two to five eggs, which incubate for about 28 days. Once hatched, baby birds covered in fluffy down waddle about their nests while waiting for their parents to return from gathering a meal of fish and crustaceans in nearby Bolinas Lagoon. (Baby egrets fly at 7 weeks, herons at 9 weeks.) Several scenic trails of varying length and challenge, including a self-guiding nature trail, lead to an overlook where telescopes are available and a ranch guide is on hand to interpret and assist. Visitors can rest on benches and observe these graceful birds as they court, establish a pecking order, build their nests, and begin rearing their young.

Exhibits in the Display Hall museum, a converted milking barn left from the days when the ranch was a dairy, give visitors detailed information about the birds as well as about the geology and natural history of the area. Nearby,

a stream-side, sod-roofed Bird Hide is designed so people can see out, but birds can't see in. Its feeders attract a variety of unsuspecting birds, including many colorful hummingbirds. A picnic area, from which the nesting site is visible, provides a scenic spot to relax and enjoy a leisurely lunch in peaceful surroundings.

## Stinson Beach

*Off Hwy. 1, (415) 868-0942; www.nps.gov/muwo/stbe. Daily 9-sunset. Free.*

This magnificent beach offers a little taste of the Southern California beach scene. Conditions often permit swimming here, though the water is cold and lifeguards are on duty usually only in summer. Since the weather here is often different from everywhere else in the Bay Area, it is wise to call and check conditions before setting out *((415) 868-1922)*. A word of caution: the waters off this stretch of coast known as the Red Triangle have suffered more shark attacks than anywhere else in the world.

### — WHERE TO STAY —

## Steep Ravine Cabins

*On Hwy. 1, 1 mi. S of town, (800) 444-7275, (415) 388-2070. 10 cabins; $. No TVs; all wood-burning stoves.*

Perched on a rocky bluff overlooking the ocean, within Mount Tamalpais State Park, each of these primitive cabins dates from the 1930s and sleeps up to four people. Each has a small wood-burning stove, a picnic table and benches, sleeping platforms, and an outdoor barbecue. They do not have running water, electricity, or shower facilities. Primitive toilets, water faucets, and firewood are nearby. Guests must provide their own bedding, cooking equipment, and light source. Paths lead down to the beach, where six primitive campsites are also available.

### — WHERE TO EAT —

## Stinson Beach Grill

*3465 Hwy. 1, (415) 868-2002. L-D daily, Sat-SunBr; $-$$. Highchairs, boosters, child menu. Reservations advised.*

This informal grill has an eclectic menu offering everything from hamburgers to osso bucco. In between are a Greek salad, an impeccably fresh salmon with tomato-basil sauce, and a spicy blackened snapper. A large selection of complementary beers from microbreweries are also available.

# Bolinas

## — A LITTLE BACKGROUND —

So shy of visitors is this tiny ocean-side hamlet that maverick residents spirit away directional signs as soon as they are posted. All visitors are hereby warned that the reception in town can be chilly.

# Point Reyes Area

## — GETTING THERE —

Located about 60 miles north of San Francisco. Take either Highway 1, or Sir Francis Drake Boulevard from Larkspur off Highway 101.

## — WHERE TO STAY —

**Reservations services**

For information on the area's B&Bs call:

• **Inns of Marin**
*(800) 887-2880, (415) 663-2000, fax (415) 669-7242; www.innsofmarin.com.*

• **Point Reyes Lodging**
*(800) 539-1872, (415) 663-1872, fax (415) 663-8431; www.ptreyes.com.*

# Olema

## — WHAT TO DO —

**Point Reyes National Seashore**
*Park Headquarters on Bear Valley Rd., W of town, (415) 464-5137; www.nps.gov/pore. Park: daily sunrise-sunset. Bear Valley Visitor Center: M-F 9-5, Sat-Sun 8-5. Free.*

Known for its beaches and hiking trails, this 71,000-acre refuge has plenty of other interesting things for visitors to do. Many activities cluster around the Park Headquarters. The Bear Valley Visitor Center houses a working seismograph and a variety of nature displays. The **Morgan Horse Ranch**, where pack and trail animals for the national parks are trained, is adjacent. (The Morgan was the first American

horse breed.) A short walk away a replica coast Miwok Indian village, **Kule Loklo**, has been re-created using the same types of tools and materials as the Native Americans themselves originally used.

Trails beginning near the headquarters include the .5-mile self-guided Woodpecker Nature Trail; the .6-mile-long self-guided Earthquake Trail, which follows the San Andreas fault and passes a spot where the Pacific plate moved 16 feet north in about 45 seconds during the 1906 earthquake; and the popular 4.1-mile Bear Valley Trail, which winds through meadows, fern grottos, and forests before ending at the ocean. The area has 147 miles of hiking trails, most of which are open to horses. Guided trail rides, buggy rides, hayrides, and overnight pack trips are available at nearby **Five Brooks Stable** *(80001 State Route #1, (415) 663-1570, fax (415) 663-8766; www.fivebrooks.com.).* Mountain bikes are permitted on some trails, and walk-in backpacking campsites are available for a fee by reservation *((415) 663-8054).*

Away from the headquarters, in the Inverness area, is the 1870 **Point Reyes Lighthouse** *((415) 669-1534. Thur-M 10-4:30. Free.).* Winds have been recorded blowing here at 133 miles per hour—the highest rate in the continental U.S. The bottom line is that it can get mighty windy, cold, and wet at this scenic spot. The lighthouse is reached by maneuvering 300 steps down the side of a steep, rocky cliff. It is a popular spot in winter for viewing migrating gray whales. **Shuttle buses** *(Sat-Sun 9-5, weather permitting; Jan-April. $4, under 16 free.)* depart regularly then from the Drake's Beach visitor center.

**Drake's Beach** offers easy beach access and has a great little short-order cafe. The **Ken Patrick Visitor Center** *((415) 669-1250. Sat-Sun 10-5.)* here has maritime history displays and a 250-gallon salt water aquarium. A herd of approximately 450 elk is often seen grazing in the **Tule Elk Reserve** on Tomales Point. The elk are descended from a group of 10 brought here in 1978. Late summer is rutting season, when the males "bugle" to attract females. The Historic **Pierce Point Ranch** is open for a self-guided tour of its buildings, including a barn, bunkhouse, and blacksmith shop. This area is dotted with historic ranches that were once part of a Mexican land grant and which now are

leased from the park. Cows are plentiful, and it is refreshing to see them out here in the wide-open green spaces instead of stuffed into a dirt feedlot.

The Point Reyes National Seashore Association offers seminars and classes in natural history, environmental education, photography, and art. To request a free catalog, call (415) 663-1200.

## Samuel P. Taylor State Park
*On Sir Francis Drake Blvd., 5 mi. E of town, in Lagunitas, (415) 488-9897; www.parks.ca.gov.*

This 2,700-acre park features redwood groves and open grassland. The most common animal in the park is the black-tailed deer, and silver salmon and steelhead trout can sometimes be seen as they migrate up Papermill Creek to spawn. A network of hiking trails and fire roads leads to the top of Mount Barnabe, and a 3-mile paved bike trail runs through the park. Devil's Gulch is perfect for a picnic, and a nearly level trail beginning there follows the old Northwest Pacific Railroad right-of-way. The park is named after gold miner and lumber baron Samuel Penfield Taylor, who came to California from Boston in 1849.

— WHERE TO STAY/EAT —

## Olema Farm House Restaurant & Bar
*10005 Hwy. 1/Sir Francis Drake Blvd., (415) 663-1264; www.olemafarmhouse.com. B Sat-Sun, L-D daily; $-$$. Highchairs, boosters, child menu. Reservations taken for D.*

This building was the town's first and has been here for over a century, since 1845. Stagecoaches used to stop here on the way to San Francisco. Now, this casual spot serves up barbecued oysters, steamed clams, and fish & chips as well as prime rib and lamb. A collection of more than 950 antique liquor bottles is displayed throughout. A full deli and bar also operate on the premises.

## Olema Inn & Restaurant
*10000 Sir Francis Drake Blvd./Hwy. 1, (415) 663-9559, fax (415) 663-8783; www.theolemainn.com. 6 rooms; $$. Continental breakfast; restaurant. No smoking; pets ok.*

Built in 1876 as a saloon, this beautifully restored inn is furnished with lovely antiques. Upstairs, **guest rooms** are outfitted with luxurious new Scandinavian beds topped with fluffy comforters.

Downstairs, the stylish **restaurant** *(L Sat, D W-M, SunBr; $$-$$$. Highchairs, boosters, child menu. Reservations advised.)* features a dining room with high ceilings, multi-paned windows, and a wood floor salvaged from a 19th-century tobacco warehouse in West Virginia. It has the pleasant feel of an updated farmhouse. The kitchen uses organic ingredients and vegetables from their own garden whenever possible, and the meats are from the esteemed local Niman Ranch. Menu items might include soup prepared with local wild mushrooms, a pork chop with a crispy corn cake, and a poached pear upside-down cake.

# Point Reyes Station

— WHERE TO STAY —

## Holly Tree Inn & Cottages
*3 Silverhills Rd., (800) 286-HOLL, (415) 663-1554, fax (415) 663-8566; www.hollytreeinn.com. 4 rooms, 3 cabins; $$-$$$. No TVs; some kitchens & wood-burning fireplaces & stoves. Hot tub. Afternoon snack, full breakfast. No smoking.*

Tucked away in its very own valley just beneath the Inverness Ridge, this rustic B&B offers four attractively appointed rooms. A spacious cottage is equipped with a wood-burning stove, a stereo and tapes, and a clawfoot tub. A stream runs picturesquely through the property, and an informal playground with a wooden plank swing invites children to play. Another of the rustic cottages is perched on stilts over Tomales Bay and features a solarium with a hot tub.

## Point Reyes Hostel
*1380 Limantour Rd., (415) 663-8811, same fax; www.norcalhostels.org. 44 beds; 1 family room.*

Nestled in a secluded valley, this former ranch house offers both a kitchen and outdoor barbecue for preparing meals. Two cozy common rooms with wood-burning stoves are also available to guests. See also page 445.

### — WHERE TO EAT —

## The Station House Cafe
*11180 Hwy. 1, (415) 663-1515, fax (415) 663-9443; www.stationhousecafe.com. B-L-D Thur-Tu; $-$$. Highchairs, boosters, booths, child menu. Reservations advised on Sat-Sun.*

Menu choices in this casual, popular spot include sandwiches, light entrees, and daily specials that always feature fresh fish and local shellfish. Hamburgers are prepared with ground chuck from cattle raised in chemical-free pastures, without hormones or antibiotics, at the Niman Ranch in Bolinas. Desserts include apple pie, devil's food cake, bread pudding, butterscotch pudding, and seasonal fruit pies. Truly all stages of hunger can be satisfied here at the same table. Additionally, service is fast and unpretentious, and a spacious patio is inviting on sunny days. Live entertainment is scheduled Friday through Sunday evenings.

# Inverness

### — WHAT TO DO —

## Johnson's Drakes Bay Oyster Company
*17171 Sir Francis Drake Blvd., (415) 669-1149, fax (415) 669-1262. M-Sat 8-4, Sun 9-4.*

A visit to this scenically situated enterprise allows viewing the various stages of the oyster-farming process. A Japanese technique of growing oysters on suspended ropes is used here, promising a sweeter meat. Oysters are available for purchase.

## Tomales Bay State Park
*Star Route, (415) 669-1140; www.parks.ca.gov. Daily 8-sunset. $5/vehicle.*

Access to the warm bay waters for swimming and wading is available at popular **Heart's Desire Beach**. The easy self-guided Indian Trail begins here and leads to a Miwok garden, where native plants used for food and medicine are labeled. It then climbs a slope that skirts the bay and ends at Indian Beach.

### —WHERE TO STAY—

## Cottages on the Beach
*(415) 663-9696; www.ptreyescountryinn.com. 2 cabins; $$. No TVs. Continental breakfast. No smoking; pets ok.*

Located down a steep driveway (directions are e-mailed upon booking), Walt's Cabin fulfills inflated expectations. The couch, breakfast table, and white comforter-covered bed all face a spectacular view of Tomales Bay. Allow time for gazing out at an amazing array of passing birds that includes hawks and small white egrets. A well-stocked pantry and fridge permit indulging in an afternoon snack of hot chocolate and preparing dinner in-house. Breakfast supplies are there, too, and they usually include locally produced Straus organic butter and Clover half-and-half. Outside, a bevy of partridges hang out in the bushes, and a walk along the beach permits examining a wrecked fishing boat.

## Manka's Inverness Lodge
*30 Callender Way/Argyle Ave., (800) 58-LODGE, (415) 669-1034, fax (415) 669-1598; www.mankas. com. 14 units; $$$-$$$+. Children free in cabins. Some TVs; some kitchens; some gas & wood-burning fireplaces/stoves. Hot tub. Restaurant; limited room service. No smoking; dogs ok.*

This rustic 1917 arts and crafts-style hunting lodge was the first place in town with a phone. During the '40s, it was a speakeasy. Cozy lodge rooms and larger cabins are available. Rooms 1 and 2 boast both a large weathered deck overlooking Tomales Bay and a clawfoot tub. Several rooms have a large four-poster bed made with unpeeled whole cypress logs: Guests climb a step stool, then sink into peaceful slumber upon its featherbed under a fluffy down comforter. Six other rooms have open-air showers.

Local game grilled in the fireplace is often on the dinner menu in the inn's intimate **dining room** *(D daily; $$-$$$. Highchairs, boosters.)*. Breakfast is optional, inexpensive, and not to be missed. Served fireside in the lobby, one such gustatory extravaganza featured eggs scrambled with local goat cheese and hand-gathered mushrooms, a side of toasted herb bread, and both homemade rhubarb purée and blood orange marmalade.

## – WHERE TO EAT –

### Priscilla's Pizza & Café
*12781 Sir Francis Drake Blvd., (415) 669-1244. L-D W-M. Highchairs, boosters.*

Pretty much the only game in town, this small cafe serves up huge salads and delicious pizzas. The "Greek," with feta, artichoke hearts, and red peppers is a favorite. Sandwiches, pastas, tempting desserts, and organic coffees are also options.

# Marshall

## –A LITTLE BACKGROUND–

A former railroad stop, tiny Marshall (its population is 394) was the site of the first wireless communications system on the West Coast. Also once a dairy center, it is now home to the first organic dairy ranch in the West. And it is also home to more than half of California's commercial oyster growers and is known additionally for its clams and mussels.

## – WHERE TO EAT –

### Hog Island Oyster Company
*20215 Hwy 1, (415) 663-9218, fax (415) 663-9246; www.hogislandoyster.com. W-Sun 9-5. Reservations required for picnic; $10/person.*

The clean water here permits growing top-notch oysters and clams. Live farm-raised oysters and clams can be purchased to take home or to eat on site. Bring a picnic, purchase some oysters, and rent a package that includes

shucking knives, a barbeque kettle, and a waterfront picnic table.

### Tony's Seafood
*18863 Hwy. 1, (415) 663-1107, fax (415) 663-1831. L-D F-Sun; $. Highchairs, boosters. No reservations. No cards.*

Many restaurants in this area offer oyster dishes made with the fresh local supply. Here, relaxing views of Tomales Bay are enjoyed from inside the wood-paneled dining room perched atop stilts over the bay. The specialty is oysters barbecued in the shell. Deep-fried oysters are also available, as are fresh local fish and a hamburger. Beer, which seems to go especially well with oysters, is available from the bar.

# Bodega Bay

## – A LITTLE BACKGROUND –

Claimed for England in 1579 by Sir Francis Drake and later discovered by Don Juan del la Bodega of Spain, this area was settled in the early 1800s when Russian explorers arrived to trap sea otters. It is the second largest salmon port on the Pacific coast and the busiest commercial fishing port between San Francisco and Eureka, but it is probably best known as the location for the 1962 Alfred Hitchcock film *The Birds*. Now a private residence, the old Potter School featured in the movie still stands in the tiny inland town of Bodega, as does **St. Theresa's Church,** a picturesque building dating from 1859 that is Sonoma County's oldest continuously active Catholic church and a state historical landmark.

## – VISITOR INFORMATION –

### Bodega Bay Area Chamber of Commerce
*575 Hwy. 1, (707) 875-3866; www.bodegabay.com.*

## – GETTING THERE –

Located approximately 75 miles north of San Francisco via Highway 1, or via Highway 101 to Highway 116 west to Highway 12 west.

## – ANNUAL EVENTS –

### Fisherman's Festival
*April. (707) 875-3422; www.bodegabay.com. $3, seniors $2, under 13 free.*

Held each year at the beginning of the commercial salmon season, this festival's highlights are a traditional parade of colorfully decorated commercial fishing boats and a Blessing of the Fleet, but bathtub races, stunt kite demonstrations, and a juried art show are also part of the fun. All proceeds benefit local nonprofit organizations.

## — WHAT TO DO —

### Chanslor Guest Ranch & Stables

*2660 Hwy. 1; www.chanslorranch.com. Stables: (707) 875-3333, fax (707) 875-9462. Daily 9-5. Horses $30+/hr., ponies $10/10 min. Must be 8 or older.*

Guided trail rides through a wetlands preserve and beach rides across sand dunes are offered at this 378-acre working guest ranch. Pony rides are available for kids under 8.

**Lodging** *((707) 875-2721. 6 rooms; $$. No smoking.)* is available.

### Osmosis Enzyme Bath & Massage

*209 Bohemian Hwy., in Freestone, 5 mi. E of town, (707) 823-8231, fax (707) 874-3788; www.osmosis. com. Daily 9-9. Enzyme bath with blanket wrap $75-$80, with massage $155-$170. Unsuitable for children. Reservations required.*

Long popular in Japan, the enzyme bath here is something like a mud bath—only lighter, more fragrant, and dry. It is said to improve circulation, break down body toxins, and relieve stress, and this is the only place in the U.S. where it is available. The experience begins in a tranquil tea garden with a soothing cup of enzyme tea to aid digestion. Then

bathers, either nude or in a swimsuit, submerge for 20 minutes in a hot mixture of Hinoki cedar fiber, rice bran, and over 600 active plant enzymes that naturally generate heat. A blanket wrap or massage follows. Private massages are given in serene outdoor Japanese pagodas nestled in a wooded area near Salmon Creek, and a Zen-inspired meditation garden is available to relax in following treatments.

### Sonoma Coast State Beach

*(707) 875-3483, fax (707) 875-3876; www.parks. ca.gov. Daily 8-sunset. Free.*

Actually a series of beaches separated by rocky bluffs, this state beach extends for 18 miles from Bodega Head to Meyers Gulch, just south of Fort Ross State Historic Park. It is accessible from more than a dozen points along Highway 1, and campsites are available.

#### • Goat Rock Beach

*Off Hwy. 1, 4 mi. S of Jenner.*

Located where the Russian River flows into the ocean, this beach is a hangout for harbor seals. March is the beginning of pupping season, when Seal Watch volunteers are on hand to interpret and answer questions for viewers. Seeing the baby seals, many people are tempted to get closer, but visitors should stay at least 50 yards away. When pups are born they depend on the mother's milk for the first 48 hours. During that critical period the mother will often go out to feed, leaving newborn pups by themselves. If a mother finds humans around her pup when she returns, she will abandon it. Seals hang around this area in large numbers through July. Then the population thins out until the following March. Driftwood collecting is encouraged, because pile-ups of wood debris are a potential fire hazard to the town. Note that swimming in the ocean is hazardous due to sleeper waves and riptides.

## — WHERE TO STAY —

### Bodega Bay Lodge & Spa
*103 Hwy.1, (800) 368-2468, (707) 875-3525, fax (707) 875-2428; www.bodegabaylodge.com. 78 rooms; $$$-$$$+. Children under 18 free. Most wood-burning fireplaces. Solar-heated pool; hot tub; sauna; health spa; fitness room. Afternoon wine; restaurant. No smoking; no pets.*

Situated at the southern end of town, overlooking the scenic wetlands marsh and sand dunes of Doran Park and the ocean beyond, this rustically attractive modern motel features rooms with stunning ocean views. A wonderful whirlpool hot tub is sheltered from the elements by glass walls, but its ceiling is open to the possibility of a light mist or rain providing a cooling touch. Golfing can be arranged at an adjacent 18-hole course.

The **Duck Club** (*B&D daily. Reservations required.*) serves elegant fare prepared with the best local ingredients: fresh Tomales Bay oysters on the half shell, Petaluma escargot with Enfant Riant truffle butter, rack of Sonoma lamb with olive-basil Zinfandel glacé and minted Sebastopol apples. Breakfast is choice here, and the ocean view is often at its best then. Delectable box lunches—packed with such goodies as marinated local fresh vegetables, herb-stuffed Petaluma game hens, and croissant sandwiches filled with Valley Ford lamb—are also available.

### The Inn at the Tides
*800 Hwy. 1, (800) 541-7788, (707) 875-2751, fax (707) 875-3285; www.innatthetides.com. 86 rooms; $$-$$$. Children under 12 free. Some kitchens & wood-burning fireplaces. Heated indoor-outdoor pool; hot tub; sauna; fitness room. Continental breakfast; 2 restaurants; room service.*

Attractive contemporary rooms with ocean views are available here. At a monthly Dinner with the Winemaker, a gut-busting five-course meal is paired with wines from a guest winery whose representative is on hand to comment.

## — WHERE TO EAT —

### The Tides Wharf & Restaurant
*835 Hwy. 1, (707) 875-3652, fax (707) 875-3285; www.innatthetides.com. B-L-D daily; $-$$. Highchairs, boosters, child menu. Reservations advised.*

Always crowded, this busy spot offers a well-priced breakfast and serves it until noon. Lunch and dinner menus are a pricier selection of seafood entrees. A Dungeness crab cocktail, though made with frozen crab, is delicious. Complete dinners come with a starter of either a potato-rich New England clam chowder, a seafood chowder, or a green salad with shrimp garnish, plus a vegetable, starch, and sourdough bread. The tasty tartar sauce is housemade, and several vegetarian items, fried chicken, and steak are options for those who don't care for fish. In addition to fish & chips, the children's menu offers a hamburger, hot dog, and grilled cheese sandwich. (One kid was overheard here saying, "It's a really good hamburger for a *nice* restaurant.") Because most tables afford sweeping views of Bodega Bay, it is worth scheduling a meal here before sunset. A more modestly priced snack bar is also open for lunch.

# Jenner

## — WHAT TO DO —

### Fort Ross State Historic Park
*19005 Hwy. 1, 11 mi. N of town, (707) 847-3286; www.parks.ca.gov. Daily 10-4:30. $6/vehicle.*

Built by Russian and Alaskan hunters in 1812 as a trading outpost, this authentically restored historic fort compound consists of two blockhouses equipped with cannons, a small Russian Orthodox chapel, a manacor's house, and a barracks. Picnic tables are available. Outside the gates, a picturesque bluff at the edge of the ocean has a path leading down to the beach. An architecturally striking Visitors Center is located adjacent to the parking area.

Held annually on the last Saturday in July, **Living History Day** allows visitors to step back in time to the 1800s. Costumed staff and volunteers perform musket drills and fire cannons, craftspeople demonstrate their skills, and a blacksmith pounds at his forge.

## Kruse Rhododendron State Reserve
*On Kruse Ranch Rd. (road to Plantation), 22 mi. N of town, at marker 42.7, (707) 847-3221; www.parks. ca.gov. Daily sunrise-sunset. Free.*

Best known for its spring floral display in April and May, depending on the weather, this 317-acre park has 5 miles of hiking trails that lead visitors over picturesque bridges and through fern-filled canyons. An easy short trail begins just above the parking area located about 1/4 -mile down a gravel road.

## Salt Point State Park
*25050 Hwy. 1, 18 mi. N of town, (707) 847-3221; www.parks.ca.gov. Daily sunrise-sunset. Visitor Center: Sat-Sun 10-3, Apr-Oct. $4/vehicle.*

A popular spot with skin divers, this park is also choice for a walk along the beach. Stump Cove has an easy, short trail down to its scenic beach. Campsites are available.

### — WHERE TO STAY —

## Fort Ross Lodge
*20705 Hwy. 1, 12 mi. N of town, (800) 968-4537, (707) 847-3333, fax (707) 847-3330; www.fortross lodge.com. 23 units; $$-$$$. Children under 12 free. Most wood-burning fireplaces. Hot tub; sauna. No pets.*

This collection of comfortable rustic-modern cabins is on a large, open, grassy bluff on the ocean side of the highway. Some units have ocean views; all have a small refrigerator, a coffee maker, a microwave oven, and a barbecue on a private patio. A beach access trail is available to guests.

## Jenner Inn & Cottages
*10400 Hwy. 1, (800) 732-2377, (707) 865-2377, fax (707) 865-0829; www.jennerinn.com. 23 units; $-$$$+. Children under 5 free. No TVs; some kitchens; some wood-burning fireplaces & stoves. Afternoon snack, continental breakfast; restaurant. No smoking; pets ok in some units.*

Tucked into a curve in the highway at the point where the Russian River runs into the Pacific Ocean, this inn offers a choice of lodge rooms, cottages, and private homes. Three rooms in the River House get unobstructed views of the estuary and share a hot tub. A cozy communal lounge has an antique wood-burning stove and a library of books and games.

## Salt Point Lodge
*23255 Hwy. 1, 17 mi. N of town, (800) 956-3437, (707) 847-3234, fax (707) 847-3354; www.saltpoint lodgebarandgrill.com. 16 rooms; $-$$. Some wood-burning stoves. Hot tub. Restaurant (seasonal). No smoking; no pets.*

Located across the street from the Pacific Ocean, this motel features a large expanse of lawn dotted with a swing set and a giant sculpted slide designed and built by local artist Bruce Johnson. Special family rooms have a queen bed and two twin bunk beds, and two rooms for couples have an ocean view and a private deck and hot tub.

## Timber Cove Inn
*21780 Hwy. 1, 14 mi. N of town, (800) 987-8319, (707) 847-3231, fax (707) 847-3704; www.timbercove inn.com. 47 rooms; $-$$$+. Unsuitable for children. No TVs; some fireplaces. Restaurant. No pets.*

Perched on a rocky seaside cliff, this inn offers many rooms with magnificent ocean views and some with sunken tubs and private hot tubs. A tall Bufano sculpture juts above the lodge, acting as a landmark, and the lobby, bar, and restaurant feature a dramatic Japanese-modern style of architecture and spectacular ocean views.

# The Sea Ranch

### — WHERE TO STAY —

## House rentals
*Rams Head Realty & Rentals, 1000 Annapolis Rd., (800) 785-3455, (707) 785-2427, fax (707) 785-2429; www.ramshead.com. 125 units; $$-$$$+. All kitchens; some fireplaces. Pets ok in some homes.*

Stunningly beautiful wind-swept coastal scenery is the backdrop for the approximately 1,500 luxury vacation homes situated in this development. Each home is unique. For example, the spectacular oceanfront Monette House has three bedrooms and a very special hot tub in an enclosed room with sliding glass doors opening to the ocean. Rustic hike-in cabins are also available. Guests have access to three recreation centers with swimming pools, as well as to hiking and jogging trails and a children's playground. An 18-hole golf course, designed in the Scottish manner by Robert Muir Graves, can be played at extra charge.

## The Sea Ranch Lodge

*60 Sea Walk Dr., (800) SEARANCH, (707) 785-2371,*
*fax (707) 785-2917; www.searanchlodge.com.*
*20 rooms; $$$-$$$+. Children under 5 free. Some*
*TVs; some wood-burning fireplaces & stoves.*
*Breakfast; restaurant; room service. No smoking;*
*no pets.*

In this rustic contemporary facility, each
room has an ocean view. Two rooms have private courtyards with hot tubs.

# Gualala

— A LITTLE BACKGROUND —

Named for an Indian word that is pronounced
"wha-LA-la" and means "water coming down
place," this town is located in a banana belt of
regularly warm weather. The area's many
celebrity property owners include singer Kris
Kristofferson and comedian Robin Williams.

— VISITOR INFORMATION —

## Redwood Coast Chamber of Commerce

*P.O. Box 199, Gualala 95445, (800) 778-LALA,*
*(707) 884-1080, fax (707) 884-9004;*
*www.redwoodcoastchamber.com.*

— WHERE TO STAY —

## The Gualala Hotel

*On Hwy. 1, (888) GUALALA, (707) 884-3441, fax (707)*
*884-1054; www.thegualalahotel.com. 19 rooms; $-$$.*
*Some shared baths. Breakfast; restaurant.*

Built by the town's founders in 1903—
when guests arrived from San Francisco by
stagecoach—this historic inn's rooms are furnished with period antiques. Five have private
baths and ocean views. Family-style dinners are
served in the restaurant, and an atmospheric
logging bar, once frequented by Jack London, is
now popular with locals.

## Mar Vista Cottages

*35101 Hwy. 1, 5 mi. N of town, (877) 855-3522, (707)*
*884-3522; www.marvistamendocino.com. 12 units; $$.*
*No TVs; all kitchens; some wood-burning fireplaces &*
*stoves. Hot tub. No smoking; pets ok.*

Most of these one- and two-bedroom cot-
tages dating from the '30s have ocean views; all
are just a short walk from a sandy beach with a
gentle surf. Recent spiffing has enlarged the

windows for better views and topped the beds
with down comforters. A Japanese-style soaking
tub is ensconced in a meadow.

## The Old Milano Hotel

*38300 Hwy. 1, 1 mi. N of town, (707) 884-3256;*
*www.oldmilanohotel.com. 9 units; $$-$$$. Unsuitable*
*for children under 16. No TVs; some wood-burning*
*stoves; some shared baths. Hot tub. Full breakfast;*
*restaurant. No smoking; pets ok in some cottages.*

Built originally in 1905 as a railroad rest
stop and pub, this elegantly refurbished cliff-
side Victorian hotel is on the National Register
of Historic Places. A garden cottage and a con-
verted caboose—complete with upstairs brake-
man's seats where occupants can watch the sun
set—are available in addition to hotel rooms,
and a cliff-top hot tub has an expansive ocean
view.

## Serenisea

*36100 Hwy. 1, 3 mi. N of town, (800) 331-3836, (707)*
*884-3836; www.serenisea.com. 23 units; $-$$$.*
*Children under 1 free. Some TVs; all kitchens; some*
*wood-burning fireplaces & stoves. Pets ok in some*
*units.*

Most of these housekeeping cabins and
vacation homes are spread over a scenic ocean
bluff with a trail leading down to the beach.
Some have private hot tubs, and one has a private sauna.

## St. Orres

*36601 Hwy. 1, 2 mi. N of town, (707) 884-3303,*
*fax (707) 884-1840; www.saintorres.com. 8 rooms,*
*12 cottages; $-$$$+. No TVs; some wood-burning*
*fireplaces; some shared baths. Hot tub; sauna. Full*
*breakfast; restaurant. No pets.*

This unusual inn has a weathered wood
exterior and a Russian style of architecture fea-
turing onion-domed turrets.

A striking 3-story-tall **dining room** *((707)*
*884-3335. D daily, SunBr; $$$. Reservations*
*advised.)* features large windows with ocean
views. Dishes often make use of locally foraged
ingredients and wild game such as boar and
venison, and a fixed-price, three-course dinner
is an option.

## Whale Watch Inn

*35100 Hwy. 1, 5 mi. N of town, (800) WHALE-42,*
*(707) 884-3667, fax (707) 884-4815; www.whale*

*watchinn.com. 18 rooms; $$$-$$$+. No TVs; some kitchens; all wood-burning fireplaces. Sauna. Full breakfast; limited room service. No smoking; no pets.*

Perched on an ocean-side cliff, this dramatic contemporary-style inn offers plenty of peace and quiet. Rooms are spread among five buildings; all have private decks and ocean views, and eight have two-person whirlpool bathtubs. The Bath Suite has a spiral staircase leading to a whirlpool bathtub for two that is positioned under a skylight and features an ocean view. The Crystal Sea offers a mesmerizing view of an ocean cove—from the couch, the bed, and another of those whirlpool tubs for two. In the morning, a delicious breakfast is brought to the room in a large willow basket tray. Guests can relax in the communal Whale Watch Room equipped with a cozy circular fireplace, panoramic view of the ocean, and telescope for whale-watching. Guests also have access to a half-mile stretch of private beach.

# Point Arena

## — WHAT TO DO —

### Point Arena Lighthouse
*At end of Lighthouse Rd., 2 mi. off Hwy. 1, (877) 725-4448, (707) 882-2777, (fax) 707-882-2111; www.pointarenalighthouse.com. Daily 10-3:30 Oct-Mar; 10-4:30 Apr-Sept. $5, under 12 $1.*

Originally built in 1870, this lighthouse was destroyed in the '06 quake and then rebuilt. It was finally automated in 1976. A museum located in the former foghorn house is filled with historical photos and features a whale-watching room. Then it's a 145-step climb (equivalent to 6 stories) up the 115-foot-tall light for a guided tour of the tower. Bargain three-bedroom, two-bath **light-keeper's homes** are located adjacent and can be rented for the night *(3 units; $$. All kitchens & wood-burning stoves. Pets ok.)*

# Manchester

## — A LITTLE BACKGROUND —

This picturesque area, with the ocean to its west and with redwood and Douglas fir forests to its east, is in the heart of Mendocino County's

dairy country. In winter, the rare whistling tundra swan flies in from Siberia.

## — GETTING THERE —

Located 5 miles north of Point Arena and 30 miles south of Mendocino.

## — WHAT TO DO —

### Manchester State Park
*(707) 882-2463; www.parks.ca.gov.*

Located where the San Andreas Fault meets the sea, this 760-acre park is the closest spot in North America to Hawaii. Campsites are available.

## — WHERE TO STAY —

### KOA Kampground
*(800) KOA-4188, (707) 882-2375, fax (707) 882-3104; www.manchesterbeachkoa.com.*

Situated within a thick grove of pine and cypress, this campground has Kamping Kottages and boasts a heated pool, a hot tub, a game room, and beach access. For more description, see page 443.

# Elk

## — A LITTLE BACKGROUND —

Measuring less than a mile from south to north, this tiny town consists of a general store, a garage (no gasoline), two restaurants, and five small inns. Much of the town is perched precariously on bluffs overlooking the Pacific. Once a logging town, it now is home to a clutch of B&Bs with access to its secluded rocky beaches.

## — GETTING THERE —

Located 14 miles south of Mendocino.

## — WHERE TO STAY —

### Harbor House Inn
*5600 S. Hwy. 1, (800) 720-7474, (707) 877-3203, fax (707) 877-3452; www.theharborhouseinn.com. 6 rooms, 4 cabins; $$$+. Unsuitable for children under 12. No TVs; some wood-burning fireplaces. Dinner & full breakfast included. No smoking; no pets.*

This Craftsman-style building was built entirely of redwood in 1916 as a lodge for lumber company executives. Throughout, traditional furnishings are mixed with antiques and accented by modern luxuries. A path leads to a private beach where guests can sun, explore tidepools, and gather driftwood, and adirondack chairs dot the property inviting lounging. Meals are taken in a beautifully appointed dining room with a spectacular ocean view, where it is a delight watching the sky fade to black. A sample four-course dinner menu might include pasta with Italian sausage and spinach, arugula salad with marinated fresh beets, a tender osso bucco alla Milanese, and a strawberry tart. Breakfast entree choices might include eggs and apple sausage, French toast with white chocolate garni, a spinach-mushroom-cheese omelet, and oatmeal with dried cranberries, toasted hazelnuts, and toasted coconut. A few tables in the restaurant are available to non-guests by reservation.

# Mendocino

## — A LITTLE BACKGROUND —

Mendocino provides a rejuvenating, quiet escape from the hectic pace of city life. Now an Historical District, this remote burg is built in a pastel Cape Cod-style of architecture and exudes the feeling that it belongs to a time past. In the early 1800s, it was a center for redwood

mills and the main shipping port for sending lumber to San Francisco. In the late 19th century, it was known as "The Town of the Water Towers." Today, some of these picturesque wooden towers are converted into lodgings, and the town is better known for its unique shops and art galleries. Visitors can slow down their systems by leaving their cars parked for the duration of a visit. Anywhere in town is easily reached via a short walk.

The nightlife here is of the early-to-bed, early-to-rise variety. Consider this itinerary: dinner out, a stroll through town, a nightcap at the Mendocino Hotel, and then off to bed.

Make lodging reservations as far in advance as possible; in-town lodging is limited and popular.

Be advised that Mendocino's volunteer fire department alarm sometimes goes off in the middle of the night. Resembling the scream of an air-raid siren, it can be quite startling, even when a person is aware of what it is.

## — VISITOR INFORMATION —

**Mendocino Coast Chamber of Commerce**
*332 N. Main St, in Fort Bragg, (800) 726-2780, (707) 961-6300, fax (707) 964-2056; www.mendocino coast.com.*

## — GETTING THERE —

Located approximately 150 miles north of San Francisco. Take Highway 101 to Highway 1, or Highway 101 to Highway 128 to Highway 1.

## — ANNUAL EVENTS —

**Mendocino Coast Whale Festival**
*March. In Mendocino & Fort Bragg; (800) 726-2780.*
In Mendocino, the fun includes wine tasting, seafood chowder tasting, and a classic rock concert. In Fort Bragg, it takes the form of a microbrewery beer tasting and a classic car show, and whale-watching cruises are available.

**Mendocino Music Festival**
*July. (707) 937-2044, fax (707) 937-1045; www.mendocinomusic.com. $18-$45; under 18 $15.*
A variety of performances—including orchestra, chamber music, opera, and jazz—are presented in a small ocean-side tent in Mendocino Headlands State Park. Master classes are scheduled, and free pre-concert

lectures educate the audience about the performances.

## — WHAT TO DO —

### Beachcombing

Follow down to the beach the little path behind the landmark **Mendocino Presbyterian Church** on Main Street. (Built in 1868 from local redwood, this American Gothic church is considered a masterpiece and is California's oldest continuously-used Presbyterian church.) While there, make a kelp horn by cutting the bulb off the end of a long, thin piece of fresh bull kelp. Rinse out the tube in the ocean so that it is hollow. Then wrap it over one shoulder and blow through the small end. The longer the tube, the greater the resonance.

### Catch A Canoe & Bicycles Too

*On Comptche-Ukiah Rd., (800) 331-8884, (707) 937-0273, fax (707) 937-0305; www.stanfordinn.com. Daily 9:30-5:30. $10+/hr.*

Drifting down calm Big River affords the opportunity to picnic in the wilderness, swim in a secluded swimming hole, and observe a variety of wildlife. Canoe rentals include paddles and life jackets. Bicycle rentals are also available.

### Ford House Museum and Visitor Center

*735 Main St., (707) 937-5397. Daily 11-4. $1 donation.*

Inside this historic 1854 home, an interpretive center focuses on the cultural and natural history of the area. During whale-watching season, a related short orientation film is shown, and information on interpretive programs at nearby **Mendocino Headlands State Park** is available. (From December through April, whales migrate close to shore and, from the headlands, can sometimes easily be seen "breaching," or jumping out of the water.) In good weather, a picnic at tables in the backyard offers a spectacular ocean view.

### Kelley House Historical Museum

*45007 Albion St., (707) 937-5791; fax (707) 937-2156; www.mendocinohistory.org. F-M 1-4; daily in summer. $2.*

A gigantic cypress tree grows in the front yard of this home built by William H. Kelley (Daisy MacCallum's father) in 1861. The restored first floor displays a collection of photos from the 1800s as well as changing exhibits of local artifacts and private collections.

### Mendocino Art Center

*45200 Little Lake St., (800) 653-3328, (707) 937-5818, fax (707) 937-1764; www.mendocinoart center.org. Daily 10-5. Free.*

Three rooms display art here. Activities related to fine arts and crafts occur year-round, and the **Mendocino Theatre Company** *((707) 937-4477; www.1mtc.org. $10-$20, under 16 $5-$10.)* stages productions in the center's theater. Cookies and coffee are sometimes available in the lobby, and an inviting courtyard garden seems the perfect place to enjoy them.

### Russian Gulch State Park

*On Hwy. 1, 2 mi. N of town, (707) 937-5804, fax (707) 937-2953; www.parks.ca.gov. Daily dawn-dusk. $5/vehicle.*

A protected beach, a 36-foot-high waterfall, and a blowhole known as the Devil's Punch Bowl are among the features of this rustic park. Picnic tables overlook an ocean cove, and campsites are available.

### Shopping

A plethora of unique boutiques makes shopping in this town a joy. The following rectanglar route hits most of the best shops. Start on Main Street at the **Golden Goose** (luxurious housewares) near the Mendocino Hotel, then continue west to **Ocean Quilts** and on down to the tiny, utterly charming shoppe known as **Mendocino Jams and Preserves**. Make a jog north/right over to Albion Street and turn east/right and continue on to **ARTicles**, inside a tiny water tower (fabulous artsy stuff), and a few doors down to **Sticks** (antique binoculars and home accessories). At Lansing Street, make a jog north/left to **Sallie Mac** (all things French).

### Van Damme State Park

*8125 Hwy. 1, in Little River, 2 mi. S of town, (707) 937-5804; www.parks.ca.gov. Daily dawn-dusk. Visitor Center: daily 10-4. $5/vehicle.*

Among the interesting features in this 1,831-acre park is a canyon wall covered with ferns and a 1/3-mile Bog Trail leading to a large area of skunk cabbage. Picnic facilities and campsites are available.

An unusual **Pygmy Forest,** where stunted trees grow in leached soil, is nearby. It has a "short" boardwalk trail, and a brochure describing the various types of trees is available at the trailhead. To reach the forest, follow Little River Airport Road approximately 3 miles inland.

## — WHERE TO STAY IN TOWN —

### Blair House Inn
*45110 Little Lake St., (800) 699-9296, (707) 937-1800, fax (707) 937-2444; www.blairhouse.com. 4 rooms, 1 cottage; $-$$$. Unsuitable for children under 6. Some shared baths. No smoking; pets ok in cottage.*

Famous as the exterior for Jessica Fletcher's house in the TV series *Murder, She Wrote,* this delightful 1888 Victorian is constructed of now absurdly expensive virgin clearheart redwood. All the rooms are decorated with antiques and hand-crafted quilts, but the Angela Suite, where Angela Lansbury actually stayed while filming, has a Victorian dip sink and a clawfoot tub. The exterior of the house is surrounded by a picket fence and a cottage garden and looks much as it did when originally built.

### Hill House Inn
*10701 Palette Dr., (800) 422-0554, (707) 937-0554, fax (707) 937-1123; www.hillhouseinn.com. 44 rooms; $$-$$$. Some wood-burning fireplaces. Restaurant; room service. Pets ok.*

Located on a 2-acre knoll above the village, this attractive lodging dates only from 1978. It has become famous as the setting for many of the early episodes of the TV series *Murder, She Wrote,* and the Bette Davis Suite is where the namesake star lodged for 6 weeks while filming her final movie. Because of this Hollywood connection, it attracts many stars as patrons. Rooms are spacious and appointed with brass beds and lace curtains.

### John Dougherty House
*571 Ukiah St., (800) 486-2104, (707) 937-5266; www.jdhouse.com. 8 units; $$-$$$. Unsuitable for children. Some wood-burning stoves. Full breakfast.*

Situated on a quiet back street, this cozy salt box-style inn, built in 1867, is one of the oldest houses in town. An adjacent water tower now serves as a charming two-room suite with an 18-foot-high beamed ceiling and fireplace, and two cottages are situated in an English garden. Most of the rooms have great ocean views.

### Joshua Grindle Inn
*44800 Little Lake Rd., (800) GRINDLE, (707) 937-4143; www.joshgrin.com. 10 rooms; $$-$$$. Unsuitable for children. No TVs; some wood-burning fireplaces & stoves. Afternoon snack, full breakfast. No smoking.*

Situated on a 2-acre knoll at the edge of town, this Victorian farmhouse was built in 1879 by the town banker. It has a New England country atmosphere, with Early American antiques furnishing each room. Guest rooms are in the main house, a cottage, and a water tower.

### MacCallum House Inn
*45020 Albion St., (800) 609-0492, (707) 937-0289; www.maccallumhouse.com. 19 rooms; $$-$$$+. Children under 10 free. 1 kitchen; some wood-burning fireplaces & stoves. Hot tub. Evening snack, full breakfast; restaurant. No smoking; pets ok in some rooms.*

Built in 1882 by William H. Kelley for his newlywed daughter, Daisy MacCallum, this converted Victorian home was one of the first B&Bs in the area. The attractively decorated rooms are furnished with antiques, many of which belonged to the original owner. A water tower suite is fitted with a bed on the first floor, a bathroom with an ocean view on the second, and another bed with an ocean view on the third. Accommodations are also available in newer cottages adjacent to the house. Some rooms have private hot tubs, and bicycles are available to rent. Non-guests can purchase breakfast, which is served in the restaurant dining rooms or, in good weather, outdoors.

In the evening, the **restaurant** *(D daily; $$$. Closed Jan-mid-Feb. Boosters. Reservations advised.)* serves elegant seafood and game entrees in the house's magnificent dining rooms. On cold nights, guests are warmed by crackling fires in two fireplaces built of smooth river stone. Light dinners and snacks are available across the hall in the cozy **Grey Whale Bar,** also operated by the restaurant. Unusual drinks include Daisy's Hot Apple Pie (a blend of apple cider, Tuaca, cinnamon, and whipped cream) and a non-alcoholic Velvet Rabbit (a frothy mix of cream, grenadine, and strawberries served elegantly in a brandy snifter).

## Mendocino Hotel & Garden Suites

*45080 Main St., (800) 548-0513, (707) 937-0511,*
*fax (707) 937-0513; www.mendocinohotel.com.*
*51 rooms; $-$$$. Children under 14 free. Some TVs &*
*fireplaces; some shared baths. 2 restaurants; room*
*service. No smoking; no pets.*

Built in 1878, this authentic Victorian
hotel dates back to when the town was a boom-
ing port for the logging trade. Its small rooms
combine 19th-century elegance with modern
convenience. Contemporary cottages, located
behind the hotel amidst almost an acre of well-
tended gardens, have luxurious suites featuring
canopied beds and marble bathrooms. Antiques
are found throughout the hotel, and one of the
most interesting is the registration desk—an
ornate teller's cage from a Kansas bank.

The casual ocean-view **Garden Room
Cafe,** built around living ficus trees established
in the ground below, is open for breakfast and
lunch. The eggs Benedict is perfect, and the
unusual potato cake wedges are delicious.
Dinner is served in the more formal **Victorian
Dining Room** (*$$$. Highchairs, boosters, child
portions. Reservations advised.*), furnished in
vintage oak. Starters include French onion soup
and a very good Caesar salad, entrees are fresh
seafood and meats, and the exciting dessert tray
always includes the house specialty—deep-dish
olallieberry pie with homemade ice cream. A
Victorian lady ghost is said to haunt tables six
and eight. The hotel's lobby **bar**, with its
stained-glass dome (believed to be a Tiffany),
is a good setting for enjoying a fancy drink
among beautiful specimens of stained glass and
antique oriental carpets.

## Mendocino Village Inn

*44860 Main St., (800) 882-7029, (707) 937-0246,*
*fax (707) 937-1549; www.mendocinoinn.com.*
*12 rooms; $-$$. Unsuitable for children under 10.*
*No TVs; some wood-burning fireplaces & stoves;*
*some shared baths. Afternoon snack, full breakfast.*
*No smoking; no pets.*

Built in 1882, this Queen Anne Victorian is
known as "the house of the doctors" because it
was originally built by a doctor, then was
bought in turn by three more doctors. All the
cozy rooms are decorated with a mix of
antiques and contemporary art. A suite with a
private deck and ocean view is available in a
converted 2-story water tower.

## Sea Gull Inn

*44594 Albion St., (888) 937-5204, (707) 937-5204,*
*fax (707) 937-3550; www.seagullbb.com. 9 rooms; $-*
*$$. 1 TV. Continental breakfast. No smoking; no pets.*

Built in 1877 as a town house, this simple
inn has a casual, friendly atmosphere. A mature
garden with giant fuchsias and a century-old
rosemary bush surrounds it. Breakfast is
brought to the room and includes hot bever-
ages, orange juice, and pastries.

## Whitegate Inn

*499 Howard St., (800) 531-7282, (707) 937-4892,*
*fax (707) 937-1131; www.whitegateinn.com. 6 rooms,*
*1 cottage; $$-$$$. Children under 2 free. Some*
*wood-burning fireplaces & stoves. Evening snack, full*
*breakfast. No smoking.*

Built in 1880, this converted Victorian
home has a view of the ocean and town and is
surrounded by a garden with a white picket
fence and gate. It is tastefully furnished with
French and Victorian antiques. Live orchids
grace every room, and lace-edged sheets and
lofty down comforters adorn every bed. Some
bathrooms feature clawfoot tubs. Homemade
cookies are always available, chocolates arrive at
bedtime, and a lavish breakfast is served on
antique china and sterling silver.

### — WHERE TO STAY NEARBY —

## Brewery Gulch Inn

*9401 Hwy. 1 N., 1 mi. S of town, (800) 578-4454,*
*(707) 937-4752, fax (707) 937-1279; www.brewery*
*gulchinn.com. 10 rooms; $$-$$$+. Unsuitable for*
*children under 12. All gas fireplaces. Afternoon snack,*
*full breakfast. No smoking; no pets.*

A rural drive leads past a 2-acre woodland
garden of native plants, up to an open meadow
and forest where this luxurious contemporary
inn is situated. Wooden Pomo Indian tepees can
be inspected on the state park land adjoining,
which also has picnic tables. Check-in occurs at
a handcrafted redwood desk topped with gran-
ite in a reception area paneled with eco-sal-
vaged redwood. The public area beyond, known
as the Great Room, has 35-foot high ceilings
and a dramatic, oversized steel-and-glass-pan-
eled wood-burning fireplace. It is the perfect
place to relax with a good book, and it is where
guests gather for the wine hour. Breakfast is
taken at one of several massive dining tables at

one end of the Great Room, where diners enjoy the spectacular view and choose from a menu that includes housemade granola, brioche French toast, and caramelized banana-and-praline pecan pancakes. Simple bacon and eggs are prepared exquisitely with eggs just laid by organically fed chickens. All this and 100% pure, sweet well water comes out of the taps, too! Upper floor guest rooms have an ocean view filtered through tall pines. The story of how owner Dr. Arky Ciancutti built the inn is fascinating. As luck would have it, he overheard some locals talking about "bottom cuts" one night in a local bar. The term refers to giant virgin redwood logs up to 16 feet in diameter that sank in Big River sludge back in the 1800s. He decided to personally salvage as many as possible. To make a long story short—and it is quite a lengthy, fascinating tale wrapped around a lot of hard work—he used this magnificent wood to build his gorgeous inn.

## Fensalden Inn

*33810 Navarro Ridge Rd., in Albion, 7 mi. S of town, (800) 959-3850, (707) 937-4042, fax (707) 937-2416; www.fensalden.com. 8 rooms; $$-$$$. Unsuitable for children under 7. 1 TV; some kitchens; some wood-burning fireplaces & stoves. Evening snack, full breakfast. No smoking; pets ok in some rooms.*

Originally a Wells Fargo stagecoach way station in the 1860s, this restful B&B sits atop 20 tree-lined acres of headlands meadow offering quiet respite. Among the rooms in the large main house is an upstairs two-room suite with a sweeping view of a pasture lined with cypress trees. Another 2-story suite is built around an 1890s water tower, and a private bungalow with an unobstructed ocean view is situated at the head of the pasture. Antique furnishings are used throughout.

## Glendeven Inn

*8205 N. Hwy. 1, in Little River, 1½ mi. S of town, (800) 822-4536, (707) 937-0083, fax (707) 937-6108; www.glendeven.com. 10 rooms; $$-$$$+. Unsuitable for children under 8. Most fireplaces. Afternoon & evening snack, full breakfast. No smoking; no pets.*

Built in 1867, this attractive New England-style farmhouse is set back from the highway on 2½ quiet acres overlooking the headland meadows and bay at Little River. Rooms are in a farmhouse as well as in a restored hay barn,

water tower, and well-designed addition. All are decorated tastefully and eclectically with antiques and contemporary art. Handmade quilts cover beds and walls, and peaceful views are seen from every window. Favorites include charming Eastlin, hidden behind a bookcase door in the main house, and Briar Rose, featuring a view of both the ocean *and* fireplace from its bed. By request, breakfast is delivered to the room.

Near the entrance, **The Gallery at Glendeven** displays the work of a cooperative of local artists.

## Heritage House

*5200 N. Hwy. 1, in Little River, 4 mi. S of town, (800) 235-5885, (707) 937-5885, fax (707) 937-0318; www.heritagehouseinn.com. 66 rooms; $$-$$$$+. Closed Jan-mid-Feb. Children under 6 free. No TVs; some wood-burning & gas fireplaces. Afternoon tea; restaurant. No smoking; no pets.*

Located on a craggy stretch of coast with magnificent ocean views and spread over 37 roomy acres of well-tended gardens, this luxurious inn offers rooms and cottages furnished either with antiques or in contemporary style. Most have ocean views and decks. If it all looks familiar, it could be because it's been seen before in the movie *Same Time Next Year*, which was filmed here. The cabin the movie was filmed in has been divided into a unit called "Same Time" and another called "Next Year." Fine dining is available in an ocean-view **restaurant** *(B M-F, D daily, Sat-SunBr; $$$. Highchairs, boosters. Reservations advised for D.).* Non-guests are welcome.

## Little River Inn

*7751 Hwy. 1, in Little River, 2 mi. S of town, (888) INN-LOVE, (707) 937-5942, fax (707) 937-3944; www.littleriverinn.com. 65 units; $$-$$$+. Children under 16 free. 1 kitchen; some wood-burning fireplaces & stoves. Health spa; 2 tennis courts (with night lights); 9-hole golf course. Restaurant; room service. Pets ok in some units.*

Built on this spectacular location in 1853 by an ancestor of the current owner, this gingerbread Victorian house became an inn in 1939 and now offers a choice of cozy attic rooms, cottages, and standard motel units. Most have expansive ocean views. On the ocean side of Highway 1, new rooms have both an indoor whirlpool tub and a private outdoor hot tub. The beach and hiking trails of Van Damme State Park are adjacent, and a spa offers pampering body treatments and restorative massage.

A lovely garden-view **restaurant** *(B M-F, D daily, Sat-SunBr. Highchairs, boosters.)* and ocean-view **bar**, which is perfect for a light meal, are open to non-guests. James Dean once hung out here and was tossed out of the dining room when he put his feet on the table.

## Mendocino Coast Reservations
*1000 Main St., in Mendocino, (800) 262-7801, (707) 937-5033, fax (707) 937-4236; www.mendocino vacations.com. 70 units; $$$-$$$+; All kitchens; some fireplaces. No smoking; pets ok in some units.*

This service arranges vacation home rentals in privately owned studio apartments, cabins, cottages, inns, and houses located on the Mendocino coast. Some units are oceanfront, some have ocean views, and some have private hot tubs.

## Stanford Inn by the Sea
*On Comptche-Ukiah Rd., in Mendocino, (800) 331-8884, (707) 937-5615, fax (707) 937-0305; www.stanfordinn.com. 33 rooms; $$$-$$$+. Children under 4 free. Some kitchens; all wood-burning fireplaces. Indoor heated pool & hot tub; sauna; fitness room. Afternoon tea, evening snack, full breakfast. No smoking; pets ok.*

Located on the outskirts of town, upon a bluff above a scenic llama farm and duck pond that is home to black swans, these luxurious yet cozy pine- and redwood-paneled contemporary rooms are decorated with antiques, fresh flowers, and the work of local artists, and many have views overlooking the gardens to the ocean beyond. Operating as a self-sufficient ecosystem, this unique property has a certified organic garden, nursery, and working farm spread over 10 acres. The greenhouse-enclosed pool and hot tub are like a tropical retreat, and mountain bikes are available for guests to borrow at no charge. Dogs get VIP treatment with special bedding, bones, biscuits, and water dishes.

The inn's exceptional, *totally* vegetarian restaurant, **The Ravens** *(B & D daily; $$. Highchairs, boosters, child menu. Reservations advised.)*, offers exciting, refined cuisine using only the freshest ingredients. In addition to serving complex dishes such as wild mushroom

galette and blackened tofu Creole, this elegant, creative gourmet venue also offers pizza, polenta, and a portabella burger.

## — WHERE TO EAT —
## Cafe Beaujolais
*961 Ukiah St., (707) 937-5614, fax (707) 937-3656; www.cafebeaujolais.com. D daily; $$. Closed Dec-Jan. Reservations advised.*

Gone are the days of great breakfasts and informal lunches in this 1893 Victorian farmhouse. Now it is dinners only, using local meats, fish, and organic produce. Wonderful breads, including a dense Austrian sunflower bread and an unusual hazelnut, are baked outside in the Brickery's wood-burning oven.

## Ledford House
*3000 N. Hwy. 1, in Albion, 7 mi. S of town, (707) 937-0282; www.ledfordhouse.com. D W-Sun; $$$. Reservations advised.*

From the highway, this inviting restaurant is visible just beyond the Shibui Sculpture Garden. Situated near the edge of a bluff overlooking the ocean, it offers delicious views from most tables and schedules live jazz nightly. In addition to an intriguing lavender lemonade, the menu lists bistro dishes such as the house specialty white bean-and-mixed meats cassoulet (a dish far too large to consume in one sitting), vegetarian dishes such as eggplant Wellington, and also more substantial entrees of steak, duckling, and prawns. Allow time to take a walk as the sun falls into the ocean, listening to the sounds of a stream sloshing beside the path and of frogs singing in the property's pond.

## Mendocino Bakery & Pizzeria
*10483 Lansing St., (707) 937-0836. Daily 8-7; $. 1 booster.*

The perfect spot for a light lunch, this super bakery dispenses tasty housemade soup and pizza warm from the oven. A hunk of fragrant, moist gingerbread makes a memorable dessert, as do chewy cinnamon twists and chocolate chip-oatmeal Cowboy Cookies. The bakery also dispenses an assortment of breads and breakfast pastries made without mixes or preservatives. Everything is exceptional.

Next door, the **Mendocino Chocolate Company** *((800) 722-1107, (707) 937-1107, fax (707) 964-8812; www.mendocino-*

*chocolate.com. Daily 10-5:30.)* purveys delicious handmade candies. Samples are always available.

Behind the bakery, tiny **Mendo Burgers** *((707) 937-1111. M-Sat 11-7, Sun to 5; $.)* dishes up the obvious in a variety of delicious renditions—beef, chicken, turkey, veggie, fish, kid-size—plus hot dogs, fresh fish & chips, housemade soups, salads, and fresh-cut fries. Sitting outdoors at roomy picnic tables is sublime on a sunny day.

### The Moosse Café

*390 Kasten St./Albion St., (707) 937-4323; www.theblueheron.com. L-D daily; $-$$. Booster seats, child items. Reservations advised.*

This sparely decorated restaurant operates inside a reconstructed house. The original structure burned to the ground in 1994, and in 1995 it was completely rebuilt in the footprint and as close to the original as possible. It features a brick fireplace in the main dining room, blond wood floors throughout, and numerous dining nooks and crannies. A few choice tables sit in front of a window overlooking a flower garden and the ocean beyond. This cafe has fed Julia Roberts, Sean Penn, and Angela Lansbury—who ate dinner here regularly during the shooting of *Murder She Wrote*. In fact, the house starred as the travel agency depicted in that TV series. These celebrities and everyone else probably choose to eat here because everything is so innovative and tasty. The lunch menu might offer a delicious electric-orange puréed yam soup; a lip-smacking-good bowtie pasta salad mixed with chicken breast, asparagus, fennel, green beans, sweet peppers, and celery tossed with a buttermilk-tarragon dressing; or a hot linguini prepared with rock shrimp, shitake and porcini mushrooms, sweet peppers, and tomatoes and tossed with an unusual, colorful butternut squash sauce. Dinners are more substantial, with cioppino, boneless roasted crispy chicken, and osso bucco among the choices. Desserts include an old-fashioned creamy chocolate pudding, a light lemon mousse, and a warm bread pudding.

**The Blue Heron Inn** *(3 rooms; $-$$. Unsuitable for children under 12. No smoking. Continental breakfast.)* operates upstairs. It features the same spare, unfussy, simple decor and is furnished with tasteful antiques and puffy comforters.

### 955 Ukiah Street

*955 Ukiah St., (707) 937-1955; www.955restaurant. com. D W-Sun; $$. Reservations advised.*

After walking down a narrow, flower-edged path, diners are seated in a room with big windows and a view of some of the town's famous water towers. Perhaps in tribute to its former life as an artist's loft, the knotty-pine walls of the large open room now hold local artwork and all of it is for sale. The restaurant is known for its seafood dishes but has an eclectic menu offering everything from a garden salad to a giant ravioli stuffed with spinach, red chard, and five cheeses. Pastas, meats, and a signature bread pudding topped with local blackberry or huckleberry compote round out the menu.

# Fort Bragg

## — A LITTLE BACKGROUND —

The largest city on the Mendocino coast, Fort Bragg also has the largest working seaport between San Francisco and Eureka. Known as Noyo Harbor, the port is home to popular seafood restaurants serving fresh fish from the daily catch. The city's cheaper rents are attracting many businesses here from quainter Mendocino.

## — GETTING THERE —

Located 10 miles north of Mendocino.

## — ANNUAL EVENTS —

### John Druecker Memorial Rhododendron Show

*May. (800) 726-2780. Free.*

One of the largest such shows in the West, this is hosted by the Noyo chapter of the American Rhododendron Society. An enormous exhibit includes everything from alpine dwarf species to huge trusses of hybrids.

### World's Largest Salmon Barbeque

*July. (800) 726-2780, (707) 964-1228; www.salmon restoration.com. $17, under 12 $10.*

In addition to feasting on king salmon, participants can look forward to music, dancing, a variety of educational salmon displays, and a fireworks show over the ocean. Proceeds benefit the non-profit Salmon Restoration Association and assist them in restocking Northern California salmon runs.

## — WHAT TO DO —

### Fort Bragg Footlighters
*248 Laurel St./McPherson St., (707) 964-3806, fax (707) 964-7055. W, Sat at 8pm; summer only. $8-$10. Reservations advised.*

Gay Nineties music and nonsense highlight a program that appeals to all ages.

### Glass Beach
*On N side of town, across from Noyo Bowl at 900 N. Main St.*

Ask for precise directions when in town, then park in the dirt lot and walk down the path to the beach. Many years ago this was a dump, but now it is the source of great joy for kids and adults alike as they scoop up bits of pottery and glass that have been smoothed into jewels. Local artists make jewelry from their finds, but anyone can easily put them in a clear glass of water at home for a fabulous free souvenir.

### Guest House Museum
*343 N. Main St., (707) 961-2840. Tu-Sun 10-4. $2 donation.*

Get a sense of this area's history by viewing the old logging photos and artifacts on display inside this beautifully restored 1892 mansion constructed entirely of redwood.

### Jug Handle State Reserve
*On Hwy. 1, 3 mi. S of town, (707) 937-5804; www.parks.ca.gov. Daily dawn-dusk. Free.*

A unique self-guided nature trail takes hikers through an ecological staircase consisting of five wave-cut terraces that demonstrate how plants and soils affect one another. During the 5-mile walk (allow 3 hours), the terrain changes from grass-covered headlands, to a pine and redwood forest, to a pygmy forest filled with full-grown trees measuring only 1 or 2 feet tall. Wear sturdy shoes, and bring water and a lunch.

### Mendocino Coast Botanical Gardens
*18220 N. Hwy. 1, 2 mi. S of town, (707) 964-4352, fax (707) 964-3114; www.gardenbythesea.org. Daily*

*9-5; Nov-Feb 9-4. $7.50, 60+ $6, 13-17 $3, 6-12 $1.*

A self-guided tour leads through 47 acres of flowering plants. Known for its rhododendrons, fuchsias, and heathers, this garden also boasts a major collection of succulents, camellias, and old heritage roses. The gift shop sells unusual perennials, and picnic facilities are available.

### Ricochet Ridge Ranch
*24201 Hwy. 1, 2 mi. N of town, across from MacKerricher State Park, (888) TREK-RRR, (707) 964-7669, fax (707) 964-9669; www.horse-vacation.com. Daily 2-hr. trail ride at 10, 12, 2, 4. $40. Must be 6 or older. Reservations required.*

Equestrian excursions vary from by-the-hour guided rides on the beach to weeklong trips with nightly stops at inns. They include treks on Fort Bragg's Ten Mile Beach and in Mendocino's majestic redwood forests. Catered trips, camping expeditions, and private tours can also be arranged.

### Shopping
A walk along Main and Laurel streets allows a look at some of the town's most interesting shops. On North Main Street, stop in at the **Mendocino Chocolate Company** at #542 for hand-dipped chocolates and truffles. Visit **Roundman's Smoke House** at #412 for smoked meat, fish, cheese, and an assortment of jerkeys. At #401, the informal **Laurel Deli** dishes up freshly made soups and sandwiches as well as gigantic blackberry muffins and delicious housemade pies. At #362 the **Northcoast Artists Gallery** displays and sells the works of local artists, and at #330 the **Hot Pepper Jelly Company** sells jars of delicious pepper jelly and many other local food products.

### Skunk Train
*Foot of Laurel St., (866) 45-SKUNK, (707) 964-6371, fax (707) 964-6754; www.skunktrain.com. Daily; schedule varies. $35-$45, 3-11 $10-$20, under 3 free if they don't occupy a seat. Reservations advised.*

This train gets its name from the fact that the original logging trains emitted unpleasant odors from their gasoline engines. Loggers said they "could smell 'em before they could see 'em." Today, a few vintage motorcars are still used in winter, but most of the trains are pulled by steam or diesel engines as they travel through dense redwood forest, through deep mountain tunnels, and over many bridges and trestles. This is the last railroad in the country to deliver mail, and so trains make a few quick stops along the way for that purpose.

— WHERE TO STAY —

### Colonial Inn
*533 E. Fir St., (877) 964-1384, (707) 964-1384, fax (707) 964-9171; www.colonialinnfortbragg.com. 10 rooms; $$. Closed part of Oct & part of spring. Children under 5 free. Some TVs; some wood-burning fireplaces. Continental breakfast. No smoking; pets ok.*

Located in a quiet residential area, this massive 1912 Craftsman wood-frame home was turned into a guesthouse in 1945. One of the tastefully decorated rooms features an oversize fireplace. Guests get free access to a local health club as well as free admission to Mendocino Coast Botanical Gardens, and a public tennis court is just a block away.

### DeHaven Valley Farm and Country Inn
*39247 N. Hwy. 1, in Westport, 17 mi. N of town, (877) DEHAVEN, (707) 961-1660, fax (707) 961-1677; www.dehavenvalleyfarm.com. 6 rooms, 3 cabins; $-$$. Children under 6 free. No TVs; some wood-burning fireplaces & stoves; some shared baths. Hot tub. Full breakfast; restaurant. No smoking; pets ok in cabins.*

Romance and family fun are both possible on this 20-acre property. For romance, request the cozy Valley View room and enjoy its private bathroom, unusual corner fireplace, and view of the valley. The spacious Eagle's Nest, with its Franklin stove and expansive windows overlooking the valley, is another winner. With kids in tow, opt for one of the Acacia cottages. One teenager who stayed here actually uttered, "Mom, you did right. This place is great!" A cozy communal living room in the traditional Victorian farmhouse holds a grand piano, the tidepools of Westport Union Landing Beach await just across the highway, and a hilltop hot tub offers a view of the valley and spectacular nighttime stargazing. Guests and non-guests alike can make reservations for a four-course dinner in the intimate **dining room**.

### The Grey Whale Inn
*615 N. Main St., (800) 382-7244, (707) 964-0640, fax (707) 964-4408; www.greywhaleinn.com. 14 rooms; $$. Some TVs; some kitchens; some wood-burning & gas fireplaces. Full breakfast. No smoking; no pets.*

Originally built as a hospital, this stately redwood building was converted into an especially spacious inn in 1976. Some of the pleasantly decorated rooms have a private deck. Others have ocean views that permit viewing the whale migration, and one has a whirlpool bathtub for two. A large communal guest area is equipped with a TV, fireplace, pool table, and plenty of board games. The elaborate breakfast buffet sometimes includes a heavenly concoction of fresh bananas and blueberries mixed with a light cream cheese sauce. A relaxing stay here can be just what the doctor ordered.

### Pine Beach Inn
*16801 N. Hwy. 1, 4 mi. S of town, (888) 987-8388, (707) 964-5603, fax (707) 964-8381; www.pinebeach inn.com. 50 rooms; $-$$. 2 tennis courts. Restaurant. Pets ok.*

This motel complex is located on 12 acres of private land. Facilities include a private beach and cove.

### Motel Row
Three traditional motels on the northern end of town offer good value and an extraordinary beachfront location.

• **Beachcomber Motel**
*1111 N. Main St., (800) 400-SURF, (707) 964-2402; fax (707) 964-8925; www.thebeachcombermotel.com. 45 rooms; $-$$$. Some kitchens & fireplaces. Fitness room. Continental breakfast. Pets ok.*

Two rooms have private hot tubs.

• **Hi-Sea Inn**
*1201 N. Main St., (800) 990-SEAS, (707) 964-5929, fax (707) 961-1094; www.hiseainn.com. 15 rooms; $-$$. Children under 13 free. Some pets ok.*

All rooms have ocean views.

• **Ocean View Lodge**
*1141 N. Main St., (800) 643-5482, (707) 964-1951; www.oceanviewlodging.com. 38 rooms; $$-$$$. Some fireplaces. No smoking; no pets.*

All rooms have ocean views.

— WHERE TO EAT —

## Cap'n Flint's
*32250 N. Harbor Dr., (707) 964-9447. L-D daily; $. Highchairs, boosters, child portions. No reservations. No cards.*

Popular with locals, the menu here offers various kinds of fish & chips, clam chowder, and the house specialty—deep-fried shrimp won tons made with a tasty cream cheese filling. Hamburgers, hot dogs, sandwiches, and wine-based drinks are also available. Though the decor consists of well-worn, mismatched furniture, the view of picturesque Noyo Harbor is excellent.

## Egghead's
*326 N. Main St., (707) 964-5005, fax (707) 961-0186; www.eggheadsrestaurant.com. B-L Thur-Tu; $. Highchairs, boosters, booths, child portions. No reservations.*

Decorated with movie photos from *The Wizard of Oz* and related knickknacks, this cheerful, popular, and tiny diner serves 40-plus varieties of crêpes and *big* omelettes. Regular breakfast items and an assortment of sandwiches are also available. Families will appreciate the privacy afforded by enclosed booths.

## Old Coast Hotel Bar & Grill
*101 N. Franklin St./Oak, (888) 468-3550, (707) 961-4488, fax (707) 961-4480; www.oldcoasthotel.com. Highchairs, boosters. L F-Sun, D Thur-Tu; $$.*

Extensively renovated and restored to its 1892 glory, this historic building features spectacular original pressed-tin walls. The airy, open dining room has an attractive bar area and beautiful original wood floors throughout. The dinner menu offers appetizers such as onion rings, popcorn shrimp, and roasted mussels. Entrees consist of seafood, pasta, pizza, and an assortment of specialties—grilled salmon, shellfish cioppino, scampi, rosemary roasted rotisserie chicken, and, on Friday and Saturday nights, prime rib.

The upstairs **hotel rooms** *(15 rooms; $-$$$. Some fireplaces. Continental breakfast.)* are simple but comfortable, and all are equipped with warm down comforters.

## The Restaurant
*418 N. Main St., (707) 964-9800; www.therestaurant fortbragg.com. D Thur-M; $$. Highchairs, boosters, booths, child menu. Reservations advised.*

An ad for this restaurant reads, "If you like to eat, you'd probably like to eat at a place where people who like to eat, eat what they like—and like it!" It's an unusual ad—just like the restaurant, which, in completely unpretentious surroundings, serves interesting food at reasonable prices. The eclectic menu changes regularly, but the emphasis is on fresh local seafood and vegetarian items. A sample lunch menu offers a variety of sandwiches, plus a hamburger, Philly cheese steak, chicken flauta, vegetable chili, and several salads and soups. Desserts are a chocolate shortcake with fresh berries and cream, a housemade ice cream, and a lemon tart. Dinner entrees the same night include Thai-style shrimp in green curry sauce, Denver lamb riblets with sweet & sour glaze, and chicken breast Amalfi topped with lemony arugula.

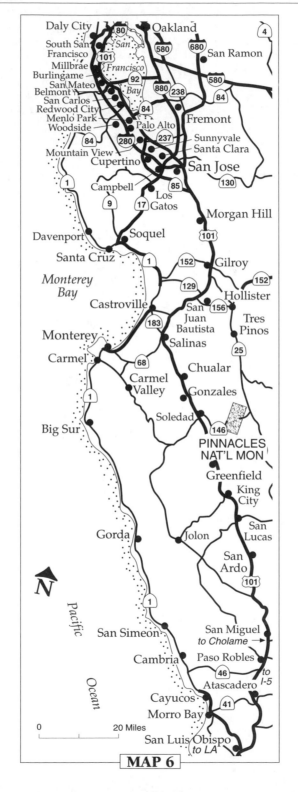

**MAP 6**

# 101 SOUTH

## Brisbane

### — WHERE TO STAY —

#### Radisson Hotel San Francisco Airport at Sierra Point
*500 Sierra Point Pkwy., 2 mi. N of airport, (800) 333-3333, (415) 467-4400, fax (415) 467-4440; www.radisson.com. 8 stories; 210 rooms; $$-$$$. Indoor pool & hot tub; fitness room. Restaurant; room service. No pets.*

This comfortable business hotel features large rooms, many with two queen beds and some with a view of the bay and airport traffic. Complimentary shuttle service is provided to and from San Francisco Airport.

Colorful, trendy **Xebec** restaurant and bar does a good interpretation of American dishes.

## Millbrae

### — WHAT TO DO —

#### San Francisco International Airport (SFO)
*800-IFLYSFO, (650) 821-8211; www.flysfo.com; www.sfoarts.org.*

SFO offers an ever-changing set of art exhibits to entertain waiting passengers. In fact,

it is the only airport in the U.S. accredited as a museum by the American Association of Museums, and each terminal has exhibits. The **Louis A. Turpen Aviation Museum** *((650) 652-2722. Sun-F 10-4:30. Free.)* in the international terminal is a replica of a 1937 airport.

### — WHERE TO EAT —

#### Fook Yuen
*195 El Camino Real/Millbrae Ave., (650) 692-8600. L-D daily; $. Highchairs, boosters. Reservations accepted.*

A branch of a chain found also in Hong Kong, Singapore, and Australia, this popular spot stands out on this Chinese restaurant row. It serves delicious, distinctive food, including dim sum at lunch and a Cantonese menu at dinner. Specialties include tank-fresh seafood, pork with pickled plums, and crispy chicken.

#### Hong Kong Flower Lounge
*51 Millbrae Ave./El Camino Real, (650) 878-8108. L-D daily; $$. Highchairs, boosters. Reservations advised.*

Authentic Hong Kong-style fresh seafood dishes, superior dim sum, and the restaurant's signature Peking duck are served in a cavernous, yet stylish, room said to seat 400.

# Burlingame

## — VISITOR INFORMATION —

### San Mateo County Convention & Visitors Bureau

*111 Anza Blvd. #410, (800) 288-4748, (650) 348-7600, fax (650) 348-7687; www.sanmateocounty cvb.com.*

## — WHAT TO DO —

### Burlingame Museum of Pez Memorabilia

*214 California Dr./Howard Ave., (650) 347-2301; www.burlingamepezmuseum.com. Tu-Sat 10-6. Free.*

Operating in the front of a computer store, this homespun exhibition includes some interactive exhibits. It displays more than 500 plastic Pez candy dispensers dating from the 1950s to the present. The rarest is a 1972 Make-a-Face. Snoopy, Bugs Bunny, and Fred Flintstone are all on display, along with Tweety Bird, who starred in a *Seinfeld* episode. A large selection of contemporary and collectible Pez dispensers is for sale, as are the hard-to-find candy refills. (The Pez mint was invented in Austria in 1927. It was introduced to the U.S. in fruit flavors and offered in a head dispenser in 1952.)

## — WHERE TO STAY —

### Embassy Suites Hotel San Francisco-Airport

*150 Anza Blvd., (800) EMBASSY, (650) 342-4600, (650) 343-8137; www.embassy-suites.com. 340 suites. Indoor pool & hot tub; fitness room. Evening snack, full breakfast; restaurant.*

Located 2 miles south of the airport and far enough from the freeway to be restive, this bay front hotel has a 9-story tropical atrium and a **Bobby McGee's** restaurant serving prime rib, steak, and fresh seafood. For more description, see page 420.

### Hyatt Regency San Francisco Airport

*1333 Bayshore Hwy., (800) 233-1234, (650) 347-1234, fax (650) 696-2669; www.sanfrancisco.hyatt.com. 10 stories; 793 rooms; $$. Unheated pool; hot tub; fitness room. 3 restaurants.*

The fabulous atrium here is filled with greenery and cascading waterfalls, objects de art, and plenty of revitalizing natural light. Amenities include a complimentary 24-hour airport shuttle.

**Knuckles Historical Sports Bar** *(L-D daily.)* has more than 20 beers are on tap, 27 TV monitors plus a large screen, and pool tables.

## — WHERE TO EAT —

### Benihana

*1496 Old Bayshore Hwy./Broadway, (650) 342-5202, fax (650) 342-6896; www.benihana.com. L M-Sat, D daily; $$. Reservations advised. Valet parking.*

The sushi bar here has a spectacular bay view. For more description, see page 58.

### Brothers Deli

*1351 Howard Ave./Primrose Rd./El Camino Real, (650) 343-2311, fax (650) 347-1866. B-L-D daily; $. Highchairs, boosters, booths.*

Transplanted Chicagoans and New Yorkers are always looking for a good deli out here. Even one that just comes close to what they were raised on is appreciated. Brothers Deli comes close. The red vinyl booths are comfy and the atmosphere casual. All the better to enjoy a lean corned beef sandwich or a hot pastrami on rye, or maybe something else from the extensive menu of sandwiches, hot plates, salads, and housemade soups. Desserts include strudel, cupcakes, and rice pudding. Everything can be packed to go.

### Copenhagen Bakery & Cafe

*1216 Burlingame Ave./Lorton Ave., (650) 342-1357, fax (650) 344-0324; www.copenhagenbakery.com. B-L daily, D W-Sun; $. Highchairs, boosters, child items.*

This combination Danish bakery and restaurant produces great six-grain and sweet French breads as well as exquisite European-style pastries. The extensive breakfast menu includes omelettes and pancakes as well as bacon and eggs and is served until 2:30 on weekends. For lunch try a delicious German bologna on sweet French bread with a side of potato salad and, of course, a dessert pastry. Or get the Royal Lunch—a collection of Danish-style open face sandwiches. Specialty coffee drinks and ice cream treats are also available. Order at the counter, then find a seat in the cheery open dining rooms with sidewalk views.

## Il Fornaio
*327 Lorton Ave., (650) 375-8000; www.ilfornaio.com. B Sat-Sun, L M-F, D daily.*
For description, see page 73.

## Isobune Burlingame
*1451 Burlingame Ave., (650) 344-8433; www.isobuneburlingame.com. L-D daily; $.*
For description, see page 73.

## Max's Opera Cafe
*1250 Old Bayshore Hwy., (650) 342-6297, fax (650) 342-2982; www.maxsworld.com. B-L-D daily.*
For description, see page 78.

## Pisces
*1190 California Dr./Broadway Ave., (650) 401-7500, fax (650) 401-8321; www.piscesrestaurant.com. D M-Sat; $$-$$$. Reservations advised.*

Operating within the town's beautifully restored and stylishly updated historic train station, this upscale yet casual spot specializes in fresh fish items. In addition to raw, seared, grilled, and smoked seafood, there is the option of the signature rotisserie-style fish dishes. For an appetizer, crispy calamari spiced with red pepper and served with a sesame-mint aioli is delicious, as is the refined New England clam chowder served with a few whole clams. Entrees might include a comforting porcini-crusted petrale sole with roasted garlic mashed potatoes or a boldly flavorful sweet miso-glazed sea bass with lobster tortellini. A few meat dishes round out the menu. Desserts are a high point and have included a layered milk chocolate mousse and a signature root beer float with warm chocolate chip cookies. Since the building is track-side, a whole lotta shakin' goes on as trains pass by.

## World Wrapps
*1318 Burlingame Ave., (650) 342-9777, fax (650) 342-9731; www.worldwrapps.com.*
For description, see page 87.

# San Mateo

### — GETTING THERE —
Located approximately 20 miles south of San Francisco.

### — ANNUAL EVENTS —
## San Mateo County Fair
*August. (650) 574-3247, fax (650) 574-3985; www.sanmateocountyfair.com. $9, 62+ & 6-12 $5.*

### — WHAT TO DO —
## Coyote Point Recreation Area
*1701 Coyote Point Dr., (650) 573-2593, fax (650) 573-3727; www.sanmateocountyparks.com. Daily 8-sunset. $5/vehicle.*

This 670-acre park is equipped with a barbecue area, several playgrounds, inviting grassy expanses, an 18-hole golf course, a rifle range, and a swimming beach with bathhouse. It is one of the best windsurfing sites in the U.S. and considered prime for beginners. As if all this isn't enough, it's also located on the descent route for the San Francisco International Airport, making it a wonderful place to just sit and watch planes land.

Bay-side and surrounded by an aromatic grove of eucalyptus trees, the architecturally impressive **Coyote Point Museum** *(1651 Coyote Point Dr., (650) 342-7755; www.coyotept museum.org. Tu-Sat 10-5, Sun 12-5. $6, 62+ & 13-17 $4, 3-12 $2; free 1st W of month.)* was the first environmental museum in the U.S. It aims to educate visitors about local ecology and the environment with numerous hands-on and multi-media displays. Exhibits inside include live colonies of termites and bees. Exhibits in the impressive outdoor Wildlife Habitats area include non-releasable live native animals (burrowing owls, a porcupine, a banana slug), a walk-through aviary of native Bay Area birds, and a colorful demonstration garden composed of plants that attract hummingbirds and butterflies. The foxes are fed daily at 11:30, the otters at 12:15. Nature's Marketplace shows how Native Americans used plants, shrubs, and trees in everyday life. Bring a lunch to enjoy in the inviting picnic area. A **Gingerbread House Contest** occurs each December.

## Central Park
*El Camino Real/5th Ave., (650) 522-7434; www.ci.sanmateo.ca.us/dept/parks. Free.*

Dating from 1922, this is the oldest municipal park in the county. Facilities include a **kiddie train** *((650) 340-1520. M-F 11-3, Sat-Sun 11-4. $1)*—a miniature version of the long-gone Southern Pacific Coast Daylight—plus a botanical garden, tennis courts, and a playground. **Victorian Days in the Park** *((650) 574-6441)* occurs annually in August.

The tidy 1-acre **Japanese Garden** *(5th Ave., (650) 522-7409, fax (650) 522-7421. M-F 10-4, Sat-Sun 11-4. Free.)* was designed by Nagao Sakurai, a former landscape architect at the Imperial Palace in Tokyo. Features include a teahouse (no tea service), a central pond divided by a narrow bridge (koi are fed daily at 11 a.m. and 3 p.m.), two waterfalls, a pagoda, and a shrine. Narrow pathways are designed to make visitors slow down and really look. Rare and unusual plants include a weeping beech and an umbrella pine.

### — WHERE TO EAT —

## Draeger's Market
*222 E. 4th Ave./B St., (650) 685-3700; www.draegers.com. Daily 7am-10pm.*

This enormous market is the largest gourmet food emporium in the U.S. More than a grocery store, this European-style facility caters to the educated palate with a sushi bar, wine tasting room, smoothie bar, deli, and bakery as well as a cooking school. It offers a vast selection of wines and beers, an expansive olive bar, and exotic meats that include alligator, turtle, and buffalo. A second-floor shop purveys an expansive selection of cookbooks, housewares, and gift items.

In a subdued, open, second-floor space drenched with light, upscale **Viognier** restaurant *((650) 685-3727, fax (650) 685-3723; www.viognierrestaurant.com. L M-F, D daily, Sat-SunBr; $$-$$$. Booths.)* serves a rustic Mediterranean menu of salads, pizzettas, grilled and rotisseried meats, and pastas. An exhibition kitchen and fireplace enhance the setting. Desserts are a high point—look for a chocolate-raspberry parfait dome that tastes as good as it sounds. The namesake wine is featured on the wine list.

## Fernando's Mexican Restaurant
*63 W. 37th Ave., (650) 345-9042. L-D daily. Highchairs, boosters, booths, child portions.*

This old-time family restaurant has a long bar on one side of the entry and an inviting open room filled with comfortable carved wooden booths on the other. Order up one of the margaritas or "mocktails" (the virgin piña colada is primo) to sip while your perusing the extensive menu. Choices include a la carte or traditional combination plates, fajitas, and house specialties—sopitos, mole enchiladas, and an assortment of seafood dishes. A three-piece mariachi band plays on Sundays from 5:30 to 8:30 p.m.

For dessert, it's just a few steps to **Romolo's Ice Cream & Cannoli Factory** *(81 37th Ave., (650) 574-0625. Tu-Sat 11-5.)* for ice cream creations, granita, tiramisu, Italian specialty cakes, and even cappuccino. Take it away or linger for a while seated on old-fashioned wire heart chairs.

## Heidi Pies
*1941 S. El Camino Real/20th Ave., (650) 574-0505. B-L-D daily; $. Highchairs, boosters, child menu. No reservations.*

The selection of freshly baked pies is replenished constantly from this old-fashioned coffee shop's own kitchen. Choices include fruit (raisin and gooseberry in addition to more common varieties), meringue (black bottom, banana), and specialty (German chocolate, pecan, cream cheese). The house specialty is hot apple pie—served plain, a la mode, with hot cinnamon sauce, with whipped cream, or with either Cheddar or American cheese. A vast selection of short-order items, including a hamburger and grilled cheese sandwich, comprise the rest of the menu. This restaurant is open around the clock, and whole pies are available to go.

## Kaimuki Grill
*104 S. El Camino Real/2nd Ave. & Crystal Springs Rd., (650) 548-9320. L Tu-F, D M-Sat; $-$$. Boosters. No reservations.*

Japanese cuisine with California and Hawaiian accents is the specialty in this simple, yet atmospheric, venue. Choose from a menu that includes Chinese-style won ton-ramen noodle soup and a large variety of sushi. Housemade noodle dishes and small appetizer items—eggplant stuffed with ground chicken, shitakes stuffed with ground beef—are particularly tasty.

## La Michoacana
*251 S. B St./3rd Ave., (650) 558-0069. L-D daily; $.*

*Highchairs, boosters. Reservations accepted.*

This tiny Mexican restaurant provides comfortable seating in its 2-story dining area. Everything is made fresh and is of exceptional taste, quality, and value, and a la carte and combination plates allow a satisfying meal whatever the stage of hunger. A selection of Salvadorean dishes includes pupusas—handmade corn tortillas stuffed with delicious cheese and flavorful seasoned pork. Horchata, Mexican hot chocolate, and wine margaritas are among the drink choices, and flan is the single dessert.

## Left Bank

*1100 Park Pl./Bay Meadows, (650) 345-2250, fax (650) 345-0770; www.leftbank.com. L-D daily.*

For description, see page 216.

## Little Sichuan Restaurant

*168 E. 4th Ave./Ellsworth St., (650) 345-9168, fax (650) 345-2167. L-D Tu-Sun; $. Highchairs, boosters.*

A large selection of delicious hot and spicy dishes is served here in light, airy rooms. Seating is comfortable, and tablecloths provide a nice touch. Dinners begin with a complimentary appetizer of boiled peanuts in shell and a kimchi-style cabbage dish. Hot-and-sour soup, kung pao chicken, and house specialty dry-cooked string beans are all particularly good. Many rice and noodle dishes—including wide chow fun rice noodles—are on the menu, along with a good selection of unspicy dishes.

## North Beach Pizza

*240 E. 3rd Ave./B St., (650) 344-5000, fax (650) 344-5233; www.northbeachpizza.com.*

For description, see page 80.

## Prince of Wales Pub

*106 E. 25th Ave./Delaware St., 1 blk. from racetrack, (650) 574-9723. L-D M-Sat; $.*

Famous for having the longest running dart tournament in the U.S. (30 years in 2001), for using the most habañero chilies per year in the U.S. (100 pounds), and for being where the Kingston Trio played before they were famous, this pub also manages to trick you into thinking you've crossed the big pond. A pleasant patio in the back boasts a 1-story-tall bird-of-paradise plant and is equipped with comfortable picnic tables. The menu offers, but of course, fish & chips and bangers (English pork sausage) as

well as a "splendid" hamburger just like the one the Duke of Windsor once enjoyed. A burger heaped with habañero chilies is also an option, and 11 beers are on draught. Waiting time can be passed playing darts, dominoes, or backgammon.

## Taxi's Hamburgers

*2700 S. El Camino, 650-377-1947, fax 650-341-8856; www.taxishamburgers.com. L-D daily; $. Child portions.*

All kinds of burgers, sandwiches, salads, a "top your own baked potato bar" with over 20 toppings, and shakes (including a low-fat version) are on the menu. The decor pays homage to taxicabs, and table-top jukeboxes play oldies but goodies.

## T.G.I. Friday's

*3101 S. El Camino Real/Hillsdale Blvd., (650) 570-4684, fax (650) 570-4663; www.tgifridays.com. L-D daily, SunBr; $-$$. Highchairs, boosters, child menu. No reservations.*

This comfortable fern bar produces tasty drinks from a massive bar dominating its center, and its vast menu offers everything from a French dip sandwich to a hamburger to a chimichanga to blackened filet mignon. The children's menu—which doubles as a coloring book and offers kids everything they love most, prepared the way they like it (for instance: a grilled cheese sandwich made with *American* cheese on *white* bread)—just might qualify as the world's most extensive. Furthering its family-friendly rep, kids are given a helium balloon as a parting gift.

## 231 Ellsworth

*231 S. Ellsworth Ave./3rd Ave., (650) 347-7231, fax (650) 347-7329; www.231ellsworth.com. L M-F, D M-Sat; $$$. Valet parking at D.*

In the sophisticated atmosphere of a darkened dining room with deep-brown walls, a surprising deep-blue ceiling, and crispy white nappery, this stylish restaurant delivers a small but palate-pleasing menu of California dishes. Chef-owner William Collier, who has worked in many kitchens, including Tavern on the Green in NYC, likes to make complex mixtures and use unusual mushrooms. Appetizers might include a delicate prawn-and-quail egg tempura presented with a spicy green papaya salad and a light, flavorful passion fruit dipping sauce, or perhaps a warm frisée and endive salad topped with goat cheese, hazelnuts, and sherry vinaigrette. Entrees have included a delicate sole with fava beans and Hon Shemiji mushrooms, as well as delicious, full-flavored lamb loin cutlets with a ragout of Black trumpets, olives, and basil gnocchetti. A five- and seven-course tasting menu is also available, along with selected wines. Desserts are divine, perhaps a milk chocolate tart with caramel sauce and cashews or a true-flavored pear sorbet with a delicate Riesling gelée. Attentive service and unobtrusive background music enhance this special-occasion dining spot. A comfortable bar area in front is worth a visit, and late-night dessert is available.

## San Carlos

### — WHAT TO DO —

**Hiller Aviation Museum**
*601 Skyway Rd., Holly St. exit off Hwy. 101, (650) 654-0200, fax (650) 654-0220; www.hiller.org. Daily 10-5. $8, 65+ & 8-17 $5.*

Recently reopened in its new home at San Carlos Airport, this huge 53,000-square-foot museum is heaven for aviation buffs. Approximately 50 aircraft and 100 exhibits span the history of aviation in California. Many displays are interactive, and fascinating videotapes show some unusual aircraft in motion. Vertical take-off and landing craft, hypersonic craft, and various wing configurations are displayed, as is a Boeing Condor that can stay in the air for 4 days—it is the largest aircraft hanging in any museum in the world. A restoration workshop viewed through giant windows allows a glimpse of the latest acquisitions. Multi-media presentations and a library enhance the experience and educate about this area's powerful influence on aviation (for example, the first "aeroplane" with three-axis control flew in this very area in 1869—3 decades *before* Kitty Hawk). Kids like visiting the 747 cockpit outdoors and climbing into the Blue Angels cockpit indoors. From 11 a.m. to 1 p.m. on the third Saturday of every month, kids age 8 through 17 are eligible to register in the Young Eagles program and take a free ride in an airplane. Flight classes for kids are scheduled regularly. Also

worth a gander, the gift shops stocks helicopter cookie cutters, pint-sized flight suits and bomber jackets, and freeze-dried pizza and ice cream.

## Redwood City

### — WHAT TO DO —

**Fox Theatre**
*2215 Broadway Ave., (650) FOX-4119, fax (650) FOX-4129; www.foxdream.com. Prices vary.*

Now completely refurbished and used as both a movie and live performance theater, this grand old art deco theater has a Vaudeville stage, a pipe organ, and a state-of-the-art audio system. Next door, the **Little Fox** theater presents live music and dancing in a 1920s-style cabaret atmosphere.

**Malibu Grand Prix/Malibu Castle**
*Grand Prix: 340 Blomquist St./Seaport Blvd., (650) 366-6463. Castle: 320 Blomquist St., (650) 367-1906. www.malibugrandprix.com; daily 10-10, to 12 on Sat-Sun & in summer; prices vary.*

Bring your daredevils to race Indy-style cars in a safe, fun environment. One- and two-seat Virage cars can be driven by ages 18 and older with a valid driver's license (younger passengers are permitted in the two-seaters), and junior drivers measuring 4'8" or taller can drive scaled-down F-50s. The adjacent Castle rounds out the fun with three 18-hole miniature golf courses, a video-game arcade, go-karts, and batting cages.

**San Mateo History Museum**
*777 Hamilton St., (650) 299-0104, fax (650) 299-0141; www.sanmateocountyhistory.com. Tu-Sun 10-4. $2, 65+ & 6-12 $2.*

The former San Mateo County Courthouse, this building boasts the largest complete stained-glass dome on the West Coast. Exhibits portray life on the Peninsula from 250 years ago through today, and include an historic courtroom. The Ships of the World gallery displays 18 scale-model ships.

### — WHERE TO STAY —

**Sofitel San Francisco Bay**
*223 Twin Dolphin Dr., 12 mi. from airport,*

*(800) SOFITEL, (650) 598-9000, fax (650) 598-9383; www.sofitel.com. 9 stories; 421 rooms; $-$$$+. Heated pool; fitness room. 2 restaurants.*

Taste France without leaving the Bay Area. This link in the sleek French hotel chain is situated near the bay among the equally glossy hi-rise headquarters of hi-tech companies. (This quiet area of waterways was the former home of Six Flags Marine World). French touches include the charming accents borne by many employees and bath mitts instead of washcloths.

## — WHERE TO EAT —

### Max's Cafe

*1001 El Camino Real, (650) 365-MAXS, fax (650) 365-8774; www.maxsworld.com. L-D daily.*

For description, see page 77.

# Woodside

## — A LITTLE BACKGROUND —

Though located just a few miles from bustling El Camino Real, Woodside feels very rural. It has been called the "horsiest community in the United States," and, indeed, it has more horses per capita than any other community in the county. Hitching posts found outside some of the town's restaurants back up the claim, and horses and wagons are often seen "parked" by them. With the recent heavy influx of people who have made their fortune in Silicon Valley, a millionaire here is now considered average— just a member of the middle class. Fortunately, the restaurant prices don't reflect this reality.

## — GETTING THERE —

Located on Highway 84, approximately 5 miles west of Highway 101.

## — WHAT TO DO —

### Filoli

*86 Cañada Rd., Edgewood Rd. exit off I-280, (650) 364-8300, fax (650) 366-7836; www.filoli.org. Guided 2-hr. tour Tu-Sat, by reservation; self-guided tour Tu-Sat 10-3:30; closed Nov-mid-Feb. $10, 7-12 $1.*

Named for the family motto—"Fight for a just cause; Love your fellow man; and Live a full life"—this 654-acre country estate surrounds a 43-room modified Georgian mansion built for William Bowers Bourn II in 1917 by his hunt-

ing buddy, architect Willis Polk. Its ballroom is gilded with gold leaf extracted from Bourn's Empire Mine in Grass Valley. (The mansion is the setting for the 1978 film *Heaven Can Wait* and is seen as the exterior of the Carrington home shown at the beginning of TV's *Dynasty*.) Tours of the house and 16 landscaped acres of European-inspired formal gardens include such delights as two manicured English knot gardens, a garden designed to resemble a stained-glass window in Chartres cathedral in France, and a practical cutting garden used to decorate the mansion. Also special is a sunken garden replicated after one on the Ireland estate the Bourns bought for their daughter. The gardens are spectacular in April, when more than 70,000 tulips and 200,000 daffodils bloom, and in May, when the rose garden is at its peak. A garden shop and cafe are near the exit; picnicking is not permitted. Special events include children's Easter parties and a Mothers' Day Champagne brunch.

### The Woodside Store

*3300 Tripp Rd./off Woodside Rd. (Hwy. 84), (650) 851-7615; www.sanmateocountyhistory.com. Tu-Thur 10-4, Sat-Sun 12-4. Free.*

Constructed of redwood in 1854, this was the first general store built between San Francisco and San Jose. It has also been a post office, a blacksmith shop, and a dental office. Meticulously restored, it now appears as it did in the 1880s.

## — WHERE TO EAT —

### Buck's

*3062 Woodside Rd./Cañada Rd., (650) 851-8010, fax (650) 851-8959; www.buckswoodside.com. B-L-D daily; $$. Highchairs, boosters, booths, child menu. Reservations advised.*

Especially popular in the morning, when local computer executives gather for power breakfasts of buckwheat pancakes and huevos rancheros, this attractive spot is filled with comfy booths and lots of windows. It's sort of like an updated old-time coffee shop, but with a full bar. Breakfast is served until 2:30 on weekends and includes all the usual suspects plus an extensive selection of omelettes and pancakes. Lunch brings on soups, salads, sandwiches, burgers, and a popular chili. American-style entrees are added at dinner along with a few more frou-frou items such as lobster ravioli with red pesto sauce or baked local halibut with pineapple salsa. Dessert portions are large enough to satisfy two or three people—the menu claims "all desserts have been tested by the American Trucking Association and found to be way too large"—and include a signature hot fudge sundae and delicious peach cobbler. Should boredom set in, just check out the mish-mash of curiosities lining the walls.

# Menlo Park

## — A LITTLE BACKGROUND —

Developed in the 1800s by two Irishmen, this peaceful tree-filled suburb is centered around its historic train station—the oldest passenger station in the state. Leland Stanford and Mark Hopkins, both rail tycoons in their time, once boarded the train here for the ride into San Francisco. Today the station is a shelter for CalTrain passengers.

## — WHAT TO DO —

### Sunset Magazine Garden
*80 Willow Rd./Middlefield Rd., (650) 321-3600; www.sunset.com. M-F 9-4:30. Free.*

A self-guided walking tour leads visitors through 7 acres of landscaped gardens surrounding an impressive 1.3-acre lawn.

## — WHERE TO STAY —

### Stanford Park Hotel
*100 El Camino Real, (800) 368-2468, (650) 322-1234, fax (650) 322-0975; www.woodsidehotels.com. 4 stories; 163 rooms; $$-$$$+. Children under 12 free. Some fireplaces. Heated pool; hot tub; sauna; fitness room. Evening snack; restaurant; room service. No smoking; no pets.*

Located just north of town, this hotel offers spacious rooms furnished with custom-made English yew wood pieces. It was one of the first hotels in the U.S. to offer the innovative computer-operated "video on command" system.

## — WHERE TO EAT —

### Allied Arts Guild Restaurant
*75 Arbor Rd./Cambridge Ave., (650) 324-2588; www.alliedartsguild.org. L M-Sat; $. Highchairs,*

boosters. Reservations required. No cards. Shops: M-Sat 10-5.

Housed in a former weaving studio and originally a tearoom, this restaurant was opened by the Palo Alto auxiliary of Children's Hospital at Stanford in 1932. In those days guild members prepared food in their homes and transported it to the premises for serving. Now a modern kitchen lets volunteers prepare three-course luncheons that include a soup, hot entree with vegetable or salad, freshly baked rolls, dessert, and choice of beverage. The menu is different each day, and all the recipes are for sale. In warm weather, an attractive patio is available for dining; request it when reserving. All profits and tips help support Children's Hospital. Allow time to wander through the attractive Spanish Colonial-style estate, once part of the vast Rancho de las Pulgas, a Spanish land grant dating back to the late 1700s. Shops invite browsing, and the peaceful 3.5-acre gardens—designed after the Alhambra Gardens in Granada, Spain—invite a leisurely stroll.

### Gaylord India
*1706 El Camino Real/Encinal Ave., (650) 326-8761, fax (650) 326-8750; www.gaylords.com. L-D daily.*

For description, see page 69.

### Left Bank
*635 Santa Cruz Ave./Doyle St., (650) 473-6543, fax (650) 473-6536; www.leftbank.com.*

For description, see page 216.

### Lisa's Tea Treasures
*1175 Merrill St./Oak Grove St., across from train station, (650) 322-5544; www.lisastea.com. Tea served M-F 11-4, Sat at 11, 1:30, 4, Sun at 12, 3; $$. Reservations advised.*

For description, see page 195.

### Picnic Pick-Ups
• **Draeger's Market**
*1010 University Dr., (650) 324-7700; www.draegers. com. Daily 7am-10pm.*

For description, see page 172.

# Palo Alto

## — A LITTLE BACKGROUND —

With wide tree-lined streets and impressive mansions on its outlying boulevards, Palo Alto historically has been home to upper-class residents. It is famous as the home of Stanford University and, more recently, for being a part of that nebulous area known as Silicon Valley. The University Avenue exit off Highway 101 leads under a canopy of magnolias, then oaks, then, upon entering the Stanford campus, palms.

## — VISITOR INFORMATION —

### Palo Alto Chamber of Commerce
122 Hamilton Ave., (650) 324-3121, fax (650) 324-1215, www.paloaltochamber.com.

## — GETTING THERE —

Located approximately 13 miles south of San Mateo, and 32 miles south of San Francisco.

## — WHAT TO DO —

### Birthplace of Silicon Valley
367 Addison Ave./Waverley St.

The product (an audio oscillator) and the company (Hewlett-Packard) that launched the high tech industry were developed in 1939 in this garage by Stanford graduates William Hewlett and David Packard. A monument beside the driveway tells the story.

### Elizabeth F. Gamble Garden
1431 Waverley St./Embarcadero Rd., (650) 329-1356, fax (650) 329-1688; www.gamblegarden.org. House: M-F 9-noon. Garden: daily dawn to dusk. Free.

Built in 1902, the Colonial Georgian Revival house here features enormous pieces of inside redwood paneling unmarred by knots. Today, volunteers maintain both the house and the manicured classic Edwardian gardens, which include small "rooms," an assortment of soothing fountains, and scattered benches for quiet reflection. Each month has its pleasures, but April's promise of a cascade of blossoms along a cherry allée might be the best. Picnicking is popular at tables sheltered by an old oak, and the lawns next door at **Bowling Green Park** are also inviting.

### Museum of American Heritage
351 Homer Ave./Waverly St., (650) 321-1004, fax (650) 473-6950; www.moah.org. F-Sun 11-4. Free.

Situated inside a charming converted, English country-style house that it rents from the city, this non-profit institution displays 19th- and 20th-century electrical and mechanical inventions. Among the 2,000-plus artifacts are obsolete typewriters, toasters, washing machines, and cameras—all arranged into themed settings such as The Kitchen, The Laundry, and The General Store. Volunteers are sometimes on hand to demonstrate a group of elevator models and the Linotype machine in The Print Shop set up in a garage out back. Special exhibits, enticing classes, and a large garden also beckon.

### Palo Alto Children's Theatre
1305 Middlefield Rd., (650) 463-4930; www.city.palo-alto.ca.us/theatre. $6, under 18 $3.

Seasonal productions here are performed by child actors ages 8 through 18 and appeal especially to children. Past shows have included such favorites as *The Tales of Beatrix Potter* and *Charlotte's Web*. Summer performances are usually staged outside, and picnics are encouraged.

### Palo Alto Duck Pond
At E end of Embarcadero Rd. Daily sunrise-sunset. Free.

Located in a quiet, unpopulated area away from town, this is one of the Bay Area's best spots to see ducks and birds. Usually the pond attracts a hefty number of ducks and seagulls, sometimes even a few swans. In winter, unusual migrating birds are also seen. A nearby small airport provides plane-watching fun.

Nearby, the **Lucy Evans Baylands Nature Interpretive Center** ((650) 329-2506. Tu-F 2-5, Sat-Sun 1-5. Free.) has exhibits that orient visitors to the area. Workshops, films, and slide shows are scheduled regularly. During daylight hours, visitors can walk out over the 120-acre salt marsh on an 800-foot-long raised wooden walkway. Naturalist-led walks are scheduled on weekends.

### Palo Alto Junior Museum & Zoo
1451 Middlefield Rd./Embarcadero, (650) 329-2111, fax (650) 473-1965; www.pajmzfriends.org. Tu-Sat 10-5, Sun 1-4. Free.

Opened in 1934, this was the first children's museum on the West Coast. Inside exhibits are hands-on and include colorful play structures; they are especially fun for children through age 10. Special programs and workshops are scheduled regularly. A well-maintained outdoor mini-zoo houses local and exotic animals—raccoons, pythons, skinks, ducks, birds, and bunnies—puts windows at kids' eye level. Adjacent **Rinconada Park** has a large, colorful playground.

## Stanford Shopping Center
*On El Camino Real, just N of Stanford campus, (650) 617-8585, fax (650) 617-8227; www.simon.com. M-F 10-9, Sat 10-7, Sun 11-6.*

Beautifully designed, this is the only shopping center in the world owned by a university. In addition to being an environmentally conscious mall, with recycling receptacles throughout, it is a showcase for California artists. Look for David Gilhooley's "Merfrog Fountain," Larry Binkley's "Flying People," and John Pugh's 180-foot-long mural of an 18th-century Parisian street scene. Among the 150 fashionable stores are: California's first **Bloomingdales; Gleim Jewelers**, where the world's largest emerald is sometimes on display; the only Northern California outlet for Dutch retailer **Oilily**; an unusual open-air **Polo/Ralph Lauren** shop; the world's first **Victoria's Secret**, which opened here in 1977. Department stores include **Macy's, Nordstrom**, and **Neiman Marcus**. Also, **The Health Library**, operated by Stanford University Hospital as a community service, provides an archive of medical information and helpful volunteer reference librarians. Food outlets include a branch of the Wine Country's **Oakville Grocery** (see page 399) filled with esoteric foods, and a branch of Berkeley's **Andronico's Market** (see page 281). Among the restaurants attracting diners at all hours are branches of **Max's Opera Cafe** (see page 78), **Palo Alto Creamery Fountain & Grill** (see page 181), and **Piatti Ristorante** (see page 386).

## The Stanford Theatre
*221 University Ave., (650) 324-3700; www.stanford theatre.org. $6, 65+ $4, under 18 $3.*

This 1,175-seat movie palace has been meticulously restored to its 1925-era grandeur by former classics professor David Packard, Jr.,

son of the computer tycoon. Plush red mohair seats, elaborate ceiling paintings, and magnificent tile work in the lobby help take audiences back in time as they view pre-1950 Hollywood films. Some movies play here that can be seen nowhere else. Retrospectives are scheduled regularly, and an organist often accompanies silent films on the theater's Wurlitzer. Box office proceeds go to film restoration and preservation.

## Stanford University Campus
*Entrance at El Camino Real/University Ave., (650) 723-2560; www.stanford.edu. Facilities sometimes closed during academic breaks.*

Founded by Leland Stanford in 1885 on what had been his family's horse farm, California's premier private university is dedicated to the memory of Stanford's son, who died of typhoid fever at the age of 15. It is fittingly nicknamed "The Farm" and is home to 13 Nobel Prize winners.

The **Quadrangle**, which is the oldest part of the campus, features buildings of Mission-style architecture. Hour-long **campus tours** *((650) 723-2560. Daily at 11, 3:15. Free.)* leave from the front steps of Memorial Auditorium. Tours of the 2-mile-long **linear accelerator** are also available *(2575 Sand Hill Rd., in Menlo Park, (650) 926-2204; www.slac.stanford.edu. M-F at 10, 1. Free. Reservation required.)*. East of the Quad is **Hoover Tower** *((650) 723-2053. Daily 10-4:30. $2, 65+ & under 13 $1.)*. Stanford's shorter version of the University of California's campanile, it stands 285 feet tall and affords a panoramic view of the area from its observation platform. At the tower's base, a museum that is part of the **Hoover Institution on War, Revolution, and Peace** *(550 Serra Mall, (650) 723-3563. Tu-Sat 11-4. Free.)* honors Stanford graduate and former president Herbert Hoover. Nearby, the **Thomas Welton Stanford Art Gallery** is home to revolving exhibitions of works by international and regional artists.

Built in 1892, the neoclassical **Iris & B. Gerald Cantor Center for Visual Arts** *(Museum Way/Lomita Dr., (650) 723-4177; www.stanford. edu/dept/ccva. W-Sun 11-5, Thur to 8; docent tour W at 12, Sat-Sun at 1, family tour 2nd Sat at 3. Free.)* is the oldest museum west of the Mississippi and the first building constructed of structurally reinforced concrete. Having suffered severe damage in the 1989 earthquake, it is repaired and once again showing its eclectic collection of extraordinary jades, Asian and Egyptian treasures, Stanford family memorabilia, and California Native American objects (a noteworthy item in this latter collection is a canoe carved by Yurok Indians from a single redwood log). The gold spike that marked the meeting of the two sections of the Transcontinental Railroad in 1869 is also displayed. An adjacent 1-acre **Rodin Sculpture Garden** *((650) 723-3469. Daily dawn-dusk; tour W at 2, Sat at 11:30, Sun at 3. Free.)* holds 20 bronzes, including "The Gates of Hell." Together the museum and garden hold the world's second-largest collection of Rodin sculpture (the largest is in Paris). All this and the fabulous **Cool Cafe** *((650) 725-4758)* providing organic fare and dramatic views of the sculpture garden, too!

## Winter Lodge
*3009 Middlefield Rd./Oregon Expressway, (650) 493-4566, fax (650) 493-3294; www.winterlodge.com. Daily 3-5, other session times vary; closed May-Sept. $7, skate rental $3.*

An *outdoor* ice skating rink in Palo Alto? Well, it's *not* on a frozen lake. Indeed, it is located in a nicely manicured residential section of town. But it *is* removed from traffic and surrounded by tall eucalyptus trees, and it's the *only* permanent outdoor rink west of the Sierra. Designed for families and children, the rink measures about two-thirds the size of an average indoor rink, making it too small for competitive skating.

### — WHERE TO STAY —
## Crowne Plaza Cabaña Palo Alto
*4290 El Camino Real/San Antonio Rd., 4 mi. from downtown, (800) 2-CROWNE, (650) 857-0787, fax (650) 496-1939; www.cppaloalto.crowneplaza.com. 8 stories; 194 rooms; $$-$$$. Children under 18 free. Heated pool; hot tub; fitness room. Restaurant; room service. Pets ok.*

This attractively renovated hotel has a curving entry hugged by 16 of its original Italian cypress trees planted in 1962. Once owned by Doris Day (and still reflecting that fact today with its pet-friendly policy) and co-owned by Jay J. Sarno (who designed and built Caesar's Palace in Las Vegas), it was popular with Rat Pack members Sammy Davis, Jr. and

Frank Sinatra. It made another big splash in 1965 when the Beatles took over the eighth floor during a concert tour, and a suite on that floor now honors them. All guest rooms have refrigerators with complimentary cold drinks, and complimentary car service is available within a 5-mile radius.

**4290 Bistro & Bar** serves Mediterranean-inspired cuisine and offers heavenly outdoor seating in nice weather.

## Garden Court Hotel
*520 Cowper St./University Ave., (800) 824-9028, (650) 322-9000, fax (650) 324-3609; www.gardencourt.com. 4 stories; 62 rooms; $$$+. Children under 12 free. Some wood-burning fireplaces. Fitness room. Restaurant; room service.*

Located just off the main street, this attractive hotel offers posh comfort. A central courtyard with fountains and flowers conveys a far-away-from-it-all feeling. The staff strives to give personal service and claims never to forget a name. Tastefully appointed guest rooms have private terraces and four-poster beds with European-style down bedding. Amenities include terry cloth robes, complimentary video tapes, shoeshine, nightly turndown, and local shuttle service.

On the ground floor directly beneath the hotel, **Il Fornaio Restaurant** *((650) 853-3888, fax (650) 853-3766; www.ilfornaio.com. B-L-D daily; $$. Reservations advised.)* serves up rustic pizzas in an elegant interior space as well as out on a sunny, peaceful courtyard. See also page 73.

## Hidden Villa Hostel
*26870 Moody Rd., in Los Altos Hills, 10 mi. from downtown, (650) 949-8648, fax (650) 948-4159; www.hiddenvilla.org. 35 beds; some private cabins. Closed June-Aug.*

Located on a 1,600-acre ranch in the foothills east of town, this facility was built in 1937 as the first hostel on the Pacific Coast. Guests sleep in rustic cabins. The property includes a working farm, organic garden, and land preserve. See also page 445.

## Sheraton Palo Alto
*625 El Camino Real/University Ave., (800) 874-3516, (650) 328-2800, fax (650) 327-7362; www.starwood. com/sheraton. 4 stories; 346 rooms; $$-$$$+.*

Children under 18 free. Some kitchens. Heated pool; fitness room. Restaurant; room service. Pets ok.

Centrally located and offering the amenities typical of the chain, this comfortable lodging has an attractively landscaped garden area with a large koi pond.

## Westin Palo Alto

675 El Camino Real, (800) WESTIN-1, (650) 321-4422, fax (650) 321-5522; www.westin.com. 5 stories; 184 rooms; $$-$$$$+. Heated pool; hot tub. Restaurant; room service. Parking $9-$12.

The Mediterranean design of this location of the luxe chain features large Etruscan-style vases in its five courtyards. It is equipped with the upscale features expected—spacious marble bathrooms and the trademark soft, down-topped Heavenly Beds.

### — WHERE TO EAT —

## Andalé

209 University Ave./Emerson St., (650) 323-2939, fax (650) 323-4270. L-D daily; $. Highchairs.

Delicious Mexican menu items include fresh fish tacos, vegetarian flautas, and seasonal fresh-fruit agua fresca drinks. After placing an order at the back counter, items are prepared to specifications using fresh ingredients and no lard. Meats sizzle continuously on the open grills. On weekends from 11 to 2, brunch items join the menu. In good weather, choice seating is on the patio just in from the sidewalk, and sometimes live music from a public square across the street provides free entertainment.

## Blue Chalk Cafe

630 Ramona St./Hamilton St., (650) 326-1020, fax (650) 326-1022. L M-F, D M-Sat; $-$$. Highchairs, boosters. Reservations accepted.

Operating within a historical building dating from 1927, this busy spot features an inviting open-air front patio and an interior equipped with pool tables. The kitchen dishes up delicious down-home Southern cuisine. Appetizers are exceptional and might include roasted Blue Lake green beans, catfish chips, and hoppin' john (black-eyed peas). Dinner is a choice of salads (a blackened chicken Caesar, a warm spinach with smoked chicken) and hefty dinner plates (house-smoked pork chops, old-fashioned meatloaf, barbecued short ribs). Don't miss a side of roasted garlic mashed potatoes or housemade buttermilk biscuits. Servers can provide a complete description of the original Southern folk art and photography decorating the premises.

## Buca di Beppo

643 Emerson St./Forest St., (650) 329-0665; www.bucadibeppo.com. L Sat-Sun, D daily.

For description, see page 60.

## Café Niebaum-Coppola

473 University Ave./Cowper St., (650) 752-0350, fax (650) 752-0359; www.cafecoppola.com. L-D daily; $$. No reservations.

This combination cafe-wine tasting bar-gift shop has a clubby feel. Styled after the cafe Les Deux Magots in Paris, it has comfortable over-size booths. The menu features pastas, pizzas, and roasted meats and fish, and the wine list includes, but of course, all the Niebaum-Coppola wines. Entertainment is via a fascinating player piano doing compositions by Francis Ford's father, Carmine. A small shop sells everything Coppola, including must-have Godfather t-shirts, and it is possible just to taste a flight of four wines ($7.50; keep the logo glass.). A branch is located in San Francisco (see page 61).

## The Cheesecake Factory

375 University Ave., (650) 473-9622. L-D daily, SunBr; $-$$. Valet parking at D.

For description, see page 63.

## Chef Chu's

1067 N. San Antonio Rd./El Camino Real, in Los Altos, (650) 948-2696, fax (650) 948-0121; www.chefchu. com. L-D daily; $$. Highchairs, boosters, booths. Reservations advised.

Chef Chu watches closely over his large kitchen staff and sees to it that excellence prevails in this well-appointed restaurant. Impressive dishes include crisp fried won tons, tasty Szechwan beef, and a magnificent hot-and-sour soup fragrant with sesame oil. Mu shu pork is served with unusual square pancakes for wrapping, and the beautifully presented lemon chicken consists of deep-fried whole chicken breasts, each glazed with lemon sauce and topped with a thin slice of lemon and a bright red maraschino cherry. A large window in the reception area provides views of the busy kitchen.

## Evvia

*420 Emerson St./Lytton St., (650) 326-0983, fax (650) 326-9552; http://evvia.net. L M-F, D daily; $$$. Valet parking.*

The welcoming open dining room of this very popular Greek restaurant features rustic beamed ceilings and an open kitchen. Colored bottles decorating the back wall glow like gemstones, and seating there is particularly comfortable. The exciting menu includes classic dishes such as spanakotiropita (phyllo stuffed with a spinach-feta mixture), Greek salad, egg-lemon soup, and moussaka, as well as delicious mesquite-grilled whole striped bass and lamb chops. Because everything is made in-house, desserts are special, and the array of baklavas—chocolate, pistachio, walnut—rate as exquisite. A sister restaurant, Kokkari, is in San Francisco (see page 74).

## Gordon Biersch Brewery Restaurant

*640 Emerson St./Forest St., (650) 323-7723, fax (650) 323-6129; www.gordonbiersch.com. L M-F, D daily, Sat-SunBr; $-$$.*

For description, see page 195.

## Hong Kong Flower Lounge

*560 Waverly St., (650) 326-3830. L-D daily.*

For description, see page 169.

## MacArthur Park

*27 University Ave./near El Camino Real, (650) 321-9990, fax (650) 321-1403; www.macpark.com. L M-F, D daily, SunBr; $$-$$$. Highchairs, boosters, child menu. Reservations advised. Valet parking.*

Situated just off the beaten path, this popular restaurant operates within an historical landmark originally designed for the U.S. War Department in 1918 by Hearst Castle architect Julia Morgan. The building is now divided into several dining areas, including two indoor balconies and a grand, barn-like room on the main floor. The kitchen is celebrated for its dry-aged steaks, California game, and baby back ribs cooked in an oak wood smoker. A menu decorated with a mouth-watering color reproduction of Wayne Thiebaud's "Two Meringues" announces dessert selections.

## Mango Cafe

*435 Hamilton Ave./Waverley, (650) 324-9443. L M-F, D daily. Highchairs. Reservations accepted.*

Traditional Jamaican, Trinidad, and Tobago cuisines dominate the menu. Chicken roti from Trinidad is a combination of curried chicken, potatoes, and veggies wrapped up burrito-style. Jamaican beef and chicken patties have a flaky crust, and vegetarian Rasta Pea Cook-Up includes a variety of beans along with unusual cho-cho. Curried goat and the house specialty, jerked chicken, are also available. The menu also offers a large selection of playful tropical smoothies, as well as a blend-your-own version—all served in humungous globe glasses with a big straw. Though the decor is simple, the dining room is comfortable and service is friendly and efficient.

## Ming's

*1700 Embarcadero Rd., (650) 856-7700, fax (650) 855-9479; www.mings.com. Dim sum daily 11-5; L-D daily; $-$$. Highchairs, boosters, booths, child menu. Reservations advised.*

Located just off Highway 101, this sedate restaurant has existed in Palo Alto since the 1950s, when it opened on El Camino Real. Ming's beef—a somewhat sweet dish prepared with wok-charred beef and a generic item on many Chinese menus—was this restaurant's invention, as was its delicately flavored chicken salad. Made with shredded, deep-fried chicken, the salad is labor-intensive to make and in such heavy demand that one chef is employed to prepare just that. Every morning another chef prepares fresh dim sum delicacies, including steamed shark's fin dumplings, delicious fresh shrimp items, and an electric-bright mango pudding in strawberry sauce. Other noteworthy dishes include dramatic drunken prawns flambé and steamed fresh garlic lobster. A full vegetarian menu is also available.

## Palo Alto Creamery Fountain & Grill

*566 Emerson St./Hamilton St., (650) 323-3131. B-L-D daily; $. Highchairs, boosters, booths. No reservations.*

Opened by the Peninsula Dairy in 1923 and featuring red leatherette booths and an authentic soda fountain, this popular diner is known for serving tasty simple food—oatmeal and buttermilk pancakes in the morning, a variety of sandwiches and hamburgers (on housemade bread and buns) at lunch, and chicken pot pies and pork chops at dinner—

at reasonable prices. Fountain items are made by "authentic soda jerks" and include their famous hand-blended milk shakes. Other favorites include sour cherry pie, housemade soups, and cherry coke. A branch is located at the Stanford Shopping Center.

## Picnic Pick-Ups

### • A. G. Ferrari Foods

*200 Hamilton Ave., (650) 752-0900; www.agferrari. com. M-Sat 10-7, Sun 11-6; and at 295 Main St., in Los Altos, (650) 947-7930. M-F 10-7, Sat 9-6, Sun 10-5.*

For description, see page 280.

### • Draeger's Market

*342 First St., in Los Altos, (650) 948-4425; www.draegers.com. Daily 7am-10pm.*

For description, see page 172.

## Saint Michael's Alley

*806 Emerson St./Homer Ave., (650) 326-2530, fax (650) 326-1436; www.stmikes.com. L-D Tu-Sat, Sat-SunBr; $$-$$$. Highchairs, boosters. Reservations advised.*

With its slate floor, sponged gold walls, and oversize central skylight, this cheery spot is primo for weekend brunch. Egg dishes are served with perfectly herbed Yukon gold potatoes that are cooked all the way through; they include a perfect St. Mike's Omelet filled with smoked bacon, sautéed mushrooms, spinach, and both cheddar and cream cheeses. A Belgian waffle, Blue Monkey pancakes dotted with banana chunks and blueberries, and an assortment of salads and sandwiches are also options. It is interesting to note that this building was once a music hall, and The Grateful Dead used to perform here before they were famous.

## Spago Palo Alto

*265 Lytton Ave./Ramona St., (650) 833-1000, fax (650) 325-9586; www2.wolfgangpuck.com. L M-F, D daily; $$$. Reservations advised. Valet parking.*

Operating within a lovely Mission-style landmark building, this is a branch of the famous Los Angeles restaurant owned by celebrity chef Wolfgang Puck. The art-filled main dining room has a view of the wood-burning oven, and an outdoor courtyard features dining under a huge oak tree. In addition to the celebrated pizzas, the menu offers items such as succulent tamarind-glazed rack of lamb,

Chinese-style roast duck, and truffled lobster-potato salad.

## Straits Cafe

*3295 El Camino Real/Lambert Ave., (650) 494-7168, (650) 494-0188; www.straitsrestaurants.com. L M-F, D M-Sat; $$-$$$.*

In warm weather, the tropical-style outside patio of this stylish restaurant is prime. Among the intriguing menu choices are Ikan Pangang, a delicious salmon filet spiced with fresh chili sauce and grilled in a banana leaf, and Mee Goreng, a spicy Indian-style noodle dish with tofu and prawns. Desserts are standouts, among them a silky banana pudding shaped like a cone. Live jazz is scheduled on Friday and Saturday nights. For more description, see page 85.

## Tamarine

*546 University Ave./Cowper St., (650) 325-8500, fax (650) 325-8504; www.tamarinerestaurant.com. L M-F, D daily; $$. Reservations advised.*

This sophisticated Vietnamese restaurant displays the work of contemporary Vietnamese artists. Semi-annual auctions are scheduled, with profits donated to a Ho Chi Minh City orphanage. The menu offers an array of delicious and dazzling small plates meant for sharing. Among the best are ginger-chicken salad (with cabbage, cashews, and caramelized onions), shaking beef (a toned-down version served on watercress salad), and delicate chili-lime aubergine (grilled white eggplants). Several kinds of flavor-infused rice, served attractively in a banana leaf wrapping, finish the main courses. Do leave space for the chocolate-filled dessert won tons.

## Taxi's Hamburgers

*403 University Ave., 650-322-TAXI, fax 650-322-6988; www.taxishamburgers.com. L-D daily.*

For description, see page 173.

## Tea-Time

*542 Ramona St./Hamilton Ave., (650) 32T-CUPS, fax (650) 32T-POTS; www.store.tea-time.com. M-F 10:30-6, Sat 11-6, Sun 11-5. Reservations accepted.*

Over 100 kinds of bulk loose-leaf teas are stocked in this little shop for tea lovers, and the menu of teatime tidbits includes crumpets and scones. Some patrons love the place so much that they leave their decorative china cup on the premises for use when they visit. In between, the cups are displayed nicely for all to enjoy. Antique cups and brand-new cozies galore are for sale along with an array of teapots, and tasting classes are scheduled regularly.

## World Wrapps
*201 University Ave./Emerson St., (650) 327-9777, fax (650) 327-8679; www.worldwrapps.com.*
For description, see page 87.

## Zao Noodle Bar
*261 University Ave./Ramond St., (650) 328-1988; www.zaonoodle.com.*
For description, see page 88.

# Mountain View

## — WHAT TO DO —

### NASA/Ames Research Center
*Moffett Field, off Hwy 101, (650) 604-6497; www.arc.nasa.gov. Visitor Center: M-F 10-6, Sat-Sun 12-4; free.*
Research in aeronautics, space technology, and more is conducted at this 430-acre facility.

## — WHERE TO STAY —

### Hotel Avante
*860 E. El Camino Real/Grant St., (800) 538-1600, (650), 940-1000, fax (650) 968-7870; www.hotel avante.com. 91 rooms; $-$$. Solar-heated pool; hot tub; fitness room. Afternoon snack, evening wine M-F, continental breakfast. No smoking; no pets.*
Decorated smartly in dark male colors, this 91-room boutique hotel is fun to wander through. A literally *cool* air-conditioned hi-fi lounge invites a visit on the third floor, and CDs can be borrowed from the front desk. Room desks are stocked with toys: a Slinky, a mini Etch A Sketch, a Rubik's Cube, a deck of Bicycle cards, and a Duncan yo-yo.

## — WHERE TO EAT —

### Lucy's Tea House
*180 Castro St./Villa, (650) 969-6365. M-Sat 11-10. No reservations. No cards.*
Entry to this Asian tea parlor is off an alley, lending a bit of mystique to the experience of dining here. Rustic twig furniture and

round paper lanterns define the atmosphere. The menu is a variety of tea drinks. Some have enticing names: the Jealous Lover is a frothy lemon-tea mixture; Sweet Memories is a fruity tea served in a cute little pitcher with a tiny cup. Also on the menu: addictive iced pearl milk tea with oversized tapioca-like balls in the bottom that are sucked up through an oversize straw; and shakes in vanilla and chocolate as well as green tea and jasmine tea flavors. A limited menu of tea snacks and sandwiches includes eggs boiled in tea, a daily rice plate special, and a kid-pleasing peanut butter toast. Leave time before or after to wander fabulously exotic **Castro Street**. Plenty of interesting shops await browsing, and the street positively teems with inexpensive Asian restaurants.

# Sunnyvale

## — VISITOR INFORMATION —

### Sunnyvale Chamber of Commerce
*101 W. Olive Ave., (408) 736-4971, fax (408) 736-1919; www.svcoc.org.*

## — WHAT TO DO —

### The Lace Museum
*552 S. Murphy Ave./El Camino Real, (408) 730-4695; www.thelacemuseum.org. Tu-Sat 11-4. Free.*
Located in a small strip mall, this tiny museum displays all manner of lace: knitted lace, bobbin lace, and nature's lace—a delicate spider web. Changing exhibits feature antique laces and related items. Lace-making materials are for sale in the shop, as is an assortment of antique hat pins and silver pillboxes, and classes are scheduled.

## — WHERE TO STAY —

### Wild Palms Hotel
*910 E. Fremont Ave./Wolfe Rd., off El Camino Real, (800) 538-1600, (408) 738-0500, fax (408) 245-4167; www.wildpalmshotel.com. 208 rooms; $$. Pool; hot tub; fitness room. Afternoon snack, continental breakfast. No smoking; no pets.*
Painted banana yellow and sporting a peachy beachy ambiance, this 2-story '50s-style motel has been converted into a tropical confection. A Hawaiian-style open-air lobby greets guests, and exotic tropical flowers and colors are

found throughout. Whimsy shines through in original murals painted on guest room doors and in the occasional chartreuse stuffed toy snake slithering across the back of a couch. Rooms surround a nicely landscaped garden courtyard with a hot tub and pool sporting bright vinyl playthings, and they are set far enough back from traffic to be quiet.

## – WHERE TO EAT –

### Picnic Pick-Ups

**• A. G. Ferrari Foods**
*304 W. El Camino Real, (408) 524-4000; www.agferrari.com. M-Sat 10-7, Sun 11-6.*
For description, see page 280.

**• C.J. Olson Cherries**
*348 W. El Camino Real/Mathilda St., (800) 738-BING, (408) 736-3726, fax (408) 736-1200; www.cjolson cherries.com. M-Sat 8-7, Sun 8-6; in winter, M-Sat 10-6, Sun 10-5.*
Owned by the Olson family and operated at this location since 1933, this old-time fruit stand is a blast from the past. It looks a lot like the overwhelmed, crowded-out dwelling in the favorite children's classic storybook *The Little House.* Let's hope it can hold out amid the urban sprawl and construction occurring every-where around it, because the 1899 farm that once stood where **P.F. Chang's Chinese Bistro** and a few other chain businesses stand now was leveled in 1999 as the heavens wept. Actually, this small stand might have a chance, because it too was torn down and completely rebuilt in 2002. Though not inexpensive, the finest fruit is found here—most especially the biggest, plumpest, juiciest cherries—and it can all be tasted before purchase. A few of the nine different types of cherries grown are available contin-uously May through August and in December and January. Most are farmed, along with apri-cots, on 13 acres the family now leases from the city. Additionally, cherry pies, chocolate-covered apricots, Medjool dates, and more are for sale.

### Tsunami Grill
*220 Capella Way, in Town and Country Village, (408) 773-8776. L M-F, D M-Sat; $. Highchairs, boost-ers. Reservations accepted.*
This casual, comfortable restaurant has a sushi chef and also serves delicious renditions of other Japanese favorites, including delicate

shrimp and vegetable tempuras. A green salad with a tasty dressing, miso soup, hot tea, and rice are included with dinner.

### Udupi Palace
*976 E. El Camino Real/Dale Ave., (408) 830-9600. L-D daily; $. No cards.*
For description, see page 283.

# Santa Clara

## – GETTING THERE –

Located off the San Tomas Expressway (G4), 2 miles west of Highway 101.

## – VISITOR INFORMATION –

### Santa Clara Chamber of Commerce & Convention-Visitors Bureau
*1850 Warburton Ave., (800) 272-6822, (408) 244-9660, fax (408) 244-9202; www.santaclara.org.*

## – WHAT TO DO –

### Intel Museum
*2200 Mission College Blvd./Burton St., (408) 765-0503; www.intel.com/go/museum. M-F 9-6, Sat 10-5. Free.*
Located in the main lobby of the Robert Noyce Building at Intel Corporation's headquar-ters (Intel is the world's largest semiconductor company and the inventor of the Pentium processor), this technology museum shows how computer chips are made and how they are used in everyday life. The museum is a self-guided experience with audio handsets available in English, Spanish, French, German, Japanese, Korean, and Chinese. Hands-on educational exhibits that appeal to both children and adults change regularly, and kids can try on "bunny suits" like those worn in actual computer chip factories.

### Mission Santa Clara de Asis
*500 El Camino Real, (408) 554-4023, fax (408) 554-4373; www.scu.edu/visitors/mission. Daily sunrise-sunset. Free.*
The original Santa Clara mission, built on a site beside the Guadalupe River in 1777, was destroyed by fire. Rebuilt in 1928, this replica of the eighth mission in the chain of California missions is on the immaculately groomed

grounds of **Santa Clara University** *((408) 554-4000, fax (408) 554-5255; www.scu.edu. Tours M-F.).* The university was built on the mission grounds in 1851 as California's first institution of higher learning and is the state's first coeducational Catholic university. Now a state historical landmark, the mission holds some interesting relics, including three bells that were a gift from the king of Spain and original artwork by professional artist Agustin Davila, who painted the original mission's interior. Extensive lush gardens showcase thousands of roses—several are classified as antique varieties—and a wide variety of trees and plants, some of which are among the oldest cultivated plants in California: olive trees planted by Franciscan friars in 1822, a giant 123-year-old Jacaranda tree, and the oldest grapevine in Northern California. Full bloom occurs April through May.

Just across from the mission, the university's **de Saissat Museum** *((408) 554-4528; www.scu.edu/deSaisset. Tu-Sun 11-4. Free.)* hosts rotating exhibits from a permanent collection featuring the work of artists such as Goya, Bonnard, and Hogarth, and of photographers such as Ansel Adams, Imogen Cunningham, and Annie Leibovitz. It also features an extensive California history collection related to the area.

### Paramount's Great America

*On Great America Parkway, off Hwys. 101 & 237, (408) 988-1776; www.pgathrills.com. Schedule varies; closed Nov.-Feb. 7-59 $45.99, 60+ $39.99, 3-6 or under 48" tall $33.99; parking $10.*

There's no question about it. The thrill rides at Northern California's most elaborate theme park are spectacular, and the roller coasters are great shocking fun: The Vortex is the West's first stand-up roller coaster; the Demon features two 360-degree loops and a double helix; and the Grizzly is a classic wooden coaster based on the extinct Coney Island Wildcat. The circa 1976 double-decker Carousel Columbia is the world's tallest, and the Drop Zone Stunt Tower free-fall ride is Santa Clara's tallest structure. The Kidzville and Splat City areas have colorful rides and attractions especially for children 12 and under. The new Boomerang Bay water park and five live shows round out the fun.

### Triton Museum of Art

*1505 Warburton Ave., across from City Hall, (408) 247-3754, fax (408) 247-3796; www.tritonmuseum.org. Daily 11-5, Thur to 9. Free.*

This small art museum is inside an award-winning building inspired by early California missions. It boasts a sculpture garden and is surrounded by 7 landscaped acres featuring several kinds of palm trees and a grove of redwoods. The permanent Austen D. Warburton Collection of American Indian Art and Artifacts displays objects illustrating the spirituality, traditions, and daily activities of Native Americans, and special exhibits are scheduled regularly.

Inside the 1913 arts and crafts-style Headen-Inman House, a charming converted farmhouse located in the park adjacent to the Triton, the **Santa Clara History Museum** *((408) 248-ARTS. Sun 1-4. Free.)* displays photographs and historic artifacts relating to the city's history. Farther back in the park, the 1866 Jamison-Brown House is famous for its porch where Jack London wrote part of *The Call of the Wild.*

### — WHERE TO STAY —

### Biltmore Hotel & Suites

*2151 Laurelwood Rd., (800) 255-9925, (408) 988-8411, fax (408) 986-9807, www.hotelbiltmore.com. 9 stories; 263 rooms; $-$$. Heated lap pool; hot tub; fitness room. 2 restaurants. No pets.*

Offering style and elegance, this business hotel is 3 miles from San Jose International Airport. A courtesy shuttle operates within a 5-mile radius. **Montague's Cafe** serves a breakfast buffet that includes traditional Japanese breakfast items.

## Embassy Suites Hotel

*2885 Lakeside Dr., (800) EMBASSY, (408) 496-6400, fax (408) 988-7529; www.embassy-suites.com. 10 stories; 257 rooms; $-$$. Children under 18 free. Indoor heated pool; hot tub; sauna; fitness room. Evening cocktails, full breakfast.*

All guests get a spacious two-room suite consisting of one bedroom plus a separate living room with sofa bed. Each suite is equipped with two TVs and a mini-kitchen with coffeemaker. The hotel is just minutes from Paramount's Great America theme park and has packages that include admission tickets. For more description, see page 420.

## Hilton Santa Clara

*4949 Great America Pkwy., (800) 321-3232, (800) HILTONS, (408) 330-0001, fax (408) 562-6736; www.santaclara.hilton.com. 8 stories; 280 rooms; $$-$$$. Heated indoor-outdoor pool; hot tub; fitness room. Restaurant; room service.*

Well-situated across the parking lot from Paramount's Great America and across the street from the Santa Clara Convention Center and a Light Rail stop, this elegant, richly-appointed new hotel serves both the business and leisure traveler. Rooms feature colorful golden granite vanities and original artwork, and some have views of Great America.

## Madison Street Inn

*1390 Madison St., (800) 491-5541, (408) 249-5541, fax (408) 249-6676; www.madisonstreetinn.com. 6 rooms; $-$$. Some shared baths. Pool; hot tub; sauna. Evening snack, full breakfast. Pets ok.*

Located just 10 minutes from the San Jose Airport, this comfy B&B is surrounded by 1/3 acre of landscaped gardens. Breakfast includes fresh fruit juice, muffins, and eggs Benedict, and the evening snack is homemade chocolate chip cookies and sherry.

## Santa Clara Marriott

*2700 Mission College Blvd., (800) 228-9290, (408) 988-1500, fax (408) 352-4353; www.santaclara*
*marriott.com. 15 stories; 759 rooms; $$-$$$. Pool; hot tub; sauna; fitness room; 4 tennis courts (with night lights). Restaurant; room service. Pets ok.*

Located adjacent to Great America and the tall, glistening towers of Sun Microsystems, this is the largest hotel in the area. It consists of one 10- and one 15-story tower, plus a 2-story wing surrounding the pool.

**Parcel 104** restaurant *((408) 970-6104, fax (408) 970-6190; www.parcel104.com. B daily, L M-F, D M-Sat. Valet parking.)* showcases celebrity chef Bradley Ogden's American regional cuisine. It's the kind of place where little forks and spoons appear between courses holding an "amuse." The accomplished kitchen produces perfectly seasoned salads and soups, and main courses have included a full-flavored housemade fettucini with spicy lamb sausage and broccoli as well as a delicious rabbit dish seasoned with aged balsamic vinegar. Dessert brings on fabulous double-chocolate spoon bread, a banana Napoleon, and homey tapioca pudding. Presentation is faultless, with each dish arranged on the perfect plate, wines poured into their complementary oversize glass, and the table set with classy Frette linens. *Yes!* An informal sushi bar adjoins, and live jazz is often scheduled.

## — WHERE TO EAT —

## Crocodile Cafe

*2855 Stevens Creek Blvd., in Valley Fair mall, (408) 260-1100, fax (408) 260-1110; www.crocodilecafe.com. L-D daily. Highchairs, boosters, child menu.*

The menu here offers a variety of salads, sandwiches, pizzas, calzones, pastas, and oak wood-grilled meats, and the kids' coloring menu has all their favorites.

## Pedro's Restaurant & Cantina

*3935 Freedom Cir., (408) 496-6777; www.pedros restaurants.com. L-D daily.*

For description, see page 369.

## Piatti

*3905 Rivermark Plaza, (408) 330-9212, fax (408) 330-9252; www.piatti.com. L M-F, D daily.*

For description, see page 386.

## Pizza & Pipes

*3581 Homestead Rd./Lawrence Expwy., (866) BEST-PIZZA, (408) 248-5680, fax (408) 248-5389;*

*www.pizzaandpipes.com. L-D daily; $. Child portions.*
This pizza parlor has a separate game room and kids' play area. In 1984, a Yamaha FX 20 electronic organ replaced the ailing antique pipe organ, but the pizza is as good as ever.

### Taxi's Hamburgers
*3139 Mission College Blvd., (408) 235-8877; www.taxishamburgers.com. L-D daily.*
For description, see page 173.

### World Wrapps
*3125 Mission College Blvd., (408) 486-9727, fax (408) 486-9774; www.worldwrapps.com.*
For description, see page 87.

# San Jose

## — A LITTLE BACKGROUND —

Touted as the "capital of Silicon Valley" (a title that seems valid considering that 24 of the area's largest computer companies have head-quarters or divisions here), San Jose—the country's 11th-largest city and California's 3rd-largest and oldest city, having been founded as a Spanish pueblo in 1777 (it also was the state capital from 1849 to 1851)—receives relatively little attention for its attractions. But that seems to be changing as the city concentrates on revitalizing its downtown area. Now, visitors to the city center can enjoy its many cultural offerings as well as its reliably mild climate—it boasts more than 300 days of sunshine annually. It also has been the number one safest large city for 4 years.

## — VISITOR INFORMATION —

### San Jose Convention & Visitors Bureau
*100 Park Center Plaza #560, (800) SAN-JOSE, (408) 295-9600, fax (408) 295-3937; www.sanjose.org.*

## — GETTING THERE —

Located approximately 50 miles south of San Francisco.

## — WHAT TO DO —

### Alum Rock Park
*End of Alum Rock Ave. (E of Hwy. 101), (408) 259-5477; www.ci.san-jose.ca.us/prns/regionalparks. Daily 8-sunset. Parking $6.*

Located in the foothills of the Diablo Range northeast of town, this 720-acre park was dedicated in 1872 and is California's very first city park. It is maintained by the city for hiking, horseback riding, bicycling, and picnicking. In some spots mineral water bubbles up from sulphur springs, a reminder of the park's past as a nationally known health spa in the early 1900s. Facilities include picnic tables, barbecue pits, and a children's playground.

The privately operated **Youth Science Institute** *(16260 Alum Rock Ave., (408) 258-4322; www.ysi-ca.org. Tu-Sat 12-4:30, also Sun in summer. 50¢, kids 25¢.)* displays live birds of prey, including hawks and owls, as well as other native animals and a large taxidermy collection. Hands-on activities are available for children.

### Cathedral Basilica of Saint Joseph
*80 S. Market St., downtown, (408) 283-8100, fax (408) 283-8110; www.stjosephcathedral.org. M-F 9:30-5. Free.*

Designed by architect Bryan J. Clinch and constructed in 1877, when it was known as St. Joseph Cathedral, this is one of downtown San Jose's most architecturally stunning buildings. It replaced the Pueblo de San Jose's first small adobe church built in 1803. The cathedral features extraordinary stained glass and murals as well as a completely restored multi-domed edifice. The choir loft holds a circa 1886 mechanical Odell organ that is one of only four in the U.S. and the only one in original condition on the West Coast.

### Children's Discovery Museum of San Jose
*180 Woz Way, in Guadalupe River Park, (408) 298-5437, fax (408) 298-6826; www.cdm.org. Tu-Sat 10-5, Sun 12-5. $7, 60+ $6.*

Children ages 1 through 10, for whom this museum was designed, are sure to be entertained. The striking, lavender-colored building housing the largest children's museum in the West was designed by Mexico City architect Ricardo Legorreta. Fortunately, he included plenty of places for adults to sit and watch while their kids have a great time doing everything from making a corn husk doll, to blowing gigantic bubbles, to climbing on a full-size fire engine. Steve Wozniak, of Apple Computer fame, sponsored the Jesse's Clubhouse exhibit named in honor of his son. Guess who the street the museum is located on—Woz Way—is named for? A snack bar serves inexpensive things that kids like to eat: hot dogs, peanut butter & jelly sandwiches, chicken nuggets.

### Emma Prusch Farm Park
*647 S. King Rd., at Hwys. 680 & 280, (408) 926-5555, fax (408) 277-3820; www.ci.san-jose.ca.us/ prns/regionalparks. Daily 8:30-sunset. Free.*

One of the things discovered when visiting this old-fashioned farm is that not all apples are computers. Deeded to the city of San Jose in 1962, this 47-acre dairy farm—surrounded now by the city—presents the opportunity to step back in time to San Jose's rural past. The restored original 19th-century white farmhouse is now the information center. The barn, which is the city's largest and the third-largest in California, is home to an assortment of domesticated farm animals that includes cows, sheep, and pigs—all thriving in spite of their closeness to the freeway. Don't miss the fruit orchard where over 100 kinds of rare fruits grow, among them limequat, pawpaw, gumi, and sapote as well as exotic varieties of cherries, guavas, persimmons, grapefruit and other citruses, and . . . apples.

### The Gaslighter Theater
*400 E. Campbell Ave., in Campbell, (408) 866-1408, fax (408) 779-4900; www.thegaslighter.com. F at 8, Sat at 2, 8. $12-$18.*

A staff member says that this cozy theater is located "in lovely downtown Campbell—Santa Clara County's fastest-growing ghost town." And, indeed, at night this seems to be the only show in town. After an exuberant greeting in the street and at the door by the cast, the whole family has fun inside hissing the villain and cheering the hero while munching on—and tossing—complimentary popcorn. The old-fashioned, two-part shows are not at all subtle, making them great for school-age children. Shows include both a melodrama (such as *Ignorance Isn't Bliss* or *No Mother to Guide Her*) and a vaudeville performance featuring dancing, singing, and comedy.

### Guadalupe River Park and Gardens
*(408) 298-7657; www.grpg.org. Daily dawn-dusk. Free.*

This narrow, 3-mile-long park follows the river. It features a **Children's Carousel** (*525 W.*

*Santa Clara St./Autumn St., (408) 999-5761. Tu-Sun 11-5; in summer, daily 10-7. $1, under 13 free on 2nd Tu.*) with 33 fiberglass animals and, just south of the airport, the renowned **Heritage Rose Garden** (*Spring St./Taylor St., 2 mi. N of downtown; www.heritageroses.us.*) with over 3,700 varieties of roses spread across 5 acres. Peak bloom occurs each May, though the show is good from April through November.

### Japantown
*N. 5th St./Jackson St., (408) 298-4303; www.japantownsanjose.org. Free.*

Dating back to the late 1800s, when bachelors from Japan migrated to the area, this historic neighborhood features streets lined with cherry trees that bloom spectacularly in the spring. It is one of only three remaining Japantowns in the U.S. Historical sites of interest include the **San Jose Buddhist Church Betsuin** (*640 N. 5th St., (408) 293-9292, fax (408) 293-0433; www.sjbetsuin.com.*), which dates from 1937 and features a Japanese garden and tile roof, the **Wesley United Methodist Church** (*566 N. 5th St., (408) 295-0367, fax (408) 295-0612.*) built in 1941, and the circa 1910 Issei Memorial Building, now housing the **Japanese-American Historical Museum** (*565 N. 5th St., (408) 294-3138, fax (408) 294-6157; www.jamsj.org. Tu-F 11-3, Sun 11-2. Free.*) and its photographic exhibits of Japanese-Americans who migrated to the Santa Clara Valley in 1890. Shops, galleries, and Japanese restaurants abound, and on Sunday mornings a bustling **Farmers' Market** unfolds. Annual festivals celebrating the changing seasons include **Nikkei Matsuri** in May, the **Obon Festival** in July, and **Aki Matsuri** in September. Japantown is just south of downtown and can be reached via the Light Rail line.

### Kelley Park
*3 mi. from downtown, (408) 27-PARKS; www.ci.san-jose.ca.us/prns/regionalparks. Daily 8-sunset. Parking $6.*

#### • Happy Hollow Park & Zoo
*1300 Senter Rd./Keyes Rd., (408) 277-3000, fax (408) 277-4470; www.happyhollowparkandzoo.org. Daily 10-5. $5.50, 65+ $5, 75+ & under 2 free.*

Children through age 10 love this mini amusement park. Spacious and shady, it offers a satisfying combination of kiddie rides and more than 150 zoo animals, including a family of endangered black-and-white ruffed lemurs. The small zoo also has a bird enclosure and a petting area, where for small change children can hand-feed animals. The zoo is known for actively breeding its lemurs and releasing them back into the wild. Five rides, daily puppet shows, and use of a concrete maze and playground equipment are included with admission. Single and double strollers can be rented, as can wagons, and picnic tables are also available.

• **Kelley Park Express Train**
*Schedule varies. $1.50.*

Boarded just outside the zoo, this miniature choo-choo train makes stops at the following two park sites.

• **History San Jose**
*1650 Senter Rd., (408) 287-2290; www.ci.san-jose.ca.us/prns/regionalparks. Tu-Sun 12-5. Tu-Sun, free; Sat-Sun, $6, 65+ $5, 6-17 $4.*

This ever-growing 14-acre complex incorporates many turn-of-the-century San Jose buildings along with structures from other periods, including a Chinese temple from the mid-1800s and a gas station from the 1920s. In all, more than 28 relocated or replicated historic homes and business buildings highlight the culture and history of San Jose and the Santa Clara Valley. Begin a visit at the Pacific Hotel, where docent-led tours commence; a self-guided tour brochure is also available. Do take time for a trolley ride and to stop in for refreshments at O'Brien's Ice Cream and Candy Store, a replica of the first place west of Detroit to serve ice cream sodas. Note that on weekdays many of the buildings are closed.

• **Japanese Friendship Garden**
*(408) 277-4192; www.ci.san-jose.ca.us/prns/regionalparks. Daily 10-sunset. Free.*

Patterned after the Korakuen Garden in San Jose's sister city of Okayama, this 6 1/2-acre garden includes four heart-shaped ponds populated with rare koi. Walk on the Moon Bridge for good luck; cross the Zigzag Bridge to get rid of evil spirits.

## Lick Observatory
*On Mount Hamilton Rd., 23 mi. E of downtown, (831) 274-5061; www.ucolick.org. M-F 12:30-5, Sat-Sun 10-5. Free.*

This observatory, built in 1887, is far from

city lights at the top of 4,372-foot-high Mount Hamilton. Now a division of U.C. Santa Cruz, it is reached via the original carriage trail—a laborious 19-mile drive up a narrow, winding two-lane road with no less than 347 curves. But its view of San Jose and the Santa Clara Valley makes the struggle worthwhile. Guided tours include seeing, but not looking through, the world's second-largest refractor telescope (it measures 120 inches), which has been in use for more than a century. Visitors get to look through a smaller 36-inch refractor scope, which has been here from the beginning and was the largest in the world at the time the observatory was built. Allow 90 minutes to reach the observatory and 2 hours to tour it. Note that no food or gas is available in the area.

## Municipal Rose Garden
*On Naglee Ave./Dana Ave., (408) 27-PARKS; www.ci.san-jose.ca.us/prns/regionalparks. Daily 8-sunset. Free.*

Located west of downtown and 2 blocks from the Egyptian Museum, this 5 1/2-acre garden began as a prune orchard in 1931. It boasts 3,500 bushes representing 189 varieties of heritage, modern, and miniature roses. Hybrid-teas comprise 75 percent of the collection. The garden is centered around a two-tiered fountain and surrounded by green lawns and tree-shaded picnic tables. Other features include a reflection pool, a sundial, concrete benches, and a natural grass stage surrounded by redwood trees. The roses are at their showy peak in May and June but continue blooming through October.

## Overfelt Gardens
*2145 McKee Rd./Educational Park Dr. (between Hwys. 680 & 101), 3 mi. from downtown, (408) 251-3323, fax (408) 251-2865; www.ci.san-jose.ca.us/prns/regionalparks. Daily 10-sunset. Free.*

Featuring expansive lawns, picnic tables, and a sometimes-gurgling stream, this peaceful 33-acre park is filled with native and exotic plants. Special features include a paved arboreal trail that meanders through the entire park, a California native plant and wildlife area, several natural wildlife sanctuaries, a fragrance garden, and three small percolation ponds that hold water for the Santa Clara Valley's water table. A 5-acre **Chinese Cultural Garden** (*www.chinese culturalgarden.org*) includes impressive statuary, including a 30-foot bronze-and-marble depiction of the ancient Chinese philosopher Confucius overlooking a reflecting pond. It has a massive white marble-and-ceramic Friendship Gate at the main entrance and displays a 15-ton piece of black marble mined in the Republic of China and presented to San Jose from Tainan City, her sister city in China.

## Peralta Adobe & Fallon House Historic Site

*175 W. St. John St./San Pedro St., downtown, (408) 993-8182; www.historysanjose.org. Sat-Sun 12-3:30. $6, seniors $5, 6-17 $4.*

Both of these historic houses are surrounded now by modern high rises. A tour of them provides a look into the daily life of two prominent early San Jose families. Built in 1797, the Peralta Adobe is San Jose's oldest structure remaining from when the city was El Pueblo de San Jose de Guadalupe and is a legacy to the city's Spanish influence. Named after Luis Peralta, who occupied the adobe from 1807 to 1851 and was one of the state's first millionaires, it has two rooms outfitted in period style—a bedroom furnished as it would have appeared in 1777 and a living room furnished to reflect the 1830s—plus an outside working horno oven. Across the street, the lavish Victorian Fallon House mansion dates from 1855. Built by an early mayor, it has 15 furnished rooms decorated in the style of the 1860s. Though its kitchen was state of the art for the times, it has no bathrooms or indoor plumbing.

## Raging Waters

*2333 S. White Rd. (Capitol Expressway/Tully Rd.), in Lake Cunningham Regional Park, (408) 238-9900, fax (408) 270-2022; www.rwsplash.com. Daily 10:30-6, June-Aug; Sat-Sun only May-Sept; closed Oct-Apr. $25.99, under 48" $19.99, 55+ $15.99; parking $6.*

This water-oriented amusement park is the Bay Area's largest and claims to have the fastest waterslides this side of the Rockies. Sliders can reach speeds up to 25 miles per hour and can be dropped 6 stories into a catchpool below. An inner tube ride, a sled ride, a rope swing, and myriad other water activities round out the fun. Importantly, an army of 40 lifeguards watches over frolickers, and facilities include free changing rooms and showers plus inexpensive lockers. Where else can a family find such good clean fun? Note that food and beverages may not be brought into the park. Food service is available, and a picnic area is provided just outside the main gate.

## Rosicrucian Egyptian Museum

*1342 Naglee Ave./Park Ave., (408) 947-3600, fax (408) 947-3638; www. egyptianmuseum.org. Tu-F 10-5, Sat-Sun 11-6. $9, 55+ $7, 5-10 $5.*

This museum houses the largest exhibit of Egyptian, Babylonian, and Assyrian artifacts in the western U.S. Highlights of the collection

include mummies, fine jewelry, and a full-size reproduction of a 4,000-year-old rock tomb—the only such tomb in the United States. Among the six human mummies is one that has a 9-inch metal pin in his knee—an exciting discovery documenting the first known attempt at knee surgery. Also in the collection are the mummies of several cats, some fish, a baboon, and the head of an ox. The stunning surrounding park is adorned with exotic trees and flowers and unusual Egyptian statuary. Baby strollers are not permitted in the museum, and picnicking is not permitted on the grounds.

## San Jose Flea Market

*1590 Berryessa Rd. (between Hwys. 680 & 101), (800) BIG-FLEA,(408) 453-1110, fax (408) 437-9011; www.sjfm.com. W-Sun dawn-dusk. Free; parking $1-$5.*

Said to be the largest in the world, bigger even than the famous Paris marketplace that started the whole thing, this outdoor flea market was the first in the U.S. It features over 2,700 vendors spread out over 120 acres. Most everything can be found here, and at bargain prices. In addition, there are more than 35 restaurants and snack stands, and a 1/4-mile-long section that is California's largest outdoor produce market. A variety of free entertainment is provided, and for a fee kids can play skee-ball and ride on a pony, a merry-go-round, and go-carts. Thursdays and Fridays are least crowded; weekends and Wednesdays are usually quite busy.

## San Jose Museum of Art

*110 S. Market St./San Fernando St., downtown (408) 294-2787, fax (408) 294-2977; www.sanjosemuseum ofart.org. Tu-Sun 11-5. Free.*

Holding a collection of primarily contemporary American art, this unusual part-1892 Romanesque sandstone/part-1991 stark modern building is said to serve as a metaphor for contemporary art's ties to tradition. A cafe is located in the original wing, and baby strollers are available to borrow at no charge.

## San Jose Museum of Quilts & Textiles

*110 Paseo de San Antonio/3rd St., downtown, (408) 971-0323, fax (408) 971-7226; www.sjquilt museum.org. Tu-Sun 10-5, Thur to 8. $5, 65+ $4, under 13 free; free 1st Thur of month.*

Focusing on 19th- and 20th-century quilts and textiles, this small gallery is the first museum in the U.S. devoted to quilts. Shows change approximately every 6 weeks.

## Santana Row

*Stevens Creek Blvd./S. Winchester Blvd. (at Hwys. 880 & 280), (408) 551-4643; www.santanarow.com. Free parking.*

The 2-block-long main drag here resembles an European shopping street. Nice touches include incorporating existing mature oak trees, adding outdoor chess tables, and using an imported Gothic chapel façade as the entry to a flower shop. This new complex combines top-end stores, branches of popular restaurants, a hotel, and apartments. Luxury merchants include Gucci, Burberry, St. John, and Escada, and branches of Sur La Table, Anthropologie, and Borders Books and Music are part of the mix. Several day spas round out the offerings, and on Sundays Santa Clara County's largest and oldest **farmer's market** operates from 10 to 3.

Rooms at sleek, sophisticated **Hotel Valencia** *(355 Santana Row, (866) 842-0100, (408) 551-0010, fax (408) 551-0550; www.hotel valencia.com. 7 stories; 213 rooms; $$-$$$+. Heated pool; hot tub; fitness room; health spa. Continental breakfast; restaurant; room service. No pets. Valet parking $15; free self-parking.)* have a masculine decor and are appointed with a stainless steel bathroom sink, a faux fur bed cover, and stylish furnishings. Mattresses are among the most comfortable ever, and a pillow menu allows for personal fine-tuning. The ultra-hip **V bar** sports a decor that includes stainless steel beaded curtains over doorways and is *the* place to be each evening.

Restaurants are numerous. Most are open daily for lunch and dinner, and most have outdoor seating that takes advantage of the generally good weather. Among the choices are:

• **Blowfish Sushi To Die For**
*#355, (408) 345-FUGU, fax (408) 345-3855; www.blowfishsushi.com.*

A row of chefs is always busy here rolling out the sushi menu. The Ritsu, with two kinds of raw tuna, and the flash-fried Crunchy California are among the most popular versions. Tempura shrimp is exquisite, and the numerous sake choices are the way to wash it all down. For dessert, try wasabe ice cream.

• **Consuelo Mexican Bistro**
*#377, (408) 260-7082, fax (408) 260-7090.*

Dishes here are not the usual Mexican items and are meant to be shared tapas-style. A satisfying meal can be composed of a crunchy jicama salad, a trio of tiny stuffed sopes, and a green pipian mole over chicken. A full bar serves an array of Latino drinks.

• **Left Bank**
*#377, (408) 984-3500' www.leftbank.com.*

For description, see page 216.

• **Maggiano's Little Italy**
*3055 Olin Ave., (408) 423-8973.*

With floors covered with tiny mosaic tiles and a large open room ringed with burgundy leather booths and filled with tables covered with red-and-white-checked cloths, this classic Italian restaurant looks like it's been here forever. Frank Sinatra convincingly sings away any doubts that might linger. Service is family-style and family-friendly, portions are large, and the menu is traditional.

• **Straits Cafe**
*#333, (408) 246-6320; www.straitsrestaurants.com.*

For description, see page 85.

**The Tech Museum of Innovation**
*201 S. Market St./Park Ave., downtown, (408) 294-TECH, fax (408) 279-7167; www.thetech.org. Tu-Sun 10-5, daily in summer; closed part of Sept. $9, 65+ $8, 3-12 $7.*

Originally called "The Garage," in whimsical reference to the garages in which many Silicon Valley inventions had their humble beginnings (the most famous being the personal computer developed by Steve Jobs and Stephen Wozniak in their garage), the nickname was dropped in favor of something more befitting the major science and technology museum it has become. Focusing on how technology affects everyday life, museum exhibits allow visitors to see how silicon chips are produced, to design a roller coaster, and to pilot an ROV (remotely operated vehicle). Volunteers are on hand to answer questions. Operating within the museum but with a separate admission fee (a combination ticket is available, and advance tickets are advised), the **IMAX Dome Theater** is a must-see. Audiences are almost completely surrounded by a film projected onto an 82-foot-diameter screen—the only one in Northern California. When leaving this electric mango-and-azure purple-colored building, don't miss the whimsical, mesmerizing autokinetic sculpture by George Rhoads located just outside the exit.

**Winchester Mystery House**
*525 S. Winchester Blvd./Stevens Creek Blvd., (408) 247-2101, fax (408) 247-2090; www.winchester mysteryhouse.com. Tours daily from 9am; last tour varies by season. $19.95, 65+ $16.95, 6-12 $13.95.*

The story goes that Sarah Winchester, heir to the $20 million Winchester rifle fortune, believed that to make amends for a past wrongdoing she had to build additions to her circa 1884 Victorian mansion continuously, 24 hours a day. Her eccentric ideas resulted in some unusual features: asymmetrical rooms, narrow passageways, zigzag stairwells, and doors opening into empty shafts. The tour of this city landmark takes in 110 of the 160 rooms, climbs more than 200 steps, and covers almost a mile. An add-on Behind the Scenes tour enters areas never before open to the public, including the stables, an unfinished ballroom, and the basement. Baby strollers not permitted on the tour.

The **Winchester Firearms Museum**, which holds one of the largest collections of Winchester rifles on the West Coast, and the **Winchester Antique Products Museum** provide an interesting way to pass time while waiting for the tour to begin. Food service and picnic tables are available. A self-guided tour of 6 acres of Victorian gardens, sprinkled liberally with fountains and statues, is included with admission. Spooky nighttime **Flashlight Tours** are scheduled annually in October and every Friday the 13th.

**Wineries**

• **J. Lohr Winery**
*1000 Lenzen Ave., (408) 288-5057 x35, fax (408) 993-2276; www.jlohr.com. Tasting daily 10-5; no tour.*

Tucked into a residential part of the city near Highway 880, this premium winery operates on the site of a former beer brewery. All wine is made on the premises, but the grapes are grown on Lohr-owned vineyards scattered from Paso Robles to St. Helena.

• **Ridge Vineyards**
*17100 Monte Bello Rd., in Cupertino, (408) 867-3233,*

*Winchester Mystery House*

fax (408) 868-1350; www.ridgewine.com. Tasting Sat-Sun 11-4; no tour.

Started by three Stanford Research Institute engineers in 1959, this destination winery is positioned high on a limestone ridge way back in the Santa Cruz Mountains and is reached via a beautiful, curvy back road. On warm days, tasting occurs outdoors, and by reservation picnics can be enjoyed at vineyard-side tables offering a magnificent view of the bay below. On cooler days, tasting occurs inside a 100-year-old barn. Known for its Cabernets and Zinfandels, Ridge has been called "the Château Latour of California," and the wines *are* good. So good, in fact, that a Zin brought to Paris as a gift to a native was personally witnessed being sniffed by that native, who expressed surprise and then swallowed with absolute delight.

— WHERE TO STAY —

### Campbell Inn

675 E. Campbell Ave., in Campbell, (800) 582-4449, (408) 374-4300, fax (408) 379-0695; www.campbell inn.com. 95 rooms; $$. Children under 13 free. Some fireplaces. Heated pool; hot tub; fitness room; 1 tennis

court (with night lights). Evening snack, full breakfast. Pets ok.

This B&B-style inn has one and two-bedroom suites. Facilities include an adjacent 16-mile jogging/bicycle/nature trail that passes through forests and alongside a stream and two lakes and that connects to a full-series par course, and the hotel provides complimentary use of 10-speed bikes. A lavish European-style hot breakfast consisting of fruits, cheeses, meats, and eggs as well as granola, croissants, and muffins is served in a poolside breakfast room (a no-cholesterol breakfast is provided upon request). The inn is close to upscale shopping, and a complimentary airport shuttle is available.

### Dolce Hayes Mansion

200 Edenvale Ave., (800) 98-DOLCE, (408) 226-3200; www.hayesmansion.dolce.com. 214 rooms; $$-$$$+. Pool; hot tub; fitness room; tennis courts. 2 restaurants; room service. No pets.

Once the largest private home in Northern California, this fabulous mansion is located about 15 minutes from downtown. It is now a conference center during the week but open to the public for weekend stays. The spacious rooms in the original house are a particular delight, but the newer rooms match the mansion's architectural style and feature contemporary comforts. It is an enjoyable challenge to find the "hidden" subterranean billiards room bar, and guests have access to volleyball courts and a jogging/walking trail running through a scenic park across the entry drive.

Dinner in the exquisite dining room that houses **Orlo's** (*L M-F, D daily. Reservations advised.*), which is furnished with antiques and features a beautiful antique crystal goblet collection, is not to be missed. The cuisine matches the setting. The **Silver Creek Dining Room**'s expansive weekend brunch is also exceptional.

## Doubletree Hotel San Jose

*2050 Gateway Pl., 5 mi. from downtown, (800) 222-TREE, (408) 453-4000, fax (408) 437-2898; www.doubletreesanjose.com. 10 stories; 505 rooms; $-$$. Children under 19 free. Heated pool; hot tub; fitness room. 3 restaurants. Pets ok.*

Located adjacent to the airport, this hotel offers convenient access to the convention center and downtown via the Light Rail. A complimentary shuttle is available to the airport. Everyone gets freshly baked cookies at check-in, and on the Executive Level guests also get a continental breakfast, terry robes, and nightly turndown.

## The Fairmont San Jose

*170 S. Market St., downtown, (800) 346-5550, (408) 998-1900, fax (408) 287-1648; www.fairmont.com. 20 stories; 805 rooms; $$-$$$+. Children under 18 free. Heated pool; 2 saunas; 2 steam rooms; fitness room. 3 restaurants; room service. Small pets ok. Valet parking $20.*

Built on the site of what was California's capitol building from 1849 to 1851, this luxury high-rise hotel has guest rooms equipped with goose-down pillows and terry robes.

Three restaurants operate off the lobby: **The Grill on the Alley** features a clubby ambiance, with dark wood paneling and black leather-upholstered booths; **The Pagoda** has striking high ceilings and gorgeous flower arrangements in addition to a Chinese menu; **The Fountain** serves casual cafe meals and a lavish Sunday brunch. Additionally, **The Lobby Lounge** serves afternoon tea and cocktails and presents live music on weekends.

## Hilton San Jose & Towers

*300 Almaden Blvd., downtown, (800) HILTONS, (408) 287-2100, fax (408) 947-4489; www.hilton.com. 17 stories; 355 rooms; $-$$$. Heated indoor lap pool; hot tub; fitness room. Restaurant; room service. Pets ok. Self-parking $10, valet $15.*

Connected via an enclosed concourse to the San Jose McEnery Convention Center, this hotel is located in the heart of the city. The **City Bar & Grill** offers regional American dishes and an extensive Sunday champagne brunch.

## Hotel De Anza

*233 W. Santa Clara St., (800) 843-3700, (408) 286-1000, fax (408) 286-0500; www.hoteldeanza.com. 10 stories; 101 rooms; $$-$$$. Fitness room. Evening snack; restaurant; room service. Pets ok. Valet parking $15.*

Referred to as the "Grand Lady of San Jose," this 1931 hotel is new again. Refurbished to its art deco grandeur, it exudes a cozy feeling and features attractively appointed, spacious rooms and well-designed tile bathrooms equipped with a phone and TV. Amenities include evening turndown, terry cloth robes, and a Raid Our Pantry nighttime snack buffet that permits bathrobe-clad guests to perch on the kitchen counter while gobbling up goodies such as chocolate chip cookies and salami cracker sandwiches. For a small additional fee, an extensive breakfast buffet can be enjoyed in a charming room that is cleverly painted to bring a cheery atmosphere into a windowless space.

**La Pastaia Restaurant** serves Italian dinners, and the **Hedley Club Lounge** presents live jazz most evenings.

## Hyatt Sainte Claire

*302 S. Market St., downtown, (800) 223-1234, (408) 885-1234, fax (408) 279-5803; www.mhotelgroup.com. 6 stories; 170 rooms; $$-$$$. Fitness room. Restaurant; room service. No pets. Parking $18.*

Designed in 1926 in a Spanish Revival Renaissance style by the same architects who did the Mark Hopkins in San Francisco, this meticulously restored hotel is a national historic landmark. It boasts beautiful original hand-painted ceiling panels and an elegant public sitting lounge. Amenities in the attractively, sometimes whimsically, decorated rooms include featherbeds and cotton kimonos. In good weather, breakfast can be taken in an inner garden courtyard featuring vibrantly colored, hand-painted Spanish ceramic tiles.

A branch of the celebrated Tuscan-style **Il Fornaio** is the hotel restaurant. For more description, see page 73.

### The Pruneyard Inn

*1995 S. Bascom Ave., in Campbell, (800) 559-4344, (408) 559-4300, fax (408) 559-9919; www.prune yardinn.com. 171 rooms; $$-$$$. Children under 13 free. Some fireplaces. Heated pool; hot tub; fitness room. Full breakfast. No pets.*

One of only three hotels in the western U.S. that is located in a shopping center, this tastefully decorated hotel is adjacent to the attractive **PruneYard** shopping complex *((408) 371-4700; www.thepruneyard.com.).* In spite of the location, it manages to provide a secluded feeling. Turndown service and a lavish European-style breakfast are included.

### — WHERE TO EAT —

### Benihana

*2074 Vallco Fashion Park, in Cupertino, (408) 253-1221; www.benihana.com. L-D daily.*

For description, see page 58.

### Britannia Arms

*173 W. Santa Clara St., downtown. (408) 278-1400.*

For description, see page 111.

### Buca di Beppo

*1875 S. Basom Ave, in Campbell, (408) 377-7722, fax (408) 377-3665; www.bucadibeppo.com. L Sat-Sun, D daily.*

For description, see page 60.

### E&O Trading Company

*96 S. First St., (408) 938-4100, fax (408) 938-4164; www.eotrading.com. L-D M-Sat.*

For description, see page 65.

### Emiles

*545 S. Second St., downtown, (408) 289-1960, fax (408) 998-1245; www.emiles.com. D Tu-Sat; $$$. Reservations advised. Valet parking.*

Owner-chef Emile Mooser grew up in the French part of Switzerland. He was trained in the wine country of Lausanne, above Lake Geneva, and now he produces a California-moderated synthesis of all that experience. In his long-lived, elegantly appointed restaurant,

the menu changes with the season. Appetizers might include a vegetable ragoût with truffle oil, baked burgundy snails, or French onion soup. Entrees include several styles of fresh fish, rack of lamb, and a seasonal game—perhaps a tender, mild moose or wild boar flavored with a classic game sauce. Prompted by the chef's own need to cut butter from his diet, lighter dishes that avoid fats—cuisine minceur—are always available. Desserts are seductive, and the signature soufflé for two, flavored perhaps with cappuccino or Grand Marnier, is definitely— excuse the expression—to die for. Adding to the overall tone of the experience, service is excellent, dishes arrive flamboyantly under silver warming domes, and chef Emile finds time to personally visit each table and chat amiably with diners.

### Gordon Biersch Brewery Restaurant

*33 E. San Fernando St./1st St., downtown, (408) 294-6785, fax (408) 294-4052; www.gordonbiersch.com. L-D daily; $-$$. Highchairs, boosters. Reservations advised.*

Seating choices include both a pleasant patio and a spacious, airy dining room overlooking stainless steel brew tanks. The eclectic menu changes regularly and features salads, sandwiches, and individual pizzas as well as more serious entrees and desserts. In addition to three styles of housemade beer, the menu offers a selection of varietal wines and coffees, and the house bread is often a delicious sourdough pumpernickel. Live jazz is sometimes scheduled outdoors on Sunday afternoon and inside in the evening. Brewmaster Dan Gordon is the only American in over 40 years to graduate from the rigorous 5-year brewing program at the Technical University of Munich in Weihenstephan, Germany.

### La Taqueria

*15 S. First St./Santa Clara Ave., (408) 287-1542. L-D daily; $.*

For description, see page 75.

### Lisa's Tea Treasures

*1875 S. Bascom Ave., #165 in The PruneYard, in Campbell, (408) 371-7377; www.lisastea.com. Tea served M-F 11-4, Sat at 11, 1:30, 4, Sun at 12, 3; $$.*

Tea is served in three intimate tearooms here at tables dressed in linen and set with fussy china and silver. Servers dressed in Victorian costume are summoned by ringing a small bell. Tea-related items are for sale in a small gift shop.

## The Old Spaghetti Factory

*51 N. San Pedro St./St. John St., downtown, (408) 288-7488, fax (408) 288-5241; www.osf.com. L M-F, D daily; $. Highchairs, boosters, child menu. No reservations.*

Oodles of noodle selections await spaghetti connoisseurs here. Choose spaghetti with regular marinara sauce, with mushroom sauce, with white clam sauce, or with meat sauce. For those who can't make up their minds, spaghetti with a sampler of sauces is an option. Meatballs, spinach tortellini, and baked chicken are also available. Complete dinners come with bread, soup or salad, drink (coffee, tea, or milk), and ice cream. The restaurant is in what was once the warehouse for the *San Jose Mercury News*. It features bordello decor and a variety of interesting seating options: an antique barber's chair in the bar, within a restored streetcar, on a brass bed converted into a booth.

# Gilroy

## — A LITTLE BACKGROUND —

Though little garlic is grown here anymore, Gilroy is still famous as "the garlic capital of the world." It holds an annual Garlic Festival in July, when the heat wilts the weak.

## — GETTING THERE —

Located 80 miles south of San Francisco.

## — VISITOR INFORMATION —

### Gilroy Visitors Bureau

*7780 Monterey St., (408) 842-6436, fax (408) 842-6438; www.gilroyvisitor.org.*

## — ANNUAL EVENTS —

### Gilroy Garlic Festival

*July. (408) 842-1625; www.gilroygarlicfestival.com. $10, 60+ & 6-12 $5.*

"The garlic capital of the world" turns into a giant open-air kitchen for this celebration of "the stinking rose." Dress in shorts, wear a visor, and bring plenty of sunscreen. A healthy appetite for all things garlic is also a good idea.

### Northern California Renaissance Fair

*September & October. At Casa de Fruta, in Hollister; (831) 252-4879; www.norcalrenfaire.org. $20, 5-11 $10; parking $10.*

Formerly known as the Renaissance Pleasure Faire, this fair morphed into its new name in 2004. Regarded internationally as the most historically correct Renaissance-period event of its kind in the U.S., this faire is an authentic re-creation of an Elizabethan village as it would have appeared over 400 years ago during a harvest festival. More than 1,200 actors, musicians, jesters, jugglers, acrobats, dancers, puppeteers, and mimes dressed in Elizabethan costume are on hand to provide authentic period entertainment and mingle with visitors. Exotic food and drink, quality crafts, and era-appropriate diversions are purveyed throughout. Visitors are encouraged to dress in Renaissance costume. Indeed, this faire has been described as "the largest costume party in the world."

## — WHAT TO DO —

### Bonfante Gardens Family Theme Park

*On Hwy. 152, 3 mi. W of Hwy. 101, (408) 840-7100; www.bonfantegardens.com. Schedule varies; closed Nov-Feb. $31.99, 65+ & 3-6 $22.99; parking $7.*

An undulating hedge leads the way into this unique, horticulturally-inspired amusement park where the theme is trees. Amazingly, the park has only one indigenous tree (located by the Artichoke Dip ride). All the rest are transplanted! The park's 19 "circus trees" date from the 1920s and were displayed at the Tree Circus in Scotts Valley in the 1940s and '50s. They are grafted into extraordinary shapes and are spread evenly throughout the park, providing great photo ops. Four themed gardens are also found here and there. In an attempt to educate children about the value of trees, Learning Sheds offering shade and short videos are scattered throughout the park. Rides are low-key and old-fashioned but fun, with the Quicksilver Mine Coaster being the fastest while the tamer Timber Twister coaster provides thrills for the little ones in its tucked-away location. Don't misses include riding the ornate 1927 M.C. Illions Supreme Carousel and driving a Chevy

Corvette or a Model T-style roadster through a tree tunnel of Italian cypresses and past more than 300 trees on the South County Backroads. Dining options are reasonably priced and include barbecue, tacos, pasta, deep-fried artichokes, orange freezes, and plenty more. Though teens will probably enjoy it here with their younger siblings, this kinder, gentler theme park is a primo experience for grade-schoolers and their parents and for senior citizens. All proceeds go back into the park and into local beautification projects.

## Gaslighter's Music Hall
*7430 Monterey St., (408) 848-3488.*
For description, see page 188.

## Mt. Madonna County Park
*7850 Pole Line Rd./Hwy. 152, 10 mi. W of Gilroy, (408) 842-2341; www.parkhere.org. Daily 8am-sunset. $4/vehicle.*

This 3,688-acre park offers stunning views of Monterey Bay and the Santa Clara Valley from its 20 miles of trails. A 1-mile self-guided nature trail winds around the crumbling ruins of cattle baron Henry Miller's summer home. White fallow deer, descendants of a pair donated by William Randolph Hearst in 1932, are displayed in an enclosed pen. A visitor center highlights the park's natural history, geology, and cultural history. On Saturday evenings in summer, live music and slide shows are presented in an amphitheater. Campsites are available.

# San Juan Bautista

## — A LITTLE BACKGROUND —
Once the largest city in central California, this town is now just a sleepy remnant of that time. It's hard to believe that at one time seven stage lines operated out of the town and that there were numerous busy hotels and saloons. Now the town holds just a few Mexican restaurants, boutiques, and antique shops.

## — VISITOR INFORMATION —
### San Juan Bautista Chamber of Commerce
*410 Third St., (831) 623-2454, fax (831) 623-0674; www.san-juan-bautista.ca.us.*

## — GETTING THERE —
Located approximately 100 miles south of San Francisco, and 45 miles south of San Jose. Take Highway 101 south, then Highway 156 east.

## — ANNUAL EVENTS —
### Early Days at San Juan Bautista
*June. (831) 623-4881.*

Visitors to the state historic park on these days witness re-enactments of 19th-century townspeople performing everyday tasks, such as tortilla-making and baking bread in a hornito oven, and the restored Plaza Hotel's famous bar is opened for business.

### El Teatro Campesino
*December. (831) 623-2444; www.elteatrocampe sino.com.*

Each year this local acting company presents a seasonal Early California folk opera in the mission. Throughout the year, they perform other productions in the new El Teatro Campesino Playhouse at 705 Fourth Street.

### La Posada
*December.*

A candlelight tour of the mission and a procession through the city streets in which Mary and Joseph are portrayed seeking shelter is scheduled.

## — WHAT TO DO —
### Fremont Peak State Park
*At end of San Juan Canyon Rd., 11 mi. from town, (831) 623-4255, fax (831) 623-4612; observatory (831) 623-2465; www.parks.ca.gov. Daily 8-sunset. $3/vehicle.*

A popular destination for picnickers and hikers, this park's summit is an easy 15-minute climb from the parking area. An observatory with a 30-inch reflecting telescope is open to the public twice each month. Campsites are available.

### Mission San Juan Bautista
*402 S. Second St., (831) 623-4528. Daily 9:30-5. By donation.*

Founded in 1797, this is 15th in the chain of 21 California missions. It is owned by the Catholic Church and has the largest church of all the missions. Thomas Doak, the first

American settler in California, painted its bright red and blue reredos and altar. If everything looks familiar, it could be because this park was a major location in the Hitchcock movie *Vertigo*.

### San Juan Bautista State Historic Park
*19 Franklin St., (831) 623-4881, fax (831) 623-4612; www.parks.ca.gov. Daily 10-4:30. $2, under 17 free.*

The restored buildings here allow visitors to see what life was like in this area in the early 1800s. A video introduction to the mission complex is presented in The Plaza Hotel, and the yard of the picturesque Castro-Breen Adobe is perfect for picnicking. Living History days occur on the first Saturday of each month.

#### — WHERE TO STAY —

### Posada de San Juan Hotel
*310 Fourth, (831) 623-4030. 34 rooms; $-$$. All gas fireplaces. Continental breakfast.*

This attractive mission-style inn makes lavish use of tiles. Situated just 2 blocks from the mission, it is connected by a breezeway to the town's main street.

#### — WHERE TO EAT —

### Jardines de San Juan
*115 Third St., (831) 623-4466, fax (831) 623-4340; www.jardinesrestaurant.com. L-D daily; $. Highchairs, boosters, child portions. Reservations accepted.*

What a wonderful fair-weather experience it is to sit outside under a sheltering umbrella on the brick courtyard here. Among the profusely flowering gardens, with autumn-colored roosters sometimes running loose, diners peruse the menu while sipping icy-cold margaritas and dipping tortilla chips in tasty salsa. Flautas consist of shredded beef rolled in a deep-fried tortilla and topped with guacamole. Tacos, enchiladas, and deliciously spicy tamales are available, as are plenty of a la carte items and veggie dishes. On weekends after 5 p.m., regional specialties join the menu. Red snapper Veracruz is available on Fridays, shrimp fajitas on Saturdays, and drunken chicken on Sundays. Limited amounts of these specialties are prepared, so diners must call to reserve their portion. Live music is scheduled on the outdoor stage each Saturday and Sunday from noon to 3:30.

### San Juan Bakery
*319 Third St., (831) 623-4570. Daily 7-7.*

Situated inside an historic building, this old-fashioned bakery makes 35 kinds of breads—including fabulous sourdough French bread and down-soft buttermilk bread—and an assortment of delicious pastries. The sugar cookies are particularly good and make a great car snack. Picnic supplies are also available.

# Salinas

#### — A LITTLE BACKGROUND —

Known as "the salad bowl of the nation," Salinas is one of the biggest cities in the Salinas Valley. This valley is where author John Steinbeck spent his formative years, and many of his novels are set here. In fact, the first working title for *East of Eden* was "Salinas Valley." Agriculturally, it is an unusual and valuable area because of its ability to grow winter vegetables—broccoli, cauliflower, head lettuce—during the summer.

#### — VISITOR INFORMATION —

### Salinas Valley Chamber of Commerce
*119 E. Alisal St., (831) 424-7611, fax (831) 424-8639; www.salinaschamber.com.*

#### — GETTING THERE —

Located approximately 20 miles south of San Juan Bautista, and approximately 100 miles south of San Francisco. It is also possible to take Amtrak *(800-USA-RAIL; www.amtrak.com.)* from Oakland or San Jose and return the same day.

#### — ANNUAL EVENTS —

### California Rodeo Salinas
*July. (800) 771-8807, (831) 775-3100, fax (831) 757-5134; www.carodeo.com. $11-$18, under 13 $1-$6.*

First presented in 1911, this outdoor rodeo is ranked fourth largest in the world. It is especially noted for its trick riders, clowns, and thoroughbred racing. Prize money totals over $200,000, attracting the best of the cowboys to the competitions.

*John Steinbeck and his sister Mary on Jill—the inspiration for* The Red Pony

### Steinbeck Festival™
*August. (831) 775-4721, fax (831) 796-3828;*
*www.steinbeck.org. $17-$60.*

Each year one of Steinbeck's many novels is emphasized at this intellectual festival honoring the town's native son. Bus and walking tours, films, lectures, and panel discussions are all part of the festivities.

### — WHAT TO DO —

### National Steinbeck Center
*One Main St., (831) 796-3833, fax (831) 796-3828;*
*www.steinbeck.org. Daily 10-5. $10.95, 62+ $8.95,*
*13-17 $7.95, 6-12 $5.95.*

The tour here begins with a 10-minute introductory film detailing highlights of Steinbeck's life. Then six galleries of interactive exhibits illustrate famous scenes from his books and his life, enhanced by selected quotes and film clips. *East of Eden* is represented by a full-size boxcar filled with faux iced lettuce—visitors actually *feel* the cool air—and clips from the movie featuring James Dean. *The Red Pony*, which Steinbeck wrote while living in his boyhood home a few blocks away, features a corral exuding the aroma of fresh hay and equipped with a replica pony that kids can mount. But the premiere exhibit seems to be the original "Rocinante"—the custom-built pick-up camper that Steinbeck drove when he traveled around the country writing *Travels with Charley*. Outside the main exhibition hall, a small Art of Writing Room invites visitors to write responses to various Steinbeck quotes and to learn a little more about writing in general.

### — WHERE TO STAY —

### Motel Row
On the east side of the freeway, the whole of North Main Street offers inexpensive generic lodging.

### — WHERE TO EAT —

### Fast-food heaven
*1300 block of N. Main St.*

### First Awakenings
*171 Main St., (831) 784-1125. B-L daily; $. Highchairs,*
*boosters, child menu.*

For description, see page 115.

## The Steinbeck House

*132 Central Ave., (831) 424-2735, fax (831) 757-5806. L M-Sat; $. Closed 2 wks. in Dec. Highchairs, boosters, child menu. Reservations advised.*

John Steinbeck was born in 1902 in the front bedroom of this beautifully renovated 1897 Victorian house. In *East of Eden* he described it as ". . . an immaculate and friendly house, grand enough but not pretentious . . . inside its white fence surrounded by its clipped lawn and roses . . ." A volunteer group now owns the house and operates a gourmet luncheon restaurant within. Serving seasonal produce grown in the Salinas Valley, the menu changes daily and includes items such as crunchy, cool gazpacho soup and tasty chicken-walnut salad. Though the dining rooms are elegantly decorated, with Steinbeck memorabilia covering the walls, the atmosphere is casual. Comfortable travel attire is acceptable, and children are welcome. After lunch, a well-priced cellar gift shop invites browsing and perhaps selecting a souvenir book by Steinbeck. Guided house tours operate on summer Sundays.

## Soledad

### — WHAT TO DO —

#### Mission Nuestra Señora de la Soledad

*36641 Fort Romie Rd., off Paraiso Springs Rd., 3 mi. W of Hwy. 101, (831) 678-2586. Daily10-4. By donation.*

This isolated mission was the 13th in the chain and was named for the Spanish word for solitude. Built in 1791, it was abandoned in 1835 and then crumbled into ruin. In 1935, volunteers rebuilt the living quarters and the chapel, which retains its original tile floor. Now it sits next to the Salinas River among peaceful green pastures and rolling hills.

#### Pinnacles National Monument

*12 mi. SE of town, take Hwy. 146 E, (831) 389-4485, fax (831) 389-4489; www.nps.gov/pinn. Park: daily 7:30-6. Visitor centers: daily 9-5. $5/vehicle.*

Formed by ancient volcanic activity, this 23,900-acre scenic area is home to craggy pinnacles and spires that are surprising to come across in an area that is otherwise so flat. Spring and fall are the best times for hiking and camping, spring being particularly popular because of the stunning display of wildflowers. At other times, the temperature can be uncomfortable. A variety of raptors—prairie falcons, red-shouldered hawks, turkey vultures, and golden eagles—nest in the rocks and are sometimes sighted, and 410 bee species make their home here—more than are found anywhere else in North America. The more developed east side of the park is reached by taking Highway 25 south, then Highway 146 west. There, a Visitor Center offers orientation, and a moderately difficult 2-mile loop trail leads to the Bear Gulch Cave.

## King City

### — ANNUAL EVENTS —

#### Eagle tours at Lake San Antonio

*January & February. (888) 588-2267, (831) 755-4899; www.lakesanantonio.net. Schedule varies. $10; parking $5. Reservations required.*

This lake is one of the largest habitats for golden and bald eagles in central California, and these 2-hour boat tours are one of the best ways to view them.

### — WHAT TO DO —

#### Mission San Antonio de Padua

*Exit at Jolon Rd. (G14) just before King City, 23 mi. SW of Hwy. 101 via Jolon Rd., in Fort Hunter Liggett, (831) 385-4478. Daily 8-6. By donation.*

Founded in 1771 by Father Serra as the third mission and known as the "Jewel of the Santa Lucias," this is one of the largest restored and rebuilt missions. Original remains at the remote, picturesque site include the well, gristmill, tannery, and parts of the aqueduct system. The imposing façade of its church is known for both the campanile located in front and its archway bells. Both the church and the quadrangle are restored to an authentic approximation of their original luster. A museum exhibits Native American artifacts, and an annual **fiesta** occurs the second weekend in June. The site is especially beautiful in the spring, when the surrounding grasslands are ablaze with a profusion of wildflowers.

# San Miguel

## — GETTING THERE —

Located approximately 65 miles south of Soledad.

## — WHAT TO DO —

### Mission San Miguel Arcangel

*775 Mission St., (805) 467-3256, fax (805) 467-2141; www.missionsanmiguel.org. Daily 9:30-4:15. By donation.*

Founded in 1797, this is 16th in the chain of California's 21 missions. The present mission building was constructed in 1816. Though the outside architecture is simple, the delicate original and unretouched neoclassical frescoes inside and the rustic wooden All-Seeing Eye of Gare are especially noteworthy. They were painted by parish Indians under the direction of professional artist Esteban Munras. The reredos feature marble pillars with intricate geometric patterns displaying a dazzling array of colors. Windows are covered by their original sheepskin drapes, and beehive ovens and olive presses are displayed in fragrant gardens. Shaded picnic tables are provided. Unfortunately, much of the mission is inaccessible due to an earthquake in 2003. A **fiesta** occurs each September on the third Sunday.

The 1846 **Rios Caldonia Adobe** *(700 Mission St., (805) 467-3357. Daily 10-4.)* is located nearby. Once part of the mission estate, this 2-story adobe has served as a hotel, stagecoach office, school, and family home. It is restored and furnished to reflect the past.

# Paso Robles

## — A LITTLE BACKGROUND —

Originally a hot springs resort in the 1800s, this "pass of the oaks" (as its name translates) is fast becoming known for its award-winning wineries. Its downtown, which borders grassy City Park, was devastated by an earthquake in 2003.

## — VISITOR INFORMATION —

### Paso Robles Visitors & Conference Bureau

*1225 Park St., (800) 406-4040, (805) 238-0506, fax (805) 238-0527; www.pasorobleschamber.com.*

## — GETTING THERE —

Located approximately 5 miles south of San Miguel.

## — WHAT TO DO —

### James Dean Memorial

*On Hwy. 46, 25 mi. E of town, in Cholame (pronounced "show-LAMB").*

Depending on a person's mood, this can be either an interesting or a bizarre side trip. This is where legendary actor James Dean crashed his racing-model Porsche 550 Spyder roadster and died in 1955 (at the intersection of Highways 46 and 41). A concrete-and-stainless steel obelisk shrine to Dean's memory stands just 900 yards from the actual death site. Constructed and maintained by a Japanese national who comes to pay homage twice a year, it is located in the parking lot of the Jack Ranch Cafe.

### Sycamore Natural Herb Farms

*2485 Hwy. 46 W., S of town, 3 mi. W of Hwy. 101, in Templeton, (800) 576-5288, (805) 238-5288; www.sycamorefarms.com. Daily 10-5.*

An enormous selection of lavenders, thymes, rosemarys, basils, and scented geraniums are gown here and can be purchased in season. Penned goats and chickens are a delight for adults and kids alike, and shaded picnic tables are provided.

In the back of a well-stocked gift shop, the **Bonny Doon Vineyard tasting room** *((805) 239-5614; www.bonnydoonvineyard.com.)* pours samples of their delicious wines. (It's *here* because the farm grows grapes for their winery Santa Cruz.) For more description, see page 100.

### Wine tasting back-roads tour

*Begin at Vineyard Drive exit off Hwy 101, just N of Templeton.*

This area's limestone soil is similar to that found in Provence in the south of France, and it produces flavorful grapes. The long, hot summers turn them into fodder for ripe, robust Merlots and Zinfandels. For this scenic drive, go west for about 8 miles through bucolic, oak-studded farmland, passing Peachy Canyon Road (which returns to the freeway). At Adelaida Road, turn right and continue for about 2 miles to **Adelaida Cellars** (*5805 Adelaida Rd., (800) 676-1232, (805) 239-8980, fax (805) 239-4671; www.adelaida.com. Tasting daily 11-5.*), a scenically situated winery specializing in producing small quantities of low-tech premium wines fermented with natural yeast. Of special interest here is an expansive walnut orchard, the bountiful fruit of which is sold in the tasting room. Continue about 10 miles east on Adelaida Road toward town, crossing 101, to **Eberle Winery** (*On Hwy. 46 East, 3.5 mi. E of Hwy. 101, (805) 238-9607, fax (805) 237-0344; www.eberle winery.com. Tasting daily 10-5, in summer to 6; tour: Sat-Sun on half-hr., M-F by request.*). The winery's excellent reds can be tasted in a room filled with medals and awards from competitions, and picnic tables are provided on a sheltered patio.

For a free map to this area's many wineries, contact the **Paso Robles Vintners and Growers Association** (*(800) 549-WINE, (805) 239-VINE, fax (805) 237-6439; www.paso wine.com.*).

### — WHERE TO STAY —

### Paso Robles Inn
*1103 Spring St., (800) 676-1713, (805) 238-2660, fax (805) 238-4707; www.pasoroblesinn.com. 100 rooms; $$-$$$. Some gas fireplaces. Pool; hot tub. 2 restaurants. No pets.*

It's rumored that in this area's chic heyday, Marilyn Monroe and Joe DiMaggio honeymooned here. And if it's good enough for them . . . In fact, guests nowadays can do something here Marilyn and Joe couldn't—book a room with a private whirlpool hot tub that fills with hot, hot water direct from the thermal springs that are found 800 feet down under most of the town. Built in 1891, the original inn was a fashionable resort popular with the wealthy and famous. It burned to the ground in 1940. (Like the Titanic was touted "unsinkable," the hotel was hailed as "absolutely fireproof.") The lobby and much of the original brick were saved and are incorporated into the inn's bungalows. Today's inn has spacious grounds with well-tended gardens, a koi pond, and convenient parking spaces right outside the door. But the main attraction is 30 comfortable, spacious spa rooms. Each has a private patio with a chocolate-brown tub and privacy curtain. The tub fills in about a half-hour with the 124-degree, stinky, rotten-egg-smelling—but-healthy-for-

what-ails-you—sulphur water that is reputed to help with skin problems, arthritis, and aching muscles and joints. Recommended soak time is 30 minutes or more. Do bring along favorite fruits and drinks to store in the room's refrigerator for after-soaking snacking. Note that the communal pool and hot tub are filled with regular water. The inn is conveniently located just across the street from the town park and a downtown area filled with shops, restaurants, and a multi-plex cinema. The inn itself has a popular bar, a vintage '40s coffee shop featuring a 50-foot circular counter with swivel stools, and a restaurant with oversize $3/4$-moon booths that is famous for its Sunday brunch.

### Motel Row
*Along Spring St.*

Best Western, Holiday Inn, Motel 6, and Travelodge are all represented.

### — WHERE TO EAT —

### Cider Creek
*3760 Hwy. 46 West, (805) 238-4144, fax (805) 238-4052. Daily 8-5.*

This tiny barn-like building purveys a collection of apple foods and permits tasting an assortment of apple juice blends made especially for them in Davis. Perhaps the best of the lot are the small, cold bottles to go, the red plastic apple "sippers" for kids, and the freshly baked pastries.

### 21st Street Drive-In
*2110 Spring St., (805) 238-0360. Daily 9-9; $. Child portions. No cards.*

An oasis off Highway 101, this old-time root beer drive-in is right out of the '50s. A carhop appears when a car's headlights are turned on, and food is served on a tray that attaches to a partially rolled-down window. Choices are simple: hamburgers, hot dogs, French fries, and *cold* root beer.

# Atascadero

### — VISITOR INFORMATION —

### Atascadero Chamber of Commerce
*6550 El Camino Real, (805) 466-2044, fax (805) 466-9218; www.atascaderochamber.org.*

## – WHAT TO DO –

### Charles Paddock Zoo
*9305 Pismo St., off Hwy. 41, 1 mi. W of Hwy. 101, (805) 461-5080. Daily 10-4; in summer to 5. $3, 65+ $2.25, 3-12 $2.*

Though small, this 5-acre zoo takes good care of its diverse population. An adjacent park has shady picnic tables and a lake with paddleboat rentals.

# San Luis Obispo

## – VISITOR INFORMATION –

### San Luis Obispo Chamber of Commerce
*1039 Chorro St., (805) 781-2670, fax (805) 543-1255; www.visitslo.com.*

### San Luis Obispo County Visitors & Conference Bureau
*1037 Mill St., (800) 634-1414, (805) 781-2531, fax (805) 543-9498; www.sanluisobispocounty.com.*

## – GETTING THERE –

Located approximately 200 miles south of San Francisco (it is the halfway point between San Francisco and Los Angeles) and 30 miles south of Paso Robles via Highway 101, and approximately 45 miles south of San Simeon via Highway 1. It is also possible to take Amtrak ((800) 872-7245).

## – WHAT TO DO –

### California Polytechnic State University (Cal Poly)
*On Grand Ave., (805) 756-1111; www.calpoly.edu. Tour: (805) 756-5734; M-F at 11; free.*

Guided walking tours of this attractive campus begin in the University Union.

### Gum Alley
*Next to 733 Higuera St.*

For several decades, gum-chewers have been depositing their product on these brick walls. Some have even taken the time to make designs. A vulgar, tacky eyesore to many, it is a cheap thrill for gum aficionados and most children. So don't get stuck here without a stick. Stock up on different colors of gum before arriving, and note that Double Bubble reputedly sticks best.

### Hot springs

#### • Avila Hot Springs
*250 Avila Beach Dr., (805) 595-2359; http://avilahot springs.com. Daily 8am-10pm. $8, 55+ & 2-12 $6.50.*

At this family-friendly spot, facilities include a large freshwater pool and a smaller 105-degree mineral pool.

#### • Sycamore Mineral Springs Resort
*1215 Avila Beach Dr., (800) 234-5831, (805) 595-7302, fax (805) 595-4007; www.sycamore springs.com. 55 rooms; $$-$$$+. Some kitchens & fireplaces. Heated pool; 23 public hot tubs, $20+/hr. Restaurant.*

Situated on a back road leading to the coast, each guest room at this inn has a private hot tub. Outdoor mineral spring hot tubs can be rented by the hour by non-guests, and massage treatments are available. The springs' history dates to 1897, when two men drilling for oil were disappointed to find sulfur-based mineral water instead. First called the "oil wells," the springs became popular in the 1920s when W. C. Fields and other celebrities who stayed at Hearst Castle stopped in.

### Mission San Luis Obispo de Tolosa
*782 Monterey St., (805) 543-6850. Daily 9-4; in summer to 5. By donation.*

Founded in 1772, this is the fifth mission in the California chain. It was the first mission to introduce the red clay roof tile, which successfully repelled the flaming arrows used in attacks by Native Americans. The extensively restored complex includes a fragrant rose garden and a museum exhibiting rare early California photos. Its charming chapel has a simple façade with a belfry and vestibule (unique among the state's missions) and is still used for services. An adjacent plaza and park provide shady trees, large grassy areas, stream-hugging paths, and inviting open-air cafes.

The nearby **San Luis Obispo County Historical Museum** *(696 Monterey St., (805) 543-0638; www.slochs.org. W-Sun 10-4. Free.)* is housed in a former Carnegie Library building and is appropriately filled with historical exhibits that include a hurdy-gurdy (or calliope) and a school bell.

## San Luis Obispo Children's Museum
*1010 Nipomo St., (805) 544-KIDS, fax (805) 545-5875. Tu-Sat 11-5, Sun 12-4. $5, under 2 free.*

Located within a transformed transmission shop, this museum is especially for kids and holds numerous hands-on exhibits that entice them to explore and interact. They can encase themselves in a giant bubble, pilot a space shuttle to the moon, and anchor a newscast. Children under age 16 must be accompanied by an adult, and baby strollers are not permitted.

### — WHERE TO STAY —

## Embassy Suites Hotel
*333 Madonna Rd., (800) 864-6000, (800) EMBASSY, (805) 549-0800, fax (805) 543-5273; www.embassy suitesslo.com. 4 stories; 196 rooms; $-$$$. Children under 18 free. Indoor heated pool & hot tub; fitness room. Full breakfast; restaurant; room service. Pets by approval.*

This branch of the all-suites hotel chain is located adjacent to a beautifully landscaped, open-air shopping mall. For more description, see page 420.

## Garden Street Inn
*1212 Garden St./Marsh St., (800) 488-2045, (805) 545-9802, fax (805) 545-9403; www.gardenstreet inn.com. 13 rooms; $$. Unsuitable for children under 16. Some fireplaces. Hot tub. Evening snack, full breakfast. No smoking; no pets.*

This enormous 1887 Italianate/Queen Anne-style mansion is beautifully restored and just a block from downtown. Fragrant old citrus trees greet guests at the front gate, and a com-

munal parlor area features an interesting browsing library.

## Hostel Obispo
*1617 Santa Rosa St., (805) 544-4678, fax (805) 544-3142; www.hostelobispo.com. 22 beds; some private rooms.*

Located just 1 block from the Amtrak station and within walking distance of downtown, this hostel has a B&B atmosphere. Bicycles are available for rental, and complimentary pancakes are served each morning. See also page 445.

## KOA Kampground
*4765 Santa Margarita Lake Rd., 10 mi. from town, (800) KOA-5619, (805) 438-5618; www.koa.com.*

For description, see page 443.

## Madonna Inn
*100 Madonna Rd., (800) 543-9666, (805) 543-3000, fax (805) 543-1800; www.madonnainn.com. 109 rooms; $$-$$$+. Children under 18 free. Some fireplaces. 2 restaurants. No smoking; no pets.*

Begun in 1958 with just 12 rooms, this sprawling pink motel now has more than 100 guest rooms. All are uniquely decorated, some more uniquely than others—like the Cave Man Room, with its stone walls, ceilings, and floors plus cascading waterfall shower; and the Barrel of Fun Room, in which all the furniture is made from barrels.

For those not spending the night, a meal in either the flamboyant **Copper Café** *(B-L-D daily; $$. Highchairs, boosters, child menu.)*— where sitting on red leather-upholstered swivel stools at an elaborately carved, horseshoe-shaped coffee bar is an option—or dinner in the more formal **Alex Madonna's Gold Rush Steakhouse** *(D daily; $$$. Highchairs, boosters, booths, child menu. Reservations advised.)*— where the menu is surf and turf and all the supporting courses are included—is a must. Also, a bakery dispenses goodies such as French cream puffs, cinnamon pull-aparts, and an assortment of pies. And don't miss the restrooms—especially the men's room featuring a stone waterfall urinal.

## Motel Inn
*2223 Monterey St.*

Opened on December 12, 1925, this is the world's very first motel. It is currently closed.

## Motel Row

A vast array of motels lines the north end of Monterey Street.

### — WHERE TO EAT —

## Benvenuti
*450 Marsh St., (805) 541-5393, same fax; www.benvenutiristorante.com. L M-F, D daily; $$. Reservations advised.*

Operating from within a transformed Victorian home, this romantic restaurant offers an extensive menu of refined northern Italian dishes. Many of the pastas are housemade, and fresh fish and lighter salads are options. Selections from the dessert tray might include a housemade light tiramisu or, in season, perfect fresh red raspberries topped with Grand Marnier.

## Farmers' Market and Street Faire
*600 & 700 blks. of Higuera St., (805) 541-0286, fax (805) 781-2647; www.downtownslo.com. Thur 6-9pm. Free admission.*

Shoppers can buy dinner fully prepared or pick up the fixings. This market is known for its delicious barbecued items, and live entertainment is provided free.

## Hobee's
*1443 Calle Joaquin, off Hwy. 101, (805) 549-9186; www.hobees.com. B-L daily; $. Highchairs, boosters, booths, child menu. No reservations.*

The secret to success here is tasty, wholesome food prepared with plenty of vegetables and tofu and served in a cheerful atmosphere in comfortable surroundings. The breakfast menu, available all day, offers a selection of omelettes and scrambles as well as whole-wheat pancakes, granola, cinnamon-orange swirl French toast, and their famous blueberry coffeecake. Lunch brings on a salad bar, housemade soups, and a variety of sandwiches and hamburgers.

## Linn's Downtown SLO
*1141 Chorro St./Marsh St., (805) 546-8444; www.linnsfruitbin.com. B-L-D daily, SunBr; $. Highchairs, boosters, child menu. No reservations.*

Known for its delicious breakfasts, expansive salad bar, and large selection of pies and desserts, this pleasant dining spot's varied menu also includes delectable pot pies, stuffed potatoes, stir-frys, and sandwiches. Everything is made from scratch in house. An adjoining shop purveys the restaurant's line of gourmet food products, which are also available through a mail-order catalogue.

## Pepe Delgado's
*1601 Monterey St., (805) 544-6660. L-D Tu-Sun; $. Highchairs, boosters, booths, child portions. No reservations.*

Comfortable booths and large, solid tables make this popular Mexican spot an especially good choice for families. The hacienda-style building features tile floors, velvet paintings, and papier-mâché parrots on perches hanging from the ceiling. Potent fruit margaritas and daiquiris come in small, medium, and large to help diners get festive. A large variety of traditional Mexican items is on the menu, and many are available in small portions. Fajitas are particularly fun to order because they arrive sizzling on raised platters and are kept warm on the table by candles.

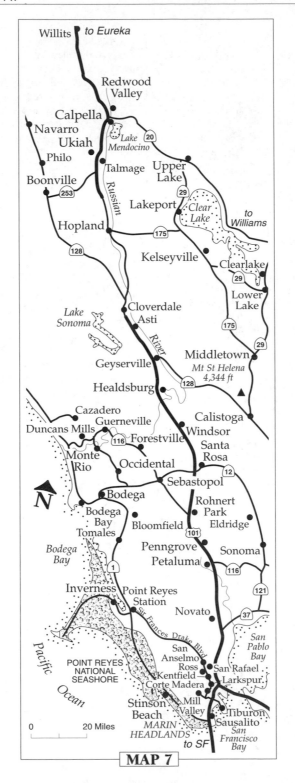

**MAP 7**

# 101 NORTH

## — A LITTLE BACKGROUND —

Just across the Golden Gate Bridge from San Francisco, spectacularly scenic Marin County comprises a number of prosperous bedroom communities. It is home to numerous rock stars and celebrities, including *Star Wars* filmmaker George Lucas, who built his studios in the hilly backcountry.

Books and films have poked fun at the generally upscale residents, presenting them as flaky New Agers with an easygoing, laid-back approach to life, who seek nothing more than to tickle each other with peacock feathers while soaking in a hot tub. The reality is, of course, something else.

Consistently fair weather makes Marin County a popular destination with Bay Area residents, especially when other areas are covered by fog.

## — VISITOR INFORMATION —

### Marin County Convention and Visitors Bureau

*1013 Larkspur Landing Cir., Larkspur, (415) 499-5000, fax (415) 461-0965; www.visitmarin.org.*

## Marin Headlands

### — A LITTLE BACKGROUND —

Converted from military to recreational use in 1972, this 12,000 acre park has its **Visitor Center** *(Alexander Ave. exit off Hwy. 101, (415) 331-1540; www.nps.gov/goga/mahe. Daily 9:30-4:30. Free.)* inside Fort Barry's old chapel. It consists of three areas: Forts Baker, Barry, and Cronkhite. Take a soul-soothing walk along Rodeo Beach. When leaving, follow McCullough Road east to Conzelman Road, which leads past some of the old bunkers and gun batteries that attest to the area's military past. The **Nike Missile Site** *((415) 331-1453. W-F & 1st Sun of month, 12-30-3:30.)*, built to protect the Bay Area against the Soviet threat during the 1950s through '70s, is restored by volunteers and has guided tours. **Hawk Hill**, at Battery 129, is considered the best site on the West Coast to view birds of prey; over 36,000 hawks and other raptors migrate over this area each year. Farther on, several twists in the road offer magnificent views of the Golden Gate Bridge, and behind it, San Francisco. A picture taken here makes the subject look as if they are standing on the edge of the earth.

## – WHAT TO DO –

### Bay Area Discovery Museum

*557 McReynolds Rd., in Fort Baker, (415) 339-3900, fax (415) 339-3905; www.baykidsmuseum.org. Tu-F 9-4, Sat-Sun 10-5. $7, under 1 free; free on 2nd Sat of month 1-5.*

This activity-oriented, hands-on museum designed especially for infants to 10-year-olds is especially nice as a rainy day outing. Themes include the bay environment, art, multimedia, and architecture. Related activities spread among eight buildings include constructing a model suspension bridge, crawling through a simulated ocean, and building a personal enclosure in the Space Maze. Kids can also climb a vinyl anthill and splash their hands in the River Fantastic, and ages 3 and under can frolic in the Tot Spot. The excitement is catching, and parents find themselves being pulled along from one activity to another by their eager children. Visitors can also explore the outdoor area immediately surrounding the museum, where a Model T is one of the play structures. For those who are caught picnic-less, a cafe serves appropriate fare, and outdoor picnic tables afford a magnificent close-up view of the Golden Gate Bridge. Special programs, festivals, and workshops are scheduled regularly.

### The Marine Mammal Center

*1065 Fort Cronkhite, (415) 289-SEAL, fax (415) 289-7333; www.tmmc.org. Daily 10-4. Free.*

Staffed by volunteers, this is one of the largest wild animal hospitals in the world. Injured, sick, and orphaned marine mammals (seals, dolphins, porpoises, whales) are brought here to be nursed back to health. When ready, they are released back into their natural habitat. Docent-led tours are available on weekends, self-guided tours during the week.

### Point Bonita Lighthouse

*(415) 331-1540; www.nps.gov/goga/mahe. Trail open Sat-Mon 12:30-3:30; tour schedule varies. Free.*

This lovely old light was the last on the Pacific Coast to be automated. The mostly dirt, 1/2 -mile trail can be scary: It includes going through a tunnel and crossing a 120-foot suspension bridge. Full moon walks are sometimes scheduled.

*The Marine Mammal Center*

## – WHERE TO STAY –

### Marin Headlands Hostel

*Bldg. 941 at Fort Barry, (415) 331-2777, fax (415) 331-6943; www.norcalhostels.org. 104 beds; private rooms.*

On the National Historic Register, this spacious, homey hostel operates in two charming turn-of-the-century buildings. See also page 445.

# Sausalito

## – A LITTLE BACKGROUND –

People come from all over the world to stroll Bridgeway, the main street of this warm and sunny town. A former fishing village, Sausalito is often referred to as California's Riviera and is now a magnet for both artists and tourists and remains a pleasure for both. Restaurants and boutiques abound, and the view across the bay to Tiburon and San Francisco is stellar. Take time to climb some of the inviting hillside stairways found throughout town. Be careful: The largest source of income for the city is parking fines. It is interesting to note that Jack London wrote the opening chapters of *The Sea Wolf* here.

## — VISITOR INFORMATION —

### Sausalito Chamber of Commerce

*10 Liberty Ship Way, Bay 2 #250, (415) 331-7262, fax (415) 332-0323; www.sausalito.org.*

## — GETTING THERE —

Take the first exit (Alexander Avenue) off Highway 101 after crossing the Golden Gate Bridge. Another exit marked "Sausalito" is 3 miles farther north. Sausalito can also be reached from San Francisco via ferry.

## — ANNUAL EVENTS —

### Floating Homes Tour

*Date varies. (415) 332-1916; www.floatinghomes.org. $25-$30.*

Approximately ten houseboats open their doors for tours during this exciting event at Kappas Marina. A portion of the proceeds benefits a local non-profit organization.

### Sausalito Art Festival

*September, on Labor Day weekend. (415) 332-3555, fax (415) 331-1340; www.sausalitoartfest.org. $20, 62+ $10, 6-12 $5.*

This juried exhibit of over 250 artists—all of whom attend in person—includes live music, fine food and wine, and a waterfront setting with magnificent bay views. It is the top-rated non-profit fine arts festival in the U.S.

## — WHAT TO DO —

### Bay Model Visitor Center

*2100 Bridgeway, (415) 332-3870, (415) 332-3871; www.spn.usace.army.mil/bmvc. Tu-F 9-4, Sat 10-5; in summer Tu-Sat 9-4. Free.*

Located on the outskirts of town, on the site of a shipyard that produced World War II Liberty Ships and tankers, this is a working hydraulic scale model of the Bay Area and Delta estuary systems. As big as two football fields, it is designed to simulate bay water conditions for research. A computerized slide show and interpretive displays help make this complex scientific project understandable to the layman. The model operates irregularly; call for upcoming dates. A small museum tells about shipbuilding here during World War II.

### Heath Ceramics

*400 Gate 5 Rd., (415) 332-3732; www.heath ceramics.com. M-Sat 10-5, Sun 12-5.*

A store adjoining this ceramics factory sells seconds of its well-known tiles and classically simple, contemporary ceramic dinnerware. The line is used in many upscale restaurants, including Chez Panisse in Berkeley, and is in the permanent collection of the Museum of Modern Art in NYC.

### Sea Trek Ocean Kayaking Center

*(415) 488-1000, fax (415) 488-1707; www.seatrek kayak.com. Guided trips $65-$95, under 13 $30-$50.*

Take a 3-hour or full-day guided trip, or rent a kayak for just an hour or the entire day. Children's classes are available, and a customized Take the Kids Sea Kayaking program includes wet suits for the whole family.

### Waldo Point

*At north end of town.*

This private houseboat colony contains both the funky and the exquisite. Visitors are not particularly welcomed by residents but are legally permitted to view the area if they respect posted no-trespassing signs. It is said that in 1967 singer Otis Redding rented a houseboat on the main dock here, which was the inspiration for his well-known song titled "(Sittin' On) The Dock of the Bay."

— WHERE TO STAY —

## Casa Madrona Hotel

*801 Bridgeway, (800) 567-9524, (415) 332-0502, fax (415) 332-2537; www.casamadrona.com. 63 rooms; $$$-$$$$+. Some kitchens & fireplaces. Hot tub; health spa. Evening snack, full breakfast; restaurant. No pets. Valet parking $20.*

Nestled against a picturesque hill above Bridgeway, this hotel offers lodging in either a converted 1885 Victorian house in back (the oldest structure in Sausalito) or in newer, tastefully decorated contemporary rooms sprinkled down the hillside amid fragrant, blooming gardens and featuring water views. Some rooms are themed. One of the most popular is the uniquely decorated Artist's Loft, but the Fireside Suite, with its clawfoot tub for two and canopy bed with harbor view, is also in heavy demand. The hotel recently expanded into the former Village Fair shopping center. Arrangements can also be made to stay on a local houseboat. The hot tub is reserved by the hour for private use. Breakfast is served to guests in the hotel's elegant restaurant, **Poggio** *(777 Bridgeway, (415) 332-7771, fax (415) 332-6589. B-L-D daily; $$. Reservations advised. Valet parking.),* which serves classic northern Italian fare.

## Hotel Sausalito

*16 El Portal/Bridgeway, (888) 442-0700, (415) 332-0700, fax (415) 332-8788; www.hotelsausalito.com. 16 rooms; $$-$$$. Continental breakfast. No smoking; no pets. Self-parking $10.*

Well-located next to the ferry landing, this small European-style boutique hotel was built in 1915 in Mission Revival style. It once served as a bordello. In his heyday, Baby Face Nelson was a regular guest, and writer Sterling Hayden once lived here. Now renovated into a bit of the French Riviera, it has a sunny decor. Colorful commissioned art decorates the halls, and handmade furniture and accents are found throughout. Most of the rooms retain their original stained-glass windows and overlook either Bridgeway or tiny Vina del Mar Park.

## The Inn Above Tide

*30 El Portal, (800) 893-TIDE, (415) 332-9535, fax (415) 332-6714; www.innabovetide.com. 30 rooms; $$$-$$$$+. Most gas fireplaces. Evening snack, continental breakfast. No smoking; no pets. Valet parking $12.*

At the only hotel *on* San Francisco Bay (some rooms jut out over the water), all rooms have spectacular views of San Francisco and of a continuous parade of vessels. Some have private decks with glass walls for even better, unobstructed gazing. Amenities include robes and binoculars, and all rooms are equipped with comfy San Francisco-made McRoskey Airflex mattresses. Evening wine and breakfast are served in the parlor but are delivered to guest rooms upon request. The ferry from San Francisco docks immediately adjacent.

## Sausalito Alta Mira

*125 Bulkley Ave., (415) 332-1350, fax (415) 331-3862; www.sausalitoaltamira.com. 22 units; $-$$$; closed Jan. Some gas fireplaces. Evening snack, full breakfast.*

Situated in the hills above town, this century-old spot offers a secluded escape. Its terrace commands a panoramic bay view and is a sublime spot to enjoy a leisurely breakfast. Many of the guest rooms and cottages also have bay views.

— WHERE TO EAT —

## Caffe Trieste

*100 Bridgeway, (415) 332-7660, fax (415) 332-7665; www.caffetrieste.com. Daily 6:30am-9:30pm.*

This is a branch of the famous North Beach coffeehouse. For description, see page 62.

## No Name Bar

*757 Bridgeway/El Portal, (415) 332-1392. Daily 10am-2am.*

Famous for its low profile, this casual spot is inside the second-oldest building in town. Stop here and relax over a pitcher of Ramos fizzes in the garden-like back room. A menu of sandwiches is available from 11 a.m. to 3 p.m. Live Dixieland jazz is performed every Sunday afternoon, and live jazz and blues are scheduled Wednesday through Saturday evenings. Chess games happen on Friday afternoons.

# Mill Valley

## — A LITTLE BACKGROUND —

Thought of by many as the quintessential Marin, this tiny town originated as an enclave of vacation cabins built by San Franciscans eager to escape the city's notoriously cool summers. It is said more professionals per capita live here than in any other community in the country. The town rests at the base of Mount Tamalpais, the county's principal landmark.

The unofficial center of town seems to be **The Depot Bookstore and Cafe** (87 Throckmorton Ave., (415) 383-2665; www.depotbookstore.com. Daily 7-7.). Once the town's Northwestern Pacific Railroad depot, it offers both indoor and outdoor seating and a plethora of reading material.

Mill Valley is also home to the original **Banana Republic** store (59 Throckmorton Ave., (415) 383-4900; www.bananarepublic.com.), now a nationwide chain. Its current location is not the original site. The town is also home to the modest original location of the **Smith & Hawken** garden-supply store (35 Corte Madera Ave., (415) 381-1800, fax (415) 381-5823; www.smith-hawken.com.).

## — VISITOR INFORMATION —

### Mill Valley Chamber of Commerce
85 Throckmorton Ave., (415) 388-9700, fax (415) 388-9770; www.millvalley.org.

## — GETTING THERE —

Located approximately 5 miles north of Sausalito. Take exit off Highway 101 and follow signs to intersection of Miller and Throckmorton avenues.

## — ANNUAL EVENTS —

### Mill Valley Film Festival
October. (415) 383-5256, fax (415) 383-8606; www.cafilm.org. Screenings $9.

Running for 11 days, this well-established festival offers screenings both of American independent cinema and foreign films, major film premières, and tributes to top filmmakers and industry leaders. Seminars are scheduled for both aspiring filmmakers and the layman in search of enlightenment. A **Children's FilmFest**, with special screenings and workshops, occurs at the same time.

## — WHAT TO DO —

### Old Mill Park
On Throckmorton Ave./Old Mill Rd., (415) 383-1370. Free.

Holding the town's namesake 1834 sawmill, this park is sheltered by an old-growth redwood grove and offers idyllic streamside picnicking. A rustic sun-speckled playground area has picnic tables, some of which are inside a circle of giant redwoods.

### Sweetwater
153 Throckmorton Ave., (415) 388-2820; www.sweetwatersaloon.com. Schedule varies. Free-$17.

This legendary nightclub schedules intimate evening performances by an array of noteworthy rock and blues musicians. Big name Bay Area residents sometimes drop in to jam.

## — WHERE TO STAY —

### Mill Valley Inn
165 Throckmorton Ave., (800) 595-2100, (415) 389-6608, fax (415) 389-5051; www.millvalleyinn.com. 25 rooms; $$-$$$+. Some fireplaces. Continental breakfast; limited room service. No smoking; no pets.

Conveniently situated downtown, this newly constructed European-style pension is tucked against a redwood covered hill. Rooms are furnished stylishly with attractive handcrafted pieces made by Northern California artists. Some have a balcony with views of the redwoods and Mount Tamalpais, and two cottages offer privacy in a creekside forest setting. Breakfast in the morning is taken on the Sun Terrace and includes an espresso bar and newspaper.

## — WHERE TO EAT —

### Buckeye Roadhouse
15 Shoreline Hwy., at Mill Valley/Stinson Beach exit off Hwy. 101, (415) 331-2600, fax (415) 331-6067; www.buckeyeroadhouse.com. L M-Sat, D daily, SunBr; $$-$$$. Highchairs, boosters, booths, child menu. Reservations advised. Valet parking.

Situated inside an updated 1937 Bavarian-style chalet, this unfussy restaurant features generous portions of tasty all-American food at reasonable prices. The main dining room has high peaked ceilings, a large stone fireplace, and dark mahogany accents. Some tables have a pleasant view over the freeway to Strawberry Point. Mixed drinks are on the menu, among them a deliciously spicy Bloody Mary. Winners at lunch include well-seasoned coleslaw, an ahi sandwich served with pesto mayo and crisp housemade potato chips, and great onion rings—sliced very thin and served with house-made ketchup. Dinner entrees include steaks, chops, and fresh seafood. If the dining room is crowded, a snack can be ordered in the bar.

## The Cantina

*651 E. Blithedale Ave./Camino Alto, in Blithedale Plaza, (415) 381-1070; www.greatmex.com. L-D daily; $$. Highchairs, boosters, booths, child menu. Reservations advised.*

It is not unusual in Marin County to find a very good restaurant located in a shopping center, as this one is. Popular at lunch, it becomes more crowded at dinner, when waits can be long. Fortunately, a variety of tangy margaritas and fresh fruit daiquiris are available, with or without alcohol, to help pass the time. The predictable Mexican items and combination plates are on the large menu, as are a few more unusual ones—green enchiladas topped with tart tomatillo sauce, an outstanding deep-fried chimichanga topped with guacamole. Chicken mole, fajitas, sandwiches, hamburgers, and steaks are also available. The patio is choice for lunch on warm days; in the evening, it is open for drinks only.

## First Crush

*24 Sunnyside Ave./E. Blithedale Ave., (415) 381-7500, fax (415) 381-7564; www.firstcrush.com. D daily; $$$. Highchairs. Reservations advised.*

Situated on the sunny side of the street, this pleasant restaurant operates inside an 1860s Victorian house. A warren of colorful interior rooms provides cozy, comfortable seating, and in good weather outdoor seating on the petite front porches is an option. The owner's mother, a ceramic artist, makes all of the tableware, and his father handcrafted the mixed-media artwork decorating the walls. The American-French menu changes regularly but has offered fried olives stuffed with fontina cheese, thick tomato-bread soup, garlicky linguini tossed with jumbo prawns and mushrooms, and macadamia-crusted Alaskan halibut. A hamburger made with house-ground beef and a creative vegetarian entree—perhaps risotto cakes with wild mushroom ragoût—are also options. Some wines are available in flights of two and three, providing the pleasure of trying a variety of vintages while still drinking the equivalent of just one glass. In season, desserts might include a delicious nectarine-peach cobbler with vanilla bean ice cream, and a cheese flight is always an option.

An enjoyable tie-in here is viewing a movie at the downtown **CinéArts@Sequoia theater** first *(25 Throckmorton Ave., (415) 388-4862; www.cinearts.com.)*, and then afterward following the sidewalk up to the charming brick pathway marked "El Paseo" and taking it through to the next street, which is Sunnyside.

## Gira Polli

*590 E. Blithedale Ave./Camino Alto, (415) 383-6040.*

For description, see page 70.

## Jennie Low's Chinese Cuisine

*38 Miller Ave., in Mill Creek Plaza, (415) 388-8868; www.jennielow.com. L M-Sat, D daily; $. Highchairs, boosters. Reservations advised.*

All items here are prepared without MSG and with Chinese brown sugar instead of white sugar, and stir-fried dishes can be prepared with low-fat chicken broth instead of oil. Co-owner, cooking teacher, and cookbook author Jennie Low has designed a menu making use of her own sauces, also available bottled to take home. The menu stresses simple, home-style food that is easy on the spicing and with many low-fat options. Among the best dishes are velvety Snow White Chicken with snow peas and large mushrooms and Hot Spicy Eggplant accented with earthy wood ear mushrooms. Most of the noodle dishes are also very good, especially the noodle soup. The house tea is a fragrant lychee-and-black leaf blend that can be purchased to take home. Because Low's favorite color is lavender, it is used for everything from the menu's type to the servers' uniforms, and it is the color of everything she herself wears. And because her lucky number is eight, all menu prices end in eight. Diners seated in the modern, clean-lined dining room can observe the busy chefs through a large glass window.

## La Ginestra

*127 Throckmorton Ave./Miller Ave., (415) 388-0224, fax (415) 388-7420. D Tu-Sun; $$. Closed 2 weeks in summer. Highchairs, boosters, booths, child portions. No reservations.*

Named for the Scotch Broom flower that is native to both Mount Tamalpais and Sorrento, Italy, this popular, casual spot specializes in Neapolitan cuisine. The ample menu includes a large selection of pastas, pizzas, and veal dishes as well as minestrone soup made with fresh vegetables and an excellent eggplant Parmesan. Fried or sautéed fresh squid is always on the menu along with potato gnocchi, saltimbocca, and housemade ravioli. Desserts include a rich housemade cannoli and a frothy white-wine zabaglione.

## Piazza D'Angelo

*22 Miller Ave., (415) 388-2000, fax (415) 388-3468; www.piazzadangelo.com. L-D daily; $-$$. Highchairs, boosters. Reservations advised.*

Designed to resemble an Italian town square, this comfortable restaurant has a retractable skylight over its main dining room and an Italian villa-style garden café for al fresco dining. Terra cotta floors, original modern art, and contemporary Italian music all help set the mood. Rotisserie-grilled meats are excellent, as are the antipastos, pastas, risotti, and innovative pizzas baked in a wood-burning oven. A rich tiramisu dessert, served in an oversize stemmed glass, is ample for two.

## Picnic Pick-Ups

• **Mill Valley Market**
*12 Corte Madera Ave./Throckmorton Ave., (415) 388-3222, fax (415) 388-8824; www.millvalleymarket.com. M-Sat 7-7:30, Sun 9-7.*

Family-owned since 1929, this small but well-stocked grocery sells everything required for a fabulous picnic. An extensive selection of honeys, mustards, green olives, vinegars, salad dressings, and jams are on the shelves, and a deli/bakery tucked in the back dispenses prepared salads and baked goods.

# Tiburon

## — A LITTLE BACKGROUND —

Smaller and less well known than Sausalito, Tiburon has a tiny Main Street lined with boutiques, galleries, and restaurants. Nearby **Belvedere**, which is Italian for "beautiful view," is Marin's smallest and most exclusive community, and its narrow, hilly roads are lined with expensive homes.

## — VISITOR INFORMATION —

**Tiburon Peninsula Chamber of Commerce**
*96 Main St., (415) 435-5633, fax (415) 435-1132; www.tiburonchamber.org.*

## — GETTING THERE —

Located 20 miles north of San Francisco. Take the Tiburon Boulevard exit off Highway 101. Follow Tiburon Boulevard 4 miles east into town.

## — WHAT TO DO —

### Angel Island State Park
*(415) 435-1915; www.angelisland.org.*

A ferry leaves from a dock behind Main Street's restaurants. For description, see page 29.

### Ark Row
*West end of Main St.*

In times past, this street was a lagoon lined with arks and houseboats. Now boutiques fill land-bound houseboats, or "arks," that are more than 100 years old. The **Windsor Vineyards tasting room** *(72 Main St., (800) 214-9463, (415) 435-3113; www.windsorvineyards.com. Tasting Sun-Thur 10-6, Fri-Sat 10-7.)* dispenses samplings of wines available for purchase only here and also sells their wines with custom messages on the labels.

### Blackie's Pasture
*On Greenwood Beach Rd., off Tiburon Blvd.; www.tiburonpeninsulafoundation.org/blackie.htm.*

Blackie was a legendary local horse that grazed here from 1938 to 1966. He was beloved by children in the area, who fed him goodies from their lunch bags on the way to school. His former pasture is paved over now and is a parking lot. Thankfully, his charming gravesite surrounded by a white picket fence was spared and can be visited at the edge of the lot, and a metal statue of his likeness now stands here.

A short walk away is **McKegney Green**, an expanse of grass overlooking the bay that is perfect for picnicking and kite-flying. The paved 2-mile **Tiburon Historical Trail**, formerly a railroad grade, starts at Strawberry Point and continues into town.

## China Cabin
*52 Beach Rd./Tiburon Blvd., in Belvedere, (415) 435-1853; www.landmarks-society.org/ chinacab.html. W & Sun 1-4, Apr-Oct. Free.*

This exquisitely restored Victorian social saloon is from the side-wheel steamer *SS China*, which provided transpacific mail and passenger service between 1866 and 1886. It features 22-karat gold-leaf trim, cut-glass accents, walnut woodwork, and oil-burning crystal-and-brass chandeliers.

## Old St. Hilary's
*201 Esperanza St./Mar West St., (415) 435-1853; www.landmarks-society.org/sthilarys.html. Church: W & Sun 1-4, Apr-Oct. Preserve: daily dawn-dusk. Free.*

Two rare wildflowers grow in the fields surrounding this also-rare white Carpenter Gothic church dating from 1888. The Black Jewel and the Tiburon Paintbrush are found nowhere else in the world. When spring wildflowers are blooming, this church displays these two and others from the 217 species protected here, all labeled for easy identification. An exhibit of wildflower photographs is also displayed.

## Paradise Beach Park
*On Paradise Dr., 1 mi. from town, (415) 499-6387. Daily 10-sunset. $5-7/vehicle.*

This sheltered, 19-acre bay-front park has a large lawn area and barbecues. The small, quiet beach is nice for wading, and license-free fishing is permitted from the pier. On warm days, the small parking lot fills early.

## Tiburon Audubon Center & Sanctuary
*376 Greenwood Beach Rd./Tiburon Blvd., (415) 388-2524, fax (415) 388-0717; www.tiburonaudubon.org. M-F 9-5; Sept-Nov, also 1st three Sat-Sun of month 9-5. Free.*

The 11 acres of land and 900 acres of bay that comprise this National Audubon Society wildlife sanctuary reflect grassland, coastal scrub, freshwater pond, and marsh habitats. A self-guided nature trail leads to a rocky beach and to a lookout spot with sweeping views of Richardson Bay and San Francisco.

Also on the property, the yellow 1876 **Lyford House** is the first and oldest Victorian home in Marin County. Once part of a dairy farm, it was barged across Richardson Bay to this location. It now displays some of John James Audubon's artwork. Call ahead for guided nature walks or house tours.

### — WHERE TO STAY —

## Tiburon Lodge
*1651 Tiburon Blvd., (800) TIBURON, (800) 762-7770, (415) 435-3133, fax (415) 435-2451; www.tiburon lodge.com. 100 rooms; $$-$$$+. Children under 12 free. Some kitchens. Heated pool. Full breakfast. No pets.*

Located just 1 block from Main Street, this inn has some rooms with private whirlpool hot tubs—the most unusual has underwater lights and is in a black-tiled bathroom with piped-in music.

## Waters Edge
*25 Main St., (877) 789-5999, (415) 789-5999, fax (415) 789-5888; www.marinhotels.com. 23 rooms; $$-$$$+. All fireplaces. Evening wine, continental breakfast; limited room service. No smoking; no pets.*

This contemporary-style hotel takes full advantage of its location on an historic dock jutting into the heart of a picturesque marina by providing almost every room with a private balcony. Comfortable chaises and cloud-soft beds with fluffy white cotton duvets beg to be plopped on for a long rest under a cozy camelhair throw. Many rooms have high-ceilings and are decorated with dark Asian-style furnishings and vintage botanical prints. Breakfast is brought to the room.

### — WHERE TO EAT —

## Guaymas
*5 Main St., (415) 435-6300, fax (415) 435-6802. L-D daily, SunBr; $$-$$$. Highchairs, boosters. Reservations advised.*

Authentic regional Mexican fare is the

specialty at this always-bustling spot. In pleasant surroundings of bleached-wood furnishings and adobe-style decor, diners enjoy a sweeping view of San Francisco. On warm days, two outdoor decks are also opened. Three styles of margarita and a variety of Mexican beers are on the menu along with approximately 30 different tequilas—each comes with a complimentary sangrita chaser (a blend of tomato and orange juices spiked with chilies). The drinks go well with the delicious complimentary house salsas and tortillas. Though a light meal can be made of just the appetizer platter, save room for the imaginative menu offering a large selection of tantalizing seafood items, three kinds of tamale, and the kitchen's forte—spit-roasted meats. Everything is made in-house from scratch.

## Picnic Pick-Ups

### • Let's Eat
*1 Blackfield Dr./Tiburon Blvd., in Cove Shopping Center, (415) 383-FOOD, fax (415) 388-3656. M-Sat 10-6, Sun 10-5.*

Choose from a continuously changing menu of delicious salads—perhaps wild rice with smoked cheese and grapes, or flavorful Mexican chicken sprinkled generously with cilantro. Sandwiches are made to order, and a delicious "panhandle pastry" is sometimes available.

### • Sweet Things
*(415) 388-8583, fax (415) 388-8581; www.sweet things.com. M-F 7:30-6, Sat 8:30-6, Sun 9:30-5.*

A few doors away, this spot specializes in great desserts that include a weighty carrot cake, a variety of interesting cookies, and the intriguingly named Fallen Angel Torte and Black Magic Layer Cake. Whole-wheat Bowser Biscuits for dogs are also available.

## Sam's Anchor Cafe
*27 Main St., (415) 435-4527, fax (415) 435-5685; www.samscafe.com. L-D daily, Sat-SunBr; $-$$. Highchairs, boosters, child menu. No reservations on deck.*

When the sun is shining, watching the boats and sea gulls while sitting outside on the deck here can be sublime. Dress is casual, and a typical weekend morning finds the rich and famous dining happily right alongside everyday people. Singles make their connections here at brunch, while parents relax with Sam's famous

Ramos gin fizz. Cranky sounds from children don't travel far, but seem instead to magically vanish in the air. The brunch menu offers a variety of egg dishes, sandwiches, and salads as well as a popular burger and fries. Unfortunately, the wait to get in can be long. This is the oldest continuously operating restaurant in town.

## Sweden House Bakery & Cafe
*35 Main St., (415) 435-9767. B-L daily; $. 1 highchair, boosters.*

This bakery cafe is a good choice for a casual breakfast or lunch enjoyed either in the cozy interior or out on a small deck with a great bay view. For lunch, open-face sandwiches are made with a choice of either German six-grain bread or Swedish Limpa—a rye bread made with molasses and grated orange peel. Soups and salads are also available. Walk-away goodies can be selected from a tantalizing housemade array that includes chocolate tortes, fruit tarts, raspberry shortbread, and chocolate chip cookies.

# Corte Madera

## — WHAT TO DO —

## Book Passage
*51 Tamal Vista Blvd., (800) 999-7909, (415) 927-0960, fax (415) 924-3838; www.bookpassage.com. M-Sat 10-9:30, Sun 10:30-9.*

This shop has the best collection of travel books and mysteries around and is a joy to browse. A cafe serves coffees and simple foods, and author events are scheduled regularly.

## — WHERE TO EAT —

## Picnic Pick-Ups

### • A. G. Ferrari Foods
*107 Corte Madera Town Center, (415) 927-4347.*
For description, see page 280.

## World Wrapps
*208 Corte Madera Town Center, (415) 927-3663, fax (415) 927-3569; www.worldwrapps.com.*
For description, see page 87.

# Larkspur

## — A LITTLE BACKGROUND —

The downtown area of charming Larkspur is listed on the National Register of Historic Places.

## — VISITOR INFORMATION —

### Larkspur Chamber of Commerce
*P.O. Box 315, Larkspur 94977, (415) 838-0038, fax (415) 925-0759; www.larkspurchamber.org.*

## — GETTING THERE —

Take the Paradise exit off Highway 101. Follow Tamalpais Drive west until it becomes Redwood.

## — WHERE TO EAT —

### Emporio Rulli
*464 Magnolia Ave./Cane St., (888) 88-RULLI, (415) 924-7478, fax (415) 924-3474; www.rulli.com. Daily 8-5:30; $.*

Offering what must be the most mouth-watering selection of sweets found this side of Milan, and displaying them in gleaming mahogany-and-glass cases worthy of jewels, this authentic Italian pasty shop is a treasure trove of exquisite confections. Among them are an enormous selection of imported chocolates and candies and ten kinds of gelato, plus Italian cakes and pastries and seasonal specialties. It is possible to select and indulge on site, along with an espresso or other beverage, and an extensive hot panini (sandwich) menu is also available.

### Lark Creek Inn
*234 Magnolia Ave., (415) 924-7766, fax (415) 924-7117; www.larkcreek.com. L M-F, D daily, SunBr; $$$+. Highchairs, boosters, child menu. Reservations advised. Valet parking.*

Situated within a landmark 1888 Victorian house beneath a cluster of tall redwoods, this destination restaurant is known for its seasonal farm-fresh American fare created by owner-chef Bradley Ogden. Seating is in an airy main dining room, in a smaller upstairs room, and on a brick patio—the venue of choice in warm weather. One dinner enjoyed on the patio here, out under the stars on a night of perfect temperature, started with a salad of heirloom tomatoes and local goat cheese. An oak-grilled salmon entree with a variety of baby vegetables followed, and the memorable conclusion was housemade coconut cake with blackberry-swirl ice cream. Ingredients are secured from local sources when possible.

### Left Bank
*507 Magnolia Ave./Ward St., (415) 927-3331, fax (415) 927-3034; www.leftbank.com. L-D daily; $$. Highchairs, boosters, child menu. Reservations advised. Valet parking F-Sat D.*

The vintage 1895 building this atmospheric Parisian-style brasserie is located within—known as the Blue Rock Inn—is in this small town's Historic District. A restaurant has operated on its ground floor since the early 1900s. The name is derived from the blue rock façade, which was quarried from the base of Mount Tamalpais. Today's airy restaurant retains the original pressed-tin ceiling and often greets diners with a welcoming fire in its massive stone fireplace. Theater posters enliven the walls, and clocks above the bar tell time locally as well as in Tahiti, Montreal, and Lyon (the chef's hometown). In good weather, outdoor dining on the veranda fronting the town's quiet main street is an option. The menu is rustic, unfussy cuisine grand-mère, or "grandma's cooking," and portions are big. Lunch is sandwiches, a hamburger Américain, salads, and a few entrees. Dinner brings on signature dishes: bouillabaisse, rotisserie chicken, steak frites. Cocktails include a Pamplemousse (grapefruit vodka with 7-Up) and 12 kinds of pastis. Apple tarte tatin, Bing cherry clafouti, and molten chocolate cake are among the scrumptious endings. Special events are often scheduled.

# San Anselmo

## — A LITTLE BACKGROUND —

With more than 130 antique dealers, this sunny town is Northern California's antique capital. But best of all, it it has *no* parking meters.

## — VISITOR INFORMATION —

### San Anselmo Chamber of Commerce
*P.O. Box 2844, San Anselmo 94979, (415) 454-2510, fax (415) 258-9458; www.sananselmochamber.org.*

## — GETTING THERE —

Located approximately 20 miles north of San Francisco. Take San Anselmo/Sir Francis Drake Boulevard exit off Highway 101 and continue west for approximately 5 miles.

## — ANNUAL EVENTS —

### Outdoor Antiques Faire
*May. (415) 457-3421. Free.*

## — WHAT TO DO —

### Marin Art and Garden Center
*30 Sir Frances Drake Blvd., in Ross, (415) 455-5260, fax (415) 454-0650; www.maagc.org.*

Operated by local volunteers, this historical 10-acre facility is planted with birch, laurel, holly, and rhododendrons and is also home to a rare dawn redwood, an unusual domed sequoia, and a spectacular magnolia tree planted in 1870. **Laurel House Antiques** *((415) 454-8472, fax (415) 454-0550. M & Thur 10-3; Tu-W, F-Sat 11-4.)* operates here selling consignment antiques. Proceeds benefit the center.

## — WHERE TO EAT —

### Bubba's Diner
*566 San Anselmo Ave./Tunstead, (415) 459-6862; www.bubbas-diner.net. B-L-D W-Sun; $. Boosters, booths. No reservations.*

Choose a comfy red-vinyl booth or a swivel-stool at the long counter—where a collection of books invites browsing. Breakfast is served all day and includes a large selection of waffles, pancakes, and omelettes, plus acclaimed house-made biscuits and gravy. Lunch brings on a hamburger made with fresh house-ground chuck, sandwiches, and salads, and dinner selections include meatloaf and rib-eye steak. With food this good, prices this low, and space this tight, there is usually a wait to get in. Pass the time checking out the local scene while lounging on one of the benches out front.

### Cucina Restaurant & Wine Bar
*510 San Anselmo Ave./Tunstead, (415) 454-2942. D Tu-Sun; $$.*

For description, see "Jackson Fillmore" on page 73. The menus are different, and this location has a wood-fired oven.

### Insalata's
*120 Sir Francis Drake Blvd./Barber Ave., (415) 457-7700, fax (415) 457-8375; www.insalatas.com. L-D daily; $$. Reservations advised.*

The airy, open interior here is filled with good tables and even a few secluded booths. Walls are decorated with large French pastels of fruits done by San Francisco artist Laura Parker. Mediterranean fare dominates the menu and has included a Tunisian seven-vegetable tagine with preserved lemons, a Syrian chicken Fattoush salad tossed with toasted pita and a lemon-herb vinaigrette, and delicious Spanish-style short ribs flavored with chocolate, sherry, and orange. All breads and desserts are made in-house, including to-die-for pecan sticky buns. Desserts are exotic: blood orange granita with vanilla bean madeleines; creamy risotto pudding with Chianti-soaked figs and a crisp almond twist. By the way, Insalata is chef-owner Heidi Krahling's maiden name. The surrounding area is filled with prime antique shops, making for great after-dining browsing.

### Taqueria Mexican Grill
*1001 Sir Francis Drake Blvd./College Ave., in Kentfield, (415) 453-5811. L-D daily; $. Highchairs. No reservations.*

Nestled under tall redwoods, this fast-food spot has tile floors, massive wooden benches and tables, a jukebox playing Mexican tunes, and plenty of piñatas. All help set the mood for the burritos, chimichangas, and tacos that are the menu mainstays. A hamburger is also available.

# San Rafael

## — A LITTLE BACKGROUND —

The oldest and largest city in Marin, San Rafael also has the best weather. It is located in Marin County's sunbelt and is an enchanting place to dine outdoors on a warm summer evening. Many artists and performers hide away here. A further claim to fame is that many old silent films were shot here, and 4th Street was the setting for director George Lucas's *American Graffiti*. For a walking tour of the historic downtown area, get a guide from the chamber of commerce and follow the plaque markers embedded in the sidewalk across the street from each site.

## San Rafael Chamber of Commerce
*817 Mission Ave., (800) 454-4163, (415) 454-4163, fax (415) 454-7039; www.sanrafael.org.*

## Italian Street Painting Festival
*June. 5th Ave./A St.; (415) 457-4878, fax (415) 457-4879; www.youthinarts.org. Free.*

Using chalk as a medium, hundreds of artists transform a downtown block into a huge canvas in homage to an Italian tradition that has survived since the 16th century. Proceeds benefit Youth in Arts.

## Marin County Fair
*July. Civic Center Fairgrounds; (415) 499-6400, fax (415) 499-3700; www.marinfair.org. $10, 65+& 4-12 $8; parking $5.*

Five days of fun include barnyard animal events, crafts competitions, and short film screenings, plus performances by big name entertainers and a low-level fireworks display. All entertainment and carnival rides are included in the admission fee. Highly regarded for its innovation and creativity, this mellow fair is a lot of fun.

## Marin Shakespeare Festival
*July-Sept. Forest Meadows Amphitheatre, Dominican College; (415) 499-1108, fax (415) 499-1492; www.marinshakespeare.org. $25, under 19 $15.*

This summer-long festival is presented in an intimate 600-seat outdoor theater.

## Artworks Downtown
*1337 4th St./C St., (415) 451-8119; www.artworks downtown.org. Tu-Sat 10-5.*

Housed in the town's 1870 opera house, **The Gallery Store** sells many of the unique items made by artists working in 30 studios in the back. Visitors are welcome to view these artists at work. The **Underground Gallery** *((415) 451-1815)* hangs changing exhibits on its natural brick walls, and art classes are regularly scheduled for both adults and children.

## China Camp State Park
*Take Civic Center exit off Hwy. 101, follow N. San Pedro Rd. E for 5 mi., (415) 456-0766; www.parks.ca.gov. Daily 8-sunset; museum 10-5. $3/vehicle.*

Once the largest fishing settlement along this shore, this spot was home to hundreds of Chinese fishermen in the late 1800s. Now all that's left is the rustic, weathered remains of the pier and buildings. A visitor center/museum displays period photographs and artifacts documenting the shrimping and fishing that occurred here until a 1911 ordinance outlawed the camp's primitive shrimp-trapping method. A small beach invites sunbathing and picnicking, and on weekends an old-time snack bar with a counter and swivel stools dispenses fast fare—including a delicious shrimp-and-cucumber sandwich (local musicians Huey Lewis and the News shot the cover for their 1980s *Sports* album inside). In addition to the village, this 1,640-acre park has hiking trails through the hills (the Turtle Nature Trail is an easy 3/4-mile loop), and campsites are available.

## Falkirk Cultural Center
*1408 Mission Ave./E St., (415) 485-3328, fax (415) 485-3404; www.falkirkculturalcenter.org. Tu, W, Thur 12-5, Sat 10-1. Free.*

Built in 1888 atop a hill just a few blocks from town and named for the lumber baron-owner's birthplace in Scotland, this 17-room Queen Anne Victorian mansion features original coffered ceilings, rich redwood paneling, decorative fireplaces, and stunning floor-to-ceiling stained-glass windows. Upstairs galleries display contemporary art, and 11 acres of formal gardens surround the house. Special events include an Alice-in-Wonderland egg hunt at Easter, a haunted house in October, and a Victorian holiday program.

## Guide Dogs for the Blind
*350 Los Ranchitos Rd., (800) 295-4050, (415) 499-4000; www.guidedogs.com. Tours M-Sat at 10:30 & 2. Free.*

Formed to help servicemen blinded in World War II, this is the largest accredited school for guide dogs in the U.S. New graduates are presented to their visually impaired partners at a monthly graduation ceremony that is open to the public. Tours include the kennels, dorms, and 11-acre campus. New foster homes are always needed to raise puppies and care for dogs in transition.

## Marin County Civic Center
*N. San Pedro Rd./Civic Center exit off Hwy. 101; www.marincenter.org. Self-guided tour: M-F 9-6. Guided tour: (415) 499-6646; W at 10:30am; $3 donation.*

The last building designed by Frank Lloyd Wright before he died, this "bridge between two hills" is a national and state historic landmark. It also is where local resident George Lucas filmed his first big movie in 1971—*THX11380*—and houses various city offices and a performing arts and convention center. A 14-acre lagoon is surrounded by grassy areas perfect for picnicking and strolling.

## Marin County Historical Society Museum
*1125 B St., in Boyd Park, (415) 454-8538, fax (415) 454-6137; www.marinhistory.org. Tu-Thur 12-3, 3rd Sat of month 1-4. Free.*

Situated within the high Victorian Gothic Boyd Gate House, built in 1880, this museum displays area memorabilia. It commemorates the life and travels of Louise Boyd, an Arctic explorer and the first woman to fly over the North Pole.

## McNears Beach Park
*201 Cantera Rd., (415) 499-6387; www.co.marin.ca.us/depts/PK/Main/pos/pdmnbch.cfm. Daily 7-8 in summer; off-season schedule varies. $4; parking $7.*

A former country club, this very popular recreation area has a heated swimming pool, a concession stand, a fishing pier, a picnic area with barbecue pits and tables, and two tennis courts. A terrific sandy wading beach fronts San Pablo Bay.

## Mission San Rafael Archangel
*1104 5th Ave., (415) 454-8141, fax (415) 454-8193; www.missionsofcalifornia.org. Daily 11-4. Free.*

Founded in 1817, this is the 20th mission. Replicated in 1949 on the approximate site of the original mission, it embodies some of that structure's characteristics—star windows modeled after those at the Carmel Mission and a bell hung from cross beams. Visitors can take a self-guided tour. A tiny adjoining museum displays vintage photos of its reconstruction and original furniture.

## Rafael Film Center
*1118 4th St./B St., (415) 454-1222; www.finc.org. $9, 65+ & under 13 $7.*

Built in 1938, this vintage film palace was renovated into a three-screen theater featuring first-run, independent, and period films. Each theater is equipped with the very best in sound and image projection (THX and Dolby sound systems are used), and each has its own personality. The lobby and richly colored main theater reflect the original art deco style, with blue velvet drapes and marvelous period chandeliers. On the second floor, theater Two has the posh feel of the '20s while the more streamlined decor of theater Three has a futuristic sense. Everything used in construction is non-toxic, so patrons needn't fear the headaches and other health problems associated with off-gassing in most new construction. A program for kids features obscure European films.

## WildCare: Terwilliger Nature Education and Wildlife Rehabilitation
*76 Albert Park Ln./B St., (415) 453-1000, fax (415) 456-0594; www.wildcaremarin.org. Daily 9-5. Free.*

This wildlife rehabilitation hospital nurses ill and orphaned native animals back to health, then returns them to their natural habitat. Visitors can view non-releasable animals in an open-air courtyard and handle a display of taxidermied animals in the education center. This organization also operates the Living with Wildlife Hotline, which provides tips on how to persuade various wild animals to take up residence elsewhere.

— WHERE TO STAY —
## Embassy Suites Hotel
*101 McInnis Pkwy., (800) EMBASSY, (415) 499-9222, fax (415) 472-1315; www.embassymarin.com. 5 stories; 235 rooms. Pool; hot tub; fitness room. Evening snack, full breakfast; restaurant; room service.*

Situated just a footbridge away from the Marin Civic Center, this hotel often has a special package for the Marin County Fair. For more description, see page 420.

— WHERE TO EAT —
## Alborz
*555 E. Francisco Blvd., near the marina.*
For description, see page 56.

## Casa Mañana
*711 D St./2nd St., (415) 456-7345; and at 641 Del Ganado Rd., (415) 479-3032. B-L-D daily; $.*

Tucked away in the unlikely interior of a small medical complex, this tiny Salvadoran/Mexican cafe serves an extensive menu of tasty, housemade classic fare—pupusas, tamales, crab enchiladas verde, flautas stuffed with mashed potatos, chalupas—as well as mussels and hamburgers and plenty of vegetarian options. Portions are large and delicious, and breakfast is served all day.

## Las Camelias

*912 Lincoln Ave./4thSt., (415) 453-5850. L M-Sat, D daily; $-$$. Highchairs, booster seats, child plate. No reservations.*

This homey spot has an interior of hardwood floors and oak furnishings. Mexican dishes are adapted from family recipes and include a variety of fish items, chicken in mole sauce, and fajitas. Generous combination plates come with the usual enchiladas and tacos, but more unusual chilies encuerados (roasted poblano pepper stuffed with caramelized onions and vegetables) and zincronizadas (flour tortilla stuffed with cheese, avocado, and veggies) are options.

## Lundy's Home Cooking

*1143 4th St./B St., (415) 456-7669. B-L daily; $. Highchairs, boosters. No reservations.*

Every breakfast item imaginable is available here, including an extensive variety of omelettes and scrambles. House specialties are huevos rancheros and huevos con chorizo. Lunch brings on a variety of excellent hamburgers as well as salads and sandwiches (the grilled MAC with sautéed mushrooms, avocado, and Swiss cheese is primo). Seating is at tiny tables or at a long counter with swiveling stools and a view of the short-order kitchen action.

## Mayflower Inne

*1533 4th St./E St., (415) 456-1011. L-D daily; $-$$. Highchairs, boosters, child portions. Reservations advised.*

This place offers the chance to experience the cozy ambiance of an English pub without leaving the country. Waitresses have been known to greet customers with a cheery "Hello, lovies" when presenting the menu. Among the traditional bland-but-hearty English items: steak and kidney pie, Cornish pasties (beef stew wrapped in a crescent pie pastry), bangers (English sausages), and fish & chips. Appetizers include a sausage roll (sausage baked in a pastry) and a Scotch egg (hard-boiled egg rolled in sausage meat and breadcrumbs and then deep-fried). English ales and beers are on tap, and dessert is a choice of fresh rhubarb pie, sherry trifle (a pudding), or chocolate cake. It is possible to relax in the English manner by indulging in a friendly game of darts or Ping-Pong.

## Panama Hotel Restaurant & Inn

*4 Bayview St., (800) 899-3993, (415) 457-3993, fax (415) 457-6240; www.panamahotel.com. B daily, L M-F, D Tu-Sun, SunBr; $-$$. Highchairs, boosters. Reservations advised.*

This charming dining room, with color-washed walls and eclectic decor, serves delicious, full-flavored renditions of Mexican-, Italian-, and Asian-influenced cuisines. Don't miss the stuffed pasilla pepper appetizer or the Tuscan toast with relish. Fresh seafood and pastas are primo. Music is on the menu Tuesday and Thursday nights, and a tropical garden patio, reminiscent of something found in Central America, is the way to go in warm weather.

**Guest rooms** *(15 rooms; $-$$. Some kitchens; some shared baths. Continental breakfast; room service.)* are also available. Some rooms have clawfoot tubs, others have canopy beds, and yet others have vine-covered private balconies. A well-known local rock musician is rumored to have kept a girlfriend lodged here for months and months. About the name. A former owner thought every town should have a Panama Hotel, and so this rambling structure, consisting of two 1910 homes connected by a patio, became San Rafael's.

## The Rice Table

*1617 4th St./G St., (415) 456-1808, same fax. D W-Sun; $$. Highchairs, boosters, booths. Reservations advised.*

The Indonesian islands were once also known as the "Spice Islands," as that area is where many spices originate. During their domination of Indonesia, the Dutch served some of the best native dishes at huge feasts called "rijsttafel" or "rice table." A West Java version of this elaborate dinner is served in this cozy, atmospheric room. The rice table dinner begins with shrimp chips and several dipping sauces, green pea vegetable soup, deep-fried lumpia (like Chinese spring rolls), a salad with lemon dressing, both white and saffron-yellow rice, pickled vegetables, and roasted coconut. Then come marinated chicken satay, shrimp sautéed in butter and tamarind, a mild chicken curry, beef sautéed in soy sauce and cloves, fried rice noodles, and fried bananas for dessert. Less elaborate meals and vegetarian selections are also available. Beer perfectly compliments the food and is available along with Indonesian-style coffee, fresh tamarind juice, and several kinds of tea.

## Yet Wah
*1238 4th St./B St., (415) 460-9883, fax (415) 460-9889; www.yetwah.com. L-D daily.*
For description, see page 88.

# Novato

— VISITOR INFORMATION —
## Novato Chamber of Commerce
*807 DeLong Ave., (800) 897-1164, (415) 897-1164, fax (415) 898-9097; http://tourism.novato.org.*

— WHAT TO DO —
## Marin Museum of the American Indian
*2200 Novato Blvd., in Miwok Park, (415) 897-4064, fax (415) 892-7804; www.marinindian.com. Tu-F 10-3, Sat-Sun 12-4. $5; under 12 free; free on last Sun of month.*
Marin County's earliest residents, the Miwok and Pomo Indians, are honored at this interactive museum. Exhibits and artifacts include tools, baskets, boats, and animal skins. Visitors can learn traditional Native American games, grind acorns with an authentic mortar, and visit a native plant garden. The 35-acre park has hiking trails, playing fields, and picnic facilities.

## Novato History Museum
*815 DeLong Ave., (415) 897-4320; www.ci.novato.ca. us/prcs/museum.cfm. W, Thur, Sat 12-4. Free.*
Built in 1850, the Victorian house this museum operates within is now home to a collection of antique dolls, toy trains, and pioneer tools that reflect the town's history.

— WHERE TO EAT —
## Jennie Low's Chinese Cuisine
*In Vintage Oaks Mall, (415) 892-8838; www.jennie low.com. L M-Sat, D daily; $.*
For description, see page 212.

# Petaluma

— A LITTLE BACKGROUND —
Located less than an hour's drive north of San Francisco, Petaluma offers an old-fashioned small town atmosphere. Perhaps this is why it was selected as the filming location for both *American Graffiti* and *Peggy Sue Got Married*. In fact, director Francis Ford Coppola is quoted as saying, "You can find any decade you want somewhere in Petaluma."

Once known as the "World's Egg Basket," this area still produces plenty of eggs but is currently better known as a dairy center.

It's pleasant to spend a day here, just walking around the downtown area. Noteworthy among the numerous antique shops is the architecturally magnificent **Vintage Bank Antiques** *(101 Petaluma Blvd. N., (707) 769-3097. Daily 10-5:30.)*, located inside a former Wells Fargo bank, and **Monarch Interiors** *(199 Petaluma Blvd. N., (707) 769-3092, fax (707) 769-0662; www.monarchinteriors.com.)*, inside the old Sonoma County National Bank. Another antique of sorts is an old-time barbershop with a swirling pole at 152 Kentucky Street. The residential area is also worth checking out for its large collection of Victorian homes.

— VISITOR INFORMATION —
## Petaluma Visitor Center
*800 Baywood Dr. #A, (877)-2-PETALUMA, (707) 769-0429, fax (707) 762-4721; www.visitpetaluma.com.*

— GETTING THERE —
Located approximately 50 miles north of San Francisco.

— ANNUAL EVENTS —
## Butter & Egg Days
*April. (707) 763-OEGG; www.butterandeggdays.com. Free.*

Celebrating this area's past as a dairy and poultry center, this festival kicks off with a hometown parade populated with giant papier-mâché cows, huge dairy trucks converted into floats, and flocks of children dressed as chickens. Other events have included an Egg Toss, a Team Butter-Churning Contest, and the Cutest Little Chick in Town Contest—when the imaginative costumes of those marching chickens, limited to ages 1 through 8, are judged.

The **Downtown Antique Faire** *((707) 762-9348; www.petalumadowntown.com.)* takes place the next day on a street blocked off to traffic.

## Ugly Dog Contest
*June. (707) 283-FAIR; www.sonoma-marinfair.org. Fair: $12, 65+ & 4-12 $8, free to those who enter a dog; parking $3.*

Just one of the many events scheduled at the annual **Sonoma-Marin Fair**, this good-spirited contest has three divisions: Pedigree Class, Mutt Class, and Ring of Champions. Every dog wins a prize, and losers get a certificate stating they "are just too beautiful to be considered ugly."

## Petaluma Summer Music Festival
*August. (707) 763-8920, fax (707) 763-8929; www.cinnabartheater.org. $14-$20.*

This festival features diverse musical events that appeal to all ages. Events are scheduled in the Cinnabar Theater, which is inside a mission-style schoolhouse, and in other locations of historical interest.

### — WHAT TO DO —

## Garden Valley Ranch
*498 Pepper Rd., 3 mi. N of town, (707) 795-0919, fax (707) 792-0349; www.gardenvalley.com. W-Sun 10-4; closed late Dec-mid-Jan. $4, under 12 $2.*

This 8-acre ranch is the largest commercial grower of garden roses in the U.S. Among their well-known customers are the late Jacqueline Onassis (for daughter Caroline's wedding), Elizabeth Taylor, Whitney Huston, Barbra Streisand, and Martha Stewart. In one garden, over 4,000 rosebushes are cultivated for cuttings. In another, plants are grown for their perfume, and some are used for potpourri. The best time for viewing is May through October, when the roses are in full bloom. The admission fee includes a self-guided tour brochure. When a private party is scheduled, the gardens are closed to the public, but the nursery and test garden remain open; call ahead to verify.

## The Great Petaluma Desert
*5010 Bodega Ave., (707) 778-8278, fax (707) 778-0931; www.gpdesert.com. F-Sun 10-4. Free.*

Featuring one of the largest selections of rare and exotic cacti and succulents in the country, this dramatic back-road nursery boasts nine greenhouses. A few of the greenhouses are off-limits except to collectors who call ahead, but those that are accessible should satisfy most people. Nearly all of the stock is propagated on site. Among the most popular plants are tillandsia, also known as "air plants" because they require no soil.

## Marin French Cheese Company
*7500 Red Hill Rd. (also known as Petaluma-Point Reyes Rd.), (800) 292-6001, (707) 762-6001, fax (707) 762-0430; www.marinfrenchcheese.com. Sales room: daily 8:30-5; tours: daily 10-4. Free.*

Located way out in the country, this cheese factory has been operating since 1865. By now, they have perfected the art of making

Camembert cheese. They also make good Brie, schloss, and breakfast cheeses—all from milk produced by a local herd of Jersey cows. Tours take visitors through the factory and explain how these special Rouge et Noir cheeses are produced, and cheeses are sampled at the end. Picnic supplies are available in an adjoining store, where these house cheeses are on sale along with picnic supplies. Two expansive grassy areas, one with a large pond, beckon, and some picnic tables are available.

## Mrs. Grossman's Paper Company
*3810 Cypress Dr., (800) 429-4549, (707) 763-1700, fax (707) 763-7121; www.mrsgrossmans.com. Tours M-F at 9:30, 11, 1:30, 3:30. Free. Reservations advised.*

The oldest and largest decorative sticker manufacturer in the U.S., Mrs. Grossman's printed 15,000 miles of stickers in 2001—enough to circle half the globe! Find out what all the fuss is about with a guided walk-through of this bright and happy printing plant. The tour begins with a video show narrated by the owner's dog, Angus, and concludes with a sticker art class and a gift bag of stickers. A gift shop sells the company's 550 sticker designs—which include everything from the original simple red heart that launched the business to a 3-D Eiffel Tower to a delicate 12-inch-long laser-cut roller coaster—plus cards and kits. Children's birthday parties can be scheduled on Friday afternoons.

After, take a walk in nearby **Shollenberger Park** *(South McDowell Blvd., (707) 778-4380; www.petalumawetlandspark.org. Daily sunrise-sunset. Free.).* A 2¼-mile walking path hugs the Petaluma River, and spotting at least a few of the more than 100 species of bird found here is almost a sure thing.

## Petaluma Adobe State Historic Park
*3325 Adobe Rd., 5 mi. E of town, (707) 762-4871, same fax; www.parks.ca.gov. Daily 10-5. $2, under 17 free.*

The boundaries of General Vallejo's vast 66,000-acre land grant once stretched from the Petaluma River on the west, to San Pablo Bay on the south, to Sonoma on the east, to Cotati and Glen Ellen on the North. This rancho, which was part of the estate, is restored to reflect life as it was here in 1840. The living quarters, a weaving shop, and a blacksmith's forge display authentic furnishings, and an

assortment of animals—including sheep and goats—roam freely. Shaded picnic tables are available beside Adobe Creek.

The most interesting times to visit are for annual events, including **Sheep Shearing** in April, **Living History Day** in May, and the **Adobe Fiesta**—with demonstrations of early California crafts and the chance for visitors to weave baskets and make hand-dipped candles—in August.

## Petaluma Historical Library & Museum
*20 Fourth St., (707) 778-4398, fax (707) 762-3923; www.petaluma.net/historicalmuseum. W-Sat 10-4, Sun 12-3. Free.*

On the National Register of Historic Places, this lovely 1903 Carnegie Library building is now in use as the town's history museum. Its interior features the original woodwork and a rare freestanding stained-glass dome. Exhibits include a Victorian dollhouse and a chicken coop. **Tours of the Historic Downtown** *(Sat-Sun at 10:30; May-Oct. Free.)* are led by docents elegantly attired in Victorian dress and include seeing the only full block of iron front buildings still standing west of the Mississippi (in the first block of Western Avenue).

### — WHERE TO STAY —
## KOA Kampground
*20 Rainsville Rd., (800) KOA-1233, (707) 763-1492; www.petalumakoa.com. Pool, hot tub.*

This branch is set on a 60-acre rural farm. Amenities include a playground, petting farm, and summer entertainment program. For more description, see page 443.

## Quality Inn
*5100 Montero Way, (800) 228-5151, (707) 664-1155, fax (707) 664-8566; www.lokhotels.com. 111 rooms; $-$$. Children under 19 free. Heated pool (seasonal); hot tub; sauna. Continental breakfast. Dogs ok.*

Located on the outskirts of town, this is a link in a chain known for its attractive Cape Cod-style of architecture and comfortable modern rooms. A generous buffet breakfast of hot drinks, pastries, cereals, and fresh fruit is served in the lobby.

## — WHERE TO EAT —

### Dempsey's Restaurant & Brewery
*50 E. Washington St., (707) 765-9694, fax (707) 762-1259; www.dempseys.com. L-D daily; $-$$. Highchairs, boosters, child menu. No reservations.*

The oldest brewery in Sonoma County, this comfortable, atmospheric brewpub serves the usual grub—cheeseburger, fries, wood-fired pizza—but also offers more sophisticated fare—magnificent flat bread with beer-spiked olives, a carnitas sandwich with tangy avocado spread, Shaken Beef served with lettuce wrappers. Full dinner entrees include roasted chicken and a pork chop. Leave room for dessert, perhaps an extraordinary fig tart with rich caramel. A beer sampler is a good way to try the wares, but Petaluma Pale Ale and Ugly Dog Stout are sure things. The housemade root beer is also very good. Organic produce used in the restaurant is grown by the chef and picked fresh every day.

### Hallie's Diner
*125 Keller St., (707) 773-1143. B-L daily; $. Highchairs, boosters, booths, child menu.*

The expansive breakfast menu at this simple cafe includes the unusual—eggs with fried plantains and black beans; fried plantain rum soufflé; cajun sausage and corncakes with eggs—as well as lattes and organic dairy products and Mickey Mouse pancakes for kids. Lunch brings on hot and cold sandwiches. So grab a seat in one of the vinyl booths or on a round swivel stool at the long counter and chow down.

### McNear's Saloon & Dining House
*23 Petaluma Blvd. N., (707) 765-2121, fax (707) 765-4671; www.mcnears.com. L-D daily, Sat-SunBr; $-$$. Highchairs, boosters, booths, child menu.*

Located inside the historic 1886 iron front McNear Building, this casual restaurant and sports bar serves an extensive eclectic menu. It is particularly popular with young adults and serves good well drinks. Diners can get great bar food, such as spicy buffalo wings and beer-batter mushrooms, as well as housemade soups, salads, sandwiches, hamburgers, barbecued chicken and ribs, pastas, and steaks. On fair weather days, windows are opened wide in the front dining area near the sidewalk, allowing for pleasant people-watching. The attached **McNear's Mystic Theatre** presents live music on Friday and Saturday nights. It was in the adjacent parking lot that the cop in *American Graffiti* lost his axel.

### Sonoma Taco Shop
*953 Lakeville St., in Gateway Shopping Ctr., (707) 778-7921; www.sonomatacoshop.com. L-D daily.*
For description, see page 228.

# Santa Rosa

## — A LITTLE BACKGROUND —

Believe it or not!, Robert Ripley was born, raised, and buried in Santa Rosa! Unfortunately, the museum that once honored him here has been dismantled.

## — VISITOR INFORMATION —

### Santa Rosa Convention & Visitor's Bureau
*9 Fourth St., (800) 404-ROSE, (707) 577-8674, fax (707) 571-5949; www.visitsantarosa.com.*
The **California Welcome Center** *(www.visitcalifornia.com)* is also at this address.

### Sonoma County Tourism Program
*520 Mendocino Ave. #210, (800) 5-SONOMA, (707) 565-5383, fax (707) 565-5385; www.sonoma county.com.*

### Sonoma County Farm Trails
*(800) 207-9464, (707) 571-8288, fax (707) 571-7719; www.farmtrails.org.*

Call for a free map of area farms that sell directly to the consumer. The map pinpoints the location of u-pick farms as well as of farms selling more unusual items such as fresh rabbits, pheasants, herbs, and mushrooms—even feather pillows and earthworms.

## — GETTING THERE —

Located approximately 10 miles north of Petaluma, and 60 miles north of San Francisco.

## — ANNUAL EVENTS —

### Luther Burbank Rose Parade Festival
*May. (707) 542-7673, fax (707) 545-6914; www.rose paradefestival.com. Free.*

Begun in 1894 as a Rose Carnival, this celebration has morphed into a parade.

## Wine Country Vintage Jazz Festival
*September. (707) 539-3494, fax (707) 778-9371;*
*www.winecountryvintagejazzfestival.org. $30-$75.*

Festivities celebrating ragtime through big band include dance parties and a free Sunday gospel presentation.

### — WHAT TO DO —

## Howarth Memorial Park
*On Summerfield Rd., access from Sonoma Ave. & Montgomery Dr., (707) 543-3282. Free. Rides: in summer, Tu-Sun 11-4; in spring & fall, Sat-Sun only; closed Nov-Jan.*

There is something for everyone in this scenic park. Children especially enjoy the free playground but, of course, also love the attractions with an admission fee: miniature train, animal barn, pony rides, and merry-go-round. Paddleboat, rowboat, and sailboat rentals are available by Lake Ralphine, and hiking trails and tennis courts round out the facilities.

## Luther Burbank Home & Gardens
*Santa Rosa Ave./Sonoma Ave., (707) 524-5445, fax (707) 543-3030; http://ci.santa-rosa.ca.us/lbhg/index.asp. Gardens: daily 8-dusk; free. Garden audio tour $3. House tours: Tu-Sun 10-3:30; Apr-Sept only; $4, 65+ & 12-18 $3. Museum: free.*

During his 50-year horticultural career, Luther Burbank developed over 800 new plants. This memorial garden displays many of his achievements, including a plumcot tree, the ornamental Shasta daisy, and a warren of spineless cacti. (He also developed the Santa Rosa plum and elephant garlic.) Burbank is buried here in an unmarked grave. Guided tours of his charming greenhouse and modified Greek Revival-style home, which retains its original furnishings, last ¹/₂ hour. The adjacent **Carriage House Museum** offers annual exhibits related to Burbank's life and work.

## Railroad Square
*4th St./Davis St., (707) 578-8478; www.railroadsquare.net.*

Now a national historic district, this area is thick with antique stores, restaurants, and specialty shops.

## Redwood Empire Ice Arena
*1667 W. Steele Ln., (707) 546-7147; www.snoopyshomeice.com. Open daily; schedule varies. $7,*

under 12 $5.50, skate rental $2.

Built in 1969, this ice-skating rink has been called "the most beautiful ice arena in the world." Since it was originally owned by the late cartoonist Charles Schulz, the Alpine decor is unexpected but the Zamboni resurfacing machine looks quite familiar. **The Warm Puppy Coffee Shop** has a few stained-glass windows depicting Snoopy and is where Schulz once ate every day (an English muffin with grape jelly for breakfast, a tuna salad sandwich for lunch).

Each December the rink becomes a theater for a special **Christmas Show**, and Snoopy always makes an appearance on ice skates. Some ice-side tables are available, and tickets sell out fast *((707) 546-2277)*.

Located adjacent, **Snoopy's Gallery and Gift Shop** *(1665 W. Steele Ln., (800) 959-3385, (707) 546-3385; www.snoopygift.com. Daily 10-6.)* purveys the largest selection of "Peanuts" merchandise in the world. Cuddly Snoopys are available in heights ranging from 4 inches to 5 feet. Copies of original "Peanuts" columns, matted and framed, are also available.

Across the street, the spacious **Charles M. Schulz Museum** *(2301 Hardies Ln., (707) 579-4452, fax (707) 579-4436; www.charlesmschulzmuseum.org. M & W-F 12-5, Sat-Sun 10-5; in summer to 5:30. $8, 62+ & 4-18 $5.)*, which is dedicated to Charlie Brown and Snoopy, displays thousands of original Schulz sketches. A highlight is an 8- by 12-foot wall from the cartoonist's Colorado home, decorated by him in 1951 and recently uncovered and extracted. Don't miss relaxing for a while watching animated cartoons in the bean bag room.

## Safari West
*3115 Porter Creek Rd., 7 mi. NE of town, (800) 616-2695, (707) 579-2551; www.safariwest.com. Tour: daily at 9, 1, & 3 (in winter at 10 & 2); $58, 3-12 $28; reservations required. Tents: $$$; no TVs; continental breakfast; no pets. Restaurant: L at 11:15 & 12, $15-$20, 3-12 $12-$15; D at 6:30, $25, 3-12 $15; reservations required.*

A visit here saves thousands of dollars in airfare and packager fees and also allows avoiding the jet lag that accompanies such a journey. This unique enterprise is run by Nancy Lang, a former curator at the San Francisco Zoo, and her husband Peter Lang, whose father Otto Lang directed *The Snows of Kilimanjaro*. The

Langs decided to devote their lives to preserving African species. Their 400-acre compound now holds more than 350 rare and endangered African animals and birds, including zebras, wildebeest, and curved-horn aoudads but no man-eating lions or body-flattening elephants to cause concern. Some, like the addax antelope and scimitar-horned Oryx, are actually extinct now in the wild. Most amazing is the herd of enormous, impressively horned Watusi cattle. (Africa's Maasai people rarely sacrifice a live cow. Instead, as their primary source of protein they prepare a "Maasai cocktail" composed of the blood, milk, and urine of these cattle.) Part of the compound tour is in an authentic safari jeep, and part is on foot—including visits to a large aviary holding rare and endangered birds plus a chance to feed the giraffes and get up close to some lemurs and cheetahs. Tour fees help pay the expenses incurred in maintaining the menagerie (the monthly feed bill runs more than $10,000). Nancy and Peter tend to sick and injured animals as lovingly as if they were their own offspring. True to Safari West's goal of propagating endangered species, eventually most of the animals move on to zoos where they help promote healthy breeding.

Consider staying the night in an authentic African safari tent-cabin. Delightfully simple in design, tents have hardwood floors, a thoroughly civilized bathroom with slate floors, a canvas ceiling, and mesh sides to let air in and keep insects out. The bed frames are constructed of whole logs and other furniture is handcrafted from local woods. Mesh "windows" permit viewing the animals and being lulled to sleep by a cacophony of crickets and the intermittent grunt from an unknown wild beast. An optional buffet barbecue dinner is taken in a vast, rustic dining room cooled by ceiling fans and furnished with massive wood-slab tables and comfy canvas chairs.

## Sonoma County Museum
*425 Seventh St., (707) 579-1500, fax (707) 579-4849. www.sonomacountymuseum.com. W-Sun 11-4. $5, 65+ & 13-19 $2.*

Located inside the city's beautifully restored 1910 post office building, this museum exhibits material relating to the county's history.

## Victorian homes
Lovely Victorian mansions line MacDonald Avenue in the older part of town.

## — WINERIES —

## Kendall-Jackson Wine Center
*5007 Fulton Rd., N of town, in Fulton, (707) 571-8100, fax (707) 569-0105; www.kj.com. Tasting daily 10-5; garden tours at 11, 1, & 3.*

Set amidst a mature walnut orchard and surrounded by 120 acres of vineyards, this château-like tasting room features new releases often not yet available in retail outlets. A large, educational Organic Demonstration Garden is planted with herbs and vegetables representing Asia, South America, France, and Italy—demonstrating the diversity as well as the similarities of these cultures. The unique Wine Sensory Gardens permit visitors to wander, wine glass in hand, sniffing and tasting the various vegetables, herbs, fruits, and flowers that compose wine-tasting descriptors, and a Viticulture Exhibit permits a self-guided tour of a 1-acre vineyard identifying 26 distinct types of grapes and illustrating the 19 grapevine trellising systems most commonly used in California.

## Matanzas Creek Winery
*6097 Bennett Valley Rd., 5 mi. E of Hwy. 101, (800) 590-6464, (707) 528-6464, fax (707) 571-0156; www.matanzascreek.com. Tasting & tours daily 10-4:30.*

Located way off the beaten track, back amid rolling foothills far away from other enterprise, this winery is the state's largest producer of lavender. It grows both the Provence variety, for cooking, and the Grosso variety, for scenting soaps and oils. Peak bloom is in June, and an assortment of products made with the bounty, including handmade soaps and sachets, are sold in the gift shop. Additionally, a beautifully maintained garden dotted with modern sculpture and several fountains surrounds the winery tasting room, and several llamas are penned in off the parking lot. A picnic area is available.

## — WHERE TO STAY —

## Flamingo Resort Hotel & Conference Center
*2777 Fourth St./Hwy. 12, (800) 848-8300, (707) 545-8530, fax (707) 528-1404; www.flamingoresort.com. 170 rooms; $-$$$. Children under 12 free. Heated pool; children's wading pool; hot tub; health spa; fitness room; 5 tennis courts. Restaurant; room service. No smoking.*

This spacious, unpretentious resort was built originally way out in the country. Now, due to urban sprawl, it is right in town. Providing all the comforts of a full-service resort, it also gives guests the convenience of a motel—parking just outside their room; not having to walk through a lobby—with the amenities of a hotel—a piano bar with live entertainment and dancing; a full-service restaurant with poolside dining. Facilities include a children's playground, shuffleboard, Ping-Pong, and a lighted jogging path. A state-of-the-art fitness center features sauna and steam rooms, racquetball and basketball courts, and a full-service spa. Childcare is also available at the health club.

## Fountaingrove Inn
*101 Fountaingrove Pkwy., (800) 222-6101, (707) 578-6101, fax (707) 544-3126; www.fountaingroveinn.com. 85 rooms; $-$$$. Pool; hot tub. Continental breakfast; restaurant.*

This sophisticated lodging features striking contemporary architecture and decor, with an equestrian theme throughout.

The hotel's piano lounge is an inviting spot to while away some time. **Equus Restaurant** *((707) 578-0149. L M-F, D daily; $$$. Reservations advised.)* offers fine dining. Vegetarian entrees include Dr. McDougall's diet, but artery-clogging standbys such as filet mignon and lobster tail are also available.

## The Gables Inn
*4257 Petaluma Hill Rd., (800) GABLES-N, (707) 585-7777, fax (707) 584-5634; www.thegablesinn.com. 7 rooms, 1 cottage; $$. Unsuitable for children under 12. No TVs; 1 kitchen; some wood-burning & gas fireplaces. Afternoon snack, full breakfast. No smoking; no pets.*

Named for the 15 gables that crown this 1877 High Victorian Gothic Revival house, this inn's spacious rooms are furnished with antiques and clawfoot tubs. Unusual features include three Italian marble fireplaces that were shipped around the Horn, a steep mahogany spiral staircase, keyhole-shaped windows, and 12-foot ceilings. In the horse-and-buggy days, governors and legislators stopped their wagons here for country hospitality. More house history is found in the parlor, where historical photos of the house and a copy of a thesis written about it by a Sonoma State professor are available for perusal and where quilt pieces made by the original owner are displayed as wall decorations. The house is set on 3½ acres in a rural area reminiscent of the south of France. The original outhouse and a 150-year-old barn remain, and a bucolic deck invites sun worship. All this and one of Northern California's best inn breakfasts, too!

## Hilton Sonoma Wine Country
*3555 Round Barn Blvd., (800) HILTONS, (707) 523-7555, fax (707) 569-5555; www.winecountry hilton.com. 246 rooms; $$. Children under 18 free. Pool (heated in summer only); hot tub; fitness room. Restaurant; room service. Pets ok.*

Sprawled across one of the few hills in town, this comfortable contemporary lodging offers guests a 7.5-mile jogging trail and a sand volleyball court as well as access to golf and tennis facilities at a nearby country club.

## Hotel La Rose

*308 Wilson St., in Railroad Square, (800) LAROSE-8, (707) 579-3200, fax (707) 579-3247; www.hotel larose.com. 4 stories; 49 rooms; $$-$$$. Children under 13 free. Hot tub. Continental breakfast; restaurant; room service. Free valet parking. No pets.*

This well-located, European-style small hotel was built in 1907 of cut stone quarried from the nearby area now known as Annadel State Park. On the National Register of Historic Places, it combines turn-of-the-century charm with modern conveniences. Rooms are stylishly decorated and furnished with English country antiques and reproductions, and they feature nice touches such as shiny marble floors and floral wallpapers. Many on the top floor have pitched ceilings, and some have private balconies. Twenty of the rooms are in a more modern annex across the street from the main hotel. A communal sun deck equipped with a hot tub is available for relaxation, and a continental breakfast is served each morning in a cheery, high-ceilinged room but can also be delivered to the room. All this and a handmade candy on the pillow at turndown each night, too!

Cozy **Josef's** French restaurant *((707) 571-8664, fax (707) 571-8760; www.josefsrestaurant. com. L Tu-F, D daily. Reservations advised.)* operates off the lobby.

## Vineyard Creek Hotel, Spa & Conference Center

*170 Railroad St., (888) 920-0008, (707) 636-7100, fax (707) 636-7277; www.vineyardcreek.com. 155 rooms; $$. Children under 13 free. Pool; health spa; fitness room. Restaurant; room service.*

A 3-story, Mediterranean-style building surrounds two large courtyards here. The back courtyard accesses a riverside walkway and features a "water wall" that serves the dual purpose of deadening freeway noise. Rooms are large and appointed with beds topped by a semi-canopy—with cotton sheets and down comforters—and with granite bathroom counters.

The **Seafood Brasserie** *((707) 636-7388. B-L-D daily; $$. Highchairs, booths, child menu.)* showcases the local bounty with a French flair. It has an exhibition kitchen, high ceilings, and a prominent bar that serves only hand-mixed drinks made without a blender.

## Vintners Inn

*4350 Barnes Rd., (800) 421-2584, (707) 575-7350, fax (707) 575-1426; www.vintnersinn.com. 44 rooms; $$-$$$+. Children under 5 free. Some wood-burning fireplaces. Hot tub. Continental breakfast; restaurant; room service. No smoking; no pets.*

The rooms in this elegant country inn are furnished with European antiques. They are spread through three separate buildings and are cozily surrounded by a 45-acre working vineyard.

The inn's highly acclaimed restaurant, **John Ash & Co.** *(4330 Barnes Rd., (707) 527-7687, fax (707) 527-1202; L M-F, D daily, SunBr; $$$. Highchairs. Reservations advised.)*, features vineyard views and dishes highlighting local products. Imaginative menu choices include creative soups and salads, small pizzas and fabulous sandwiches, and exceptional desserts made in-house by a special pastry chef. (Note that founding chef John Ash no longer owns the restaurant or cooks here, but current chef, Jeffrey Madura, was well trained by him.)

### — WHERE TO EAT —

Santa Rosa is where John A. McDougall, author of *The McDougall Plan for Super Health and Life-Long Weight Loss* and promoter of heart-healthy eating, makes his home. It is interesting to note his influence on this area. Most, if not all, of the restaurants have at least one heart-healthy item on the menu. Many have more. Surprisingly, even small fast-food spots such as the **Sonoma Taco Shop** *(100 Brookwood St./2nd St., in Creekside Center, (707) 525-8585; www.sonomatacoshop.com. L-D daily; $. Child portions.)*, with its impressive 33 heart-healthy options (a complete nutrient breakdown of each item is available), can be counted on to satisfy this need.

## The Cantina

*500 4th St., in Courthouse Square, (707) 523-3663; www.greatmex.com. L-D daily.*

For description, see page 212.

## Downtown Wednesday Night Market

*On 4th St. & B St., (707) 524-2123; www.srdowntown market.com. W 5-8; June-Sept only. Free.*

At this festive event, local restaurants serve up inexpensive portions of barbecued turkey legs, sausage, kebobs, burgers, and oysters along with salads, calzone, chili, and burritos. Farmers are on hand with fresh produce, arts-and-crafts artists display their wares, and plenty of street entertainers do their thing.

### Flying Goat Coffee

*10 4th St., in Railroad Square, (707) 575-1202, fax (707) 433-0704; www.flyinggoatcoffee.com. M-F 7-6, Sat-Sun 8-6.*

Fresh-roasted specialty coffees can be sipped either inside, in the laid-back atmosphere of a tall-ceilinged shop, or outside, where the sport is train-watching. Housemade pastries are also available.

### Mixx

*135 4th St., in Railroad Square, (707) 573-1344, fax (707) 573-0631; www.mixxrestaurant.com. L M-F, D M-Sat, SatBr; $$-$$$. Highchairs, boosters, booths, child menu. Reservations advised.*

This restaurant is oversize in every way: seating, ceiling (20 feet high), wine glasses, food seasoning. Sitting beneath the drooping lily light fixtures at one of the substantial tables here feels great. Drinks can be ordered from a full bar, which as it happens is not just *any* bar. Built in the late 1800s in Italy, it was shipped around Cape Horn in 1904 and has been here ever since. In fact, the building has been either a bar or restaurant since that opening date. And then there is the food. Prepared by owner-chef Dan Berman and his wife Kathleen, who is the pastry chef, the delightful eclectic menu satisfies all stages of hunger. Appetizers might be a spicy, complexly flavored puréed soup of guajillo chili, roasted tomato, and smoked chicken, or a perfect house salad composed of local greens accented colorfully with edible flowers. With preference given to ingredients available locally, the dinner menu features some relatively unusual items such as venison and free-range veal (prepared memorably in the past with a whole-grain mustard sauce and side of garlicky, crisp Yukon gold potatoes). The restaurant is deservedly famous for its housemade ice creams and sorbets, and the crème brulee just might be the world's best.

### Omelette Express

*112 4th St., in Railroad Square, (707) 525-1690; www.omelette.com. B-L daily; $. Highchairs, boosters, child items. No reservations.*

Diners sit on pressed-back chairs at old-fashioned oak tables in this popular spot. All omelettes are available with egg whites only, and hamburgers, sandwiches, and a variety of salads are also on the menu.

### Peter Rabbit's Chocolate Factory™

*2489 Guerneville Rd./Fulton Rd., (800) 4-R-CANDY, (707) 575-7110, fax (707) 579-5663. M-Sat 10-6.*

Located on the outskirts of town, in a building that belies the cute name, this candy store is worth seeking out. Visitors can usually observe some yummy or other being whipped up on huge marble slabs located adjacent to the retail area. Among the over 120 goodies produced are nut brittles, saltwater taffy, and caramel corn that seems to get better with age. At Christmas, life-size 5-foot-tall chocolate Santas join the menu. There are even chocolate-dipped prunes. Should addiction occur, everything is available by mail order.

### Willie Bird's Restaurant

*1150 Santa Rosa Ave./Barham Ave., (707) 542-0861; www.williebird.com. B-L-D daily; $-$$. Highchairs, boosters, child menu.*

This casual, old-time restaurant celebrates Thanksgiving every day by serving their own natural brand of tasty turkey in varied forms. Try the Willie Bird Special—a traditional turkey feast with giblet gravy and celery-onion bread stuffing—or something more unusual, such as turkey scallopini or turkey sausage. The motto here is "Turkey always and turkey all ways." Children's portions include a turkey hamburger and turkey hot dog. Plenty of non-turkey items are also available.

# Guerneville and Russian River Area

## — A LITTLE BACKGROUND —

Once upon a time, in 1809, a party of Russians and Aleuts from the Russian-American Fur Company in Sitka, Alaska, landed at the mouth of what is now the Russian River. They named it "Slavianka," or "little beauty." In recognition of the Russian influence in the area, it became referred to as the "Russian" River.

In the '20s and '30s the area became a summer resort favored by wealthy San Franciscans who traveled here by ferry and train. Then it faded in popularity and became a pleasant and uncrowded retreat. Today, slowly recovering from a state of decay, it is regaining some of its former popularity and is known nationally for its resorts catering to gays. The atmosphere is easygoing, and it is acceptable to dine anywhere in casual clothing.

Guerneville, the hub of the Russian River resort area, is surrounded by many smaller towns. The area has numerous public beaches, even more privately-owned ones, and also some unofficial nude beaches. Inquire in town about how to find, or avoid, them.

### — VISITOR INFORMATION —

#### Russian River Chamber of Commerce Visitor Center
*16209 First St., (877) 644-9001, (707) 869-9000, fax (707) 869-9215; www.russianriver.com.*

#### Russian River Wine Road
*(800) 723-6336, (707) 433-4335, fax (707) 433-4374; www.wineroad.com.*

A free map provides details on wineries and lodgings stretching from Forestville to Cloverdale.

### — GETTING THERE —

Located approximately 75 miles north of San Francisco. Exit Highway 101 at Highway 12 west, following it to Highway 116. For a more scenic route, take the River Road exit just north of Santa Rosa and follow it west. Located approximately 15 miles west of Santa Rosa.

### — ANNUAL EVENTS —

#### Russian River Wine Road Barrel Tasting
*March. (800) 723-6336, (707) 433-4335, fax (707) 433-4374; www.wineroad.com/events/ barreltasting.asp.*

Participants are permitted to get behind the scenes in wine making and sample special wines that aren't usually available for tasting. Wineries provide tastes of wines still in the barrel as well as of some new vintages and old library treasures.

#### Apple Blossom Festival
*April. In Sebastopol; (877) 828-4748, (707) 823-3032, fax (707) 823-8439; www.sebastopolapple blossom.org. $6, 62+ & 10-17 $4.*

Scheduled each year to occur when the area's plentiful apple orchards are snowy-white with blossoms, this festival includes a parade down Main Street and plenty of booths purveying apple-related crafts and foods.

#### Bohemian Grove
*Last 2 wks. of July.*

Many of the world's most powerful political, military, and corporate leaders have been getting together at this 2,700-acre private resort since 1873. The public is not invited.

#### Gravenstein Apple Fair
*August. In Sebastopol; (800) 207-9464, (707) 824-1765, fax (707) 571-7719; www.farmtrails.org. $8, 65+ $6, 6-16 $4. No pets.*

Held on and off since the turn of the century, this old-time country fair is staged amid the large, shady oak trees and rolling hills of Ragle Ranch Park. The fair specifically celebrates the flavorful, crisp, early-ripening Gravenstein apple—an old German variety dating from 1790 that is indigenous to the area and well known for making the best juices and pies. In fact, this area is known as the world's Gravenstein capital. Fun at the fair is of the down-home variety, with opportunities to taste apples, observe beekeepers in action, and pet a variety of farm animals. Apples and related foods and products are available for purchase directly from farmers. Proceeds fund the printing of the Sonoma County Farm Trails map.

#### Jazz on the River
*September. (510) 655-9471; www.jazzontheriver.com. $40+, under 11 free. No pets.*

Music festivals don't get much more casual than this one. Audience members can actually float in the placid river on an inner tube while listening to a range of jazz. It's a good idea to pack an ice chest and picnic basket, but food and drink are available for sale. Note that bottles and cans are not permitted.

### — WHAT TO DO —

#### Armstrong Redwoods State Reserve
*17020 Armstrong Woods Rd., (707) 869-2015,*

*fax (707) 869-5629; www.parks.ca.gov. Daily 8am-1 hr. after sunset. $5/vehicle.*

A Visitors Center orients hikers to the trail system within this 700-plus-acre park of thousand-year-old redwood groves. A free parking lot is located just outside the tollgate, and no admission fee is charged for parking there and walking in.

The **Armstrong Woods Pack Station** *((707) 887-2939; www.redwoodhorses.com. Schedule varies. $60+. Reservations required. Must be 10 or older or have guide's permission.)* offers trail rides and full-day lunch rides among the mammoth trees found here. Overnight trail rides and longer pack trips are available May through October.

Almost 4 miles farther, at the end of a narrow, steep, winding road, **Austin Creek State Recreation Area** *((707) 869-2015, www.parks. sonoma.net/austin.html.)* offers 20 miles of hiking trails, plus rustic camping facilities and four hike-in campsites.

## Duncans Mills
*On Hwy. 116, 10 mi. W of Guerneville, (888) 422-6736, (707) 865-2024, fax (707) 865-1466; www.duncans millscamp.com.*

Once a lumber village, this tiny town is now home to a collection of shops, a deli, a restaurant, a riverside campground with private beach, and a horseback-riding concession.

## J's Amusements
*16101 Neeley Rd., (707) 869-3102. Daily in summer; Sept & Mar-June, Sat-Sun only; closed in winter. $2-$4/ride.*

Various kiddie rides and entertainments await families in search of cheap thrills. Among them are a creaking mini-roller coaster, a tilt-a-whirl, a waterslide, and a 36-hole miniature golf course.

## Kozlowski Farms
*5566 Hwy. 116 N., in Forestville, (800) 4-R-FARMS, (707) 887-1587, fax (707) 887-9650; www.kozlowski farms.com. Daily 9-5.*

This scenic farm is planted with 25 acres of apple trees and assorted berries. Homemade juices, berry vinegars, wine jellies, berry jams and fruit butters made without sugar, and much more are sold year-round at a store in the farm's barn. A mail-order catalogue is available.

## River swimming
Almost anywhere along the banks of the Russian River is a nice place to lay a blanket. A prime spot is under the **Monte Rio bridge**, where parking and beach access are free. Another choice spot is **Johnson's Beach** (see page 232). Canoe and paddleboat rentals and snack stands are available at both. The riverbed and beaches are covered with pebbles, so waterproof shoes are advised.

A good game to play with children here is "Find the Siamese Twin Clam Shells." Be prepared with a special prize for the kid who finds the largest number of intact pairs.

## — WINERIES —

## Korbel Champagne Cellars
*13250 River Rd., (707) 824-7000, fax (707) 869-2981; www.korbel.com. Tasting daily 10-4; tours daily 10-3, on the hr.; more frequent tours in summer. Rose garden tours: Tu-Sun at 11, 1, 3; Apr-Oct only; free.*

The nation's oldest producer of méthode champenoise champagne, this century-old winery also produces brandy and wine. Eight kinds of champagne can be tasted, and chilled splits and deli items can be purchased for impromptu picnics.

The grounds are landscaped with beautifully maintained flower gardens. An **Antique Rose Garden**, faithfully restored to its turn-of-the-century beauty, is filled with old-time flowers such as coral bells, primroses, and violets, as well as some more unusual plants. Among the more than 250 varieties of rose are rare specimens such as the original Burbank Tea, the Double Musk celebrated in Shakespeare's plays, and the True Ambassador, which was once thought to be extinct.

## — WHERE TO STAY —

## Applewood Inn and Restaurant
*13555 Hwy. 116, (800) 555-8509, (707) 869-9093, fax (707) 869-9170; www.applewoodinn.com. 16 rooms; $$-$$$+. Unsuitable for children under 21. Some gas fireplaces. Heated pool (seasonal); hot tub. Full breakfast; restaurant. No smoking; no pets.*

Built in 1922 as a private home, the Mission Revival-style mansion is now a county historical landmark. Two newer Mediterranean-style villas are part of the 6-acre complex featuring an idyllic pool area surrounded by mature vineyards and tall redwood trees. The hot tub is wonderful at night, especially when all the stars are out. Public tennis courts, located adjacent to the property, are a short walk away through a valley still populated with apple trees that once comprised an orchard. The inn's decor is tasteful and unfussy, with aesthetically pleasing touches. Rooms are spacious and comfortable, and some have private patios or balconies overlooking the vineyards and peaceful pastures beyond. Breakfast is simple, yet special—perhaps a sectioned grapefruit topped with a perfect red maraschino cherry, followed by beautifully presented eggs Florentine prepared with tender baby spinach fresh from the inn's own garden—and on warm days can be enjoyed outdoors by the pool.

Enticing, sophisticated California-Provençale dinners are served in the **restaurant** *(D Tu-Sat; $$$. Reservations advised.).* Designed to resemble a French Barn, the dining room has two river rock fireplaces, lofty beamed ceilings, and windows looking out over tall redwoods.

## Creekside Inn & Resort

*16180 Neeley Rd., (800) 776-6586, (707) 869-3623, fax (707) 869-1417; www.creeksideinn.com. 17 units; $-$$$. Children under 2 free. Some kitchens, & wood-burning fireplaces; some shared baths. Unheated pool (seasonal). Full breakfast (B&B rooms only). No smoking; pets ok.*

Located a short stroll from town, just across the historical bridge, this quiet resort dates back to the '30s. Guests have a choice of lodgings. The main house operates as a B&B, with six rooms sharing two bathrooms. Of the nine modernized housekeeping cottages, which all feature attractive half-timbered exteriors, a favorite is the Tree House—named for the fact that trees can be observed from every window. RV spaces are also available. Facilities include a large outdoor pool area with a barbecue, horseshoe pit, pool table, Ping-Pong table, croquet lawn, and lending library. When rains are normal, Pocket Canyon Creek provides the soothing sound of running water as it meanders through the property.

## The Inn at Occidental

*3657 Church St., in Occidental, (800) 522-6324, (707) 874-1047, fax (707) 874-1078; www.innatocci dental.com. 16 rooms, 1 cottage; $$-$$$+. Unsuitable for children under 10. Some fireplaces. Evening snack, full breakfast. No smoking; pets ok in cottage.*

Not your average B&B, this exquisite, yet cozy, beauty of an inn presents guests with the very best in food and hospitality. A restored Victorian, it is the town's oldest residential structure and sits tucked among tall redwoods on a hillside just above town. Outside, covered porches are furnished with wicker and the garden features a fountain and walled courtyard. Inside, special features include fir floors, wainscotted hallways, and themed guest rooms—one with a private hot tub. The inn is furnished delightfully with the owner's vast and ever-growing antique and art collection. Multi-course Winemaker Dinners held in the formal dining room provide the chance to dine with some of the area's local food providers, whose products are featured in the meal. Best of all, the owner's collection of beautiful china, which must rival that of Martha Stewart, is used for these events.

## Johnson's Beach & Resort

*16241 First St., (707) 869-2022, fax 707-869-8282; www.johnsonsbeach.com. 10 rooms; $. Closed Nov-Apr. Some kitchens. No smoking; no dogs.*

These bargain old-time hotel rooms are adjacent to the river. Only weeklong rentals are reservable; shorter stays are first-come, first-served. Facilities include two rustic wooden swings, a large-tire sandbox, both pool and Ping-Pong tables, and access to a beach with a snack bar and both boat and beach paraphernalia rentals. Campsites are also available.

## Ridenhour Ranch House Inn

*12850 River Rd., (888) 877-4466, (707) 887-1033, fax (707) 869-2967; www.ridenhourranchhouse inn.com. 8 rooms; $$. Children under 5 free. Some TVs; 1 gas fireplace & 1 wood-burning stove. Hot tub. Afternoon snack, full breakfast. No smoking; dogs ok in some rooms.*

Built of redwood in 1906, this canary-yellow ranch house was constructed by the first settlers in the area. Decorated with English and American antiques, the house has six guest rooms. Two more rooms are in an adjacent cottage dating from 1934. Recreational facilities include a hot tub pleasantly situated beneath sheltering trees, a badminton area, and a croquet lawn. Across the highway, secluded beaches are reached via a short walk down a lane lined with blackberry bushes. An expansive breakfast is prepared each morning in a restaurant-style kitchen by the Austrian owner-chef, who warns his guests, "If you don't eat well in the morning, you don't look well at the wineries." So he offers wonderful treats such as homemade Gravenstein applesauce and fruit preserves, gigantic croissants, a fruit smoothie with a touch of brandy from neighboring Korbel winery, a wonderfully light bread pudding, and a dish made with eggs collected from the ranch's own hens. Fresh cookies and sherry are always out in the living room, which is also well equipped with games and reading matter.

## Rio Villa Beach Resort

*20292 Hwy. 116, in Monte Rio, (707) 865-1143, fax (707) 865-0115; www.riovilla.com. 12 rooms, 2 cabins; $-$$. Children under 2 free. Some kitchens, & wood-burning fireplaces. Continental breakfast on weekends.*

Some of the rooms in this peaceful spot have private balconies with river views. Guests can relax both on a large deck surrounded by manicured grounds overlooking the river and on a private beach.

## Riverlane Resort

*16320 First St., (800) 201-2324, (707) 869-2323, fax (707) 869-1954; www.riverlaneresort.com. 12 cabins; $-$$$. Children under 3 free. All kitchens; some wood-burning fireplaces & stoves. Heated pool (seasonal), hot tub. No pets.*

Located by the river, this pleasant enclave of cabins offers river access.

## Village Inn

*20822 River Blvd., in Monte Rio, (800) 303-2303, (707) 865-2304, fax (707) 865-2332; www.villageinn-ca.com. 11 rooms; $-$$. Some rooms suitable for children; children under 2 free. Some TVs; 1 kitchen; some shared baths. Continental breakfast; restaurant; room service. Small dogs ok.*

Built as a summer home in 1906, this rustic structure was turned into a hotel in 1908 and has remained one ever since. A worthy claim to fame is that *Holiday Inn*, starring Bing Crosby, was filmed here. Lodging facilities vary from small sleeping rooms to suites with a riverfront deck. In summer, the **restaurant**

serves a popular Sunday brunch outdoors on a pleasant deck overlooking the river.

## House rentals

Call the Visitors Bureau for the names of realty companies that rent private homes to vacationers.

## — WHERE TO EAT —

### Ace-In-The-Hole Cider Pub

*3100 Hwy. 116 N., in Sebastopol, (707) 829-1ACE, fax (707) 829-1157; www.acecider.com. L-D daily; $.*

Taste refreshing hard ciders made from local ingredients at America's very first cider pub. They're made from fermented apple juice (5% alcohol), are said to be an "exhilarating" alternative to the heaviness of beer and the high alcohol content of wine, and come in four flavors: apple, pear, apple-honey, and berry. Can't decide? Try a sampler. The large, open interior is welcoming on dreary days, while the ample patio is prime in sunny weather. Tours of the cider mill behind the pub are available upon request, and live music is scheduled on Friday and Saturday nights.

### CazSonoma Inn

*1000 Kidd Creek Rd., in Cazadero, 3 mi. W of town, (888) 699-8499, (707) 632-5255, fax (707) 632-5256; www.cazsonomainn.com. D daily, SunBr; $$; closed Dec-Apr. Highchairs, boosters, child portions. Reservations advised.*

Nestled between two creeks in a protected valley, this 1926 lodge is reached via a 1-mile-long dirt road. The dining room serves California cuisine and offers great views of the tranquil forest setting. In warm weather, a large deck out under the redwoods is irresistible. Live music is usually scheduled on weekends.

**Cabins and lodge rooms** *(4 rooms, 2 cabins; $$. Children under 12 free. No TVs; some kitchens & wood-burning fireplaces. Unheated pool (seasonal). Evening snack, continental breakfast. Pets ok in cabins.)* are also available. A man-made waterfall and 2 miles of hiking trails are among the features found on the 147 acre site.

### Mom's Apple Pie

*4550 Hwy. 116 N./near Hwy. 12, in Sebastopol, (707) 823-8330, fax (707) 823-5482; www.momsapple pieusa.com. Daily 10-6; $. 1 highchair.*

Located beside an 8-acre apple orchard, this cheery bakery is always worth a stop. Pies are made by hand and include not just the famous apple but banana cream, peach, raspberry, pecan and more, including mini pies—all available to take home as well. Fried chicken, tasty soup, and sandwiches are also available.

Next door, Mom's original site has morphed into **Stella's Cafe** *((707) 823-6637. L W-Sat & M, D W-M; $$. Highchairs, boosters. Reservations advised.)*, a cozy spot serving impressive dinners.

## The Occidental Two

*In Occidental.*

Both of these restaurants serve bountiful multi-course, family-style Italian dinners. They have highchairs, boosters, and a reasonable plate charge for small children. Prices are moderate, and inexpensive ravioli and spaghetti dinners with fewer side dishes also are available. Reservations are advised at prime dining times during the summer, and on weekends and holidays year-round. People come to these restaurants to eat BIG. Picking a favorite can prove fattening.

### • Negri's
*3700 Main St., (707) 823-5301, fax (707) 874-2158. L-D daily.*

Meals here start with a steaming bowl of minestrone soup, rounds of moist salami, and a hunk of crusty Italian bread. Then come more plates bearing pickled vegetables, marinated bean salad, creamy large-curd cottage cheese, and a salad tossed with Thousand Island dressing. When tummies begin to settle, the ravioli arrives—stuffed with spinach and topped with an excellent tomato-meat sauce. Then the entree arrives: a choice of crispy, moist fried chicken, saucy duck, or grilled porterhouse steak. (Seafood entrees are available on weeknights.) Entrees are served with a side of thick French fries and heavy zucchini pancakes. Then come the doggie bags. For those with room, apple fritters are available at additional charge.

### • Union Hotel
*3731 Main St., (707) 874-3444, fax (707) 874-3662; www.unionhotel.com. L-D daily.*

In operation since 1876, this restaurant seats 400 people in three enormous dining rooms and on an outdoor patio. Simplicity seems to be the key to its success. The entree choice is limited to roasted chicken or duck, chicken cacciatora, or steak. Side dishes include an antipasto plate of marinated kidney beans, cheese, and salami, plus minestrone soup, a delicious salad with light Thousand Island dressing, hand-rolled ravioli, a fresh vegetable, and bread and butter. Dessert—apple fritters, spumoni ice cream, or apple pie—and coffee are extra. A bakery, pizzeria, and cafe adjoin.

## River Inn Restaurant
*16141 Main St., (707) 869-0481; www.theriverinn.net. B M-Thur, L-D daily; $-$$; closed Nov-Mar. Highchairs, boosters, booths, child portions. No reservations.*

It's unusual to find the owner-chef of your average coffee shop strolling past the booths asking customers, "How's your meal today?" But that's just what happens here. And the chef considers using anything canned to be "a cardinal sin." The all-American breakfast menu includes crisp waffles, thin Swedish pancakes, perfect French toast, omelettes, oatmeal, and fresh fruit. At lunch and dinner, just about everything imaginable is available, including vegetarian items.

## Topolos at Russian River Vineyards Restaurant

*5700 Hwy. 116 N., in Forestville, (707) 887-1562, fax (707) 887-1399; www.topolos.net. L-D daily in summer, SunBr; closed M-Tu rest of year; $$. Highchairs, boosters, child portions. Reservations advised.*

In good weather, diners are seated outdoors and shaded by grape arbors and umbrellas. In colder weather, seating is inside the century-old farmhouse that is now the restaurant. Greek dishes are the specialty, but a hamburger is on the lunch menu. Extensive use is made of local products as well as of fresh organic herbs and vegetables grown on site, and a large selection of the winery's own vintages are available by the glass. This is the only family-owned and -operated winery/restaurant in the state.

Organically-grown wines can be sampled in the adjacent **Topolos at Russian River Vineyards Winery** tasting room *((800) TOPO-LOS, (707) 887-1575; www.topolos.net. Tasting daily 11-5; tours by appt.).* The Zinfandel is described by winemaker Michael Topolos as "very American. It's forward and gutsy just like we are." The unusual, rich Alicante Bouschet varietal is also noteworthy. Children are served sparkling apple cider while their parents taste.

# Healdsburg

### — A LITTLE BACKGROUND —

Small town America is alive and well in Northern California. When visitors arrive in this charming old-fashioned town, they sometimes are shocked to find cars stopping *willingly* as they wait in a crosswalk to cross the street. Even the cars in the far lane sometimes wait! And parking places are usually easy to find, even around the popular town square. All this plus the weather is generally sunny.

Healdsburg was incorporated in 1867 and then slowly rose around a central Spanish-style plaza. It is one of the few examples remaining of a planned early California town. The plaza's original owner gave it to the town as a gift with the provision that it be used forever as a "pleasure ground" free from public buildings. Nowadays, a free **Summer Sunday Concert Series** is scheduled on the plaza June through August. Historic homes and buildings are sprin-

kled around the square and throughout the surrounding neighborhood, adding greatly to the town's turn-of-the century flavor.

The surrounding area is home to over 50 premium wineries, a few of which have tasting rooms right in town. Visitors can spend the day driving or biking the back roads, happily hopping from winery to winery, or can opt to just stay in town antiquing and shopping.

### — VISITOR INFORMATION —

## Healdsburg Chamber of Commerce & Visitors Bureau

*217 Healdsburg Ave., (800) 648-9922, (707) 433-6935, fax (707) 433-7562; www.healdsburg.org.*

### — GETTING THERE —

Located 75 miles north of San Francisco, and 12 miles north of Santa Rosa.

### — WHAT TO DO —

## Healdsburg Veterans Memorial Beach

*13839 Old Redwood Hwy., (707) 433-1625; www.sonoma-county.org/parks/pk_hvet.htm. Daily 7am-8pm; June-Sept only. $3-$4/vehicle.*

This is a choice spot to swim in the warm Russian River, which in summer has an average water temperature of 70 to 75 degrees. A lifeguard is on duty from 10 a.m., and canoe and inner tube rentals are available. Facilities include a diving board, a children's wading area, a picnic area with barbecues, and a snack bar. Sunbathers have a choice of a large sandy beach or a shady lawn area.

## W.C. "Bob" Trowbridge Canoe Trips

*20 Healdsburg Ave., (800) 640-1386, (707) 433-7247, fax (707) 433-6384. Check-in daily 8-12:30, Apr-Oct only. $45/canoe/half day, $55/full day. Must be 6 or older. Reservations necessary.*

The canoe fee for these unguided trips includes life jackets, paddles, and canoe transport. An after-canoeing barbecue is an option each weekend at additional cost, and a 2-day trip is also available. Trowbridge has five other rental sites along the river.

## Windsor Waterworks & Slides

*8225 Conde Lane, in Windsor, 6 mi. S of town, (707) 838-4195, fax (707) 838-7690. Daily 11-7, June-Aug; Sat-Sun only, May & Sept.; closed Oct-Apr. $17.95, under 4 free.*

In addition to several waterslides, this water-oriented facility holds a swimming pool, a wading pool, a volleyball court, a snack bar, and shaded picnic facilities.

### — WINERIES —

## Belvedere Vineyards & Winery

*4035 Westside Rd., (707) 431-4442, fax (707) 431-0826; www.belvederewinery.com. Tasting daily 11-5.*

Call ahead to reserve a tour of the elegant, manicured **Aroma Garden.** Dotted with koi ponds and waterfalls and always open for strolling, it is both relaxing and educational. Sections are devoted to white wines, red wines, and to attracting butterflies and hummingbirds, with the occasional redwood rocking chair invitingly punctuating the landscape. Plans call for this winery to specialize in organic wines.

## Dry Creek Vineyard

*3770 Lambert Bridge Rd., 3 mi. W of Hwy. 101, (800) 864-WINE, (707) 433-1000, fax (707) 433-5329; www.drycreekvineyard.com. Tasting daily 10:30-4:30; no tour.*

Known for its Fumé Blancs and Chenin Blancs, this winery has a cool, shady picnic area under a canopy of old pine and maple trees. An annual December **Open House** (*$15*) celebrates the season with live music, wine tasting, and plenty of good food.

## Ferrari-Carano Vineyards & Winery

*8761 Dry Creek Rd., (800) 831-0381, (707) 433-6700, fax (707) 431-1742; www.ferrari-carano.com. Tasting daily 10-5; tour M-Sat at 10, reservation required.*

Designed like an elegant Italianate villa, the visitor center here is surrounded by flower gardens modeled after Victoria, B.C.'s Butchart Gardens. The gardens spread over 5 acres and are enhanced by bridges, brooks, and gazebos, and in spring 18,000 tulips burst into bloom. The winery is known for its Chardonnays and Fume Blancs.

## Foppiano Vineyards

*12707 Old Redwood Hwy., (707) 433-7272, fax (707) 433-0565; www.foppiano.com. Tasting daily 10-4:30; self-guided tour.*

Established in 1896, this family-owned winery offers a self-guided tour through its Chardonnay, Cabernet Sauvignon, and Petite Sirah vineyards. It takes about 30 minutes, and a free explanatory brochure is available in the tasting room.

## Hop Kiln Winery

*6050 Westside Rd., (707) 433-6491, fax (707) 433-8162; www.hopkilnwinery.com. Tasting daily 10-5; no tour.*

This unique winery is reached by taking a quiet back road through miles of scenic vineyards. Wine tasting occurs inside a landmark 1905 hops-drying barn built by Italian stonemasons (it once supplied San Francisco breweries). Known for its big Zinfandels, the winery also produces unique Big Red and A Thousand Flowers blends. Two appealing picnic areas are available: one overlooks a duck pond and vineyards; the other rests in the shade of a gigantic Kadota fig tree planted in 1880.

## J Wine Company

*11447 Old Redwood Hwy., (888) J WINE CO, (707) 431-5400, fax (707) 431-5410; www.jwine.com. Tasting daily 11-5; tour by appt.*

The lines of this elegant, ultra-modern winery are softened with attractive landscaping and a lily pond moat. Now producing an array of sparkling wines, it has plans for adding still wines soon. At a bar enhanced by a massive metal-and-glass sculpture backlit in fibre optics (it is symbolic of diamonds and champagne bubbles and certain to provoke discussion), tasters can try wines by the glass or sample an entire flight accompanied by foods designed to complement them. A stop here allows killing the proverbial two birds with one stone. Park once, taste twice: Rodney Strong Vineyards is located just across the way. And speaking of birds, blue herons—as well as otters—are sometimes seen in the pond.

## Preston Vineyards

*9282 W. Dry Creek Rd., (800) 305-9707, (707) 433-3372, fax (707) 433-5307, bread hotline (707) 433-4720; www.prestonvineyards.com. Tasting daily 11-4:30; no tour.*

This small family-owned winery produces terrific Rhone-style wines and good Fumé Blancs. Outside the tasting room, a shaded brick patio holds comfy wicker chairs and numerous resident cats. Bread baked on the premises in an Italian-style forno oven can be purchased; call ahead to find out what Lou, the winery owner, is baking and when it's available for sale. Picnic tables are shaded by an old walnut tree, and courts for Italian bocce ball and French petanque are available. On the way in or out, an inviting roadside creek invites frolicking.

## Rodney Strong Vineyards

*11455 Old Redwood Hwy., (800) 678-4763, (707) 431-1533, fax (707) 433-0939; www.rodneystrong.com. Tasting daily 10-5; tours daily at 11, 3.*

A self-guided tour circles the tasting room, where the winery's delicious Chardonnays and Cabernet Sauvignons can be sampled. Picnic tables are available, and special events are scheduled regularly in summer.

## Simi Winery

*16275 Healdsburg Ave., (800) 746-4880, (707) 433-6981, fax (707) 433-6253; www.simiwinery.com. Tasting daily 10-5; tours daily at 11, 1, 3.*

Opened in 1890, this friendly winery pours samples of reserve wines, and on Tuesdays the tours include barrel tasting. An inviting redwood-shaded picnic area is available.

## — WHERE TO STAY —

## Best Western Dry Creek Inn

*198 Dry Creek Rd., (800) 222-5784, (707) 433-0300, fax (707) 433-1129; www.drycreekinn.com. 102 rooms; $$. Children under 16 free. Heated pool (seasonal); hot tub; fitness room. Continental breakfast; restaurant. Pets ok.*

At this attractive contemporary motel, all guests are greeted with a complimentary bottle of wine in their room.

## Camellia Inn

*211 North St., (800) 727-8182, (707) 433-8182, fax (707) 433-8130; www.camelliainn.com. 9 rooms; $$-$$$. Children under 2 free. No TVs; some gas fireplaces. Heated pool (seasonal). Afternoon snack, full breakfast. No smoking.*

Situated just 2 blocks from the town square, this 1869 Italianate Victorian townhouse is a quiet retreat. The surrounding grounds are planted with over 50 varieties of camellia, some of which were given to the original owner by Luther Burbank. In keeping with the theme, each room is named for a camellia variety. The tastefully furnished, high-ceilinged Royalty Room—originally the home's dining room—boasts an antique Scottish high bed with a step stool and a ceiling-hung canopy as well as an unusual, ornate antique-brass sink fitting. Several rooms have whirlpool bathtubs for two. An afternoon spent out in the oak-shaded, villa-style pool area is incredibly relaxing. Breakfast is served buffet-style in the dining room, where guests are seated at a large clawfoot mahogany table.

## Healdsburg Inn on the Plaza

*110 Matheson St., (800) 431-8663, (707) 433-6991, fax (707) 433-9513; www.healdsburginn.com. 10 rooms; $$-$$$. Some fireplaces. Unsuitable for children. Some gas fireplaces. Afternoon & evening snack, full breakfast. No pets.*

Located right on the town square, this 1900 Victorian was once a stagecoach stop. Rooms, situated mostly on the second floor and reached via a grand staircase, are furnished with authentic Victorian antiques and have generously-sized bathrooms with resident rubber duckies. The Early Light Room was the town's first photography studio and features a spectacular skylight. It just can't get any cozier than being in the peach-colored Sonnet Room on a rainy morning, with the fireplace flickering and the church bells across the plaza ringing out the hour. A champagne breakfast is served in a second-floor solarium overlooking a row of trees with the town plaza behind; in summer it moves to an outside deck. A bottomless jar of cookies and a fridge full of cold drinks are always available. The work of local artists decorates each room and is for sale in a small shop operating in the hotel lobby.

## Honor Mansion

*14891 Grove St., (800) 554-4667, (707) 433-4277, fax (707) 431-7173; www.honormansion.com. 13 units; $$-$$$+. Some gas fireplaces. Pool; tennis courts.*

*Afternoon & evening snack, full breakfast. No smoking.*

Sporting an ancient sequoia tree in a front yard surrounded by a white picket fence, this Italianate Victorian built in 1883 was a family home for 108 years before it was restored and converted into a B&B. A well-treated staff of 14 keeps things humming, and their attention to detail delights guests in the form of dishes filled with candies and jars filled with cookies. Many rooms have fireplaces requiring just the flip of a switch to deliver a full-blown blaze, and some rooms have clawfoot tubs with mommy and baby rubber duckies ready to float. Room choices include a 2-story converted water tower suite, a detached cottage furnished with an oak buffet fitted with a small refrigerator and a wet bar, and several suites in the main house with a private patio and Jacuzzi. Recreational facilities include a six-hole putting green, a 1/4-mile jogging track, several bocce ball courts, and a full-size croquet lawn. After a swim in the pool or a nap atop a fluffy bed or a long soak in a deep tub with copy of *Millionaire* and *Billionaire* magazines to dream over, it's time for the evening hors d'oeuvres and wine service designed to keep guests from feeling any hunger until dinner. In the morning, indulge in a sobering espresso or frothy cappuccino from the automatic maker that is available to guests at any time, or arrange for delivery of a pot of coffee or tea. A sumptuous breakfast is served in the Victorian's dining room on elegantly arranged fine china. It includes a fruit plate, a hot entree—perhaps caramel-apple French toast or spice pancakes with lemon sauce—and plenty of cherry-orange scones. Allow time before packing up to hand-feed the colorful, hungry koi in the "kissing koi pond" just outside the dining room.

## Hotel Healdsburg

*25 Matheson St., (800) 889-7188, (707) 431-2800, fax (707) 431-0414; www.hotelhealdsburg.com. 3 stories; 55 rooms; $$$-$$$+. Pool; health spa; fitness room. Continental breakfast; restaurant; room service.*

Featuring a stylish minimalist decor and with a collection of Tibetan rugs accenting its polished wood floors, this luxurious new hotel fronts on the plaza. Subdued rooms are appointed with the best linens and oversize soaking tubs, and breakfast is delivered to the room. The spa offers a wine-and-honey wrap among many relaxing options. In summer, movies are screened outdoors under the stars, and live jazz also is sometimes presented.

The lobby **Grappa Bar** serves refreshments fireside or on a screened porch, weather permitting, and the casual **Café Newsstand** dispenses espresso, panini, and housemade gelato. Celebrity chef Charlie Palmer's **Dry Creek Kitchen** *(317 Healdsburg Ave./Matheson St., (707) 431-0330. L-D daily; $$$+.)* uses the best local ingredients for its innovative menu, which changes daily. Past items have included the delicious likes of baby beet salad with goat cheese, tortellini stuffed with roasted cauliflower in a browned butter-Cabernet sauce, and duck with pomegranate-molasses glaze. A tasting menu is also available. Seating in the sophisticated dining room is comfortable, and diners get a glimpse of the busy kitchen through a frosted glass wall.

## Madrona Manor

*1001 Westside Rd., (800) 258-4003, (707) 433-4231, fax (707) 433-0703; www.madronamanor.com. 23 rooms; $$-$$$+. Unsuitable for children under 12. No TVs; some wood-burning & gas fireplaces. Heated pool (seasonal). Full breakfast; restaurant. No smoking.*

Featuring an unusual mansard roof, which makes it look moody in spite of its cheery cream-and-baby blue exterior, this majestic mansion is situated off a side road running through rural vineyards. An imposing archway frames a long driveway leading up to the 8-acre estate, built in 1881 as a country retreat and now a protected historic site. Five rooms feature furniture original to the house, and a public music room boasts an unusual square rosewood piano. Room number 202 has a particularly charming decor of floral wallpaper, a dark-wood dresser and matching cozy double bed, and a very high ceiling. Its spacious bathroom holds a dramatic, unexpected giant cactus and an old-fashioned deep clawfoot tub. Four newer outer structures hold more rooms. Breakfast here is reminiscent of a typical European morning spread, with juice, coffee, breakfast breads, housemade jams, seasonal fruits, meats and cheeses, soft-boiled eggs (in a chicken-shaped basket), vegetable frittata, fabulous light bread pudding, and housemade granola among the choices.

For dinner, guests need only to enter the elegant dining rooms known as **Restaurant at Madrona Manor** *(D W-Sun. Reservations advised.)*, where dishes often feature produce from the estate's own gardens and orchards. Both a fixed-price, three-course dinner and an a la carte menu are offered. One dinner enjoyed here featured a delicious soft-shell crab tempura and a peachy-keen dessert sampler of peach shortcake, peach crisp, and peach ice cream. The wine list features local Sonoma vintages. Outside seating is available on a heated terrace.

## — WHERE TO EAT —

## Bear Republic Brewing Co.

*345 Healdsburg Ave., (707) 433-BEER, fax (707) 433-2205; www.bearrepublic.com. L-D daily; $. Highchairs, boosters, child menu. No reservations.*

Though the dining room is wide-open so diners can view the brewing vats, this warehouse-like spot still manages to feel cozy. Or perhaps it just seems that way because of the warm greeting provided by its owner. Get acquainted with the house brews—including the award-winning Red Rocket Ale—with a sampler, or try a delicious house-brewed root beer or cream soda. Burgers, sandwiches, and salads are all choice, but more substantial entrees and smaller appetizer plates—including addictive garlic-chili fries—are on the menu as well.

## Flying Goat Coffee

*324 Center St., (800) 675-3599, (707) 433-3599, fax (707) 433-0704; www.flyinggoatcoffee.com. M-F 7-6, Sat-Sun 8-6.*

For description, see page 229.

## Picnic Pick-Ups

### • Costeaux French Bakery & Cafe
*417 Healdsburg Ave., (888) 355-0217, (707) 433-1913, fax (707) 433-1955; www.costeaux.com. B-L Tu-Sun; $. Highchairs, child portions. No reservations.*

Family-owned and -operated since 1923, this spot is choice for picking up picnic supplies and even ribbon-tied box lunches. Huge sandwiches are made to order on a choice of light deli rolls or other housemade breads, and wonderful housemade soups, deli salads, sandwiches, and pizzas are more options. The awe-inspiring selection of desserts includes a caramel-macadamia nut tart, several cheesecakes, and an assortment of fresh fruit tarts and French pastries. Seating is either in the airy, high-ceilinged interior or outside on a pleasant sidewalk-side patio. Don't miss seeing the restroom, papered attractively with authentic wine labels.

### • Downtown Bakery and Creamery
*308-A Center St., (707) 431-2719, fax (707) 431-1579; www.downtownbakery.net. M-F 6am-5:30, Sat 7-5:30, Sun 7-4. No cards.*

Co-owner Lindsey Shere did time in the kitchen at Berkeley's renowned Chez Panisse. She also wrote the best-selling cookbook *Chez Panisse Desserts*. So the exceptional hand-shaped, slow-rise breads and the pastries and ice creams produced in her kitchen here are not a complete surprise. When available, the focaccia, sticky buns, fruit turnovers, and fig newtons are not to be missed. On warm Wine Country days, it is a refreshing pleasure to indulge in one of the shop's old-fashioned milkshakes or sundaes, and it's always a good idea to purchase to-go cookie dough to bake at home. Organically grown, freshly milled flours are used, and produce and dairy products are organic and locally produced whenever possible.

### • Dry Creek General Store
*3495 Dry Creek Rd., (707) 433-4171, fax (707) 433-9569; www.dcgstore.com. Daily 6-6, in summer to 7.*

This old fashioned general store/deli opened in 1881 and is now a state historical landmark. Claiming to be "the best deli by a dam site!," it *is* located by a dam site (the Warm Springs Dam) and it sure *does* dispense good picnic fare! Sandwiches are made to order, and plenty of housemade salads and garnishes are available.

### • Jimtown Store
*6706 Hwy. 128, (707) 433-1212, fax (707) 433-1252; www.jimtown.com. M-F 7-5, Sat-Sun 7:30-5; closed 2 wks. in Jan.*

Dating back to the late 1800s, this landmark general store specializes in preparing great picnics to enjoy right on their patio or take along to a winery. Order 24 hours in advance, or take a chance on what's available at the last minute. Among the eclectic gourmet sandwiches: Brie with olive salad, lamb with fig tapenade, roast turkey with balsamic onions. But ham and cheese, chicken salad, and peanut butter & jelly are also available. Picnic hampers are available for loan, and suggestions are provided about where to find the perfect picnic spot. Antiques, folk art, and local products are also for sale.

• **Oakville Grocery**
*124 Matheson St., on the plaza, (707) 433-3200, fax (707) 433-2744; www.oakvillegrocery.com. Sun-Thur 7-7, F-Sat to 8:30.*

For description, see page 399.

## Restaurant Charcuterie
*335 Healdsburg Ave., (707) 431-7213. L-D daily; $-$$. 1 highchair. Reservations accepted for D.*

With a light, French-influenced menu, this casual spot is perfect for a quick meal. Particularly tasty salads—the item of choice in this generally warm area— include one with strips of blackened chicken breast served over a lightly dressed Caesar salad, and another with toasted walnuts, cubes of apple, golden raisins, and Gorgonzola over baby greens with poppy seed dressing. Sandwiches and pastas are available at lunch, and more substantial entrees— such as baked chicken and rabbit fricassée—are added at dinner.

## Zin Restaurant & Wine Bar
*344 Center St., (707) 473-0946, fax (707) 473-0642; www.zinrestaurant.com. L-D daily. Reservations advised.*

Located just a few blocks from the Plaza, this stylish yet casual restaurant has an open dining room with an industrial-style decor featuring cement walls and open rafters. Natural wood trim and paintings of rural scenes add to the warm and cozy feeling. What makes this spot really unique is that menu items are designed to pair with hearty, all-American Zinfandels. The slow-braised lamb shank is a hands-down winner, but in addition to the expected Zin-friendly meats, lighter fish items and roasted chicken are also on the menu. For a starter the deep-fried beer-battered green beans with mango salsa is choice, and for dessert the coffee ice cream with Kahlua chocolate sauce should not be passed up. The wine list, but of course, is dominated with Zins.

# Geyserville

— VISITOR INFORMATION —
**Geyserville Chamber of Commerce**
*P.O. Box 276, Geyserville 95441, (707) 857-3745; www.geyservillecc.com.*

— GETTING THERE —
Located approximately 8 miles north of Healdsburg.

— ANNUAL EVENTS —
**Fall Colors Festival**
*October. (707) 857-3745; www.geyservillecc.com. Free.*

The whole town celebrates the end of the grape harvest with this festival.

— WHAT TO DO —
**Lake Sonoma**
*3333 Skaggs Springs Rd., (707) 433-9483, fax (707) 431-0313; www.parks.sonoma.net/laktrls.html. Free.*

This scenic spot hosts all manner of water activities—fishing, boating, water-skiing, swimming. Everything from a canoe to a patio boat or houseboat can be rented from the **Lake Sonoma Resort** *(Stewarts Point Rd., (707) 433-2200.).* A Visitors Center displays the area's wildlife and provides a self-guided tour through the **Don Clausen Fish Hatchery**. When the steelhead trout and salmon run here, usually from November through April, they can be observed using a man-made fish ladder.

— WINERIES —
**Château Souverain**
*400 Souverain Rd., at Independence Lane exit off Hwy. 101, (888) 80-WINES, (707) 433-8281, fax (707) 433-5174; www.chateausouverain.com. Tasting daily 10-5; no tour; closed first 2 wks. in Jan.*

Tucked into a vineyard-covered hill and featuring distinctive towers reminiscent of the area's once-common hop kilns, this winery is known for producing award-winning Cabernets.

The aptly named **Alexander Valley Grille** *((707) 433-3141. L daily, D F-Sun; $$-$$$. Highchairs, boosters. Reservations advised.)* presents a menu of refined cuisine designed to complement the wine list. The dining room features a beamed ceiling and oversize fireplace and has spectacular views of the scenic Alexander Valley. In good weather, diners can sit outdoors on the Garden Terrace.

## Geyser Peak Winery
*22281 Chianti Rd., 1 mi. N of town at Canyon Rd. exit off Hwy. 101, (800) 255-WINE, (707) 857-9400, fax (707) 857-9402; www.geyserpeakwinery.com. Tasting daily 10-5; no tour.*

Shaded patio picnic tables here overlook Alexander Valley.

## Lake Sonoma Winery
*9990 Dry Creek Rd., (877) 850-WINE, (707) 473-2999, fax (707) 543-2301; www.lakesonomawinery.net. Tasting daily 10-5; tour by appt.*

Featuring a dramatic view of the Dry Creek Valley, this winery is known for its Zinfandels, Cabernet Sauvignons, and Chardonnays and was the first in the country to produce the rich Zinfandel-like Cinsault varietal. The winemaker makes "wines I like to drink," as does everyone else who tastes them. Tasters can picnic on a porch with a dramatic view overlooking the vineyards.

## Trentadue Winery
*19170 Geyserville Ave., (888) 332-3032, (707) 433-3104, fax (707) 433-5825; www.trentadue.com. Tasting daily 10-5; no tour.*

Plan a picnic here in the welcoming shade of a grape arbor. Known for its spicy red Carignane and Sengoviese, this small family enterprise also sells picnic supplies in its tasting room. Children get soft drinks, cookies, and candy to keep them happy while their parents taste.

### — WHERE TO STAY —

## The Hope-Merrill Bed & Breakfast Inn
## The Hope-Bosworth Bed & Breakfast Inn
*21253 Geyserville Ave., (800) 825-4BED, (707) 857-3356, fax (707) 857-4673; www.hope-inns.com. 12 rooms; $$-$$$. One child free in Hope-Bosworth House. Some TVs; some wood-burning & gas fireplaces. Heated pool (seasonal). Full breakfast. No smoking; no pets.*

The 1870 Eastlake Stick Victorian Hope-Merrill house is restored exquisitely to that period with antique furnishings and authentic Bradbury & Bradbury silk-screened wallpapers.

In fact, the owner's restoration efforts won a first place award from the National Trust for Historic Preservation. Should this lovely inn be booked, opt for the charming Queen Anne Victorian Hope-Bosworth house located across the street. Under the same ownership, these two houses share some facilities. When the temperature permits, a dip in the attractively situated pool is sublime, and in the morning a full breakfast is served in the formal dining room. Guests at either house can reserve a gourmet picnic lunch for two featuring local foods.

A special two-part "Pick and Press" package is perfect for wannabe wine-makers. Participants check in at harvest time in September for a round of grape picking and pressing, plus, of course, some tasting and dining. They return in the spring for a bottling and labeling session, plus, of course, more tasting and dining, and then depart with two cases of their own wine sporting personalized labels.

# Anderson Valley

### — A LITTLE BACKGROUND —

Once famous for apple orchards, this area is now best known for its grapes and wines. In Boonville, a town that has yet to install a stop sign or traffic light, the townspeople speak an unusual 19th-century slang known as "Boontling." Here public telephones are labeled "Buckey Walter" and quail are called—after the sound they make—"rookie-to."

### — VISITOR INFORMATION —
## Anderson Valley Chamber of Commerce
*P.O. Box 275, Boonville 95415, (707) 895-2379; www.andersonvalleychamber.com.*

## Anderson Valley Winegrowers Association
*(707) 895-WINE, same fax; www.avwines.com.*

This organization provides free information on the valley's wineries.

### — GETTING THERE —

Take Highway 128 north. Boonville, the valley's largest town, is about 50 miles north of Geyserville and 115 miles north of San Francisco. This spectacular winding route is a rural two-lane back road that follows the Navarro River through oak-wooded hills dotted with sheep peacefully grazing in meadows. After Philo, it enters the Navarro River Redwoods and passes through an 11-mile corridor of tall trees known as the "tunnel to the sea." Gas up before heading out, and avoid this route after dusk.

— ANNUAL EVENTS —

## California Wine Tasting Championships
*July. (707) 895-2002, fax (707) 895-2001. Free for spectators.*

Held at **Greenwood Ridge Vineyards** *(5501 Hwy. 128, in Philo; www.greenwood ridge.com. Tasting daily 10-5, in summer to 6; no tour.)*, this unique and festive event includes good food, live music, chocolate and cheese tasting contests, and novice, amateur, and professional wine tasting competitions.

## Woolgrowers Barbecue and Sheep Dog Trials
*July. In Boonville, at Mendocino County Fairgrounds; (707) 895-3011. Free.*

In addition to the sheep dog trials, visitors see sheep-shearing, wool spun into yarn, and related crafts. A barbecued lamb feast and a sheep weight-guessing contest are also part of the fun.

— WHAT TO DO —

## Anderson Valley Historical Museum
*Hwy. 128/Anderson Valley Way, in Boonville, (707) 895-3207; http://andersonvalley museum.org. F-Sun 1-4; in summer from 11; closed Dec-Feb. Free.*

This old-fashioned, one-room red schoolhouse located just west of town is a worthwhile stop.

## The Apple Farm
*18501 Greenwood Rd., in Philo, (707) 895-2461, fax (707) 895-2333. Fruit stand: Daily 9-5; later in summer & fall. Weekend: $225/person + lodging ($$-$$$).*

One part of this enterprise is a 30-acre certified organic farm with over 80 varieties of apples ripening at different times from August through October. The bounty and related products are for sale at the farm's **fruit stand**.

The other part is a **cooking school** operated by the original proprietors of the highly acclaimed French Laundry in Yountville. The school strives to simplify everyday cooking

and to get participants back in their kitchens preparing daily meals and enjoying it. On Farm Weekends everyone get hands-on experience, preparing and consuming Friday dinner, Saturday lunch and dinner, and Sunday brunch. According to owner Sally Schmitt, it is "like a house party with some cooking lessons thrown in." Schmitt teaches students to use what is already in their garden and panty and encourages using the best ingredients while doing the least possible to them. Participants get 3 hours off on Saturday afternoon to hike, bike, or visit local wineries on their own. Currently one guest room and three cabins are available on the premises.

## Hendy Woods State Park
*On Greenwood Rd., just off Hwy. 128, 8 mi. NW of Boonville, (707) 937-5804; www.parks.ca.gov. $5/vehicle.*

Situated along the Navarro River, this 850-acre park holds two groves of old-growth redwoods, a riverside picnic area with tables under a grove of sprawling walnuts, and a 1-mile self-guided nature Loop Trail. Campsites and four cabins with wood-burning stoves are available.

— WINERIES —

## Husch Vineyards
*4400 Hwy. 128, in Philo, (800) 55-HUSCH, (707) 895-3216, fax (707) 895-2068; www.huschvineyards.com. Tasting daily 10-5, in summer to 6; no tour.*

The tasting room here is inside a charming rose-covered cabin. Don't miss the delicious Carignane and Muscat Canelli. Picnic tables under a vine-sheltered arbor invite lingering.

## Navarro Vineyards
*5601 Hwy. 128, in Philo, (800) 537-WINE, (707) 895-3686, fax (707) 895-3647; www.navarrowine.com. Tasting daily 10-5, in summer to 6; tours by appt.*

Known for its varietal grape juices—which children get to sample—and varied Gewurztraminers, this winery is situated within a striking Craftsman-style redwood building. Its wines are available only at the winery. Attractive picnic areas are provided on a deck overlooking the vineyard and under a trellis in the vineyard.

## Roederer Estate
*4501 Hwy. 128, in Philo, (707) 895-2288, fax (707)*

895-2120; www.roedererestate.net. Tasting daily 11-5; tour by appt.

Boasting state-of-the-art methode champenoise wine-making facilities, this winery has a tasting room with beautiful valley views. It produces all of its own grapes, which are pressed gently and then aged elegantly in carved French oak barrels.

## — WHERE TO STAY —

### Highland Ranch
*18941 Philo-Greenwood Rd., in Philo, (707) 895-3600, fax (707) 895-3702; www.highlandranch.com. 11 cabins; $$$+; closed mid-Dec. Children under 2 free. No TVs; all wood-burning fireplaces. Unheated pool (seasonal); 2 tennis courts. All meals included. Pets ok.*

Guests at this secluded dude ranch can enjoy the rural pleasures of fishing, swimming, and canoeing in three ponds, plus clay pigeon shooting, mountain biking, hiking, and, of course, horseback riding—all at no additional charge. Lodging is in modern redwood cabins.

### Wellspring Renewal Center
*8550 Rays Rd./Hwy. 138, in Philo, (707) 895-3893; www.wellspringrenewal.org. 9 cabins; $. Children under 3 free. No TVs; some kitchens & wood-burning stoves; some shared baths. No smoking.*

Founded in 1979 as an interfaith center, this 50-acre facility located adjacent to Hendy Woods State Park offers programs focused on deepening spirituality and engendering creativity. Regularly scheduled programs include planting and harvesting weekends, meditation and healing retreats, an arts and crafts week, and storytelling workshops. A variety of lodging is available: lodge rooms; both rustic and improved cabins; a campground at which guests can either pitch their own tent or rent a tepee or tent cabin. All guests are asked, but not required, to donate 1 hour of their time each day to a needed chore, and guests must bring their own towels and bedding. Individuals, families, and groups are welcome.

## — WHERE TO EAT —

### Boonville Hotel
*14050 Hwy. 128/Lambert Ln., in Boonville, (707) 895-2210, same fax; www.boonvillehotel.com. D Thur-M; closed 1st 2 wks. in Jan. Highchairs, boosters.*

*Reservations advised for D.*

Owner-chef Johnny Schmitt did his internship at his parent's former restaurant, the French Laundry in Yountville, and he displays his expertise in every dish. Here he uses the local bounty for salads, soups, upscale pizza, hearty entrees, and wonderful desserts, and he features local Anderson Valley wines. All-inclusive regional dinners are scheduled regularly and worth going out of the way for.

**Lodging** *(12 rooms; $-$$$; closed 1st 2 wks. in Jan. Children under 1 free. No TVs. Continental breakfast. No smoking.)* is also available. Eight light, airy rooms and two bungalows have a clean-lined contemporary style, with light woods and sumptuous tiled bathrooms, and are furnished with simple pieces handmade by local craftspeople (many items are available for purchase). Beds are made with all-cotton sheets and boldly-striped down comforters, and unusual, attractive floral arrangements—perhaps white hydrangia balls mixed with wispy blue forget-me-nots—add a touch of whimsy.

### Picnic Pick-Up
- **Boont Berry Farm**
*13981 Hwy. 128, in Boonville, (707) 895-3576. M-Sat 10-6, Sun 12-6.*

This tiny health food store has a cozy, old-fashioned atmosphere and is well-stocked with deli items, locally-grown organic produce, pastries, breads (including the town's famous Bruce Bread), and homemade ice cream.

# Hopland

## — A LITTLE BACKGROUND —

Tiny Hopland is easy to overlook as a getaway destination. Located just 1½ hours from the Bay Area and about 45 minutes north of Santa Rosa, this 3-block-long slow-down in the road seems too soon to stop for the night. But it is well equipped to provide a satisfying weekend escape.

Prior to the arrival of white settlers in the mid-1800s, this area was home to Pomo Indians, who were accomplished basket weavers. Hopland was named after the hops that still grow wild here, and which have been cultivated since 1860 for brewing beer. Though hops were once the area's primary crop, they were displaced in the 1940s by fruits, and now wine grapes. And while this low-key area is slowly transforming from a farming community into a recreational destination, it has a long way to go.

## — GETTING THERE —

Located approximately 25 miles north of Geyserville, and 110 miles north of San Francisco.

## — ANNUAL EVENTS —

### Redwood Run
*June. (707) 247-3424; www.redwoodrun.com.*
Hopland's answer to the Rose Parade, this event finds thousands of motorcycles and their riders making the run from the Bay Area to the Garberville-Piercy area on the Eel River and back again. Most seem to stopover mid-way, mid-day in Hopland, making for quite a sight. The group has a reputation for not causing trouble and is certainly an exciting mass to witness.

## — WHAT TO DO —

### Sho-Ka-Wah Casino
*13101 Nokomis Rd., (877) 546-7526, (707) 744-1395; www.shokawah.com. Open 24 hours.*

Offering a tiny bit of nightlife, this Native American-run casino operates in a magical rural area just a few miles east of Highway 101.

### Solar Living Center
*13771 S. Hwy. 101, (707) 744-2100, fax (707) 744-1682; www.solarliving.org. M-Sat 10-6, Sun 10-5. Guided tour F-Sun at 11 & 3. Free.*
Pick up a self-guided tour brochure at the entrance to this surprising, impressive 12$\frac{1}{2}$ -acre complex, or time your visit for a guided tour. An especially refreshing stop on a hot day (it can soar to 110 degrees around here in summer, and the town claims 300 days of sunshine every year), this small oasis has an Agave Cooling Tower dispensing a refreshing mist, and a Children's Play Area with an optional pipe-tunnel entrance, a sandbox, and a water pump. The symbolic center of the site is formed by the Central Oasis, a sort of a mini-Yellowstone fountain of dancing geysers, and the Solar Calendar, a sort of mini-Stonehenge designed to reconnect visitors to the changing seasons. Once inside the cool shop, double-entendre intended, browse the useful merchandise and check out a wall cutaway showing the building's unusual straw-bale construction. On the way out, a sign urges, "Turn inspiration into action."

## — WINERIES —

### Brutocao Cellars Tasting Room
*13500 S. Hwy. 101, (800) 433-3689, (707) 744-1664; www.brutocaoschoolhouseplaza.com. Tasting Sun-Thur 10-5, F-Sat to 6.*
This tasting room operates inside an historic building that formerly served as the town's high school. An adjacent garden with 5,000 roses forming a rainbow, some bocce ball courts, a concert area, and several shops are also part of the package.

### Fetzer Vineyards Tasting Room & Visitor Center
*13601 Eastside Rd., (800) 846-8637, (707) 744-7600, (707) 744-7488; www.fetzer.com. Tasting daily 10-5. Self-guided garden tour: Daily 9-5; free. Guided garden tour: Daily; schedule varies; May-Sept only; $6+. Cooking classes: (707) 744-7604.*
Fetzer Vineyards is reached by taking Highway 175 east about a mile through lush meadows. After driving down the elm-lined lane leading into this property, visitors can taste

wine, take a tour of the extensive organic gardens, participate in a cooking class, and even spend the night. Fetzer is the industry leader in farming organic grapes, is heavy into recycling, and is the only U.S. winery that builds its own oak barrels on site. The tasting room offers free samplings of all Fetzer wines, including their famously well-priced Sundial Chardonnay, and its **Valley Oaks Deli** dispenses freshly prepared salads, soups, sandwiches, and other picnic goodies. Guided tours of the impressive and beautiful 5-acre **Bonterra Organic Gardens**, filled with riotously colorful flowers and fragrant herbs and even mulberry trees, are a sensory delight. Special events and cooking classes are scheduled regularly in a well-equipped culinary center overlooking a bucolic pond.

Located in the property's converted carriage house, each of the contemporary-style rooms in the **Fetzer Inn** *(6 rooms; $$-$$$. Pool (seasonal). No smoking; no pets.)* has a vineyard view. Several also have whirlpool tubs.

## – WHERE TO STAY –

### Hopland Inn
*13401 S. Hwy. 101, (800) 266-1891, (707) 744-1890; fax 707-744-1219; www.hoplandinn.com. 21 rooms; $$. Unsuitable for children. Unheated pool (unavail Oct-Apr.). Continental breakfast; restaurant. No smoking; no pets.*

Around since 1890, this inn is the oldest building in town and on the discerning National Historic Register. It is authentically restored, down to the original exterior colors and period furnishings sprinkled throughout. Large, high-ceilinged guest rooms feature coordinated wallpapers and bedspreads, and some have couches or large bathrooms with tubs. Each is named for a local pioneer family and decorated with fascinating historical black-and-white photos of the family. Though situated right on Highway 101, its back rooms are quiet, and as evening descends or as the sun rises, the crowing of a crazed rural rooster might be heard somewhere beyond the busy-ness of the highway. Staying here permits walking just about anywhere in town. In warm weather, a small pool provides respite from the heat, and breakfast is served then on an outdoor patio under an enormous 500-year-old oak. A grand, marble-topped bar, with racks of liquor bottles on either side of a gargantuan mirror and a

rolling ladder for reaching them, is original to the building and a gathering spot for evening refreshment (the bar is open only to inn guests). Then it is just a mosey on into the elegant **dining room** for a tasty meal *(D W-M; $$. Highchairs. Reservations advised.)* prepared by the skilled innkeepers.

## – WHERE TO EAT –

### Bluebird Cafe
*13340 S. Hwy. 101, (707) 744-1633. B-L daily, D F-Sun. Highchairs, boosters, child items.*

It's cool and comfortable inside this restored 1870s commercial building decorated with lace curtains and featuring original light fixtures. Choose from five types of grape juice and five types of burger—ostrich, salmon, turkey, garden, or regular—as well as stir-frys, pastas, and salads. Attractive paintings—all for sale—and a stuffed moose head hang on the walls.

# Clear Lake Area

## – A LITTLE BACKGROUND –

Believed to be the oldest lake in North America, spring-fed Clear Lake is the largest natural fresh-water lake that is totally within California (Lake Tahoe is partially in Nevada). It measures 19 miles by 8 miles. The 90-mile drive around the perimeter takes $2^{1}/_{2}$ to 3 hours.

From the 1870s into the early 1900s, this area was world-famous for its health spas and huge luxury resort hotels. Then, for various reasons, it fell into a state of disrepair and slowly lost its acclaim. Now it is a reasonably priced family resort area.

Lake County's first traffic light was installed in 1982. There are now seven, but it still has no parking meters.

Clear Lake is situated on volcanic terrain, giving it an unusual physical appearance and a profusion of hot springs. According to a Pomo Indian legend, when there is no snow on 4,200-foot Mount Konocti in April, the volcano will erupt. Those who heed legends should check the April snowfall before making vacation plans.

## Lake County Visitor Information Center
*6110 E. Hwy, 20, in Lucerne, (800) LAKESIDE, (707) 274-5652, fax (707) 274-5664; www.lakecounty.com.*

— GETTING THERE —

Located approximately 19 miles east of Hopland via Highway 175.

An alternate route follows Highway 29 north from St. Helena. This scenic route goes through the heart of the Wine Country. The rolling hills are strewn with blooming wild flowers in spring and with brilliantly colored foliage in fall. Make the drive during daylight; this winding two-lane road is tedious to drive at night, and, of course, the lovely scenery cannot be enjoyed then.

— ANNUAL EVENTS —

## Summer Concert Series
*June-August. In Lakeport, in Library Park. Free.*

A little bit of everything is on the program at this casual event. In the past, the mostly-California bands have included Joe Louis Walker and Country Joe and the Fish.

— WHAT TO DO —

Fishing, swimming, boating, rock hunting, golfing, and water-skiing are the big activities here. Fishing is the biggest. The lake is reputed to be the best bass-fishing spot in the West—maybe even the best in the entire country. The lake's nutrient-rich waters are credited with producing plenty of 10-pounders, and the lake record is a 17.52-pounder!

Lakefront public parks and beaches are located in Lakeport and Clearlake.

## Anderson Marsh State Historic Park
*8825 Hwy. 53, between Lower Lake & Clearlake, (707) 994-0688; www.parks.ca.gov. Tu-Sun 10-5. $2/vehicle.*

Acquired by the state in 1982, this 1,065-acre park contains an additional 470 acres of tule marsh. An 1855 ranch house is open to visitors during special events, and tree-shaded picnic tables are provided.

The annual **Blackberry Festival** *(August; (707) 995-BERY. $2-$3.)* features a variety of entertainment and plenty of homemade blackberry pie.

## Clear Lake State Park
*5300 Soda Bay Rd., in Kelseyville, 3.5 mi. NE of town, (707) 279-4293; www.parks.ca.gov. Daily sunrise-sunset. $5/vehicle.*

Located on the shores of the lake, this park offers swimming, fishing, a boat-launching ramp, picnic facilities, campsites, and miles of hiking trails—including the ¼-mile Indian Nature Trail and 3-mile Dorn Nature Trail. A Visitor Center provides a slide show introduction to the area and a Touch Corner for children. Displays include local wildlife dioramas, a native fish aquarium, an erupting volcano, and exhibits on the area's Pomo Indian history.

## Lake County Historic Courthouse Museum
*255 N. Main St., in Lakeport, (707) 263-4555; www.lakecounty.com. W-Sat 11-4, Sun 12-4. Free.*

Formerly a courthouse, this 1871 brick building now holds a renowned collection of Pomo Indian baskets, stone arrowheads, and tools, plus historical records.

## Lower Lake Historic Schoolhouse & Museum

*16435 Morgan Valley Rd., in Lower Lake, (707) 995-3565; www.lakecounty.com. W-Sat 11-4.*

The restored Lower Lake Grammar School houses a reconstructed turn-of-the-century classroom. Museum exhibits include an extensive geological display, a scale model of the dam on Cache Creek, and collections from pioneer families.

## — WHERE TO STAY —

### Jules Resort

*14195 Lakeshore Dr., in Clearlake, (707) 994-2129, fax (707) 994-4814; www.julesresort.com. 18 units; $. Some kitchens. Pool. No pets.*

Lodging here is in pleasant vintage cabins. Facilities include a lakefront pool, private beach, and fishing pier. This place is so popular in the summer that many guests book a year in advance.

### Konocti Harbor Resort & Spa

*8727 Soda Bay Rd., in Kelseyville, (800) 660-LAKE, (707) 279-4281, fax (707) 279-9205; www.konocti harbor.com. 250 rooms; $-$$$+. Children under 12 free. Some kitchens. 2 heated pools; 2 children's wading pools; health spa; fitness room; 8 clay tennis courts (with night lights). Restaurant. No pets.*

Nestled in the shadow of Mount Konocti on the rim of the lake, this beautifully landscaped resort enjoys a superb setting. Reminiscent of luxury resorts in Hawaii, it is a lot easier to reach and much less expensive. The list of facilities and services is extensive: pro tennis lessons, a children's playground, a recreation room, a jogging trail, a bar with live music in the evenings, a miniature golf course, and a marina that rents fishing boats, water-skiing equipment, and pedal boats. Babysitting can be arranged, and tennis, spa, concert, and fishing packages are available. The spa and fitness center offer an additional indoor pool and hot tub, a sauna and steam room, a gym, and a variety of pampering treatments. The **Classic Rock Cafe** offers fun and innovative American meals in a rock museum setting.

A **Classic Concerts by the Lake** series, which has both dinner and cocktail seatings, brings in big name entertainment year-round. In good weather, shows are held in an outdoor amphitheater.

## Skylark Shores Resort Motel

*1120 N. Main St., in Lakeport, (800) 675-6151, (707) 263-6151, fax (707) 263-7733; www.skylark shoresmotel.com. 40 rooms, 5 cabins; $-$$. Children under 1 free. Some kitchens. Heated pool (seasonal). No smoking; no pets.*

These modern motel rooms and cabins are located lakefront. The spacious, well-maintained grounds feature an expansive lawn, swings, and a wading area in the lake.

## — WHERE TO STAY NEARBY —

### Wilbur Hot Springs Health Sanctuary

*3375 Wilbur Springs Rd., near intersection of Hwys. 16 & 20, 25 mi. E of lake, 22 mi. W of Williams, (530) 473-2306; www.wilburhotsprings.com. 20 rooms; $$-$$$. Children under 3 free. No TVs; all shared baths. Pool; 4 hot tubs; sauna. No smoking; no pets. Day use: $40, 4-12 $17.50; reservations required.*

Soaking in one of the four tubs filled with hot sulfurous spring water and then plunging into the cool water of the outdoor pool is the main activity here. Clothing is optional in pool and tub areas only. Several styles of massage are available, and the ambitious can take walks in the surrounding hills. Lodging is in both private rooms and dormitory-style shared rooms; campsites are also available. Rooms have no electrical outlets, so kerosene and solar-powered lamps light the night. A parlor is equipped with a pool table and piano for entertainment, and guests can prepare their own meals in a large communal kitchen (the nearest restaurant is 20 miles away).

## — WHERE TO EAT —

### Park Place

*50 Third St., in Lakeport, (707) 263-0444. L-D daily; $-$$. Highchairs, boosters, child portions. Reservations advised.*

Located lakefront and across the street from Library Park, this cafe offers incredible views from its outdoor rooftop dining area. For starters, don't miss the magnificent bruchetta— a baguette topped with pesto and sun-dried tomatoes and then grilled. The menu has a large selection of fresh pastas, including several kinds of tortellinis and raviolis, plus fresh fish, steaks, and hamburgers.

# Ukiah

— VISITOR INFORMATION —
**Greater Ukiah Chamber of Commerce**
*200 S. School St., (707) 462-4705; www.ukiah chamber.com.*

— GETTING THERE —

Located approximately 15 miles north of Hopland, and 110 miles north of San Francisco.

— WHAT TO DO —

**Grace Hudson Museum** and **Sun House**
*431 S. Main St., (707) 467-2836, fax (707) 467-2835; www.gracehudsonmuseum.org. W-Sat 10-4:30, Sun 12-4:30; tour of house on the hr., 12-3. By donation: $2, $5/family.*

Named for the prominent painter who specialized in doing portraits of the area's Pomo Indians, this museum displays Native American games, musical instruments, and baskets as well as some of Ms. Hudson's personal paraphernalia. Her six-room home, the California Craftsman-style Sun House, is adjacent to the museum. Built of redwood in 1911, it still holds most of its original furnishings. Picnic facilities are available in a park area within the 4½-acre complex.

— WHERE TO STAY —

**Orr Hot Springs**
*13201 Orr Springs Rd., 13 mi. W of Hwy.101, (707) 462-6277, fax (707) 463-2516. 3 rooms, 14 cottages; $$. Children under 3 free. No TVs; some kitchens + communal kitchen; some wood-burning stoves; some shared baths. Unheated mineral water pool; 4 private & 2 communal hot tubs; sauna; steam room. No smoking. Day use: $15-$22, under 18 half price.*

In the 1850s, when this mineral springs resort was built, patrons reached it via stagecoach. Now they get here by driving a scenic, winding, two-lane road. A natural rock swimming pool built into the hillside is filled with cool mineral spring water, and several underground springs are tapped to fill—with body-temperature water—four porcelain Victorian tubs in an 1863 bathhouse. A gas-fired sauna features a stained-glass window and a clear skylight. Note that this is a clothing-optional establishment. Guests sleep in either dormitories, guest rooms, or cottages built in the 1940s from locally milled redwood, and must bring their own food. Campsites are also available. **Montgomery Redwoods State Park**, which offers two loop trails for hiking, is just 1 mile down the road.

**Vichy Springs Mineral Springs Resort**
*2605 Vichy Springs Rd., 3 mi. E of Hwy. 101, (707) 462-9515, fax (707) 462-9516; www.vichysprings.com. 12 rooms, 3 cottages; $$-$$$. Children under 1 free. No TVs; some kitchens & gas fireplaces. Unheated pool & natural hot springs pool; hot tub. Full breakfast. No smoking; no pets. Day use: $35/person.*

Founded in 1854, this 700-acre resort still has three cottages that were built then—two are the oldest still-standing structures in Mendocino County—and a hotel built of redwood in the 1860s. It is the only naturally carbonated warm mineral baths in North America and is named for the famous French springs, which has the same kind of alkaline waters and was discovered by Julius Caesar. In its heyday, the resort attracted guests from San Francisco who endured a day's journey to get here—by ferry across the bay, then by train to Cloverdale, then by stagecoach to the resort. They came in search of curative powers attributed to the waters. Among the famous guests were writers Mark Twain, Jack London, and Robert Louis Stevenson, and presidents Ulysses S. Grant, Benjamin Harrison, and Teddy Roosevelt. The resort's 130-year-old concrete "champagne" tubs are filled with 90-degree, tingling, naturally carbonated water and situated in a shady area overlooking a creek. Swimsuits are required. Guests can swim in an unchlorinated Olympic-size pool, schedule a treatment in the massage cottage, or get in some more rigorous activity with a hike to a 40-foot-high waterfall or a mountain bike ride over dirt roads. Picnic lunches can be arranged, and the resort's own Vichy Springs Mineral Water is available bottled for drinking.

# Willits

— A LITTLE BACKGROUND —

The old-time sign over Main Street, welcoming visitors to the "Gateway to the Redwoods," is Reno's second arch recycled. It was over Virginia

*Mark Twain taking the waters*

Street in Reno, Nevada from 1964 through 1987 and has been here since 1990. (Reno retains its first and third arches.)

## — VISITOR INFORMATION —

### Willits Chamber of Commerce

*239 S. Main St., (707) 459-7910, fax (707) 459-7914; www.willits.org.*

## — GETTING THERE —

Located approximately 25 miles north of Ukiah, and 140 miles north of San Francisco. Heading north after here, it begins getting mountainous and scenic.

## — WHERE TO STAY —

### Emandal Farm

*16500 Hearst Rd., 16 mi. NE of town, (707) 459-5439, fax (707) 459-1808; www.emandal.com. Open for 1-wk. stays during Aug; weekends in spring & fall. 19 cabins; rates vary according to age & include 3 meals per day. No TVs; all shared bathrooms.*

On weekend visits to this 1,000-acre working farm, guests arrive for Friday night dinner. Families are assigned a table for their stay and then spend some blissful hours there chowing down superb home cooking prepared with the farm's own organically grown produce. Days are filled with leisurely activities—perhaps a short hike down to a sandy beach on the magnificent Eel River for a swim, or maybe a hike up the steep hill behind the barn to Rainbow Lake. Some folks just doze in the hammocks outside each of the rustic one-room redwood cabins dating from 1916. Others get involved with farm chores: milking the goats, collecting eggs, feeding the pigs. In fall, the farm's very special jams, relishes, and baking mixes are available by mail order for the holidays.

### KOA Kampground

*1600 Hwy. 20, (800) KOA-8542, (707) 459-6179, fax (707) 459-1489; www.koa.com.*

In a setting of rolling hills and trees, this campground has an Old West theme. Facilities include a swimming pool, fishing pond, petting zoo, mini golf, playground, arcade, rental bikes, and more. In summer, special activities include hayrides and ice cream socials. For more description, see page 443.

## — WHERE TO EAT —

### Fast food

It's all here. Families with small children will favor **Burger King**, **Fosters Freeze**, and **McDonald's**—all of which have colorful playgrounds attached to their dining areas.

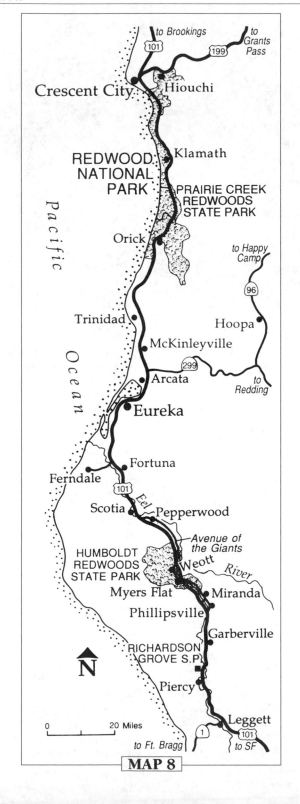

to Brookings
101
to Grants Pass
199

Crescent City
Hiouchi

REDWOOD NATIONAL PARK
Klamath

PRAIRIE CREEK REDWOODS STATE PARK

Pacific

Orick

to Happy Camp
96

Trinidad
Hoopa

McKinleyville
299

Ocean

Arcata
to Redding

Eureka

Fortuna

Ferndale
101

Scotia
Eel
Pepperwood

Avenue of the Giants

HUMBOLDT REDWOODS STATE PARK
Weott
River

Myers Flat
Miranda

Phillipsville

Garberville

N

RICHARDSON GROVE S.P.

Piercy

0        20 Miles

Leggett
1
101

to Ft. Bragg
to SF

**MAP 8**

# The Avenue of the Giants

## — A LITTLE BACKGROUND —

*The redwoods, once seen, leave a mark or create a vision that stays with you always . . . It's not their stature nor the color that seems to shift and vary under your eyes; no, they are not like any other trees we know, they are ambassadors from another time.*
— John Steinbeck, 1962

This spectacularly scenic drive officially begins at Phillipsville, though the scenery begins farther south around Leggett. Actually the old Highway 101, The Avenue of the Giants parallels the freeway and Eel River and is a breathtaking route that winds through grove after grove of huge sequoia sempervirens redwoods. In fact, this route is home to 60 percent of the tallest trees in the world. It continues for 32 miles to Pepperwood, where it rejoins the busier new Highway 101. Unusual sights along this unique stretch of road are numerous. In spots, it juxtaposes nature's best and most majestic with humankind's most kitchy and trite. Fortunately, the number of shops displaying chainsaw-carved redwood souvenirs is small, with plenty of long stretches of uninterrupted tall trees in between.

Millions of years ago, when dinosaurs roamed the earth, forests of gigantic redwoods were plentiful. After the Ice Age, the redwood—which has a life span of 400 to 800 years but sometimes lives beyond 2,000 years—survived only in a narrow 540-mile-long by 40-mile-wide strip along the northern coast of California. Before the logging days on the north coast, it is estimated this area contained $2^{1}/_{2}$ million acres of redwoods. Now only 100,000 acres of ancient old-growth redwoods remain—most preserved in the state and national park systems. Approximately half of these huge old trees are found in Humboldt Redwoods State Park.

## — GETTING THERE —

Phillipsville is 78 miles north of Willits, and 214 miles north of San Francisco.

## — ANNUAL EVENTS —

### Reggae on the River
*August. In Piercy; (707) 923-4583; www.reggae ontheriver.com. $150. No pets.*

Held on the banks of the Eel River, this is considered one of the best reggae music festivals in the world. Only 3-day tickets are available, and it sells out every year.

## — WHAT TO DO —

### Confusion Hill
*75001 N. Hwy. 101, in Piercy, (707) 925-6456. Daily 10-5. House: $5, 4-12 $4. Train (summer only): $7, 4-12 $5.*

Water runs uphill here, appearing to defy gravity, and a miniature train takes passengers on a ride through a tree tunnel to the crest of a hill in the redwoods. This is also home to the world's tallest redwood chainsaw carving.

### Drive-through trees

• **Drive-Thru Tree Park**
*67402 Drive-Thru Tree Rd., in Leggett, (707) 925-6363, fax (707) 925-6455; www.drivethrutree.com. Daily 8-dusk. $3/car.*

Most average-size cars can squeeze through the hole in this 315-foot-high, 21-foot-diameter, 2,400-year-old giant redwood known as the Chandelier Tree. Bring a camera. Nature trails and lakeside picnic tables are available.

• **Shrine Drive-Thru Tree**
*13078 Avenue of the Giants, in Myers Flat, (707) 943-3154. $1.50, under 7 free.*

This 275-foot-tall, still-living tree has a circumference of approximately 64 feet. A natural fire cavity has been widened to accommodate cars, providing the opportunity to take an unusual picture. The site also has a drive-on log and a children's walk-through stump and 2-story tree house, plus each car gets a free postcard.

### Humboldt Redwoods State Park
*In Weott; www.parks.ca.gov. Daily dawn-dusk. $6/vehicle. Visitor Center: 2 mi. S of town, next to Burlington Campground, (707) 946-2409, fax (707) 946-2326; daily 10-4, in summer 9-5.*

This 51,222-acre park straddles the two-lane road, and parts are so dense with trees that sunlight barely filters through. Campsites are available.

The 10,000-acre **Rockefeller Forest** *(Near Weott; accessed from Mattole Rd., (707) 946-2311.)* is the world's largest grove of old-growth virgin redwoods. The entire forest has never been cut, a rarity in these parts. Also referred to as "the world's finest forest," it features hiking trails leading to the Flatiron Tree (shaped like an old-fashioned flat iron), the Giant Tree (which, based on a combination of height, circumference, and crown size, is considered the champion redwood by the American Forestry Association), and the 356-foot-high Tall Tree. In fact, believe it or not!, 10 of the 16 tallest trees in the world stand in this single grove. Easy, baby stroller-friendly trails include Founders Grove Loop and Giant Tree Loop.

The **Children's Forest**, a 1,120-acre memorial to children, is located across the south fork of the Eel River. It is reached by a moderate 2.4-mile round-trip trail beginning at Williams Grove. **Williams Grove** features picturesque picnic and swimming sites on the river.

### Richardson Grove State Park
*1600 Hwy. 101, 8 mi. S of Garberville, (707) 247-3318, fax (707) 247-3300; www.parks.ca.gov.*

This park holds the ninth-tallest coast redwood and a walk-through tree, both of which are easily accessible. Campsites are available.

— WHERE TO STAY —

### Benbow Inn
*445 Lake Benbow Dr., in Garberville, (800) 355-3301, (707) 923-2124, fax (707) 923-2897; www.benbow inn.com. 55 rooms; $-$$$+; closed Jan-Mar. Some TVs & wood-burning fireplaces. Afternoon tea, evening snack; restaurant. No smoking; no pets.*

This magnificent English Tudor inn, which opened to the public in 1926, offers a variety of rooms—all furnished with antiques. Some rooms have lake views and private patios; all are equipped with a basket of mystery novels and a carafe of sherry. A majestic communal lounge with fireplace and library invites socializing, and game tables are set with chessboards and jigsaw puzzles. Interesting art prints decorate the walls throughout. This spot enjoys perfect summer temperatures. Outside pleasures that make the most of it include colorful English gardens with grassy expanses, a small private beach and lake, a putting green, lawn games,

and free bicycles. Off premises, a 9-hole golf course and heated swimming pool are within walking distance. A complimentary tea is served each afternoon at 3 p.m. (non-guests may partake for a small charge), and classic films are screened each evening. Special events are often scheduled, and holiday festivities occur throughout December.

The elegant **restaurant** *(B-L-D daily; $-$$$.)* has an expansive menu, with both simple dishes and more sophisticated fare. In fair weather, a well-priced Sunday champagne brunch buffet is served outdoors on a large terrace overlooking the lake. Additionally, a cozy taproom bar dispenses good cheer and live entertainment on some evenings, and guests can order picnic baskets.

### Miranda Gardens Resort
*6766 Avenue of the Giants, in Miranda, (707) 943-3011, fax (707) 943-3584; www.mirandagardens.com. 16 units; $-$$$. Some kitchens & fireplaces. Heated pool (seasonal). Continental breakfast. No smoking; some pets ok.*

Lodging here is a choice of either motel rooms or redwood cottages. A children's playground and plenty of outdoor games—croquet, shuffleboard, horseshoes—are available out under the redwoods.

# Scotia

— A LITTLE BACKGROUND —

Scotia is one of the last company-owned lumber towns in the United States. Owned by the Pacific Lumber Company, which has its headquarters here, the town was founded in 1869. Today it still caters to workers, providing them with homes and facilities.

— WHAT TO DO —

### Demonstration Forest
*On Hwy. 101, 5 mi. S of town, (707) 764-2222. Daily 8-4; summer only. Free.*

To educate the public about modern forestry practices and permit seeing how a forest grows back after harvest, the Pacific Lumber Company offers self-guided tours through a part of its forest that was harvested in 1941. Picnic tables are available.

## Pacific Lumber Company Lumber Products Tour

*On Main St., (707) 764-4247, fax (707) 764-4150; www.palco.com. M-F 8-1:30. Free.*

Though the world's largest redwood lumber mill closed in 2001, a self-guided tour is available through the company's lumber manufacturing factory. A fisheries exhibit with an indoor aquarium and fish ponds adjoins. Get a pass for the hour-long tour at the **Scotia Museum**, located inside the old Greek Revival-style First National Bank building.

### — WHERE TO STAY —

## Scotia Inn

*100 Main St., (707) 764-5683, fax (707) 764-1707; www.scotiainn.com. 10 rooms; $$-$$$. Children free. Some TVs. Continental breakfast; restaurant. No smoking.*

The hotel that stood on this site in 1888 accommodated travelers waiting for the stagecoach south. The current hotel, built in 1923, greets guests with a magnificent lobby featuring walls of burnished redwood. Rooms are furnished with antiques, and bathrooms feature clawfoot tubs. A splurge on the Bridal Suite is worthwhile just for its impressive private Jacuzzi room. Dinner is served daily in the **Redwood Room** and **Pub**.

# Ferndale

### — A LITTLE BACKGROUND —

Composed of well-preserved and restored Victorian buildings, this tiny village was founded in 1852. It remains largely unchanged since the 1890s—except that then it had 9 churches and 9 saloons and now it has 6 churches and 3 saloons—and is now a state historical landmark. Of special note are the many "butterfat palaces," a local nickname for the elaborate Victorian homes paid for by the area's rich dairy industry.

Now, in addition to the dairy farming, the town prospers as an artists' colony and is filled with galleries and antique shops. Shops of particular interest include the old-time **Ferndale Meat Company** at 376 Main Street, which uses old-fashioned curing and smoking techniques and sells deli items, and the **Golden Gait**

**Mercantile** department store at 421 Main Street, which has creaky floorboards and sells penny candy and other vintage items associated with the good old days. It is so civilized here, that the town bookstore leaves bargain used books out at night in its entryway; anyone who wants to purchase one is on the honor system to slip a dollar through the mail slot.

The scenic pioneer cemetery on a hill behind the old Methodist church is also interesting to visit, and don't miss the circa 1860 gumdrop-shaped coast cypress trees on Ocean Avenue. A great way to get the lay of the land is via a surprisingly well-priced horse-drawn carriage tour with the **Ferndale Carriage Company** *((877) 879-1423. $8+. Reservations advised.).*

In 1994, the whole town starred in the film *Outbreak*.

### — VISITOR INFORMATION —

## Ferndale Chamber of Commerce

*P.O. Box 325, Ferndale 95536, (707) 786-4477, same fax; www.victorianferndale.org/chamber.*

### — GETTING THERE —

Located approximately 265 miles north of San Francisco, 15 miles south of Eureka, and 5 miles west of Highway 101. The exit that leads through Fernbridge permits crossing the Eel River over an historic 1911 bridge that is the oldest reinforced concrete bridge still in existence.

### — ANNUAL EVENTS —

## Cross Country Kinetic Sculpture Race

*May; on Memorial Day Weekend. (707) 845-1717; www.kineticsculpturerace.org. Free.*

In this unusual competition, bizarre and artistic people-powered sculptures race 38 miles over dunes and rivers from Arcata to Ferndale. Cheating is encouraged, and the prizes are questionable. Founder Hobart Brown created this event to promote "adults having fun so kids want to grow up."

## Fortuna Rodeo

*July. In Fortuna; (707) 725-3959; www.fortuna rodeo.com. $7, kids $3.*

The oldest professional rodeo in the West, this event includes a chili cook-off, street games, a parade, a carnival, and more.

## Humboldt County Fair
*August. (707) 786-9511; www.humboldtcountyfair.org.*
*$6, 62+ $3, 6-12 $2; parking $2.*

The oldest uninterrupted county fair in California, this event has happened annually since 1897 and includes carnival rides, horseracing, a goat-calling contest, and more.

## America's Tallest Living Christmas Tree
*December. (707) 786-4477.*

Heralding the Christmas spirit, this village annually rekindles its 125-foot Sitka spruce in a ceremony that has been a tradition since the 1930s.

## Lighted Tractor Parade
*December. (800) 346-3482, (707) 786-4116.*

Area farmers decorate their antique and modern tractors, trailers, and wagons with Christmas lights and holiday scenes.

— WHAT TO DO —

## Ferndale Museum
*515 Shaw Ave., (707) 786-4466; www.gingerbread-*
*mansion.com/ferndalemuseum.html. W-Sat 11-4,*
*Sun 1-4; also Tu in summer; closed Jan.*

Exhibits here include Victorian room settings, a crosscut of a 1,237-year-old redwood, and a working turn-of-the-century seismograph. An annex displays farming, logging, and dairy equipment.

## Kinetic Sculpture Museum
*393 Main St., (707) 786-9634. Daily 10-5. Free.*

Human-powered vehicles designed to travel over roads, mud, sand, and water are on display at this unstaffed museum.

## Loleta Cheese Factory
*252 Loleta Dr., in Loleta, (800) 995-0453, (707) 733-*
*5470, fax (707) 733-1872; www.loletacheese.com.*
*Daily 9-5.*

Known for their Monterey Jacks and smoked salmon Cheddar, this factory has big windows through which the cheese-making process can be observed. Arrive before noon to assure seeing some action. Cheeses are made from the rich milk of cows grazed on the grass and clover pastures of the Eel River Valley, and more than 24 kinds can be tasted, including white cheddars. A note of interest is that part of

*Halloween II* was filmed across the street in the Familiar Foods building.

## Lost Coast
The wildly scenic area of Cape Mendocino—the westernmost point in the continental U.S.—was given this name because of its remoteness. Beginning just south of town, it is reached via steep Wildcat Road. Dating back to the 1870s, Wildcat begins off Ocean Avenue 1 block west of Main Street, then twists and turns for 30 scenic miles to the treacherous waters of the ocean. Look for the sign to "Cape Town—Petrolia." Not many redwoods grow here, as they are repelled by the salt air, but dense Douglas fir forests and unspoiled farmlands make up for that. Make a day of it by traveling all the way to Petrolia, which was the home of California's first oil well in 1865 and where there are campsites and a few inns; and on to Honeydew, to the Rockefeller Forest; then on to Highway 101 to return to Ferndale. Pack in food, a good map, and a full tank of gas, as there are few, if any, concessions along the way. Campsites are available.

— WHERE TO STAY —

## Gingerbread Mansion Inn
*400 Berding St., (800) 952-4136, (707) 786-4000,*
*fax (707) 786-4381; www.gingerbread-mansion.com.*
*11 rooms; $$-$$$+. Unsuitable for children under 9.*
*Some TVs; some wood-burning & gas fireplaces.*
*Afternoon high tea, full breakfast. No smoking.*

Originally built in 1899 as a doctor's home, this carefully restored, cheery peach-and-yellow Queen Anne-Eastlake Victorian mansion boasts gables and turrets and elaborate gingerbread trim. Rooms are furnished with Victorian antiques, and each has its own charm. The Gingerbread Suite features antique "his" and "hers" clawfoot tubs perched toe to toe right in the bedroom, with framed art of bathing babies hanging on the wall above. Several other rooms have spectacular spacious bathrooms equipped with wood-burning fireplaces and twin clawfoot tubs placed side by side. The third-floor attic is the opulent Empire Suite, with a dramatic 12-foot ceiling and marble floor. Guests are pampered: with bathrobes and bubble bath; with breakfast served in the grand dining room and enhanced by use of the owner's collection of green cameo Depression glass; and with a

proper afternoon tea served in the four guest parlors. All food is made on premises, including hand-dipped chocolates that announce bedtime. Guests can stroll or sit in the formal English garden and marvel at its unusual topiaries, 2-story-high camellia bushes, and variety of fuchsias; they can also sit on the second-floor porch and watch the very limited street action.

### Shaw House Inn

*703 Main St., (800) 557-SHAW, (707) 786-9958, fax (707) 786-9758; www.shawhouse.com. 8 rooms; $-$$. Afternoon tea, full breakfast. No smoking; no pets.*

Built in 1854 by the town founder, this white-and-blue gabled Carpenter Gothic Victorian farmhouse, set on park-like grounds way back from the street behind a white picket fence, is the oldest house in town. It is so old that it predates the town of Ferndale. In fact, its original name was Ferndale. Made entirely of redwood, and with unusual paneled ceilings, it is listed on the National Register of Historic Places. Public spaces include a library, two parlors, a dining room, and balconies, and antique furnishings are used throughout. The expansive surrounding garden is designed to reflect the house's era and includes vintage wildflowers, old roses, and fragrant wisterias.

### Victorian Inn

*400 Ocean Ave., (888) 589-1808, (707) 786-4949, fax (707) 786-4558; www.a-victorian-inn.com. 12 rooms; $-$$$. Some fireplaces. Full breakfast; restaurant. No smoking.*

Built in 1890 of local redwood, this massive, high-ceilinged hotel features beautifully appointed rooms with vintage fixtures and furnishings. Some rooms have clawfoot tubs and window alcoves overlooking Main Street.

## — WHERE TO EAT —

### Curley's Grill

*400 Ocean Ave., in the Victorian Inn, (707) 786-9696, fax (707) 786-9697. B Sat-Sun, L-D daily; $-$$. Highchairs, boosters. Reservations advised.*

Extremely popular with locals, this comfortable spot serves generous portions of consistently good food at fair prices. The atmosphere is bright and cheery, with a collection of vintage salt-and-pepper shakers adding a touch of whimsy to each table. Highly touted dishes include a tortilla-and-onion cake and a Caesar salad. More sure things include the housemade soup of the day and the delicate fresh snapper sautéed with lemon and white wine. In addition to full dinners, a hamburger, a vegetarian burger, and several sandwiches and salads are available.

### Ferndale Pizza Company

*607 Main St., (707) 786-4345. L-D Tu-Sun; $. Highchairs, boosters.*

Operating out of a converted vintage gas station, this modest, cozy spot serves up delicious hand-thrown pizza and sandwiches served on housemade rolls. The owner grinds his meats and hand-forms the meatballs.

## Eureka

### — A LITTLE BACKGROUND —

Eureka was founded in 1850 as a gold rush supply base for inland mines. By 1865 it had shifted into harvesting lumber for shipbuilding and housing. Over time, ambitious logging activity has changed the scenery here quite a bit. The best of the remaining virgin redwoods are in this area's state parks, all of which were established in the 1920s.

A small town with a welcoming attitude and atmosphere, Eureka is known as "the coolest city in the nation." The average temperature in July ranges from 52 to 60 degrees. In January, it drops to between 41 and 53 degrees. In fact, the highest temperature ever recorded in Eureka was 87 degrees on October 26, 1993. The average annual rainfall is 37 inches, and fog can sometimes be heavy even in summer.

The winter off-season is an uncrowded time to visit the north coast redwood country around Humboldt Bay. Visitors then should pack warm clothing and kiss the sunshine good-bye as they prepare to enjoy the stunning beauty of this quiet, often misty area.

Eureka and nearby Arcata are both known for their brightly painted, well-preserved Victorian houses. In fact, Eureka has more Victorian buildings than any other city in the U.S. See an interesting selection by driving down Hillsdale Street between E and C streets.

Be warned that gas is expensive here. That's because it is brought in by barge.

## – VISITOR INFORMATION –

### Humboldt County Convention & Visitors Bureau
*1034 2nd St., (800) 346-3482, (707) 443-5097, fax (707) 443-5115; www.redwoods.info.*

### The Greater Eureka Chamber of Commerce
*2112 Broadway, (800) 356-6381, (707) 442-3738.*

## – GETTING THERE –

Located approximately 130 miles north of Willits, and approximately 280 miles north of San Francisco.

## – ANNUAL EVENTS –

### Independence Day Humboldt Bay 4th of July Festival
*July. (707) 442-9054. Free.*

For this old-fashioned celebration, a street festival takes over four city blocks with live entertainment, train rides, and children's activities. It culminates with a fireworks extravaganza over Humboldt Bay.

### A Coastal Christmas
*November-December. (800) 346-3482.*

The whole town is decorated elaborately for the season, and lodgings book up fast. Call for a brochure.

### Truckers Christmas Light Convoy
*December. (800) 346-3482, (707) 442-5744. Free.*

Each year over 150 18-wheel big rigs— decorated with thousands of twinkling lights and loaded with "candy cane" logs—are seen truckin' through town in a slow procession. A crane carries the manger scene, carolers sing from a hay hauler, and cows pull Santa's sled.

## – WHAT TO DO –

### Blue Ox Millworks
*Foot of X St., 3 blks. N of 4th St., (800) 248-4259, (707) 444-3437, fax (707) 444-0918; www.blueox mill.com. M-Sat 9-4. $7.50, 65+ $6.50, 6-12 $3.50.*

Dozens of antique woodworking machines are seen in this working museum on a self-guided, 1-hour tour. The oldest dates back to 1860, the newest to 1948. Many of the Victorian-era machines are pedal-powered and currently used to reproduce gingerbread trim for renovated Victorian homes. Of special interest are several cabins built on sleds, or "skids," so they could be pulled through the snow to new logging sites. Kids particularly enjoy

*Carson Mansion*

meeting the assortment of farm animals, including two resident blue oxen weighing in at 2,000 pounds each.

## Carson Mansion
*143 M St./2nd St.*

Built between 1884 and 1886, this is said to be the most photographed Victorian house in the world and is the "queen" of Victorian architecture. It is a mixture of several building styles—including Queen Anne, Italianate, and Stick-Eastlake—and took 100 men more than 2 years to build. Pioneer lumber baron William Carson, a failed gold miner, privately financed it in order to avoid laying off his best men during a depression. It now houses a private club and can be viewed only from the exterior.

## Clarke Historical Museum
*240 E St./3rd St., in Old Town, (707) 443-1947, fax (707) 443-0290; www.clarkemuseum.org. Tu-Sat 11-4. Free.*

An important collection of local Indian baskets and ceremonial regalia is on display here along with an extensive collection of 19th-century regional artifacts and pioneer relics. The palatial 1912 building is also the backdrop for displays of antique weapons and Victorian furniture and decorative arts.

## Covered bridges
*Take Hwy. 101 S to Elk River Rd., then follow Elk River Rd. to either Bertas Rd. (2 mi.) or Zanes Rd. (3 mi.).*

These two all-wood covered bridges were constructed of redwood in 1936. **Berta's Ranch bridge** is the most westerly covered bridge in the U.S. **Zane's Ranch bridge** is the second-most westerly covered bridge in the U.S. Both are 52 feet long.

## Fort Humboldt State Historic Park
*3431 Fort Ave., at S end of town, (707) 445-6567; www.parks.ca.gov. Daily 8-5. Free.*

U.S. Grant was posted here in 1854. The hospital, which dates to 1863, is restored and now used as a museum. Exhibits within the park include some locomotives, a restored logger's cabin, and displays of pioneer logging methods. An excellent view of Humboldt Bay makes this a nice spot for a picnic. The Junior Ranger Program operates in summer (see page 445).

At the annual **Dolbeer Donkey Days**, held in April, antique equipment is put into action. Steam donkeys are operated, and logging techniques are demonstrated. Train rides are part of the fun.

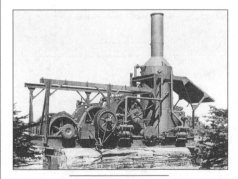

*Dolbur steam donkey*

## Humboldt Bay Harbor Cruise
*Foot of C St., (707) 445-1910, fax (707) 445-0249. Tu-Sat at 1 & 2:30, W-Sat also at 4; closed Nov-Apr. $12.50, 60+ & 13-17 $10.50, 5-12 $6.50. Additional charge for cocktail cruise Thur-Sat at 5:30 & SunBr every other wk. at 11.*

The 75-minute cruise aboard the tiny 40-passenger *M/V Madaket*—which once ferried workers to the lumber mills across the bay in Samoa—allows a view of the bustling activity and native wildlife of the bay. Built in 1910 in nearby Fairhaven, it is the oldest operating passenger vessel in the U.S. and has the smallest licensed bar in the state.

## Morris Graves Museum of Art

*636 F St./7th St., (707) 442-0278, fax (707) 442-2040; www.humboldtarts.org. Thur-Sun 12-5. Free.*

Located within the historic Carnegie Library building, which was the state's first free public library in 1904, this new museum features beautifully restored woodwork and a magnificent tile floor. It displays local and traveling exhibitions and has an outdoor sculpture garden and a small performance space. Kids have their own art program and gallery downstairs.

## Old Town

*1st St./2nd St./3rd St., from C St. to G St., (707) 443-5097.*

This waterfront area consists of restored commercial and residential Victorian buildings. Many restaurants, boutiques, and antique shops are located here, including the original **Restoration Hardware**. The **Romano Gabriel Sculpture Garden**—a folk art garden constructed from vegetable crates by the late artist Romano Gabriel—can be viewed at 315 2nd Street. A new Boardwalk along the waterfront stretches for 4 blocks and is a great place to stroll, sit, and just watch people and wildlife.

## Sequoia Park Zoo

*3414 W St./Glatt St., (707) 442-6552; www.eureka webs.com/zoo. Tu-Sun 10-5; May-Sept to 7. Free.*

The backdrop for this combination zoo/playground/picnic area is a 77-acre forest of old-growth redwoods. Local Roosevelt elk, brown bears, and river otters are displayed, and a petting zoo is open in summer from 11:30 a.m. to 3:30 p.m. The forest has hiking trails and a duck pond.

## — WHERE TO STAY —

## Abigail's "Elegant Victorian Mansion"

*1406 C St., (707) 444-3144, (707) 442-5594; www.eureka-california.com. 4 rooms; $-$$. Unsuitable for children. Some shared baths. Sauna. Afternoon snack, continental breakfast. No smoking; no pets.*

A National Historic Landmark, this spectacular 1888 Queen Anne-influenced Eastlake Victorian was built originally for the town mayor. It is located in a residential neighborhood overlooking Humboldt Bay. Opulently decorated with many of the innkeeper's family heirlooms, its public spaces include two parlors, a library, and a sitting room. Guests are entertained by such nostalgic pleasures as listening to the Victrola and watching silent movies. Each guest room is unique, but the Van Gogh Room is exceptional in that it displays an original watercolor by the artist as well as several original works by Dali. The afternoon snack here is old-time lemonade, or maybe an ice cream soda, but certainly *not* contemporary wine and cheese. The house is set on a tranquil, park-like estate complete with manicured Victorian flower gardens and a croquet lawn, and bicycles can be borrowed. Perfectly accenting the inn's splendor is the spirited innkeepers' enthusiasm for sharing information about anything that might intrigue a guest. Town tours from the rumble seat of a lovingly restored Model T can be arranged, with the dramatic innkeeper dressed in charming era garb and donning a straw hat. A visit here offers a step back in time to a more gracious era; it is a sort of Victorian living history experience. A lavish, formal breakfast is served at an elegantly set table and includes the house coffee—a fragrant blend with hints of chocolate and hazelnut.

## Carter House Inns

*(800) 404-1390, (707) 444-8062, fax (707) 444-8067; www.carterhouse.com. $$-$$$+. Children under 12 free. Afternoon & evening snack, full breakfast; restaurant; room service. No smoking; no pets.*

Looking like it has been here forever, the weather-darkened redwood inn that is the **Carter House** *(1033 3rd St./L St. 4 stories; 6 rooms. Unsuitable for toddlers. 1 fireplace.)* was actually built by owner Mark Carter in 1982. It is a replica of an 1884 Eastlake Victorian design of two San Francisco architects, one of whom designed Eureka's famous Carson Mansion. (The original house stood on the corner of Bush and Jones streets in San Francisco and was destroyed in the fire following the 1906 earthquake.) Rooms are all oversize and elegantly furnished.

Across the street, the **Hotel Carter** *(301 L St. 24 rooms. Some gas fireplaces.)* was built in 1984 to replicate a long gone Victorian inn originally in the area. It provides casual, tasteful lodging amenable to families. Some large suites have showers built for two and in-room hot tubs large enough for a family of four, and a video library of almost 300 films is available at minimal charge. An impressive **wine shop** operates off the lobby.

**Bell Cottage** *(1023 3rd St. 3 rooms. Shared kitchen; some wood-burning & gas fireplaces.)* is adjacent to the Carter House. The romantic Victorian **Carter Cottage** *(1027 3rd St. 1 room. Kitchen; 2 gas fireplaces.)* features a deep marble spa tub and fireplaces in both the sleeping and living areas.

The owner's substantial collection of original local art is displayed throughout the inns. In the evening wine and hors d'oeuvres are available, and at bedtime cookies and tea appear. Interested guests may visit the herb and vegetable garden that supplies the restaurant. It is the most extensive inn kitchen garden on the West Coast.

**Restaurant 301** *(In Hotel Carter. B-D daily. Highchairs. Reservations advised.)* offers an elegant dinner menu showcasing the region's finest seasonal delicacies, including Kumamoto oysters and Pacific salmon. Designed to please both the eye and the palate, entrees are arranged artistically on oversize plates and garnished with such delights as fresh flowers and herb sprigs. Past menu selections have included flavorful squash cakes, chicken cacciatora with creamy polenta, and grilled pork loin with both housemade chutney and applesauce. A well-priced five-course, fixed price dinner is available with optional selected wine pairings. In addition to an extensive, carefully chosen wine list, bar drinks are available. Breakfast for the inns is provided here and includes a pastry buffet and a hot egg dish served to the table.

### The Daly Inn
*1125 H St., (800) 321-9656, (707) 445-3638; www.dalyinn.com. 5 rooms; $-$$$. Unsuitable for children under 12. Evening snack, full breakfast. No smoking; no pets.*

Built in 1905, this elegantly restored Colonial Revival mansion is furnished with interesting antiques and decorated with an array of exquisite wallpaper patterns. Public spaces include a sun porch and TV room.

### KOA Kampground
*4050 N. Hwy 101, 4 mi. N of town, (800) KOA-3136,*

*(707) 822-4243, fax (707)822-0126; www.koa.com. Pool & hot tub (seasonal); sauna.*

For description, see page 443.

### Motel Row
Last-minute accommodations can usually be found along both 4th and 5th streets and Broadway.

### — WHERE TO EAT —

### Bon Boniere
*215 F St., in Old Town, (707) 268-0122. M-F 11-9, Sat-Sun to 11; $. Child menu.*

The most kid-friendly place in Old Town, this old-fashioned ice cream parlor operates inside an atmospheric brick-walled room with high ceilings, marble-topped tables, and a long counter topped with jars of sweets. It's been serving up goodies since 1898. The best lunch just might be a hot dog with all the trimmings and a black cherry milkshake prepared with housemade ice cream. Before leaving, stock up on golf ball-size jawbreakers and long red licorice whips. Cones and frozen bananas to go are also an option.

### Café Waterfront
*102 F St., in Old Town, (707) 443-9190; www.cafe waterfront.com. B-L-D daily; $-$$. Highchairs, boosters.*

Operating within a Queen Anne Victorian, this restaurant has one cozy room with a very high ceiling and a tall bar that provides additional seating. The menu offers tasty fresh seafood dishes as well as simple soups, salads, and burgers. Two beautifully decorated **guest rooms** are available upstairs.

### Los Bagels
*403 2nd St., in Old Town, (707) 442-8525; www.losbagels.com. B-L W-M; $. Highchairs, boosters.*

This attractive, high-ceilinged building is the place to go for a quick snack or meal of house-made bagels and other freshly baked goods. Mexican hot chocolate, fresh juices, and smoothies are also on the limited menu.

### Lost Coast Brewery & Cafe
*617 4th St., in Old Town, (707) 445-4480, fax (707) 445-4483; www.lostcoast.com. L-D daily; $.*

Situated within an historic building, this is the first brewery in the U.S. founded and operated by women. Among the several kinds of handcrafted microbrews, the hands-down favorite seems to be the Downtown Brown Ale. Inexpensive pub fare is available—some prepared with the house beers as an ingredient—and goes well with a pint.

## Samoa Cookhouse

*On Cookhouse Dr. (from Hwy. 101 take Samoa Bridge to end, turn left on Samoa Blvd., then take first left turn), (707) 442-1659, fax (707)442-1699; www.humboldtdining.com/cookhouse. B-L-D daily; $. Highchairs, boosters, child prices (under 5 free). No reservations.*

Originally built in the 1890s by the Georgia-Pacific Corporation to feed its loggers, this is the last surviving cookhouse in the West. There is no menu. Just sit down at one of the long, boarding house-style tables and a hearty, delicious, family-style meal starts arriving. Though the menu changes daily, a typical breakfast consists of biscuits and gravy, fluffy scrambled eggs, pancakes, sausage, and coffee or tea. Lunch might consist of marinated three-bean salad, long-simmered and flavorful Florentine tomato soup, fresh-baked bread with butter and assorted jams, green salad with ranch dressing and croutons, rice pilaf, lemon-pepper chicken, saucy beans, peas, chocolate cake with chocolate pudding frosting and whipped cream topping, and coffee or tea. A fantastic value! Most dishes are prepared from scratch with fresh ingredients. The only items not included in the fixed price are milk and sodas.

After dining, wander through the free **mini-logging museum** of artifacts and historic photos. Work up an appetite before, or work off some calories after, with a walk along the area's driftwood-strewn beaches. To find them, follow any of the unmarked turnoffs from Samoa Boulevard.

# Arcata

Home to Humboldt State University, this small city is centered around an old-fashioned town square lined with bookstores, coffeehouses, and inexpensive restaurants. It is a birder's paradise;

enthusiasts can call (707) 822-LOON for a run-down on the current rare-bird sightings in the area.

— VISITOR INFORMATION —

## Arcata Chamber of Commerce

*1635 Heindon Rd.., (707) 822-3619, fax (707) 822-3515; www.arcatachamber.com.*

This is also the location of the **California Welcome Center**.

— GETTING THERE —

Located 5 miles north of Eureka.

— ANNUAL EVENTS —

## Godwit Days

*April. (800) 908-WING, (707) 822-4500; www.god witdays.com. Free-$40.*

Named for the Marbled Godwit—a large brown shorebird with a long, slightly upturned bill—this fair celebrates the spring bird migration with seminars and exhibits.

## Arcata Bay Oyster Festival

*June. (707) 822-4500.*

Humboldt Bay produces 90% of California's oysters. Most local restaurants feature them on their menus, and this annual festival celebrates the bounty.

— WHAT TO DO —

## Arcata Marsh and Wildlife Sanctuary

*600 S. G St., (707) 826-2359. Interpretive center: daily 9-5; tour Sat at 8:30am. Free.*

Home and temporary refuge to more than 200 species of bird, this is a breeding area for ducks and other waterfowl and a feeding area for fish-eating birds such as osprey, herons, grebes, and egrets. At low tide, people flock here to view the thousands of shore birds foraging on the mud flats of Humboldt Bay. Though birds are here year-round, the largest variety is seen during the fall and spring migrations. Facilities include 4$^{1/2}$ miles of trails, observation blinds, an interpretive center, and a picnic area. After that description, it is amazing to learn that this thriving, scenic wetlands preserve is positioned over the former city dump and currently treats and recycles the city's wastewater and sewage.

### Fire & Light Originals
*45 Erickson Ct., (800) 844-2223, (707) 825-7500, fax (707) 825-7700; www.fireandlight.com. Tour W at 10; free; reservations required.*

Every month U.S. citizens throw away enough bottles and jars to fill a giant skyscraper. Doing its bit to stem that tide, this unusual enterprise makes beautiful, high quality tableware from hand-poured recycled glass.

## — WHERE TO EAT —

### Jacoby's Storehouse
*791 8th St., on the plaza.*

Built in 1857, this fireproof stone storehouse once supplied the mule trains headed to the gold mines. It is the oldest masonry building in Humboldt County. Interesting features include pressed-tin ceilings and unusual stained-glass light fixtures.

On the first floor, **Abruzzi** *((707) 826-2345, fax (707)826-0514; www.abruzzi catering.com. $$-$$$.)* is a popular spot to celebrate a special occasion. With crisp white nappery and a romantic atmosphere, the restaurant specializes in housemade breads and pastas and serves fine Italian cuisine.

On the second floor, amid a pathway of interesting boutiques, the **Bon Boniere** ice cream parlor *((707) 822-6388. Daily 10-10.)* dishes up everything cold and creamy. For more description, see page 259.

On the third floor, the **Plaza Grill** *((707) 826-0860. D daily; $. Child menu.)* is a casual spot that is good with kids. A barkeep mixes up cocktails, and the menu offers sandwiches, salads, and grilled fresh fish and steaks. The fireplace here came from actor Humphrey Bogart's house in Los Angeles, and beautiful etched glass-and-grillwork windows hail from the Plaza Hotel in New York City.

### Los Bagels
*1061 I St., (707) 822-3150; www.losbagels.com.*
For description, see page 259.

# Trinidad

## — A LITTLE BACKGROUND —

Older than Eureka by about 4 months, this scenic fishing village was a supply port for gold miners in the 1850s and later became a whaling port. Its circa 1860 lighthouse still operates, and it boasts a very nice beach.

## — VISITOR INFORMATION —

### Greater Trinidad Chamber of Commerce
*P.O. Box 356, Trinidad 95570, (707) 677-1610; www.trinidadcalif.com.*

## — GETTING THERE —

Located 23 miles north of Eureka.

## — WHAT TO DO —

### Humboldt State University Marine Laboratory
*570 Ewing St., (707) 826-3671, fax (707) 826-3682; www.humboldt.edu/~marinelb. M-F 8-5, Sat-Sun 10-5; closed Sat-Sun in summer. Free.*

This research facility has a small aquarium exhibit and a touch tank that are open to the public. A 30-minute guided tour is available by reservation.

### Patrick's Point State Park
*4150 Patrick's Point Dr., 6 mi. N of town, (707) 677-3570; www.parks.ca.gov. $5/vehicle.*

Whale-watching and weddings are both prime at Wedding Rock, where some grey whales have become year-round residents off shore. A few years ago, stargazing was part of the scene, too, literally, when *The Lost World* was filmed here. Agate Beach Trail leads to its namesake beach via a steep, winding trail with lots of stairs, and Octopus Trees Trail passes by Sitka spruces, whose odd roots cause them to resemble octopuses. This 632-acre park is also home to an authentically re-created Yurok Indian village, and a Visitor Center has relevant displays. Campsites are available.

## — WHERE TO STAY —

### Bishop Pine Lodge
*1481 Patrick's Point Dr., (707) 677-3314, fax (707) 677-3444; www.bishoppinelodge.com. 12 cabins; $-$$. Some kitchens. Fitness room. No smoking; pets ok.*

These cozy one-room and two-bedroom cabins are tucked among redwoods. Built in the 1920s, they are renovated and feature modern amenities. Charming shutters with pine tree cutouts frame the multi-paned windows on the rustic exteriors, while knotty-pine paneling warms up interiors. A few swings and a basketball area are available for children on the spacious, well-maintained grounds, and one unit has a semi-private sunken hot tub on its redwood deck.

### The Emerald Forest
*753 Patrick's Point Dr., (707) 677-3554, fax (707) 677-0963; www.cabinsintheredwoods.com. 12 cabins; $-$$. Dogs ok in some cabins.*

Set back in a deep, dark forest of tall trees, this spacious old-time property has a campground as well as rustic cabins. A three-bedroom, two-bath family cabin that sleeps eight is available, or parents of older children can rent one cabin for themselves and a separate, smaller one nearby equipped with bunk beds for the kids. Facilities include a children's playground with wooden structures, a rec room, and a small general store.

### The Lost Whale Inn
*3452 Patrick's Point Dr., (800) 677-7859, (707) 677-3425, fax (707) 677-0284; www.lostwhaleinn.com. 8 rooms, 3 houses; $$-$$$+. Children under 3 free. No TVs. Hot tub. Afternoon snack, full breakfast. No smoking; no pets.*

Set back on a bluff above the ocean, this contemporary Cape Cod-style farmhouse inn features spacious rooms—five with spectacular ocean views. Guests often wake up to the sound of sea lions barking out on Turtle Rock, and migrating whales are sometimes seen from the dining room or deck while eating breakfast. A steep, scenic wooded trail leads to the inn's private beach, and Patrick's Point State Park is just down the road. Children, who are especially welcomed and well cared for here, can look forward to picking berries, fantasizing in a playhouse, frolicking on a playground, and feeding the inn's ducks and goats. Two suites have special sleeping lofts for children.

### — WHERE TO EAT —
### Seascape Restaurant
*1 Bay St., (707) 677-3762. B-L-D daily; $$. Highchairs, boosters, booths, child menu.*

Owned and operated by the Cher-Ae Heights Indian Community of the Trinidad Rancheria, this casual spot at the base of the pier has rustic stone walls, comfy booths, and big windows with views of the scenic cliff-edged bay. Breakfast is served until 4 p.m. The menu stresses fresh seafood, and lunches are a particular bargain.

# Klamath

### — VISITOR INFORMATION —
### Klamath Chamber of Commerce
*P.O. Box 476, Klamath 95548, (800) 200-2335, (707) 482-7165, fax (707) 482-2251; www.klamathcc.org.*

### — GETTING THERE —
Located approximately 60 miles north of Eureka, and approximately 40 miles south of the Oregon border.

### — WHAT TO DO —
### Klamath River Jet Boat Tours
*On Hwy. 101 S., (800) 887-JETS, (707) 482-5822; www.jetboattours.com. Schedule & rates vary; May-Oct only.*

This invigorating journey begins at the Klamath estuary called "Rekwoi"—the Native American word for where fresh water meets the Pacific Ocean. From there, the boat turns upriver for a closer look at the area's natural wildlife. With flat bottoms and no rudder or propeller, jet boats provide a smooth and safe, yet fast and exciting, ride. Some trips include an optional barbecue dinner, and overnighting at a remote wilderness lodge can be arranged.

### Prairie Creek Redwoods State Park
*On Hwy. 101, 6 mi. N of Orick, (707) 464-6101 x5301; www.parks.ca.gov. Daily 9:30-5. $5/vehicle.*

The 8-mile unpaved gravel road to Gold Bluffs Beach and Fern Canyon—where a short, easy 1.5-mile loop trail awaits—passes through a beautiful forest into an area of vertical cliff walls carpeted with ferns and mosses. Steven Spielberg filmed part of *The Lost World: Jurassic Park II* here. This 14,000-acre park is a refuge for one of the few remaining herds of native Roosevelt elk, which are the largest mammals in California. Viewing is prime from mid-September to mid-October at the Elk Prairie section on Newton Drury Scenic Parkway. Campsites are available.

## Redwood National Park
*Visitor Centers in Orick (1 mi. S of town) & Hiouchi (summer only), (707) 464-6101, fax (707) 464-1812; www.nps.gov/redw. Daily 9-5. Free.*

This magnificent, sprawling national park encompasses 105,000 acres. It has numerous entrances, so take time to stop at a visitor center to get oriented and to inquire about borrowing Family Adventure Packs to use with children. Ranger-led interpretive programs are scheduled daily June through August. **Ladybird Johnson Grove** (*On Bald Hills Rd., off Hwy. 101.*) is an easy, level 1-mile loop. Permits are required for visiting the **Tall Trees Grove**, which contains the world's tallest tree (367.8 feet) as well as the second, third, and fifth tallest trees. The walk takes about 4 hours and covers 3.2 miles. The permits are free at the Orick Visitor Center. Roosevelt elk are often seen in the Elk Meadow section of the park on Davison Road, south of Prairie Creek Redwoods State Park

## Trees of Mystery
*15500 Hwy. 101 N., (800) 638-3389, (707) 482-2251, fax (707) 482-2005; www.treesofmystery.net. Daily 9-5, in summer 8-8. $12, 60+ $10, 4-10 $5.*

As visitors approach this privately owned grove of redwoods, they are greeted by a 50-foot-tall Paul Bunyan and a 32-foot-tall Babe. This is fun for kids, and they can pose free for a picture on Paul's boot without entering the park. The 8/10 -mile trail inside, which is steep in parts, passes through a tunnel made from a hollowed-out log and continues on past a well-maintained group of unusual trees. In a setting at times reminiscent of Disney meets Ripley's Believe It or Not!, visitors see the Candelabra Tree with new trees growing off its fallen trunk,

the famous Cathedral Tree with nine trees growing from one root structure, and similar natural wonders. A section displays intricate redwood carvings that tell the tale of Paul Bunyan along with a recorded narration. The silent 1/4-mile SkyTrail aerial gondola ride through the redwood forest canopy lets riders get off at the top to view the panorama through binoculars provided on an observation deck.

The world's largest private collection of Native American artifacts is displayed in the back of the gift shop in the **End of the Trail Museum**; admission is free. Displays include colorful beaded-leather clothing, arrowheads, dolls, and baskets. Two snack bars and picnic facilities are available.

## — WHERE TO STAY —

## Redwood National Park Hostel
*14480 Hwy. 101 N., 7 mi. N of town, 12 mi. S of Crescent City, (800) 909-4776 x74, (707) 482-8265, fax (707) 482-4665; www.norcalhostels.org. 30 beds; 1 private room. Closed Dec-Feb.*

This northernmost link in the California coast hostel chain is located within national park boundaries. Operating within the historic circa 1890s pioneer DeMartin House, it has a full kitchen and spectacular ocean views. See also page 445.

## Requa Inn
*451 Requa Rd., (866) 800-8777, (707) 482-1425, fax (707) 482-0844; www.requainn.com. 10 rooms; $-$$. Closed Jan-Feb. Unsuitable for young children. No TVs. Full breakfast; restaurant. No smoking; no pets.*

This restored historic hotel dating from 1885 has comfortable, pleasantly decorated rooms. The dining room serves a surf-and-turf menu. Fishermen particularly favor the location at the scenic mouth of the Klamath River in the center of Redwood National Park.

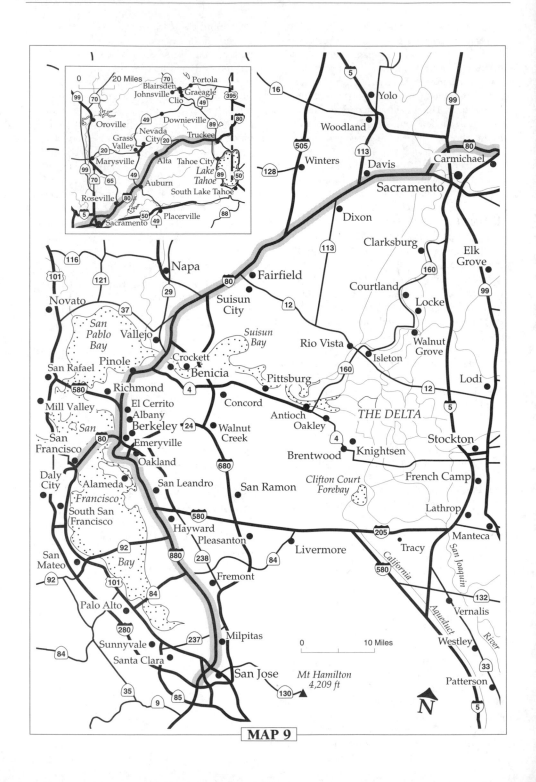

**MAP 9**

# I-80 NORTH

## Emeryville

### – A LITTLE BACKGROUND –

This industrial city is home to **Pixar Studios**, famous for animation movies like *Toy Story* and *Finding Nemo*.

### – WHAT TO DO –

**Bay Street Emeryville**
*Bay St./Christie Ave., (510) 655-4002; www.baystreet emeryville.com. Most shops: M-Sat 10-8, Sun 11-6.*
Built above a large Indian burial ground, this shopping center has shops and restaurants galore plus a 16-screen **AMC movie complex**.

### – WHERE TO EAT –

**Emeryville Public Market**
*5959 Shellmound St./Powell St., (510) 652-9300; www.emerymarket.com. B-L-D daily.*
In this cavernous building's food court, just about every ethnic cuisine imaginable is purveyed at bargain prices. Middle Eastern items from **Sara Deli** and Chinese items from **The Crispy Fry** are especially delicious. People-watching is prime, and a **Borders** bookstore and a movie multi-plex are adjacent.

**Hong Kong East Ocean Seafood Restaurant**
*3199 Powell St., (510) 655-3388 or (510) 655-3389, fax (510) 654-5349. Dim sum M-F 11-2:30, Sat-Sun 10-2:30; D daily; $-$$. Highchairs, boosters. Reservations accepted for D.*
Surprisingly, this out-of-the-way restaurant, reached via a scenic waterfront drive, serves up dim sum every bit as good as that found in San Francisco's Chinatown and has waits almost as long. Except here a gorgeous bay view can be enjoyed while waiting and dining. Light Cantonese seafood and vegetable dishes are also available. Dim sum is not brought around on carts or trays here. Instead, diners mark their selections on a menu form.

## Berkeley

### A LITTLE BACKGROUND

The always-fascinating community of Berkeley is a study in contrasts. Visitors arrive with a variety of expectations. Some seek the intellectual climate associated with a community built around the University of California, the state's most prestigious public university. Others expect to see weird people and hippie communes. Those who know their food come seeking the acclaimed restaurants, and those who know one of the town's nicknames, Berserkley, expect to see a bit of that. Then there is the well-known ultra-liberal political climate, in which someone who would be thought a liberal elsewhere is here considered a conservative, which explains another nickname—the People's Republic of Berkeley. In reality, Berkeley is all these things, and, making any stereotype impossible, it also is the place where the word "yuppie" was coined. Berkeley has also pioneered many frontiers. It was the first city in the nation with a public health department, the first to have a lie-detector machine, the first with curb cuts for wheelchairs, the first to ban Styrofoam, and the first to rename Columbus Day the more politically correct "Indigenous Peoples Day" (it's listed that way under "holidays" on parking meters). And it is the place where plutonium and berkelium—the 97th element—were discovered.

### — VISITOR INFORMATION —

**Berkeley Convention & Visitors Bureau**
*2015 Center St., (800) 847-4823, (510) 549-7040, fax (510) 644-2052; www.visitberkeley.com.*

### — GETTING THERE —

Cross the Bay Bridge and follow the signs to I-80 north. The central Berkeley exit is University Avenue.

### — ANNUAL EVENTS —

**Spring House Tour**
*April. (510) 841-2242; www.berkeleyheritage.com. $20-$25.*

   Sponsored by the Berkeley Architectural Heritage Association, this tour provides access to some of the city's many architecturally interesting homes. Related talks are usually scheduled.

**Live Oak Park Fair**
*June. (510) 898-3282; www.liveoakparkfair.com. Free.*

   This has evolved into a first-rate juried arts-and-crafts show, with live entertainment and some food booths. The park itself—with its mature shade trees, rolling lawns, and meandering creek—is inviting to visit any time.

**Berkeley Kite Festival & West Coast Kite Championships**
*July. In Cesar E. Chavez Park at Berkeley Marina. (510) 235-KITE; www.highlinekites.com. Free.*

   Tell someone to "go fly a kite" at this exhilarating event. Or better yet, tag along and see kites galore, plus Japanese-style Rokkaku kite battles and taiko drummers.

**How Berkeley Can You Be? Parade**
*September. Along University Ave., (510) 654-6346; www.howberkeleycanyoube.com. Free.*

   Bizarre marching groups wear their Berkeleyest costumes. Parade includes puppets, floats, and art cars.

**Solano Avenue Stroll**
*September. (510) 527-5358, fax (510) 548-5335; www.solanostroll.org. Free.*

   This mile-long block party is the oldest and largest free street festival in the East Bay. Strollers can munch their way from one end to the other.

**International Taiko Festival**
*November. At U.C. Berkeley, Zellerbach Hall. (415) 928-2456, same fax; www.taikodojo.org. $22-$36.*

   It's hard to imagine something more exhilarating than witnessing one muscle-bound taiko drummer after another beating out an intoxicating primal rhythm. Dating back 2,000 years, the thunderous sound of these drums was once used to stimulate rain and then, later, to signal Japanese armies into battle. It is said to be the heartbeat of the Japanese people. San Francisco's internationally acclaimed Taiko Dojo usually performs on a 1-ton, 12-foot-high drum—the largest in the western hemisphere.

### — WHAT TO DO —

**Adventure Playground**
*160 University Ave., in Shorebird Park, (510) 981-6720, fax (510) 981-6725; www.ci.berkeley.ca.us/parks. Sat-Sun 11-4; in summer M-F 9-5, Sat-Sun 11-5. Free for children accompanied by adults, or $5/3 hrs.*

   The story goes that in Europe after World War II a designer built a series of modern playgrounds. But the children continued, indeed *preferred*, to play in bombed-out buildings and to construct their own play equipment from the plentiful rubble and debris. Taking that cue, he designed the first Adventure Playground. This

U.S. version offers a storage shed full of tools and recycled wood that children can use to build forts and clubhouses and other things, and then leave them up or tear them down when they are done. The playground also has a tire swing, climbing net, and fast-moving trolley hanging from a pulley. A more traditional play area is just outside the fence.

Next door, **Shorebird Park Nature Center** *((510) 981-6720; www.ci.berkeley.ca.us/marina. Tu-Sat 1-5.)* has a 100-gallon aquarium. Marina tours and walks are scheduled by appointment.

Nearby, at the bay end of University Avenue where the Berkeley Pier begins, is a sculpture depicting a bow-and-arrow-wielding Native American astride his horse. Artist Fred Fierstein is said to have placed it here himself in 1985 when he got tired of waiting for Berkeley politicians to decide to do it for him. He had offered "The Guardian" to the city at no cost, but after long deliberation it was rejected as too aggressive—not to mention that the animal appears to urinate when it rains. Berkeley residents then voted to keep it here, but their decision might not be final. See it now.

## Berkeley Iceland
*2727 Milvia St./Derby St., (510) 647-1620, fax (510) 647-1616; www.berkeleyiceland.com. Schedule varies. $7, 5-18 $6, under 5 $4, skate rental $3.*

Measuring 100 by 200 feet, this rink ranks as one of the largest ice skating surfaces in the country.

## Berkeley Rose Garden
*On Euclid Ave./Bayview Pl., (510) 981-5150; www.ci.berkeley.ca.us/parks. Daily sunrise-sunset. Free.*

Planted at the turn of the century, this terraced garden was originally conceived as a classical Green arboretum. It is a particular delight in late spring and summer, when the 250 varieties of rose are in full bloom. Benches sheltered by arbors covered with climbing roses make for pleasant picnicking and provide gorgeous views of the bay and San Francisco. Tennis courts adjoin. The garden is a popular spot for weddings, and a knot of people is found at the top most evenings watching the sun set. Across the street, **Codornices Park** is equipped with a playground, a basketball court, and a long, exciting, and potentially dangerous (be careful!)

concrete slide. Trails follow the creek and pass the oldest grove of dawn redwoods found outside of China.

## Blake Garden
*70 Rincon Rd./Arlington Ave., in Kensington, (510) 524-2449; www.laep.ced.berkeley.edu/laep/ blakegarden. M-F 8-4:30. Free.*

Surrounding the residence of the president of the University of California, this enormously varied 10½-acre hillside garden was designed in the 1920s by one of the first students in the landscape architecture department at U.C. Berkeley. The garden is used by both U.C. and other area educational institutions as an outdoor laboratory and educational facility. It divides more than 1000 plant species into five areas: a formal Italianate garden with reflecting pool; a redwood canyon with under plantings of ferns, gingers, and other woodland exotic species; a drought-tolerant garden; a flower cutting garden; and an undeveloped Australian Hollow. Benches positioned throughout invite quiet reflection, and picnic tables are available. A Carmelite Monastery is adjacent on what was once part of the original lot.

## Downtown Arts District
Works by local artists and 100 cast-iron panels imprinted with poetry are displayed here.

### • Aurora Theatre
*2081 Addison St./Shattuck Ave., (510) 843-4822, fax (510) 843-4826; www.auroratheatre.org. $28-$40.*

In this intimate venue, no seat is more than 4 rows from the stage.

### • Berkeley Repertory Theatre
*2025 Addison St./Shattuck Ave., (510) 647-2949, fax (510) 647-2976; www.berkeleyrep.org. $10-$55.*

This Tony Award-winning company has established a national reputation for its ambitious programming and dynamic productions. It is well known for its presentation of important new dramatic voices and its fresh adaptations of seldom-seen classics.

### • Capoeira Arts Café
*2026 Addison St./Shattuck Ave., (510) 666-1349; www.capoeiraarts.com. Daily 7:30am-7pm; $.*

This atmospheric cafe filled with colorful original art dispenses simple coffees, smoothies, and sweets, plus soups, salads, and sandwiches.

Brazilian martial arts classes sometimes provide delightful free entertainment.

## Fourth Street
*1800 block, (510) 644-3002, fax (510) 649-9095; fourthstreetshops.com. Shop schedules vary.*

Surprisingly in a city of Berkeley's size and income level, there are no department stores or traditional shopping malls. This trendy block featuring a 1920s industrial style of architecture is as close to one as the city comes. It is a shopping mall done Berkeley-style. Designed, built, and owned by a Berkeley developer/architectural firm, the street's buildings are kept at 2 stories. The owner controls leasing of the entire block and hand picks the unusual stores. A variety of restaurants offers delicious fare and spectacular people-watching.

• **Builders Booksource** *(#1817, (510) 845-6874, fax (510) 845-7051; www.buildersbooksource.com.)* stocks books on architecture and design as well as "nesting" books on interior design and gardening.

• **The Gardener** *(#1836, (510) 548-4545; www.thegardener.com.)* specializes in elegant accessories for the garden and home.

• **George** *(#1844, (510) 644-1033; www.georgesf.com.)* stocks everything tempting for cats and dogs, including fresh-baked treats.

• **Hear Music** *(#1809, (510) 204-9595; www.hearmusic.com.)* permits listening before buying.

• **Lighting Studio** *(#1808, (510) 843-3468, fax (510) 843-1846; www.lightingstudio berkeley.com.)* displays the very best and latest in lighting fixtures.

• **Miki's Paper** *(#1801, (510) 845-9530)* has an impressive selection of handmade Japanese papers.

• **The Pasta Shop** *(#1786, (510) 528-1786)* is a spacious branch of the mother ship in Oakland (see page 310).

• **Sur La Table** *(#1806, (510) 849-2252, fax (510) 849-1980; www.surlatable.com.)* purveys fine kitchen equipment at fair prices.

## The Judah L. Magnes Museum
*2911 Russell St./College Ave., (510) 549-6950, fax (510) 849-3673; www.magnes.org. Sun-Thur 10-4; in summer Sun-W 11-4, Thur 11-8. By donation: $4, seniors $3, under 12 free.*

The first Jewish museum established in the western U.S., this institution exhibits Jewish ceremonial and fine arts from communities around the world. It is housed in a converted 1908 mansion, the gardens for which were landscaped by John McLaren, designer of San Francisco's Golden Gate Park.

## Ohlone Dog Park
*Hearst St./Grant St., (510) 843-6221; www.ci.berkeley. ca.us/parks. Daily 6am-10pm. Free.*

Established as an experiment in 1979, this was the first leash-free dog park in the nation. Located within Ohlone Park, it has 4-foot-high fences that foil even the most gifted jumpers. A concrete walkway is equipped with seating areas alongside, and a lawn with wood chips is on either side of the walkway. Water taps are provided at both ends of the park. Because it is partially paved, the park is a particularly good choice in wet weather, and dogs like to run here. Owners must clean up after their dogs, and plastic bags are provided.

## Takara Sake USA Tasting Room and Sake Museum
*708 Addison St./4th St., (800) 4-TAKARA, (510) 540-8250, fax (510) 486-8758; www.takarasake.com. Tasting daily 12-6. Free.*

Sample several kinds of sake and plum wine in the spacious tasting room of this nation's largest sake brewery. A raised tatami room invites removing shoes and relaxing for a bit. Upon request, an informative video tells about the history and making of sake. The country's only sake museum displays artifacts related to this subtle beverage.

## Telegraph Avenue
*4 blks. betw. Bancroft Way & Dwight Way, S of campus, (510) 649-9500, fax (510) 649-9518; www.telegraphberkeley.org.*

Fondly referred to as "the Ave" or "Tele" by locals, this famous, or perhaps infamous, avenue is probably best known for its role as a gathering spot and point of confrontation during the 1960s Free Speech Movement. It has now slipped into a more peaceful state, but still appears stalled in the '60s. On weekdays rushing students crowd the sidewalks, and on weekends shoppers crowd its many boutiques. A stroll here passes a street bazaar of crafts stalls selling souvenirs such as colorful tie-dyed t-shirts and peace symbol jewelry. Thoroughly modern chain stores are also well represented.

**People's Park** *(bounded by Telegraph Ave., Haste St., Hillegass Ave., & Dwight Way)* was the rallying place for some anti-war and free speech protests in the '60s and '70s.

• **Annapurna** *(#2416, (510) 841-6187)* is a psychedelic "head shop" left over from the turbulent 1960s.

• **Bookstores** in the 2400 block include **Cody's** *(#2454, (510) 845-7852; www.codys books.com.)*, which stocks new obscure tomes along with the latest best-sellers and holds Sunday evening poetry readings; **Moe's Books** *(#2476, (510) 849-2087; www.moesbooks.com.)*, which is said to be the biggest used bookstore west of the Hudson; and **Shakespeare & Co.** *(#2499, (510) 841-8916.)*, which sells unusual used editions.

### Tilden Regional Park
*Off Grizzly Peak, along Wildcat Canyon Rd., (510) 562-PARK; www.ebparks.org/parks/tilden.htm. Daily 8am-10pm. Free.*

This beautiful, well-developed 2,077-acre park has 35 miles of hiking trails as well as numerous picnic spots, many with barbecues.

• **Environmental Education Center**
*(510) 525-2233, fax (510) 526-2393. Tu-Sun 10-5. Free.*

This is a good place to get oriented and obtain current information about park attractions. Exhibits stress local natural history. Educational programs and naturalist-guided walks, many designed especially for families and children, are scheduled regularly.

• **Golf Course**
*(510) 848-7373. Daily sunrise-sunset. M-Thur $32, F $47, Sat-Sun $55; reduced twilight rates.*

This scenic 18-hole course has all types of holes permitting all types of shots.

• **Lake Anza**
*(510) 848-3028. Daily 11-6, Apr-Oct only. $3.50, 62+ & 1-15 $2.50.*

This low-key swimming area has lifeguards on duty, and a snack bar is available.

• **Little Farm**
*(510) 525-2233. Daily 8:30-4. Free.*

This brightly painted, well-maintained farm is home to cows, donkeys, sheep, ducks, chickens, goats, rabbits, pigs, and assorted other barnyard animals.

• **Merry-Go-Round**
*(510) 524-6773. Sat-Sun 11-5; daily in summer. $1.*

One of only four classic 4-row carousels remaining in Northern California, this antique gem is located in the center of the park. Built in 1911 by the Herschel-Spillman firm in New York, it spent time before it settled here at Urbita Springs Park in San Bernardino, at Ocean Beach in San Diego, and at Griffith Park in Los Angeles. It was restored in 1978. In addition to horses, it sports an assortment of colorful animals, including a stork, a dragon, and a frog. Its large band organ operates like a player piano and is regarded as one of the finest examples of its kind.

• **Pony Rides**
*(510) 527-0421. Sat-Sun 11-5, spring & fall, weather permitting; in summer also Tu-F 11-4. $3.*

Children age 2 and older are strapped securely into a saddle with a back support and given an exciting ride in the pony wheel. Children 5 and older can ride horses on the fast track in a larger ring.

• **Regional Parks Botanic Garden**
*(510) 841-8732; www.nativeplants.org. Daily 8:30-5. Free.*

Located across from the carousel, this 10-acre garden was begun in 1940. It offers the opportunity for a leisurely, quiet walk. Over 3,000 drought-resistant species and subspecies are displayed, and native plants are also featured.

• **Steam Train/Redwood Valley Railway**
*Grizzly Peak Blvd./Lomas Cantadas, (510) 548-6100. Sat-Sun 12-5, weather permitting; daily in summer. $1.75.*

Started in 1952 by the late Erich Thomsen, a career railroad man, and now operated by his daughter Ellen, this miniature train concession is described as "a hobby that got out of hand." The replica 15-inch gauge, 5-inch scale narrow-gauge, oil-burning miniature steam train (whew!) follows a scenic route that includes one tunnel and two trestles. The ride covers 1¼ mile and lasts 12 minutes.

## University of California
*Telegraph Ave./Bancroft Way, (510) 642-6000; www.berkeley.edu.*

The foremost attraction here is, of course, higher learning. Known for academic excellence, U.C. Berkeley boasts a faculty distinguished by 17 Nobel Prize winners. Many noteworthy facilities on this 1,232-acre campus are open to the public.

### • Berkeley Art Museum
*2626 Bancroft Way/College Ave., (510) 642-0808, fax (510) 642-4889; www.bampfa.berkeley.edu. W-Sun 11-5, Thur to 7. $8, 65+ & 13-17 $5; free 1st Thur of month.*

Many visitors think that this building itself is as interesting and unusual as its contents. Built in a cubist style of architecture, it is strikingly reminiscent of New York's Guggenheim— except that it is angular instead of circular. The permanent collection stresses modern and Asian art and includes a large collection of paintings by Modernist Hans Hofmann.

The **Pacific Film Archive** *(2575 Bancroft Way/College Ave., (510) 642-1124, fax (510) 642-4889; www.bampfa.berkeley.edu/pfa. Daily programs. $8, 65+ & under 12 $5.)* is one of five world-class public archival film collections in the U.S. It has the largest collection of Japanese titles outside of Japan and one of the world's largest collections of silent and early films from the former Soviet Union and pre-1960 Eastern Europe, plus hundreds of experimental movies by West Coast filmmakers. The theater is clean, the sound system excellent, and the audience well mannered. No snacks are available.

### • Botanical Garden
*200 Centennial Dr., (510) 643-2755, fax (510) 642-5045; http://botanicalgarden.berkeley.edu. Daily 9-5; in summer also W-Sun to 8; closed on 1st Tu of month. $3, 65+ $2, 3-18 $1; free every Thur.*

Located behind the campus in lush Strawberry Canyon, this "library of living plants" covers 34 acres and contains over 13,000 different types of plants organized by continent of origin. Of special interest are the herb garden, rhododendron dell, redwood grove, California native plants area (which includes more than half of the state's native species), old rose garden, and Chinese medicinal herb garden stocked with more than 90 rare plants. Children particularly enjoy the greenhouse filled with carnivorous plants and the lily pond stocked with colorful koi. Grassy areas perfect for picnicking are scattered throughout this peaceful spot.

### • Cal Day Open House
*Annually in April. (510) 642-5215; www.berkeley.edu/calday. Free.*

Most of the university departments sponsor exhibits and events.

### • Cal Performances
*(510) 642-9988, fax (510) 643-2359; www.calperfs.berkeley.edu. Free-$125.*

Acclaimed internationally for presenting extraordinary talent, this series is famous for showcasing the latest works of established artists and the debuts of new talent.

### • Campanile
*In center of campus; www.berkeley.edu/visitors/campanile.html. Elevator: M-F 10-; $2, seniors & under 19 $1.*

*DNA Model at Lawrence Hall of Science*

Modeled after the slightly taller campanile in St. Marks Square in Venice, this campus landmark stands 307 feet tall—the equivalent of 30 stories. When classes are in session, 10-minute mini-concerts are hand-played on its 61-bell carillon three times each weekday at 7:50 a.m., noon, and 6 p.m. On Sundays, a 45-minute recital is performed at 2 p.m.—the perfect time to enjoy a picnic on the surrounding lawn. An elevator takes visitors up 200 feet to an observation platform for a 360-degree view of the area.

### • Campus Tour
*2200 University Ave./Oxford St., Visitors Center, 101 University Hall, (510) 642-5215; www.berkeley.edu/visitors. M-Sat at 10, Sun at 1; confirm time and departure location. Free.*

This guided tour is a good way to get an overview of the campus. A self-guiding tour brochure is also available here.

### • Lawrence Hall of Science
*On Centennial Dr., below Grizzly Peak Blvd., (510) 642-5132; www.lawrencehallofscience.org. Daily 10-5. $8.50, 62+ & 5-18 $6.50, 3-4 $4.50; planetarium +$3, 6-18 $2.50, must be 6 or older; parking $1/hr.*

Located high in the hills behind the campus, this button-pusher's paradise was established by the university in 1958 as a memorial to Ernest Orlando Lawrence, who developed the cyclotron and was the university's first Nobel laureate. Exhibits are of special interest to school-age children and include educational games, a seismic recorder, and the small Holt

Planetarium. The hall's permanent exhibits include the popular Within the Human Brain (an assortment of intriguing activities that explain how our brains function) and Math Rules (puzzles and mathematical challenges that defy the popular notion that math isn't fun). On weekends, a Biology Lab permits experimenting with animal mazes and learning about a variety of small animals. Outside on the entry plaza, kids can play on a life-size fin whale and a DNA molecule climbing structure. The short-order **Bay View Cafe** provides a magnificent panoramic view of the bay and San Francisco.

### • Museum of Paleontology
*Near Oxford St./University Ave., 1101 Valley Life Sciences Bldg., (510) 642-1821, fax (510) 642-1822; www.ucmp.berkeley.edu. M-Thur 8am-10pm, F 8-5, Sat 10-5, Sun 1-10. Free.*

Initiated in the 1860s, this collection of fossils is one of the largest and oldest in North America. Among the displays are a complete Tyrannosaurus rex skeleton, the largest Triceratops skull ever found, a frozen mammoth, ancient bacteria, and the skeleton of a saber-toothed tiger—California's state fossil.

In the same building, the **Museum of Vertebrate Zoology** (*Rm. 3101; (510) 642-3059, fax (510) 643-8238; www.mip.berkeley.edu/mvz. M-F 8-noon & 1-5. Free.*) holds one of the largest and most important collections of vertebrates in the world.

• **Phoebe A. Hearst Museum of Anthropology**
*Bancroft Way/College Ave., 102 Kroeber Hall, (510)
643-7648, fax 510-642-6271; http://hearstmuseum.
berkeley.edu. W-Sat 10-4:30, Sun 12-4. $4, 55+ $3,
under 12 free; free every Thur.*

Part of the campus since 1901, this
museum stores the largest anthropological
research collection (over 4 million artifacts) in
the western U.S.

— **WHERE TO STAY** —

**Bancroft Hotel**
*2680 Bancroft Way/College Ave., (800) 549-1002,
(510) 549-1000, fax (510) 549-1070; www.bancroft
hotel.com. 22 rooms; $$. Children under 12 free.
Continental breakfast. No smoking; no pets. Self-park-
ing $10.*

Located directly across from the campus,
this landmark 1928 arts and crafts-style hotel
was designed by Walter T. Steilberg, an associate
of Julia Morgan. It offers peaceful, airy rooms
with sweeping views of San Francisco Bay and
the Berkeley hills. Many also have large bal-
conies or decks

**Berkeley City Club**
*2315 Durant Ave./Dana St., (510) 848-7800, fax (510)
848-5900; www.berkeleycityclub.com. 6 stories;
40 rooms; $$-$$$. No TVs. Indoor heated pool; fit-
ness room. Continental breakfast; restaurant. No
smoking; no pets.*

Opened in 1930 as the Berkeley Women's
City Club, this magnificent historical landmark
building was designed by Julia Morgan—the
well-known architect who designed Hearst
Castle. Featuring Moorish and Italian Gothic
elements, it is decorated with oriental rugs and
tasteful vintage furniture that enhance the Old
World beauty of its lead-paned windows and
aged redwood trim. Free **tours** are given on the
fourth Sunday of each month. Rooms are com-
fortably furnished, and all have views of either
the San Francisco Bay or the campus and hills.
A bar and restaurant are available to guests
only, and a beauty salon and massage service
operate on site. An intimate **theater** venue often
schedules performances that are open to the
public.

**Claremont Resort & Spa**
*41 Tunnel Rd., at Ashby Ave./Domingo Ave., (800)
551-7266, (510) 843-3000, fax (510) 848-6208;*
*www.claremontresort.com. 6 stories; 279 rooms;
$$$+. Children under 18 free. 2 heated pools; hot tub;
4 saunas; 2 steam rooms; health spa; fitness room;
10 tennis courts (fee; 6 with night lights). 2 restaurants; room service. Self-parking or valet $17.50.*

Built originally by a Kansas farmer who
struck it rich and wanted to fulfill his wife's
dream of living in a home resembling an
English castle, the first incarnation of this hotel
burned to the ground in 1901. The current
Victorian hotel, built in 1915, once charmed
architect Frank Lloyd Wright into describing it
as ". . . one of the few hotels in the world with
warmth, character and charm." The hotel now
provides all the amenities of a resort, but in an
urban setting. Lobby and hallways are decorated
with a collection of contemporary art (the
largest private collection of contemporary
Pacific Northwestern artists in the U.S.), and
wine tasting and food sampling occur there on
Saturday afternoons. Some rooms boast Jacuzzi
tubs for two and views of San Francisco, others
have charm from the past—a deep closet here, a
vintage tub there. The hotel's two pools and hot
tub are surrounded by several long rows of
chaise lounges—looking like something out of
sunny Southern California or Hawaii, but certainly *not* Berkeley. A full-service European-style
spa offers a variety of revitalizing treatments
and packages and features a hot tub with a view
of San Francisco and the Golden Gate Bridge, a
sauna and steam room, 2 silent flotation tanks,
a cascading Deluge shower, and 32 treatment
rooms. Additionally, a kids' activity center permits dropping them off for a few hours of fun
and games.

In addition to fresh fish and meats,
romantic **Jordan's** *((510) 549-8510, fax (510)
549-8553. B-L-D daily, SunBr; $$$. Highchairs,
boosters, reduced child price. Reservations
advised. Valet parking.)* provides a menu of
Lifestyle Cuisine—California fare with a touch
of the Pacific Rim—and a fixed-price four-
course tasting menu. Comfortable chairs invite
sitting back and enjoying the spectacular bay
view. Sunday brunch here is an extravagant buf-
fet of salads, fresh fruit, seafood, and meats. It
includes a design-your-own-omelette station
and a dessert table laden with fine cakes, choco-
late éclairs, chocolate fondue, and several flavors
of mousse. Live music is scheduled on Sunday
evenings.

*The Claremont Hotel*

**Paragon Bar & Café** *((510) 549-8585; www.paragonrestaurant.com. L-D daily; $$. Valet parking.)* is more casual, with a comfortable bar area providing entertainment Wednesday through Sunday evenings. Among the potent and colorful specialty cocktails are Bermuda's famous Dark and Story and a pale yellow Rain Drop. The bar also pours more than 50 vodkas. The dining room has a transitional area of communal tables, with traditional unshared tables in the back—all with impressive bay views. The American brasserie menu items have included a flavorful roasted beet salad, a delicate pan-seared sea bass over basmati rice, and a tasty, satisfying orecchiette consisting of house-made fennel sausage, cauliflower, and cute little cap-shaped pasta. A burger is always on the menu and a reliably good choice. When available, don't miss the triple chocolate mousse cake.

### Doubletree Hotel Berkeley Marina

*200 Marina Blvd., (800) 222-TREE, (510) 548-7920, fax (510) 548-7944; www.doubletree.com. 373 rooms; $$. 2 indoor heated pools & 2 hot tubs; sauna; fitness room. Restaurant; room service. Pets ok.*

Situated in a tranquil setting on the marina, this comfortable low-rise lodging provides marina views and easy parking. All rooms have either a patio or balcony.

### The French Hotel

*1538 Shattuck Ave./Cedar St., (510) 548-9930, same fax. 18 rooms; $-$$. Cafe; room service. No smoking; no pets.*

In this European-modern hotel situated just across the street from Chez Panisse, all rooms have a private patio. Just off the lobby, the hotel's coffeehouse has sidewalk tables that are popular with locals.

### Hotel Durant

*2600 Durant Ave./Bowditch St., (800) 2-DURANT, (510) 845-8981, fax (510) 486-8336; www.hotel durant.com. 6 stories; 144 rooms; $$. Children under 12 free. Restaurant; room service. No pets. Self-parking or valet $10.*

Particularly popular with parents in town to visit their children at the university, this atmospheric hotel is just 1 block from the university. Historic photographs of the campus hang in the hallways, and some of the attractively appointed rooms feature campanile views.

**Henry's Publick House & Grille** *(B-L-D daily; $-$$.)* has a cozy, comfortable pub atmosphere and authentic Tiffany lamp fixtures. Food is well prepared and includes a good hamburger, fresh fish items, and a variety of inexpensive sandwiches and salads.

## Rose Garden Inn

*2740 Telegraph Ave./Ward St., (800) 992-9005, (510) 549-2145, fax (510) 549-1085; www.rosegardeninn. com. 40 rooms; $$-$$$. Children under 4 free. 1 kitchen; some wood-burning & gas fireplaces. Full breakfast. No smoking; pets ok.*

Situated 7 blocks from the university, this charming lodging complex includes two landmark Tudor-style mansions, a carriage house, and a garden house. Rooms are attractively decorated and comfortable, and some have views of San Francisco. Families are accommodated comfortably in the larger junior suites. The buildings open onto a central garden oasis filled with fountains, patios, and hundreds of rose bushes, and the cookie jar is never empty.

## — WHERE TO EAT —

Berkeley was the first city in the state to introduce legislation regulating smoking in public places. It was also the first city to require non-smoking sections in restaurants. Now California is the first state in the nation to require that all restaurants and bars in the state are 100% non-smoking. Smoking in workplaces is also prohibited.

## Ajanta

*1888 Solano Ave./The Alameda, (510) 526-4373, fax (510) 526-3885; ajantarestaurant.com. L-D daily; $$. Highchairs, boosters. Reservations advised.*

With an ever-changing menu of creative, complex regional Indian dishes, this simple restaurant is always a delight. Complete dinners are well priced, but ordering a la carte doesn't cost much more and offers the opportunity to try some unusual items. Presentation is part of the pleasure. All dinners begin with papadam—a crisp lentil wafer served with dipping sauce. Condiments include mango chutney, housemade spicy carrots, and lime pickles. Alu tikki (deep-fried potato-and-pea patties) is a popular appetizer. Entrees change regularly and include curries, tandoori meats (including their signature lamb-rib chops) and fish, and a selection of vegetarian and vegan dishes; all can be ordered in any degree of spiciness. Plates are attractively arranged with three scoops of saffron-laced rice

anchored in the middle by a mound of spinach purée. A light mango mousse and liquidy kulfi rice pudding are especially delicious desserts. This restaurant is named for the site of ancient Buddhist cave temples that is a famous tourist attraction in western India. Reproductions of some of the cave paintings appear on wall murals that were painted in India.

## Au Coquelet

*2000 University Ave./Milvia St., (510) 845-0433. B-L-D daily; $$. Highchairs, boosters. No reservations.*

This spot is popular with students and night owls and is as Berkeley as you can get. It is a great spot for a coffee and pastry anytime, since it stays open until 1 a.m., and its regulars have been described as "defying description." Indeed, it attracts a cross-section. The cafe menu is simple—omelettes, cold and hot sandwiches, burgers, salads, soups—but the selection of housemade tortes and tarts and coffee drinks is outstanding.

## Berkeley Thai House

*2511 Channing Way/Telegraph Ave., (510) 843-7352. L M-Sat, D daily; $$. Highchairs, boosters. Reservations advised at D.*

In good weather, a table on the spacious wooden deck here is a choice spot to relax with a cooling, sweet Thai iced tea. On nippier days and in the evening, the cozy inside dining room decorated with Indonesian artifacts is an inviting option. Specials chalked on a board by the entrance are usually a good bet. Favorite dishes include spicy-hot basil chicken, full-flavored cashew nut chicken, moo-prik-khing (a superb stir-fry with pork and fresh green beans in a spicy sauce), panang neur (beef and sweet basil in a spicy red curry sauce with a coconut milk base), and pad thai (a sweet, orange-colored noodle dish accented with ground peanuts, bean sprouts, bean cake, and a few tiny shrimp).

## Bette's Oceanview Diner

*1807 4th St./Hearst Ave., (510) 644-3230. B-L daily; $$. Boosters, booths. No reservations.*

It's fun to sit on a counter stool (a purse hook is provided underneath) and watch the cooks hustle in this casual, noisy diner featuring a 1950s truck-stop decor and a menu of traditional American food. A jukebox provides more entertainment with an eclectic mix of everything from '50s classics to reggae. Breakfast is served all day beginning at 6:30 a.m., and choices include spicy scrambled eggs, steak and eggs, omelettes, griddle cakes with real maple syrup, delicious French toast, and some combination plates—The New York (smoked salmon, bagel, cream cheese, red onion, and tomato) and The Philadelphia (scrapple, poached eggs, toast, and grilled tomato). Blintzes are also sometimes available. Lunch is a satisfying assortment of well-prepared classic sandwiches (the Reuben and meatloaf are particularly good), housemade soups, and homey items such as grilled bockwurst and potato pancakes. Thick old-fashioned milkshakes are available, too, but oddly no hamburger or fries. By the way. About that ocean view. There is none. Oceanview is the name of the neighborhood in which the restaurant is located.

Next door, **Bette's To Go** *((510) 548-9494. M-F 6:30-5, Sat-Sun 8-5.)* has take-out pastries, sandwiches, salads, pizza by the slice, and other goodies.

## Blakes on Telegraph
*2367 Telegraph Ave./Durant Ave., (510) 848-0886, fax (510) 540-8831; www.blakesontelegraph.com. L-D daily; $. Highchairs, boosters, booths. Reservations accepted.*

A campus hangout since 1940, this restaurant serves a large variety of hamburgers and snacks. On weekdays, lunch is served both downstairs in the funky rathskeller, with its sawdust-covered floor and old wooden booths, and upstairs, where diners get excellent views of the sidewalk parade outside. A cover charge is levied on the live music scheduled most evenings.

## The Blue Nile
*2525 Telegraph Ave./Dwight Way, (510) 540-6777. D daily; $. Reservations advised Sat-Sun.*

Delicious, spicy Ethiopian stews (wat) are served here atop traditional spongy bread (injera). Favorites include boneless chicken tibs and the saucier, spicier, juicer doro wat made with chicken on the bone. Many vegetarian dishes are available, and all entrees come with sides of steamed carrots and green salad. Diners may eat in the traditional Ethiopian manner, with fingers, wrapping injera around the

various foods, but plastic forks are available for those who prefer the traditional American way. Sweet honey wine and housemade fruit drinks perfectly complement the cuisine. Downstairs seating, within cozy beaded-curtain alcoves, is prime.

## Boran Thai
*1892 Solano Ave./The Alameda, (510) 525-3625. L M-Sat, D daily; $. Highchairs, boosters. Reservations taken.*

After selecting seating either at regular tables or in the area where diners remove their shoes and sit on floor cushions with feet dangling under the table, complimentary shrimp chips and dipping sauce are brought for munching on while perusing the menu. Winners include delicate basil chicken, tasty cashew nut chicken, crispy-fried fresh red snapper glazed with a hot-and-sweet tamarind sauce, and flavorful Panang beef in peanut-curry sauce. A good selection of vegetarian options is available, and at lunch all entrees include cabbage soup, steamed rice, and fresh steamed vegetables.

## Breads of India
*2448 Sacramento St./Dwight Way, (510) 848-7684. L-D daily; $. Highchairs. No reservations. No cards.*

In spite of having only a few tables and almost no ambiance, this popular spot usually has a line waiting to get in. A sign-up sheet is posted outside. The teeny kitchen stuffed with cooks produces dishes such as jumbo prawns in a complexly spiced, tomato-based masala sauce, and organic Yukon gold potatoes in a mild fresh spinach purée. The garlic naan is exceptional, and more delicious exotic bread options—all prepared with organic flour—include roomali roti (a thin unleavened bread prepared with a blend of white and wheat flours) and tawa daal paratha (stuffed with spicy chickpeas). Entrees are served on one American-style plate with trimmings of basmati rice and dahl. The kitchen uses the best ingredients, blends their own spices, and never freezes or microwaves anything (indeed, there doesn't seem to be any room for these appliances in the tiny kitchen). Only olive oil is used—none of that fattening Indian ghee. The menu changes daily, and always among the choices are a tandoori-cooked meat item and two vegetarian dishes. With 300 recipes for entrees and 140 for breads, this restaurant aims to surprise.

## Brennan's
*720 University Ave./4th St., (510) 841-0960. L-D daily; $; closed part of July. 1 highchair, boosters. No reservations.*

Reminiscent of a shamrock, with its dark green exterior and bright green interior, this Berkeley institution's hall-like dining room is dominated by an enormous rectangular bar. Two large-screen TVs are tuned perpetually to sporting events. Always crowded and boisterous, it has a variety of beers and microbrews on tap and is furnished with decidedly untrendy Formica tables. The hofbrau-style food is generous portions of meat and potatoes, and each night has its hot-plate special. Hot sandwiches come with made-from-scratch mashed potatoes smothered in gravy, and side dishes include tasty stuffing, macaroni salad, potato salad, and coleslaw. Service is cafeteria-style: pick a table, wait in line, chow down.

## Bua Luang
*1166 Solano Ave./Cornell Ave., in Albany, (510) 527-8288. L-D daily; $. Highchairs, boosters. Reservations accepted.*

Though this tiny dining room is a treat any time, it is especially delightful as a refuge on a warm afternoon or as a cozy retreat on a cool evening. Ingredients are fresh, spicing is simple, and portions are generous. Stars on the menu include deep-fried curry puffs, red Panang beef curry, and an unusual, tasty pumpkin curry. Dark brown rice and a large selection of seafood and vegetarian items are also available.

## Cactus Taqueria
*1881 Solano Ave./The Alameda, (510) 528-1881, fax (510) 528-2425. L-D daily; $. Highchairs, boosters. No reservations.*

Mexican fast food at its best is served cafeteria-style in this popular taqueria. Burritos are custom made, with a choice of several kinds of flavored tortillas, black or pinto beans, and a variety of well-seasoned fillings. Tacos and tamales are also available. Tortillas are lard-free, meats are the best, and tortilla chips are fried in safflower oil. Housemade drinks include several fresh fruit agua frescas and horchata (a sweet rice drink), and several addictive salsas are available—including a tangy green tomatillo and a smoky mole. Seating is at colorfully-stained wooden tables, and an indoor water fountain provides restive background sound.

## Café de la Paz
*1600 Shattuck Ave./Cedar St., in Cedar Center, (510) 843-0662, fax (510) 843-0669; www.cafedelapaz.net. L M-F, D daily, Sat-SunBr; $$. Highchairs, boosters. Reservations advised.*

Popular with locals, this exciting spot serves authentic traditional and contemporary Latin American cuisine, with many vegetarian and vegan options. Specialties include cachapas from Venezuela (corn pancakes topped with a sweet pepper sauce), tamal de pollo from Guatemala (corn masa with chicken mole and a spicy chili sauce), and carne asada fajitas con salsa barbacoa (beef topped with a spicy smoky-sweet sauce). Personal favorites are the chicken and vegetable enchiladas topped with either a rich mole sauce or piquant tomatillo sauce, and fabulous corn bread made with whole corn kernels. Portions are generous and served festively on Fiestaware. The welcoming second-floor dining room, with its large windows overlooking the street and soothing fountain, add to the experience.

## Café Fanny
*1603 San Pablo Ave./Cedar St., (510) 524-5447. B-L daily; $. No reservations.*

Operated by the venerable Alice Waters, this simple spot, named for her daughter (who was named for the beautiful fishwife's daughter in Marcel Pagnol's film trilogy about life on the waterfront in Marseille), is an outpost of tonier Chez Panisse. Bread and wine comes from next-door neighbors—the Acme Bakery and Kermit Lynch. Breakfasts are simple, but the boiled egg—perhaps a blue or green Araucana—is perfect and the toast is, too. Lunch is a selection of several sandwiches. Limited seating is available outside with a view of a noisy parking lot, but no one seems to mind.

## Cafe Panini
*2115 Allston Way/Shattuck Ave., in Trumpetvine Court, (510) 849-0405; www.cafe-panini.com. L M-F; $. No reservations.*

Popular with university students and staff, this tiny spot produces divine gourmet sandwiches. Diners order at the counter, then select a seat either in the brick-walled interior or out in a sheltered courtyard—the top choice on a sunny day. Sandwiches are made with magnificent Semifreddi Bakery sweet baguettes and topped with enticing combinations. A personal favorite is the mushroom-pesto topped with sun-dried tomato and melted mozzarella. As at Chez Panisse—where this cafe's owner was once a waitress and then a wine buyer—all ingredients are fresh. Tuna is not from a can. Meats are cooked in-house. Mayonnaise is made from scratch. Herbs are fresh. A soup, a pasta salad, and some great housemade desserts are also available.

## Cancun Taqueria

*2134 Allston Way/Shattuck Ave., (510) 549-0964. L-D daily; $. Highchairs, boosters, child menu. No reservations.*

Meats here are broiled over open flames, seafood is grilled, and there are plenty of vegetarian specials. Lard and MSG are not used, but purified water is. Everything—soft and crispy tacos, burritos, quesadillas, tostadas—is super tasty, especially when tarted up with delicious selections from the extensive complimentary salsa bar.

## César

*1515 Shattuck Ave./Cedar St., (510) 883-0222. L-D daily; $-$$. No reservations.*

Casual and cozy, this tapas bar is operated by a group that includes Alice Waters' husband and is located in the Gourmet Ghetto next door to Chez Panisse. A true bar, its menu offers a large selection of spirits and wines, and food is served until 11 p.m. The short menu changes daily but always includes some delicious options: a tiny plate of two tasty red piquillo peppers filled with melted cheese; a more substantial stack of flat, thin fried potatoes seasoned with rosemary and whole sage leaves; rock cod with a spicy red romesco sauce; a bocadillo (sandwich) of spicy tuna and egg. Chewy Catalan almond cookies and dessert wines provide fine finishes. The open room has a large communal table in the center made from floorboards brought in from an old London warehouse.

## Cha-Am

*1543 Shattuck Ave./Cedar St., (510) 848-9664; www.chaam-berkeley.acbox.com. L-D daily; $. Highchairs, boosters. Reservations advised.*

The current leader in the informal ranking of this city's best Thai restaurants, this gem features a festive atmosphere, an attentive staff, and chefs who produce complex flavors and interesting combinations. Among the winners on its exciting menu are laap-gai (a chopped chicken salad tossed with fresh mint and coriander), pad-makua-yao (chicken sautéed with basil, chilies, and eggplant), and pad-ped-gung (prawns sautéed with sweet curry sauce, fresh Thai herbs, and green beans).

## Chez Panisse

*1517 Shattuck Ave./Cedar St.; www.chezpanisse.com. M-Sat. Boosters, booths, child menu M-Thur. Cafe: L-D; $$-$$$; reservations advised; accepted up to 1 month in advance; (510) 548-5049. Restaurant: D; $$$+; reservations essential; accepted up to 1 month in advance; (510) 548-5525.*

Opened in 1971 by U.C. graduate Alice Waters as a hangout for her friends, this fabulously famous restaurant inside a converted art deco-style house features the definitive California cuisine—simply prepared food made with the freshest ingredients. A different fixed-price menu is served each night in the legendary downstairs dining room. A less expensive upstairs cafe serves a seasonal menu of simple items such as baked goat cheese salad, Spanish-style grilled chicken with lentils, and almond cake with poached Bosc pears and sour cherries. Meals in both venues are usually a perfect 10. A 15% service charge is automatically added to the bill and divided by the entire staff, so no need to tip more unless service was above and beyond. The area surrounding this restaurant is known as the "Gourmet Ghetto." Allow time to explore.

## FatApple's

*1346 Martin Luther King Jr. Way/Rose St., (510) 526-2260, fax (510) 526-1253. B-L-D daily; $-$$. Highchairs, boosters, child menu. No reservations.*

This popular restaurant's forte is good food made from scratch using basic ingredients: The lean ground chuck used for hamburgers is ground on the premises; soup is made fresh; blue cheese salad dressing is made with the real stuff; robust Peet's coffee is freshly ground and served with heavy whipping cream. The famous hamburger is served on a housemade wheat or white bun, and just-right milkshakes (the olallieberry is outstanding) are served in the metal mixing canister. For dessert, it's impossible to go wrong with a slice of the puffy apple pie the restaurant is named for, but the chocolate velvet and lemon meringue pies are also delicious. Breakfast features fresh-squeezed orange juice, crisp waffles served with pure Vermont maple syrup, omelettes, buckwheat or whole-wheat pancakes, and freshly baked pastries.

## Grégoire
*2109 Cedar St./Shattuck Ave., (510) 883-1893, fax (510) 883-1894; www.gregoirerestaurant.com. L-D daily.*

This upscale hole-in-the-wall produces accomplished French take-out fare, and it *must* be good because California Cuisine guru Alice Waters is a customer. Chef Grégoire makes everything from scratch using fresh local ingredients. A few tables are available for dining, but it's more fun to fax in an order and pick it up dressed in delightful eight-sided corrugated boxes made of recycled material (this *is* Berkeley). The monthly menu is posted conveniently at the website with a downloadable, faxable order form. A recent dinner started with thick, tasty mushroom soup, moved on to falling-off-the-bone-tender braised lamb shank Provençal and crispy round potato puffs, and ended with a flaky housemade apple tarte tatin. Have merci!

## Inn Kensington
*293 Arlington Ave./Amherst, in Kensington, (510) 527-5919. B-L daily; D M-Sat; $. Highchairs, boosters. Reservations advised for D. No cards.*

Situated amid a strip of shops (a stylish flower shop, a small grocery store, a drug store with great gift items and a post office branch, a hardware store), this popular local spot has been here since 1981. Breakfast features dozens of omelettes and scrambles, plus excellent homefries and gigantic housemade buttermilk biscuits. At lunch, the enticing selection of tasty international dishes includes items such as Santa Fe pita pizzetta, Moroccan-style deep-fried lemon-ginger chicken breast with salsa, and East Indian curried chicken in filo dough. Desserts

include housemade ice cream and a bargain oversize cookie.

## Juan's Place
*941 Carleton/9th St., (510) 845-6904. L M-F, D daily; $. Highchairs, boosters. No reservations.*

Always bustling, this family-friendly spot is reminiscent of a Mexican roadhouse. All the usual traditional Mexican food suspects are on the menu: burritos, tacos, tostadas, quesadillas, tamales, fajitas, flautas. Enchiladas come stuffed with the usual, as well as with crab or shrimp, and are topped with a variety of sauces, including a deep, smoky mole. Heavier meat entrees and several chilis are also options, as is a horchata rice drink and a caramel flan dessert.

## Kathmandu
*1410 Solano Ave./Santa Fe Ave., in Albany, (510) 526-3222. D Tu-Sun; $$. 1 booster. Reservations advised.*

Tibetan and Napalese fare—a cross between Chinese and Indian cuisines—is served in this tiny space. A good selection of vegetarian items is available, and various kinds of sprouted beans add a pleasing crunch to many dishes. Lamb items are a specialty, and khashi ya chhwela, a spicy stew served at room temperature, is choice. Though entree dishes come with condiments, rice, and bread, do also try chatmari—a soft rice-flour bread stuffed with curried chicken. Beer and either cinnamon or banana lassi yogurt drinks are good accompaniments. A pot of chai, a spiced tea served with milk, makes a nice ending.

## King Tsin
*1699 Solano Ave./Tulare Ave., (510) 525-9890; www.kingtsin.com. L-D daily; $$. Highchairs, boosters. Reservations advised.*

The first Mandarin Chinese restaurant in town, this popular spot recently remodeled its dining room and now has hardwood floors and big windows looking out on the street. No MSG is used in preparing the tasty items that include hot-and-sour soup, juicy pot stickers, spiced prawns (coated with batter, deep-fried, and served in a spicy-sweet sauce), Mongolian beef (smothered in green onions and served on a bed of crisp rice noodles), vegetarian green beans, and dramatic sizzling meat and fish plates. Soft-shell crab and Peking duck are also on the menu. Mixed drinks can be ordered from a full bar.

## King Yen

*2995 College Ave./Ashby Ave., (510) 845-1286. L-D daily; $-$$. Highchairs, boosters. No reservations.*

The high-ceilinged main dining room here, with its generous flower arrangements and potted plants, is as delightful as the cuisine. Dishes include Szechwan beef (batter-dipped meat is deep-fried, then stir-fried with a spicy-sweet sauce), General's chicken (lots of crunchy water chestnuts), and delicately seasoned mu shu pork. Exotic beggar's chicken and Peking duck are available by advance order. Good vegetarian items include crispy spring rolls, dry-cooked string beans, and bean curd with black bean sauce. Chow mein and hot-and-sour soup also can be requested without meat. Both white and brown rice are available, and the kitchen uses no MSG.

## Kirala

*2100 Ward St./Shattuck Ave., (510) 549-3486, fax (510) 549-0165; www.kiralaberkeley.com. L Tu-F, D daily; $$. No reservations.*

Pass the inevitable wait in this festive spot's tiny bar, where a dish of edamame (soybeans) and a bottle of sake or Japanese beer speed it along. The Japanese fare includes appetizers (delicate seafood or pork gyoza/pot stickers; light-as-air tempura), robata grill items (spicy sardines; baby lobster tail with tiny red caviar; silky shitake mushrooms), an array of sushi (fresh water or sea eel among them) and sashimi, and full meals with soup, salad, and rice. A la carte portions are delicious but small, so do request a side of rice.

Before or after, **Berkeley Bowl Market-place** *(2020 Oregon St., (510) 843-6929; www.berkeleybowl.com. M-Sat 9-8, Sun 10-6.)* is just a block away. This grocery store is legendary for its produce section and also has a large take-out selection.

## La Méditerranée

*2936 College Ave./Ashby Ave., (510) 540-7773, fax (510) 540-0665; www.cafelamed.com. B-L-D daily. Highchairs, boosters. No reservations.*

This is the perfect place for refreshment during a shopping spree in the low-key Elmwood neighborhood. If unfamiliar with Middle Eastern cuisine, try a sampler plate. Cinnamony chicken Cilicia in phyllo dough and succulent chicken pomegranate are both out-standing. Soups and salads are options for lighter appetites, and a selection of coffees and sweets provide the perfect dessert or snack.

## La Note

*2377 Shattuck Ave./Channing Way, (510) 843-1535, fax (510) 843-1517; www.lanoterestaurant.com. B-L M-F, D Thur-Sat, Sat-SunBr; $-$$. Highchairs, boosters. Reservations not accepted for Sat-SunBr.*

Touching just the right culinary notes, this charming restaurant delivers the Provence dining experience without the native negatives of small dogs and cigarette smoke. On the patio on a warm, sunny day, while sipping a cafe au lait from a big bowl as they do in France, it's possible to fantasize about actually being in the south of France. Winning items on the breakfast menu include lemon-gingerbread pancakes with poached pears, fluffy scrambled eggs, and perfectly fried rosemary potatoes. Omelettes, hot cereals, and French toast made with cinnamon brioche soaked in orange water batter and drizzled with lavender honey are also available. Lunch brings on les salades, les soupes, and les sandwiches, and dinner les bagnats (traditional Provençale open-face sandwiches), les poissons (fish), and les viandes (meats). Bon appetit!

## La Val's

*1834 Euclid Ave./Hearst Ave., (510) 843-5617; www.lavals.com. L-D daily; $. Highchairs, boosters, booths. No reservations.*

Located on the quieter north side of the U.C. campus, this long-popular student hangout has good pizza, pastas, and brew—all at great prices. The super-casual seating inside is enhanced with overhead TVs broadcasting sporting events, but on warm afternoons sitting at a picnic table in the courtyard beer garden is hard to beat. Waiting time can be spent playing video games.

## The Med (iterraneum Caffe)

*2475 Telegraph Ave./Haste St., (510) 549-1128. Daily 7am-11:30pm; $. No reservations. No cards.*

With a casual atmosphere and untidy decor, this coffeehouse seems to have been serving students forever. It catered the Free Speech Movement activists back in the '60s as they planned their moves, including Jerry "You can't trust anybody over 30" Rubin. But, as everyone knows, times change. Now it has an ATM on the premises and serves smoothies and ice cream cones. Don't miss the Berliner—a sort of coffee-ice cream float—and the fabulous chocolate layer cake with rum custard filling. Short-order breakfast and lunch items are available.

## O Chame Restaurant & Tea Room

*1830 4th St./Hearst Ave., (510) 841-8783. L-D M-Sat; $$. 1 highchair. Reservations advised for D.*

Reminiscent of Chez Panisse in its simplicity and use of the freshest ingredients, this soothing, tranquil spot has a refined menu that changes weekly. Among the offerings are whimsical presentations (a "tower" salad composed of stacked slices of daikon radish, smoked salmon, and mango) as well as more traditional presentations (soup prepared with king salmon, mustard greens, fresh shitake mushrooms, and soba noodles). The restaurant is known for its noodle dishes, one of the most popular being udon noodles with smoked trout. A variety of sakes, including the Hakusan brand produced domestically in the Wine Country, and an extensive list of teas are also available. Dessert can be simple but exquisite: fresh sweet cherries served chilling amid ice cubes. Beautiful bento box lunches are available to go.

## Peet's Coffee & Tea

*2112 Vine St./Cedar St., (510) 841-0564; www.peets. com. M-Sat 7-7, Sun 7-6.*

It was here in 1966 that now-retired owner Alfred Peet, a Dutch émigré, became the first in the U.S. trade to import specialty varieties of coffees and to dark-roast whole coffee beans—a radical move at the time that touched off a revolution among coffee drinkers. A Berkeley institution, this coffee boutique dispenses an impressive variety of coffees and teas and, though it has no place to sit down, is the gathering spot each morning for large numbers of coffee freaks. Holding their hot cups of java, they spill right into the street. Professionals in three-piece suits mingle here with blue-collar workers, all chatting happily. Sometimes it seems that almost everyone in this town, no matter what kind of work they do, has a curious, educated mind. Perhaps they would like to mull this over: Starbucks owned Peet's from 1984 to 1987. But Peet's is now an independent company once again, with a plethora of outlets throughout the Bay Area.

## Phoenix Next Door

*1786 Shattuck Ave./Francisco St., (510) 883-0783, same fax. B-L M-Sat; $. No cards.*

Operating as an adjunct to the **Phoenix Pastificio** pasta shop, which provides creative organic pastas to many Bay Area restaurants, this simple cafe's changing menu permits trying some of the finished wares on site. After lunching on delicious potato bread rolls and olive bread panini, a perfectly dressed organic mixed green salad, and a plate of whole wheat spaghettini with basil-arugula pesto and slow-roasted tomatoes, one happy customer who just couldn't get enough stopped by the retail counter and purchased cut-to-order porcini pappardelle to take home for dinner the next evening.

## Picante

*1328 6th St./Gilman St., (510) 525-3121, fax (510) 526-7486; www.picantecocina.citysearch.com. L M-F, D daily, Sat-SunBr; $. Highchairs, boosters, booths, child menu. No reservations.*

Claiming to be the largest taqueria in the Bay Area, this casual spot has two large indoor dining rooms and an outside area with a soothing wall fountain. Menu choices include the expected burritos, tamales, tacos (prepared with handmade corn tortillas), quesadillas, and tostadas. Especially good fillings include carnitas (slow-cooked pork), pollo asado (grilled chicken with fresh salsa), rajas (roasted Poblano chilies with sautéed onions and Mexican cheese), and chorizo y papas (spicy Mexican sausage and potatoes). Special vegetarian and vegan items are also available. Among the drinks are aguas frescas (fresh fruit drinks), margaritas made with agave wine, and a large selection of Mexican beers.

## Picnic Pick-Ups

• **A. G. Ferrari Foods**
*2905 College Ave./Ashby Ave., (510) 849-2701; and 1843 Solano Ave., (510) 559-6860; www.agferrari. com.*

Dine in or take away a picnic from this totally Italian deli. Housemade fresh pastas include a delectable pappardelle that is even better topped with the housemade meat sauce. A specialty olive bar holds particularly good black olives with almonds, and the deli case always has an assortment of tempting salads and entrees.

• **Andronico's Market**
*1550 Shattuck Ave./Cedar St., (510) 841-7942, fax (510) 841-3042; www.andronicos.com. Daily 7:30am-midnight.*

This upscale supermarket carries delicious take-out fare and locally-made gourmet treats, and boxed lunches are available by 24-hour advance reservation. It is located within what was once the consumer-owned Co-op, a supermarket that operated here from 1938 to 1988 and was the country's largest urban cooperative.

• **Campus food stalls**
*At the campus entrance, on Bancroft Way/Telegraph Ave. M-F 11-3, more or less; $. No cards.*

These informal stands offer simple fast foods such as donuts, soft pretzels, fresh juices and smoothies, falafel (a Middle Eastern vegetarian sandwich made with pocket bread), and other ethnic dishes. Nearby benches, steps, and grassy areas offer impromptu picnic possibilities. And because this famous intersection attracts all kinds of entertainers—jugglers, musicians, revivalists, you-name-it—an amazing floor show is free.

• **Monterey Market**
*1550 Hopkins St./Monterey Ave., (510) 526-6042; www.montereymarket.com. M-F 9-7, Sat 8:30-6.*

This low-key, much-heralded produce market caters to the sophisticated Berkeley palate with an impressive assortment of produce, including tender baby vegetables, exotic melons, and wild mushrooms. The market also supplies the area's fine restaurants, and prices are unexpectedly low.

• **Noah's Bagels**
*1883 Solano Ave./The Alameda, (510) 525-4447, fax (510) 525-4408; www.noahs.com. M-F 6:30-6, Sat-Sun 7-5.*

The very first Noah's store opened in nearby Emeryville. This branch was among the first in what has now become a very large chain. Promising "a taste of old New York," this shop delivers a bagel that is described by the founder as "crusty outside, chewy inside, tasty and big." They come in many varieties, including "super onion" and "multi-grain," and a selection of freshly made cream cheese "shmears" make the perfect topping. Bagel sandwiches are made to

order, and plenty of supporting items and cold drinks are also available. Noah says, "Protect your bagels . . . put lox on them!"

• **Whole Foods Market**
*3000 Telegraph Ave./Ashby Ave., (510) 649-1333, fax (510) 649-1474; www.wholefoodsmarket.com. Daily 8am-10pm.*

This Texas-based natural foods retailer purveys an amazing selection of good-for-you foods, and its busy bakery and deli-coffee bar offer the makings for a great picnic. Seating is also available inside and at sheltered tables outside. Special child-size shopping carts are fun for kids.

## Plearn
*2050 University Ave./Shattuck Ave., (510) 841-2148. L-D daily; $-$$. Highchairs, boosters. No reservations.*

Very popular and with a "Thai-tech" decor, this restaurant's best dishes include yum-nua (a yummy mixture of beef slices seasoned with onion, ground chilies, fragrant fresh mint, and lime juice), him-ma-pan (chicken with cashew nuts and chilies), and pat-prik-king (pork with chilies and string beans). For a pittance more, an entree is served with both rice and an iceberg lettuce salad topped with an exotic bright yellow, tangy-sweet dressing. For dessert, a crispy deep-fried banana topped with a light coconut sauce can be pleasant.

## Pyramid Alehouse, Brewery & Restaurant
*901 Gilman St./6th St., (510) 528-9880, fax (510) 528-9921; www.pyramidbrew.com. L-D daily; $-$$. Booths, child menu. Reservations accepted.*

Situated within one gargantuan room, this massive, very noisy operation can still feel cozy for diners seated in one of the comfy, private booths. But for those in the mood to mingle, tables and chairs and bar-tables abound. Fifteen beers are on tap, all brewed on the premises in huge vats visible from the dining room. Try the popular traditional Amber Lager, the Hefeweizen wheat beer served with a lemon wedge, or the Weizen Berry—Hefeweizen flavored with raspberry. Can't decide? Get a sampler of four. Light drinkers will like that single 4-ounce sample sizes can be ordered. The expansive, eclectic menu offers snacks, soups, pizzas, sandwiches, burgers, and salads, as well as heftier entrees of fish & chips, baby back ribs, and assorted steaks. The chicken-fried steak pub plate is particularly good. A tasty, spicy-sweet housemade mustard is served with many items. For dessert, be daring and order up an Espresso Stout float. **Brewery tours** are given Monday through Friday at 5 p.m., and Saturday and Sunday at 2 and 4 p.m. On Saturday nights in summer, movies are screened outdoors in the parking lot.

## Rick & Ann's

*2922 Domingo Ave./Ashby Ave., (510) 649-8538, fax (510) 649-8568; www.rickandanns.com. B-L daily, D Tu-Sun; $. Highchairs, boosters, child menu. Reservations accepted for D only.*

The extensive breakfast menu at this cozy neighborhood spot is served until 2:30 p.m. and features both the usual and the unusual—gingerbread waffles, hash prepared with beets, lacy corn cakes, French toast made with challah dipped in orange-cardamom batter. Superb homefries are prepared using fresh potatoes that are fried until they are *done* and served topped with sour cream and chopped green onions. At lunch, hamburgers, salads, and a variety of sandwiches join the menu, and dinner brings on American classics such as meatloaf and macaroni and cheese. Good pie is available anytime. Banquettes along the wall, Shaker-style chairs, and tables with hammered metal tops lend a solid feeling. Kids get a coloring place mat and a basket of crayons to keep them occupied.

## Ristorante Raphael

*2132 Center St./Oxford St., (510) 644-9500, fax (510) 644-9597; www.ristoranteraphael.com. L Tu-F, D Tu-Sun. Highchairs, boosters. Reservations advised.*

Colorful faux-painted walls, cherub frescoes, and sidewalk views enhance the Italian-Jewish fare dished up at this bustling restaurant. Its owner, Noah Alper, founded Noah's Bagels (he sold that company in 1996). Certified kosher, the menu is mostly vegetarian with some fine fish selections—similar to the kosher dairy restaurants found in New York City. Pastas and desserts are prepared on site. Appetizers include a stuffed artichoke, soup of the day, and organic salads. Thin-crusted, wood-fired pizzas include the simple, ever-popular tomato-mozzarella Margherita and the enticingly named mozzarella-oregano-olive oil bianca neve (or "snow white"). A delicious calzone stuffed with eggplant, mushrooms, olives,

and more is also on the menu. Pasta dishes—including a great conchiglie with a sautéed sauce of eggplant, garlic, smoked mozzarella, capers, and tomato—are prepared vegan upon request, as are pizzas. The full bar serves wines from around the world, including some kosher wines, and also a tasty red-hued Moretti La Rossa Italian beer.

The **Landmark Act 1 & 2** movie theater (*(510) 464-5980; www.landmarktheatres.com.*) is right next door, making dinner and a movie quite convenient.

## Saul's Restaurant & Delicatessen

*1475 Shattuck Ave./Cedar St., (510) 848-DELI, fax (510) 848-8366; www.saulsdeli.com. B-L-D daily; $. Highchairs, boosters, booths, child menu. No reservations.*

Boasting a NYC deli feel and some very comfortable booths, this casual spot presents popular traditional Jewish deli dishes: chicken soup with matzo balls or noodles, long-simmered brisket with carrots and onions, crispy latkes, delicious egg creams, and creamy rice pudding. The pita bread and hummus are especially good. A complimentary bowl of addictive whole, crisp cucumber pickles are brought to munch on while perusing the menu. The deli prepares everything to go.

## Skates

*100 Seawall Dr., at foot of University Ave., (510) 549-1900; www.skatesonthebay.com. L M-F, D daily, Sat-SunBr; $$. Highchairs, boosters, booths, child menu. Reservations advised.*

Window tables take best advantage of the stunning three-bridge view here. Brunch items include an omelette and frittata, French toast, a shellfish Benedict with lemon-dill scones, and macadamia nut-banana sourdough pancakes. The extensive lunch menu offers deep-fried Cajun shrimp in coconut beer batter, a hamburger on focaccia bun, and a variety of soups, salads, and pastas, and the dinner menu features fresh fish items. Desserts are traditional and include a hot fudge sundae, a burnt-cream custard, and, in season, a giant strawberry shortcake.

## Smokey Joe's Cafe

*1620 Shattuck Ave./Cedar Ave., no phone. B-L daily. No "plastic."*

The owner of this tiny hole-in-the-wall diner—basically a counter with stools plus several small tables—has been dishing up noteworthy breakfasts since 1973. Smokey is famous for his homefries and delicious omelettes. Everything is made to order, and the fresh organic OJ is squeezed *after* it is ordered. The all-vegetarian menu says this is "where the elite meet to eat no meat" and includes a vegan tofu scramble and a holy mole frijole bowl. Decor consists of '60s memorabilia—tie-dyed things, a large peace symbol brick—and live music is sometimes scheduled. It's a trip!

### Spenger's Fresh Fish Grotto

*1919 4th St./University Ave., (510) 845-7771, fax (510) 845-7778; www.mccormickandschmicks.com. L-D daily; $$-$$$. Highchairs, boosters, booths, child menu. Reservations advised.*

Begun in 1890 as a country store, Spenger's evolved into a fish market and then morphed again after Prohibition into a bar and restaurant. Now part of the McCormick & Schmick seafood chain, it serves the very freshest fish in a vast variety of styles. The menu changes daily and includes favorite standards as well as more unusual items. The restaurant remains one of Berkeley's most popular. Seating includes comfy booths and "snugs" (semi-closed-off private areas) in a warren of rooms decorated with everything sea-related—it's a veritable maritime museum. Don't miss viewing the extensive collection of model ships or the massive 34-carat Star of Denmark canary diamond once owned by Hawaii's Queen Kapiolani and now displayed in the Diamond Bar. A well-stocked fish market adjoins.

### Taiwan

*2071 University Ave./Shattuck Ave., (510) 845-1456. L-D daily, Sat-SunBr; $. Highchairs, boosters. No reservations.*

Taiwanese specialties and representative dishes from most of the Chinese provinces are served here. Portions are generous, and a vegetarian menu is available. Favorites include kuo teh (pot stickers), spinach with garlic, dry-braised green beans, vegetable chow fun, General Tsao's chicken, spicy fish-flavored chicken, beef a la Shangtung (deep-fried pieces of battered beef in a tasty sauce), showy sizzling beef and sizzling chicken platters, Mongolian beef, and spicy prawns. Exotic items include Taiwan pickle cabbage with pork tripe soup, boneless duck web, and numerous squid dishes. Beggar's chicken and Peking duck are available when ordered 1 day in advance. On weekends, a Chinese breakfast is served. The fortune cookies here are unusually prophetic. The strip inside mine once read, "You would make an excellent critic."

### Top Dog

*#1: 2534 Durant Ave./Telegraph Ave., (510) 843-5967; #2: 2503 Hearst Ave./Euclid Ave., (510) 843-1241; www.topdoghotdogs.com. L-D daily; $. No reservations.*

Hot dogs are the extent of the menu at this atmospheric hole-in-the-wall. Twelve different kinds are available, including a veggie version. The most popular dog is the namesake kosher Top Dog. Topped off with sauerkraut and hot mustard, it's one of the best dogs on the West Coast. To dine, grab one of the few counter stools, sit on the bench outside, or just stomp and chomp.

More small restaurants are in this dining mini-mall. One of the best is **Aki** *((510) 848-0208. L-D Sun-F; $.)*, with a full Japanese menu and a greaseless tempura.

### Udupi Palace

*1901-1903 University Ave./Martin Luther King Blvd., (510) 843-6600. L-D daily; $. Highchairs. No cards.*

A cog in a chain that stretches to Toronto, Canada, this all-vegetarian cafe serves up the pancakes and other dishes that comprise South Indian cuisine. Thin, rolled, rice-flour crêpes known as dosas are especially good and include a gargantuan paper dosa that measures almost 2 feet long and is filled with a yellow split peas, a triangular mysore masala dosa filled with spicy potatoes, and a lacy rava masala dosa made with two kinds of onion and filled with potatoes. Uthappam are smaller and fatter—more like Western pancakes—and topped with various mixtures. Rice dishes, curries, and a daily special 10-item thali flesh out the focused menu.

### VIK's Chaat Corner

*724 Allston Way/4th St., (510) 644-4412; www.vik distributors.com. L Tu-Sun; $. No reservations.*

Operating within a wide-open former

garage-warehouse, this casual Indian cafe is described as reminiscent of a New Delhi bazaar. Excited diners line up out the door waiting to order at the counter and then volley for space at the charmless tables. The limited menu is handwritten on a board and changes daily. Food is served unceremoniously on paper plates with plastic utensils. Chaat translates as "small snacks," and deliciously spiced choices include a variety of appetizer-sized items that make a nice meal when shared. Consider pakori chaat (lentil dumplings with tamarind chutney), sev puri (potatoes and onions with garlic chutney), and samosas topped with spicy garbanzo curry. Both a meat and a vegetarian plate complete with rice and bread are also available. Drinks include a delicious creamy mango lassi and a thick guava nectar, and for dessert Indian sweets can be selected from a glass case. Next door, a related shop sells exotic Indian cooking staples.

### Walker's Restaurant & Pie Shop
*1491 Solano Ave./Curtis St., in Albany, (510) 525-4647. B-L Tu-Sat, D Tu-Sun, SunBr; $. Highchairs, boosters, child portions. No reservations.*

Most everyone in these parts has been here at some point for one of the famous home-style meals. The surroundings are simple, but the food is fresh, ample, and all housemade. The old-fashioned menu hasn't changed much over the years. Breakfast choices include omelettes and French toast, while lunch is burgers, sandwiches, and hot plates. Complete dinners include soup, a green salad, popovers, an entree with a fresh vegetable and either baked or mashed potato, and a slice of their celebrated pie (the banana cream and sour cherry are fabulous). Entrees include fish, fried chicken, ham, New York steak, prime rib, and daily specials.

## Crockett

### — WHERE TO EAT —

### The Nantucket
*At foot of Port St., (510) 787-2233. L-D daily; $$. Highchairs, boosters, child portions. Reservations advised.*

Situated at the end of a twisting road under the Carquinez Bridge, on the other side of the tracks, this unpretentious restaurant specializes in New England-style fresh fish items.

Most are available either charcoal-broiled or pan-fried. Shellfish is available lightly breaded and deep-fried Cape Cod-style as well as in casseroles with Newburg or Mornay sauce. Shellfish cioppino, a house specialty, is prepared either old-fashioned style (in the shell) or lazy man's style (out of the shell). Lobster and steak comprise the higher-priced end of the menu. All dinners come with a choice of either creamy white clam chowder or a green salad topped with shrimp, with Parmesan cheese-topped French bread, with a fresh vegetable prepared with flair, and with a choice of either French fries or seasoned rice. All tables have a water view. Should there be a wait, drinks and seafood appetizers can be ordered from the bar and enjoyed either indoors or out on the pier. Crockett is the major center for sugar production on the West Coast. Driving back to the freeway, the large red brick building seen to the east is the circa 1906 C&H Sugar refinery.

## Benicia

### — A LITTLE BACKGROUND —

Founded in 1847 by General Vallejo and named for his bride, this low-key town was the state capital for a short time in 1853. Situated on the Carquinez Strait, about 30 miles northeast of San Francisco, it was also a very busy port. Now it is known for its many antique shops (located along First Street) and the **Benicia Glass Studios** consortium of glass-blowing factories *(675 & 701 E. H St., (707) 745-2614; beniciaglass.com. M-Sat 10-4, Sun 12-5. Free.).* Note that many town shops are closed on Mondays and Tuesdays.

### — VISITOR INFORMATION —

### Benicia Chamber of Commerce
*601 First St., (800) 559-7377, (707) 745-2120, fax (707) 745-2275; www.beniciachamber.com.*

### — GETTING THERE —

Located about 35 miles from San Francisco, and 7 miles east of Vallejo via I-780.

### — WHAT TO DO —

### Benicia Capitol State Historic Park
*115 W. G St., (707) 745-3385; www.parks.ca.gov.*

*Daily 10-5. $2, under 16 free.*

Historic information, artifacts, and period furniture await visitors inside this restored 2-story, red brick Greek Revival building that served as the state capitol from February 4, 1853 to February 25, 1854. Also in the park is the 1858 Federal-style Victorian **Fischer-Hanlon House,** a renovated Gold Rush hotel. It holds an impressive collection of period furniture, and tours are sometimes available.

## — WHERE TO STAY & EAT —

### The Union Hotel

*401 First St., (866) 445-2323, (707) 746-0110, fax (707) 745-3032; www.unionhotelbenicia.com. 12 rooms; $$. Full breakfast Sat-Sun; restaurant. No smoking; pets ok.*

Located right on the main street, in the part of town reflecting the ambiance of a quieter era, this 1885 Victorian hotel offers individually decorated rooms.

For a gourmet dinner, hotel guests need just catch the elevator down to the attractive **restaurant** *(L-D daily, Sat-SunBr. Highchairs, boosters, child portions. Reservations advised.).* For a relaxing after-dinner drink, it's just a few steps over to a cozy **lounge** with an impressive 110-year-old mahogany bar and stained-glass windows.

# Vallejo

## — VISITOR INFORMATION —

### Vallejo Convention & Visitors Bureau

*495 Mare Island Way, (800) 4-VALLEJO, (707) 642-3653, fax (707) 644-2206; www.visitvallejo.com.*

This bureau also provides information on Benicia.

## — GETTING THERE —

Located 30 miles northeast of San Francisco.

## — WHAT TO DO —

### Mare Island Historic Park

*(707) 557-1538, fax (707) 552-3266; www.mareisland hpf.org. Tour: (707) 644-4746; by donation, $10, 6-12 $5; reservations required.*

Historic Mare Island, the West Coast's first Naval base and shipyard, was founded in 1854 to fend off pirates who were then roaming the local seas. Interestingly, it is named after a female horse that swam to the island. Over a period of 142 years, 513 ships were built here. The base also launched the first U.S. submarine, and the movie *Sphere*—starring Sharon Stone—was filmed here. Because the island still has a guarded security gate, the only way to see it is via a guided tour. The 2-hour tour includes seeing world-famous **St. Peter's Chapel,** built in 1901 and featuring beautiful Tiffany stained-glass windows and an inverted-keel redwood ceiling (it was the Navy's first inter-denominational chapel); the historic cemetery (burial place of Anna Turner, daughter of Francis Scott Key); and Officer's Row mansions and gardens. The **Admiral's Mansion** can be toured for an additional fee ($4). Participants also see Alden Park, which is home to a cannon from the War of 1812, torpedoes from the Civil War, and a German Marder suicide submarine from 1944.

### Six Flags Marine World

*Marine World Parkway/Hwy. 37, (707) 643-6722; www.sixflags.com. F-Sun spring & fall, daily in summer, closed in winter; opens at 10, closing time varies. $45.99, 60+ $35.99, children 48" tall & under $24.99; parking $10.*

Just a few years ago, this theme park completely reinvented itself by adding rides to its world-famous collection of wildlife shows. It is now the nation's only combination wildlife park, oceanarium, and theme park. The exciting animal shows feature dolphins, sea lions, elephants, tigers, and exotic birds, and a spectacular water-skiing show is put on by daredevil humans. Visitors can walk through animal habitat areas to see African animals and ride an

Asian elephant *($5)*. The Looney Tunes Acme Foam Factory—with slides and climbing structures and hundreds of orange foam balls for kids to toss or shoot from air cannons—and the Gentle Jungle petting area are particularly popular with young children. Butterfly Habitat is the first walk-through free-flight butterfly enclosure in the western U.S., and the walk-in Lorikeet Aviary provides up-close observation of these brightly colored birds and the opportunity to feed them. Now adding thrills to the mix are five monster roller coasters, the world's first 3-D motion simulator ride, and an assortment of other wild rides. Consider taking the ferry from San Francisco—the Blue & Gold Fleet *((415) 705-5555; www.blueandgoldfleet.com.)* departs from Pier 39—or BART *((415) 992-2278; www.bart.gov; runs M-Sat.)*.

### Vallejo Naval and Historical Museum
*734 Marin St./Virginia St., (707) 643-0077, fax (707) 643-2443; www.vallejomuseum.org. Tu-Sat 10-4:30. $2, seniors $1, under 13 free.*

Operating inside the town's former City Hall, this museum's treasures include a working submarine periscope that pokes through the roof and provides a view of Mare Island.

# Fairfield

## – WHAT TO DO –

### Anheuser-Busch Brewery Tour
*3101 Busch Dr., (707) 429-7595. Tu-Sat 10-4, on the hr., Sept-May; also M June-Aug. Free.*

The tour here starts with a short video explaining how a Bud is made. Then visitors don plastic safety glasses and head out to see

the beer bottled and capped—or canned—and then boxed. Back in the Hospitality Room everyone gets free samples and snacks. All ages are welcome.

### Jelly Belly Candy Company
*One Jelly Belly Lane, Abernathy Rd. east exit off I-80, (707) 428-2838, (800) 9-JELLY-B; www.jellybelly.com. Tours: Daily 9-5; free.*

Family-run since 1898, this company has been making candy corn since around 1900 and the famous, flavorful Jelly Belly® jelly bean since 1976. After taking the 40-minute Candyland factory tour (baby strollers are permitted), everyone gets a souvenir bag of the company's jelly beans. Though tours are given daily, on weekends the workers are off and the factory isn't operating. The gift shop sells Belly Flops (rejects) at bargain prices when available, and an exhibition candy kitchen lets visitors view the making of an array of sweets (the company makes over 100 other kinds of candy). A cafe offers Jelly Belly-shaped pizzas and hamburgers, and birthday party rooms, a picnic area, and a dog walk are also available.

### Western Railway Museum
*5848 Hwy. 12, in Suisun City, between Fairfield & Rio Vista (exit Hwy. 80 at Hwy. 12, then drive 12 mi. E), (707) 374-2978, fax (707) 374-6742; www.wrm.org. Sat-Sun 10:30-5; W-Sun in summer. $8, 65+ $7, 2-14 $5.*

Located between two sheep pastures in the middle of a flat, arid no-man's land, this very special museum displays and actually operates its collection of historic electric streetcars and interurban trains. Among the dozen or so operating electric cars are both a bright red car from the Peninsular Railway and an articulated car, which is hinged so it can go around corners and which ran on the Bay Bridge from 1939 to 1958. Several cars operate each weekend, running along a 10-mile stretch of track with overhead electric trolley wires. Cars are operated by the same volunteers who spent countless hours lovingly restoring them. Stationary cars awaiting repair can be viewed in several large barns. An oasis-like picnic and play area is available to visitors, and a bookstore offers a large collection of railroad books and paraphernalia. All fees collected are used to restore and maintain the streetcars. (It costs about $170,000 to restore a

car and, because the labor is volunteer, it can take as long as 10 years!) The museum also operates theme trains over the Sacramento Northern Railway. Pumpkin Patch Trains run at Halloween, and Santa Claus Specials sometimes operate during December.

# Sacramento

## — A LITTLE BACKGROUND —

*It is fiery summer always, and you can gather roses, and eat strawberries and ice-cream, and wear white linen clothes, and pant and perspire at eight or nine o'clock in the morning.*

—Mark Twain

Gold was discovered in 1848 just 30 miles east of Sacramento, and the rest is history. As news of the discovery spread like wildfire around the globe, fortune hunters came here before setting out for the mining fields. Sacramento has been the state capital since 1854. In 1866, Mark Twain was a special news correspondent with the *Sacramento Union Newspaper*.

Most of the major historic attractions are concentrated in the downtown area. This flat, central part of town was laid out in a grid of lettered and numbered streets by town founder John Sutter's son, John Sutter, Jr., making it easy to get around even now.

As in New York City, the streets here are almost empty on Sunday, and they are pretty quiet on Saturday. So surprisingly, on weekends it is a great destination for avoiding crowds.

## — VISITOR INFORMATION —

**Sacramento Convention & Visitors Bureau**
*1608 I St., (800) 292-2334, (916) 808-7777, fax (916) 808-7788; www.discovergold.org.*

## — GETTING THERE —

Located approximately 90 miles northeast of San Francisco.

### —By Train—

**Amtrak**
*(800) USA-RAIL; www.amtrak.com.*
    Capitol Corridor trains leave for Sacramento daily from San Jose, San Francisco (via bus connection to Oakland), and Oakland. Family fares are available. Overnight train-hotel packages can be booked through **Amtrak Vacations** *((800) 440-8202).*

### —Scenic Route by Car—

Take Highway 160 through the Delta (see page 375).

## — ANNUAL EVENTS —

**Sacramento Jazz Jubilee**
*May; Memorial Day weekend. (916) 372-5277, fax (916) 372-3479; www.sacjazz.com. $9-$40.*

This is the world's largest traditional jazz festival. Styles include zydeco, blues, Latin jazz, Western swing, and gospel.

## Waterworld USA

*Mid-May to mid-September. 1600 Exposition Blvd., (916) 924-3747, fax (916) 924-1314; www.sixflags.com. Daily 10:30-6. Over 4' tall $21.99, under 4' $16.99, 60+ $12.99, under age 3 free; parking $7.*

Located adjacent to the state fair site, this attraction features the largest wave pool in Northern California, the highest waterslides in the West, and an assortment of other attractions.

## California State Fair

*August. 1600 Exposition Blvd.; (877) 225-3976, (916) 263-FAIR; www.bigfun.org. $10, 62+ $8, 5-12 $6; parking $7.*

There's something for everyone at the oldest state fair in the West, which is also the largest agricultural fair in the U.S. Pleasures include monorail and carnival rides, thoroughbred racing, educational exhibits, and live entertainment. Special for children are a petting farm, pony rides, and a nursery where baby animals are born each day.

### — WHAT TO DO —

## American River Parkway

*(916) 366-2072, fax (916) 855-5932; www.sacparks. net. Daily sunrise-sunset. $4/vehicle.*

This is 23 miles of water fun. Call for a free map and more information about facilities.

• **Effie Yeaw Nature Center**
*6700 Tarshes Dr., in Ancil Hoffman County Park, in Carmichael, (916) 489-4918, fax (916) 489-4983; www.effieyeaw.org. Daily 9-5, Mar-Oct; 9:30-4, Nov-Feb. Free.*

Displays and hands-on exhibits bring the area's natural and cultural history to life. A Maidu Indian Village and a 77-acre nature preserve with three self-guided nature trails are also part of the center.

• **Fishing**
The best month for salmon and steelhead is October. Favorite spots are the Nimbus Basin below the dam and Sailor Bar. A state license in required.

• **Jedediah Smith National Recreation Trail**
This paved pathway runs for 23 miles along the American River.

• **Raft trips**
Trips begin in the Upper Sunrise Recreation Area, located north of the Sunrise Boulevard exit off Highway 50. In summer, several companies rent rafts and provide shuttle bus return.

## Bridges

Located near Old Sacramento, the Tower Bridge—a lift span drawbridge—sometimes can be observed going up. To the right of it, the I Street Bridge is one of the few remaining pedestal bridges in the country; sometimes it can be observed turning.

## The B Street Theatre

*2711 B St./27th St., (916) 443-5300, fax (916) 443-0874; www.bstreettheatre.org. $17.50-$21.50.*

Founded by actor Timothy Busfield—who starred in TV's memorable *Thirty-Something*—and his brother Buck, this small non-profit professional theater company presents only world premieres. None of their productions has been performed anywhere else. The theater itself is small, and seating in the round means performances are in-your-face intimate. The audience is close enough to the actors to see their warts, wrinkles, and other human imperfections. Everything is in place for a satisfying night of theater.

## California State Capitol tour

*10th St./L St., (916) 324-0333; www.statecapitol museum.com. Tours daily 9-4. Free.*

Restored now to its turn-of-the-century decor and earthquake-safe—a job that cost $68 million and is said to have been the largest restoration project in the history of the country—the Capitol is quite a showcase. Free tickets are available in the basement a half-hour before each tour, and a small **museum** with a 10-minute orientation film entertains visitors during any wait. A short-order cafeteria operates in the basement for meals and snacks, and a full-service cafe is open weekdays on the sixth floor.

The surrounding park is the largest **arboretum** west of the Mississippi and home to over 300 varieties of trees and flowers from all over the world as well as to one of the largest camellia groves in the world. Tours are scheduled daily in summer at 10:30 a.m. The circular **California Vietnam Veteran's Memorial** *(15th*

*St./Capitol Ave.)* is located by the rose garden at the park's east end. The 22 shiny black granite panels of this privately funded monument are engraved with the 5,822 names of California's dead and missing. **The International World Peace Rose Garden** *((800) 205-1223; www.world peacegardens.org.)* here displays more than 800 roses.

## California State History Museum

*1020 O St./10th St., (916) 653-7524, fax (916) 653-7134; www.castatehistory.org. Tu-Sat 10-5, Sun 12-5. $5, 55+ $4, 6-13 $3.50.*

Arranged by topics, this museum tells the state's story in four exhibit galleries: the Place, People, Promise, and Politics of California. The collection includes authentic documents, films, an inviting reconstructed cafe, a ghostly holo-gram, and the occasional car and bus. An audio guide for self-touring is included with admis-sion. The museum occupies the first two floors of the California Archives building. Before leav-ing, visit the 6-story-tall interior courtyard sculpture known as "Constitution Wall."

## Crocker Art Museum

*216 O St./3rd St., (916) 264-5423, fax (916) 264-7372; www.crockerartmuseum.org. Tu-Sun 10-5, Thur to 9. $6, 65+ $4, 7-17 $3.*

Located within a magnificent Italianate building dating from 1874, this is the oldest public art museum west of the Mississippi. Collection highlights include Master drawings, 19th-century American and European paintings, and contemporary Northern California art in all media. Family activities occur every week-end, and lectures, films, and Sunday afternoon concerts are often scheduled. Picnic tables are available across the street in lovely Crocker Park.

## Governor's Mansion State Historic Park

*1526 H St./16th St., (916) 323-3047; www.parks. ca.gov. Tours: Daily 10-4, on the hr. $2, under 17 free.*

Built in 1877, this 30-room Victorian mansion was purchased by the state in 1903 for $32,500. During the next 64 years, it was home to 13 governors and their families. It remains just as it was when vacated by its last tenant— Governor Ronald Reagan. Now serving the public as a museum, it displays 15 rooms of furnishings and personal items left behind by

each family. Visitors see Governor George Pardee's 1902 Steinway piano, Earl Warren's hand-tied Persian carpets, and Hiram Johnson's plum velvet sofa and chairs. Among the inter-esting artifacts are marble fireplaces from Italy and gold-framed mirrors from France. The official State of California china, selected by the wife of Goodwin Knight in the late 1950s, is also on display.

## Old Sacramento Historic District

Situated along the Sacramento River, Old Sacramento was the kickoff point for the gold fields during the Gold Rush. It was the western terminus for both the Pony Express and the country's first long distance telegraph, and the country's first transcontinental railroad started here. Said to be the largest historic preservation project in the West, Old Sacramento is a 28-acre living museum of the Old West. Vintage build-ings, wooden walkways, and cobblestone streets recall the period from 1850 to 1880. Restau-rants, shops, and historic exhibits combine to make it both an entertaining and educational spot to visit.

Information on tours can be obtained at the **Visitor Information Center** *(1004 2nd St./ J St., (916) 442-7644, fax (916) 264-7286; www.oldsacramento.com. Daily 9-5.).* Horse-drawn carriages can be hired for rides from Old Sacramento to the Capitol.

● **California State Railroad Museum**
*111 I St./2nd St., (916) 445-6645; www.csrmf.org.*
*Daily 10-5. $4, under 17 free; ticket good on same day*
*for admission to Central Pacific Passenger Depot.*

This gigantic 3-story building holds the largest interpretive railroad museum in North America. Inside, 21 beautifully restored, full-size railroad locomotives and cars representing the 1860s through the 1960s are on display. Among them are an apartment-size, lushly furnished Georgia Northern private car complete with stained-glass windows, and a Canadian Pullman rigged to feel as if it is actually moving. A film, a 30-projector multi-image slide show, and assorted interpretive displays tell the history of American railroading. Docent-led tours are available, and well-trained, railroad-loving volunteers, wearing historically authentic railroad workers' garb, are always on hand to answer questions. Upstairs, great views of the trains below are afforded from an oversize catwalk. A large collection of toy trains—including a 1957 pastel pink Lionel train designed especially for little girls—is also displayed.

Nearby, the **Central Pacific Passenger Depot** *(930 Front St./J St.)* displays nine more locomotives and cars. Visiting this reconstructed

train depot provides the opportunity to step back in time to 1876—an era when riding the train was the chic way to travel. A free audio tour wand picks up recorded descriptions of displays. The **Sacramento Southern Railroad** excursion steam train departs from the depot for a 6-mile, 40-minute round-trip *(Sat-Sun 11-5, on the hr.; Apr-Sept only. $6, 6-12 $3.)*.

● **Discovery Museum History Center**
*101 I St., (916) 264-7057, fax (916) 264-5100;*
*www.thediscovery.org. Tu-Sun 10-5; daily July-Aug. $5,*
*60+ & 13-17 $4, 4-12 $3.*

This 3-story brick building is a replica of Sacramento's first public building—the 1854 City Hall. A 113-foot freestanding fiberglass flagpole in front is said to be the tallest in the entire country. The museum brings Sacramento's history and the 1849 Gold Rush to life with an extensive collection of gold specimens (worth $1 million and including a 13-pound gold nugget), historical photos, and historic farm equipment. Among the exhibits are a replica mineshaft and an antique poultry incubator. Children especially enjoy a kid-sized log cabin and story area with rocking chair, as well as coloring stations located throughout.

The nearby **Discovery Museum Science & Space Center** *(3615 Auburn Blvd., (916) 575-3941, fax (916) 575-3925. Tu-F 12-5, Sat-Sun 10-5; daily 10-5, July-Aug. $5, 60+ & 13-17 $4, 4-12 $3.)* has the area's only planetarium, plus live animals and a nature trail.

● **Eagle Theatre**
*925 Front St./J St., (916) 323-6343, fax (916) 327-0953; www.csrmf.org. Performances sometimes presented F-Sat at 8pm; $10-$12. Tour: Schedule varies; free.*

A reconstruction of California's first theater building built in 1849, the Eagle now presents Gold Rush-era plays and musicals. Children's programs are also sometimes scheduled.

● **Old Sacramento Schoolhouse**
*1200 Front St./L St., (916) 483-8818. M-F 10-4, Sat-Sun 12-4. Free.*

Now a museum, this 1800s one-room schoolhouse has a play yard with old-fashioned board swings kids can still use.

● **Riverboat cruises.**
*110 L St., (800) 433-0263, (916) 552-2933, fax (916) 552-2942; http://spiritofsacramento.com. Schedule*

*varies. $10-$67.50. Reservations required.*

Two paddle wheelers, the *Spirit of Sacramento* and the *Matthew McKinley*, ply the waters here offering sightseeing, brunch, lunch, dinner, sunset, and happy hour cruises.

## State Indian Museum State Historic Park

*2618 K St./26th St., (916) 324-0971; www.parks.ca. gov. Daily 10-5. $1, under 17 free.*

Established in 1940, this museum displays interesting examples of bark clothing and a permanent basket collection featuring colorful Pomo feather baskets. Films are shown throughout the day. Picnicking is particularly pleasant beside a duck pond across from the museum.

## Sutter's Fort State Historic Park

*2701 L St./27th St., (916) 445-4422, fax (916) 442-8613; www.parks.ca.gov. Daily 10-5. $3, under 17 free.*

A reconstruction of the settlement founded in 1839 by Captain John A. Sutter—who originally arrived with 10 Hawaiians and lived in a grass hut built by them out native grasses—this is the first permanent interior settlement built in California and the oldest restored fort in the West. The central building is the original built by Sutter and Native Americans. Exhibits include carpenter, cooper, and blacksmith shops as well as prison and living quarters. An audio tour is included with admission. On Living History Days, demonstrators stay in character for 1846: The man portraying James Marshall, who was a carpenter before he discovered gold, might be working on wood projects and will look startled if asked about gold since it wasn't discovered in this part of California until 1848. Blacksmithing, musket and cannon demos, and military drills are also part of the show. On monthly Pioneer Demonstration Days, interpreters dress in character but recognize that it is 2002. Then, visitors can participate in some of the crafts, including rope-making, corn husk doll-making, basketry, and baking. In summer, interpreters dress in period garb, demonstrate crafts, and give historical information daily. As part of the Environmental Living program, school groups take over the fort on Tuesday and Thursday from November through June, dressing in period clothing and doing demonstrations.

## Towe Auto Museum

*2200 Front St., (916) 442-6802, fax (916) 442-2646; www.toweautomuseum.org. Daily 10-6. $7, seniors $6, 5-18 $2-$3.*

This cavernous museum displays more than 150 antique cars depicting the history of the American automobile. In addition to the cars, the museum has a Mighty Wurlitzer Theater Pipe Organ with 1,200 pipes. Mini-concerts are presented on Sunday afternoons in the spring and fall. Call for directions; this museum is difficult to find.

## Victorian houses

Elaborate Victorian homes are found between 7th and 16th streets, from E to I streets. Don't miss the Heilbron house at 740 O Street and the Stanford house at 800 N Street.

## William Land Park

*On Freeport Blvd. betw. 13th Ave. & Sutterville Rd., (916) 277-6060.*

This 236-acre park has a supervised playground, children's wading pool, 9-hole golf course, and fishing pond for children under 16. It also incorporates:

### • Fairytale Town

*3901 Land Park Dr., (916) 264-5233; www.fairytale town.org. Schedule varies. $3.50-$4, under 3 free.*

Nursery rhymes and fairy tales come to life in this 2½-acre amusement park.

### • Funderland

*1350 17th Ave., Sutterville Rd./S. Land Park Dr., (916) 456-0115, fax (916) 383-7735; www.funder landpark.com. Schedule varies; closed most of Dec-Jan. $1-$1.50/ride.*

In operation since 1948, this old-fashioned amusement park for young children delights them with an assortment of rides. Pony rides are available adjacent.

### • Sacramento Zoo

*3930 W. Land Park Dr./Sutterville Rd., (916) 264-5888, fax (916) 264-5887; www.saczoo.com. Daily 9-4; Nov-Jan 10-4. $6.75-$7.25, 3-12 $4.50-$5.*

This modest 15-acre zoo is home to over 150 exotic and native species, 40 of which are endangered or threatened. It holds just enough exhibits to keep visitors busy for a pleasant few hours. A snack bar dispenses a limited, but appropriate and satisfying, menu, and baby strollers can be rented.

## — WHERE TO STAY —

Motels abound. Call a favorite chain for reservations, or contact the Convention & Visitors Bureau for a list of lodgings.

### Delta King

*1000 Front St., in Old Sacramento, (800) 825-KING, (916) 444-KING, fax (916) 444-5314; www.deltaking. com. 5 stories; 44 rooms; $$. Children under 6 free. Continental breakfast; restaurant. No smoking; no pets. Valet parking $12.*

Launched in 1927, this flat-bottomed riverboat plied the waters between Sacramento and San Francisco in the late 1920s and '30s. After having spent 15 months partially submerged in the San Francisco Bay, she received years of restoration work costing $9.5 million and is now appropriately moored dockside in Old Sacramento. All guest rooms have private bathrooms with an old-fashioned pedestal sink and tall-tank toilet with pull-chain, and a few have clawfoot tubs. The vessel's wheelhouse is converted into a room with a private second-story observation deck.

An elegant dinner with a river view can be enjoyed in the **Pilothouse Restaurant** (*(916) 441-4440. L M-Sat, D daily, SunBr. Highchairs, boosters, child menu. Reservations advised.*), located on the Promenade Deck. Entrees include luxury items such as prawns, steak, and rack of lamb. A well-executed Caesar salad is dramatically prepared tableside and not to be missed, and an enticing dessert tray is also available. Live music is performed on a grand piano most evenings in a cozy lounge-style bar adjoining the restaurant.

On Friday and Saturday night an interactive murder mystery dinner show is presented in the **Mark Twain Salon**, a lively bar overlooking the boat's 17-ton paddle wheel. Live performances are also scheduled Thursday through Sunday down on the Cargo Deck in the intimate **Delta King Theatre**. Intermissions are long, allowing plenty of time to visit the lobby bar. Dinner-theater and overnight packages are sometimes available.

### Hyatt Regency Sacramento

*1209 L St./12th St., (800) HYATT-CA, (916) 443-1234, fax (916) 321-3099; http://sacramento.hyatt.com. 15 stories, 503 rooms; $$$. Heated pool; hot tub; fitness room. 2 restaurants; room service. No pets.*

*Self-parking $15, valet $18.*

Situated across the street from the Capitol and adjacent to both the convention center and the pedestrian K Street Mall, this well-located luxury hotel features a Mediterranean architectural style, an atrium lobby, and marble floors. A charming topiary hedge fence in the shape of people and animals defines its front entrance.

### KOA Kampground

*3951 Lake Rd., in West Sacramento, (800) KOA-2747, (916) 371-6771, fax (916) 371-0622; www.koa.com.*

For description, see page 443.

### Radisson Hotel Sacramento

*500 Leisure Ln., (800) 333-3333, (916) 922-2020, fax (916) 649-9463; www.radisson.com/sacramentoca. 309 rooms; $-$$$. Children under 18 free. Heated pool; hot tub; fitness room. Restaurant.*

Located on the outskirts of downtown, this low-rise hotel complex operates much like a vacation resort. Rooms are spacious and comfortable, and some overlook a natural spring-fed lake and koi pond. On weekends throughout the summer, jazz and orchestra performances are scheduled in the property's own amphitheater and are free to guests. Bicycle rentals are available for rides along the scenic Jedediah Smith bike trail, which runs along the American River Parkway adjacent to the hotel. (The 35-mile trail runs along the river from Old Sacramento to Folsom. The hotel is about 5 miles from the Old Sacramento end.) A courtesy shuttle takes guests to the grand, indoor Arden Fair Shopping Mall located nearby.

### Sacramento Hostel

*925 H St./10th St., (800) 909-4776 #40, (916) 443-1691, fax (916) 443-4763; www.norcalhostels.org. 80 beds; 5 private rooms.*

Operating within an 1885 Victorian mansion, this jewel is centrally located and convenient to major attractions. It features a restored drawing room, luxurious parlor, recreation room, and patio with barbecue as well as verandahs and gardens. See also page 445.

### Sterling Hotel

*1300 H St./13th St., (800) 365-7660, (916) 448-1300, fax (916) 455-6102; www.sterlinghotel.com. 16 rooms; $$. Continental breakfast; restaurant. No smoking; no pets. No parking.*

Located just 3 blocks from the Capitol, this converted Victorian mansion claims to be the only hotel in the country with private, oversize Jacuzzis in each all-marble bathroom. Room 303, furnished with a posh oriental carpet and with a balcony overlooking the front yard's magnolia trees, is especially nice. The hotel's highly rated restaurant, **Chanterelle**, serves California cuisine.

## — WHERE TO EAT —

### Buca di Beppo
*1249 Howe Ave./Hurley Way, (916) 92-AMORE, fax (916) 922-6671; www.bucadibeppo.com. L-D dailly.*
For description, see page 60.

### Buffalo Bob's Ice Cream Saloon
*110 K St., in Old Sacramento, (916) 442-1105. Daily 10-6; $. Highchairs, boosters. No cards.*
A variety of sandwiches and hot dogs are available here, as is old-time sarsaparilla to wash it all down. Ice cream concoctions dominate the menu and include exotic sundaes such as Fool's Gold (butter brickle ice cream topped with butterscotch and marshmallow, whipped cream, almonds, and a cherry) and Sierra Nevada (peaks of vanilla ice cream capped with hot fudge, whipped cream, almonds, and a cherry).

### Fanny Ann's Saloon
*1023 2nd St., in Old Sacramento, (916) 441-0505. L-D daily; $. Boosters. No reservations.*
This narrow, four-level restaurant has a raucous ambiance and funky decor that provide the makings for instant fun. Children and adults alike enjoy the casual atmosphere and American-style fare: good half-pound hamburgers, assorted styles of 9-inch hot dogs, curly French fries, and large bowls of housemade soup. A variety of sandwiches and salads are also available. After placing orders with the cook at the back window, diners can relax with a game of pinball or get a downright cheap drink at the old bar. When one mother inquired whether there were booster seats, the cheerful hostess replied, "I'll hold the kids on my lap."

### Fat City Bar & Grill
*1001 Front St., in Old Sacramento, (916) 446-6768; www.fatsrestaurants.com/fatcity. L M-F, D daily, Sat-SunBr; $$. Highchairs, boosters, child menu. No reservations.*

This high-ceilinged brick building was constructed around 1849 by Samuel Brannan as a general merchandise store. It was the first store established after the City of Sacramento was laid out. Now it holds a popular restaurant featuring Tiffany-style lamps, stained-glass windows, and Victorian-style furnishings. Delicious specialty drinks are served at an ornate old mahogany bar, or with meals at dining tables overlooking sidewalk traffic. Appetizers such as Southern fried chicken strips and French onion soup are on the menu along with a variety of pasta dishes and hamburgers. Old-fashioned desserts such as strawberry shortcake and hot fudge sundaes wind things up.

### Fox & Goose Public House
*1001 R St./10th St., (916) 443-8825; www.foxand goose.com. B daily, L M-F, D M-Sat; $. Highchairs, boosters, booths, child menu. No reservations.*
Located within a 1913 building that was once the Fuller Paint and Glass Company, this English-style pub features high ceilings, rustic unfinished floors, multi-paned windows, and roomy booths. Breakfast doesn't get any better. The menu then offers British-style grilled tomatoes, bangers, and crumpets, as well as American standards and a large variety of omelettes. Many items are prepared on the premises—granola, scones, muffins, and thoroughly-cooked homefries—and free-range chicken eggs are available. Lunch items include Cornish pasties, Welsh rarebit, English tea sandwiches, and a classic ploughman's plate, plus desserts of rich burnt cream custard and layered trifle. Live music is scheduled most evenings, when pub grub is served until 9:30. Over 15 English and Irish beers are on tap, and a good selection of California wines is available.

### Hard Rock Cafe
*7th St./K St., in Downtown Plaza, (916) 441-5591; www.hardrock.com. L-D daily.*
For description, see page 71.

### Ikedas
*6200 Folsom Blvd. /61st St., (916) 457-6940; www.ikedas.com/sacramento.htm. Daily 9-7.*
For description, see page 346.

### Los Nopales
*106 J St., in Old Sacramento, (916) 443-6376,*

*fax (916) 443-6998. L-D daily; $-$$. Highchairs, boosters, booths, child portions. No reservations.*

The lovely old brick walls of this festively appointed restaurant are decorated with paintings of the California missions. Mexican fare includes nachos, quesadillas, and homemade tamales and sopes. Both full meals and less expansive, less expensive a la carte items are available. For dessert try the deep-fried ice cream. Live music is scheduled on Saturday night.

## Max's Opera Cafe
*1735 Arden Way, in Market Square Plaza at Arden Fair Shopping Mall, (916) 927-6297.*

For description, see page 78.

## The Old Spaghetti Factory
*1910 J St., near Old Town, (916) 443-2862, fax (916) 443-4753; www.osf.com.*

Located within a former Western Pacific Depot outside the main tourist area, this is a link in the popular noodle chain. For more description, see page 196.

## Piatti
*571 Pavilions Lane, (916) 649-8885, fax (916) 649-8907; www.piatti.com. L-D daily.*

For description, see page 386.

## Pyramid Alehouse, Brewery & Restaurant
*1029 K St., downtown, (916) 498-9800; www.pyramid-brew.com. L-D daily.*

For description, see page 281.

## T.G.I. Fridays
*1229 Howe Ave., (916) 925-5766, fax (916) 925-4151; www.tgifridays.com.*

For description, see page 173.

## Virgin Sturgeon
*1577 Garden Hwy., (916) 921-2694. B Sat-Sun, L M-F, D daily; $-$$. Boosters, child portions. No reservations.*

This funky, often raucous spot is reached via a ramp through a converted truck rig. It's popular with politicians and "river rats" (people with boats). Situated atop a barge, it has outdoor deck seating overlooking the placid Sacramento River—a great idea in warm weather—as well as cozy interior seating, and it is famous for serving great Cuban black beans and rice, steamed clams, barbecued pork ribs, and mushroom cheeseburgers. Several other wildly popular restaurants are also found in this area.

# Truckee

### – A LITTLE BACKGROUND –
Much of the original architecture in this old mining town is well preserved, and many shops and restaurants on the main street operate within interesting, sometimes beautifully restored, historic buildings. The town's yellow Victorian Southern Pacific Depot dates from 1896 and is now the Amtrak and Greyhound station as well as the Visitors Center.

### – VISITOR INFORMATION –
**Truckee Donner Chamber of Commerce and Visitor Information Center**
*10065 Donner Pass Rd., in the train depot, (530) 587-2757, fax (530) 587-2439; www.truckee.com.*

### – GETTING THERE –
Located approximately 185 miles northeast of San Francisco, and 100 miles northeast of Sacramento. Located approximately 55 miles northwest of North Lake Tahoe via Highway 267.

### –WHAT TO DO –
**Donner Memorial State Park**
*12593 Donner Pass Rd., off Hwy. 40, 2 mi. W of town, (530) 582-7892; www.parks.ca.gov. Daily 8-dusk. $6/vehicle. Museum: daily 9-4; $3, 6-16 $1.*

Located on Donner Lake, this park is a monument to the tragic Donner Party stranded here by blizzards in 1846. Picnic facilities, lake swimming, hiking trails, nature programs, and campsites (June through September only) are available. The **Emigrant Trail Museum** features exhibits on the area's history, including a video telling the Donner Party story and also the very Hawken Rifle that William Eddy used in 1846 to shoot an 800-pound grizzly bear.

### – WHERE TO STAY –
**The Truckee Hotel**
*10007 Bridge St., (800) 659-6921, (530) 587-4444, fax (530) 587-1599; www.thetruckeehotel.com.*

4 stories; 37 rooms; $-$$. Children under 4 free. Some TVs; some shared baths. Afternoon snack Sat-Sun, continental breakfast. No smoking; no pets.

Originally built as a stagecoach stop in 1868, this beautifully renovated Victorian offers stylish period lodging.

**Moody's Bistro** ((530) 587-8688, fax (530) 587-8831; www.moodysbistro.com. L-D daily, Sat-SunBr; $$. Booths.) is known for good food, good music, and occasional great surprises: In 2004, Paul McCartney stopped in as a customer and sang a few tunes with the jazz trio.

### — WHERE TO EAT —

**Squeeze In**
10060 Donner Pass Rd., (530) 587-9814. B-L daily; $. Highchairs, boosters. No reservations.

At breakfast in this long, narrow cafe, diners have a choice of 57 kinds of omelettes. A variety of other breakfast items and sandwiches are also on the menu.

# Plumas County

### — A LITTLE BACKGROUND —

Boasting an abundance of national forest land, this area is noted for its outdoor recreation. Visitors can fish, ride horses, take pack trips, hike, camp, ride bikes, white water raft and kayak, and golf on five courses (including Whitehawk Ranch, the only course in the country that permits players to wear jeans). Birdwatching is prime on man-made Lake Davis, where campsites are also available, and wildlife spotting is generally good throughout the area. The Lakes Basin Recreation Area, a former gold-mining hideaway, now offers all the sports mentioned above plus stays in historic, rustic lodging. Over 30 natural mountain lakes are hidden in this remote, unspoiled terrain located within the Plumas National Forest. North of old-time **Wiggin's Trading Post** (In Chilcoot, (530) 993-4721), where everything from worms to chapstick to Daniel Boon fur hats are for sale, Frenchman Lake is reached via a scenic drive through Little Last Chance Creek canyon and its unique geological formations of volcanic rock. The lake is known for giving up trophy trout. In October and November, the entire area puts on a dazzling display of fall foliage color.

The main drag in the charming town of Graeagle is lined with red cottages that were once the homes of lumber mill workers and now are converted into unique shops. It is one of the area's larger towns and a convenient spot to settle in. The town's Mill Pond has paddleboat and kayak rentals.

### — VISITOR INFORMATION —

**Eastern Plumas Chamber of Commerce**
73136 Hwy. 70, in Portola, (800) 995-6057, (530) 836-6811, fax (530) 836-6809; www.easternplumas chamber.com.

**Plumas County Visitors Bureau**
550 Crescent St., in Quincy, (800) 326-2247, (530) 283-6345, fax (530) 283-5465; www.plumas county.org.

### — GETTING THERE —

Follow Highway 89 north for 50 miles into Graeagle. This route passes through the Sierra Valley, which is the largest alpine valley in North America and which has scenery varying from conifer and aspen forests to pastures and wildflowers. Alternatively, travel here via Highway 5, to Highway 99, to Highway 70, following Highway 70 to north of Oroville and then along the 130-mile Feather River National Scenic Byway through the spectacularly scenic Feather River Canyon, and on to Hallelujah Junction at Highway 395, just east of Chilcoot. The route crosses vintage railroad bridges and passes through tunnels. This area is 240 miles northeast of San Francisco.

### — ANNUAL EVENTS —

**Mohawk Valley Independence Day Celebration**
July. In Graeagle; (530) 832-5444; www.graeagle. com/events.

Festivities include a small parade with marching bands and bagpipers, fireworks over the town pond, a pancake breakfast, live music in the park, and dancing in the streets.

**Railroad Days**
August. In Portola; (530) 836-6811; www.ci.portola. ca.us/railroaddays.htm.

This festive event celebrates the railroad, mining, and logging industries that shaped

*Charming cottage shop in Graeagle*

Portola's past. Train rides, music, arts and crafts, and kids' activities are part of the fun.

### — WHAT TO DO —

**Graeagle Stables/Reid Horse & Cattle Co.**
*On Hwy. 89, in Graeagle, (530) 836-0430; www.reid horse.com. June-Oct only. $29/1 hr.*

In addition to trail rides, pack trips can be arranged ((530) 283-1147). Stables are also located at Gold Lake and Bucks Lake.

**Jim Beckwourth Museum**
*2180 Rocky Point Rd., E of Portola, (530) 832-4888. Sat-Sun 1-4, summer only. Free.*

Also known as the Beckwourth Cabin, this refurbished 1850s log cabin was once a trading post and hotel. It now honors African-American frontiersman James P. Beckwourth, who discovered in 1851 the lowest pass through the Sierra Nevada. The trail named for him begins in Reno, runs through this area, and ends in Oroville.

**Plumas-Eureka State Park and Museum**
*310 Johnsville Rd., 5 mi. W of Graeagle, (530) 836-2380; www.parks.ca.gov. Daily 8-4, summer only. $2, under 17 free.*

Situated on the site of one of the region's largest quartz-mining operations, the museum here is located in a former bunkhouse. It features an exhibit on longboard ski racing, which originated nearby, and displays a majestic stuffed golden eagle and a ceramic foot warmer. An outdoor complex includes a restored stamp mill, miner's home, blacksmith shop, and assayer's office. During summer, a supervised gold-panning program and Junior Ranger Program (see page 445) are offered. Also in summer on the last Saturday of each month, Living History Days features costumed docents and hands-on pioneer activities. Picnic tables, campsites, and ranger programs are available.

**Portola Railroad Museum**
*700 Western Pacific Way, off Commercial St., in Portola, (530) 832-4131, fax (530) 832-1854; www.wplives.org. Daily 10-5, Mar-Oct only. By donation. Train rides: $5, under 12 $2, family $12; Sat-Sun, June-Aug only. Run-A-Locomotive: (530) 832-4532; $95+.*

Housed in a former Western Pacific diesel shop, this hands-on museum features one of the largest and most historic collections of diesel locomotives in the nation. It also has 95 freight and passenger cars, 12,000 feet of track, and displays assorted photos and artifacts. Visitors can climb aboard the cars outside, though a few rarer cars stored inside require a guided tour. This facility is world-famous for its unique Run-A-Locomotive program, allowing visitors to actually drive a diesel engine. A ride on a train of cabooses is offered on summer weekends along a 1-mile balloon track.

## — WHERE TO STAY —

### Feather River Inn
*On Hwy. 70, W of Blairsden, (888) 324-6400, (530) 836-2623, fax (530) 836-0927; www.feather riverinn.com. 100+ rooms; $-$$; closed Nov-Apr. Heated pool; tennis courts; 9-hole golf course. Restaurant. No smoking; pets ok in cabins.*

Built in 1914, this charmingly rustic Swiss-style resort was once a destination for the Bay Area's elite, who arrived by train and disembarked at the facility's own depot. It is now a private camp and conference center, with a golf course, communal cabins, and a chalet-style lodge and restaurant. A prime spot for family reunions, it also hosts a family camp and Elderhostel program. Some rooms are available to the public, as are summer Friday night prime rib dinners and an extensive Sunday brunch. Recreation includes basketball, sand volleyball, and horseshoes.

### Gray Eagle Lodge
*5000 Gold Lake Rd., in Lakes Basin Recreation Area, 5 mi. S of Graeagle, (800) 635-8778, (530) 836-2511, fax (530) 836-0916; www.grayeaglelodge.com.*

*18 cabins; $$-$$$; closed mid-Oct-mid-May. No TVs. Unheated swimming hole. Includes full breakfast & dinner; restaurant. Pets ok in cabins.*

This rustic, remote, and very inviting complex includes a massive log lodge with an open, log-beam ceiling. Comfortably appointed cabins with knotty pine interiors are spread along Graeagle Creek and Falls, which provides Graeagle's drinking water and feeds into the town's Old Mill Pond. Some cabins have sleeping lofts or second bedrooms, making them particularly attractive to families. Others permit casting a fishing line right from their deck.

Fine dining is available to non-guests in **Firewoods** *(D daily; $$$. Child menu. Reservations required.)*, which serves California mountain cuisine and housemade soups and breads. Anglers who catch a fish can arrange for the chef to clean and cook it.

### Pullman House Inn
*256 Commercial St., in Portola, (530) 832-0107; www.psln.com/pullman. 6 rooms; $. Continental breakfast. No smoking; no pets.*

Built in 1910 as a boarding house for railroad workers, this B&B sports a railroad theme. A model train runs on tracks attached to the perimeter of the breakfast room ceiling, and stunning locomotive paintings done by local artist Ken Roller hang on the walls. Pullman memorabilia is displayed throughout. A deck permits sitting and watching the arrivals and departures of trains on the nearby tracks.

### River Pines Resort
*8296 Hwy. 89, in Blairsden, (800) 696-2551, (530) 836-0313, fax (530) 836-0815; www.riverpines.com. 65 units; $-$$. Continental breakfast in winter; restaurant. Heated pool (seasonal); hot tub. Pets ok in off-season.*

This old-fashioned motel is the kind of place where guests gather fallen pinecones and line them up in a row beside the door of their cabin. Guests can park right in front of their unit, and rooms have knotty-pine paneling and soothing views of the surrounding pines. Housekeeping cottages require a 3-night minimum stay.

The adjacent **Coyote Bar & Grill** *((530) 836-2002, fax (530) 836-0815. D Tu-Sun; $$; closed Jan-Feb.)* serves Southwestern-style cuisine.

## Sardine Lake Resort

*Off Gold Lake Rd., 15 mi. S of Graeagle; summer (530) 862-1196; winter (916) 645-8882. 9 cabins; $$. Pets ok.*

Once upon a time this spectacularly scenic spot was called Emerald Lake—until a mule named Sardine fell in, and miners renamed it in her honor. It offers a dramatic view of the craggy Sierra Buttes. Though the cabins here are so popular that it is neigh on impossible for new guests to get a reservation—there is a story that one family that was going through divorce negotiations considered their annual reservation here more important than their dog—it *is* possible to come here and fish from the window of the open-air bar, or to rent a boat, or to have an elegant dinner in the cozy **dining room** *(D mid-May-mid-Oct. Reservations required.)*.

### — WHERE TO EAT —

## Grizzly Grill

*250 Bonta St., in Blairsden (530) 836-1300; www.grizzlygrill.com. D daily; closed M-Tu in winter; $$. Highchairs, boosters, child menu. Reservations advised.*

Contemporary American cuisine is the specialty in this tasteful, upscale venue. A particularly good baby greens salad with honey-roasted walnuts and crumbled bleu cheese is among the appetizers, and assorted pastas, meats, and fish comprise the entrees. An antique bar and comfortable lounge area furnished with lodgepole pine furniture invites lingering.

## The Log Cabin

*64 E. Sierra Ave., in Portola, (530) 832-5243. D W-M; $$. Highchairs, boosters, booths, child portions. Reservations accepted.*

German and American cuisines are the specialties, with particularly good schnitzel, sauerbraten, and steaks. The knotty-pine interior is cozy, with china plates decorating the walls and comfortable wooden booths for seating.

## The Village Baker

*340 Bonta St., in Blairsden, (530) 836-4064. Tu-Sun 6-2, Sun to noon; in winter W-Sun. Highchairs, boosters.*

This spacious old-time bakery is definitely the place to go for delicious European-style pastries and breads, not to mention espresso drinks.

# I-880 SOUTH

## Oakland

### — A LITTLE BACKGROUND —

Though this much-maligned city usually loses in the struggle with San Francisco for media attention, it does have a "there there." (Although Gertrude Stein, who lived here as a child, is often quoted as having said about this city, "There is no there there," in reality it seems that she was referring to what remained of her demolished childhood house.) Interesting facts about this surprising city: It is the West Coast headquarters for the federal government; it has the country's third-largest Chinatown (or Asia Town as it is called here); the Human Wave— the synchronized movement of sports fans in stadiums—was "invented" in Oakland during the seventh-inning stretch of the final playoff game between the Oakland Athletics and New York Yankees on October 15, 1981; it is the most ethnically diverse city in the U.S., with at least 81 different languages and dialects spoken; the largest cookie producer in the U.S.— Mother's Cake & Cookie Company—has been located here since 1914.

### — VISITOR INFORMATION —

**Oakland Convention & Visitors Bureau**
*463 11th St., (510) 839-9000, fax (510) 839-5924; www.oaklandcvb.com.*

### — GETTING THERE —

Located approximately 10 miles east of San Francisco. From San Francisco, cross the Bay Bridge, taking Highway 580 south into Oakland.

### — ANNUAL EVENTS —

**Tulip Bloom at Mountain View Cemetery**
*March-April. 5000 Piedmont Ave., (510) 658-2588, fax (510) 652-2726; www.oaklandhistory.com/files/hmvc1.html. Tour: 2nd Sat of month, 10am; free.*

More than 22,000 Dutch tulips bloom each spring in the cemetery gardens here. Drive or take a stroll through this 220-acre classic cemetery designed in 1863 by Frederick Law Olmsted, designer of Golden Gate Park. In 1865, Jane Waer, in plot 1, was the first person buried here. Since then, more than 165,000 people have joined her, and there's room for more. Serpentine paved walkways thread through the picturesque tombstones, including those of architects Julia Morgan and Bernard Maybeck and artist Thomas Hill. Don't miss either the ornately decorated main mausoleum or

"Millionaires' Row," where steel magnate Henry J. Kaiser, banker Charles Crocker, and several Ghirardelli chocolatiers rest in small Victorian family mausoleums with spectacular views of San Francisco and Oakland. Two pyramids and an assortment of stone angels round out the visual delights. This is also a bird-watcher's paradise and home to plenty of feral cats.

## Open Studios
*June. (510) 763-4361, fax (510) 763-9470; www.pro artsgallery.org. Free.*

For this combination gallery exhibit and self-guided tour of artists' workplaces throughout the East Bay, more than 500 artists open the doors to their studios, workshops, lofts, and homes to meet with the public. Many offer works for sale.

## Woodminster Summer Musicals
*June-September. In Joaquin Miller Park, (510) 531-9597, fax (510) 531-0671; www.woodminster.com. $17-$31, children under 16 free with an adult paying full price; parking $2.*

It's difficult to imagine a more pleasant way to spend a balmy summer evening than at a live performance here. Witnessing the deepening of the evening and the slow appearance of the stars adds to the overall enjoyment of the production on stage. The amphitheater seats approximately 1,500 people on individually molded seats, all with good views. Pre-theater picnic tables are set up in redwood groves outside the theater.

## Black Cowboy Parade
*October. On 14th St. near City Hall; (510) 531-7583. Free.*

The only such event in the U.S., this parade commemorates the contributions made by African Americans and other minorities to building the American West. A festival follows in De Fremery Park.

## Lighted Yacht Parade
*December. At Jack London Square;(510) 814-6000; www.jacklondonsquare.com. Free.*

Festivities include a parade of twinkling vessels plus holiday music and children's activities.

## – WHAT TO DO –

## Chabot Space & Science Center
*10000 Skyline Blvd., in Joaquin Miller Park, (510) 336-7300, fax (510) 336-7491; www.chabotspace.org. Full facility: F 5-10, Sat 10-10, Sun 12-5; in summer Tu-Thur 10-5, Fri-Sat 10-10, Sun 12-5. $13, 65+ & 4-12 $9.*

Begun in 1883 as the Oakland Observatory, this facility was originally located downtown. It served as the official timekeeping station for the entire Bay Area from 1885 through 1915, measuring time with its transit telescope. Now it has the largest, most technologically advanced planetarium west of NYC. Facilities include a domed-screen MegaDome theater, an assortment of hands-on exhibits, and an observatory with three telescopes (the observatory is open free on Fridays and Saturday nights from dusk to 10 p.m.).

## Dunsmuir Historic Estate
*2960 Peralta Oaks Ct., near 106th St. exit off I-580 east, (510) 615-5555, fax (510) 562-8294; www.dunsmuir.org. House and grounds: 1st Sun 12-3; house tours: W at 11 & 12; Easter-Sept only; $5, 62+ & 6-13 $4. Grounds open for strolling year-round, Tu-F 10-4; free.*

Built in 1899, this renovated 37-room neoclassical Revival mansion is furnished with period antiques. It features a Tiffany-style dome and 10 fireplaces. Visitors can picnic and stroll on the 50 acres of grounds. Of special interest are a grotto, a drained but rustically beautiful

swimming pool, and a peaceful duck and swan pond. The horror film *Burnt Offerings* and the James Bond thriller *A View to a Kill* were both filmed here.

Cultural entertainment is scheduled on Family Sundays. Each December the grounds are transformed into a wonderland for **Christmas at Dunsmuir**, and the house is decked out in appropriate finery. Other annual special events include a **Spring Festival** and a **Scot's Faire** the first weekend in July with Highland games and more.

### Fortune Cookie Factory Tour
*261 12th St./Harrison St., (510) 832-5552, fax (510) 832-2565. M-F 10-3. $1.*

The A&K Wong Inc. bakery still hand-folds its cookies. It also makes unusual fruit-flavored fortune cookies and permits customers to insert their own original messages. Drop-in tours last about 15 minutes and include a small bag of cookies.

### Jack London Square
*(866) 295-9853, (510) 645-5968, fax (510) 645-9363; www.jacklondonsquare.com.*

Situated on the inlet of the Oakland Estuary, this entertainment complex borders the city's huge commercial shipping area. People come here to stroll the spacious modern walkways closed to cars, to browse a variety of shops, and to dine in myriad restaurants. Also, boat-watching on the estuary is enjoyable, slow-moving trains pass regularly on the tracks at the area's northern edge, and nightlife is lively.

#### • Alameda/Oakland Ferry
*510-522-3300; www.eastbayferry.com,). Schedule & fares vary.*

Board the ferry here for Alameda. San Francisco destinations are the Ferry Building, Pier 39, the Giants' SBC Park, and Angel Island State Park.

#### • Heinold's First and Last Chance Saloon
*48 Webster St., (510) 839-6761; www.heinoldsfirstand lastchance.com. Daily noon-midnight. Age 21+ only.*

Built in 1883 from the remnants of a whaling ship, this informal, funky bar with a tilted floor pays tribute to the area's waterfront past. Jack London, a longtime Oakland resident, was a regular customer during the period when he was an oyster fisherman here. Though somewhat menacing in appearance (it is impossible

to see in through the thick windows), this saloon makes a good spot to wet a dry whistle and is a National Literary Landmark. While here, notice the still-functioning gas lamps and a clock that stopped at 5:18 a.m. during the 1906 earthquake.

**Jack London's Cabin** is across the way. Moved here in 1970, this rustic one-room hovel is believed to have housed London when he prospected in Canada's Yukon Territory during the 1897 Klondike gold rush.

#### • Port of Oakland Tours
*(510) 627-1188; www.portofoakland.com. May-Oct; schedule varies. Free. Reservations required.*

Sponsored by the Port of Oakland, these 90-minute tours take participants alongside port operations in the Oakland Estuary.

#### • USS Potomac
*Berthed at N end of Jack London Square. Visitor Center at 540 Water St./Clay St., (510) 627-1215, fax (510) 839-4729; www.usspotomac.org. Dockside tour: W & F 12-3, Sun 12-4; $3, 60+ $2, 6-17 $1. Narrated history cruise: 1st & 3rd Thur, 2nd & 4th Sat of month, mid-April - mid-Nov, weather permitting; $35, 60+ $30, 6-17 $15; advance purchase advised.*

This 165-foot-long, all-steel vessel served as President Franklin Delano Roosevelt's "floating White House." Having undergone a 12-year, $5 million restoration, it is now a National Historic Landmark. The 2-hour ride begins ashore with a background video and the chance to study some historical photos, including one

of Elvis Presley—who once owned the yacht—presenting it to his friend Danny Thomas for St. Jude's Hospital. More photos testify to its degeneration from its original purpose of chasing rumrunners into being used for drug running, and its eventual sinking near Treasure Island. Ronald Reagan passed legislation to restore her and, happily, with the help of the Port of Oakland and many dedicated volunteers, she now operates as a public museum. FDR, who was confined to a wheelchair and suffered from sinusitis, preferred the *Potomac* to the White House on sultry summer days. He relaxed on this simple, but comfortable, ship as he led the country through the Great Depression and World War II. Aboard, visitors can see his surprisingly small and simply furnished cabin and his private elevator mounted within a false smokestack (it may be used by visitors in wheelchairs). The radio room, pilothouse, and various guest rooms are also open for inspection. The cruise goes out of the estuary, past the gigantic maritime crane horses reputed to have inspired George Lucas for his similar-looking *Star Wars* characters, on past Treasure Island, and then around Alcatraz. Complimentary snacks include coffee, soft drinks, and juices as well as cookies. A favorite spot to settle in is the lower fantail deck lounge in back, with a seat so deep that the legs of loungers must be stretched out straight.

## Lakeside Park/Lake Merritt

*Entrance at Grand & Bellevue aves., (510) 238-7275; www.oaklandnet.com/parks. Free; parking $2 Sat-Sun.*

This beautiful expanse of water is the hub of a variety of activities and is encircled in the evening by a lovely necklace of lights. Fed by both salt water from the bay and fresh water from streams in the hills, it is approximately 18 feet deep.

### • Boating Center

*568 Bellevue Ave./near Grand Ave., (510) 238-2196, fax (510) 238-7199; www.oaklandnet.com/parks. Daily 10-3:30, later in summer. Boat rentals $6+/½-hr.-$12/hr.*

A variety of vessels are for rent, including rowboats, sailboats, and pedal boats. Gondolas operated by opera-singing gondoliers can also be hired for about half the price they'd go for in Venice through **Gondola Servizio** *((866) SERVIZIO, (510) 663-6603, fax (510) 238-7199; www.gondolaservizio.com. $45+/couple. Reservations required.).*

### • Camron-Stanford House

*1418 Lakeside Dr./14th St., (510) 444-1876; www.cshouse.org. Tours W 11-4, Sun 1-5. $5, seniors $4, 12-18 $3, under 12 free; free 1st Sun of month.*

Restored and furnished in period fashion, this 1876 Italianate-style Victorian is on the western edge of Lake Merritt. Tours begin with a short film on Oakland's history.

### • Children's Fairyland

*699 Bellevue Ave./Grand Ave., (510) 452-2259, fax (510) 452-2261; www.fairyland.org. Daily 10-4 in summer; W-Sun in spring & fall; F-Sun in winter; puppet shows at 11, 2, 4. $6, under 1 free; magic key $2.*

Designed especially for children age 8 and under, this non-profit facility was the country's first educational storybook theme park when it opened in 1950. In fact, Disneyland is patterned after it. Mother Goose rhymes and fairy tales come to life in more than 30 fantasy sets, some of which hold live animals. Among the attractions are an Alice in Wonderland card maze, a variety of slides (including one down a dragon's back), and rides on a mini-carousel and -Ferris wheel. Kids can also steer a mini-motor boat, and all ages can watch an award-winning puppet show. Mature trees provide shade, and a picnic area, fast-food stand, and packaged birthday party are also available. No adults are admitted without a child, and no child is admitted without an adult. For the annual Halloween **Jack-O-Lantern Jamboree**, families are encouraged to come in costume.

• **Lakeside Garden Center**
*666 Bellevue Ave., at N end of lake, (510) 763-8409; www.oaklandnet.com/parks. W-F 11-3, Sat 10-4, Sun 12-4. Free.*

In addition to fuchsia and bulb gardens, a Japanese garden, citrus garden, and herb garden for the blind and disabled are found here. A Bonsai and Suiseki Display Garden exhibits an assortment of suiseki viewing stones and 50 bonsai trees—among them a 400-year-old Japanese black pine that was brought to the U.S. for the 1915 Panama Pacific International Exposition in San Francisco, and a Dalmyo oak that is the oldest in cultivation in the U.S. A community garden is available free to anyone who wants to grow their own pesticide-free produce.

• **Rotary Nature Center/Lake Merritt Wildlife Refuge**
*600 Bellevue Ave./Perkins St., at N end of lake, (510) 238-3739, fax (510) 238-7962; www.oaklandnet.com/parks. Center open daily 10-5. Free.*

The nature center has a nature/science library and computers for children to use when researching school reports. The wildlife refuge dates to 1870 and is the first and oldest in the country. Among the birds seen here regularly are egrets, mallards, Canada geese, and herons. Daily feeding is at 3:30 p.m.

## Morcom Amphitheater of Roses
*700 Jean St./Grand Ave., (510) 238-3187; www.oak landnet.com/parks. Daily dawn-dusk. Free.*

Not far from Lake Merritt, this peaceful garden is designed in traditional Florentine style with terraces and a classic reflecting pool. Special sections are devoted to pastel roses and antique roses, and a children's garden features miniature roses. A wedding site designed with a color scheme of white, beige, and pink is reputed to bring good luck. Bloom is best June through October, and benches positioned throughout invite picnicking.

## Museum of Children's Art (MOCHA)
*538 Ninth St./Washington St.,(510) 465-8770, fax (510) 465-0772; www.mocha.org. Tu-F 10-5, Sat-Sun 12-5. Free.*

This gallery displays East Bay children's art as well as the occasional national and international exhibit. Drop-In Art classes are scheduled regularly for parents and kids.

## Oakland Ice Center
*519 18th St./San Pablo Ave., (510) 268-9000; www.oaklandice.com. M-F 12-5, Sat-Sun 1-5; evening schedule varies. $7.50, 55+ & under 13 $6.50, skate rental $2.50.*

This Olympic-size rink has a variety of programs and packages.

## Oakland Museum of California
*1000 Oak St./10th St., (510) 238-2200, (888) OAK-MUSE, fax (510) 238-2258; www.museumca.org. W-Sat 10-5, Sun 12-5, 1st F to 9; free 2nd Sun of month. $8, 65+ & 6-17 $5; parking $1/hr.*

This beautifully designed tri-level museum is the only one in the state focusing on the art, natural sciences, and history of California. Built in 1969, it is celebrated for both its innovative shows and its architecture featuring terraced gardens with a center courtyard. The Natural Sciences Gallery walks visitors across a miniature representation of the state, complete with appropriate plant and animal life. Near the gift shop, visitors can rest in a surprisingly comfortable circular, banquette-style chair fashioned from a large slice of a giant redwood burl and view multi-colored koi in a lily pond outside. An airy cafe, with huge picture windows overlooking the gardens, serves reasonably priced lunches and snacks.

Each March, the museum is benefited by a **White Elephant Sale** *((510) 839-5919. Free.)*. This truly mammoth rummage sale offers just about anything imaginable, as well as many things unimaginable. In April or May, volunteers collect hundreds of specimens for display at the annual **California Wildflower Show**. In December, the annual **Fungus Fair** celebrates the beauty, tastes, and fragrances of fungi with a display of more than 1,000 local specimens.

## Oakland Zoo
*9777 Golf Links Rd., off Hwy. 580, in Knowland Park, (510) 632-9525, fax (510) 635-5719; www.oakland zoo.org. Daily, 10-4, weather permitting; rides open at 11. $9, 55+ & 2-14 $5:50; parking $5.*

Be sure to see the state-of-the-art Malayan sun bear exhibit (the largest in the U.S.) and the

*Three "kids" get acquainted at the Petting Zoo*

naturalistic habitats: the Tropical Rainforest, Australian Outback, and African Savanna. The Skyride chairlift offers a good view of the outstanding African Veldt enclosure, with its watering hole for giraffes and several species of crane, and provides at its crest a magnificent panoramic view of the bay. A kiddie ride area includes a roller coaster, carousel, and train. Special events are scheduled regularly.

## Paramount Theatre

*2025 Broadway/21st St., (510) 465-6400, fax (510) 893-5098; www.paramounttheatre.com. Tours: (510) 893-2300; 1st & 3rd Sat at 10am; $1; must be 10 or older. Movies: at 8pm; $6.*

Built in 1931, this magnificently renovated, ravishingly beautiful landmark is at its best during an actual performance. Try to come for the Organ Pops series, when silent films are accompanied live by a magnificent old Wurlitzer organ (the second largest west of the Mississippi), or for the Movie Classics series, which features the best vintage films. Movies are preceded by a World War II-era newsreel, a vintage cartoon, and a rousting round of prize giveaways. Ballet, symphony, and theater performances are also scheduled.

## Pardee Home Museum

*672 11th St./Castro St., across from Preservation Park, (510) 444-2187, fax (510) 444-7120; www.pardeehome.org. Tours W, F, Sat at 12, 1, 2, 3. $5, under 13 free. Reservations advised.*

Home to three generations of the Pardee family, this house was lived in by Enoch Pardee (mayor of Oakland in the mid-1870s) and his son, George C. Pardee (mayor of Oakland in the early 1890s and then governor of California from 1903 to 1907). More than 50,000 pieces of family memorabilia and historical artifacts are displayed just as they were left when the home was donated, and all the furniture is original to the house. A unique Carleton Watkins light fixture hangs in the downstairs hallway. The expansive grounds hold a lovely mature coastal redwood.

## Parkway Speakeasy Theater

*1834 Park Blvd./E. 18th St., near Lake Merritt, (510) 814-2400; www.picturepubpizza.com. Daily; schedule varies. $5; must be 21 or older. No cards.*

In this classic movie house, viewers sit on comfortable couches while munching on thin-crust pizza and enjoying a brew with a view of first-run, second-run, and classic flicks. Popcorn with *real* butter is also on the menu. Mondays are Baby Brigade night, when infants under 1 year are admitted free and their attendant noises are welcome.

## Preservation Park
*13th St./Martin Luther King Jr. Way, (510) 874-7580, fax (510) 268-1961; www.preservationpark.com. Free.*

This group of 16 exquisite Victorian houses was originally scheduled to be demolished by Highway 980, but they were saved when a public outcry caused the freeway to be moved over a block. They represent five distinct domestic architectural styles from 1870 to 1910. Those on the north side of the street are in their original positions, while the rest were moved in from other parts of the city. Rented out by the city to non-profits for office space, the houses are restored only on the outside. The area is blocked off to traffic and is beautifully landscaped with posh lawns, palms, and pines plus one gorgeous 19th-century fountain. A cafe in one house serves weekday lunch.

## Redwood Regional Park
*7867 Redwood Rd., (510) 562-PARK; www.ebparks.org /parks/redwood.htm. Daily 5am-10pm. $4/vehicle; $1/dog.*

This unassuming park is full of surprises. It holds a grove of second-growth redwood trees—a remnant of the solid redwood forest that was harvested long ago to build homes in San Francisco—and has the only fish ladder in the Bay Area, where rainbow trout spawn. A Forest Festival is sometimes held in the fall.

## Spectator sports
*At Oakland Coliseum, Hegenberger Rd. exit off I-880.*

• **Baseball. Oakland Athletics**
*(510) 638-GOAS; www.oaklandathletics.com. Apr-Oct.*

• **Basketball. Golden State Warriors**
*(888) GSW-HOOP; www.warriors.com. Nov-Apr.*

• **Football. Oakland Raiders**
*(510) 864-5000; www.raiders.com. Aug-Sept.*

## Temescal Regional Park
*6500 Broadway Terrace/Hwys. 13 & 24, (510) 652-PARK; www.ebparks.org/parks/temescal.htm. Daily 5am-10pm. $4/vehicle Sat-Sun; $1/dog. Swim area: (510) 652-1155; daily 11-6 in summer, Sat-Sun Apr-Oct; $3, 62+ & under 16 $1.*

Opened as a recreation area in 1936, this scenic 48-acre park offers swimming, fishing, jogging, and hiking. Facilities include a rose garden, two children's play areas, and a 13-acre artificial lake with a roped-off swimming area and raft. A lifeguard is on duty at the swim area, and vending machines, picnic tables and barbecue pits are available.

## USS *Hornet* Museum
*At Pier 3, Alameda Point, in Alameda, (510) 521-8448, fax (510) 521-8327; www.uss-hornet.org. W-M 10-5. $14, 65+ $12, 5-17 $6.*

Stretching the length of three football fields and reaching 11 stories high, this immense vessel served as an aircraft carrier from 1943 to 1970. Now a National Historic Landmark, during World War II, when she was known as the "Grey Ghost," this oil-fired ship could outrun anything. The legendary Lt. Col. "Jimmy" Doolittle did all his raids from this ship. The *Hornet* holds an unequaled combat record for destroying enemy aircraft and sinking enemy ships. She survived 59 air attacks without getting hit, and was the primary recovery vessel for the Apollo 11 and 12 moon missions in 1969. Nowadays, vets lead fascinating tours, and a dynamite view of San Francisco is enjoyed from the flight deck. Great photo ops abound; do bring a camera. On Living Ship Day (the third Saturday of the month) the radar tower turns, the loud-speakers spit out messages, and the extraordinarily fast airplane elevator carries fighter planes up and down from the hold to the deck. Big Band Dance programs are sometimes scheduled.

## Yoshi's
*510 Embarcadero West/Washington St., (510) 238-9200; www.yoshis.com. M-Sat at 8 & 10, Sun at 2 & 8. $10-$28; no age min.*

Though this contemporary space holds a California-Japanese restaurant complete with a tatami room and separate sushi bar, the music in the jazz club far eclipses the food. In the club, which attracts the circuit elite, the audience can order light snacks and sushi.

— **WHERE TO STAY** —

## Oakland Marriott City Center
*1001 Broadway, (800) 228-9290, (510) 451-4000, fax (415) 835-3466; https://marriott.com. 21 stories, 491 rooms; $$-$$$+. Children under 19 free. Heated pool; hot tub; fitness room. Restaurant. No pets. Self-parking $12, valet $23.*

Casting a dramatic profile on the downtown skyline, this centrally located, angular building is Oakland's only high-rise, full-service luxury hotel. It connects to the Oakland Convention Center and is one of the few hotels in the Bay Area with a kosher kitchen.

## Washington Inn
*495 10th St./Washington St., (510) 452-1776, fax (510)-452-4436; www.thewashingtoninn.com. 47 rooms; $$. Full breakfast M-F, continental Sat-Sun; restaurant. No smoking; no pets. No parking.*

Located across the street from the Oakland Convention Center, this landmark building was Oakland's first hotel. It features turn-of-the-century decor, and photos of old Oakland hang in the welcoming, high-ceilinged lobby.

**Twist** *((510) 832-7449. L-D M-F; $$. Reservations accepted.)* operates off the lobby in another high-ceilinged room with gorgeous high-gloss wood floors and a bank of windows looking out onto the street. Cool stage lighting sets the mood, and a menu of contemporary Mediterranean cuisine tempts the palate.

## Waterfront Plaza Hotel
*10 Washington St., at Jack London Square, (800) 729-3638, (510) 836-3800, fax (510) 832-5695; www.waterfrontplaza.com. 5 stories; 145 rooms; $$$-$$$+. Heated pool; sauna; fitness room. Restaurant; room service. No pets. Valet parking $9.*

Situated next door to the ferry boarding dock, this contemporary hotel offers an atmosphere of casual luxury and features a glass-enclosed swimming pool deck overlooking the estuary. More than half of the rooms have water views.

**Jack's Bistro** *(1 Broadway, (510) 444-7171; www.jacksbistro.com. B-L-D daily, Sat-SunBr; $$. Highchairs, boosters, booths. Reservations accepted.)* offers an eclectic menu, patio dining, and more splendid water views. Evening entertainment is scheduled regularly.

### — WHERE TO EAT —

## À Côté
*5478 College Ave./Taft Ave., (510) 655-6469; www.citron-acote.com. D Tu-Sun; $$. Highchairs. No reservations.*

Who doesn't like sitting in a dimly lit room buzzing with excitement? Choose the bar, some smaller side tables, or a central communal table in this casual bistro. The ever-changing menu consists of rustic French and Spanish small plates meant to be shared. All seem to be winners, but the don't-misses include pommes frites with aioli, house-marinated olives, and any of the flatbreads. A selection of cheeses and a long list of wines and spirits add to the hum. Designated drivers aren't denied drink delights—try a tasty Gewurztraminer grape juice served up in a martini glass. Delicious desserts might include a Meyer lemon-curd tart or a plate of profiteroles stuffed with banana-nut ice cream.

## Bay Wolf
*3853 Piedmont Ave./40th St., (510) 655-6004, fax (510) 652-0429; www.baywolf.com. L M-F, D daily; $$$. Highchairs, boosters. Reservations advised.*

One of the region's very best restaurants, this veteran bistro has been around for more than 25 years now. Serving a Mediterranean-inspired menu and famous for its duck dishes, it operates out of a simple but cozy remodeled Victorian house sporting paintings by internationally recognized local artists. The menu changes every 3 weeks, highlighting the food of a different region and making use of the season's bounty. Starters might include a subtly spiced puréed cauliflower soup or a vibrantly colored citrus-beet salad. The sublime, silky, duck liver flan that is the kitchen's signature is always available. Entrees have included a satisfying swordfish steak served with French lentils, and a magnificent ravioli stuffed with butternut squash purée and topped deliciously with sautéed onions, bacon, and fresh sage leaves. Desserts are worth saving space for, but when little room remains, try a plate of sweets that hopefully will include a chocolate-covered, liqueur-soaked cherry and a tiny gingerbread angel. Brunch is served only once each year, on Mother's Day.

## Cactus Taqueria
*5642 College Ave., (510) 658-6180, fax (510) 658-6181. L-D daily.*

For description, see page 276.

## Caffé 817
*817 Washington St./9th St., downtown, (510) 271-7965, fax (510) 271-0778; www.caffe817.com. B-L M-Sat; $.*

For breakfast, this sleek, modern, very Italian paninoteca (sandwich bar) prepares a perfectly poached blue Aracauna hen egg, squeezes a vibrantly colorful glass of blood orange juice, and brews superb coffees using a state-of-the-art espresso machine and Illy beans imported from Trieste. Note that "a latte" is made with filtered coffee and served French-style in a big bowl, whereas "a regular latte" is made with espresso and served in a tall glass. Lunch items include assorted housemade soups, polentas, salads, and panini. Add to these choices sun-brewed iced tea, Tuscan wines, fresh juices, and Italian Moretti beer from the Tyrolian area of Udine, and life is good. A picnic box can be prepared with a call by 4 p.m. the day before needed. All this and walls graced by the work of local artists, too!

### Caffé Verbena
*1111 Broadway/11th St., downtown, (510) 465-9300, fax (510) 465-9302; www.restaurantverbena.com. L-D M-F; $$. Booths. Reservations advised.*

Tucked away in an office building lobby, this spot features a low-key bar and a wide-open, comfy dining room. The busy kitchen whips up some tasty fare. Artichoke fritters with lemon aioli and a wild mushroom pizza both make great starters. Main courses include bouillabaisse, achiote roasted chicken, and flat iron steak with green peppercorn sauce. To wash it down, choose from cocktails and a large selection of wines and beers.

### Everett & Jones Barbeque
*126 Broadway/2nd St., near Jack London Square, (510) 663-2350, fax (510) 663-8856; http://super-que.com. L-D daily; $. Highchairs, boosters. Reservations accepted.*

This family-owned and -run, full-service restaurant is a sit-down-and-stay-a-while branch of a popular take-out storefront. Former Oakland Raiders coach John Madden says it's "the greatest"; Mayor Jerry Brown calls it "the premier restaurant in Oakland"; and Whoopi Goldberg says,"Ummm—goood!" Lunch portions of chicken, ribs, homemade beef links, and the house-specialty beef brisket come with potato salad, wheat bread, and the tasty, award-winning house sauce in a choice of mild, medium, or hot (and they *do* mean *hot*). Dinner portions are bigger and include a choice of fresh housemade greens, yams, potato salad, and baked beans, plus either corn bread or

wheat bread. It all washes down nicely with a Brothers Brewing Company beer produced locally by the only African American-owned microbrewery in the country. Desserts include sweet potato, pecan, and peach pies, and lemon, chocolate (actually white cake with chocolate frosting), and "sock-it-to-me" cakes.

### Fentons Creamery
*4226 Piedmont Ave./Entrada Ave., (510) 658-8500, fax (510) 658-5300; www.fentonscreamery.com. Daily 11-11; $. Highchairs, boosters, child menu. No reservations.*

Enormous portions of housemade 14% butterfat ice cream is the name of the game at this well-established ice cream parlor, in business here since 1922 and remodeled in 2003 after a devastating fire. Favorite flavors for Fentons freaks looking for a fix are toasted almond and Swiss milk chocolate. Many of the sundaes are big enough to share among several people. If all those people eating out of one bowl is unappealing, ask for extra bowls. Drinks include milkshakes served in old-fashioned metal canisters as well as sodas, floats, and sherbet freezes. Fizzes are made by blending juice, sherbet, carbonated water, and an egg into a froth. The menu also offers soups and salads, a hamburger, and an assortment of sandwiches, including the delicious house specialty—fresh crab salad on grilled sourdough.

### Huynh
*381 15th St./Franklin St., (510) 832-5238; www.huynh restaurant.com. L M-F, D M-Sat; $. Highchairs, boosters. No reservations.*

The large, open, butterscotch-colored dining room here is furnished with jack wood tables and chairs made by the owner's family in Viet Nam. (Customers can place special orders.) Portions are large and service is fast. Among the outstanding Vietnamese items on the menu are deep-fried imperial rolls, lotus root salad topped with peanuts and served with shrimp crackers, hot-and-sour soup, shrimp with coconut milk over rice vermicelli, and a vegetarian special consisting of tofu sautéed with eggplant and onions. Pho noodle dishes, rice plates, and all kinds of drinks and teas—including exotic French iced black coffee and lotus leaf hot tea—are also on the exceptional menu.

## Il Pescatore
*57 Jack London Square, (510) 465-2188, fax (510) 465-0238; www.ilpescatoreristorante.com. Highchairs, boosters. L-D daily, Sat-SunBr; $$. Reservations advised.*

This atmospheric, bustling, remotely ark-shaped restaurant serves a variety of garlic-laden Italian seafood dishes. Though waiters don spiffy white shirts with black vests and ties, customers dress casually. Garlicky baked Dungeness crab, positioned attractively on large clamshells, is a great appetizer. Entrees include a delicious, delicate fresh filet of sole covered in a light egg batter and sautéed with white wine, lemon juice, and capers. The extensive, mouth-watering menu also offers plenty of other seafood choices, plus meats, pastas, and vegetarian items—all accompanied by steamed fresh chard and pasta tubes in a light tomato sauce. A slab of liquor-soaked housemade tiramisu provides a just right, not-too-sweet ending.

## Isobune Sushi
*5897 College Ave./Chabot St., 510-601-1424. L-D daily.*
For description, see page 73.

## Italian Colors
*2220 Mountain Blvd./Park Blvd., Montclair area, (510) 482-8094. L M-F, D daily; $$. Highchairs, boosters, child portions. Reservations advised.*

This attractively decorated neighborhood restaurant features warm peach-colored walls and a large, high-ceilinged, open dining room. Outdoor patio dining, with a view of the hills, is an option in warm weather. Diners young and old alike are given crayons with which to express themselves on the butcher paper-covered tables—after all, this *is* California. This amenity is also a nod to the restaurant's name and to the fact that this is a great place with kids. Though the menu of Italian-style California cuisine changes seasonally, particularly delicious items have included: a bruchetta starter topped with a variety of mushrooms; a delicate Green Scarves lasagna made with thin layers of pasta atop a cheese-cream sauce; a perfect sea bass; and a succulent herb-roasted chicken. Sicily is the focus of the menu specials on Monday nights. Pizzas and housemade desserts—order the gooey warm chocolate cake in advance as it takes 20 minutes to prepare—are also on the menu.

## Jade Villa
*800 Broadway/8th St., (510) 839-1688, fax (510) 839-5779. Dim sum daily 9:30-3, D daily; $. Highchairs, boosters. No reservations.*

There are many excellent dim sum restaurants in San Francisco's Chinatown, however difficult parking and long waits for seating can be a deterrent. This spot in Oakland's smaller Chinatown combines enjoying a meal of these tasty appetizers with easier parking and a shorter wait. Especially good among the approximately 100 kinds of dim sum served are deep-fried sweet taro balls, nicely spiced pork-filled bows, delicate steamed shrimp dumplings, and exquisite deep-fried shrimp toasts topped with a pea. The Cantonese-style dinner menu features fresh fish dishes and several family-style dinners.

## King Yen
*4080 Piedmont Ave./41st St., (415) 652-9678. L-D daily.*
For description, see page 279.

## Kinkaid's
*1 Franklin St., at Jack London Square, (510) 835-8600, fax (510) 835-2032; www.r-u-i.com/kin. L-D daily, Sat-SunBr; $-$$. Highchairs, boosters, child menu. Reservations accepted.*

The ideal spot for lunch here is at a water-side table in the room fitted with a magnificent 15-foot-tall teak bar. Kayakers, canoers, and motorboaters outside provide constant entertainment. Delicious wedges of housemade sesame pan bread come with meals.

## Le Cheval
*1007 Clay St./10th St., downtown (510) 763-8957, fax (510) 763-0555. L M-Sat, D daily; $. Highchairs, boosters. Reservations advised.*

This cavernous dining room positively roars with animated diners. Large windows open to the street, providing an even more open feeling, and namesake horses are prominent in the decor. Especially tasty selections on the classic French-Vietnamese menu include lemon grass chicken, curry-spicy Singapore-style thin noodles, and clay pot prawns. Bananas flambé makes a spectacular, satisfying dessert. Service is super fast.

## L.J. Quinn's Lighthouse
*51 Embarcadero Cove (16th Ave. exit off I-880),*
*(510) 536-2050; www.quinnslighthouse.com. L-D daily,*
*SunBr; $$. Highchairs, boosters, child menu.*
*Reservations advised.*

Quinn's operates out of the attractively remodeled Oakland Harbor Lighthouse. Built in 1903 and replaced by an automatic beacon in 1966, it was purchased from the Coast Guard for just $1. The novelty of the setting makes dining here fun. Roasted peanuts are complimentary in the casual Upper Deck Pub, and, much to the delight of children, it's okay to throw the shells on the floor. Sitting on the upstairs deck overlooking the quiet estuary with a fancy drink and some garlic bread is highly recommended. In the downstairs Yacht Club Dining Room, lunch items include pastas, seafood, and a hamburger, and brunch offers a Jambalaya omelette.

## Max's Diner
*500 12th St./Broadway, downtown, (510) 451-MAXS,*
*fax (510) 451-5838; www.maxsworld.com. L M-F.*

For description, see page 77.

## Nan Yang
*6048 College Ave./Claremont Ave., (510) 655-3298. L-D Tu-Sun; $. Highchairs, boosters. Reservations for 4+.*

The Bay Area's first Burmese restaurant (opened in 1983), this restive spot includes the refined touch of cloth napkins. The particularly good selection of vegetarian items includes a crunchy Burmese ginger salad composed of 16 ingredients—among them shredded ginger and cabbage, toasted yellow split peas, fava beans, and peanuts—all mixed together at table by the server. Also exceptional on the enticing menu are a green papaya salad with Burmese dressing, a savory curried smoked eggplant, an appetizer of batter-fried tropical squash served with a tomato-garlic sauce, and flavorful curried garlic noodles served with succulent chicken and crisp lettuce.

## Oakland Grill
*301 Franklin St./3rd St., near Jack London Square,*
*(510) 835-1176, fax (510) 835-1804. B-L-D daily; $.*
*Highchairs, boosters. No reservations.*

Situated in the produce district, this down-to-earth spot is a cheery haven for a satisfying meal and a good cup of coffee. The excellent breakfasts are served all day. Three-egg omelettes and two-egg "scramlets" are available with an extensive choice of fillings and are prepared with egg whites upon request. They come with a side of baking powder biscuits and home-fried potatoes. Hot cakes, French toast, crêpes, and eggs Benedict are also options. Lunch brings on a hamburger and veggie burger, a French dip sandwich, and a variety of salads, while dinner concentrates on steaks and a few chicken and fish dishes. Being selected by *Travel & Leisure* as one of the country's top 100 restaurants in 1995 obviously refers to the food, not the ambiance.

## The Old Spaghetti Factory
*61 Webster St., at Jack London Square, (510) 893-0222, fax (510) 893-0288; www.osf.com. L M-F, D daily; $.*

For description, see page 196.

## Oliveto
*5655 College Ave./Shafter Ave., (510) 547-5356;*
*www.oliveto.com. L M-F, D daily; $$$. Highchairs,*
*boosters. Reservations advised.*

Preparing delicious, simple dishes made with the freshest seasonal ingredients is the creed of the kitchen here. Perhaps that shouldn't be a surprise, since the well-known chef, Paul Bertolli, honed his skills at Chez Panisse. Sample dishes include a blood orange-avocado-butter lettuce salad and a flavorful pan-roasted halibut entree. A seasonal soup, freshly made pastas, and an assortment of side dishes are always available at dinner. Do leave room for dessert, as they are exceptional: warm rhubarb and candied-orange pastry, Meyer lemon éclairs with lemon-caramel sauce and pistachios, simple tangelo sherbet. Should the classy upstairs restaurant be completely booked, as it often is, opt for a less expansive, and less expensive, meal in the cozy downstairs **cafe**.

## Picnic Pick-Ups
### • A. G. Ferrari Foods
*4001 Piedmont Ave., (510) 547-7222; www.agferrari. com; also at 6119 La Salle Ave., (510) 339-9716.*

For description, see page 280.

### • G. B. Ratto & Co. International Grocers
*821 Washington St./9th St., (510) 832-6503.*
*M-Sat 9-6.*

Don't expect to just dash in and out of this Old World-style wonderland of international foods. Family-operated since 1897, this turn-of-the-century brick building is literally stuffed to the rafters with goodies. There are bins of grains and pastas, bulk spices, hanging sausages, garlic braids, and fresh breads. There is sauerkraut from Germany, pepper from India, and morel mushrooms from France. A long deli counter provides countless sandwich possibilities, and a picnic box will be pre-packed by reservation.

• **Rockridge Market Hall**
*5655 College Ave., (510) 655-7748; www.rockridge markethall.com. Open daily.*

Specialty shops include **The Pasta Shop** for deli foods and a vast variety of fresh pastas, as well as a produce shop, wine shop, and flower shop.

## Scott's Seafood Grill & Bar
*2 Broadway, at Jack London Square, (510) 444-3456, fax (510) 444-6917; www.scottseastbay.com. L-D daily, SunBr; $$$. Boosters, booths. Reservations advised. Valet parking.*

With window tables overlooking the estuary and live background music emanating from the bar, this upscale fish house is a great place for a celebration. In addition to fresh seafood, the extensive menu also offers some pastas and steaks. A New Orleans-style Sunday brunch features complimentary champagne and live jazz.

## Szechwan Restaurant
*366 8th St./Franklin St., in Chinatown, (510) 832-7878. L M-F, D daily; $. Highchairs, boosters. Reservations accepted.*

All the usual suspects are found on this extensive menu: crispy fried won tons, noisy sizzling rice soup, spicy hot-and-sour soup, Chinese burrito-like mu shu dishes, and dramatic sizzling iron platters. Personal favorites include crispy dry-braised green beans in a garlicky sauce with minced pork, and the house special chow fun—a colorful, fragrant hodgepodge of meats and vegetables mixed with addictive wide, flat rice noodles. Chinese brunch items are also on the lunch menu. Different than the more common dim sum breakfast specialties, they include Chinese-style donuts, onion pancakes, and almond jelly.

## T.G.I. Friday's
*450 Water St., at Jack London Square, (510) 451-3834, fax (510) 451-7304; www.tgifridays.com. L-D daily.*

For description, see page 173.

## Tin's Teahouse
*701 Webster St./7th St., in Chinatown, (510) 832-7661, fax (510) 832-5049. Dim sum daily 9-3, D W-M; $. Highchairs, boosters. Reservations advised.*

The first restaurant to serve dim sum in the area, this small, bright dining room is filled with mirrors and plants and positively bustles with activity as the delightful items are brought around on trays. The selection is large and includes plenty of seafood, and a vegetarian menu is also available. The dinner menu features a good hot-and-sour soup and crispy roasted duck.

## TJ's Gingerbread House
*741 5th St./Brush St., (510) 444-7373, fax (510) 444-2204; www.tjsgingerbread.com. Br-L-D & afternoon tea Tu-Sat; $$-$$$. 1 highchair, boosters, child portions. D reservations required.*

The first step to enjoying a Cajun-Creole dinner at this unique restaurant is requesting that a menu be faxed or mailed. Then call to reserve a date and to place an entree order—an unusual procedure that leaves people anticipating the experience. Arrival at the colorful little empire that is TJ's meets expectations. The three dining rooms consist of two delightful rooms in the original Victorian house, each boasting an extensive doll collection, plus a newer gazebo annex. Appetizers include shrimp rémoulade and escargots. Among the 20-plus main courses is the house specialty—a tasty, mildly spicy "spoon" jambalaya heavy with ham, Louisiana hot sausage, and prawns. Other entrees include Bayou catfish Étouffée, whiskey-stuffed lobster, and sautéed quail. Complete dinners include "sassy" corn bread, marinated steamed vegetables, Cajun "come back" dirty rice, and a dessert bowl of vanilla ice cream garnished with a tiny frosted gingerbread man and a large ginger cake cookie studded with walnuts, raisins, and chocolate chips. A teeny, tiny shop tucked under the front porch purveys everything gingerbread: dolls, bubble bath, fresh cookies.

*Horse-drawn, narrow-guage railroad at Ardenwoood*

# Fremont

## — A LITTLE BACKGROUD —

In its heyday, from 1912 to 1916, the Niles district of town was the largest film studio in Northern California. Charlie Chaplin made some of his earliest silent films here—*The Champion* and *The Tramp*. More recently, Fremont has been declared the best city in America to raise a child in.

## — ANNUAL EVENTS —

### Broncho Billy Film Festival

*June. (510) 494-1411, (510) 796-1940; www.nilesfilm museum.org. $2.50-$10.*

Screenings of movies filmed in the area are enhanced by film seminars and tours of historic Niles.

## — WHAT TO DO —

### Ardenwood Historic Farm

*34600 Ardenwood Blvd., off Hwy. 84, (510) 796-0663; www.ebparks.org/parks/arden.htm. Thur, F, Sun 10-4; $5, 62+ $4, 4-17 $3.50; admission includes horse-drawn railroad & house tour. Also open Tu, W, Sat 10-4 with no special activities; $1.50, 4-17 75¢. House*

*tour: (510) 791-4196; Thur-Sun 11-3; get tickets at train station; additional fee on Sat; must be 6 or older.*

Situated in a fragrant eucalyptus grove, this 205-acre farm was named after a forested area described in Shakespeare's *As You Like It*. It is one of the few historic farm parks in the West and allows visitors to step back in time for a view of 1880s farm life. The old farm buildings, crop fields, and antique farm equipment have all been restored, and on some days the admission fee includes rides on a novel horse-drawn, narrow-gauge railroad as well as on several hay wagons and surreys. Hourly tours are given of the restored **Patterson House**—a white gingerbread Victorian farmhouse furnished with period antiques that are original to the house. Throughout the park, staff in period costumes demonstrate typical Victorian farm chores that vary with the season but might include shoeing a horse, shearing a sheep, constructing a barrel, thrashing wheat, milking a goat, washing clothes, or making cheese. Visitors are encouraged to pitch in. A blacksmith demonstrates his craft daily. Children especially enjoy rolling around on the grassy expanses. Sometimes they can see baby farm animals, and sometimes rugs are hung out on the line for them to beat clean.

Supplement a picnic with farm fare from the **Farmyard Cafe** and, in season, with organic vegetables sold at the park entrance. See also photo on page 299.

## Coyote Hills Regional Park
*8000 Patterson Ranch Rd., (510) 795-9385; www.ebparks.org/parks/coyote.htm. Daily 8-8; Nov-Mar, 8-6. Visitor Center: Tu-Sun 9:30-5. $4/vehicle, $1/dog.*

The Visitor Center features an Ohlone Indian display, and an Indian archaeological site is sometimes accessible. The park has 15 miles of trails, plus a boardwalk trail through a fresh-water cattail marsh. Picnic tables are available, and dogs can be off leashes unless otherwise posted.

## Mission San Jose De Guadalupe
*43300 Mission Blvd./Washington Blvd., (510) 657-1797. Daily 10-5. By donation.*

Marking the center of the oldest community in the East Bay, this mission was founded in 1797 and is 14th in the chain of California missions. It is also known as Old Mission San Jose and was the only mission built in the East Bay. Though little remains of the original structure, part of the original adobe monastery wing now holds exhibits. Of particular note are the peaceful graveyard and the beautiful interior of the 1809 New England Gothic-style St. Joseph's Church.

## Niles Canyon Railway Museum
*6 Kilkare Rd., in Sunol, (925) 862-9063; www.ncry.org. Every Sun Apr-Sept; 1st & 3rd Sun, Jan-Mar, Oct, Nov; 10-4. By donation: $9, 62+ $7, 3-12 $4.*

Operating on abandoned Southern Pacific Lines rail, refurbished oil-burning and steam engines and World War II-era diesel locomotives follow the original route of the 1869 transcontinental railroad. They hiss and chug through a woodsy gorge while pulling a variety of vintage cars between Sunol and Niles. The 12½-mile round trip takes an hour. A "museum" displays old train cars and locomotives in the process of being meticulously restored by members of the Pacific Locomotive Association. Just a caboose or the entire train can be chartered for a special occasion. Wildflower Trains run in April, and decorated Santa Trains run some evenings in December.

## — WHERE TO EAT —

### Alborz
*39935 Mission Blvd., (510) 440-1755.*
*For description, see page 56.*

### Fellini-O
*3900 New Park Mall Rd./Mowry Ave., in Newark, (510) 792-6600, fax (510) 713-0501. L M-F, D M-Sat; $$. Highchairs, boosters. Reservations advised.*

The Italian arias play at just the right decibel, the attentive servers have Italian accents, and the food is European Italian. Dining is, in fact, reminiscent of feasting beside Lake Como, except the view here is of a shopping mall. Oh well, back to that food. The kitchen is accommodating about splitting orders, so try sharing a delicious housemade pasta and perhaps a meat or fish dish.

### Fernando's Mexican Restaurant
*494 Mowry Ave., (510) 796-4750.*
A mariachi band plays on Friday nights. For more description, see page 172.

### Little Sichuan Express
*34420-G Fremont Blvd., (510) 608-0585, fax (510) 608-5777.*
For description, see page 173.

### Pearl's Cafe
*4096 Bay St., (510) 490-2190; www.pearls-cafe.com. L Tu-F, D Tu-Sat; $$-$$$. Highchairs. Reservations advised.*

When you finally find this enticing spot in sprawling Fremont, which is one of the 10 largest cities in square miles in the country, the sense of euphoria is much the same as that experienced when discovering a rare pearl in an oyster. No wonder Clint Eastwood hangs here after hours, though he is probably also influenced by the fact that his wife is a friend of the owner. A sample menu might offer up delicious deep-fried artichoke and sweet potato fritters with a garlicky aioli dip as a starter, and pork loin with a tasty balsamic vinegar-strawberry sauce or a pan-roasted salmon with lemon-scented mashed potatoes as main courses. Desserts here are killers, and the best way to die is eating the Snickers ice cream pie.

## Salang Pass

*37462 Fremont Blvd./Central St., (510) 795-9200. L-D Tu-Sun; $$. Highchairs, boosters. Reservations accepted.*

Fremont has the largest population of Afghanis outside of Afghanistan. Located in an area known as "Little Kabul," this comfortable restaurant specializes in the cuisine. Seating is on the floor in a tented area with maroon-colored floor cushions or at regular Western tables. Particularly tasty entrees include ground-meat or lamb kabobs, fish curry, mantoo (a sort of ravioli filled with ground beef), and an eggplant dish. All dinners come with a western salad and bolani (traditional unleavened Afghan flat bread served with a delicious cilantro dipping sauce). Dough—a yogurt drink flavored with cucumber and mint—makes a tart and refreshing accompaniment, and baklavah is the perfect dessert.

## Tyme for Tea & Co.

*37501 Niles Blvd., (510) 790-0944; www.tyme fortea.com. W-F 12-3, Sat-Sun 11-5; $. Reservations advised.*

Henry James once said, "There are few hours in life more agreeable than the hour dedicated to the ceremony known as afternoon tea." True. Sydney Smith said, "Thank God for tea! What would the world do without tea?—how did it exist? I am glad I was not born before tea." True again. Operating in an alcove within an antique shop and making good use of doilies, mismatched vintage silverware, and charming bone china tea cups, this tearoom offers respite from the day's tribulations. The full Victoria Tea includes loose leaf tea (herbals and decafs available) or coffee (this *is* the U.S., *not* England), a scone with crème frâiche plus lemon curd and preserves, and assorted tea sandwiches and pastries. Smaller spreads are also available. Should there be a wait, browsing the shop's well-priced collection is time well spent. Allow time to browse the myriad antique shops lining the street for several blocks.

## Udupi Palace

*5988 New Park Mall Rd., in Newark, (510) 770-4008. L-D daily; $.*

For description, see page 283.

## Vung Tau

*6092 Mowry Ave., in Cedar Shopping Center, in Newark, (510) 793-8299, fax (510) 793-8427. L-D Tu-Sun; $. Highchairs, boosters, booths. Reservations accepted.*

Located in a mall filled with Asian restaurants and shops, this spot serves authentic Vietnamese cuisine in a comfortable coffee shop atmosphere. Delicious options from the extensive menu include a flat sheet rice noodle topped with butterflied grilled prawns, and a specialty red curry chicken. Noodle soups and rice plates are good one-plate choices. Fresh-squeezed orange juice and unusual shakes—durian, avocado, green bean—should not be overlooked.

# Milpitas

### — WHERE TO STAY —

## Embassy Suites

*901 E Calaveras Blvd., (408) 942-0400, fax (408) 262-8604; ww.embassysuites.com. 9 stories; 266 rooms. Indoor pool & hot tub; sauna. Restaurant.*

This atrium-style hotel has a tropical-Mediterranean design, with a soothing waterfall, a koi pond, and natural lighting from a glass skylight. For more description, see page 420.

### — WHAT TO DO —

## BFI's The Recyclery

*1601 Dixon Landing Rd. (W of I-880), (408) 262-1401, fax (408) 262-0603; www.bfisanjose.com/recyclery. html. M-F 9-5. Free.*

Sponsored by Browning Ferris Industries, this $1 million Education Center at their solid waste management facility has interactive displays that teach all about garbage—perhaps more than most people really want to know. See the 100-foot-long Wall of Garbage, which graphically illustrates the amount of garbage tossed out each year by the average family of four and demonstrates how much waste is produced every second in the U.S. Learn about the problems of waste and the positive role recycling can play. An observation deck features windows overlooking the area where trucks dump recycled items and where workers sort them.

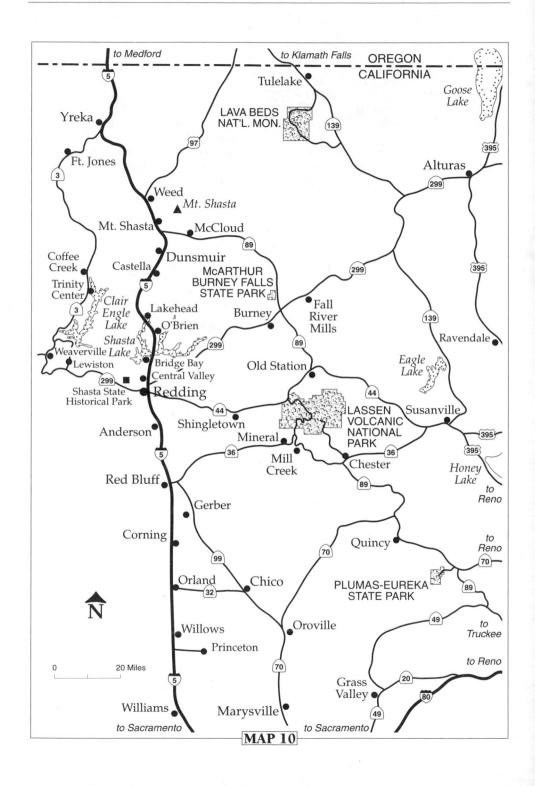

to Medford    to Klamath Falls    OREGON
CALIFORNIA

Tulelake

Goose
Lake

Yreka

LAVA BEDS
NAT'L. MON.

Ft. Jones

Alturas

Weed

Mt. Shasta

Mt. Shasta    McCloud

Coffee
Creek    Castella    Dunsmuir

McARTHUR
BURNEY FALLS
STATE PARK

Trinity
Center

Clair
Engle
Lake    Lakehead    Burney    Fall
River
Mills

O'Brien

Shasta
Weaverville Lake    Ravendale

Lewiston    Bridge Bay
Central Valley    Old Station    Eagle
Lake

Shasta State
Historical Park    Redding

Anderson    Shingletown    LASSEN
VOLCANIC
NATIONAL
PARK    Susanville

Mineral

Mill
Creek    Chester    Honey
Lake    to
Reno

Red Bluff

Gerber

Corning    Quincy    to
Reno

Orland    Chico    PLUMAS-EUREKA
STATE PARK

N

Willows    Oroville    to
Truckee

Princeton    to Reno

0    20 Miles

Grass
Valley

Williams    Marysville

to Sacramento    to Sacramento

**MAP 10**

I-5 NORTH

## Williams

### — WHERE TO EAT —

**Granzella's**

*451 Sixth St., (800) 759-6104, (530) 473-5583, fax (530) 473-2957; www.granzellas.com. B,L,D daily; $.*

Popular with travelers and locals alike, this complex consists of an Italian restaurant, a deli (which claims to have the largest selection of imported beer in Northern California), and a shop selling baked goods and bargain-priced local olives. The bar holds a large collection of mounted trophies, including a giant polar bear.

The **Inn** *((530) 473-3310. 43 rooms; $. Children under 18 free. Pool (seasonal), hot tub. Continental breakfast.)* is particularly popular with duck hunters in season.

## Willows

### — WHAT TO DO —

**Wildlife refuges**

• **Colusa National Wildlife Refuge**

*Hwy. 20 exit, 15 mi. S of town, just N of Williams.*

This refuge is about 7 miles off the freeway. It has a 3½-mile gravel loop drive.

• **Sacramento National Wildlife Refuge**

*Norman Rd./Road 68 exit, 5 mi. S of town, (530) 934-2801, fax (530) 934-7814; http://sacramentovalley refuges.fws.gov. Visitor Center: daily 7:30-4 during migration, Oct-Mar; M-F Apr-Sept.*

This refuge has a 6-mile auto tour, a viewing platform, and a walking trail.

## Chico

### — A LITTLE BACKGROUND —

Though many residents of this charming small town prefer to play it down, Chico is most famous for its party school, Chico State—the second-oldest university in the state. Both *Playboy* and MTV have acknowledged this claim to fame. And indeed, lots of students are seen around town, which is not particularly surprising since downtown streets dead-end at the campus. Still, in spite of the fact that Chico is first and foremost Party Central, much more to see and do awaits visitors here. Chico is also referred to as "the crown jewel of the north valley," and many movies were filmed here, among them *Gone with the Wind* and Clint Eastwood's *The Outlaw Josey Wales*.

## Chico Chamber of Commerce
*300 Salem St., (800) 852-8570, (530) 891-5556, fax (530) 891-3613; www.chicochamber.com.*

— GETTING THERE —

Located 85 miles north of Sacramento via Highway 99, and 180 miles northeast of San Francisco via I-5 to Highway 32 east, and 22 miles east of I-5.

— ANNUAL EVENTS —

## Endangered Species Faire
*May. (530) 891-6424, fax (530) 891-6426; www.bec net. org.*

Educational programs, live animal presentations, and musical performances combine to make this an enjoyable event.

— WHAT TO DO —

## Bidwell Mansion State Historic Park
*525 The Esplanade, downtown, (530) 895-6144; www.parks.ca.gov. Mansion tours: W-F 12-4, Sat-Sun 10-4, on the hr. $1, children free.*

General John Bidwell, who founded the town in 1860 and was a member of the first overland wagon train to reach California, used his Gold Rush earnings to build this 3-floor, 26-room Italianate Victorian mansion in 1865. Designed by Henry W. Cleveland, who also designed the Palace Hotel in San Francisco, its cavernous rooms have 14-foot ceilings and provide a cooling break in summer. Interesting features include eight slate fireplaces painted to look like marble and a third-floor ballroom that, because the owners were Presbyterians, was never used for that purpose. Shockingly, the house once was used as a Chico State dormitory. A gigantic Southern magnolia tree planted out front in 1863 is now taller than the house, and an adjacent carriage house displays several antique coaches and wagons.

## Bidwell Park
*(530) 895-4972; www.ci.chico.ca.us/parks/Bidwell_ Park.asp. Daily 11-sunset. Free.*

The third-largest city park in the U.S. (Phoenix's South Mountain Park is the largest, Los Angeles' Griffith Park is second), this 3,670-acre park was the movie stand-in for Sherwood Forest in the original 1938 *Adventures of Robin Hood.* Among its numerous trails is the ½ mile-long World of Trees Independence Trail nature path that winds through a former U.S. Forest Service tree nursery; it is accessible to both the physically and visually challenged. Most of the park is closed to cars and so is particularly enjoyable on a bicycle, which can be rented downtown. In summer, Chico Creek is dammed to form several swimming holes. The imaginative Caper Acres playground located at the south end has a nursery rhyme theme, and a stables rents horses.

**Chico Creek Nature Center** (*1968 E. 8th St., (530) 891-4671; www.chico.com/naturecenter. Tu-Sun 11-4. By donation.*) displays living examples of area wildlife and operates a children's program.

## California State University, Chico
*2nd St./Hazel St., (800) 542-4426, (530) 898-6835, fax (530) 898-6456; www.csuchico.edu. Guided campus tours M, W, F at 11:30; free; reservations advised.*

Founded in 1887, this beautiful campus has several art galleries, an anthropology museum, and a rose garden.

## Chico Museum
*141 Salem St., (530) 891-4336. W-Sun 12-4. Free.*

Housed in an architecturally interesting former Carnegie Library dating from 1904, this gem of a museum focuses on Chico's history and culture. Collection highlights include the town's original Chinese Taoist Temple and some exceptional Maidu and Yahi Indian baskets.

## National YoYo Museum
*320 Broadway, in Bird in Hand store, (530) 893-0545, fax (530) 893-0797; www.nationalyoyo.org. M-Sat 10-6, Sun 12-5. Free.*

More than 2,000 yo-yos are displayed here. Among them is the world's largest—a 256-pound wooden behemoth that requires an 80-foot crane to operate.

## Satava Art Glass Studio
*819 Wall St., (530) 345-7985, fax (530)345-9014; www.satava.com. W-F 10-5:30, Sat 9-4. Free.*

Using ancient techniques to create nature-themed glass pieces, Richard Satava has been blowing vividly colored artworks at his studio here since 1977. His ethereal jellyfish pieces sell for between $400 and $10,000. Less expensive items are also available in the gift shop inside a converted house. Watching him in action out back in his cool, open-air studio is fascinating. There, surrounded by mature black bamboo and a giant fig tree, Rick and crew perform their finely orchestrated glass-blowing dance to vintage Beatles tunes and squawking jays.

## — WHERE TO STAY —

### The Grateful Bed

*1462 Arcadian Ave./E. 5th Ave., (530) 342-2464, fax (530) 342-5500; www.chico.com/grateful. 4 rooms; $$. No TVs. Full breakfast. No smoking; no pets.*

On a tree-lined residential street near downtown, this lovely 1905 Italianate farmhouse Victorian features beautifully decorated rooms. Suite Dreams is a standout with its king-size iron bed and oversize bath with clawfoot tub and twin pedestal sinks. The three-course candlelight breakfast sometimes includes decadent white chocolate scones.

### Holiday Inn

*685 Manzanita Ct., 4 mi. from downtown, (800) 310-2491, (530) 345-2491, fax (530) 893-3040. 5 stories; 172 rooms; $. Evening snack M-Thur; restaurant. Pool; hot tub; fitness room. Pets ok.*

Located in the quieter outskirts of town, this full-service hotel provides a complimentary shuttle to the airport.

### Music Express Inn

*1091 El Monte Ave./Hwy. 32, 2 mi. from downtown, (530) 891-9833, fax (530) 893-8521; http://now2000. com/musicexpress. 9 rooms; $-$$. Full breakfast. Pool. No smoking; no pets.*

Out on the edge of town near where Highways 32 and 99 intersect, this simple inn combines the best of a B&B and motel. Rooms are in several converted houses. The design permits guests to park in front of their room motel-style and also to enjoy a made-to-order breakfast B&B-style. Rooms are equipped with whirlpool tubs and ceiling fans, and the fence out front is usually loaded with gorgeous roses. The owner conducts music lessons in the main house and operates a popular music camp here in summer, hence the name. Don't miss seeing her 1916 Steinway reproducing grand that plays 500 pieces of music just as the artist originally

performed them (Martha Stewart has a 1926 model).

## — WHERE TO EAT —

### Shubert's Ice Cream and Candy Store

*178 E. 7th St./Main, (530) 342-7163. Daily to 10pm; $.*

On a hot summer day in Chico, nothing beats an ice cream cone. Family-owned since 1938 and now a town landmark, this shop dispenses to-die-for housemade ice cream and candies. There's no place to sit inside, but get a cone—consider a simple Chico mint, a Mount Shasta (chocolate ice cream with coconut and marshmallow swirls), or a fabulous Turtle (caramel ice cream with pecans and chocolate swirl)—and sit on a bench out front, just licking lazily and watching the world go by.

### Sierra Nevada Taproom & Restaurant

*1075 E. 20th St., just W of Hwy. 99 at 20th St. exit, (530) 345-2739; www.sierranevada.com. L-D Tu-Sun, SunBr; $. Child menu. No tasting; tour M-F & Sun at 2:30 pm, Sat continuously 12-3; self-guided tour daily 10-6.*

This renowned brewery is the country's ninth largest. It has a stylish taproom and restaurant situated inside a large room accented with polished copper and gleaming wood. This brewpub serves up its famous Pale Ale and other housemade beers (a sampler is available) as well as a deliciously executed, modestly priced menu featuring expected items such as beer-battered fish & chips and a hamburger. More exotic fare is also available, including an Asian noodle salad and an assortment of wood-fire oven pizzas with chi-chi toppings. In nice weather, the outside patio is primo and the perfect place to try a milkshake made with the brewery's own malt. Mustards and malt vinegar made with house beers make good souvenirs.

### Thursday Night Market

*Broadway/3rd St., downtown, (530) 345-6500. Thur 6-9pm; Apr-Sept only.*

For this weekly event, the streets are lined with vendors displaying handmade goods and farm-fresh produce, and shops and restaurants stay open later than usual. Children's activities and entertainers provide diversion for everyone.

## Tres Hombres Restaurant

*100 Broadway/1st St., downtown, (530) 342-0425, fax (530) 342-0528. L-D daily. Highchairs, boosters, child menu.*

Popular with students, this restaurant serves a selection of Mexican items in John Bidwell's former storehouse and office. In a large, open, brick-walled room with comfy booths and roomy tables, this happening place's menu offers the expected as well as more imaginative items such as tequila-lime paella and pasta. The excellent fajitas dish is large enough for two people with average appetites to share. A cheeseburger is an option, and margaritas come in many styles, including non-alcoholic fresh fruit versions.

# Paradise

## — GETTING THERE —

From Chicoo, this mountain hamlet is an easy 11-mile drive up a scenic hill via Skyway/ Highway 134. On the way, watch both for fields dotted with big rocks left from when Mt. Lassen blew in prehistoric times and for historical Chinese walls fitted together without mortar. The town sign reads, "May you find Paradise to be all its name implies."

## — ANNUAL EVENTS —

### Johnny Appleseed Days

*October. (530) 877-9356. Free.*

Though only one orchard is left in this former apple producing area, people come from all over to celebrate everything apple. Demonstrations, crafts, a pancake breakfast, and, of course, lots of apple pie are part of the fun.

## — WHAT TO DO —

### Antiquing

This town has more than 20 well-priced antique shops, most of them on the main drag. Some are in old historical houses sporting spoiled resident cats and atmospheric old-time music. One of the most extensive inventories is in the **Skyway Antique Mall** (*6118 Skyway, (530) 877-6503; www.skywayantiquemall.com. M-Sat 10-5, Sun 12-5.*), where 25 dealers display their finds.

## Gold Nugget Museum

*502 Pearson Rd., (530) 872-8722. W-Sun 12-4. Free.*

Visitors here can walk through a replica mine and view a reproduction of the largest gold nugget ever discovered in North America—a 54-pound monster found here in 1859. A miniature covered bridge and a one-room schoolhouse are found on the shady grounds outside, and a blacksmith shop and gold panning sluices operate on summer weekends. Days of Living History occurs each year in September and includes crafts demonstrations, hands-on activities, and food booths.

## Honey Run Covered Bridge

*Take downhill road directly across street from Skyway Antique Mall at 6118 Skyway.*

Built across Butte Creek in 1894, this is the only covered bridge in the U.S. with three different roof levels. Though closed to traffic, it provides a lovely stroll. (A horse and buggy scene was shot here for the 1955 film *Friendly Persuasion.*) From here, it's 5 miles back to Chico on a road that passes through 1,000-foot-deep Butte Creek Canyon gorge—called "Little Grand Canyon" by locals.

An annual fund-raising **Pancake Breakfast** (*June; on 1st Sun. (530) 342-9197.*) raises money for a local school and museum and permits the opportunity to dine on the bridge. Arts and crafts projects and live music are part of the down-home atmosphere.

## — WHERE TO EAT —

### Stirling City Hotel

*16975 Skyway, 11 mi. from town, up scenic Skyway, in Stirling City, (530) 873-0858; www.stirlingcity.info. Schedule varies; $.*

This picturesque mountain town retains its original wooden walkways from when it was action central for gold and silver mining, then logging. Though it has a population of only 371, gold mining still goes on. Afternoon tea is served in this 1904 building on Thursdays, brunch is scheduled one Sunday each month, and dinners are by reservation. Owner-chef-cookbook author Charlotte Ann Hilgeman says she only makes stuff she likes "because I might have to eat the leftovers."

The **B&B** part of the hotel consists of six simple, cozy, and blessedly un-cutesy guest rooms. They are decorated with vintage furniture and chenille bedspreads and share bathrooms.

Across the street, manicured **Clotilde Merlo Park** *((530) 873-1658. Thur-Sun 10-7; May-Oct only. Free.)* has several koi-filled ponds, nature trails, and a lovely outdoor chapel.

# Corning

## — GETTING THERE —

This small town is 170 somewhat flat, dreary miles from San Francisco, punctuated only by the occasional sighting of an unusual migrating bird.

## — WHAT TO DO —

### Olive Pit
*2156 Solano St., (800) OLIVE-PIT, (530) 824-4667, fax (530) 824-4702; www.olivepit.com. Daily 7am-7:30, in summer to 8:30.*

In the town that is the center of the olive industry in Northern California, everything olive is found here. Taste a vast variety of flavored olives (the best being the greens stuffed with pimento and almond), pick up some car snacks, or chow down on fast food.

# Red Bluff

## — VISITOR INFORMATION —

### Red Bluff/Tehama County Chamber of Commerce
*100 Main St., (800) 655-6225, (530) 527-6220, fax (530) 527-2908; www.redbluffchamberof commerce.com.*

## — ANNUAL EVENTS —

### South Shasta Model Railroad
*April-May; Sat-Sun. In Gerber, 12 mi. S of town, (530) 385-1389. $4, 5-12 $3.*

This miniature ¼-inch O-gauge reproduction of the 100-mile Southern Pacific Railroad line from Gerber to Dunsmuir operates in the basement of a private farmhouse. It includes 16 handmade steam locomotives, 100 cars, and over 900 feet of track. Visitors can also ride on a 2-foot-gauge steam train and visit a museum of antique farm equipment.

## — WHAT TO DO —

### Kelly-Griggs House Museum
*1248 Jefferson St., (530) 527-1129. Thur-Sun 1-4. By donation.*

This restored 1880s Victorian is just off the freeway. While here, pick up a self-guiding map to local Victorian homes.

### William B. Ide Adobe State Historic Park
*21659 Adobe Rd., (530) 529-8599, fax (530) 529-8598; www.parks.ca.gov. Daily 8-5. $3/vehicle.*

Located on the outskirts of town beside the Sacramento River, this authentically furnished one-room adobe house was the home of early California settler William B. Ide—the Republic of California's first and only president. Other buildings in the 3-acre park are an adobe smokehouse, a carriage shed for old buggies, and a small corral. This is a great spot for a picnic.

# Lassen Volcanic National Park and Area

## — A LITTLE BACKGROUND —

Now a dormant volcano, imposing 10,457-foot Lassen Peak last erupted in 1915. (It is one of only two active volcanoes on the U.S. mainland. The other is Mt. St. Helens in Washington, which last erupted in 1980. A curious fact is that they both erupted in the month of May.) It is thought to be the largest plug dome volcano in the world. The best time to visit is July through September, when the 35-mile road through the park is least likely to be closed by snow. Visitors can take several self-guided nature walks, and guided hikes and campfire talks are scheduled in summer. Children age 7 through 12 can participate in the Junior Ranger program (see page 445), and those age 4 through 6 can participate in the Chipmunk Club (contact the Loomis Museum for information). Wooden catwalks supplement the trail through popular Bumpass Hell (it is named after its discoverer Kendall Bumpass, who lost a leg after he fell into a boiling mud pot), which is the largest geothermal feature in the park and features geological oddities such as boiling springs and mud pots, pyrite pools, and noisy fumaroles. The trail covers 3 miles and takes about 3 hours round trip. The park also offers over 150 miles of backcountry trails, including a 17-mile section of the Pacific Crest Trail. The park's **Loomis Museum** *((530) 595-4444 x5180. Daily 9-5; June-Aug only. Free.)*, which is located inside a lovely old stone building at Manzanita Lake, has an orientation video and exhibits dramatic photos of the 1914 eruption. A free park newsletter/map orients visitors and lists daily activities. Eight campgrounds are available on a first-come, first-served basis. For skiing information, see page 430.

Park admission is $10 per vehicle.

### – VISITOR INFORMATION –

**Park Headquarters**
*38350 Hwy. 36, in Mineral, (530) 595-4444, fax (530) 595-3262; www.nps.gov/lavo. M-F 8-4:30.*

**Lassen County Chamber of Commerce**
*84 N. Lassen St., in Susanville, (530) 257-4323, fax (530) 251-2561; www.lassencountychamber.org.*

### – GETTING THERE –

Take Highway 36 east from Red Bluff, or Highway 44 east from Redding.

### – WHAT TO DO –

**Fort Crook Museum**
*43030 Fort Crook Museum Rd., on Hwy. 299, in Fall River Mills, (530) 336-5110. M-F 10-4, Sat-Sun 1-4; May-Nov only. $5, 6-12 $3.*

Composed of a 3-story main building and five outer buildings, this large museum complex displays six rooms of antique furniture, a collection of early farm implements and Native American artifacts, the old Fall River jail, a one-room schoolhouse from Pittville, and a pioneer log cabin.

**McArthur-Burney Falls Memorial State Park**
*24898 Hwy. 89, in Burney, (530) 335-2777; www.parks.ca.gov. Daily 8-4; Apr-Sept to 11. $5/vehicle.*

A lovely 1-mile nature trail winds past the soothing rush of the 129-foot waterfall here (Theodore Roosevelt called it the eighth wonder of the world), allowing for closer inspection of the volcanic terrain for which this area is known. Paddleboats can be rented at man-made Lake Britton, where facilities include picnic tables, a sandy beach, and a wading area for children. Swimming is allowed only in designated areas, as the lake has a steep drop-off. Campsites are available.

A boat is needed to reach isolated **Ahjumawi Lava Springs State Park**, which features one of the largest systems of freshwater springs in the world. Descendants of the Native American Ahjumawi tribe reside in the area.

Twelve miles away, the town of Burney offers motels and supermarkets.

**Spattercone Crest Trail**
*1/2 mi. W of Old Station, across from Hat Creek Campground. Free.*

This 2-mile, self-interpretive trail winds past a number of volcanic spatter cones, lava tubes, domes, and blowholes. It takes about 2 hours to walk and is most comfortably hiked in early morning or late afternoon.

**Subway Cave**
*1 mi. N of Old Station, near junction of Hwys. 44 & 89, (530) 335-2111. Free.*

Lava tubes formed here about 2,000 years ago, when the surface of a lava flow cooled and hardened while the liquid lava beneath the hard

crust flowed away. This cave, which is actually a lava tube, winds for about 1/4 mile. Always a cool 46 degrees, it makes a good place to visit on a hot afternoon. However, it is completely unlighted inside, so visitors are advised to bring along a powerful lantern. Allow time for a picnic in the lovely surrounding woods. Just north of here, Mt. Lassen starts showing up in the rearview mirror, and Mt. Shasta looms ahead.

— WHERE TO STAY —

Little lodging is found here, but many forest campsites are available on a first-come, first-served basis. Visitors should bear in mind that this area is remote and does not offer big-city facilities such as supermarkets.

### Drakesbad Guest Ranch

*At end of Warner Valley Rd., 17 mi. from Chester, (530) 529-1512 x120, fax (530) 529-4511; www.drakesbad.com. 19 units; $$$; closed Oct-May. Child rates; under 2 free. No TVs. Hot springs pool. Includes 3 meals. Dogs ok.*

Located at the end of the road in a secluded, scenic mountain valley within the national park, this rustic resort was a hot springs spa in the mid-1800s. It has been a guest ranch since the turn of the century and is now the only one located within a national park. Most of the rustic cabins, bungalows, and lodge rooms have no electricity, so kerosene lanterns provide light. The ranch is within easy hiking distance of some of Lassen's thermal sights: 1 mile from the steaming fumaroles at Boiling Springs Lake; 2 miles from the bubbling sulfurous mud pots at Devil's Kitchen. Guests can rent horses from the ranch stables for guided rides into these areas. All this and a good trout fishing stream, too! Day visitors should call ahead for horse or dining reservations, which include complimentary use of the 90- to 100-degree hot springs-fed pool. Overnight guests should book a year in advance.

### Hat Creek Resort

*On Hwy. 89 just N of Hwy. 44, in Old Station, 11 mi. from N entrance to Lassen Park, (530) 335-7121, fax (530) 335-7031. 17 units; $. Cabins closed in winter. Some kitchens.*

These bargain motel rooms and old-time housekeeping cabins—with linoleum floors and homemade curtains—are located beside rushing Hat Creek, which is considered to be one of the finest fly-fishing streams in the western U.S. Guests can fish in the creek, roast marshmallows over an open fire, and check out the stars at night.

— WHERE TO STAY NEARBY —

### KOA Kampground

*7749 KOA Rd., in Shingletown, 5 mi. S of Hwy. 44, 21 mi. from Lassen, (800) KOA-3403, (530) 474-3133.*

Facilities include a playground, pool, petting zoo, and general store. For more description, see page 443.

**Wild Horse Sanctuary**

*On Wilson Hill Rd., in Shingletown, 5 mi. S of Hwy. 44, 21 mi. from Lassen, (530) 335-2241, same fax; www.wildhorsesanctuary.org. 5 cabins; 1 night/$295/ person, 2 nights/$395/person; trips Apr-Oct only; viewing year-round, W & Sat 10-3. Unsuitable for children under 14. No TVs; shared bath house. All meals included.*

This protected preserve for wild mustangs and burros is the only wild horse sanctuary in the nation. Guests ride out of a base camp to observe the 200-plus population in their natural habitat. Meals are served by an open campfire, and overnight accommodations are in new, but rustic, cabins overlooking Vernal Lake. Prices include everything.

# Lava Beds National Monument

## — A LITTLE BACKGROUND —

It doesn't hurt to be warned ahead of time that this 46,000-acre national monument is located in the middle of nowhere. In fact, this could be where the expression "out in the tules" originated.

The monument has a campground, but the nearest motels and restaurants are far away in Tulelake. It's a good idea to pack-in picnic supplies, as there is nowhere to buy food within many miles of the monument. The area also buzzes with insects, is a haven for rattlesnakes, and sometimes has plague warnings posted. Still, it is an unusual place that is well worth a visit.

The Visitors Center at the southern entrance offers a good orientation. Historically, this area was the site of the 1872 Modoc War— the only major Indian war fought in California. Geologically, the area is of interest because of its concentration of caves.

Park admission is $10 per vehicle.

## — VISITOR INFORMATION —

**Monument Headquarters**

*(530) 667-2282, fax (530) 667-2737; www.nps.gov/ labe.*

## — GETTING THERE —

Go north from Lassen Volcanic National Park on Highway 89 to Highway 299. Continue northeast to Highway 139, taking it north through sparsely populated forest and farmland. The monument is approximately 115 miles northeast of Mt. Shasta City/Highway 5.

## — WHAT TO DO —

**Caves**

Located a short walk from the **Visitors Center** *(Daily 8-5; in summer to 6.)*, Mushpot Cave has interpretive displays and is the only lighted cave here. A 2-mile loop road leads to 20 caves developed for easy access, including some with descriptive names such as Blue Grotto, Sunshine, and Natural Bridge. The 71-step staircase at Skull Cave descends 80 feet to an ice floor, and some of Catacombs must be crawled through. Lanterns are available to borrow.

**Tule Lake** and **Lower Klamath National Wildlife Refuges**

*4 mi. S of Oregon border, (530) 667-2231, fax (530) 667-3299; www.klamathnwr.org. Visitor Center: 4009 Hill Rd., in Tulelake; M-F 8-4:30, Sat-Sun 10-4; free.*

The gravel road north out of the monument passes through the Tule Lake portion of this scenic area, which is the largest wetlands west of the Mississippi. These refuges are home to a variety of interesting birds that are easily viewed from a car. In winter, they have the densest concentration of bald eagles in the U.S. south of Alaska.

# Redding

## — A LITTLE BACKGROUND —

Built on the Sacramento River, this down-to-earth city anchors the area's outdoor recreation venues. Its stores are convenient for stocking up before heading out on a boating, fishing, hunting, or hiking trip. Redding is also home to the country's largest covered street mall. Note that it gets hot here in summer. *Real* hot.

## — VISITOR INFORMATION —

**Redding Convention & Visitors Bureau**

*777 Auditorium Dr., (800) 874-7562, (530) 225-4100, fax (530) 225-4354; www.visitredding.org.*

## Shasta-Cascade Wonderland Association

*1699 Hwy. 273, in Anderson, 7 mi. S of town,*
*(800) 474-2782, (530) 365-7500, fax (530) 365-1258;*
*www.shastacascade.org.*

### — GETTING THERE —

Located 30 miles north of Red Bluff, and 210
miles north of San Francisco.

### — WHAT TO DO —

## Coleman National Fish Hatchery

*24411 Fish Hatchery Rd., in Anderson, 11 mi. SW of I-5*
*(Deschutes Rd. E exit), 20 mi. SW of town, (530) 365-*
*8622, fax (530) 365-0913; http://fisheries.fws.gov.*
*Free.*

The huge Chinook, or king salmon, flap
their way out of Battle Creek and up the fish
ladder here four times each year. See the fall
run spawn October through mid-December; the
late fall run spawn January through March; the
winter run spawn May through July; and the
spring run spawn August through September.
Steelhead trout spawn January through March.
Fingerlings can be seen in holding tanks in the
hatchery building. This is the largest salmon
hatchery in the U.S. A **Salmon Festival** occurs
here each October.

## Shasta State Historic Park

*On Hwy. 299, 10 mi. W of I-5, in Old Shasta,*
*(530) 243-8194; www.parks.ca.gov. Free. Courthouse*
*Museum: W-Sun 10-5; $2, 6-12 $1; includes same-day*
*admission to Weaverville Joss House S.H.P.*

Prosperous and bustling during the Gold
Rush, this gold-mining ghost town is now an
interesting museum of restored buildings and
picturesque ruins located on either side of the
highway. In the 1861 **Courthouse Museum**, a
lovely eclectic collection of California art spanning 1850 through 1950 is displayed Louvre-
like—all crowded together tightly on the walls.
A collection of Modoc Indian baskets and of
antique weapons is also displayed. A gallows is
just outside the completely restored courtroom,
and a basement jail with heavy-duty ironwork
and a ghost hologram is 13 steps down. A large
picnic area with tables, a barn, and grassy
expanses are adjacent, and across the highway
the old Blumb Bakery, though no longer operating commercially, still has its massive brick
oven and sometimes serves up inexpensive

baked goods and drinks. Also across the street,
the delightful Litsch Store is refitted and
stocked to look as it did way back when and is
sometimes open for tours. More than 30% of
the objects displayed are original to the store,
and the rest are convincing replicas.

## Turtle Bay Exploration Park

*800 Auditorium Dr., (800) TURTLEBAY, (530) 243-*
*8850, fax (530) 243-8898; www.turtlebay.org. Tu-Sun*
*9-5; daily in summer. $11, 65+ $9, 4-15 $6.*

This fascinating complex situated on the
banks of the Sacramento River is composed of
several venues—all focusing on life along the
river. Resembling a 19th-century logging mill,
Paul Bunyan's Forest Camp center has exhibits
about the region's logging days plus an extensive collection of living California snakes. A creative outside play area has a tree stump maze,
an osprey nest climbing structure, and a giant
log slide; a live butterfly exhibit is open May
through September. The **Turtle Bay Museum**'s
displays run the gamut from a bevy of Wintu
Indian baskets to a collection of atmospheric
aquariums filled with local river fish and turtles.
Particularly popular with kids is the reproduction of an oak tree with a window in the floor
through which they can peer down at its root
structure. A cafe with outdoor seating overlooks
the new harp-shaped, pedestrians-only **Sundial
Bridge** designed by avant-garde Spanish architect Santiago Calatrava—one of the world's premier bridge designers. Made from steel, glass,
and granite, it is environmentally sensitive and
has no supports in the water. It features a
translucent surface, and its pylon forms the
world's largest working sundial. Stop in at the
Visitor Center for an orientation to this spread-
out facility.

### — WHERE TO STAY —

## Best Western Hilltop Inn

*2300 Hilltop Dr., (800) 336-4880, (530) 221-6100,*
*fax (530) 221-2867; www.thehilltopinn.com. 114 rooms;*
*$-$$. Heated pool; children's pool; hot tub. Full break-*
*fast; 2 restaurants.*

This contemporary motel provides guests
with passes to a nearby health club.

A step above the usual motel restaurant,
**C. R. Gibbs American Grill** *(www.crgibbs.com)*
operates off the lobby. Items on the expansive

menu include pizza from a wood-fired oven and rotisserie chicken, as well as a superb French-dip sandwich and delicious fish tacos. The bar is known for its selection of beers and martinis but also serves up sodas and milk-shakes and features live music in the evening April through October. The patio is primo in good weather.

## Motel 6
*1640 Hilltop Dr., 3 mi. SE of town, (800) 4 MOTEL 6, (530) 221-1800, fax (530) 221-6175; www.motel6.com. 80 rooms; $. Unheated pool (closed in winter).*
This chain has three branches in town.

## Motel Row
*Along Hilltop Drive.*

### — WHERE TO EAT —

## The Keep
*21968 Old 44 Dr./Deschutes, in Palo Cedro, 9 mi. E of town, (530) 547-2068. L Tu-F, D Tu-Sun; $$. Reservations advised.*
Named for a castle's central stronghold, where in medieval times valuables and royalty were kept, this unique "restaurant and mead hall" serves the largest selection of meads in the world. Made from fermented honey, mead is the world's oldest fermented beverage. Here it is offered in flavors that include fruits, such as blackberry, and specialty honeys, such a Black Oak honey. In low-key keeping with the theme, antlers decorate the walls paneled with honey-pine wainscoting. The lunch menu offers prime rib and roast pork sandwiches as well as stuffed yams and potatoes. Dinner brings on shepherd's pie, a delicious vegetable-rich stout pork stew, and some pasta and seafood choices, too. Marvelous dark, sweet bread made from a medieval recipe is included along with either soup or salad. It makes sense that this unique eatery is in this rural suburb of small farms and ranches spread along Cow Creek, because Palo Cedro is the honeybee queen capital of the world. It ships out more queen bees from its post office than any other town in the world.

## Nannette's Grill
*1777 Market St., (530) 241-4068. B-L M-Sat, D Tu-Sat; $-$$. Child portions.*
A large lunch selection of scrumptious salads, sandwiches and burgers, crepes, and

quiches make a quick decision here difficult. The Thai chicken salad and the chicken-marinated artichoke-brie hot sandwich are both highly recommended. Desserts include a cream puff and éclair that make good use of the housemade chocolate ganache.

# Trinity Alps

### — A LITTLE BACKGROUND —

Densely forested and home to 55 alpine lakes, this is the largest wilderness area in the U.S. It is prime camping country, and there's not much to do here except relax and perhaps fish, boat, or hike. It's also the only county in the state with no freeway and no stop lights. Promisingly, James Hilton, author of *Lost Horizon*, said in 1941 that Weaverville was as close as he had come to a real-life Shangri-La.

### — VISITOR INFORMATION —

## Trinity County Chamber of Commerce
*211 Trinity Lakes Blvd., in Weaverville, (800) 487-4648, (530) 623-6101, fax (530) 623-3753; www.trinitycounty.com.*

### — WHAT TO DO —

## Jake Jackson Museum & History Center and Trinity County Historical Park
*508 Main St., in Weaverville, (530) 623-5211, fax (530) 623-5053; www.tcoek12.org/~museum. Daily 10-5, May-Oct; Tu-Sat 12-4, Nov-Apr. By donation.*
This museum traces Trinity County's history using mining equipment, old bottles, and photographs. Exhibits include a reconstructed blacksmith shop and miner's cabin. Outside, a creek-side picnic area beckons, and a full-size steam-powered stamp mill, located on the block just below the museum, is operated on holidays.

## Weaverville Joss House State Historic Park
*404 Main St., in Weaverville, (530) 623-5284; www.parks.ca.gov. Tours W-Sun 10-4; on hr. $2, under 17 free. Includes same-day admission to Courthouse Museum at Shasta S.H.P.*
Located in a shaded area beside a creek, this Chinese Taoist temple provides cool respite on a hot summer day. Built in 1874 on the site of a previous temple that burned to the ground, it is still used for worship and is the oldest continuously used Chinese temple in the state.

## — WHERE TO STAY —

### Coffee Creek Ranch

*Off Hwy. 3, in Coffee Creek, 40 mi. N of Weaverville, (800) 624-4480, (530)266-3343, fax (530) 266-3597; www.coffeecreekranch.com. 15 cabins; $$$+. Child rates. No TVs; wood-burning fireplaces & stoves. Heated pool (seasonal); children's wading pool; hot tub; fitness room. Includes all meals; restaurant. No smoking.*

Private one- and two-bedroom cabins here are surrounded by trees. Activities include horse-drawn hayrides, movies, steak-frys, outdoor games, square and line dancing, archery, gun practice on a rifle range, panning for gold, and supervised activities for children 3 to 17. Horseback riding is included in the price in spring and fall; in summer, there is an additional charge. Cross-country skiing, sleigh rides, and dog-sled rides are available in winter.

### Trinity Alps Resort

*1750 Trinity Alps Rd., in Trinity Center, 12 mi. N of Weaverville, (530) 286-2205, same fax; http://trinity alpsresort.com. 43 cabins; $$; closed Oct-Apr. No TVs; all kitchens. 1 tennis court. Restaurant. Pets ok.*

Arranged especially to please families, this 90-acre resort is composed of rustic 1920s cabins with sleeping verandas—all scattered along rushing Stuart Fork River. Guests provide their own linens or pay additional to rent them. Simple pleasures include crossing the river on a suspension bridge, hanging out at the general store, and enjoying dinner on a patio overlooking the river at **Bear's Breath Bar & Grill**.

Scheduled activities include square dancing, bingo, and evening movies. Hiking and fishing are popular activities, and kids can ride their bikes endlessly.

### Trinity Lake Resorts & Marinas

*45810 Hwy. 3, in Trinity Center, 15 mi. N of Weaverville, (800) 982-2279, (530) 286-2225, fax (530) 286-2665; www.trinitylakeresort.com. 12 cabins; $-$$; closed Nov-Feb. No TVs; all kitchens. Restaurant. Dogs ok.*

This quiet spot offers lodging in a cabin in the woods or on a houseboat on Trinity Lake. Guests provide their own bedding and linens. The marina also rents boats, houseboats, and slips, and the bar and restaurant offer a terrific view of the lake.

# Shasta Lake Area

## — GETTING THERE —

Located approximately 235 miles north of San Francisco.

## — WHAT TO DO —

### Lake Shasta Caverns

*20359 Shasta Caverns Rd., in O'Brien, (800) 795-CAVE, (530) 238-2341, fax (530) 238-2386; www.lakeshastacaverns.com. Tours daily; schedule varies. $18, 65+ $16, 4-12 $9.*

Discovered in 1878, these caverns didn't open for tours until 1964. The 2-hour tour begins with a 15-minute catamaran cruise across the McCloud arm of Lake Shasta. Then visitors board a bus for a scenic, winding ride up the steep mountainside to the caverns. In this case, getting there really is half the fun. Nature trails, picnic facilities, and a snack bar are available.

### Shasta Dam

*16349 Shasta Dam Blvd., in Shasta Lake City, 5 mi. off Hwy. 5, (530) 275-4463; www.mp.usbr.gov. Tours daily at 9, 11, 1, 3. Free.*

Built in 1938, this is the second-largest dam in the U.S. and the highest center-overflow dam in the world (it's three times higher than Niagara Falls!). The guided 1-hour tour includes seeing a film showing how dams are built and viewing an exhibit room. For security reasons, tours no longer include the base of the dam or the power plant.

## Houseboats

Lake Shasta has the largest fleet of houseboats west of the Mississippi. For more information, see page 441.

## Motel Row

Inexpensive motels are located at Bridge Bay and in the Lakehead area.

---

# Dunsmuir

Surrounded by a million acres of forest and wilderness, this wildly scenic town is touted as "the home of the best water on Earth." And, indeed, pure spring water from Mt. Shasta glaciers is delivered to the city via lava tubes and then piped to every tap in town. One of the hamlet's 10 always-flowing public drinking fountains is in a sheltered spot by the side of the two-lane road through town. It is reminiscent of restorative fountains seen in small spa towns in Germany's Black Forest.

The town's history is the railroad. At the turn of the 19th century, it was a division point on the railroad and a popular resort area. By the 1920s, things were really booming. Celebrities stopped here by the trainload, including Clark Gable and Babe Ruth, and the town's California Theatre was a movie palace. Then, in the 1950s steam locomotives were phased out, drastically hurting the area's economy. And in 1961, I-5 bypassed Dunsmuir—a mixed blessing that allowed the town to retain its charm.

## Dunsmuir Chamber of Commerce

*411853 Pine St., (800) DUNSMUIR, (530) 235-2177; www.dunsmuir.com.*

## Brown Trout Gallery & Cafe

*5841 Sacramento Ave., (800) 916-4278, (530) 235-0754; www.browntroutgallery.com. Shop: Daily 10-5. Cafe: Daily 7-4; $.*

This boutique purveys interesting crafts and art. Of special note is a stream running underneath that can be seen and heard through a hole in the floor. A cafe serves up coffee and.

## Castle Crags State Park

*Castle Creek Rd., in Castella, 10 mi. S of town; (530) 235-2684, fax (530) 235-2684; www.parks.ca.gov. Daily sunrise-sunset. $4/vehicle.*

Mile-high, snaggle-tooth granite peaks dominate this 6,000-acre park. Hiking trails, picnic areas, and swimming holes are available. For a smashing picnic spot with a view of the crags and Mt. Shasta, drive up the narrow one-lane road leading to Vista Point. The 1-mile Indian Creek Nature Trail loop has gentle slopes and provides an easy leg-stretch. Campsites are available.

## Enchanted Forest Porcelain Doll Factory

*4100 Pine St., (530) 235-0441. Tu-F 10-4, Sat 10-3.*

Between them, Marian and Loren Anderson make about 1,600 expensive dolls each year for collectors. Marian sews all the outfits and will duplicate a wedding dress.

## Hedge Creek Falls

*On Dunsmuir Ave., at N end of town. Free.*

The short, easy path leading to the falls follows the Sacramento River. Once there, it is possible to walk behind the base of the falls, and picnicking is lovely. A table and gazebo are provided at the trailhead. Legend has it that the notorious Gold Rush-era bandit Black Bart once used the area as a hideout.

## Upper Sacramento River Center

*5819 Sacramento Ave., (530) 235-2012, fax (530) 235-2439; www.riverexchange.org. Tu-M 9-5. Free.*

A 1991 Southern Pacific tanker car derailment here spilled 18,000 gallons of pesticide into the Sacramento River, killing everything in its path for 40 miles. It was the worst inland water spill in the state's history. After a lot of effort, the river is back to normal, and this center was built as part of a resulting settlement. Part hands-on museum and part river information center for those who want to fish, raft, hike, or mountain bike in the area, it has a variety of river-related exhibits. Among them are a 6-foot by 16-foot map of the Upper Sacramento River watershed, a stuffed black bear, and great activities for kids.

## — WHERE TO STAY —

### Cave Springs Resort
*4727 Dunsmuir Ave., (888) 235-2721, (530) 235-2721; www.cavesprings.com. 25 units; $. Pool; hot tub; 1 tennis court. Restaurant. Pets ok.*

Situated on the outskirts of town, just above the river, this old-time mountain resort seems like something out of a time warp. It offers simple motel rooms, cabins, and RV accommodations, and facilities on the spacious, cedar-sheltered grounds include a playground and bocce ball court.

### Railroad Park Resort
*100 Railroad Park Rd., 1 mi. S of town, (800) 974-RAIL, (530) 235-4440, fax (530) 235-4470; www.rrpark.com. 28 units; $-$$. Some kitchens. Unheated pool; hot tub. Restaurant (closed Nov-Mar). Pets by approval.*

Guests here can sleep in an authentic antique caboose or in a deluxe, handicapped-equipped boxcar unit. Each is furnished with antiques and has a clawfoot tub, and family units have bunk beds. Three cabins and some creek-side campsites are also available. The nearby Cascade Mountains and their granite Castle Crags Spires can be viewed while frolicking in the pool, and prime rib and seafood dinners are served inside an authentic McCloud River Railroad car that is converted into a restaurant.

## — WHERE TO EAT —

### Cafe Maddalena
*5801 Sacramento Ave., (530) 235-2725, fax (530) 235-0639; www.cafemaddalena.com. D Thur-Sun; $$; closed Jan-Mar. Highchairs, boosters. Reservations advised.*

Located across the street from the old train station, this well-loved restaurant has a cozy interior lined with knotty-pine walls. The talented chef-owner hails from Sardinia and takes pride in whipping up authentic, well-executed Italian dishes that would be extraordinary anywhere, but seem especially so here, so far from a major city.  One menu choice is housemade ravioli stuffed with ricotta and artichokes and topped with fresh tomato; another is a superb pizza topped with a mixture of spinach, oyster mushrooms, garlic, eggplant, and mozzarella. (Sometimes the chef even makes *fresh* mozza-

rella.) Among the desserts are tiramisu and an unusual egg-less bitter lemon flan that is heaven for those watching their cholesterol.

---

# McCloud

## — A LITTLE BACKGROUND —

Set in the shadow of Mt. Shasta, this scenic mill town was owned by the McCloud Lumber Company from 1897 to 1965. It looks now much as it did then. The streets here are wide, with boardwalks fronting the commercial buildings, and there is little traffic and lots of trees.

## — VISITOR INFORMATION —

### McCloud Chamber of Commerce
*205 Quincy St., (530) 964-3113, fax (530) 964-2808; www.mccloudchamber.com.*

## — GETTING THERE —

From I-5, follow Highway 89 for 10 miles into town.

## — WHAT TO DO —

### Shasta Sunset Dinner Train
*(800) 733-2141, (530) 964-2142, fax (530) 964-2250; www.shastasunset.com. Schedule varies; Jan-Aug only. $80. Excursion train: Schedule varies; June-Aug only; $12-$18, under 12 $8-$12.*

Refurbished 1915 coach cars are used on the 3-hour, 40-mile dinner trip, which includes a gourmet meal served on elegant white linen set with china and silver. On the scenic hour-long excursion to Signal Butte, passengers sit in open-air cars.

## — WHERE TO STAY AND EAT —

### McCloud Guest House
*606 W. Colombero Dr., (877) 964-3160, (530) 964-3160; www.mccloudguesthouse.com. 5 rooms; $$. Continental breakfast. No smoking.*

Sitting on a hill above town amid 6 acres of gardens, this 1907 California Craftsman-style house has a large veranda. Its antique furnishings include an ornate pool table in the lounge.

### McCloud Hotel
*408 Main St., (800) 964-2823, (530) 964-2822, fax (530) 964-2844; www.mccloudhotel.com.*

*16 rooms; $$-$$$. Full breakfast; restaurant. No smoking.*

A registered national landmark, this hotel was built in 1916 on the same foundation as a prior hotel that burned down that same year. It once had 96 rooms and provided housing for mill workers and teachers, and its basement was the town library until the 1960s. Now meticulously restored, its old-fashioned lobby invites lingering over a board game or book. The individually decorated rooms are spacious and furnished with rescued and restored pieces original to the hotel and area. A canopy bed, a whirlpool tub for two, or a private balcony are options, and breakfast can be delivered to the room.

## Mount Shasta City

### — A LITTLE BACKGROUND —

A 14,161-foot-tall volcanic mountain that last erupted in 1786, Mount Shasta holds five glaciers and is where the Sacramento River originates. It is climbed in summer and skied in winter. Poet Joaquin Miller, who considered it the most beautiful mountain in the West, described it as "lonely as God and white as a winter moon." New Agers rank it up there with Stonehenge and the Egyptian pyramids, apparently because of its unusual energy fields. Peculiar stories, involving UFOs and Bigfoot, abound in this area.

### — VISITOR INFORMATION —

**Mt. Shasta Chamber of Commerce/ Visitors Bureau**
*300 Pine St., (800) 926-4865, (530) 926-4865, fax (530) 926-0976; www.mtshastachamber.com.*

**Siskiyou County Visitors Bureau**
*P.O. Box 1138, Mount Shasta City 96067, (877) 847-8777, (530) 926-3850, fax (530) 926-3680; www.visitsiskiyou.org.*

### — GETTING THERE —

Located 50 miles north of Redding, and 290 miles north of San Francisco.

### — WHERE TO STAY —

**KOA Kampground**
*900 N. Mt. Shasta Blvd., (800) KOA-3617, (530) 926-4029.*

This picturesque campground has majestic Mt. Shasta as a backdrop. Recreational facilities include a swimming pool, volleyball courts, horseshoe pits, and a game room. For description, see page 443.

**Motel Row**
*Along Mt. Shasta Blvd.*

### — WHERE TO EAT —

**Fast-food Row**
*At Central Mt. Shasta exit.*

Even with the various logo signs fighting it out amidst the trees, the view here is weepingly beautiful. On a clear day the mysterious mountain dominates the scene, and on a cloudy day it plays peek-a-boo—tantalizing the imagination. Alas, it seems the locals take this awesome sight for granted, so in the **Burger King** they often leave empty the corner tables boasting a million-dollar view.

## Yreka

### — VISITOR INFORMATION —

**Yreka Chamber of Commerce**
*117 W. Miner St., (530) 842-1649, fax (530) 842-2670; www.yrekachamber.com.*

### — GETTING THERE —

Located approximately 50 miles north of Mount Shasta, and 22 miles south of the Oregon border. This small town is positioned halfway between San Francisco and Portland, Oregon.

### — WHAT TO DO —

**Blue Goose Steam Excursion Train**
*300 E. Miner St., (800) YREKA-RR, (530) 842-4146; http://users.snowcrest.net/yrekawesternrr. Sat-Sun at 11; May-Oct only. $14, 60+ $11, 3-12 $7.*

A ride on this **Yreka Western Railroad** excursion train, pulled by a restored 1915 Baldwin steam locomotive that had a role in the movie *Stand by Me*, treats passengers to spectacular views of Mount Shasta. (The locomotive is nicknamed "Pancho" because it was punctured by bullets during a battle in Mexico with Pancho Villa.) After the hour ride to Montague, there is an hour layover during which passengers can tour the historic town and enjoy a treat in an old-fashioned ice cream parlor. Seats in the steam engine cab and caboose are available at additional charge. A 1,000-square-foot model railroad is displayed in the old depot, now operating as a **railroad museum**.

## Siskiyou County Museum
*910 S. Main St., (530) 842-3836; www.co.siskiyou.ca. us/museum. Tu-F 9-5, Sat 9-4. By donation.*

This small museum emphasizes local artifacts and history. Of special interest is the occasional exhibit featuring a local pioneer family, one of which was the Terwilligers. A 2$^{1}/_{2}$-acre **Outdoor Museum** *(9:30-4:30; May-Sept only.)* is located adjacent. Among its original and replica historic buildings are a schoolhouse, a Catholic church, a blacksmith shop, a miner's cabin, and an operating general store.

## The Yreka Historic District
*Along Miner St.*

More than 75 19th-century homes are seen here, with most situated on the four blocks of Third Street located between Lennox and Miner. The Chamber of Commerce provides a descriptive tour brochure.

### — WHERE TO EAT —

## Grandma's House
*123 E. Center St., 530-842-5300; B-L-D daily; $. Booths.*

Cozy and welcoming, with Tiffany-style lamps and floral wallpaper, Grandma's House is just like, well, Grandma's house. It's been family-run since 1977. The breakfast menu offers goodies such as buttermilk hot cakes with housemade boysenberry syrup and is served until 1 p.m. The lunch menu, which is a large selection of sandwiches and a salad bar, is available through dinner, when housemade biscuits, fried chicken, grilled pork chops and more substantial items are also options. Do save room for a slice of housemade pie. A cookbook featuring simple recipes used in the restaurant makes a great souvenir.

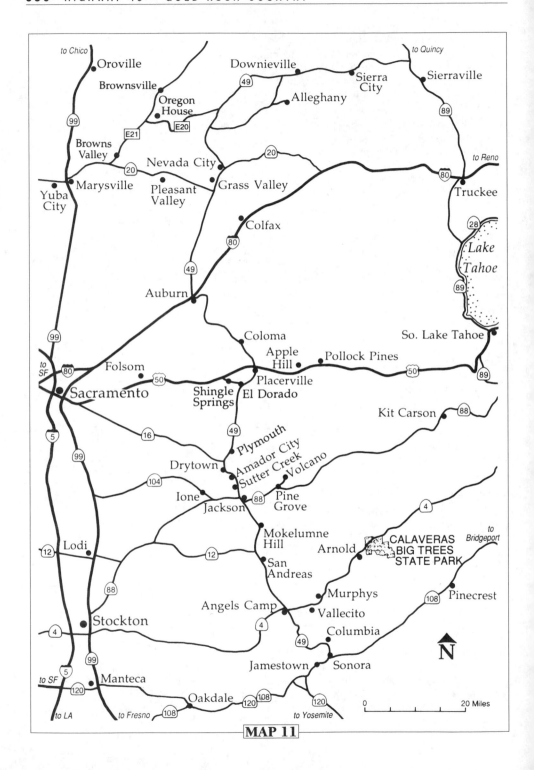

to Chico
Oroville
Brownsville
Oregon House
E21
E20
Browns Valley
99
20
Nevada City
Marysville
Pleasant Valley
Grass Valley
Yuba City
Downieville
49
Alleghany
Sierra City
Sierraville
to Quincy
89
20
to Reno
80
Truckee
Colfax
80
49
Lake Tahoe
28
89
Auburn
Coloma
Apple Hill
Pollock Pines
So. Lake Tahoe
Folsom
50
Sacramento
Shingle Springs
Placerville
El Dorado
50
89
to SF
80
16
49
Plymouth
Amador City
Sutter Creek
Volcano
Kit Carson
88
5
99
Drytown
104
Ione
88
Pine Grove
Jackson
4
to Bridgeport
Lodi
12
Mokelumne Hill
Arnold
CALAVERAS BIG TREES STATE PARK
12
San Andreas
88
Murphys
Pinecrest
108
Angels Camp
Vallecito
4
Stockton
49
Columbia
4
99
Jamestown
Sonora
N
Manteca
120
to SF
5
Oakdale
120
108
120
to LA
to Fresno
108
to Yosemite
0     20 Miles

**MAP 11**

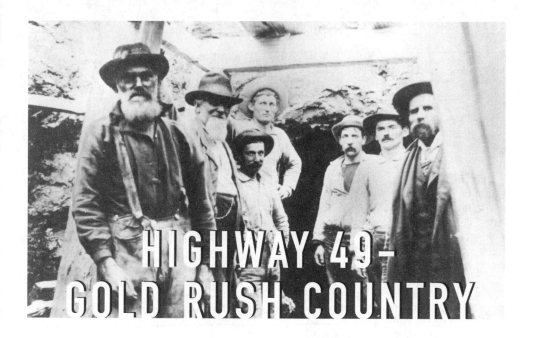

# HIGHWAY 49 – GOLD RUSH COUNTRY

## — A LITTLE BACKGROUND —

The Mother Lode, as this area is sometimes referred to (a term that is derived from a Spanish word for "riches"), stretches along the entire route of Highway 49, south from Mariposa and north through Nevada City, ending in Downieville. (On the other hand the Mother Lode *veins*, which run from Northern California to South America, surface in the area between Jamestown and Auburn and again in Nevada City.)

All the main Gold Rush towns can be visited by driving along Highway 49. But many scenic side roads lead to tiny hamlets with intriguing names such as Fiddletown and Rescue, inviting exploration.

This area provides history, adventure, and scenic beauty. Not yet heavily promoted and

packaged, it also provides many low-key and inexpensive vacation joys for the hype-weary traveler. A thorough visit could take weeks, but a satisfying one takes only a few days. For a weekend visit, don't attempt to drive the entire route. Visit one portion and then go back another time to see more.

Because the area is steeped in history, consider reading for more background information. Two classic books about the area that are also good for reading aloud are *The Celebrated Jumping Frog of Calaveras County*, by Samuel L. Clemens (Mark Twain), and *The Luck of Roaring Camp*, by Bret Harte.

Currently there is said to be another gold rush on. Many nervous people are staking claims, so caution is advised when doing any unguided panning or prospecting.

During the Gold Rush this area was filled with wineries. Its rich soil and high elevations produce excellent grapes and bold, deeply flavored wines. So be on the lookout for the nearly 100 wineries that have popped up here.

## — GETTING THERE —

Located approximately 135 miles east of San Francisco. Take Highway 80 to Highway 580 to Highway 205 to Highway 120 to Highway 49.

# Jamestown

## – A LITTLE BACKGROUND –

Filled with architecturally interesting old buildings, this historical boom town's economy is now fueled by myriad antique shops.

## – WHAT TO DO –

### Railtown 1897 State Historic Park

*Fifth St./Reservoir St., (209) 984-3953, fax (209) 984-4936; www.railtown1897.org/railtown. Daily 9:30-4:30, Apr-Oct; 10-3 Nov-Mar. Train: Sat-Sun 11-3, on the hr.; Apr-Oct only; $6, 6-12 $3. Tour: daily 10-3, on the hr.; $2, 6-12 $1.*

Be sure to allow time to watch the hubbub that surrounds preparing the train for departure. The depot is full of excitement as the huge steam train rolls in and out, sounding its screaming whistle and belching a mix of fire, smoke, and steam. The Mother Lode Cannonball, an historic steam train, takes passengers on a 40-minute, 6-mile round trip to Woods Creek Siding. Several other trips are available. A tour is given of the old six-stall roundhouse turntable and machine shop, where the trains are still serviced. If it all looks familiar, that could be because many TV shows and movies have been filmed here, including *Bonanza, Little House on the Prairie, The Virginian, High Noon*, and *Pale Rider*.

## – WHERE TO STAY –

### Jamestown Hotel

*18153 Main St., (800) 205-4901, (209) 984-3902, fax (209) 984-4149; www.jamestownhotel.com. 11 rooms; $-$$. Unsuitable for children under 7. Full breakfast; restaurant. No smoking; no pets.*

Built in the 1850s, this hotel is furnished with Victorian antiques and has many spacious suites with sitting rooms.

The **Cafe on the Patio** (*L-D Thur-M, SunBr; $-$$. Highchairs, boosters, child portions.*) has indoor and outdoor seating and serves an eclectic lunch menu of soups, salads, sandwiches, and pastas. Dinner brings on heartier entrees, including prime rib, scampi, rack of lamb, and several chicken dishes. A welcoming adjacent saloon specializes in fancy drinks, California wines, and tasty appetizers.

### The National Hotel

*18183 Main St., (800) 894-3446, (209) 984-3446, fax (209) 984-5620; www.national-hotel.com. 9 rooms; $-$$. Unsuitable for children under 10. TVs upon request. Full breakfast; restaurant; room service. No smoking; pets ok.*

A sense of history awaits at this really *old* hotel. Built in 1859, it has been in continuous operation ever since. In fact, it is one of the oldest continuously operating hotels in the state and is now an official historical landmark. Until 1978, rooms were rented to men only and went for $4 a night. Indoor plumbing was added in 1981. Much of the antique furniture is original to the hotel, and that which isn't is right in tune with the era. A private Soaking Room with a clawfoot tub for two—sort of an 1800s hot tub—is available to all guests. Overall, everything is far more luxurious now than anything those gold miners ever experienced.

The hotel's **restaurant** (*L-D daily, SunBr. Highchairs, boosters, child menu. Reservations advised.*) is an especially inviting spot for dinner after the drive in. On warm evenings, diners are seated outside on a pleasant patio. Strong points of the menu include fresh fish with creative sauces, a wine list with the largest selection of Gold Country wines available *anywhere*, and exceptional desserts. Just off the parlor, an old-time saloon features its original redwood long bar with brass rail and an 1881 cash register and is the perfect spot for a nightcap.

## – WHERE TO EAT –

### Smoke Cafe

*18191 Main St., (209) 984-3733; www.thesmoke cafe.swbd.net. L-D daily; $-$$. Highchairs, boosters, child menu. No reservations.*

Located within a modern Santa Fe-style building with soft stucco edges and lots of tile, this popular spot specializes in Mexican cuisine. Among the many items on the menu are pollo de mole poblano, chili verde, and a hamburger.

# Sonora

## – A LITTLE BACKGROUND –

Once known as the "Queen of the Southern Mines," when it was the richest and wildest town in the southern Mother Lode, this city still bustles and is a popular stopover spot for skiers and other travelers on their way to vacation cabins and recreation. Because it is a crossroads, it has been built up more than most Gold Rush towns and is far from quiet. But off the main thoroughfares, a taste of the old Sonora of Victorian homes and quiet streets can still be found. It is interesting to note that in Spanish "tuolumne" means "stone houses."

## – VISITOR INFORMATION –

### Tuolumne County Visitors Bureau
*542 W. Stockton Rd., (800) 446-1333, (209) 533-4420, fax (209) 533-0956; www.thegreatunfenced. com.*

## – WHAT TO DO –

### Autumn colors drive
Take Highway 108 about 30 to 35 miles east of town for a dazzling display of fall leaf colors. This entire area is populated with aspen and is usually vibrant with color after the first frost, which generally happens in early October. Beginning in late October, colorful leaves are seen right in town.

### Mark Twain's Cabin
*Off Hwy. 49, midway between town & Angels Camp.*
Built on Jackass Hill, this rickety replica of Twain's cabin is constructed around the original chimney. It can be viewed from the outside only. Twain lived here in 1864 and '65, when he wrote *The Celebrated Jumping Frog of Calaveras County* and *Roughing It.*

### Tuolumne County Museum & History Center
*158 W. Bradford Ave., (209) 532-1317; www.tchistory. org. Sun-F 10-4, Sat 10-3:30. Free.*
Located inside a jail built in 1866, this museum displays Gold Rush-era relics that include pioneer firearms and gold samples. Picnic tables are available.

## – WHERE TO STAY –

### Gunn House Motel
*286 S. Washington St., (209) 532-3421; www.gunn househotel.com. 20 rooms; $-$$. Solar-heated pool. Continental breakfast; restaurant. Pets ok.*

Built in 1850, this adobe house was once the residence of Dr. Lewis C. Gunn. It later became the offices for the *Sonora Herald*—the area's first newspaper. Rooms are restored and furnished with antiques. The cozy office is staffed with helpful personnel, and a poolside cocktail lounge is available to guests.

# Columbia State Historic Park

## – A LITTLE BACKGROUND –

In her prime, with over 6,000 people calling her home, Columbia was one of the largest mining towns in the southern Mother Lode. Her nickname, "Gem of the Southern Mines," was reference to the $87 million-plus in gold mined here (a figure calculated when gold was $35 an ounce).

This reconstructed Gold Rush town has been a state historic park since 1945. It is open daily from 9 to 5, and admission is free. Streets are blocked off to all but foot traffic and an occasional stagecoach. A museum introduces visitors to the town's history, and more exhibits are scattered among the many restored historic buildings.

In fact, the whole town is basically a living museum. Private concessionaires operate modern versions of businesses that were here in the 1800s. The town saloon pours cold mugs of beer and old-fashioned, root beer-like sarsaparilla. A blacksmith ekes out a living practicing his craft in a ramshackle shed, and a candy kitchen uses 100-year-old recipes and antique equipment to turn out such old-time favorites as horehound, rocky road, and almond bark. Customers in the photography studio don Gold Rush-era clothing for portraits, which are taken with vintage camera equipment but developed with quick modern processes. Visitors can even tour a still-operating gold mine and learn to pan for gold in a salted sluice.

If it all looks familiar, note that *High Noon* and episodes of *Little House on the Prairie* were filmed here.

## – VISITOR INFORMATION –

### Columbia State Historic Park
*22708 Broadway, (209) 532-0150; www.parks.ca.gov.*

## Columbia California Chamber of Commerce

*P.O. Box 1824, Columbia 95310, (209) 536-1672; www.columbiacalifornia.com.*

— ANNUAL EVENTS —

## Victorian Promenade and Egg Hunt

*March or April; on Easter Sunday.*

Participants don their best 1880s attire and fanciest hat for this historical Easter parade.

## Fireman's Muster

*May.*

Volunteer fire crews from the western U.S. test their skills in historical fire fighting.

## A Miners Christmas

*December; first 2 weekends.*

St. Nick arrives by stagecoach each day, and roasted chestnuts, hot camp coffee, and hot apple cider are among the culinary treats.

— WHAT TO DO —

## A. N. Fisher & Co. Stage Line & Livery Stable

*(209) 588-0808. Schedule varies. Stage: $5-$6.50. Stable: pony rides $10/10 min.; horse $18/¹/₂-hr., must be 8 or older, reservations advised.*

Ride in an authentic stagecoach and experience travel as many gold-seekers did years ago. Or take a trail ride into the back woods through limestone canyons. Guides walk the gentle ponies.

## Fallon House Theatre

*(209) 532-3120, fax (209) 532-7270; www.sierra rep.com. W-Sat at 8; W, Sat, Sun at 2. $15-$22. Advance purchase advised.*

Located in the rear of the Fallon Hotel, this historic theater has been operating since the 1880s. The second-longest continually operating playhouse in California, it stages both first-run and classic dramas and musicals and employs both professional and student talent. The semi-professional Sierra Repertory Theatre stages eight major productions each year.

— WHERE TO STAY —

## City Hotel

*On Main St., (800) 532-1479, (209) 532-1479, fax (209) 532-7027; www.cityhotel.com. 10 rooms; $$; closed M Oct-May. Children under 4 free. No TVs; all shared baths. Full breakfast; restaurant; limited room service. No smoking; no pets.*

This 1856 hotel provides overnight lodging in keeping with the town's flavor. Rooms are restored and furnished with Victorian antiques from the collection of the California State Parks Department. Eager-to-please students from the Columbia College Hospitality Management program dress in period clothing and supplement the full-time staff by performing such esoteric duties as fluffing pillows and, in the beautifully appointed restaurant downstairs, de-crumbing tables. Guests are encouraged to congregate in the parlor in the evening for sherry, conversation, and games. To make the trek down the

hall to the bath more civilized, guests are loaned a wicker basket packed with shower cap, slippers, robe, soap, and shampoo.

The hotel **restaurant** (*D Tu-Sun, SunBr; $$. Highchairs, boosters, child portions. Reservations advised.*) serves elegant regional cuisine, and fixed-price, four-course seasonal dinners are available. The cozy **What Cheer Saloon**, which retains its original cherry-wood bar that traveled around the Horn from New England, adjoins.

## Columbia Gem Motel

*22131 Parrotts Ferry Rd., 1 mi. from park, (866) 436-6685, (209) 532-4508; www.columbia gem.com. 11 units; $-$$. Pets ok.*

Small log cabins are scattered here in an attractive pine tree setting. Motel rooms are also available.

## Fallon Hotel

*On Washington St., (800) 532-1479, (209) 532-1470, fax (209) 532-7027; www.cityhotel.com. 14 rooms; $-$$; closed M-W Oct-May. Children under 4 free. No TVs; many shared bathrooms. Full breakfast; restaurant. No smoking; no pets.*

This historic hotel, dating from 1857, has undergone a $4 million renovation and is beautifully restored to its Victorian grandeur. Many of the furnishings are original to the hotel. Several large second-floor rooms with balconies are perfect for families. The hotel is operated in similar style as the City Hotel and is under the same management. The **Fallon Ice Cream Parlor** dishes up goodies on the main floor, and packages that include lodging, dinner at the City Hotel, and a performance in the Fallon House Theatre are available.

# Murphys

— A LITTLE BACKGROUND —

Nicknamed "Queen of the Sierra," the town once was the source of gold strike after gold strike and made the founding Murphy brothers rich, and it is believed that Joaquin Murieta began his outlaw ways here. Nowadays it is definitely a happening place, with lots of boutiques, art galleries, restaurants, and winery tasting rooms. A map to the town's sights and buildings—many of which were constructed of lava

stone and stucco after a tragic fire in 1859—is available from merchants and at the check-in desk in Murphys Hotel.

— ANNUAL EVENTS —

## Bear Valley Music Festival

*July. In Bear Valley; (800) 458-1618, (209) 753-2574, fax (209) 753-2576; www.bearvalleymusic.org.*

Held high in the Sierra in a circus-style red-and-white-striped tent, this festival presents a musical smorgasbord.

— WHAT TO DO —

## Calaveras Big Trees State Park

*1170 E. Hwy. 4, in Arnold, 15 mi. E of town, (209) 795-2334; www.parks.ca.gov. Daily sunrise-sunset. Visitor Center: Daily 11-3; in winter, Sat-Sun only. $5/vehicle.*

This ancient forest houses the mammoth, and now rare, giant sequoia variety of redwood. The Big Trees Nature Trail is a choice trek for families with young children and provides the chance to see the Discovery Tree stump that once was used as a dance floor. Other trails are available, as are campsites and picnic tables and barbecue facilities. A cross-country ski trail is maintained in winter, and a horseback-riding concession operates in summer. Also in warm weather, the Beaver Creek Picnic Area has a good wading area for children. Picnic provisions can be picked up in Arnold, where there are delis, markets, and restaurants.

## Mercer Caverns

*1665 Sheep Ranch Rd., off Hwy. 4, 1.5 mi. N of town, (209) 728-2101; www.mercercaverns.com. Daily 10-4:30; in summer, Sun-Thur 9-5, F-Sat 9-6. $10, 5-12 $6.*

Discovered more than 100 years ago in 1885, this well-lighted, 55-degree limestone cavern takes about an hour to tour. It is said to be the longest continually operating commercial cavern in the state. The tour descends stairs to a depth of 161 feet and stops in 10 rooms. Tours begin every 20 minutes. Baby strollers are not permitted.

## Moaning Cavern

*5350 Moaning Cave Rd., in Vallecito, 5 mi. W of town, (866) 762-2837, (209) 736-2708, fax (209) 736-0330; www.caverntours.com. Daily 10-5; in summer 9-6. $12, 3-13 $6.*

The 45-minute tour descends a 100-foot-high spiral staircase into the largest public cavern chamber in California. It is big enough to hold the Statue of Liberty! The cavern was originally discovered by Native Americans, many of whom are thought to have fallen to their death here. In fact, the oldest human remains in the U.S. were found here. A **rappel tour** *($45. Must be 12 or older. Reservations required.)* allows a 165-foot rope descent into the cave. Nature trails, picnic tables, and campsites are available. Baby strollers are not permitted.

## Murphys Black Bart Theatre
*580 S. Algiers, (209) 728-8842; www.blackbart players.com. Sat-Sun in Apr, Aug-Sept, Nov; 8pm. $7.50. Reservations advised.*

The Black Bart Players perform musicals, melodramas, mysteries, comedies, and classics here.

## Old Timers Museum
*470 Main St., (209) 728-1160. F-Sun 11-4; in winter Sat-Sun only. Free.*

Dating from 1856, this is the oldest stone building in town, and it is interesting to note that the stones were fitted together without mortar. The museum it houses displays Gold Rush-era memorabilia.

## Wineries
Prior to Prohibition, there were more wineries in this area than anywhere else in the state.

### • Ironstone Vineyards
*1894 Six Mile Rd., (209) 728-1251, fax (209) 728-1275; www.ironstonevineyards.com. Tasting daily 10-6; tours daily at 11:30, 1:30, 3:30.*

A replica of an 1859 gold stamp mill, this modern winery is the largest in the area and is known for its Chardonnays and Merlots. It features a showplace tasting room constructed of oak and stone, with windows overlooking the vineyards. An operating sluice that once was used to separate gold from gravel is situated by the parking lot, and a small museum displays a 44-pound gold piece and Gold Rush artifacts that include a mining car and gold scales. Guided half-hour tours visit the aging caverns blasted from the hard rock after which the winery is named. In winter programs, an historic 769-pipe theater organ in the fifth floor ballroom accompanies silent films, and in spring, visitors can view a stunning display of 100,000 daffodils. A deli will pack up box lunches to go or to eat on site in the dramatic lakeside picnic area.

### • Milliaire Winery
*276 Main St., (209) 728-1658, fax (209) 736-1915; www.milliairewinery.com. Tasting daily 11-5; no tours.*

Operating out of a converted carriage house/gas station, this tiny winery is known for its intense, full-bodied wines. It also produces three delicious dessert wines: a late harvest Zinfandel, a Zinfandel Port, and a Semillon.

### • Stevenot Winery
*2690 San Domingo Rd., 4 mi. from town, 1 mi. past Mercer Caverns, (209) 728-3436, fax (209) 728-3710; www.stevenotwinery.com. Tasting daily 10-5; tours by appt.*

Located back in a canyon on the site of the first swimming pool in Calaveras County, this winery operates in a series of vintage buildings. The tasting room was once the home of founder Barden Stevenot, and it features a large native-limestone fireplace surrounded by windows overlooking the ranch and winery. The rustic Alaska House—a replica Gold Rush cabin with a sod roof and split-log walls—is now a private tasting room. The winery is famous for its Merlots and white Zinfandels. Picnic tables are sheltered under a grape arbor and have a view of the surrounding vineyards. In summer, live outdoor performances by **Murphys Creek Theatre** *((866) 463-8659, (209) 728-8422; www.murphyscreektheatre.org. $13-$20.)* are presented in an intimate grassy amphitheatre.

## — WHERE TO STAY —

### Dunbar House, 1880

*271 Jones St., (800) 692-6006, (209) 728-2897, fax (209) 728-1451; www.dunbarhouse.com. 4 rooms; $$-$$$. Unsuitable for children under 10. All gas-burning stoves. Afternoon snack, full breakfast. No smoking; no pets.*

Surrounded by a white-picket fence, this restored Italianate-style house was the filming location for the TV series *Seven Brides for Seven Brothers*. Rooms are decorated with antiques, lace, and down comforters. Guests are greeted each afternoon with cookies, munchies, and assorted beverages, and a complimentary bottle of wine and an evening appetizer plate awaits in each room's refrigerator. The aim here is to surprise and please guests at every turn. It is a bit like being welcomed back into the womb. Among the pleasures: towel warmers, candles, ceiling fans, a CD player, live orchids, bathrobes and slippers, and the comfiest of pillows and bedding. A large, well-tended century-old garden features native roses and is equipped with a soothing fountain, couch swing, and hammock. Robins, blue jays, hummingbirds, big black bumblebees, and even woodpeckers frequent it. Horse-drawn buggy rides through town can be arranged.

### Murphys Historic Hotel

*457 Main St., (800) 532-7684, (209) 728-3444, fax (209) 728-1590. 29 rooms; $. Children under 12 free. Some TVs & shared baths. Continental breakfast; restaurant.*

Built in 1856 and a historical landmark since 1948, this very old hotel provided lodging for such Gold Rush-era luminaries as U.S. Grant, J.P. Morgan, Mark Twain, Horatio Alger, and Black Bart—each of whom has a room he actually stayed in named after him. Modern motel rooms, with no legends attached, are available adjacent to the hotel. Though the hotel rooms are immeasurably more interesting, they have one big drawback: The noisy hotel bar, reputed to be the best in the Mother Lode, is kept jumping until the wee hours by townspeople and travelers alike. Those who want to sleep should opt for a less interesting, but quiet, motel room.

The hotel **restaurant** *(B-L-D daily; $-$$. Highchairs, boosters, child menu. Reservations advised.)* is popular with locals. Menu choices consist of hearty, made-from-scratch American country and continental fare—the specialty of the house is prime rib and fried chicken—and portions tend to be large.

## — WHERE TO EAT —

### The Peppermint Stick

*454 Main St., (209) 728-3570. Sun-Thur 11-8; daily in summer; $. Highchairs, boosters, child portions. No reservations. No cards.*

When it was built in 1893, this building served as the town icehouse. Now it is a cheerful ice cream parlor serving old-fashioned sodas and sundaes, trendy coffees, candies, and soups and sandwiches. Everything can be packed to go.

# Angels Camp

## — A LITTLE BACKGROUND —

Taking its name from George Angel, who founded it as a trading post in 1848, this quiet little burg is thought to be the town Bret Harte wrote of in *Luck of Roaring Camp*, and it is where Mark Twain first heard the story that he fabricated into *The Celebrated Jumping Frog of Calaveras County*. The sidewalks sport plaques celebrating high-jumping frogs from past competitions, and, of course, all kinds of souvenir frogs are available in gift shops. It is interesting to note that in Spanish "calaveras" means "skulls."

## — VISITOR INFORMATION —

### Calaveras County Chamber of Commerce

*1211 S.. Main St., (209) 736-2580, fax (209) 736-2576; www.calaveras.org.*

### Calaveras Visitors Bureau

*1192 S. Main St., (800) 225-3764, (209) 736-0049, fax (209) 736-9124; www.visitcalaveras.org.*

### Jumping Frog Jubilee

*May; 3rd weekend. (209) 736-2561, fax (209) 736-2561; www.frogtown.org. $5-$9.*

Most contestants bring their own frog to enter in this historic contest, but rental frogs are also available on site. In 1986, Rosie the Ribiter set the current world's record by landing—after three leaps—21 feet 5³/4 inches from the starting pad. She earned her jockey $1,500. The prize money is usually won by frog jockeys who are serious about the sport and bring 50 to 60 frogs. So far, a rental frog has never won. The **Calaveras County Fair** is part of the fun and features carnival rides, livestock exhibits, a rodeo, a destruction derby, headliner entertainers, and fireworks.

### Angels Camp Museum & Carriage House

*753 S. Main St., (209) 736-2963; www.angelscamp. gov/museum.htm. Daily 10-3, Mar-Dec; Sat-Sun only, Jan-Feb. $3, 6-12 $1.*

A repository of Gold Rush memorabilia, this museum displays a blacksmith shop, an extensive mineral and rock collection, and a carriage barn filled with vintage wagons and buggies.

There is only one recommended restaurant for this town. Could this have something to do with Mark Twain's description of some "day-before-yesterday dishwater" coffee and "hellfire" soup suffered long ago at the Hotel Angels?

### Picnic Pick-Up

**• The Pickle Barrel**
*1225 S. Main St., (209) 736-4704. Tu-Sun 10-6.*

This friendly Italian deli packs picnic supplies to go and provides tables for those who decide to stay. Informal picnic areas are found by the river, and scenic **Utica Park** has sheltered picnic tables and a large children's play area.

# San Andreas

Progress has stripped this town of most of its historic character. Now many locals work in a cement plant whose gravels just a century ago yielded gold to the town's original Mexican settlers. The town is also home to the state's largest cashmere goat ranch, which is the only custom cashmere dehairer in the U.S.

### Calaveras County Museum

*30 N. Main St., (209) 754-1058. Daily 10-4. $2, 60+ $1, under 12 50¢.*

Items on display upstairs in this restored 1867 courthouse include Miwok Indian and Gold Rush artifacts. Among the nicely organized exhibits is a full-size display of a Gold Rush-era general store. The jail cell Black Bart once occupied is downstairs in a rustic courtyard landscaped with native California plants and trees.

### California Cavern

*9565 Cave City Rd., off Mountain Ranch Rd., in Mountain Ranch, 10 mi. E of town (call for directions), (866) 762-2837, (209) 736-2708, fax (209) 736-0330; www.caverntours.com. Daily 10-4 Jan & Apr-Dec; call for Feb-Mar. $12, 3-13 $6.*

First opened to the public in 1850, this cavern is now a state historic landmark. The nearly level Trail of Lights tour takes 60 to 80 minutes and follows the footsteps of John Muir, Mark Twain, and Bret Harte. Baby strollers are not permitted. The more strenuous **spelunking tour** (*$99. Must be 8 or older. Reservations required.*) through the unlighted portion of the cavern "involves climbing rocks and a 60-foot ladder, squeezing through small passages, crossing 200-foot-deep lakes on rafts, and viewing breathtaking formations unequaled in any other cavern in the West."

— **WHERE TO STAY** —

**Black Bart Inn & Motel**
*55 W. Saint Charles St., (800) 225-3764 x331, (209) 754-3808, fax (209) 754-5755; www.blackbartinn.com. 65 rooms; $; some shared baths. Unheated pool. 2 restaurants.*

This lodging facility is named after the infamous highwayman, Black Bart, whose career ended in this town. He robbed 29 stagecoaches between 1875 and 1883, always using an unloaded gun. Rooms are available in both a vintage hotel and in a more modern motel located adjacent.

# Mokelumne Hill

— **WHERE TO STAY** —

**Hotel Leger**
*8304 Main St., (209) 286-1401, fax (209) 286-2105; www.hotelleger.com. 13 rooms; $-$$. Some wood-burning fireplaces & shared baths. Unheated pool. Continental breakfast; restaurant. No smoking; pets ok.*

Once considered among the most luxurious of Gold Rush hotels, this 1879 lodging still provides comfortable rooms with period antiques and cozy comforters. Many have sitting areas, and all are furnished with tasteful period pieces. ("Leger" is now pronounced here "legger," although a while back French owners pronounced it "la-JAY.")

**Shadows** restaurant (*L-D Thur-M*), a historic saloon, and a billiards parlor operate on the ground floor.

# Jackson

— **A LITTLE BACKGROUND** —

Two important gold-bearing quartz mines are located just north of this busy town. The Argonaut and Kennedy mines had some of the deepest vertical shafts in the world, extending over 5,000 feet into the ground.

— **VISITOR INFORMATION** —

**Amador County Chamber of Commerce & Visitors Bureau**
*125 Peek St., (800) 649-4988, (209) 223-0350, fax (209) 223-4425; www.amadorcountychamber.com.*

It is interesting to note that in Spanish "amador" means "lover of gold."

— **ANNUAL EVENTS** —

**Italian Picnic and Parade**
*June; first weekend. At Italian Picnic Grounds; (209) 267-0206. Admission fee.*

Every year since 1882, the public has been invited to this festive event sponsored by the Italian Benevolent Society of Amador County. The fun includes kiddie rides, dancing, a parade down Highway 49 in Sutter Creek, and an all-you-can-eat barbecue.

— **WHAT TO DO** —

**Amador County Museum**
*225 Church St., (209) 223-6386. W-Sun 10-4. By donation. Scale models operate Sat-Sun 11-3, on the hr.; $1, under 8 free.*

Located within the 1859 red brick Armstead Brown House, this museum displays scale models of the Kennedy Mine tailing wheels and head frame and of the North Star Mine stamp mill. A brightly painted wooden train engine, which was once a prop on TV's *Petticoat Junction*, is parked permanently out back.

**Jackson Rancheria Casino, Hotel & Conference Center**
*12222 New York Ranch Rd., (800) 822-WINN, (209) 223-1677, fax (209) 223-9444; www.jacksoncasino.com. Open 24 hours.*

Gambling and big name entertainment are the draws at this windowless behemoth owned by the Jackson Rancheria Band of Miwuk

Indians. A Minor's Camp Arcade welcomes children ages 12 through 17 (and children 7 through 11 who are with a parent or guardian), and the **Raging River Restaurant** offers dining beside a soothing, man-made river running right through the casino. Note that no alcohol is allowed, or served, on the premises. The **hotel** *(4 stories; 100 rooms; $-$$$. No pets.)* offers convenient lodging.

### Kennedy Gold Mine

*Near intersection of Hwys. 49 & 88, (209) 223-9542; www.kennedygoldmine.com. Tours Sat-Sun 10-3, Mar-Oct only. $9, 6-12 $5.*

One of the richest gold mines in the world, this mine produced over $34.2 million worth of gold from 1880 to 1942. At 5,912 feet deep, it was once also the deepest mine in North America. During the guided surface tour, visitors can try panning for gold and view several mining buildings, the 125-foot-high metal head frame, and a display of mining equipment.

### Kennedy Mine Tailing Wheels Park

*On Jackson Gate Rd., 1 mi. N of town. Daily dawn to dusk. Free.*

Unique to the Gold Country, four huge 58-foot-diameter wheels—built in 1912 to lift waste gravel, or "tailings," into flumes so that they could be carried to a holding area—can be viewed by taking a short walk on well-marked trails on either side of the road. Two of the wheels have already collapsed. Better hurry to see this site before time takes its toll on the other two. The Kennedy Mine can be seen from here. Picnic tables are available.

### Wine tasting

#### • Amador Vintners' Association

*(888) 655-8614, (209) 267-2297, fax (209) 267-2298; www.amadorwine.com.*

Many wineries are located in this area, with a heavy concentration occurring around the nearby town of Plymouth.

### — WHERE TO STAY —

### National Hotel

*2 Water St., (209) 223-0500, fax (209) 223-4845, 4 stories; 25 rooms; $-$$. Some TVs & shared baths. Restaurant.*

This hotel claims to be the oldest in con-tinuous operation (since 1862) in California. Some room decor is modest, as are the prices, while others are a little more flamboyant—the Bordello Suite, the John Wayne Suite—and a tad more expensive. Prior guests have included every California governor since 1862, two Presidents (Garfield and Hoover), and John Wayne. The ancient bar has a cheery pub atmosphere.

### Roaring Camp

*In Pine Grove, 10 mi. from town, (209) 296-4100, fax (209) 296-4101; www.volcano.net/~pineacre/roaring_camp.htm. 20 cabins; $440/wk./couple; closed Oct-Apr. Shared modern bath house. Restaurant.*

Guests leave their cars behind and make the 1-hour trip into the remote canyon here via truck. They stay in this former mining camp in rustic prospector cabins without electricity and must bring all their own gear and food. Recreation consists of swimming, fishing, and panning for gold in the Mokelumne River, as well as hiking and perhaps collecting rocks. Guests may keep all found gold. A saloon, short-order restaurant, and general store are available when guests get tired of roughing it. Weekly stays run Sunday to Sunday. One-day tours are also available. On Saturday evenings, a group of diners is trucked in for a riverside steak cookout; weekly guests are invited to join this event at no charge.

# Sutter Creek

### — A LITTLE BACKGROUND —

Seven gold mines were once located on this quiet Main Street. Now it is lined with modern gold mines—antique shops.

### — VISITOR INFORMATION —

### Sutter Creek Visitor's Center

*(800) 400-0305, (209) 267-1344, fax (209) 267-1898; www.suttercreek.org.*

### — WHAT TO DO —

### Sutter Gold Mine

*13660 Hwy. 49, toward Amador City, (866) 762-2837, (209) 736-2708, fax (209) 736-0330; www.sutter*

gold.com. Daily 10-4; in summer 9-5. Tours on the hr.; $14.95, 4-13 $9.95. Gold-panning $5. Must be 3 or older for tour.

Made up of 16 historic mines that produced over 1.3 million ounces of gold, this is the first active gold-mining operation in the area since the Central Eureka Mine closed in the late 1940s. After donning hard hats, a "boss buggy"—a jeep-like safari-car shuttle—takes participants down Indiana-Jones style about 450 feet underground into the belly of the beast for a walking tour, and later returns everyone to the surface. Panning for gold can be done without taking the tour, and a movie about gold mining is free. Picnic facilities are available.

## — WHERE TO STAY —

### The Foxes
77 Main St., (800) 987-3344, (209) 267-5882, fax (209) 267-0712; www.foxesinn.com. 7 rooms; $$-$$$. Some wood-burning fireplaces. Full breakfast. No smoking; no pets.

Built in 1857, this New England-style farmhouse is located in the center of town. Guests are welcomed in the kitchen by a serious collection of silver tea services—upon which breakfast is served in the morning—and a refreshing glass of strawberry lemonade. Rooms are comfortable and decorated unfussily with a mixture of antiques, canopied beds, and contemporary comforts. Baths are large and tastefully tiled, and some have clawfoot tubs. As might be expected, a tasteful leitmotif of foxes occurs throughout. Breakfast is cooked-to-order and delivered to the room.

### Grey Gables Inn
161 Hanford St., (800) GREY-GABLES, (209) 267-1039; www.greygables.com. 8 rooms; $$-$$$. Unsuitable for children under 12. All fireplaces. Afternoon tea, evening snack, full breakfast. No smoking; no pets.

Bringing a touch of England to the area, this inn is designed to look like an English country manor. Guest rooms are named for English poets such as Byron, Browning, and Shelley. Each is furnished with antiques and an armoire, and some have clawfoot tubs. In English fashion, afternoon tea is served on lovely china in the formal parlor, and breakfast can be taken either in the social atmosphere of the dining room or in the privacy of the guest room.

### Sutter Creek Inn
75 Main St., (209) 267-5606, fax (209) 267-9287; www.suttercreekinn.com. 17 rooms; $-$$. Unsuitable for children. Some TVs & wood-burning fireplaces. Afternoon snack, full breakfast. No smoking; no pets.

Opened as an inn in 1966, this 1859 Greek Revival structure was one of the first B&Bs west of the Mississippi and has staked its claim as the first in California. Rooms are available in the house as well as in an adjacent carriage house. As guests arrive each day, homemade lemonade and cookies are served in the garden. In the morning coffee is served by the fireplace, and then at 9 a.m. sharp a full sit-down breakfast is served family-style at long trestle tables in the dining room and kitchen. Each room has its own charm—one with a closet filled with books, another with a clawfoot tub. For those who have been longing to spend the night in a bed suspended from the ceiling by chains, this inn fulfills that and other yearnings (the guests really swing here). Some visitors have even seen a friendly ghost, although it has been more than 25 years since the last sighting. Croquet and hammocks beckon from the garden, and handwriting analysis and both foot and body massage are available by appointment for an additional fee.

## — WHERE TO EAT —

### Susan's Place Wine Bar & Eatery
15 Eureka St., (209) 267-0945, fax (209) 267-1201; www.susansplace.com. L-D Thur-Sun.

Situated just off Main Street, this popular spot has a welcoming vine-covered courtyard that is especially inviting on a warm day. The unusual menu features build-your-own pastas, cheese-sausage boards, and Amador County wines.

### Sutter Creek Ice Cream Emporium
51 Main St., (209) 267-0543, fax (209) 295-3782. Sun-Thur 10-8, F-Sat 9-10; in winter Sun-Thur 10-6, F-Sat 9-9; $. 1 highchair.

This old-fashioned soda fountain sells ice cream specialties and over ten kinds of housemade fudge. Sandwiches, tamales, and corn dogs are also available, plus a wall full of candy. The owner sometimes bangs out a ragtime tune or two on a 1919 Milton Piano, and the annual **Sutter Creek Ragtime Festival** occurs here on the second weekend in August.

### Zinfandels at Sutter Creek
*51 Hanford St., (209) 267-5008, fax (209) 245-5260; www.zinfood.com. D Thur-Sun; $$. Reservations advised.*

Operating inside a cozy converted house, this is a polished, white tablecloth-and-candles kind of place. The California cuisine menu here changes monthly, and wines are paired with each dish. A whimsical touch is added to the decor by using wine bottle corks glued to the walls as trim.

# Volcano

## – A LITTLE BACKGROUND –

The scenic, rural drive here from Sutter Creek is ill marked, poorly paved, and best maneuvered during daylight. And experience indicates that directions and information obtained around these parts are often vague or misleading, leaving plenty of room for error and making a good map worth its weight in gold.

Because this tiny town is built in a depression on top of limestone caves, it is green year-round. Sleepy and quiet now, during the Gold Rush it was a boomtown well known for its boisterous dance halls and saloons. It also opened the state's first public library.

## – ANNUAL EVENTS –

### Daffodil Hill
*Mid-March until bloom is over in April. 18310 Rams Horn Grade, off Shake Ridge Rd., 3 mi. N of town, (209) 296-7048. Schedule varies. Free.*

Originally planted in the 1850s by a Dutch settler, then added to and maintained by Grandma McLaughlin, this 6-acre garden boasts more than 300 varieties of bulb. There are many, many daffodils, with a few tulips and hyacinths mixed in, too. McLaughlin's grandchildren and great-grandchildren plant additional bulbs every year. Currently more than 300,000 bloom together each spring, making for a spectacular display. Peacocks, chickens, and sheep wander the grounds, and there is a picnic area with tables. It is a pleasant surprise that this seasonal extravaganza of bloom is so non-commercial.

## – WHAT TO DO –

### Black Chasm
*15701 Pioneer-Volcano Rd., (866) 762-2837, (209) 736-2708, fax (209) 736-0330; www.caverntours.com. Daily 10-4; in summer 9-5. $12, 3-13 $6.*

The cave tour visits the Colossal Room, which measures 100 feet across and 150 feet deep and has giant rock bridges over deep lakes, and the Landmark Room, which features twisting, looping helictite crystals.

### Indian Grinding Rock State Historic Park
*14881 Pine Grove-Volcano Rd., in Pine Grove, (209) 296-7488; www.parks.ca.gov. Park: Daily dawn-dusk. Museum: M-F 11-3, Sat-Sun 10-4. $6/vehicle.*

The largest of the grinding rocks here is a huge flat bedrock limestone measuring 175 feet by 82 feet. It has over 1,185 mortar holes and approximately 363 petroglyphs (rock carvings)—all made by Native Americans who ground their acorns and other seeds here with pestles. A reconstructed Miwok village contains a ceremonial roundhouse, a covered hand-game area, several cedar-bark houses, and an Indian game field. Additional facilities include a self-guided nature trail and **Chaw'se Regional Indian Museum**, which orients visitors with a video show and interpretive displays. Picnic facilities and campsites are available. A **"Big Time" Miwok Celebration** is scheduled each September.

### "Old Abe" Volcano Blues Cannon
Located in the center of town in a protected shelter, this cannon helped win the Civil War without firing a single shot! Cast of bronze and brass in Boston in 1837 and weighing 737 pounds, it somehow reached San Francisco and was smuggled to Volcano in 1863. The town used it to control renegades drawn here in search of quick wealth. For the complete story, ask around town.

### Soldiers' Gulch Park
Rocky terrain, a gurgling stream, and scenic stone ruins—including the façades of several ancient buildings—provide a picturesque backdrop against which to enjoy a picnic or just a few moments of quiet contemplation.

## Volcano Theatre Company

*(209) 296-2525; www.volcanotheatre.org. F-Sat at 8 & some Sun at 2; Apr-Nov. $7-$12. Reservations required.*

The first little theater group to form in California was the Volcano Thespian Society in 1854. Performances are held in the intimate 50-seat Cobblestone Theater, except in summer, when they occur in an outdoor amphitheater. Children are welcome.

### — WHERE TO STAY —

## St. George Hotel

*16104 Main St., (209) 296-4458, fax (209) 296-4457; www.stgeorgehotel.com. 20 rooms; $-$$; closed part of Jan. No TVs; some shared baths. Continental breakfast; restaurant. No smoking; pets ok in 1 rm.*

Rooms are available in either the solidly constructed main hotel, built in 1862, or in bungalows built almost a hundred years later in 1961. For safety reasons, families with children under 12 must stay in the newer rooms located around the corner, their consolation being a private bathroom. In the hotel, a cozy memorabilia-crammed saloon *(Thur-Sun)* and a parlor area with fireplace and games invite relaxing. The hotel **restaurant** *(D Thur-Sun, SunBr; $-$$. Reservations advised.)* serves creative California cuisine.

# Amador City

### — A LITTLE BACKGROUND —

With a population of 202, this is the smallest incorporated city in the state. Basically it is a crook in the road lined with a series of interesting antique shops inside atmospheric historical buildings—some with brick walls and iron doors.

### — WHERE TO STAY —

## Imperial Hotel

*14202 Hwy. 49, (800) 242-5594, (209) 267-9172, fax (209) 267-9249; www.imperialamador.com. 6 rooms; $-$$. Unsuitable for small children. Breakfast; restaurant; room service. No smoking; no pets.*

This beautifully restored historic brick building opened as a hotel in 1879, closed in 1927, then reopened in 1988. Outside it features iron doors and shutters, and the attractively decorated, high-ceilinged interior conveys a touch of artistic flair with contemporary art, colorful fabrics, and an assortment of lovely antiques. A secluded stone patio provides a restful garden retreat.

The cozy **restaurant** *(D Tu-Sun, SunBr. Reservations advised.)* offers a brief, eclectic menu of delicious Mediterranean-style fare and mostly local wines. Sunday brunch is taken in the sun on a small patio and is primo. The completely restored old-time **Oasis Bar** is especially inviting for an after-dinner drink.

## Mine House Inn

*14125 Hwy. 49, (800) MINE-HSE, (209) 267-5900; www.minehouseinn.com. 13 rooms; $-$$. Unsuitable for children under 12. No TVs; some gas fireplaces. Heated pool (seasonal); hot tub. Full breakfast. No smoking; no pets.*

Built in 1881 as the headquarters for the Keystone Mine, this attractive restored brick building now houses guest rooms furnished with Gold Rush-era antiques. Each room is named for its original function: the Vault Room, the Retort Room, the Assay room. In the morning, guests can have breakfast in the dining room or just push a buzzer and have it delivered to the door. Five luxury suites are also available in a newer annex.

### — WHERE TO EAT —

## The Buffalo Chips Emporium

*14179 Hwy. 49, (209) 267-0570. B-L W-Sun; $. 1 highchair, 1 booster. No cards.*

Some folks just buy a simple cone here and then sit outside on one of the weathered benches to leisurely watch the busy world drive by. Others prefer to sit inside what was once the town's Wells Fargo Bank and indulge in a fancy fountain item.

# Drytown

### — A LITTLE BACKGROUND —

Once home to 27 saloons, Drytown is now known for its equally abundant antique shops—and not much else.

# Shingle Springs

## – A LITTLE BACKGROUND –

Named for a cool spring that surfaced near a shingle mill here in 1849, this rural area is now—just as it was then—the perfect spot to set up camp.

## – VISITOR INFORMATION –

### Shingle Springs/Cameron Park Chamber of Commerce
*3300 Coach Lane #B7, in Cameron Park, (530) 677-8000, fax (530) 676-8313; www.sscpchamber.org.*

## – WHERE TO STAY –

### KOA Kampground
*4655 Rock Barn Rd., (800) KOA-4197, (530) 676-2267; www.koa.com.*
   Facilities include a fishing pond. For more description, see page 443.

# El Dorado

## – WHERE TO EAT –

### Poor Red's
*6221 Main St., (530) 622-2901. L M-F, D daily; $. Highchairs, boosters, child portions. No reservations.*
   Judging just from the outside of this 1852 building, which looks to be an unsavory bar, this former Wells Fargo stage stop might easily be passed by. But then weary travelers would miss the experience of dining on exquisite ham, ribs, chicken, and steak—all cooked over an open oak-wood pit and served in generous portions. Because this restaurant is very popular and also very small, weekend dinner waits can run over an hour. Some patrons pass that time downing Gold Cadillacs at the old-time horse-shoe bar. (It is interesting to note that Poor Red's is the largest user of Galliano in North America, Galliano being the main ingredient in those Gold Cadillacs invented here in 1948.) Some pass it studying the mural behind the bar that depicts the town as it appeared in the late 1800s. Others pass it feeding the jukebox. And some beat the wait by ordering take-out.

# Placerville

## – A LITTLE BACKGROUND –

Placerville, which in Spanish means "the golden one," was once known as Hangtown because hangings here were so common. This is where the Hangtown Fry—made with eggs, bacon, and oysters—originated. The town's **Hangman's Tree** bar *(305 Main St., (530) 622-3878.)* is built on top of the legendary hanging tree's stump and sometimes has a controversial, lifelike dummy hanging from a rope out front. Railroad magnate Mark Hopkins, meat-packer Philip Armour, and automobile-maker John Studebaker all got their financial starts here.

## – VISITOR INFORMATION –

### El Dorado County Visitors Authority
*542 Main St., (800) 457-6279, (530) 621-5885, fax (530) 642-1624; www.visit-eldorado.com.*

## – ANNUAL EVENTS –

### Wagon Train celebration
*June. (916) 621-0607; www.hwy50wagontrain.com.*
   Horse-drawn wagons travel to town down Highway 50 from Carson City via Lake Tahoe.

### Apple Hill
*September-December. (530) 644-7692; www.apple hill.com. Daily 9-6.*
   On a mountain ridge east of town, the Apple Hill tour route follows an historic path originally blazed out in 1857 by Pony Express riders. Each fall, 42 apple ranches along this route sell 22 varieties of tree-fresh apples at bargain prices, and they're *crunchy*, because they're *fresh!* An impressive selection of homemade apple goodies can also be purchased: fresh-pressed apple cider, hard cider, apple wine, spicy apple butter, caramel apples, apple jelly, dried apples, apple cake, apple sundaes, apple syrup, and, of course, apple pie. Many of the farms have picnic facilities, and some have snack bars. A few also have hiking trails, fishing ponds, pony rides, train rides, and live jazz. Three wineries are also located here. Several apple varieties are available into December.
   Cherry season begins on Father's Day weekend, when the **West Coast Cherry Pit-Spitting Championships** occur, and nine

Christmas tree farms open the day after Thanksgiving.

## — WHAT TO DO —

### El Dorado County Historical Museum
*104 Placerville Dr., at El Dorado County Fairgrounds, 2 mi. W of town (530) 621-5865, fax (530) 621-6644; www.co.el-dorado.ca.us/museum. W-Sat 10-4, Sun 12-4. By donation.*

Historic exhibits in this "great hall" include a Wells Fargo stagecoach and a wheelbarrow made by John Studebaker in the days before he manufactured cars.

### Fountain-Tallman Museum
*542 Main St., (530) 626-0773. F-Sun 12-4; Sat-Sun only, Nov-Feb. Free.*

Located in an atmospheric 1852 soda works building, this museum documents the town history. Downstairs are Gold Rush artifacts; upstairs is Victorian furniture.

### Gold Bug Mine
*Off Bedford Ave., 1 mi. N of town, (530) 642-5232, fax (530) 642-5236; www.goldbugpark.org. Daily 10-4, mid-Apr-Oct; Sat-Sun 12-4, Nov-mid-Apr. $3, 5-16 $1; audio tour +$1.*

Visitors here can take a self-guided tour through a cool ¼ mile-long lighted mine shaft, see a working model of a stamp mill inside an authentic stamp mill building (these were used to crush granite to extract the gold), picnic at creek-side tables, and hike in rugged 61-acre Gold Bug Park.

### Wineries

#### • Boeger Winery
*1709 Carson Rd. (Schnell School Rd. exit off Hwy. 50), (800) 655-2634, (530) 622-8094, fax (530) 622-8112; www.boegerwinery.com. Tasting daily 10-5; no tours.*

The stone cellar tasting room here is part of the original winery that operated from the 1860s through the 1920s. During Prohibition the winery became a pear farm, becoming a winery again in the early 1970s. Shaded streamside picnic tables beckon, and a sandbox awaits children.

#### • Sierra Vista Vineyards and Winery
*4560 Cabernet Way, (800) WINE-916, (530) 622-7221, fax (530) 622-2413; www.sierravistawinery.com. Tasting daily 10-5; tours by appt.*

Enjoy a magnificent view of the entire Crystal Range of the Sierra Nevada while picnicking at this pleasant winery.

# Coloma

## — A LITTLE BACKGROUND —

This is where James Marshall, a sawmill foreman who worked for Captain John Sutter, discovered gold in 1848. The entire town is now a National Historic Landmark.

## — WHAT TO DO —

### Marshall Gold Discovery State Historic Park
*On Hwy. 49, (530) 622-3470, fax (530) 622-3472; www.parks.ca.gov. Park: Daily 8-5; $5/vehicle. Museum: Daily 10-4:30; free.*

This lovely 265-acre park encompasses 70 percent of the town. It contains a reconstruction of the original **Sutter's Mill** (where the Gold Rush began) as well as picnic facilities, nature trails, and Gold Rush-era buildings and artifacts. An exact replica of the piece of gold Marshall found is displayed in the museum (the original is at the Smithsonian in Washington, D.C.). The **James W. Marshall Monument** is located on a hill overlooking the town.

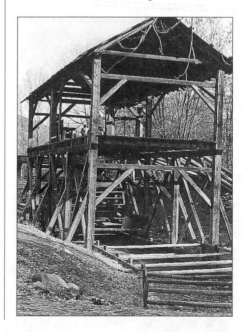

Marshall's grave is here, and a statue depicts him pointing to the spot where he discovered gold.

## Whitewater Connection.

*See page 442.*

The office and base camp for this white water rafting outfit is located adjacent to the state park. Participants on American River trips can camp out at the outfitter's riverside facility. Half- and full-day trips are scheduled Monday through Saturday from mid-April through September; longer trips are also available.

# Auburn

*See page 442.*

## – VISITOR INFORMATION –

### Auburn Area Chamber of Commerce

*601 Lincoln Way, (530) 885-5616, fax (530) 885-5854; www.auburnchamber.net.*

### Placer County Visitors Council

*13411 Lincoln Way, (866) PLACER-1, (530) 887-2111, fax (530) 887-2134; www.visitplacer.com.*

It is interesting to note that in Spanish "placer" means "surface mining."

## – WHAT TO DO –

### Bernhard Museum Complex

*291 Auburn-Folsom Rd., (530) 888-6891; www.placer.ca.gov/museum/bernhard.htm. Tu-Sun 11-4. Free.*

Docent-led tours are available of the Greek Revival-style Bernhard Residence, a restored Victorian farmhouse built in 1851 and furnished with Victorian antiques. A restored historic winery and reconstructed carriage barn are also on the site.

### Gold Country Museum

*1273 High St., at Gold Country Fairgrounds, (530) 887-0690; www.placer.ca.gov/museum/goldctry.htm. Tu-Sun 11-4. Free.*

Located within a building constructed of logs and stones, this old-time museum emphasizes mining exhibits. Visitors can walk through a 48-foot-long mine shaft and view a working model of a stamp mill. Local Maidu Indian artifacts and an extensive doll collection are displayed.

### Placer County Museum

*101 Maple St., (530) 889-6500; www.placer.ca.gov/museum/courthou.htm. Tu-Sun 11-4. Free.*

Located on the echoing first floor of the landmark Placer County Courthouse (the entrance is at ground level under the formal steps that are reminiscent of an Aztec temple), this museum's exhibits include a Native American habitat, a restored circa 1915 sheriff's office, and the Pate Collection of Native American Art featuring over 400 artifacts from throughout the U.S. The jail serves as a gallery, and a spectacular 52-piece gold collection worth more than $350,000 is displayed in a vault in the gift shop. Kids particularly enjoy a hands-on telegraph and telephone display.

## – WHERE TO STAY –

### KOA Kampground

*3550 KOA Way, (800) KOA-6671, (530) 885-0990; www.koa.com. Pool (seasonal); hot tub.*

For description, see page 443.

### Motel Row

Many motels are located at the top of the hill on Lincoln Way and across the freeway on Bowman Road.

## – WHERE TO EAT –

### Awful Annie's

*160 Sacramento St., (530) 888-9857; http://awfulannies.com. B-L daily; $. Highchairs, boosters, child menu. Reservations for 5+.*

Everything about this tiny spot is appealing—the lace-covered windows, the large outdoor deck, the all-day breakfast menu. The lunch menu includes scads of salads, sandwiches, and burgers. Truth be told, Annie's is awful good.

### Cafe Delicias

*1591 Lincoln Way, (530) 885-2050. L-D W-M; $. Highchairs, boosters, booths, child portions.*

Located in one of the town's oldest buildings, this casual Mexican restaurant serves especially good flautas and housemade tamales.

### Ikedas

*13500 Lincoln Way (¼ mi. E of Auburn Ravine-Foresthill exit off I-80), (530) 885-4243, fax (530) 885-6215; www.ikedas.com. Daily 8-7; Sat-Sun & in summer to 9; $. Highchairs, child portions. No cards.*

Since the 1950s, the casual Burger Bar here has been serving travel-weary diners fast-food fare: fresh-ground hamburgers, hot dogs, rice bowls, burritos, deep-fried whole mushrooms, fruit pie, fresh fruit salad, frozen yogurt, ten flavors of hot chocolate, and thick fresh fruit milkshakes. An adjacent produce market sells terrific car snacks, among them giant cashews and pistachios, both of which are grown in the area.

## Shanghai
*289 Washington St., (530) 823-2613. L-D, irregular schedule; $. Highchair, child portions. No cards.*

The oldest family-owned bar and restaurant in the state and the setting for the movie *Phenomenon*, this atmospheric spot has been serving Cantonese fare since 1906. Burgers, fresh fish, and steaks are also on the menu. The intriguing 1850s building has very high pressed-tin ceilings and an ancient interior decor. Vintage photos depict early Auburn and the Gold Rush, and colorful paper lanterns and fans add atmosphere. Live music is scheduled Thursday through Sunday.

# Grass Valley

## — A LITTLE BACKGROUND —

It was here, in what was once the richest gold-bearing region in the state, that gold mining became a well-organized industry. Many advanced mining techniques were developed and first used here.

## — VISITOR INFORMATION —

### Grass Valley/Nevada County Chamber of Commerce
*248 Mill St., (800) 655-4667, (530) 273-4667, fax (530) 272-5440; www.grassvalleychamber.com. M-F 9-5, Sat 10-3.*

Because of its location inside a replica of the home once occupied by scandalous Gold Rush personality Lola Montez, this office is worth visiting in person.

## — ANNUAL EVENTS —

### Bluegrass Festival
*June. (209) 293-1559; www.grassvalleychamber.com/ bluegrass_festival.htm. $20+.*

### Cornish Christmas
*December. (530) 272-8315; www.grassvalleychamber. com/cornish_christmas.htm. Free.*

Experience an old-time Christmas at this event celebrating the traditions of the Cornish miners who settled this Gold Rush town. Visitors can dance in the downtown streets, which close to traffic, and ride in a horse-drawn carriage.

## — WHAT TO DO —

### Bridgeport Covered Bridge
*Take Hwy. 20 W 10 mi. to Pleasant Valley Rd., turn right (N) and follow S fork of Yuba River 9 mi. to Bridgeport; (530) 432-2546, fax (530) 432-4182.*

Built over the south fork of the Yuba River in 1862 and in use until 1971, this is the longest (256 feet) single-span wood-covered bridge in the world. It is now a state historical landmark and part of **South Yuba River State Park**. Not currently maintained and in shaky condition, it should be walked across with caution. Facilities include a scenic picnic area on the riverbank and several hiking trails. Those who have witnessed it claim the wildflower display here in March is spectacular.

### Empire Mine State Historic Park
*10791 E. Empire St., (530) 273-8522; www.parks. ca.gov. Daily 10-5; in summer 9-6. $2, under 17 free. Cottage & mineyard tours, each +$1.50; cottage tour, Sat-Sun 12-3:30, May-Oct; mine yard tour, schedule varies.*

Once the largest and richest hard rock mine in the state, the Empire Mine operated for over a century—from 1850 to 1956. Though it still holds millions of dollars worth of gold, the ore is too expensive to extract. The mine is now a 805-acre state park. Of special interest is the stone **Bourn Cottage** (also known as the Empire Cottage), which was designed and built as a summer home for William Bowers Bourn II by his hunting buddy, Willis Polk, in 1897. It is in the style of an English country manor and features hand-planed heart-redwood walls. The surrounding 13 acres of formal gardens feature an antique rose garden planted in 1905, several fountains, and a reflecting pool. The mineyard illustrates many facets of the business and allows visitors to look down a lighted mine shaft. Among the approximately 12 miles of hiking trails are self-guided

backcountry paths and an easy 2-mile loop Hardrock Trail. Picnicking is not permitted in the park.

## Grass Valley Museum
*410 S. Church St./Chapel St., (530) 273-5509.*
*Tu-F 12:30-3:30. By donation.*

Built in 1863 as Mount Saint Mary's Convent and Orphanage, this was the state's first orphanage for non-Indian children. The building now displays Gold Rush memorabilia and furnishings as well as a fully equipped doctor's office, classroom, parlor, and music room from that era.

## North Star Power House Mining Museum
*On Allison Ranch Rd./S end of Mill St., (530) 273-4255. Daily 10-4; closed Oct-Apr. By donation.*

Once the power house for the North Star Mine, this rustic stone building houses a collection of old photographs, mining dioramas and models, and a 30-foot-diameter, 10-ton Pelton water wheel dating from 1896—the largest such wheel ever constructed. It also displays the largest operational Cornish pump in the country. A grassy picnic area is located across adjacent Wolf Creek.

## Oregon House
*35 mi. W of town (take Hwy. 20 W to Browns Valley, then Hwy. E21 N to Oregon House, then E20 E).*

### • Collins Lake Recreation Area
*On Collins Lake Rd., (800) 286-0576, (530) 692-1600, fax (530) 692-1607; www.collinslake.com. Daily sunrise-sunset. $6-10/vehicle.*

Popular with fishermen, this 1,000-acre lake has lakefront campsites, RV hook-ups, and cabins, and boat rentals are available.

### • Renaissance Vineyard & Winery
*12585 Rices Crossing Rd., (800) 655-3277, (530) 692-2222, fax (530) 692-2497; www.rvw.com. Tasting & tour F-Sat at 11, by appt.*

The drive through the scenic Sierra Nevada foothills required to reach this isolated valley would be worthwhile even if this special winery weren't waiting at the end. Operated by the Fellowship of Friends, a non-denominational religious group, the winery is atop a scenic hillside terraced with grapevines.

**The Bistro** *((530) 692-2938. L W-Sat; $ 1 highchair, 1 booster, 1 booth, child portions. Reservations advised.)* serves a seasonally changing menu of entrees designed to pair well with Renaissance wines. When the weather is warm, deck seating is available. On hotter days, the air-conditioned interior of the dining room brings welcome relief.

### – WHERE TO STAY –

## Holbrooke Hotel
*212 W. Main St., (800) 933-7077, (530) 273-1353, fax (530) 273-0434; www.holbrooke.com. 28 rooms; $-$$. Some gas fireplaces. Continental breakfast; restaurant.*

Established in 1851, this meticulously restored Victorian grand hotel has hosted four presidents (Grant, Garfield, Cleveland, and Harrison), stagecoach robber Black Bart, and author Mark Twain. Current guests can step back in time in beautifully appointed rooms featuring brass beds and the original clawfoot tubs. Most rooms hold only two people, but a few larger rooms can accommodate a child on a rollaway bed. A century-old wrought-iron elevator cage lifts guests from floor to floor. This lodging complex, which consists of both the hotel and the 1874 **Purcell House** behind it, is conveniently located in the center of town.

Both the **Golden Gate Saloon**—the oldest

bar in the state and featuring an ornate bar that was shipped around the Horn—and the elegant **212 Bistro** *(L-D daily, SunBr.)*, with full family amenities, operate on the main floor.

## Sivananda Ashram Yoga Farm
*14651 Ballantree Ln., (800) 469-9642, (530) 272-9322, fax (530) 477-6054; www.sivananda.org/farm. 8 rooms; $. Children under 12, half-price. No TVs; all shared bathrooms. Meals included. No smoking.*

The bell rings here at 5:30 each morning to awaken guests. Attendance at scheduled meditation and yoga classes is mandatory. In between, guests dine on vegetarian meals and have plenty of free time to enjoy the natural surroundings of the 80-acre farm. Lodging is simple, almost austere, consisting of both dormitories and single and double rooms, and during the summer guests may bring their own tents.

## — WHERE TO EAT —

### Marshall's Pasties
*203 Mill St., (530) 272-2844. M-F 9:30-6, Sat 10-6; $.*

Meat-and-potato turnovers were once popular lunch fare among the area's Cornish miners, who dubbed them "pasties" and carried them down into the mines in their pockets. At lunchtime, they reheated their pasties on a shovel held over candles secured in their hard hats. How about a hasty tasty pasty picnic? (Actually, "pasty" rhymes with "nasty.") Though town resident William Brooks invented the pasty-making machine now used throughout the world, here the pastries are made by hand.

### Tofanelli's
*302 W. Main St., (530) 272-1468. L-D daily; $. Highchairs, boosters, child portions.*

Salads, sandwiches, and several kinds of hamburgers—including a tofu burger and a veggie burger—are on the lunch menu. The brick-and-oak decor is attractive and restful.

# Nevada City

## — A LITTLE BACKGROUND —

Reputed to be the best privately preserved and restored small city in the state, this picturesque mining town is also said to contain residential and commercial buildings representative of all the major 19th-century architectural styles. Scenically situated on seven hills, the town boasts a particularly fine assortment of lovely gingerbread-style Victorian homes, and the entire downtown district is on the National Register of Historic Places. It is interesting to note that in Spanish "nevada" means "snow-covered."

## — VISITOR INFORMATION —

### Nevada City Chamber of Commerce
*132 Main St., (800) 655-NJOY, (530) 265-2692, fax (530) 265-3892; www.nevadacitychamber.com.*

## — ANNUAL EVENTS —

### International Teddy Bear Convention
*April. (530) 265-5804, fax (530) 478-0728; www.teddybearcastle.com. $5, seniors $3, under 12 & bears free.*

Bears from all over the world come out of hibernation for this warm, fuzzy event. Bearaphernalia and bear necessities—and luxuries—abound, and all kinds of bears are available for adoption.

### 4th of July Parade
*July. (800) 655-NJOY, (530) 272-8315; www.nevada citychamber.com/events_fourth.htm. Fairgrounds: $5, under 13 free; parking $2.*

Held in Nevada City on even years and in Grass Valley on odd, this old-fashioned celebration begins with a parade. Diversions follow— food stalls, competitions, entertainment—at the fairgrounds and, as might be expected, it culminates in a fireworks extravaganza.

### Constitution Day Parade
*September. (800) 655-NJOY, (530) 265-2692; www.nevadacitychamber.com/events_constitution.htm.*

The signing of the U.S. Constitution is honored at this oldest and largest celebration in the West with marching bands, drill teams, floats, fire engines, and equestrians. Pre-parade activities include a re-enactment of the signing.

### Fall colors
*Mid-October to mid-November. (800) 655-NJOY, (530) 265-2692; www.nevadacitychamber.com/ events_fallcolors.htm*

## Victorian Christmas
*December; on the 3 Wed eves & on the Sun aft.*
*before Christmas. (800) 655-NJOY, (530) 265-2692;*
*www.nevadacitychamber.com/events_victorian.htm.*
*Free.*

### – WHAT TO DO –

## Firehouse No. 1 Museum
*214 Main St., (530) 265-5468. F-Sun 11:30-4; daily in*
*summer. By donation.*

Located inside a charming 1861 Victorian firehouse, this museum is said to be haunted. Among the intriguing pioneer memorabilia on display are a Chinese altar, snowshoes made for a horse, relics from the Donner Party, and a noteworthy collection of Maidu Indian baskets.

## Nevada Theatre
*401 Broad St., (530) 265-6161, fax (530) 265-2294;*
*www.nevadatheatre.com.*

Opened in September of 1865 and lectured in twice by Mark Twain, this is the oldest original-use theater building in California. It is refurbished to appear as it did when it first opened and is used year-round for plays, concerts, films, and other performing arts events.

## Wineries

• **Nevada City Winery**
*321 Spring St., (800) 203-WINE, (530) 265-WINE,*
*fax (530) 265-6860; www.ncwinery.com. Tasting*
*M-Sat 11-5, Sun 12-5; tour on Sat at 11:30.*

Housed now in an historic foundry building, this winery is located only 2 blocks from where it originated a century ago. It is known for its Cabernets, Merlots, and Zinfandels.

• **Indian Springs Vineyards Tasting Room**
*303 Broad St., (800) 375-9311, (530) 478-1068,*
*fax (530) 478-0903. Tasting daily 11-5.*

Taste premium wines produced from grapes grown in Nevada County and other parts of Northern California.

### – WHAT TO DO NEARBY –

## Independence Trail
*Off Hwy. 49, 6 mi. N of town, in South Yuba River*
*State Park, (530) 272-3823. Free.*

This 4-mile nature trail follows the Excelsior Canal and Flume, which was built in 1856 to carry water 25 miles downstream through the mountains to Smartville for hydraulic gold mining. The trail is level and easy for both wheelchairs and baby strollers to navigate. One section permits hikers to cross flumes suspended over deep crevices and a waterfall. This area features an outstanding display of wildflowers in April and May.

## Malakoff Diggins State Historic Park
*23579 N. Bloomfield Rd., off Hwy. 49, 26 mi. NE of*
*town, (530) 265-2740, same fax; www.parks.ca.gov.*
*Museum: Sat-Sun 10-4; daily May-Sept. $5/vehicle.*

Inhabited by over 1,500 people in the 1870s, when it was the largest hydraulic gold-mining operation in the world, North Bloomfield is now a ghost town. Several buildings are restored, but there are no commercial shops. The park museum is in a former dance hall and has an interpretive display on hydraulic mining. Visitors can hike on numerous trails and fish in a small lake, and picnic facilities are available. Primitive cabins and both walk-in and regular campsites are available. Note that the drive from Nevada City takes just under an hour, and the last mile into North Bloomfield is dirt road.

## Oregon Creek swimming hole
*On Hwy. 49, 18 mi. N of town.*

Located in the middle fork of the Yuba River, this popular spot has sandy beaches, both deep swimming and shallow wading spots, and picnic facilities.

### – WHERE TO STAY –

## Grandmere's Inn
*449 Broad St., (530) 265-4660, fax (530) 265-4416;*
*www.grandmeresinn.com. 6 rooms; $$-$$$.*
*Afternoon snack, full breakfast. No smoking; no pets.*

This 1856 Colonial Revival home was built by Aaron Sargent, who wrote the 19th constitutional amendment granting women the vote. (The author of the 15th amendment, which freed former slaves, also lived in Nevada City.) On the National Register of Historic Places, it is decorated beautifully in French country style with antique pine furnishings and gorgeous floral fabrics, and it is conveniently located at the Top of Broad Street—one of the town's earliest residential areas.

## National Hotel

*211 Broad St., (530) 265-4551, fax (530) 265-2445; www.thenationalhotel.com. 42 rooms; $-$$. Children under 12 free. Some kitchens; 1 gas fireplace; some shared baths. Unheated pool. Restaurant; room service. No pets.*

Located on the town's main street, this claims to be the oldest continuously operating hotel west of the Rockies—maybe even west of the Mississippi. Luminaries who have been guests here include Herbert Hoover, who stayed here when he was a mining engineer for the Empire Mine, and Mark Twain. Built in 1856, it is a state historical landmark and features high ceilings, cozy floral wallpapers, and old-time furniture. Families of four are accommodated in two separate rooms with a bath in between.

Plush, old-fashioned **Hoover's** (*B-L-D daily, SunBr; $-$$. Highchairs, boosters, child portions. Reservations advised.*) features a steak and lobster dinner menu.

## Northern Queen Inn

*400 Railroad Ave., (800) 226-3090, (530) 265-5824, fax (530) 265-3720; www.northernqueeninn.com. 86 units; $-$$. Some kitchens & wood-burning stoves. Heated pool; hot tub. Restaurant.*

Located on the outskirts of town beside Gold Run Creek, this pleasant lodging complex has modern motel rooms, cottages, and 2-story chalets. A small collection of full-size trains is displayed on the property, including a 1920s railbus, a 1910 wood-burning locomotive, and another engine that had roles in several classic western movies.

The **Nevada County Traction Company** (*402 Railraod Ave., (800) 226-3090, (530) 265-0896, fax (530) 265-0869. Schedule varies. $10, 2-12 $7.*) operates a 1½-hour, 3-mile train ride in open-top excursion cars.

## Piety Hill Cottages

*523 Sacramento St., (800) 443-2245, (530) 265-2245, fax (530) 265-6528; www.pietyhillcottages.com. 9 cottages; $-$$. Children under 3 free. All kitchenettes; 1 wood-burning stove. Hot tub (seasonal). Continental breakfast. No smoking; no pets.*

This 1930s auto court motel has one- and two-room cottages with antique furnishings. A breakfast basket is delivered to the room.

## Red Castle Inn

*109 Prospect St., (800) 761-4766, (530) 265-5135; www.redcastleinn.com. 4 stories; 7 rooms; $$. Unsuitable for children under 10. No TVs. Full breakfast. No smoking.*

Situated on a hilltop above town, this beautifully restored and poshly furnished Gothic Revival mansion was built in 1860. Said to be one of only two of this style left on the West Coast, it features gingerbread and icicle trim and has old-fashioned double brick walls. Rooms are decorated deliciously, and breakfast is an occasion. Some guests have reportedly seen the spirit of Laura Jean, who was once a governess here.

### — WHERE TO EAT —

## Cafe Mekka

*237 Commercial St., (530) 478-1517. Sun-Thur 8am-10pm, F-Sat to midnight; $.*

Mix-matched furniture here includes some stuffed couches and chairs, making for a casual atmosphere. Art that is part of regularly changing shows hangs on the tall walls. Divine desserts and pastries made by the cafe's own baker include the White Bronco—chocolate cake with whipped cream filling topped with white chocolate swirls and raspberry sauce (guess what famous trial it is named for), and a board full of coffee selections keeps things perking right along.

## Country Rose Café

*300 Commercial St., (530) 265-6252. L-D daily, SunBr; $-$$. Boosters, booths, child portions. Reservations advised.*

The charming dining room in this 1860s brick building features wooden booths and rose print tablecloths. In summer, diners can also sit in a bucolic outdoor area with a creek running through it. The inviting country-French menu includes delicious housemade soups and sandwiches, French hot chocolate, and a great lemon chiffon pie. Classically prepared fresh fish is a house specialty.

## Friar Tuck's

*111 N. Pine St., (530) 265-9093, fax (530) 265-9777; www.friartucks.com. D daily; $$. Highchairs, boosters, booths, child portions. Reservations advised.*

Operating in a building dating back to 1857, this popular restaurant burned to the ground in 2002. It has reopened with a new take on its old look and features lots of cozy booths, s huge state-of-the-art kitchen, and locally made fiber-optic lighting. The extensive menu offers a variety of casual fondue items—including a chocolate dessert version—as well as grilled fresh fish, rack of lamb, roasted duck, ribs, and steak. The wine list runs the gamut from inexpensive local labels to expensive rare vintages, and varietals are available by the glass.

**Posh Nosh**
*318 Broad St., (530) 265-6064. L-D Tu-Sun; $$. Child menu. Reservations advised.*

Operating within an historic stone building, this restaurant offers a cozy downstairs room for winter dining. In summer, a pleasant patio out back is choice. The eclectic menu offers something for everyone. Lunch consists of plenty of sandwiches and salads, while dinner brings on steak, ribs, and fresh fish.

# Downieville

## – A LITTLE BACKGROUND –

One of the Gold Country's best-preserved mining towns, this scenic mountain enclave is known as the gateway to the Lost Sierra and is a surprise to come upon as Highway 49 winds through, narrowing to one lane over the town's northern bridge. It is situated where the North Yuba River and the Downie River merge, known as the Forks. Early miners found big gold nuggets here by the bucketful. The rustic town retains its 19th-century charm with wood plank sidewalks, original brick buildings that include a white steeple church, and the ever-present soothing sound of the Downie River. Main Street still has a mining supply shop and saloon, and the 1885 town gallows, used only once, still stands outside the County Courthouse. Downieville is considered the least changed of California's Gold Rush towns.

The best way to enjoy a quick stop is with a picnic among the Gold Rush artifacts in riverside Lions Memorial Park; sandwich and pizza shops are adjacent. And pick up a copy of *The Mountain Messenger* newspaper. It is the state's oldest continuously published weekly—since 1853. Nowadays the town is a popular destina-

tion with mountain bikers, who enjoy riding on the plentiful dirt roads.

## – GETTING THERE –

Located 55 miles northeast of Nevada City.

## – WHAT TO DO –

**Downieville Museum**
*(530) 289-3423. Daily 11-4, mid-Apr-mid-Oct. By donation.*

This small museum operates within a circa 1852 fire-repellant stone building made with thick walls of mortar-less schist and with iron shutters and doors. It was originally a Chinese store and gambling house. Displays include historical photographs, artifacts, and clothing from the 1800s.

## – WHERE TO STAY –

**Sierra Shangri-La**
*On Hwy. 49, (530) 289-3455; www.sierrashangrila. com. 11 units; $-$$$. Children under 2 free. No TVs; some kitchens & wood-burning fireplaces & stoves. No smoking.*

There is little to do here except commune with nature. Guests can relax, do some fishing and hiking, and enjoy the sight and sound of the Yuba River rushing past their cabin door. Some units are perched right over the river, allowing guests to fish from their deck. Eight housekeeping cottages and three B&B units are available.

# Sierra City

## – VISITOR INFORMATION –

**Sierra County Chamber of Commerce**
*P.O. Box 436, Sierra City 96125, (800) 200-4949, (530) 862-0308; www.sierracounty.org.*

## – GETTING THERE –

Located 60 miles northeast of Nevada City.

## – WHAT TO DO –

**Sierra County Historical Park and Museum**
*100 Kentucky Mine Rd., off Hwy. 49, (530) 862-1310. W-Sun 10-5, June-Sept; Sat-Sun only in Oct; closed Nov-May. Mill tour at 11 & 2. $5, 7-17 $2.50. Museum only: $1; under 6 free.*

A 45-minute guided tour through the reconstructed 1850s **Kentucky Mine Stamp Mill** located here permits viewing the original machinery, which is still intact and operable. The museum is inside a reconstructed wood-frame hotel dating from the mid-19th century. Picnic tables and barbecue facilities are available under a canopy of oak trees.

The eclectic **Kentucky Mine Concert Series** is held on Saturday evenings in July and August in an amphitheater within the complex.

### — WHERE TO STAY —

#### Herrington's Sierra Pines Resort
*On Hwy. 49, (800) 682-9848, (530) 862-1151; www.herringtonssierrapines.com. 21 units; $-$$; closed Dec-Mar. Some kitchens & wood-burning fireplaces. Restaurant. Pets ok.*

Located on the north fork of the Yuba River, this lodging facility consists of duplex units and one cabin. The **restaurant** *(B-D daily. Highchairs, boosters.)* is known for its baked goods and rainbow trout, which are caught fresh each morning from the property's own trout pond.

#### Packer Lake Lodge
*3901 Packer Lake Rd., 10 mi. N of town, (530) 862-1221, same fax. 14 cabins; $; closed Nov-Apr. Children under 2 free. No TVs; some kitchens & wood-burning stoves; some shared baths. Restaurant. Pets ok.*

Located at the end of a road in a remote corner of the Sierra Nevada, this rustic resort has eight housekeeping cabins with sun decks overlooking Packer Lake. They are rented by the week and include use of a rowboat. (No motorboats are permitted on the lake.) Six sleeping cabins are available by the night. Summer dates here are usually booked up several years in advance. The **restaurant** is open for dinner to non-guests by reservation.

#### Salmon Lake Lodge
*On Gold Lake Rd., 10 mi. N of town, (530) 757-1825; www.salmonlake.net. 14 cabins; $-$$; 1-wk. min. June-Oct; closed Nov-Apr. No TVs; some kitchens & wood-burning fireplaces & stoves; some shared baths. Dogs ok.*

Located in the glaciated high country of Sierra County, this remote resort has been in continuous operation for almost a century. Guests park their cars at the east end of Salmon Lake and are transported by a staff-operated barge across the lake. There they sleep in one of the cabins or tent-cabins and are provided free access to an assortment of boats. Some cabins are fully equipped, but guests in tent-cabins must provide their own bedding, kitchen utensils, and supplies. The experience is like luxurious camping. To ease cooking chores, guests are invited twice each week to a catered barbecue (additional fee) held on an island in the center of the lake.

# Sierraville

### — GETTING THERE —

Located 80 miles northeast of Nevada City, where Highway 49 meets Highway 89. Highway 89 continues north to Plumas County and south to Truckee and Lake Tahoe.

### — WHAT TO DO —

#### Sierra Hot Springs
*1 Campbell Hot Springs Rd., off Hwy. 89, (530) 994-3773, fax (530) 994-3479; www.sierrahotsprings.org. Baths open 24-hours daily. Day-use: $12-$15, 5-12 half-price. No smoking; no pets.*

Swimsuits are optional in the indoor and outdoor hot springs at this secluded spa. Open since the 1850s, it has three pools (one hot, two cool) positioned inside a copper geodesic dome with stained glass and skylights; a deck and swimming pool are outside.

**Lodging** includes five private rooms and a dormitory in a rustic lodge by the springs, plus hotel rooms in town in its renovated 1909 **Globe Hotel** *(20 rooms; $.)* Campsites are also available. Rates include unlimited use of the springs.

An organic vegetarian **restaurant** serves nightly buffet dinners *(F-Sun, winter only.).*

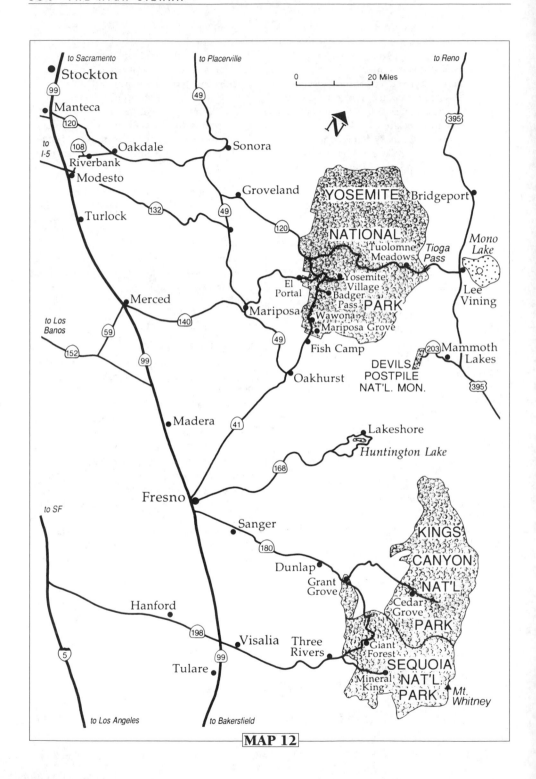

to Sacramento

to Placerville

to Reno

Stockton

99

Manteca

120

to I-5

108 Oakdale

Riverbank

Modesto

Turlock

132

Sonora

49

Groveland

49

120

YOSEMITE

Bridgeport

NATIONAL

Tuolomne Meadows

Tioga Pass

Mono Lake

395

El Portal

Yosemite Village

Merced

140

Mariposa

Badger Pass

PARK

Wawona

Lee Vining

to Los Banos

59

152

99

49

Mariposa Grove

Fish Camp

Oakhurst

DEVILS POSTPILE NAT'L. MON.

203 Mammoth Lakes

395

Madera

41

Lakeshore

Huntington Lake

168

to SF

Fresno

Sanger

180

KINGS

CANYON

NAT'L

Hanford

198

Dunlap

Grant Grove

Cedar Grove

PARK

to Los Angeles

5

99

Visalia

Tulare

Three Rivers

Giant Forest

Mineral King

SEQUOIA NAT'L PARK

Mt. Whitney

to Bakersfield

0          20 Miles

**MAP 12**

# THE HIGH SIERRA

## Yosemite National Park

— A LITTLE BACKGROUND —

*Yosemite Park is a place of rest. A refuge . . . in which one gains the advantage of both solitude and society . . . none can escape its charms. Its natural beauty cleanses and warms like fire, and you will be willing to stay forever . . .*

*—John Muir*

Yosemite is worth returning to in every season. Doing so permits enjoying the spectacular beauty of the park's dramatic seasonal changes. Most visitors see this grand national park in the summer, when it is at its busiest—with congested roads and accommodations filled to capacity. All this makes it difficult to focus on what was the original draw—the scenic, natural beauty of the High Sierra. To catch a glimpse of the Yosemite described by Muir, it is essential to visit in the off-season: in fall when the colorful foliage change is spectacular; in winter when snow blankets the valley floor; in spring when the falls are at their fullest.

Yosemite's high country was designated a national park in 1890. The valley, which was under state supervision, was added to the national park in 1906. (It is amazing to realize that the valley comprises just 1% of the park's terrain. In fact, Yosemite is as big as the state of Rhode Island.) Among the park's scenic wonders are El Capitan—the largest piece of exposed granite in the world—and Yosemite Falls—the tallest waterfall in North America and the fifth tallest free-falling waterfall in the world.

Bear in mind that falls and rivers can be dangerous as well as beautiful. Be careful, especially when hiking with children.

A $20 per vehicle admission fee, which is good for 7 days, is collected at all park entrances. Visitors receive a copy of the *Yosemite Guide* activities newsletter and a park map. For more information, see www.YosemitePark.com.

— VISITOR INFORMATION —

### National Park Service
*Yosemite National Park 95389, (209) 372-0200, fax (209) 372-0220; www.nps.gov/yose.*

### Yosemite Sierra Visitors Bureau
*41969 Hwy. 41, in Oakhurst, (559) 683-4636, fax (559) 686-5697; www.go2yosemite.net.*

Request a free *Visitors Guide* covering areas outside the national park.

## — GETTING THERE —

Located approximately 240 miles east of San Francisco. Take Highway 80 to Highway 580 to Highway 205 to Highway 120. To minimize the need for chains in winter, take low-elevation Highway 140 in from Merced.

## — ANNUAL EVENTS —

### Chefs' Holidays

*January & February. At The Ahwahnee.*

Guest chefs give cooking presentations and prepare gala banquets.

### Vintners' Holidays

*November & December. At The Ahwahnee.*

Two days of wine seminars hosted by esteemed wine-makers culminate in a sumptuous feast in The Ahwahnee Dining Room. Courses are designed especially to complement wines sampled in the seminars.

### Bracebridge Dinner

*December. At The Ahwahnee; (559) 253-5635. Not appropriate for children under 8.*

Since 1927, the fare at this 3-hour mock-medieval feast has been seven courses of elegant Christmas dishes. Pageantry, carols, and jesters entertain diners in between. Attending this memorable, and expensive, dinner is a pleasure not many get to enjoy.

## — STOPS ALONG THE WAY —

Attractions are listed in the order encountered driving in from the San Francisco Bay Area.

### Manteca Waterslides at Oakwood Lake RV Campground

*874 E. Woodward Rd., in Manteca, (877) OAKWOOD, (209) 249-2500, fax (209) 239-2060; www.oakwood lake.com. Daily in summer; Sat-Sun only, May & Sept; schedule varies. $25, under 42" tall free; parking $6.*

This was North America's first waterslide park, and it is where the world's first fiberglass waterslide was invented in 1976. Now its more than 1 mile of fiberglass waterslides include the state's tallest speed slide—the 8-story-high V-MAX—as well as three Thunder Falls thrill slides. Most slides have over 400 feet of enclosed flume and multiple 360-degree turns. Other attractions include the inner tube-maneuvered River Rapids and the two-person

inner tube ride Jet Scream. The giant Castaway Bay children's slide and activity pool provides fun for the little ones, too. Campground facilities are available year-round and include a fishing lake, a playground, and acres of shady barbecue and picnic areas.

### Knight's Ferry Covered Bridge

*12 mi. E of Oakdale, (209) 881-3517, fax (209) 881-3203. Visitor center M-F 8-4, Sat-Sun 10-2. Free.*

Built in 1863 and measuring 330 feet long, this bridge is the longest and oldest covered bridge west of the Mississippi. It is closed to cars now, but pedestrian traffic is still permitted. A park on the highway side of the Stanislaus River provides picnicking and fishing spots. On the other side of the river is a rustic Gold Rush-era town with a general store, several restaurants, and another park.

Unguided raft, canoe, and kayak rentals can be arranged through **River Journey** *((800) 292-2938, (209) 847-4671, fax (209) 847-1300; www.riverjourney.com.).*

### Groveland

This rustic mountain town is home to the **Iron Door Saloon** *(18761 Main St. (Hwy. 120), (209) 962-8904; www.iron-door-saloon.com.),* which was built in 1853 and claims to be the oldest saloon in the state. It also serves lunch and dinner in its Grill and dishes up ice cream treats from its Soda Fountain.

In summer, the **Groveland Motel & Indian Village** *(18933 Main St., (888) 849-3529, (209) 962-7865, fax (209) 962-0664; www.grove*

*landmotel.net. 27 units; $-$$$. No pets.)* gives pooped parents the option of renting a cabin for themselves and an adjacent carpeted tepee for the kids. Mobile home units are also available.

## — WHAT TO DO —
## PARK ACTIVITIES

### The Ansel Adams Gallery
*In Yosemite Village, (209) 372-4413; www.ansel adams.com. Daily 9-5.*

Special edition photographs by this well-known photographer are for sale here.

### Bicycle rentals
*Yosemite Lodge: (209) 372-1208. Curry Village: (209) 372-8319. Schedule varies. $5.50/hr., $21/day.*

All rental bikes are old-fashioned one-speeds. A map to the 8.7-mile Yosemite Valley bike path loop is provided, and helmets are available at no charge. Child carriers are not available.

### Big Trees Tram Tour
*On Hwy. 41, in Wawona, 35 mi. from valley, (209) 375-1621. Daily; schedule varies; June-Oct only. $11, child $5.50. Reservations advised.*

Approximately 500 giant sequoias are located in the 250-acre **Mariposa Grove of**

**Giant Sequoias.** Some measure 15 to 25 feet in diameter, and some are over 2,000 years old. Open-air trams take visitors on a guided 1-hour tour of a 6-mile scenic loop. A 7-mile hiking trail also loops through the grove, but it is not necessary to walk the entire distance—several impressive trees are seen within the first mile. In winter, this is a choice spot for cross-country skiing.

### Bus tours
*(209) 372-1240. Valley floor: $20.50, child $15.50. Grand Tour: $55, child $27.50; June-Oct only.*

The Grand Tour includes Glacier Point, from which gazers enjoy a 270-degree view of the high country and a bird's-eye view of the valley 3,214 feet below.

### Hiking
Participate in a ranger-guided walk or take any of the many self-guided trails. Maps can be purchased in park stores. The most popular trail is the Mist Trail to Vernal Fall, which features breathtaking vistas and a close-up view of the 317-foot-tall waterfall.

### Junior Ranger Program
This program is available June through August for children ages 8 through 12. Consult the *Yosemite Guide* for details. For more description, see page 445.

### Movies
Scenic movies and slide shows are scheduled some evenings. Check the *Yosemite Guide* for times and locations.

### Pioneer History Center
*On Hwy. 41, in Wawona, 25 mi. from valley. Daily dawn-dusk. Free.*

This village of restored historic pioneer buildings dating from the late 1800s is reached by walking across an authentic covered bridge. Originally located in different areas around the park, the various structures were moved here in the 1950s and '60s. In summer, history comes to life with demonstrations of soap making, yarn spinning, rail-splitting, and other pioneer crafts, and horse-drawn carriage rides are sometimes available.

### Rafting

*Rentals: At Curry Village, (209) 372-8319. June-July only. $13.50, under 13 $11.50.*

Scenic and calm is the area on the Merced River between Pines Campground and Sentinel Bridge. Raft rentals include personal flotation devices, paddles, and return shuttle.

### Winter activities

See pages 435 to 437.

### Yosemite Chapel

*In the Valley.*

Built in 1879, this charming structure is the oldest building in the park.

### Yosemite Mountaineering School

*(209) 372-8344. Year-round. $117+. Must be 14 or older.*

Learn rock climbing at one of the finest schools in the world. Beginners learn the safety essentials for dealing with this area's granite rock and can expect to climb as high as 80 feet in the first lesson. Oddly, snow and ice climbing are offered only in summer.

### Yosemite Museum

*In Yosemite Village, next to Valley Visitor Center, (209) 372-0304. Daily 9-12 & 1-4. Free.*

Visitors learn about the Awaneechee Indians through artifacts, cultural demonstra-

tions, and recorded chants. A reconstructed Indian Village located behind the museum features a self-guided trail that points out plants used by the Native American residents for food, clothing, and shelter.

### Yosemite Valley Stables

*(209) 372-8348. Schedule varies; Apr-Oct only. Guided 2-hr. horse rides $51+. Must be 7 or older.*

Said to have the largest public riding stock in the world, this concession can arrange a custom pack or fishing trip. Mule rides are also available.

## ACTIVITIES OUTSIDE THE PARK

The first three destinations are reached via the Tioga Pass, which at 9,945 feet is the highest motor vehicle pass in California. The route winds through Yosemite's high country past magnificent mountain vistas, deep blue lakes, and soaring glacier-carved granite monoliths. Note that this pass closes in winter.

### Bodie State Historic Park

*8 mi. S of Bridgeport, (760) 647-6445; www.parks.ca.gov. Daily 8-dusk. Museum: Daily, summer only. Stamp mill tour: Schedule varies, June-Oct only. $2, under 17 free.*

Located at the end of a 13-mile side road off Highway 395, the last 3 miles of which are unpaved, this 486-acre park is the largest unrestored ghost town in the West. In 1879, when 10,000 people lived here, there were 2 churches, 4 newspapers, and 65 saloons. It was reputed to be quite rowdy. A little girl who moved here in its heyday wrote in her diary, "Good, by God! We're going to Bodie." This passage has also been interpreted as "Good-bye God! We're going to Bodie." Due to fires in 1892 and 1932, only about 5% of the town structures remain. No food service or picnic facilities are available.

## Devil's Postpile National Monument

*(760) 934-2289; www.nps.gov/depo. Daily 7am-7:30pm; June-Oct only. Shuttle bus: $7, 3-15 $4.*

This 60-foot-high formation is constructed of polygonal basaltic columns formed long ago by quickly cooling lava. Visitors can take a pleasant 1-mile walk through the monument, and a short hike leads to 101-foot-high Rainbow Falls. The road in is closed to vehicles. Visitors are required to ride a shuttle bus from the Mammoth Mountain Ski Area.

## Mono Lake

*Off Hwy. 395, (760) 647-3000; www.monolake.org. Dining & lodging information: (760) 647-6629.*

John Muir described this desolate area as, "A country of wonderful contrasts, hot deserts bounded by snow-laden mountains, cinder and ashes scattered on glacier-polished pavement, frost and fire working together in the making of beauty." Mark Twain called it the "Dead Sea of the West." An ancient Ice Age lake, estimated to be at least 1 million years old, Mono Lake features an unusual terrain of pinnacles and spires formed by calcium-rich mineral deposits that spurt up from the lake bottom. It is filled with water that contains almost three times the salt found in ocean water and holds not a single fish—though tiny brine shrimp flourish. Perhaps this is what attracts the 50,000-plus vacationing seagulls that flock in during April to nest, stay into August, and then head back to the coast. Situated at over 7,000 feet above sea level, it is one of the largest lakes in the state. Fall is the ideal time for a visit. Campsites are available.

### • Mono Basin National Forest Scenic Area Visitor Center

*Off Hwy 395, on W shore just outside Lee Vining, (760) 647-3044; www.fs.fed.us/r5/inyo. Daily 9-4:30 in summer; Sat-Sun rest of year. Guided nature walks: Daily at 10 & 1 in summer; Sat-Sun at 1 rest of year. Free.*

Overlooking the lake, this center has interpretive displays that provide insight into the area.

• **Mono Lake Committee Information Center**
*On Hwy. 395/Third St., in Lee Vining, (760) 647-6595,
fax (760) 647-6377. Daily 9am-10pm in summer;
closes earlier rest of year. Free.*

Get oriented here with a brief slide show
about the lake. In summer, a free hour-long
sunset walk is led daily at 6 p.m., and a naturalist-led canoe tour is offered on weekends (small
charge for use of equipment).

## Yosemite Mountain Sugar Pine Railroad
*56001 Hwy. 41, in Fish Camp, 4 mi. S of park's south
entrance, 1-hr. drive from valley, (559) 683-7273;
www.ymsprr.com. Schedule varies. Train: $14, 3-12 $7;
Jenny rail cars: $10, 3-12 $5.*

A reconstruction of the Madera Sugar Pine
Co. Railroad that made its last run in 1931, this
narrow-gauge steam train takes passengers on a
45-minute, 4-mile scenic excursion through the
Sierra National Forest. Passengers get a live narration on the area's history while sitting in
open-air touring cars upon logs carved out to
form long benches. A stopover at the midway
point to picnic or hike is an option. Moonlight
rides, which include a steak barbecue and
campfire program, are scheduled on Saturday
evenings in summer. Smaller Jenny rail cars,
powered by Model A engines, take passengers
on shorter 30-minute rides along the same
route when the train is not operating. A picnic
area and snack shop are available.

— **WHERE TO STAY** —

### PARK LODGING: IN THE VALLEY

*(559) 252-4848; www.yosemitepark.com. Reservations
essential. Some facilities open year-round. Children
under 13 free. No pets.*

It is especially difficult to obtain accommodations in summer and on holiday weekends. Rates for two range from $60 to $822. A
bargain Midweek Ski Package is available in
winter.

### The Ahwahnee
*123 rooms; $$$+. Some fireplaces. Pool (seasonal);
tennis courts. Afternoon tea; restaurant; room service.
No smoking. Free valet parking.*

Built in 1927 of granite blocks and con-
crete beams, this sedate luxury hotel is a
National Historic Landmark. Its decor includes
priceless Native American baskets and oriental

rugs, and interesting historic photos and art-
work hang on the walls. The grand Great
Lounge, with a walk-in fireplace at either end, is
delightful to sit in. Some cottages are available.

### Campgrounds
*(800) 436-7275; http://reservations.nps.gov. $.
Most Apr-Oct only; several open year-round.*

### Curry Village
*628 units; $-$$. No TVs; some fireplaces; some
shared baths. Unheated pool. Restaurant.*

Accommodations include standard rooms,
cabins, and inexpensive tent-cabins located
along the Merced River that sleep up to six people. The pool can be used by non-guests for a
small fee.

### Housekeeping Camp
*266 units; $. No TVs; some fireplaces.*

Cook on an outdoor pit grill and experience camping beside the Merced River without
the bother of setting up a tent. Units sleep up to
six people and consist of three concrete walls, a
concrete floor, a canvas roof, and a canvas curtain closure. Basic furniture is provided.

### Yosemite Lodge at the Falls
*245 rooms; $-$$. No TVs; some shared baths. Heated
pool (seasonal). 3 restaurants.*

Accommodations are comfortable modern
hotel rooms. The pool can be used by non-
guests for a small fee.

### PARK LODGING: ELSEWHERE

### High Sierra Camps
*(559) 253-5674. 204 beds; $$; summer only.
Unsuitable for children under 7. No TVs; communal
bath house. Breakfast & dinner included; dining tent.*

Five camps provide dormitory-style tent
accommodations and include two meals. Guests
must bring their own linens. Reservations are
assigned by lottery.

### Tuolumne Meadows Lodge
*At park's east entrance, (209) 372-8413. 69 units; $;
summer only. No TVs; all wood-burning stoves; com-
munal bath house. Dining tent; D reservations
required.*

This is an all tent-cabin facility.

## Wawona Hotel

*On Hwy. 41, in Wawona, 30 mi. from valley, 6 mi. inside park's south entrance. 104 rooms; $-$$; open Apr-Nov & Christmas vacation; weekends only Jan-Easter. No TVs; some shared baths. Unheated pool; 1 tennis court; 9-hole golf course. Restaurant.*

Built in 1879, this Victorian hotel is located near the Mariposa Grove of Giant Sequoias. A National Historic Landmark, it is said to be the oldest resort hotel in the state. Most rooms accommodate only two people; a few in the annex, added in 1918, accommodate three. Facilities include a "swimming tank" built in 1917.

A special **Christmas program** is scheduled annually. Details vary from year to year, but in the past it has included a stagecoach ride across the covered bridge leading to the Pioneer History Center, where all the cabins were decorated for the holidays. Santa might arrive in a horse-drawn wagon dating from the 1800s, and a special Christmas Eve and New Year's Eve dinner is always served.

## White Wolf

*At Tioga Pass, 31 mi. from the valley. 28 cabins; $; summer only. No TVs; shared bath house. Dining tent.*

This complex consists of tent-cabins and a few cabins with private baths. Breakfast and dinner are available.

## LODGING UNAFFILIATED WITH THE PARK

### The Redwoods In Yosemite

*In Wawona, 4 mi. inside park's south entrance, (888) 225-6666, (209) 375-6666, fax (209) 375-6400; www.redwoodsinyosemite.com. 124 units; $$-$$$+. Children under 4 free. Some TVs; all kitchens; most wood-burning fireplaces or stoves. Pets ok in some units.*

These rustic cabins and modern homes come equipped with linens and kitchenware.

### Tenaya Lodge at Yosemite

*1122 Hwy. 41, in Fish Camp, 2 mi. outside park's south entrance, (800) 635-5807, (559) 683-6555, fax (559) 683-8684; www.tenayalodge.com. 4 stories; 244 rooms; $$-$$$+. Children under 18 free. 1 indoor heated pool & hot tub, 1 outdoor heated pool & hot* *tub; 2 saunas; 2 steam rooms; fitness room. 2 restaurants; room service. No pets.*

Built in 1990, this plush lodge is a cross between the park's Yosemite Lodge and Ahwahnee hotel. A majestic public reception area features 3-story-tall beamed ceilings, and all guest rooms have forest views. Guided nature walks are scheduled most mornings, weather permitting. In winter, ski and snowshoe rentals are available at the hotel, and guests can strike out on a scenic cross-country ski trail through adjacent Yosemite National Forest. In summer, campfire programs, wagon rides, and rentals of mountain bikes are added to the roster. Spa services are available year-round, and Camp Tenaya children's program operates some evenings for ages 5 through 12 *($35)*.

## — WHERE TO EAT -

### PARK DINING

All of these valley facilities are open daily and equipped with highchairs and booster seats.

## The Ahwahnee Dining Room
*(209) 372-1489. B-L M-Sat, D daily, SunBr; $-$$$. Child portions. Reservations essential for D.*

The best time to dine in the rustic splendor of this magnificent dining room is during daylight hours, when the spectacular views of the valley afforded by the floor-to-trestle-beamed ceiling, 34-foot-tall leaded-glass windows can be fully enjoyed. Dinner is expensive, and men are requested to wear a sport coat or dress sweater and women to dress accordingly. Guests of the hotel get first choice at reservations, so non-guests often must settle for either an early or late seating. Children fit in best at breakfast or lunch.

## Cafeterias
*Curry Pavilion, at Curry Village; Food Court, at Yosemite Lodge. B-L-D; $.*

Meals here are quick and informal.

## Mountain Room Restaurant
*At Yosemite Lodge. D; $$-$$$. Child portions.*

The walls in this stunning room are papered with striking black-and-white photomurals of mountain climbers, and floor-to-ceiling windows look out on Yosemite Falls. The menu features broiled fresh fish and aged beef as well as smoked trout, sautéed button mushrooms, and warm cheese bread. Get rid of the kinks developed on the long ride in with a drink in the adjacent Mountain Room Lounge.

## Picnic Pick-Ups

Box lunches can be reserved at hotel kitchens the evening before they are needed. Supplies can also be picked up at **Degnan's Deli** in Yosemite Village.

## Wawona Dining Room
*(209) 375-1425. B-L-D, SunBr; $-$$. Child portions. Reservations advised for D.*

The inexpensive Sunday brunch is highly recommended. Served in the hotel's wonderful traditional Victorian dining room, where expansive multi-paned windows provide views of the surrounding pines, it consists of simple, satisfying fare. Breakfast or lunch during the rest of the week is also particularly pleasant.

### DINING OUTSIDE THE PARK

## Erna's Elderberry House
*48688 Victoria Ln. (Hwy. 41), in Oakhurst, 15 mi. outside park's south entrance, (559) 683-6800, fax (559) 683-0800; www.chateausureau.com. D daily; $$$+; closed 1st 3 wks. of Jan. Highchairs, child portions. Reservations essential.*

This stellar venue is similar to the destination restaurants found in the countryside of France. The staff prepares a different six-course, fixed-price meal every night. One meal enjoyed here in the elegantly appointed front room began with a flute of elderberry-flavored champagne. It continued with a scallop and sorrel timbale artistically positioned on a nest of pasta, and was followed by corn and cilantro soup and then fresh pears poached in Riesling. The main course was alder wood-smoked chicken sausages served with wild rice and a colorful array of vegetables. A simple, elegant salad followed. Dessert, which is served outside on a candle-lit garden terrace, was a duo of Chocolate Decadence in fresh mint sauce and puff pastry filled with caramelized apples and creamed gourmand. Three wines selected to complement each dinner are offered by the glass.

Elegant lodging is available in the property's castle-like **Chateau du Sureau** *((559) 683-*

6860, fax (559) 683-0800. 10 rooms; $$$+, 12% gratuity added to bill. Unsuitable for children under 7. TVs by request; all wood-burning fireplaces. Unheated pool. Afternoon snack, full breakfast; restaurant; room service. No smoking.), which features a giant outdoor chess court and serene walking paths. Maids wearing long black dresses topped with white ruffled aprons keep things spiffy. ("Sureau" is the French word for "elderberry.")

# Sequoia and Kings Canyon National Parks

## — A LITTLE BACKGROUND —

Though located just south of Yosemite National Park, about a 3-hour drive away, these two scenic national parks often are overlooked. It's a shame because they, too, offer spectacular scenery and are much less crowded.

Sequoia National Park was established in 1890. It was California's first national park and is the country's second-oldest national park (Yellowstone is the oldest). Kings Canyon National Park was established in 1940. Combined, they encompass over 860,000 acres.

The main attraction at these parks is the enormous sequoia trees, with their vibrant cinnamon-colored bark. The trees can be viewed in both Sequoia Park's Giant Forest and Kings Canyon's Grant Grove. The largest is the **General Sherman Tree** in Sequoia National Park. It towers 275 feet high, measures 36$^{1/2}$ feet in diameter, and is approximately 2,100 years old. This makes it higher than Niagara Falls, as wide as a city street, and the largest living tree on the planet.

**Mt. Whitney** is also located in Sequoia park and, at 14,494 feet, is the highest point in the United States outside of Alaska. It can't be viewed from the park without a long hike. From the east side of the Sierra, it is a 1- to 3-day hike to its peak; from the west side it is a 7- to 9-day hike.

Admission to the parks is $10 per vehicle.

## — VISITOR INFORMATION —

**Sequoia and Kings Canyon National Parks**
47050 Generals Hwy., Three Rivers 93271-9700, (559) 565-3341, fax (559) 565-3730; www.nps.gov/seki.

## — GETTING THERE —

Located approximately 250 miles southeast of San Francisco. Take Highway 80 to Highway 580 to Highway 99 south, to either Highway 180 east or Highway 198 east.

## — ANNUAL EVENTS —

### Trek to the Tree
December. (559) 875-4575, fax (559) 875-0745; www.sanger.org/events.html.

Since 1926, the 267-foot-tall **General Grant Tree** in Kings Canyon National Park has been the site of a special Christmas service. In honor of its official status as the Nation's Christmas Tree, a wreath is placed at its base each year by members of the National Park Service. A car caravan leaves from the tiny town of Sanger, and seats are also available by reservation on a chartered bus.

*General Grant Tree*

## — WHAT TO DO —

## Caves

### • Boyden Cavern

*74101 E. Kings Canyon Rd, in Sequoia National Forest, just outside Kings Canyon N.P., (866) 762-2837, (209) 736-2708, fax (209) 736-0330; www.cavern tours.com. Tours daily 10-5, June-Sept; 11-4 Apr-May & Oct-Nov. $10, 3-13 $5.*

This cave is located in spectacular 8,000-foot-deep Kings River Canyon—the deepest canyon in the United States. The guided tour takes about 45 minutes. Baby strollers are not permitted.

### • Crystal Cave

*In Sequoia N.P., (559) 565-3759, fax (559) 565-3728; www.sequoiahistory.org/cave/cave.htm. Tour schedule varies; May-Nov only. $10, seniors $8, 6-12 $5.*

This 48-degree marble cavern (bring a jacket) is reached via a steep 1/4-mile trail. The guided tour takes about 45 minutes. Note that there are no restrooms. Tickets must be purchased at the Foothills or Lodgepole visitor center; they are not sold at the cave entrance. Allow at least 1 1/2 hours to reach the cave. Strollers and baby backpacks are not permitted.

## Fishing

The most popular spots are along Kings River and at the forks of the Kaweah River. A California fishing license is required. Ask about fishing regulations at park visitor centers.

## Horse rentals

*In Cedar Grove, Grant Grove, & Mineral King; www.nps.gov/seki/stables.htm. Closed late fall-spring.*

## Junior Ranger Program

Kids can earn a patch while discovering the parks' resources and learning how to protect them. Ages 5 through 8 earn the Jay Award, ages 9 through 12 the Raven Award. To get started, purchase a Junior Ranger booklet in any visitor center, and follow the instructions. The program operates year-round. For more description, see page 445.

## Trails

Over 900 miles of hiking trails are in these parks. The Big Trees Trail is an easy 2/3-mile loop with interpretive exhibits.

## Unusual trees

Many of these trees are encountered on the drive along the 46-mile **Generals Highway** connecting the two national parks. Some require either a short walk to reach or a drive down a side road. From December through May, this highway occasionally is closed by snow.

### • Auto Log

Cars can be driven onto this fallen sequoia for a photograph.

### • Senate Group and House Group of Sequoias

These are among the most symmetrically formed and nearly perfect of the sequoias. They are reached via the Congress Trail, an easy 2.1-mile walk that begins at the General Sherman Tree.

### • Tunnel Log

Cars can drive through this tunnel carved in a tree that fell across the road in 1937. Note that the upright drive-through-tree, which was actually in Yosemite National Park, went down in a 1969 snowstorm.

## Visitor Centers

*Lodgepole: (559) 565-4436; www.nps.gov/seki/ lpvc.htm; daily, Sat-Sun only in winter; schedule varies. Grant Grove: (559) 565-4307; www.nps.gov/ seki/ggvc.htm; daily 9-5, in summer 8-6, in winter 9:30-4:30. Foothills: (559) 565-3135; www.nps. gov/seki/amvc.htm; daily 8-4:30, in summer to 5.*

See exhibits on the area's wildlife as well as displays on Native Americans and the sequoias. Inquire here about the schedule for nature walks and evening campfire programs.

## — WHERE TO STAY —

## Montecito-Sequoia Lodge

See pages 436 and 441.

## Park Lodging

*Sequoia N.P.: (888) 252-5757, (559) 253-2199; www.visitsequoia.com. Kings Canyon N.P.: (866) K-CANYON, (559) 452-1081; www.sequoia-kingscanyon.com. $-$$$. Children under 12 free. No TVs; some shared baths. Restaurant. Campgrounds: (800) 365-2267.*

At Sequoia, the new 102-room **Wuksachi Lodge** *(64740 Wuksachi Way. Restaurant.)* offers deluxe hotel rooms in three price categories.

Ranger programs are scheduled several nights each week.

Arrangements can be made to backpack 11 miles into the **Bearpaw High Sierra Camp**, where facilities are tent-cabins with canvas sides and wood floors. Hot showers, cots, and linens are provided, and dinner and breakfast are included. Reservations are necessary.

Kings Canyon has both deluxe hotel rooms and rustic cabins.

Campsites are available on a first-come, first-served basis. In summer, reservations are accepted for Lodgepole and Dorst campgrounds in Sequoia National Park.

For more information, request a park brochure that explains the various options in detail.

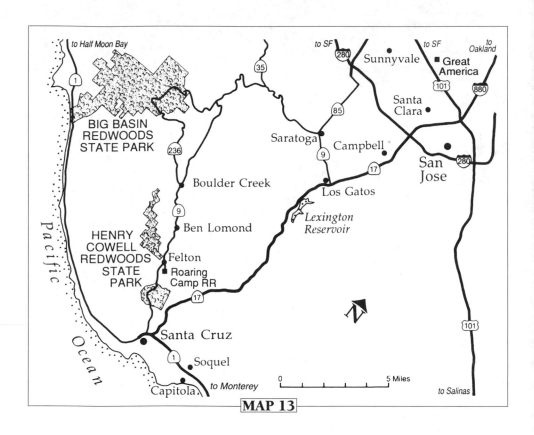

to Half Moon Bay

to SF    to SF    to Oakland

(280)

Sunnyvale    ■ Great America

(1)

(35)

(101)

(880)

Santa Clara ●

BIG BASIN REDWOODS STATE PARK

Saratoga

(85)

Campbell ●

San Jose

(280)

(236)

(9)

(17)

Boulder Creek

Los Gatos

*Pacific*

(9)

Lexington Reservoir

HENRY COWELL REDWOODS STATE PARK

Ben Lomond

Felton

■ Roaring Camp RR

(17)

(101)

Santa Cruz

*Ocean*

(1) Soquel

0    5 Miles

to Monterey

Capitola

to Salinas

**MAP 13**

SANTA CRUZ MOUNTAINS

## Los Gatos

— A LITTLE BACKGROUND —

Tucked in the lush, green Santa Cruz mountains, this upscale community is known for its many antique shops on Main Street and the many boutiques and restaurants lining Santa Cruz Avenue. Another popular shopping and restaurant street is University Avenue. Originally a logging town, its name is Spanish for "the cats," in reference to the mountain lions that once roamed the hills in large numbers.

### — VISITOR INFORMATION —

**Los Gatos Chamber of Commerce**
349 N. Santa Cruz Ave., (408) 354-9300,
fax (408) 399-1594; www.losgatosweb.com.

### — GETTING THERE —

Located approximately 55 miles south of San Francisco, and 10 miles south of San Jose. Take Highway 101 to Highway 17 to the Los Gatos exit.

### — WHAT TO DO —

**Mountain Charley's Saloon**
15 N. Santa Cruz Ave., (408) 395-8880; www.mountaincharleys.com. Tu-Sat noon-2am. Cover varies.

Situated on the second floor of a vintage building and featuring attractive mountain views through a wall of high arched windows, this old-fashioned saloon opened as one of the area's first music bars in 1972—when nearby Palo Alto was a "dry" city. A live band performs nightly, making a visit to this gigantic, jumping saloon an exciting experience. Age minimum is 21.

**Museums of Los Gatos**
(408) 395-7375, fax (408) 395-7386. W-Sun 12-4. Free.

• **Art Museum of Los Gatos**
4 Tait Ave./W. Main St., (408) 354-2646.
Housed in a Spanish-style building dating from 1907, this small museum displays contemporary fine arts and hosts juried shows.

• **History Museum of Los Gatos**
75 Church St./E. Main St., (408) 395-7375.
Located inside the remains of the Forbes Mill flour mill dating from 1854, this tiny venue focuses on town history.

**Parks**

• **Oak Meadow Park**
Off Blossom Hill Rd., (408) 354-6809. $4/vehicle.
This 12-acre park has picnic facilities, baseball diamonds, hiking trails, a 1910

hand-carved English clockwise **carousel** *($1.50)*, a well-equipped playground with an authentic fire engine and airplane to climb on, and a train pulled by a steam locomotive at the narrow-gauge **Billy Jones Wildcat Railroad** *((408) 395-7433; www.bjwrr.org. Sat-Sun 11-3; in summer, daily 10:30-4:30. $1.50, under 2 free.)*.

• **Vasona Lake County Park**
*Off Blossom Hill Rd., (408) 356-2729. Daily 8-dusk. $4/vehicle.*

This 151-acre park is dominated by a huge reservoir where visitors can fish and rent rowboats or paddleboats. At the **Youth Science Institute** *(296 Garden Hill Dr., (408) 356-4945, fax (408) 358-3683; www.ysi-ca.org. M-F 9-5. Free.)*, visitors can see exhibits on water ecology and conservation and use barbecue facilities and a playground.

## — WHERE TO STAY —

### Garden Inn
*46 E. Main St., (866) 868-8383, (408) 354-6446, fax (408) 354-5911; www.gih4me.com. 28 rooms; $$. Some kitchens. Heated pool (seasonal). Breakfast dining voucher.*

These rustic Spanish-style bungalows are in a quiet area just 2 blocks from town. Complimentary use of a nearby health club is available to guests. It is claimed that Marilyn Monroe and Joe DiMaggio honeymooned here.

### Hotel Los Gatos
*210 E. Main St., (866) 335-1700, (408) 335-1700, fax (408) 335-1750; www.hotellosgatos.com. 72 rooms; $$-$$$+. Heated pool; hot tub; sauna; health spa; fitness room. Restaurant; room service. No smoking; no pets.*

Located just down the street from a Ferrari/Bentley showroom, this luxurious hotel has a rustic Italian-country style. Public spaces are decorated with Mexican tiles and pottery, studded leather chairs, and ornate wood-inlayed Moroccan tables. A sort of Mediterranean hacienda, it melds the two architectural styles with a terracotta-tiled roof and spacious interior courtyards with palm trees and fountains. Traditional art is displayed throughout. Guest rooms are furnished luxuriously with colorful silk drapes and comforters, soft Egyptian cotton linens, and tile-and-granite bathrooms, and they are equipped with high-speed internet connections and DVD and CD players. Movies and music can be borrowed at no charge.

**Kuleto's** *((408) 354-8290)* restaurant features Italian fare. For more information, see page 74.

### La Hacienda Inn
*18840 Saratoga-Los Gatos Rd. (Hwy. 9), (800) 235-4570, (408) 354-9230, fax (408) 354-7590; www.lahaciendainn.com. 20 rooms; $$. Children under 6 free. Some kitchens; some wood-burning & gas fireplaces. Heated pool (seasonal); indoor hot tub; fitness room. Continental breakfast; restaurant; room service. No smoking.*

Tucked away from the main highway at the base of the Santa Cruz Mountains, this pleasant inn was founded in 1901 by a former representative of the China-Japan Trading Company who designed it to incorporate a Japanese style. Now this newer inn, built in 1961, has cozy rooms with 12-foot-tall redwood-beamed ceilings and pine and oak furnishings. The 4-acre site features a lushly landscaped garden with colorful flowerbeds and an expansive lawn area.

The adjacent **La Hacienda Restaurant** *((408) 354-6669, fax (408) 354-6764; www.lahaciendaonline.com. L M-Sat, D daily, SunBr.)* offers Italian and continental cuisine.

### Los Gatos Lodge
*50 Saratoga Ave., (800) 231-8676, (408) 354-3300, fax (408) 354-5451; www.losgatoslodge.com. 123 rooms; $$. Children under 12 free. Some kitchens & fireplaces. Heated pool (seasonal); hot tub. Restaurant; room service. Dogs ok.*

Located on attractive, spacious grounds, this contemporary motel provides a putting green and shuffleboard area.

## — WHERE TO EAT —

### Andalé
*6 N. Santa Cruz Ave., (408) 395-4244; also at 21 N. Santa Cruz Ave., (408) 395-8997, fax (408) 399-5564.*

The #21 location is large and spacious, while the founding location at #6 is quite small. For more description, see page 180.

### The Chart House
*115 N. Santa Cruz Ave., (408) 354-1737, fax (408) 395-4553; www.chart-house.com. D daily; $$-$$$. Highchairs, boosters, child portions. Reservations advised.*

Located inside a stately old Victorian mansion, this popular restaurant features an a la carte menu of prime rib, steaks, and fresh seafood. Salads include housemade dressing, and both hot sourdough and squaw breads are available.

### Fleur de Cocoa
*39 N. Santa Cruz Ave., (408) 354-3574, fax (408) 354-9544; www.fleurdecocoa.com. Tu-Sat 7:30-6, Sun 8-4.*

This authentic French pâtisserie presents a case full of croissants, éclairs, and other pastries, plus housemade chocolate. A great hot chocolate is another option.

### Pedro's Restaurant & Cantina
*316 N. Santa Cruz Ave., (408) 354-7570, fax (408) 395-8578; www.pedrosrestaurants.com. L-D daily; $$. Highchairs, boosters, booths, child menu. Reservations advised.*

This popular spot features an adobe-style interior with a bank of highly desirable enclosed booths in back. The delicious Mexican dishes are served in hefty portions. Especially tasty items include chimichangas (deep-fried flour tortillas filled with chicken and topped with guacamole and sour cream), quesadillas (large flour tortillas filled with Jack cheese and topped with guacamole and sour cream), and chicken enchiladas topped with a fabulously tasty mole sauce made with 36 ingredients. Flautas, several tostadas, and an assortment of seafood dishes are also available, and fried ice cream is among the desserts.

# Saratoga

## — A LITTLE BACKGROUND —

Saratoga is a smaller, quieter, and even more picturesque town than Los Gatos.

## — VISITOR INFORMATION —

### Saratoga Chamber of Commerce
*14485 Big Basin Way, (408) 867-0753, fax (408) 867-5213; www.saratogachamber.org.*

## — WHAT TO DO —

### Garrod Farms Stables
*22647 Garrod Rd., (408) 867-9527, fax (408) 741-1169; www.cgv.com. Daily 8:30-4:30; M-F by reservation, Sat-Sun first-come first-served. Horses $30/hr., must be 8 or older; ponies $20/¹/₂-hr.*

Horse trails roam over 200 acres. Shetland ponies are available for children under 8; an adult must walk them with a lead rope.

The **Cooper-Garrod Estate Vineyards** winery *(22645 Garrod Rd., (408) 867-7116, fax (408) 741-8090; www.cgv.com. Tasting M-F 12-5, Sat-Sun 11-5; tour by appt.)* is also located here. It produces estate Chardonnay and Cabernet Sauvignon on 21 acres farmed by the family for over a century. Tasting occurs in the historic Fruit House.

### Hakone Gardens
*21000 Big Basin Way (Hwy. 9), (408) 741-4994, fax (408) 741-4993; www.hakone.com. M-F 10-5, Sat-Sun 11-5. By donation; parking $7. Tea ceremony: 1st Thur of month, by reservation; & 1st Sun of month, Mar-Oct, no reservations; small fee.*

Originally a private garden but now a city park, this is the oldest authentic Japanese-style residential garden in the western hemisphere. It is typical of a mid-17th-century residential garden and is composed of four separate areas: a Hill and Pond Garden, a Tea Garden, a Zen Garden, and a Bamboo Garden (it boasts the largest collection of Japanese bamboo in a public park in the western world). Special features include a Japanese-style house built without nails or adhesives, a pond stocked with eye-catching koi, and three authentic tea ceremony rooms. A simple tea is served in the garden on summer weekends for a small fee, and a picnic area with tables is available.

### Montalvo Center for the Arts and Arboretum
*15400 Montalvo Rd., (408) 961-5800, fax (408) 961-5850; www.villamontalvo.org. Arboretum: Daily 9-5. Gallery: Schedule varies. Free.*

Once the summer home of Senator James Phelan, this majestic 1912 Mediterranean-style estate is now the county center for fine arts. It also serves as a bird sanctuary. Self-guided nature trails wind through the 175-acres of gardens. Performing arts events—some especially for children—are presented June through

September in a natural outdoor amphitheater and year-round in an indoor Carriage House.

## Savannah Chanelle Vineyards
*23600 Congress Springs Rd./Hwy. 9, (408) 741-2934, fax (408) 867-4824; www.savannahchanelle.com. Tasting daily 11-5; tour by appt.*

Established in 1892, this winery has original plantings dating from 1910 and 1920. Its rustic tasting room is located at the end of a steep, woodsy back road, and it is surrounded by tall redwoods and 14 acres of vineyards that include the oldest Cabernet Franc vineyard in the state. Picnic tables are available.

### — WHERE TO STAY —

## The Inn at Saratoga
*20645 Fourth St., (800) 543-5020, (408) 867-5020, fax (408) 741-0981; www.innatsaratoga.com. 5 stories; 46 rooms; $$-$$$+. Children under 18 free. Afternoon snack, continental breakfast. No smoking; no pets.*

Combining an old-time Victorian feeling with modern luxurious amenities and a contemporary decor, this hotel is set in a quiet canyon behind busy Highway 9. Guest rooms all face a forest of old eucalyptus through which winds gurgling Saratoga Creek. Afternoon wine and appetizers are served either in the cozy lobby or outdoors on a sylvan patio. Families will appreciate that Wildwood Park, with its ample playground, is just across the creek.

## Sanborn Park Hostel
*15808 Sanborn Rd., (408) 741-0166; www.sanborn parkhostel.org. 39 beds; private rooms.*

Constructed of logs, this rustic arts and crafts-style building dates from 1908. It is located in a secluded redwood grove in the area's foothills. The naturally fragrant, quiet setting has plenty of hiking trails, plus a volleyball court and barbecue facilities.

Just down the road in Sanborn-Skyline County Park are campsites, picnic tables, and the **Youth Science Institute** *(www.ysi-ca.org. Tu-Sat 12-4:30, also Sun in summer. Free.)*. For more description, see page 368.

# San Lorenzo Valley

### — A LITTLE BACKGROUND —

Tucked into a dense redwood forest, this area has simple motels and cabins that are mostly relics left from a long ago heyday. Still, the abundance of tall trees, trails, and swimming holes, as well as reasonable prices, make it a choice destination for bargain-hunting vacationers.

Traveling is best done in daylight. Though the back roads are lightly traveled, they are also curvy and slow. And, of course, the forest scenery is part of the reason for coming here.

### — VISITOR INFORMATION —

## San Lorenzo Valley Chamber of Commerce
*P.O. Box 67, Felton 95018, (831) 335-2764.*

### — GETTING THERE —

Located approximately 70 miles south of San Francisco. Take Highway 280 to Highway 84 to Highway 35 to Highway 9. It is a beautiful drive over sun-dappled two-lane roads. On weekends, the roads are filled with bicyclists, but on weekdays, it is smooth sailing.

### — WHAT TO DO —

## Ben Lomond Park
*9525 Mill St., in Ben Lomond, (831) 454-7956, fax (831) 464-7950; www.scparks.com. Daily 8am-sunset. $1.*

This dammed-up, deep-water swimming hole has a sandy beach, a playground, and shaded picnic tables with barbecue facilities. In summer, equipment rentals are available, and lifeguards are on duty.

## Big Basin Redwoods State Park
*21600 Big Basin Way, in Boulder Creek, 8 mi. from town, (831) 338-8860, fax (831) 338-8863; www.parks.ca.gov. Daily sunrise-sunset. $5/vehicle.*

California's first and oldest state park, Big Basin has over 80 miles of hiking and equestrian trails in its 20,000 acres of redwood forest. The easy, canopy-shaded .6-mile Redwood Loop Trail is self-guiding and relatively flat. It leads to the park's most interesting redwoods: Mother-of-the-Forest (tallest in park at 329 feet); Father-of the-Forest (with a 66-foot circumference); and Zoo Tree (imagined animals are seen within). The trail also has a lovely stone water fountain and is dotted with log benches. Other hikes include the 10.3-mile trail leading to 65-foot-high Berry Creek Falls, and the especially popular Skyline to the Sea backpacking trail. The Nature Lodge museum features an assortment of exhibits, and a woodsy log cabin Visitor Center built in 1938 by the CCC provides general information. Campfire programs are often scheduled in a huge outdoor amphitheatre with seats carved into logs. A dramatic bloom of wild azaleas and rhododendrons is seen each spring, when globe lilies and hairy star tulips are also seen. A Junior Ranger Program for children operates here (see page 445). Inexpensive tent cabins can be reserved *((800) 874-TENT, (831) 338-4745; www.calparks co.com.)*; an optional package includes food and bedding. Traditional campsites and hike-in campsites are also available.

### Felton Covered Bridge Park
*Off Graham Hill Rd./Mt. Hermon Rd., in Felton, (831) 425-1234, fax (831) 462-8330; www.scparks. com. Daily 8am-sunset. Free.*

Built over the San Lorenzo River in 1892, this redwood bridge is restored to its original condition and can be walked on. A state historical landmark, it measures 34 feet high and is the tallest covered bridge in the U.S. Facilities include a nice grassy area with picnic tables, barbecues, and a playground.

### Hallcrest Vineyards
*379 Felton Empire Rd., in Felton, (800) OWW-WINE, (831) 335-4441, fax (831) 335-4450; www.webwinery. com/hallcrest. Tasting daily 12-5; tour by appt.*

Hidden behind a ridge of mansions, this winery is noted for its Estate White Riesling. All wines in their **Organic Wine Works** division are made from organically grown grapes. No sulfites are used, and wines are approved for vegans. This division is one of only two federally licensed organic wine processors in the United States. Picnic tables are provided on a shady deck just outside the tasting room.

### Henry Cowell Redwoods State Park
*101 N. Big Tree Park Rd., off Hwy. 9, in Felton, 2 mi. S of town, (831) 335-4598; www.parks.ca.gov. Daily sunrise-sunset. $5/vehicle.*

A number of trails lead through this park's redwood groves, including the easy, mile-long Redwood Circle Trail that visits the hollow General Fremont Tree within which the general is said to have once camped. Trail guides are available at the Nature Center. Campsites are available.

### Highlands Park
*8500 Hwy. 9, in Ben Lomond, (831) 454-7956; www.scparks.com. Daily 8-dusk. Free.*

The grounds of this old estate have been transformed into a park with a playground, a skate park, two softball diamonds, three tennis courts, a volleyball court, and picnic tables. Nature trails lead to a sandy river beach.

### Roaring Camp & Big Trees Narrow-Gauge Railroad
*On Graham Hill Rd., in Felton, (831) 335-4484, fax (831) 335-3509; www.roaringcamp.com. Schedule varies. $18, 3-12 $12; parking $6.*

This 6-mile, hour-long steam train ride winds through virgin redwoods and crosses over a spectacular trestle. About the time passengers start feeling a little restless, the train makes a short stretch stop at Cathedral Grove— an impressive circle of tall, 800-year-old redwoods said to have a 3,000-year-old root system! Another stop is made at Bear Mountain, where riders may disembark for a picnic or hike and then return on a later train. Bring warm wraps. Though this area enjoys warm to hot weather in the summer, it can get chilly on the train ride. Picnic facilities are available. Another train, the **Big Trees & Pacific Railway** (*$20, 3-12 $15.*), makes two trips each day between Roaring Camp and the Santa Cruz Beach

Boardwalk. The round-trip excursion takes 3 hours.

An outdoor **chuck wagon barbecue** *(Sat-Sun 12-3; May-Oct only.)* operates near the depot, and the **Red Caboose Saloon** dispenses short-order items. Be sure to save some tidbits for hungry ducks and geese in the lake.

Special events include the **Civil War Encampment and Battles** in May and a chocolate **Easter egg hunt** for kids during spring vacation.

## San Lorenzo Valley Museum
*12547 Hwy. 9, in Boulder Creek, (831) 338-8382, fax (831) 338-8332; www.slvmuseum.com. W, F, Sat, Sun 12-4. Free.*

Situated within a church built completely of precious heart of redwood in 1885, this museum shows rare photographs of the area's early logging days. A recreated early-1900s kitchen and a Victorian parlor are also displayed. A self-guided walking tour of historical Boulder Creek is available here.

### — WHERE TO STAY —

## Econolodge
*9733 Hwy. 9, in Ben Lomond, (800) 676-1456, (831) 336-2292, fax (831) 336-0554; www.stayinthe redwoods.com. 21 rooms, 1 cottage. $-$$$. 1 kitchen. Heated pool (seasonal). Continental breakfast.*

These standard motel rooms are set back against a strand of tall redwoods. A pretty garden surrounds the large pool area, and the property is peaceful and well maintained.

## Felton Crest Inn
*780 El Solyo Heights Dr., in Felton, (800) 474-4011, (831) 335-4011, fax: 831-335-4011; www.felton crest.com. 4 rooms; $$$+. Unsuitable for small children. 1 wood-burning stove. Continental breakfast. No smoking; no pets.*

Situated up a hill, at the end of a private road in a rural residential area, this B&B is surrounded by an acre of redwoods. A contemporary brown-shingled mountain house with mustard-yellow trim, it is reminiscent of lodgings found in Germany's Black Forest. Public spaces include a big sundeck, a sheltered tea area with a hammock, and a cheery breakfast room. Beds are made with soft featherbeds and topped with pouffy white duvets—all covered with lovely cut-lace linens. It's like being on

Mick's cloud. The third-floor Treetop Penthouse has a knotty-pine cathedral ceiling with exposed rafters, a stained glass window, and a private deck open to the fragrant tall trees. Deeply dark, silent nights are part of the deal.

## Fern River Resort Motel
*5250 Hwy. 9, in Felton, (831) 335-4412, fax (831) 335-2418; www.fernriver.com. 14 cabins; $-$$. Children under 3 free. Most kitchens; some gas fireplaces. Hot tub. No smoking.*

These modernized knotty-pine cabins are located on the river across from Henry Cowell Redwoods State Park. The 5-acre lot features a redwood-shaded outdoor recreation area with volleyball, tetherball, and Ping-Pong. Guests have use of a private beach on the river, and riverside picnic tables are provided.

## Jaye's Timberlane Resort
*8705 Hwy. 9, in Ben Lomond, (831) 336-5479; www.jayestimberlane.com. 10 cabins; $-$$. All kitchens; some fireplaces. Solar-heated pool (seasonal).*

These renovated cabins are scattered on spacious grounds shaded by redwoods.

## Merrybrook Lodge
*13420 Big Basin Way, in Boulder Creek, (831) 338-6813. 8 rooms; $. Some kitchens; some wood-burning fireplaces & stoves. Dogs sometimes ok.*

Tucked among towering redwoods, some of these cottages and motel-style units overlook Boulder Creek.

### — WHERE TO EAT —

## The Brook Room
*11570 Hwy. 9, in Brookdale, (831) 338-6433, fax (831) 338-3066; www.brookdalelodge.com. D W-Sun, SunBr; $-$$$. Child menu.*

A natural brook flows right through the center of this unique dining room that has been around almost forever. Once mentioned in "Ripley's Believe It or Not!" it must be seen to be believed. Diners sit streamside, enjoying the pleasant, continuous sound of water rushing over stones and viewing the occasional trout. A well-priced champagne brunch buffet is available on Sundays, while dinner brings on a more expensive surf-and-turf menu. Prime Rib is a bargain on Thursdays, and live jazz begins at 5 p.m. on Sundays.

**Brookdale Lodge** *(46 rooms; $-$$$. Children under 13 free. Indoor heated pool. Restaurant. No pets.).* Built as the headquarters for a lumber mill in 1870 and converted into a hotel in 1900, this complex features standard '50s-style motel rooms and cottages. Some family rooms and two theme suites—the Marilyn Monroe Suite and the Enchanted Forest Suite—are available. Pool hours vary by season and are subject to lifeguard availability.

## Ciao! Bella!!

*9217 Hwy. 9, in Ben Lomond, (831) 336-9221, fax (831) 336-4561. L-D daily; $$. Reservations advised.*

"We are the people our parents warned us against," promises the menu. That might be referring to the slightly off-center waitstaff. They sing. They dance. They have tattoos. Funky is an understatement, but fun isn't, what with parking spaces reserved for Elvis and Fonzie and the gang. Though seating inside is cozy and atmospheric, dining outside on the deck within a natural cathedral circle of tall, tall redwood trees is not to be missed. But most importantly the food is tasty, and each meal begins with bread and an addictive dipping sauce of fresh garlic mixed at table with olive oil and balsamic vinegar. Menu items include pasta aplenty, plus an assortment of salads and heavier meat dishes.

## Picnic Pick-Up

• **New Leaf Community Market**
*13159 Hwy. 9, in Boulder Creek, (831) 338-7211; also at 6240 Hwy. 9, in Felton, (831) 335-7322.*

Everything needed for a delicious, healthy picnic—and more—is found in this popular local grocery.

## Scopazzi's Restaurant

*13300 Big Basin Way, in Boulder Creek, (831) 338-4444. L-D Tu-Sun; $$. Highchairs, boosters, child menu. Reservations advised.*

This spacious, rustic mountain lodge has operated as a restaurant since 1902. Known for its Italian meals, the menu offers cannelloni, veal scaloppine, and chicken cacciatora along with fried prawns, pepper steak flambé, and quail en cocotte. Children should be pleased to see the options of a hamburger, a grilled cheese sandwich, pizza, and spaghetti.

## Tyrolean Inn

*9600 Hwy. 9, in Ben Lomond, (831) 336-5188, fax (831) 336-2804; www.tyroleaninn.com. D Tu-Sat, SunBr; $$. Highchairs, boosters, child menu. Reservations advised.*

Appearing as something right out of Germany's Black Forest, this family-operated restaurant prepares exquisite Austrian-German cuisine. An interesting assortment of imported beers is available, including a refreshing Weiss Bier cloudy with yeast and served in a tall glass over a wedge of lemon. The expansive entree selection includes sauerbraten and schnitzels, and among the desserts are housemade fresh apple strudel and Black Forest cake. With 24 hours notice, the kitchen will prepare any venison, hare, or duck specialty dish desired. In good weather, brunch is available on a patio sheltered by mature redwoods. Dinner is served in a romantic, cozy dining room heated by two fireplaces.

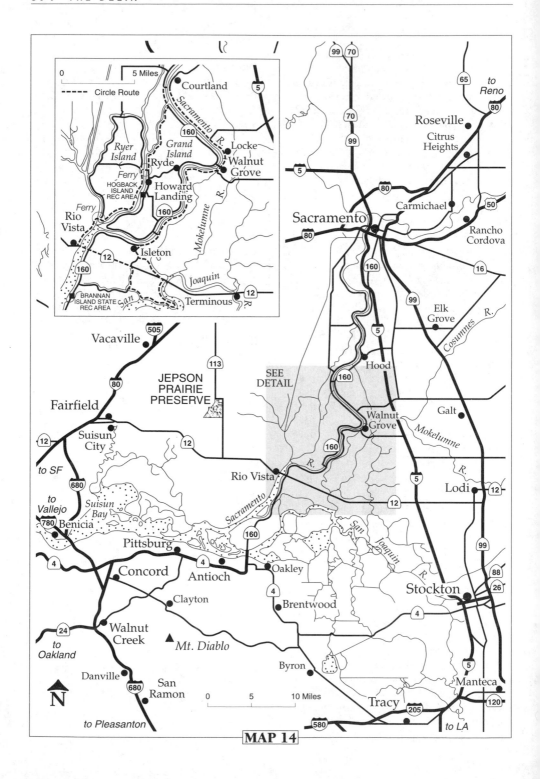

### Inset map

0 — 5 Miles
- - - Circle Route

Courtland
Sacramento R.
160
Locke
Ryer Island
Grand Island
Ryde
Walnut Grove
Ferry
HOGBACK ISLAND REC AREA
Howard Landing
160
Mokelumne R.
Ferry
Rio Vista
12
Isleton
160
San Joaquin R.
BRANNAN ISLAND STATE REC AREA
Terminous
12

### Main map

99  70
65
to Reno
80
70
Roseville
99
Citrus Heights
5
80
Carmichael
50
Sacramento
Rancho Cordova
80
160
16
99
Elk Grove
Cosumnes R.
Vacaville
505
Hood
113
SEE DETAIL
160
Galt
JEPSON PRAIRIE PRESERVE
80
Fairfield
Walnut Grove
Mokelumne R.
12
Suisun City
12
160
R.
to SF
Rio Vista
5
Lodi
12
680
to Vallejo
Suisun Bay
Sacramento R.
12
780  Benicia
San Joaquin R.
99
Pittsburg
160
88
4
4
Oakley
Stockton
26
Concord
Antioch
Clayton
4
24
Brentwood
4
Walnut Creek
to Oakland
▲ Mt. Diablo
Byron
Manteca
Danville
680
San Ramon
0    5    10 Miles
5
to Pleasanton
Tracy
120
205
580
to LA

**N**

**MAP 14**

# THE DELTA

## — A LITTLE BACKGROUND —

Composed of flat land, crisscrossed by more than 700 miles of rivers and sloughs (pronounced "slews"), this agricultural area is filled with scenic roads running along raised levees. The Delta is formed by five major rivers and many more sloughs, cuts, and canals. The two largest rivers—the Sacramento and the San Joaquin—join here and flow on out to the Pacific Ocean via San Francisco Bay. Bridges abound (there are at least 70), and many can be raised to accommodate large boats. Popular for a houseboat vacation (see page 441), this area is also pleasant for just a day trip. Pack along a good detailed map, as the roads here are maze-like, and try to avoid driving at night, when the levee roads can be dangerous.

Trendy hasn't yet hit this area and probably never will. Food is basic, and wine is sometimes mistreated. However, people in the area enjoy a good time, and many eating establishments book live entertainment in the evening.

## — VISITOR INFORMATION —

### California Delta Chambers & Visitors Bureau
*P.O. Box 6, Isleton 95641, (209) 367-9840; www.californiadelta.org.*

### Hal Schell's Delta Map and Guide
*P.O. Box 9140, Stockton 95208, (209) 951-7821; www.californiadeltadawdling.com. $3.*

This indispensable aid is available in many Delta stores. To secure one in advance, send $4 to the above address.

## — GETTING THERE —

Located approximately 60 miles east of San Francisco. Take Highway 80 north to Highway 4 east. Continue following Highway 4 as it turns into Highway 160 (River Road) and crosses the gigantic arch that is the John A. Nejedly Bridge. Highway 160 continues north into Sacramento.

## — ANNUAL EVENTS —

### Pear Fair
*July; last Sun. In Courtland; (916) 775-2000; www.pearfair.com. Free; parking $5.*

The Delta is the foremost pear-growing area in the country. This annual celebration of the harvest features a parade, kiddie rides, and, of course, plenty of pear foods. Contests include pear bobbing, pear pie eating, and pear peeling—in which the longest continuous peel after 10 minutes wins. A competition to find the area's largest pear is also part of the fun.

The following towns are listed in the order in which they appear on the circle tour highlighted with broken lines on the map on page 374. It is possible to start the tour at any point. Following it takes drivers through the area's most scenic towns, across several different types of bridges, and on two car ferries.

# Isleton

## — A LITTLE BACKGROUND —

Located at the geographic center of the Delta, this picturesque, isolated town is one of the larger in the area. Once a bustling port city with a population of more than 2,000, it is now home to only 830 people.

## — VISITOR INFORMATION —

**Isleton Chamber of Commerce**
*308 Second St., (916) 777-5880, fax (916) 777-4330; www.isletoncoc.org.*

## — ANNUAL EVENTS —

**Asian Celebration**
*March. (916) 777-5880; www.isletoncoc.org. Free.*
  The town celebrates its Asian heritage with the Great March of China, lion dancers, an Asian gift bazaar, ancient cultural rites, Asian foods, and the Invitational Rickshaw Races.

**Crawdad Festival**
*June; Father's Day weekend. (916) 777-5880; www.isletoncoc.org. Free.*
  Benefiting the town Children's Fund, this festival features live music and entertainment, activities such as a Crawdad Race and a Crawdad Petting Zoo, and a mess of cooked crawdads for eating.

## — WHERE TO EAT —

**Hotel Del Rio**
*209 2nd St., (916) 777-6033, fax (916) 777-6123; www.hoteldelrio.com. D Tu-Sun; $$. Child portions. Reservations advised.*
  The specialty of the house here is prime rib in three sizes: petite, regular, and double. Broasted chicken and deep-fried prawns round out the menu, and big plates of Cajun-style crawdads are sometimes available. All entrees include visits to the salad bar. Live music is scheduled in the bar on Saturday and Sunday nights. Inexpensive **rooms** furnished attractively with antiques are available upstairs.

# Walnut Grove

## — A LITTLE BACKGROUND —

This town, which grew up on both sides of the river, is linked by the first cantilever bridge built west of the Mississippi. Most of the decaying east side of town, which holds the remnants of a Chinatown, is on the National Register of Historic Places. The west side is a well-maintained residential area.

## — VISITOR INFORMATION —

**Walnut Grove Area Chamber of Commerce**
*14195 River Rd., no phone; www.walnutgrove.com.*

## — WHERE TO EAT —

**Giusti's**
*14743 Walnut Grove Rd., 4 mi. W of town, (916) 776-1808; www.giustis.com. L-D Tu-Sat, SunBr; no D Jan-Feb; $$. Highchairs, boosters, child portions. No reservations. No cards.*
  In a rustic landmark building standing at the junction of the North Fork of the Mokelumne River and Snodgrass Slough, this restaurant has been dishing up family-style Italian dinners since 1896. For lunch, it's burgers, pastas, and steaks. The dining room overlooks the river, and the bar ceiling is covered with more than 950 baseball caps.

# Locke

## — A LITTLE BACKGROUND —

Said to be the only town in the country that was built entirely by and for Chinese immigrants, this tiny town dates back to 1915. Its narrow Main Street is lined with picturesque weathered wooden buildings, many of which are still inhabited. In its prime, it had more than 3,000 residents. Now the aging Chinese residents, down to only about 50, are often seen sitting on benches on the wooden walkways, just watching. When leaving here, continue the circle tour as indicated or backtrack to Walnut Grove, cross the river, and continue south to Ryde.

*The Real McCoy*

## — WHAT TO DO —

### Dai Loy Museum
*On Main St., (916) 776-1661; www.locketown.com/ museum.htm. Thur-F 11-4:30, Sat-Sun 11-5. $1, children 50¢.*

Located within what was the town gambling hall from 1916 to 1951, this museum fills visitors in on the town's history as a Chinese outpost. The Central Gaming Hall, with its original furniture and gaming tables, and the low-ceilinged dealers' bedrooms, located upstairs, can be viewed, and interesting era photographs hang on the walls throughout.

## — WHERE TO EAT —

### Al's Place
*13936 Main St., (916) 776-1800; www.locketown. com/als.htm. L-D daily; $. Highchairs, boosters. No reservations. No cards.*

Once a speakeasy, this restaurant's unsavory looks might cause many people to pass it by. But once through the bar, which can be rowdy even at lunchtime, diners enter a windowless back room and can seat themselves at simple Formica picnic tables with benches. In addition to a steak sandwich served with a side of tasty grilled garlic bread, which used to be the only thing on the menu, hamburgers and chicken sandwiches are now available. Jars of peanut butter and apricot jam adorn each table and are meant to be used with the steak. Parents can sometimes strike a deal with a waitress to bring extra bread so their kids can make peanut butter & jelly sandwiches. At dinner, when the place gets more crowded, the steak goes up a bit in price and is served with sides of fries, pasta, French bread, and grilled mushrooms. Chicken and pasta are also available. When leaving, stop by the bar to find out how dollar bills get stuck to the 2-story-high ceiling. It costs only $1 to find out. Stuck without a buck? An ATM is on the premises.

# Ryde

## — WHAT TO DO —

### Car ferries
*Free.*

Catch the old-time diesel-powered, cable-guided **Howard's Landing Ferry**, also known as the *J-Mack*, off Grand Island Road. It holds about six cars, and waits are usually short. (Note that it closes down for lunch from 12 to 12:30.) Once on Ryer Island, take Ryer Road south to the **Ryer Island Ferry**, also known as *The Real McCoy*. After crossing, follow the road into Rio Vista.

## Hogback Island Recreation Area
*On Grand Island Rd., www.sacparks.net. $4/vehicle.*

A grassy picnic area is bounded on one side by Steamboat Slough and on the other by a boat-launching lagoon. This isn't a good swimming area, but there are access spots that are fine for getting feet wet.

### — WHERE TO EAT —

## Grand Island Mansion
*13415 Grand Island Rd., in Walnut Grove, (916) 775-1705; www.grandislandmansion.com. SunBr; $$. Boosters, child portions. Reservations required.*

Across the island, this spot is open only on Sunday for an opulent champagne brunch. Diners are welcome to tour the mansion and grounds.

## Ryde Hotel
*14340 Hwy. 160, 3 mi. S of Walnut Grove, (888) 717-RYDE, (916) 776-1318, fax (916) 776-1195; www.rydehotel.com. SunBr; seasonal schedule; $$. Highchairs, boosters, child portions. Reservations advised.*

Built in 1926 and once owned by actor Lon Chaney, this colorful pink stucco, art deco hotel operated a basement speakeasy during Prohibition. It is claimed that Herbert Hoover, who was a Prohibitionist, announced his presidential candidacy in 1928 in this very hotel while standing, ironically, above a large stash of bootleg booze. Now beautifully restored, the hotel once again serves elegant dinners in its dining room. Live music accompanies Saturday night dinner. **Guest rooms** *(4 stories, 32 rooms; $-$$. Continental breakfast Sat-Sun. No smoking.)* are also available.

# Rio Vista

### — VISITOR INFORMATION —

## Rio Vista Chamber of Commerce
*75 Main St., (707) 374-2700, fax (707) 374-2424; www.riovista.org.*

### — WHAT TO DO —

## Brannan Island State Recreation Area
*17645 Hwy. 160, 3 mi. S of town, (916) 777-6671; www.parks.ca.gov. Daily sunrise-sunset. Visitor Center: Sat-Sun. $4/vehicle.*

Located on a knoll, this 336-acre park offers slough-side picnic and swimming areas and a short nature trail. Campsites are available.

## Victorian homes
*On Second St.*

Second Street is also known as Millionaires' Row.

### — WHERE TO EAT —

## Foster's Big Horn
*143 Main St., (707) 374-2511. L-D Tu-Sun; $-$$. Highchairs, boosters, booths, child menu. Reservations accepted. No cards.*

Opened in 1931, this restaurant features walls lined with more than 250 mounted big game heads—including a full-grown elephant that is the largest mammal trophy in any collection in the world, the largest mounted moose head in the world, and a rare giraffe head. Gathered by the late hunter William Foster, who shot most of the wild animals himself, it is the world's largest collection of big game trophies. An attractive bar area in front leads to an open dining room with high ceilings and comfortable booths. Sandwiches and hamburgers are on the lunch menu, and steak and seafood on the dinner menu.

## The Point Waterfront Restaurant
*120 Marina Dr., in Delta Marina, (707) 374-5400, fax (707) 374-2542; www.pointrestaurant.com. L Tu-Sat, D Tu-Sun, SunBr; $$. Highchairs, boosters, booths, child menu.*

Overlooking the Sacramento River at its widest point, this comfortable, well-maintained restaurant has many roomy booths. The lunch

menu features housemade soups and sandwiches. Dinner entrees include prime rib,
scampi, and chicken Dijon. Photos illustrating
Humphrey the Whale's well-publicized visit to
the area are displayed in the entryway.

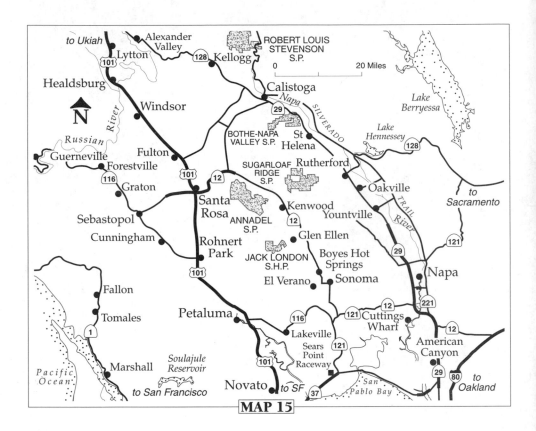

MAP 15

# WINE COUNTRY

## – A LITTLE BACKGROUND –

California's first wineries were appendages of the 21 Franciscan missions that were built a day's ride by horseback from each other in a chain reaching from San Diego to Sonoma. The missions produced the wine for sacramental use. Eventually the church gave up making wine, and the art passed into the realm of private enterprise.

Presently Sonoma County and Napa County are literally erupting with new small family wineries. Winemaking has become a hobby with many city folks who have bought themselves modest vineyard retreats.

The most popular route for wine tasting is in the Napa Valley along Highway 29 between Oakville and Calistoga. Not far behind is scenic Highway 12 in the Sonoma Valley. When visiting these stretches of highway, which are heavily concentrated with wineries, try to remain selective. Experts suggest not planning to taste at more than four wineries in one day.

Though a visit to the Wine Country is enjoyable at any time of year, fall just might be the most beautiful season. This is when the grapevine leaves turn brilliant hues of gold and red, and "the crush" is in full swing. Workers are seen in the fields, and gondolas laden with grapes move slowly down the highway delivering their bounty to the wineries. But because everyone is working to beat the clock, winery personnel are less available to give visitors quality time. However, at this time of year the crowds, like the hot temperatures, have subsided, making it the perfect time for sampling some wine, doing a little feasting, and relaxing amid this area's beauty.

Young children can be difficult on a winery tour. Out of courtesy to the other tour participants—a noisy child interferes with the guide's presentation—parents might consider having a member of their party stay with the children while the others go on a tour. Most wineries don't require taking a tour before tasting. Or visit a winery with a self-guided tour. It's a nice idea to bring along some plastic wine glasses and a bottle of grape juice so children can "taste," too.

Many wineries have picnic areas. An ideal itinerary is to tour a winery, taste, and then purchase a bottle of wine to drink with a picnic lunch.

A wrinkle in the pleasure of wine tasting is that many wineries now charge for tasting. Sometimes the charge permits tasters to keep their glass as a souvenir or is applied to a wine purchase. Tasting fees tend to be imposed by smaller wineries with expensive vintages, and their purpose seems to be to keep the less serious tasters away. Some wineries don't charge for tasting their less expensive wines but do impose a charge for their premium wines. Charges change regularly, and occasionally a winery will charge one day but not the next. It's best to call ahead to determine the charge or just to expect that a fee of around $5 to $10 will be levied when tasting premium wines. A few wineries now also charge for tours.

Some tasting rooms provide vertical tastings, which portray the aging process of a varietal, and cross tastings, which show the different results that varied treatment of the same grapes can cause. To arrange a special tasting, call ahead.

### — GETTING THERE —
#### —By Cruise Ship—
**Clipper Cruise Line**
*(800) 325-0010, (314) 655-6700, fax (314) 655-6670; www.clippercruise.com.*

### — ANNUAL EVENTS —
**Carols in the Caves**
*December. (925) 866-9559; www.carolsinthe caves.com. $38; unsuitable for children under 10.*

In spectacular settings, David Auerbach performs seasonal music selections using rare and unusual instruments he has collected from around the world: the panpipes of South America, the Celtic harp of Ireland, the steel drums of Trinidad. Instruments and winery sites change each year. Mr. Auerbach also performs in winery caves during the summer and fall.

### — WHAT TO DO —
**California Wine Tours**
*22455 Broadway, in Sonoma, (800) 294-6386, (707) 939-7225, fax (707) 939-7240; www.california winetours.com.*

Customized winery tours to any region of the wine country can be arranged. Riders just sit back and relax in a stretch limo, sipping something cool from the complimentary beverage bar while leaving the driving to a classy tuxedoed professional. Printed itineraries are provided. Round-trip ferry rides from Pier 39 in San Francisco can be included for an additional fee.

# Sonoma

### — VISITOR INFORMATION —
**Sonoma Valley Visitors Bureau**
*453 First St. East, (707) 996-1090, fax (707) 996-9212; www.sonomavalley.com.*

### — GETTING THERE —
Located approximately 45 miles north of San Francisco. Take Highway 101 to Highway 37 to Highway 121 to Highway 12.

### — ANNUAL EVENTS —
**Valley of the Moon Vintage Festival**
*September. (707) 996-2109; www.sonomavinfest.com. Free.*

Begun in 1887 as a celebration of the harvest, this old-time event kicks off in the historic Barracks each year with an evening tasting of elite Sonoma Valley wines. Free daytime events include a Blessing of the Grapes, several parades, and a re-enactment of the Bear Flag Revolt (during the revolt American soldiers seized the town from General Vallejo, taking down the Mexican flag and raising the bear flag—which later became California's state flag). Messy grape-stomping competitions, in which one person stomps while the other holds a bottle under the spigot, are also part of the fun.

### — WHAT TO DO —
**Depot Park Museum**
*270 First St. West, (707) 938-1762; www.vom.com/ depot. W-Sun 1-4:30. Free.*

Operated by volunteers from the Sonoma Historical Society, this tiny museum is housed in the restored Northwestern Pacific Railroad Depot and features changing historical and railroad exhibits. Adjacent Depot Park has a playground and picnic area. A bicycle path following the old railroad tracks here originates at Sebastiani Winery.

**Infineon Raceway**
*At intersection of Hwys. 37 & 121, (800) 870-RACE, (707) 938-8448, fax (707) 938-8430; www.infineon raceway.com. Schedule & ticket prices vary; closed Dec-Jan; under 12 free.*

Facilities for car races here include a 2.52-mile course with 12 turns and a $1/4$-mile drag strip. Concession stands dispense fast food, and grassy hillsides provide perfect picnic perches.

## Ramekins
*450 W. Spain St., (707) 933-0450 x10, fax (707) 933-0451; www.ramekins.com.*

Newly constructed in a semi-rural setting, this unusual building of solid, 2-foot-thick rammed-earth walls holds a delightful cooking school. It features subtle, whimsical, food-related decorative touches—such as stair railings resembling asparagus stalks—and is furnished with rustic light-pine pieces. Students dice and measure and stir while learning new techniques in a well-equipped teaching kitchen. Short classes are scheduled year-round in all styles of cooking, and eating the results with fellow students is a big part of the fun.

Spacious, tastefully decorated **guest rooms** *((707) 933-0452. 5 rooms; $$-$$$. Continental breakfast.)* are available upstairs. Some have high four-poster beds. Bathrooms are particularly interesting. Some are equipped with an unusual raised stone sink placed so that its bottom is flush with the counter top, and some have contemporary-style open showers. Stainless steel soup ladles double as towel racks.

## Sonoma Plaza

This town square—the largest in the state and a National Historic Landmark—was designed by General Vallejo in 1834 for troop maneuvers. Basically an old-fashioned park, it is great for picnics and has a playground and tiny duck pond. City Hall, which is located here, acted as the Tuscany County Courthouse on TV's *Falcon Crest.*

## Sonoma State Historic Park
*On the plaza, along Spain St., (707) 938-1519; www.parks.ca.gov. Daily 10-5. $2, under 17 free.*

This extensive park preserves structures dating from the early 1800s, when General Mariano Guadalupe Vallejo, founder of Sonoma, was Mexico's administrator of Northern California.

### • Barracks
This 2-story, whitewashed adobe building once housed Vallejo's soldiers. It now contains historical exhibits. Vallejo drilled his soldiers across the street in what is now the town square.

### • Mission San Francisco Solano de Sonoma
This re-created mission is next door and across the street from the Barracks. Founded in 1823 and the most northerly and last in the chain of California missions, this historic site has been through a lot. It burned to the ground twice, was the victim of a Native American uprising, and sustained serious damage in the 1906 earthquake. Then it went through a period as a saloon, a winery, and even a hennery. It now houses a museum and an 1840s parish church. A collection of watercolors depicting each of California's 21 missions is on permanent display. The paintings were done in 1903 by Chris Jorgensen, who traveled from mission to mission by horse and buggy. An adobe section of the mission's original quadrangle is located near the church, which is said to host a ghost, and an impressive old prickly pear cactus forest graces the courtyard.

### • Toscano Hotel
*20 E. Spain St., on the plaza, (707) 938-5889; www.sonomahistoricpreservation.org. Tours: Sat-M 1-4.*

This beautifully restored mining-era hotel was built in 1858.

### • General Vallejo's Home
*At W. Third St./W. Spain St., (707) 938-9559. Self-guided tour daily; docent tours: F-Sun at 1 & 2.*

Located at the end of a long, tree-shaded lane 1/2 mile west of the plaza, this classic 2-story Victorian Gothic has its original furnishings. Shaded picnic tables and another giant prickly pear cactus garden are found here.

## Sonoma Train Town
*20264 Broadway, (707) 938-3912; www.traintown.com. F-Sun 10-5; daily in summer. Train $3.75, other rides $1.75.*

A miniature steam train (a diesel engine is used on weekdays) winds through 10 acres during the 20-minute ride here. It passes through forests and tunnels and crosses both a 70-foot double-truss bridge and a 50-foot steel-girder bridge. During a 10-minute stop at a miniature 1800s mining town, where the train takes on water, riders detrain at a petting zoo inhabited by sheep, goats, ducks, and llamas. An antique merry-go-round, full-size Ferris wheel, airplane ride, snack bar, and picnic area are available at the station.

## Vasquez House

*129 E. Spain St., in El Paseo de Sonoma, (707) 938-0510; www.sonomahistoricpreservation.org. W-Sun 1:30-4:30; $. Free admission.*

Built in 1856, this refurbished wood-frame house features a tearoom where visitors can relax over homemade pastries and a pot of tea.

## Vintage Aircraft Company

*23982 Arnold Dr., off Hwy. 121 at Sonoma Valley Airport, 2 mi. N of raceway, in Schellville, (707) 938-2444; www.vintageaircraft.com. W-M. $130+. Reservations advised.*

A pilot here claims an aerobatic ride in an authentic 1940 Stearman biplane, once used to train World War II combat pilots, "tops any roller coaster ever built." Calmer scenic rides and glider rides are also available, and antique planes can be viewed at the airport.

— WINERIES —

## Bartholomew Park Winery

*1000 Vineyard Ln., (707) 935-9511, fax (707) 938-9460; www.bartholomewparkwinery.com. Tasting daily 11-4:30; tour by request.*

Situated in the heart of peaceful 400-acre Bartholomew Memorial Park, this winery is a newcomer to the area. Though wine grapes were planted on the property in the early 1830s and the land once was owned by Agoston Haraszthy, known as the father of the California wine industry (and connected with the Vallejo family), this winery has been in business just since 1994. The winery makes only 100% varietal wines and produces just 4,000 cases each year. Because production is so small, the flavorful premium wines are sold only at the winery. Just off the tasting room, a small but interesting museum chronicles the property's history and current grape-growing practices. It also holds a fascinating topographical map and photographic displays of both contemporary area winemakers and of images by Victorian photographer Eadweard Muybridge dating back to the early 1870s. Visitors can picnic in a spacious area with a vineyard view, and a 3-mile hiking trail leads through a fragrant old-growth conifer forest with the promise that on a clear day you can see forever—or at least to San Francisco. Monthly jazz concerts are scheduled, and visitors are invited to help punch down the grapes during harvest.

## Buena Vista Winery

*18000 Old Winery Rd., (800) 926-1266, (707) 938-1266, fax (707) 939-0916; www.buenavistawinery.com. Tasting daily 10-5; tour daily at 11, 2, reservations advised.*

Founded in 1857, this is California's oldest winery. Visitors park among the grapevines, and, after a short, pleasant walk in, taste wines in the welcoming old Press House. Don't miss the nutty cream sherry, available only at the winery. Selecting a bottle for a picnic is highly recommended. Take it outside to enjoy at one of the tables shaded by stately old eucalyptus trees growing on the banks of a tiny brook. The winery's shop sells a variety of picnic supplies. If kids are along, do purchase a chilled bottle of Gewurztraminer grape juice for them.

## Cline Cellars

*24737 Hwy. 121, 2 mi. S of plaza, (800) 546-2070, (707) 940-4000, fax (707) 940-4034; www.clinecellars.com. Tasting daily 10-6; tour at 11, 1, 3.*

Situated on the original site of Mission San Francisco Solano, this winery is known for its Rhone-style wines. Grapes for the wines are grown on the family ranch in Oakley. Six thermal pools filled by underground mineral springs dot the property. Once warm, they have been cool since the last big earthquake, and some are populated now with fish and turtles. A picnic area surrounded by rose bushes and three of the ponds is located behind the farmhouse tasting room.

## Gloria Ferrer Champagne Caves

*23555 Hwy. 121, (707) 996-7256, fax (707) 996-0378; www.gloriaferrer.com. Tasting daily 10:30-5:15; tour at 12, 2, 4.*

Located back from the highway, atop a hill in a Catalan hacienda-style building, this tasting room provides views across the vineyards. In warm weather, tasters can relax on a patio; in cooler weather, they can gaze at the view from inside, warmed by a large fireplace. The winery is part of Spain's Freixenet family, which has been making wine since the 12th century. The tour visits the man-made caves and provides insight into the making of sparkling wine.

## Gundlach Bundschu Winery

*2000 Denmark St. (another entrance is on Thornsberry Rd.), 3 mi. E of plaza, (707) 938-5277,*

*"If you can't say 'Gundlach-Bundschu Gewurztraiminer', you shouldn't be driving!"*

fax (707) 938-9460; www.gunbun.com. Tasting daily 11-4:30; self-guided tour.

Located off a winding, backcountry road, this pioneer winery was established in 1858. Now the great-great grandson of German founder Jacob Gundlach's partner continues the tradition. Jim Bundschu, who has been referred to as the "clown prince of wines," and his merry wine-makers produce wines they like to drink themselves—wines with intense varietal character. White wines here are dry and flavorful, reds dark and complex. The Kleinberger varietal, a kind of Riesling, is produced by vines brought over in 1860. It is unique to the winery and can only be purchased here. Picnic tables perch on a small hill overlooking a pond and vineyards. When leaving, be sure to take the alternate road out. Each route provides different scenery.

### Ravenswood

18701 Gehricke Rd., (888) 669-4679, (707) 933-2332, fax (707) 938-9459; www.ravenswood-wine.com. Tasting daily 10-5; tour daily at 10:30.

A prime producer of Zinfandel, this winery's bold slogan is "no wimpy wines." A picnic area overlooks the vineyards, and a festive barbecue with live music purveys picnic lunches on summer weekends.

### Sebastiani Vineyards & Winery

389 Fourth St. East, (800) 888-5532, (707) 933-3230, fax (707) 933-3390; www.sebastiani.com. Tasting daily 10-5; tour daily at 11 & 3, Sat-Sun also at 1.

This winery has been owned continuously by the same family since 1904—longer than any other in the country. It is home to Northern California's first vineyard, planted in 1825 by Franciscan padres and purchased from them by Sebastiani in 1904. The winery is best known for its Symphony and Pinot Noir Blanc, which are available only at the winery. While here, stroll through the museum and view the world's largest collection of carved oak wine casks. Educational tastings and a trolley tour of town are sometimes options, and a pleasant picnic area is available.

### Viansa Winery

25200 Arnold Dr. (Hwy. 121), 5 mi. S of plaza, (800) 995-4740, (707) 935-4700, fax (707) 996-4632; www.viansa.com. Tasting daily 10-5; tour at 11 & 2.

Built on top of a hill commanding magnificent views of the area, this winery opened in 1990. Owned by Sam Sebastiani and his wife Vicki—the name comes from merging the first two letters of each of their first names—this beautifully crafted Tuscan-style winery building was inspired by a monastery near Farneta, Italy. Noteworthy wines include Barbera Blanc—a light blush wine perfect for picnics—and Cabernet Sauvignons. They are sampled in the tasting room featuring a magnificent "wall of wines" behind two tasting bars. Wines are available for purchase only at the winery and by mail order.

The **Italian Marketplace** food hall is designed after the mercato in Lucca, Italy, and the extraordinary food offerings *almost* overshadow the wines. Using Vicki's recipes, the kitchen staff prepares wonderful things for picnics: country pâté, torta rustica, hot-sweet mustard, focaccia bread, panini (Italian sandwiches), a triple-chocolate chunk cookie, tiramisu. More goodies include porcini mushroom tomato sauce (made with Viansa Cabernet Sauvignon) and spiced figs (made with Sonoma black mission figs and Viansa Cabernet Sauvignon using Vicki's grandmother's recipe). Some of the items are prepared with produce from the winery's own vegetable garden. On nice days, picnics can be enjoyed at a bevy of tables situated on a knoll with a panoramic view of the Sonoma and Napa valleys. On cooler days, tables are available inside.

January through March are the prime months to view birds here at the expansive **Viansa wetlands** (*Guided tour Feb-May, every other Sun at 8:30am. $15.*). That is when the greatest numbers are in transit on their southward trek.

## — WHERE TO STAY —

### El Dorado Hotel
*405 First St. West, on the plaza, (800) 289-3031, (707) 996-3030, fax (707) 996-3148; www.hotel eldorado.com. 26 rooms; $$. Heated pool. Restaurant; room service. No smoking; no pets.*

Built in 1843, this historic inn was gutted and remodeled with plenty of Mexican paver tiles and beveled glass. Each of the contemporary rooms contains handmade furnishings—including iron four-poster beds and large mirrors softened by rustic twig frames—and a goose-down comforter to chase the chill.

On the first floor of the hotel, appealing **Piatti** (*(707) 996-2351; www.piatti.com. L-D daily; $$-$$$. Boosters, child portions. Reservations advised.*) offers outside seating at heavy marble tables on a rustic tiled patio dominated by a majestic old fig tree. On cooler days, the large inside dining room is equally inviting. The menu of deliciously innovative Italian cuisine changes regularly and always has several daily specials plus a risotto. A variety of unusual pizzas are baked in a wood-burning oven, and most of the pastas are made by hand in house. Piatti oil—a delicious dipping sauce for bread made with virgin olive oil, balsamic vinegar, salt, pepper, garlic, red pepper flakes, and chopped parsley—is served gratis upon request. Both local and imported Italian wine varietals are available by the glass, and trendy tiramisu is always on the dessert menu.

### The Fairmont Sonoma Mission Inn & Spa
*18140 Hwy. 12, in Boyes Hot Springs, 3 mi. N of plaza, (800) 441-1414, (707) 938-9000, fax (707) 938-4250; www.fairmont.com/sonoma. 228 rooms; $$$-$$$+. Children under 18 free. Some wood-burning fireplaces. 3 heated mineral pools; 3 mineral hot tubs; sauna; health spa; fitness room; 18-hole golf course. 2 restaurants; room service. No smoking.*

Built in 1927 and surrounded by 13 acres of beautifully landscaped, fragrant grounds, this sedate luxury resort's pink adobe architecture is reminiscent of the town mission. Its immense lobby is outfitted with comfortable oversize furniture and features beautifully tiled floors and massive ceiling beams. Vintage rooms in the original building sport enormous closets, and the completely round turret—the most requested room—has a view of the pool and gardens. Newer contemporary-style rooms and luxury suites are also available. Though children are welcome, this is an adult-oriented resort: Children under 18 are not permitted in the well-equipped, full-service spa, but can use the hotel pool.

People have been coming to this spot for the therapeutic 135-degree mineral waters long before the hotel was built, so it is fitting a fabulous spa should take form here. An entire day can be used to good advantage. Start by decompressing with the Bathing Ritual: Soak first in the 92-degree Tepiderium Roman Bath; then move on to the 102-degree Caldarium hot pool; cool off under 2-foot-wide Mega showerheads; and finally enter the herbal steam room and then the sauna. That ought to do it! An array of treatments is available, including the fabulous Wine Country Kur. Nicknamed "the scrub, tub, and rub," it consists of an exfoliation rub with local grape seed crush, a soak in a hot grape seed-enhanced bath, and then a massage with rich grape seed oil and lotion. Men might especially enjoy the facial designed just for them. The spa also has an outdoor pool and several private outdoor hot tubs.

The gorgeous **Santé Restaurant** *(B-D daily; $$$.)* operates just off the lobby. The seasonal menu changes regularly but might include a tasty salad with spicy pecans and blue cheese as a starter, and perhaps a horseradish-crusted grouper or a black pepper-and-coriander-crusted rack of lamb. If available, opt for the dessert of fireside s'mores, which includes housemade marshmallows, Valrhona chocolate, and a trip to the outdoor fire pit or huge lobby fireplaces. The spacious, casual dining room of the **Big 3 Diner** *(18140 Hwy. 12, (707) 938-9000. B-L-D daily, Sat-SunBr; $-$$. Highchairs, boosters, booths, child menu. Reservations advised.)* offers seating at tables and in comfy booths. The restaurant is well known for its extensive and delicious breakfast menu, which has everything from oatmeal with raisins and brown sugar to eggs Benedict. At lunch and dinner, the menu features eclectic American foods such as sandwiches, soups and salads, a delicious hamburger, and trendy pizzas. During the week before Christmas, **Breakfast with Santa** is scheduled each morning, when Santa visits each table with gifts for children. Make reservations by calling (707) 939-2410. Low-fat spa cuisine options are available in both restaurants.

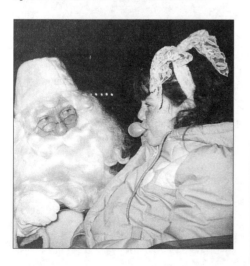

## MacArthur Place

*29 E. MacArthur St., (800) 722-1866, (707) 938-2929, fax (707) 933-9833; www.macarthurplace.com. 64 rooms; $$-$$$+. Children under 13 free. Heated pool; hot tub; health spa; fitness room. Continental breakfast; restaurant; room service. No pets.*

Featuring a combination of restored Victorian buildings and newly constructed units, this historic estate has been transformed into a luxurious country inn. Rooms are decorated sumptuously with splendid fabrics and furniture, and bathrooms have oversize open showers. Guests can stroll through 6 acres of manicured gardens and view the original sculptures ensconced throughout, get a relaxing treatment in the spa, or borrow a bike and see the sights. Upon leaving the property, a sign indicates New York is 3,562 miles thataway and Sonoma Plaza is 4 blocks straight ahead. It's a no-brainer which way to go.

**Saddles** *((707) 933-3191. L M-F, D daily, Sat-SunBr; $$-$$$. Highchairs, boosters.)* is situated in a beautifully transformed 100-year-old barn said to be fashioned after Thomas Jefferson's at Monticello. It has saddles for chairs in the waiting area and serves good grub, including delicious potato skin cups filled with salsa, exquisite garlic bread, and really good salads. Entrees include an assortment of prime steaks plus baby back ribs, roasted chicken, a vegetarian pasta, and fresh fish. At "The Finish Line," as the dessert menu is called, don't miss the signature brownie mousse parfait wrapped in a cowboy kerchief.

## Sonoma Hotel

*110 W. Spain St., on the plaza, (800) 468-6016, (707) 996-2996, fax (707) 996-7014; www.sonoma hotel.com. 16 rooms; $-$$$. Unsuitable for children under 12. No TVs; some shared baths. Continental breakfast; restaurant. No pets.*

Dating from the 1870s, when it was the town theater, this hotel's rooms are furnished in carefully selected turn-of-the-century antiques and have private bathrooms with clawfoot tubs. The friendly resident ghost, a Chinese man named Fred who dresses in coolie-style clothing, is said to roam the third floor and has been seen late at night sweeping the sidewalk outside.

## The Coffee Garden

*415-421 First St. West, on the plaza, (707) 996-6645. B-L daily; $. Highchairs. No reservations.*

Located within the historic 1830s Captain Salvador Vallejo Adobe, this inviting cafe offers salads, sandwiches, and coffees. Order in front, then find a chair out back in the casual patio garden planted with a large variety of native flora.

## The General's Daughter

*400 W. Spain St., (707) 938-4004, fax (707) 938-4099; www.thegeneralsdaughter.com. L M-Sat, D daily, SunBr; $$. Highchairs, boosters, booths. Reservations advised.*

General Vallejo's third daughter, Natalia, built this Victorian in 1864 with her husband, Attilla Haraszthy, whose family grew grapes in the valley. Situated just 3 blocks from the plaza, the house has been beautifully renovated, and its warm-colored walls are adorned with striking farm-themed paintings by Rod Knutson. Diners have a choice of several seating spaces, plus a patio area in good weather. And the food lives up to the surroundings. Starters might include crisp buttermilk-and-cornmeal-coated onion rings with lemon-pepper aioli, or a flavorful salad of Sonoma County mixed greens with roasted goat cheese, sun-dried tomatoes, and hazelnuts dressed lightly with a roasted garlic-balsamic vinaigrette. Main courses include light sandwiches—the curry lamb-Feta cheese on cracked wheat is particularly tasty and served with a delicious potato salad—and a vegetarian mixed grill, as well as more substantial meat and fish items. Desserts are made on site by a full-time pastry chef. Ending a meal with a cigar on the west porch is an intriguing possibility.

## Picnic Pick-Ups

### • Cucina Viansa

*400 First St. East, on the plaza, (707) 935-5656, fax (707) 935-5651; www.cucinaviansa.com. Daily 11-9.*

This simple self-service deli is operated by Viansa Winery. Delicious sandwiches and salads—eggplant on focaccia, spinach-ricotta ravioli with sun-dried tomato sauce—are among the items available for take-out or to eat on the premises. Desserts include a tasty and good-for-

you housemade fig newton. Boxed lunches are available by advance order. Seating on high stools at a window counter overlooking the Sonoma Mission is particularly appealing. Wine tasting is available.

### • Sonoma Cheese Factory

*2 W. Spain St., on the plaza, (800) 535-2855, (707) 996-1931, fax (707) 935-3535; www.sonomajack.com. Daily 8:30-5:30.*

This crowded shop stocks hundreds of cheeses (including their famous varieties of Sonoma Jack made from old family recipes) plus cold cuts, salads, and marvelous marinated artichoke hearts. Sandwiches are made to order. A few tables are available inside, and more are outside on a shaded patio. The workings of the cheese factory can be observed on weekdays through large windows in the back of the shop, and cheese samples are provided for tasting.

# Glen Ellen

*Like the curve of a scimitar blade, the Valley of the Moon stretched before them, dotted with farm houses and varied by pasture-lands, hay-fields, and vineyards. The air shimmered with heat and altogether it was a lazy, basking day. Quail whistled to their young from thicketed hillside behind the house. Once, there was a warning chorus from the foraging hens and a wild rush for cover, as a hawk, high in the blue, cast its drifting shadow along the ground.*

— Jack London, *Burning Daylight*, 1910

Contrary to popular belief, Jack London, a man with an eye for landscapes, didn't coin the name "Valley of the Moon." The valley stretching north from Sonoma was referred to as "Valle de la Luna" as early as 1841. But London, who lived on a ranch here when he wasn't on the road, popularized the term—and the place—in his novels.

Now, almost a hundred years later, there are still no high-rise buildings or shopping malls here. Instead visitors are treated to unimpeded views of tree-covered hills and vineyards that appear to stretch forever. It is the perfect antidote to the congestion of civilization, and it is where food guru M.F.K. Fisher spent her last

20 years and where actress Sharon Stone is rumored to have a vacation home.

## — GETTING THERE —

Located on Arnold Drive, 7 miles north of Sonoma via Highway 12.

## — WHAT TO DO —

### Jack London Bookstore
*14300 Arnold Dr., (707) 996-2888, fax (707) 996-4107. Thur-M 12-4:30.*

To get in the mood for visiting this area, read a London classic such as *The Call of the Wild* or *Martin Eden*. Or stop in at this wee shop, which in addition to stocking rare and out-of-print books, especially those by Jack London, also has a good selection of mysteries. The proprietor can provide assistance in selecting a London title.

### Jack London State Historic Park
*2400 London Ranch Rd., (707) 938-5216; www.parks. ca.gov. Park: Daily 10-5, in summer to 7. Museum: Daily 10-5. $5/vehicle.*

Jack London, who wrote 191 short stories and 51 books, was once one of the highest paid authors in the country. This 830-acre park contains the ruins of his 26-room Wolf House (reached via a pleasant 1/2-mile trail), his grave, and **The House of Happy Walls**—a museum built in his memory by his widow. Beauty Ranch includes the cottage he actually lived in as well as Pig Palace, a deluxe piggery designed by London. London's nephew donated it all to the state.

### Jack London Village
*14301 Arnold Dr.*

This bucolic, rustic, quiet, low-key complex has a creek-side location with an operating waterwheel and a few picnic tables. It holds several gift shops purveying unusual merchandise, a few restaurants, and **The Olive Press** *((800) 9-OLIVE-9, (707) 939-8900, fax (707) 939-8999; www.theolivepress.com. Daily 10-5:30.)*, where olives are custom-pressed. The process can only be viewed in fall, but the product can be tasted and purchased year-round.

## — WINERIES —

### Benziger Family Winery
*1883 London Ranch Rd., (888) 490-2739, (707) 935-3000, fax (707) 935-3016; www.benziger.com. Tasting daily 10-5; self-guided tour daily; tram tour daily, schedule varies.*

Just up the hill from the little crook in the road that is Glen Ellen, this family-operated winery provides a 30-minute tram tour through the vineyards and hands-on experience with vines, grapes, and trellising techniques. The tour is followed by tasting a wide selection of wines. Additional diversions include a gallery displaying original art from which various of their wine labels are designed, some caged peacocks, and extensive picnic facilities.

### B.R. Cohn Winery
*15000 Sonoma Hwy. 12, (800) 330-4064, (707) 938-4064, fax (707) 938-4585; www.brcohn.com. Tasting daily 10-4:30; no tour.*

Originally part of a Spanish land grant and a dairy during the '40s and '50s, this 65-acre estate is now a winery owned by the manager of the Doobie Brothers. All of the old farm buildings have been converted into winery buildings, and Sonoma Valley's largest olive orchard—8 acres of French picolinei trees planted over 125 years ago—is now farmed for premium extra-virgin olive oil. The winery's distinctive, intense Cabernets are credited to the area's unique microclimate. Several picnic areas are available, and music and theater performances are sometimes scheduled in an amphitheater.

## — WHERE TO STAY —

### Gaige House Inn
*13540 Arnold Dr., (800) 935-0237, (707) 935-0237, fax (707) 935-6411; www.gaige.com. 15 rooms; $$-$$$+. Unsuitable for children under 10. Some gas fireplaces. Heated pool (seasonal); hot tub. Afternoon & evening snack, full breakfast. No smoking; no pets.*

Because of this inn's 1890 Queen Anne-Italianate exterior, most guests are surprised by its fresh, understated, clean-lined, definitely un-Victorian interior. With Asian touches and gorgeous orchids throughout, the simple but elegant style is refreshing and easy to become accustomed to. Perfect afternoon relaxation is provided by a sheltered creek-side deck and by a gorgeous pool and hot tub area with a perfectly manicured half-acre of lawn lined with flowering oleander trees. Among the most interesting rooms are the Gaige Suite, with a 12-foot ceiling, four-poster lace-canopy bed, and wraparound balcony; and the Creek Side Suite, with a Jacuzzi for two and a double-headed shower, a private porch overlooking Calabasas Creek, and a stunning tree-filled view from the bed. A gourmet two-course breakfast is served at private tables in an airy, open room. It might include an appetizer plate of ripe fruits plus a hot plate of polenta and goat cheese topped with perfectly poached eggs and mild salsa—all served on beautifully glazed, Japanese-style rectangular plates. Coffee is the best—Peet's—and orange juice is fresh-squeezed.

## — WHERE TO EAT —

### Glen Ellen Inn Restaurant

*13670 Arnold Dr., (707) 996-6409; www.glenellen inn.com. L F-Tu, D daily; $$. Highchairs, boosters. Reservations advised.*

This modest, charming place is sort of a California-style roadhouse. Diners are seated in one of several small rooms, and in warm weather more tables are tucked into an outside sunken herb garden with a koi pond and mini-waterfall. Husband Christian Bertrand produces a non-stop parade of delicious California-fusion fare. Dinner begins with a basket of scones fresh from the oven, often delivered to the table by co-owner and wife Karen, who sometimes waits tables all by herself. Items on the dinner menu have included an exquisitely light puff pastry pocket filled with mushrooms and sausage in a brandy cream sauce, and a late harvest ravioli stuffed with the unexpected taste sensation of a mixture of pumpkin, walnuts, and sun-dried cranberries served on a bed of oven-glazed butternut squash. Save room for one of the killer desserts: perhaps a vertical chocolate mousse contained within a tall chocolate "basket," or maybe housemade vanilla ice cream topped with a marvelous caramel-toasted coconut sauce.

Newly constructed creek-side **Secret Cottages** *((707) 996-1174. 5 cottages; $$-$$$. All fireplaces.)* are painted in warm earth colors and have whirlpool tubs for two surrounded in natural stone tile.

### Picnic Pick-Up

#### • Glen Ellen Village Market

*13751 Arnold Dr., (707) 996-6728; www.sonoma-glenellenmkt.com. Daily 6am-9pm.*

The perfect place to select a picnic lunch, this full-service deli prepares sandwiches to order and offers a variety of salads and desserts. Fresh local produce, cold drinks, and the usual market staples are also available.

# Kenwood

## — GETTING THERE —

Located 3 miles north of Glen Ellen on Highway 12, which continues on into Santa Rosa.

## — ANNUAL EVENTS —

### World Pillow Fighting Championships

*July. (707) 833-2440; www.kenwoodpillowfights.com. $6, under 13 free. No pets.*

This very serious all-day competition takes place on a greased pipe positioned over a muddy morass into which losers, and sometimes winners, are buffeted.

## — WHAT TO DO —

### Morton's Warm Springs Resort

*1651 Warm Springs Rd., (805) 692-2807; www.mor tonswarmsprings.com. Sat-Sun 10-4; summer only. $8, 55+ & 2-11 $7.*

Long ago, these mineral springs were used by Native Americans to heal their sick. Nowadays, two large pools and one toddler wading pool are filled each day with fresh mineral water averaging 86 to 88 degrees. Lifeguards are on duty. Facilities include picnic tables and barbecue pits shaded by large oak and bay trees, a snack bar, a large grassy area for sunbathing, a softball field, horseshoe pits, a basketball court, and two volleyball courts. A teenage rec room is equipped with a jukebox, Ping-Pong tables, and pinball machines, and dressing rooms and lockers are available.

### Sugarloaf Ridge State Park

*2605 Adobe Canyon Rd., (707) 833-5712; www.parks.ca.gov. Daily dawn-dusk. $5/vehicle.*

Here await 25 miles of wilderness trails, a horseback-riding concession, and campsites.

## — WINERIES —

### Château St. Jean Vineyards and Winery

*8555 Sonoma Hwy. (Hwy. 12), (800) 543-7572, (707) 833-4134, fax (707) 833-4200; www.chateau stjean.com. Tasting daily 10-5; tour at 11 & 3, when staff is available.*

This winery specializes in white varietals. The tasting room is inside a 1920s château, and the grassy, shaded picnic area has several fountains and fishponds.

### Kunde Estate Winery & Vineyards

*10155 Sonoma Hwy. (Hwy. 12), (707) 833-5501, fax (707) 833-2204; www.kunde.com. Tasting daily 10:30-4:30; tours F-Sun, on the hr.*

Tucked between expansive vineyards and the Sugarloaf foothills, this fourth-generation family-owned and -operated winery produces a spicy Zinfandel from gnarled vines growing in a 28-acre vineyard planted over 113 years ago. Tours are given of the half-mile-long aging caves, which are camouflaged by a hill planted with Chardonnay grapes, and a picnic area is situated by a fountain and pond under a shady grove of oak trees.

### The Tasting Room

*9575 Sonoma Hwy. (Hwy. 12), (707) 833-6131, fax (707) 833-1000; www.the-wine-room.com. Tasting daily 11-5; no tour.*

Tommy Smothers says, "Making wine is so close to show business. Wine, like comedy, is subjective. Either people like your wine—or your songs, or your comedy—or they don't. Each is a creative process and you're only as good as your last effort." His wines—**Smothers Winery/Remick Ridge Vineyards**—and several others are available here for tasting. Children get grape juice and pretzels while their parents taste, and a small shaded area is equipped with picnic tables.

## — WHERE TO STAY —

### Kenwood Inn & Spa

*10400 Sonoma Hwy. 12, (800) 353-6966, (707) 833-1293, fax (707) 833-1247; www.kenwoodinn.com. 30 rooms; $$$+. Unsuitable for children under 21. No TVs; all wood-burning fireplaces. 2 unheated pools; hot tub; health spa. Full breakfast; D F-Sat for guests only. No smoking.*

Hugging a hillside covered with olive trees, this sensual, aesthetically pleasing Tuscan-style inn looks very much like an old Italian villa. Guests are greeted at the desk by an inviting arrangement of seasonal fruits. Painted in gray and ochre tones, the various buildings enclose a center courtyard and mix attractively with the green of the garden and the seasonal punch of color provided by orange globes hanging from persimmon trees and yellow orbs ripening on lemon bushes housed in terra-cotta pots. Fountains and archways are everywhere. Rooms are furnished with a combination of antiques and comfortable newer pieces, and the blissful beds are covered with both a feather bed and a lofty down comforter.

# Napa

## — A LITTLE BACKGROUND —

Considered by most tourists to be the center of the Wine Country, this town is more accurately referred to as the "Gateway to the Wine Country." The center of its charming old town features interesting vintage churches and buildings and is currently being renovated and developed. A group of wineries is found south of town, but the Wine Country's heaviest concentration of wine estates is farther north. Film buffs will be interested to know that the Napa River stood in for the Mekong Delta in Francis Ford Coppola's *Apocalypse Now*.

## — VISITOR INFORMATION —

**Napa Valley Conference & Visitors Bureau**
*1310 Napa Town Center, (707) 226-7459; www.napavalley.com.*

## — GETTING THERE —

Located approximately 50 miles north of San Francisco. Take Highway 101 to Highway 37 to Highway 121 to Highway 12 to Highway 29.

## — ANNUAL EVENTS —

**Napa Valley Mustard Festival**
*February-March. (707) 259-9020, fax (707) 938-0123; www.mustardfestival.org.*

Designed to bring visitors into this area at a beautiful, unhurried time of year, this festival includes a variety of unusual events held around the Napa Valley. Events include tastings as well as art, sporting, and recipe competitions.

**Napa Valley Wine Auction**
*June. Events held throughout the valley; (800) 982-1371 x402, (707) 963-3388, fax (707) 963-3488; www.napavintners.com. $600-$2,5000/2.*

Though tickets are pricey, this 4-day event usually sells out early. Tickets to individual are sometimes available at the last minute. Its pop-

ularity might be explained by the fact that many wine makers open their homes and wineries to unique public events in the interest of helping to raise money for local health centers. For example, one year the Rutherford Hill Winery hosted a refined candlelight dinner in their hillside caves, while Stag's Leap Wine Cellars hosted a festive Greek dinner and dancing extravaganza on their courtyard. A Friday night Vintner Dinner and Saturday afternoon auction take place at the lush Meadowood Resort.

## — WHAT TO DO —

**COPIA**
*500 First St., E of Hwy.29, (888) 51-COPIA, (707) 259-1600; www.copia.org. W-M, 10-5. $12.50, 62+ & students $10, 6-12 $7.50; half-price on W.*

Someone made the delicious comment that without food we cannot live, without wine we cannot endure, and without art we cannot evolve. Here to cover all the bases is COPIA: The American Center for Wine, Food & the Arts. Situated on 12 acres beside the Napa River, this new center is named for the goddess of abundance and celebrates American achievements in the culinary, winemaking, and visual arts. It was founded and mostly funded by Robert and Margrit Mondavi. Among interesting exterior architectural features are random-patterned fitted stone walls representing the past and a metal crescent representing the future. Admission includes daily educational programs and garden tours (see over 40 varieties of lavender). Though it has no permanent art collection, works on loan are displayed throughout. A long-term exhibition, "Forks in the Road: Food, Wine and the American Table," offers a light-hearted yet serious look at the place of food and wine in American life today and provides many interactive opportunities. Cooking classes, dinners, concerts, and Friday Flicks are scheduled at additional charge. Visitors need not pay admission to visit **Julia's Kitchen** (the late Julia Child was an honorary trustee) *((707) 265-5700. L W-M, D Thur-Sun; $$$. Reservations advised.)*, the **American Market Cafe** (perfect for picking up picnic supplies), or the cleverly named **Cornucopia** gift shop. All proceeds benefit this non-profit center.

## Di Rosa Preserve

*5200 Carneros Hwy. (Hwy. 121)/near Duhig Rd., 6 mi. W of town, (707) 226-5991, fax (707) 255-8934; www.dirosapreserve.org. Schedule varies. $12; free 1st & 3rd W of month. Reservations required.*

The show at this expansive 215-acre museum complex begins in the parking lot, where wrought-iron sheep greet visitors. This is one of the largest regional art collections in the country—perhaps because owner Rene di Rosa has never sold a work of art he's acquired—and tours last 2¹⁄₂ hours. So extensive is the collection of more than 1600 pieces of local contemporary art that a tram is used to shuttle guests between the four gallery buildings: a 19th-century stone winery building that was converted into a house and now into a gallery; a tractor barn; two new architecturally striking structures. Art is also displayed outdoors among the meadows and rolling hills. With its towering oaks, 100-year-old olive orchard, and 35-acre lake, the property is also a bit of a nature preserve. It has its own flock of peacocks and is a stopping point for migratory birds.

## Napa Valley Opera House

*1030 Main St., downtown, (707) 22-OPERA, fax (707) 226-5392; www.nvoh.org. Schedule & prices vary.*

After being closed to public performances since 1914, this revitalized 1879 Italianate-style opera house now features informal cabaret seating in the first-floor Cafe Theatre. Upstairs, a small, contemporary-style theater has fixed seats allowing everyone a good view.

## Napa Valley Wine Train

*1275 McKinstry St., (800) 427-4124, (707) 253-2111, fax (707) 251-5264; www.winetrain.com. Daily; schedule varies; closed 1st wk. in Jan. $40-$140. Reservations required.*

This leisurely 3-hour, 36-mile excursion takes passengers through the heart of the Wine Country. The train boasts opulently restored vintage lounge cars and a 1916 Pullman converted into a kitchen complete with a stainless-steel galley and a window-wall allowing chefs to be viewed in action. Tickets are available for brunch, lunch, or dinner served in richly appointed dining cars outfitted with the refined pleasures of damask linen, bone china, and silver flatware. Almost everything is prepared right on the train using fresh ingredients, and the menu offers several choices in each category. One lunch enjoyed aboard included a tasty baby lettuce salad with Cambozola cheese and hazelnut-sherry vinaigrette, filet mignon with Cabernet-Roquefort sauce, and a creamy tiramisu served cutely in an oversize cappuccino cup. A deli car that is perfect for families with young children offers an inexpensive a la carte menu. Some runs make a stop at a winery, and special events such as private winery tours and murder mystery dinners are often scheduled.

## — WINERIES —

## Artesa Winery

*1345 Henry Rd. (call for directions), off Hwy. 121, (707) 224-1668, fax (707) 224-1672; www.artesa winery.com. Tasting daily 10-5; tour at 11, 2.*

This spectacular Spanish-owned winery can be difficult to find but is well worth the effort. Its stunning minimalist architecture has it set right into a grassy hill that acts as a sod roof, helping insulate wines stored beneath. Visitors reach the tasting room by walking up a pyramid-like staircase on either side of a cascading man-made waterfall. Stunning panoramic views are enjoyed at the top. In the spirit of the Codorniu family's creation of the first methode champenoise sparkling wine in Spain in 1872, the winery creates a distinctly California sparkling wine here. After sampling in the spacious tasting room or outside on the inviting deck, a mini-museum of wine-related artifacts awaits leisurely perusal.

## Domaine Carneros

*1240 Duhig Rd., just off Hwy. 121, 6 mi. SW of town, (707) 257-0101, fax (707) 257-3020; www.domaine carneros.com. Tasting daily 10-6; tours 11-4, on the hr.*

Sitting atop a hill surrounded by vineyards, this imposing classic French château is inspired by the Château de la Marquetterie—an historic 18th-century residence in Champagne, France owned by the winery's principal founder. After climbing a *lot* of steps, visitors reach the elegant tasting salon and garden terrace. Here, information is dispensed both about the methode champenoise procedure that produces the champagnes of French founder Taittinger and about their local sparking wines made in the same tradition. Flavored mineral water is given to children while their parents taste.

## Hakusan Sake Gardens

*One Executive Way (at intersection of Hwys. 12 & 29; enter at N. Kelly Rd.), (800) KOHNAN-1, (707) 258-6160, fax (707) 258-6163; www.hakusan.com. Tasting daily 10-5; self-guided tour.*

Situated on the southern outskirts of town, this Wine Country oddity can be passed by in a flash. Be vigilant in looking for the turn-off. After a self-guided exterior tour of the factory, stroll through the tranquil Japanese Zen Garden. Conclude with a tasting of premium sakes, including delicious plum and pretty pink raspberry versions. All are made using Sacramento Valley rice and contain no sulfites, sulfates, or preservatives.

## The Hess Collection

*4411 Redwood Rd., (877) 707-HESS, (707) 255-1144, fax (707) 253-1682; www.hesscollection.com. Tasting daily 10-4; self-guided tour; gallery admission free.*

Located on the slopes of Mt. Veeder, off a road that winds first through the suburbs and then through scenic woods, this unusual winery is owned by Swiss entrepreneur Donald Hess. He grows grapes here in rocky soil on steep, terraced hillsides and turns them into premium wines. Built in 1903, the winery was once the original Napa Valley home for the Christian Brothers. Extensively remodeled, it retains the original stone walls and features an impressive 13,000-square-foot art gallery. Among the eclectic collection of contemporary paintings and sculptures are works by Robert Motherwell and Frank Stella and a stunning portrait by Swiss artist Franz Gertsch titled "Johanna II." At various points, portholes look into rooms where steel fermentation tanks and bottling machines are located. Visitors can also view a 12-minute narrated slide presentation of the winemaking operations. The winery is known for its Chardonnays and Cabernet Sauvignons, and its Mt. Veeder Estate Merlot is available for purchase only at the winery. Valser mineral wasser (water) from Switzerland—available nowhere else in the U.S.— is provided to tasters and to children.

## Trefethen Winery

*1160 Oak Knoll Ave./Hwy. 29, (800) 556-4847, (707) 255-7700, fax (707) 255-0793; www.trefethen.com. Tasting daily 10-4:30; tour by appt.*

Built in 1886, this historic building is a superb example of a wooden gravity-flow winery. Though it can be a bit difficult to find, it is worth the effort just to drive through the majestic gates and down an impressive private road through expansive vineyards to the tasting room.

## — WHERE TO STAY —

## Blackbird Inn

*1755 First St./Jefferson St., near downtown, (888) 567-9811, (707) 226-2450, fax (707) 258-6391; www.foursisters.com. 8 rooms; $$-$$$. Children under 6 free. Some fireplaces. Afternoon snack, full breakfast. No smoking; no pets.*

Situated inside a completely gutted and reworked 1920s arts and crafts-style house, this new inn provides a refreshing change from frou-frou. All rooms have the same subdued, masculine-style decor of dark plaid, striped, and floral fabrics. Dark mahogany wood trim is used throughout, and bathrooms are appointed with marble vanities and shiny white tiles. Iron-frame beds hold a charming row of blackbirds atop the foot end. For dinner, an easy option is just to cross the inn's back parking lot for a French meal at **La Boucane**.

## The Carneros Inn

*4048 Sonoma Hwy. 12, (800) 888-400-9000, (707) 299-4900, fax (707) 299-4950; www.thecarneros inn.com. 96 cottages; $$$+. All wood-burning fireplaces. Heated pool (year-round); hot tub; health spa; fitness room. Restaurant; room service. No smoking; no pets.*

Each unit here is a private cabin, and, due to an odd building code restriction and perhaps in homage to the site's former trailer park, all are built on wheels. Each has a private deck with heater, a yard, and plenty of space in between. Fixtures are top-of-the line—including an oversize shower with three heads and a hand-held, a second outdoor shower with sunflower head, limestone tiles, and a heated slate floor—and the decor simple—lovely cherry wood floors, puffy beds, and a flat-panel TV. The spa has two saunas and steam rooms—fresh herbs are put in daily—and offers a menu of treatments that includes their signature Red Flower Body Massage Ritual using a line of exclusive Japanese-inspired products (*www.red*

flower.com). Celebrities are finding out about this hideaway, including singers Jessica Simpson and Nick Lachey, who spent their second anniversary here.

The **Hilltop Restaurant** is for guests only. The more casual **Boon Fly Cafe** (B,L,D daily; $-$$.) is open to the public. Consisting of a one-room, barn-like dining room with a wood floor, it serves up simple diner fare.

## Embassy Suites Napa Valley

1075 California Blvd., 1/2-mi. from downtown, (800) 400-0353, (800) EMBASSY, (707) 253-9540, fax (707) 253-9202; www.embassynapa.com. 205 suites; $$$+. Children under 12 free. All kitchens. Indoor heated pool; hot tub; sauna. Evening drinks, full breakfast; restaurant; room service. Pets welcome.

This branch offers suites equipped with a bedroom, a front room with hide-a-bed, a kitchenette, and two TVs. Breakfast is the all-you-can-eat variety with eggs cooked to order, bacon, sausage, pancakes, fried potatoes, toast, fresh fruit, muffins, cereals, and beverages, and it can be enjoyed either in a pleasant indoor atrium or outside by a pond inhabited by ducks and both black and white swans. For more description, see page 420.

## Hennessey House

1727 Main St., (707) 226-3774, fax (707) 226-2975; www.hennesseyhouse.com. 10 rooms; $$-$$$. 1 TV; some wood-burning & gas fireplaces. Sauna. Afternoon & evening snack, full breakfast. No smoking; no pets.

Listed in the National Register of Historic Places, this 1889 Eastlake Queen Anne Victorian's exterior is painted stylishly in five different colors. Six rooms are in the main residence, four more in a carriage house. Some have oversize whirlpool tubs or clawfoot tubs, others have featherbeds. Breakfast is served under what is claimed to be Napa County's finest 19th-century, hand-painted, stamped-tin ceiling, and it is indeed magnificent.

## La Residence

4066 St. Helena Hwy. N (Hwy. 29), 4 mi. N of town, (800) 253-9203, (707) 253-0337, fax (707) 253-0382; www.laresidence.com. 23 rooms; $$-$$$+. Some fireplaces. Heated pool (seasonal); hot tub. Evening snack, full breakfast.

Set back on a spacious site amid a tiny groomed vineyard, this inn's guest rooms are spread among three buildings and are decorated uniquely with designer fabrics and quality furnishings. The 1870 farmhouse Mansion features late 18th-century Revival architecture and rooms decorated with American antiques, while the French Barn additionally holds the reception area and breakfast room. A newer Cellar House has large suites with fireplaces and French doors opening onto a patio. Breakfast is simply prepared and made with the best ingredients—fluffy scrambled eggs, monster buttery croissants, a perfect fresh fruit cup.

### — WHERE TO EAT —

## Alexis Baking Company and Cafe

1517 Third St., (707) 258-1827. B-L daily; $. Highchairs, boosters.

This combination bakery/cafe is a must-stop for breads and pastries to take home, but most people wind up staying for a casual meal, too. Breakfast offerings include Dutch babies and hot cinnamon rolls. Lunch is a selection of pastas, sandwiches, soups, and salads.

## Cole's Chop House

1122 Main St./Pearl St., downtown, (707) 224-MEAT, fax (707) 254-9692; coleschophouse.citysearch.com. D daily; $$$. Booths. Reservations advised. Valet parking F-Sat.

Situated inside a vintage building made with hand-hewn native stone, this stunning space dates to 1886 and retains its original 80-foot-high open truss ceiling and Douglas fir floors. The golden-hued plaster walls are trimmed with mahogany and brightened with antique French posters. To allow sampling more of the menu, consider sharing, especially the 16-ounce U.S.D.A. Prime, corn-fed, 21-day Chicago dry-aged New York steak—it might just be the very best steak ever. Garlic mashed potatoes and a wickedly delicious chocolate pecan pie are also share-worthy, but do order separate cups of cappuccino.

## Downtown Joe's

902 Main St./Second St., downtown, (707) 258-2337; www.downtownjoes.com. B-L-D daily; $. Highchairs, boosters, child menu.

Situated within an historic building constructed in 1894, then updated in 1926 with an art deco tile façade, this centrally located brew-pub serves up housemade soups, salads, pizzas, steaks, and seafood, plus a burger, ribs, and a pulled pig sandwich. Beers include Golden Thistle Bitter Ale (an English-style bitter) and a dark, full-bodied Slipknot Stout; a refreshing housemade root beer is also available. Seating is inside at a comfortable bar and outside on a patio overlooking the west bank of the Napa River. Live music is scheduled Thursday through Saturday evenings.

## Tuscany

*1005 First St./Main St., downtown, (707) 258-1000, fax (707) 256-3575. L M-F, D daily; $$-$$$. High-chairs, boosters. Reservations advised.*

This inviting restaurant operates inside a substantial, wide-open space that retains the 1855 building's original hardwood floors and brick walls. It has no trouble mixing modern and new with cozy and warm. Servers wear casual blue work shirts, and tables are covered with butcher paper. The restaurant is wildly popular with locals, and lots of families dine here. Indeed, animated diners are content to eat in the bar when the main room is full. The Mediterranean menu includes pizzas made in a wood-fired oven and both grilled and rotisserie meats. Among the possibilities for starters are a fig-and-walnut salad with baby arugula or a butter lettuce salad with fresh pears and candied walnuts; for entrees, a superb half-moon ravioli in a light sage cream sauce or a spice-rubbed rotisserie chicken with perfect, creamy baby Yukon potatoes.

# Yountville

— VISITOR INFORMATION —

## Yountville Chamber of Commerce

*6516 Yount St., (707) 944-0904, fax (707) 944-4465; www.yountville.com.*

— WHAT TO DO —

## Hot air balloon rides

Tour the Napa Valley via hot air balloon. Trips average 1 hour in the air; altitude and distance depend on which way the wind blows.

## • Adventures Aloft

*6525 Washington St., in Vintage 1870, (800) 944-4408, (707) 944-4408, fax (707) 944-4406; www.napavalleyaloft.com. $185-$250, 6-16 $160-$200. Reservations required.*

This is the Wine Country's oldest balloon company, with the most experienced pilot team available. The adventure includes pre-flight coffee and pastry and a post-flight sit-down breakfast enhanced with a local sparkling wine.

## • Napa Valley Balloons

*6975 Washington St., (800) 253-2224, (707) 944-0228, fax (707) 944-0219; www.napavalley balloons. com. $185. Children must be at least 48 inches tall.*

This business offers a similar experience, plus an enamel balloon lapel pin and a photo of either the launch or landing.

## Vintage 1870

*6525 Washington St., (707) 944-2451, fax (707) 944-2453; www.vintage1870.com. Daily 10-5:30.*

Once a winery, this lovely old brick building now houses specialty shops and restaurants. Hot air balloons can often be seen from the children's play area outside.

— WINERIES —

## Domaine Chandon

*1 California Dr., (707) 944-2280, fax (707) 944-1123; www.chandon.com. Tasting daily, May-Oct 10-6, Nov-Apr 11-5; tours M, Thur-F, Sun at 11, 1, 3, Sat also at 5.*

This attractive French-owned winery specializes in sparkling wines produced by the traditional methode champenoise. It is reached by crossing a wooden bridge spanning a scenic duck pond surrounded by beautifully landscaped grounds. Built with stones gathered on the site, its arched roofs and doorways are inspired by the caves of Champagne, France. The Tasting Salon features a tasting bar overlooking the valley and provides tables and chairs both inside and outside on a terrace. Visitors can purchase a taste, a glass, or a bottle, as well as hors d'oeuvres.

Though the spacious, elegant dining room in the winery **restaurant** *((800) 736-2892, (707) 944-2892, fax (707) 944-1123. L-D Thur-M; closed Jan; $$$. Reservations advised.)* is lovely, in good weather the terrace is the première spot to be seated. Menu items are designed especially to complement the winery's sparkling and varietal wines, which are available by the glass. A signature tasting menu pairs four courses at lunch and seven at dinner with Chandon wines. In support of the elegant atmosphere, men are requested to wear jackets at dinner.

## — WHERE TO STAY —

### Bordeaux House
*6600 Washington St., (800) 677-6370, (707) 944-2855, fax (707) 945-0471; www.bordeauxhouse.com. 8 rooms; $$. Some wood-burning fireplaces. Afternoon snack, full breakfast. No smoking; no pets.*

This ultra-modern building features a curved, red brick exterior and lush French- and English-style gardens.

### Burgundy House
*6711 Washington St., (707) 944-0889; www.burgundy house.com. 6 rooms; $$. Unsuitable for children under 11. No TVs; 1 wood-burning fireplace. Full breakfast. No smoking; no pets.*

Built in 1890 as a brandy distillery, this house was constructed of local fieldstone and river rock and has walls that are 22 inches thick. Lace-covered windows and antique pine and oak furniture complement the rustic interior construction. An inspired breakfast is served in either the downstairs lobby or the backyard rose garden, depending on the weather.

### Maison Fleurie
*6529 Yount St., (800) 788-0369, (707) 944-2056, fax (707) 944-9342; www.foursisters.com. 13 rooms; $$-$$$. Children under 2 free. Some gas fireplaces. Heated pool (seasonal); hot tub. Afternoon snack, full breakfast. No smoking; no pets.*

The rustic, vine-covered main building was built in the center of town as a hotel in 1873. It has 2-foot-thick brick walls, lots of terra cotta tile, and romantic multi-paned windows. Rooms, some of which are located in two adjacent buildings, are decorated in French country style. Amenities include oversize pool towels, complimentary use of mountain bikes, evening turndown, and a morning newspaper. Cookies, fruit, and beverages are always available, and wine and hors d'oeuvres are served in the afternoon. Though breakfast is delightful taken in the cozy dining room, it is delivered to the room upon request.

### Napa Valley Lodge
*2230 Madison St., (800) 368-2468, (707) 944-2468, fax (707) 944-9362; www.woodsidehotels.com. 55 rooms; $$$-$$$+. Some fireplaces. Heated pool (year-round); hot tub; sauna; fitness room. Afternoon snack, continental breakfast. No smoking; no pets.*

Located on the outskirts of town, this Spanish-style motel is across the street from a park and playground. Each room has a private patio or balcony, and breakfast includes champagne.

### Napa Valley Railway Inn
*6503 Washington St., (800) 520-0206, (707) 944-2000. 9 units; $-$$. Children under 7 free. No TVs. No pets.*

Railroad enthusiasts are sure to enjoy a night in a brass bed here. Three cabooses and six rail cars—authentic turn-of-the-century specimens sitting on the original town tracks—have been whimsically converted into comfortable suites complete with private bath, sitting area, and skylight.

### Vintage Inn
*6541 Washington St., (800) 351-1133, (707) 944-1112, fax (707) 944-1617; www.vintageinn.com. 80 rooms; $$$-$$$+. Children under 1 free. All wood-burning fireplaces. Heated pool (year-round); hot tub; 2 tennis courts. Afternoon snack, continental breakfast. Pets ok.*

This attractive contemporary inn is centrally located next to Vintage 1870. Rooms feature sunken spa tubs and 18th-century antiques, and bicycle rentals are available.

## — WHERE TO EAT —

### Brix

7377 St. Helena Hwy. (Hwy. 29), (707) 944-2749, fax (707) 944-8320; www.brix.com. L-D daily, SunBr; $$-$$$. Highchairs, boosters, booths. Reservations accepted.

Comfortable booths and tables here have views both of the expansive kitchen garden and vineyard as well as of the action in the open kitchen. Tasty sesame cracker bread is provided for munching and served in a sculpted metal basket with a grapevine design that is echoed throughout the restaurant in lighting fixtures and furnishings. The menu emphasizes grilled meats and seafood and makes use of seasonal herbs and vegetables from the kitchen's garden.

### The French Laundry

6640 Washington St., (707) 944-2380; www.french laundry.com. L F-Sun, D daily; $$$; closed part of Jan. Reservations essential.

Indeed once an actual French laundry, this rustic old stone building now holds one of the Wine Country's most popular culinary gems. England's *Restaurant* magazine calls it the best restaurant in the world. Owner-chef Thomas Keller offers diners either a five-course or seven-course menu, as well as a five-course vegetarian menu. The kitchen specializes in freshly prepared, innovative, labor-intensive dishes. Among the great desserts: a tarte tatin made with peaches and topped with sour cream ice cream, and "coffee and doughnuts"—a cappuccino semifreddo plus a cinnamon-sugar doughnut. The noteworthy wine list concentrates on Napa Valley vintages. Reservations are accepted 2 months in advance to the day. But be warned: this tiny restaurant is so popular and so difficult to get a reservation at that one busy San Francisco executive is said to have hired a temporary worker to spend the day on the phone trying to get him one!

### Mustards Grill

7399 St. Helena Hwy. (Hwy. 29), (707) 944-2424, fax (707) 944-0828; www.mustardsgrill.com. L-D daily; $$. Boosters. Reservations advised.

The best place to be seated at this popular bar and grill is on the cool, screened porch. Though tables are set with crisp white napery, the atmosphere is casual and chic and the menu imaginative. Selections include soups, salads, and sandwiches—the grilled ahi tuna with basil mayonnaise and the hamburger are particularly tasty—as well as entrees such as barbecued baby back ribs, mesquite-grilled Sonoma rabbit, and marinated skirt steak. Fresh fish specials are also available. Onion rings are thin, light, and superb, and housemade ketchup can be ordered with them. Garlic lovers will be pleased with a roasted head to spread on the complimentary baguette. Varietal wines are available by the glass, and rich desserts and specialty coffees invite lingering.

The **Cosentino Winery** (*7415 St. Helena Hwy. (Hwy. 29), (707) 944-1220, fax (707) 944-1254; www.cosentinowinery.com. Tasting daily 10-5:30.*) is located just next door. Built in 1990, this winery is known for producing the country's first designated Meritage wine. Referred to as The Poet, this wine is composed of a marvelous blend of Cabernet Sauvignon, Cabernet Franc, and Merlot.

# Oakville

## — WINERIES —

### Opus One

7900 St. Helena Hwy. (Hwy. 29), (800) 292-6787, (707) 944-9442, fax (707) 944-2753; www.opusone winery.com. Tasting daily 10-4; tour daily at 10:30, reservations required.

The gated entrance to this exceptional winery is just north of town. A merging of American (Robert Mondavi) and French (Baron Philippe de Rothschild) winemaking skills, this exclusive label boasts a facility that is as impressive as its wine. Though from the highway it looks like a squat pyramid, up close and personal it resembles more a contemporary monastery. Constructed of Texas limestone and landscaped with a softening planting of olive trees, the winery uses gentle gravity-flow production and plants its vines in dense French Bordeaux style. This requires costly handwork and helps explain the $150 tab attached to its young bottles of Cabernet Sauvignon. A highlight of the tour is seeing the immense barrel room, which is somehow reminiscent of the pods lined up waiting to hatch in *The Body Snatchers*, only here it is great wine aging in French oak barrels that is waiting patiently to be born.

### Robert Mondavi Winery

*7801 St. Helena Hwy. (Hwy. 29), (888) RMONDAVI, (707) 226-1395; www.robertmondaviwinery.com. Tasting daily 9:30-4:30; tours 10-4, reservations advised.*

In addition to ordinary tasting and tours, this long-lived winery offers all kinds of specialty tastings and tours. Call for details.

At the annual **Summer Festival at Robert Mondavi Winery** *(July & Aug.)*, the entertainers (who in the past have included Ella Fitzgerald, Al Hirt, and the Preservation Hall Jazz Band— on the *same bill*!) probably enjoy the dusk concerts as much as their audience. After an intermission for wine and cheese tasting, the concerts conclude under the stars. Picnics are encouraged, and catered repasts are available by advance reservation. Ah, the pleasure of sitting on a lawn, surrounded by vineyards and rolling foothills, while listening to great jazz.

### — WHERE TO EAT —

### Picnic Pick-Ups

• **Oakville Grocery Co.**
*7856 St. Helena Hwy. (Hwy. 29), (707) 944-8802, fax (707) 944-1844; www.oakvillegrocery.com. Daily 9-6.*

Everything needed to put together a fantastic gourmet picnic can be found here. Select from a vast variety of mustards, vinegars, jams, fresh fruits, imported beers, and natural juices, as well as cheeses, sandwiches, salads, sausages, and other deli items, plus a large assortment of enticing desserts. If the choices seem overwhelming, call 48 hours in advance to order a pre-packed picnic box, and let them pick the contents.

# Rutherford

### — WINERIES —

### Beaulieu Vineyard

*1960 St. Helena Hwy. (Hwy. 29), (800) 264-6918, (707) 967-5230, fax (707) 963-5920; www.bvwines.com. Tasting daily 10-5; no tour.*

Founded in 1900 by Frenchman Georges deLatour, this winery is known for its Cabernet Sauvignons and Chardonnays. It is said to be the oldest continuing winery in California.

### Niebaum-Coppola Estate Winery

*1991 St. Helena Hwy. (Hwy. 29), (800) RUBICON, (707) 968-1161, fax (707) 963-9084; www.niebaum-coppola.com. Tasting daily 10-5; vineyard tour at 11; chateau tour at 10:30, 12:30, 2:30.*

Founded in 1879 by a Finnish sea captain who made his fortune in the Alaskan shipping trade, this is one of the oldest wineries in the Napa Valley. It is now owned by legendary film director Francis Ford Coppola, who has owned a home on part of the property since the 1970s, and who, when the winery was up for sale, made an offer they couldn't refuse. Now, after driving down a long lane, through some iron gates and past newly planted vineyards, visitors arrive at an impressive vintage estate. A gift shop extraordinaire purveys such essentials as *The Godfather* t-shirts and enormous macaroni. This winery is known for its premium red Rubicon wine, which goes for $50 to $70 a bottle, but more affordable everyday wines are also available. In addition to a traditional tasting bar, the winery has a small cafe where wines can be tasted by the glass, and a terrace provides space for picnicking. Coppola's five Oscars and an authentic Tucker automobile are on view on the floor above the tasting room, and the **Centennial Museum** documents the winery's history.

### Sequoia Grove

*8338 St. Helena Hwy. (Hwy. 29), (800) 851-7841, (707) 944-2945, fax (707) 963-9411; www.sequoiagrove.com. Tasting daily 10:30-5; tour Sat-Sun at 11:30 & 2.*

Family-owned and -operated, this small winery gets its name from the 100-year-old cluster of tall sequoia redwoods its tasting room sits beneath. Known for its Rutherford-style Cabernet Sauvignons, it claims to be the only winery with underground production facilities. Things are *real* casual here, with several mellow dogs lounging about while tasters sample the wares. In 2003, the tasting room was damaged when lightening struck and toppled one of the sequoias, so visitors will be sampling in a tent until repairs are completed.

## St. Supery Winery

*8440 St. Helena Hwy. (Hwy. 29), (800) 942-0809,*
*(707) 963-4507, fax (707) 963-4526; www.stsupery.*
*com. Tasting daily 10-5; tour daily at 1 & 3.*

This French-owned winery's **Wine Discovery Center** is a super place to get an introduction to wine-making. The tour here includes a viewing of the Queen Anne Victorian **Atkinson House**, once occupied by the winery's founder and now furnished with unusual Victorian pieces representative of the era, and an educational visit to a 1-acre demonstration vineyard where, in season, varietal grapes can be tasted. A highlight of the tour is a SmellaVision display that permits a whiff of the various scents used to describe wines (grassy, peppery, etc.). This winery produces award-winning Sauvignon Blancs and bottles a French-produced Viognier as well as several premium kosher wines. Children get a coloring book and crayons to occupy them while parents taste.

# St. Helena

### — A LITTLE BACKGROUND —

Downtown's Main Street is lined with upscale clothing and housewares boutiques, and most are inside atmospheric vintage buildings.

### — VISITOR INFORMATION —

St. Helena Highway, Main Street, and Highway 29 are all the same road.

## St. Helena Chamber of Commerce

*1010 Main St., (800) 799-6456, (707) 963-4456,*
*fax (707) 963-5396; www.sthelena.com.*

### — GETTING THERE —

Located approximately 15 miles north of Yountville via Highway 29.

### — WHAT TO DO —

## Bale Grist Mill State Historic Park

*3369 Hwy. 29, 3 mi. N of town, (707) 942-4575;*
*www.parks.ca.gov. Daily 10-5; tour Sat-Sun at 11:30,*
*1, 2:30, 3:30. $3, children $1, under 6 free.*

Reached via a shaded, paved, stream-side path, this gristmill ground grain for farmers from the 1840s through the turn of the century. The damp site and slow-turning millstones are reputedly responsible for the exceptional corn-meal produced here. Interpretive displays are located inside the gable-roofed granary, and the 36-foot-diameter waterwheel is restored to full operation. Corn and wheat are ground at 1 and 3 p.m. on weekends and are available for purchase. Picnic tables are provided in several shaded areas, and a 1-mile loop History Trail leads through the woods to a pioneer cemetery.

## Cameo Theater

*1340 Main St., (707) 963-9779; www.cameo*
*cinema.com. $7, 55+ & under 13 $4.*

This tiny first-run movie theater is equipped with posh velvet seats and Dolby digital sound, making it well worth a visit. Special performances are sometimes scheduled. When offered, *Silverado Squatters*, based on the book by Robert Louis Stevenson and performed live by local resident Donald Davis, is a don't-miss.

## Silverado Museum

*1490 Library Ln., (707) 963-3757, fax (707) 963-0917;*
*www.silveradomuseum.org. Tu-Sun 12-4. Free.*

Situated on the edge of a scenic vineyard, this museum contains over 8,500 pieces of Robert Louis Stevenson memorabilia. There are paintings, sculptures, and manuscripts as well as his childhood set of lead toy soldiers. Consider a family read-in of *A Child's Garden of Verses* or *Treasure Island* before or after this visit.

### — WINERIES —

## Beringer Vineyards

*2000 Main St., just N of town, (707) 963-7115,*
*fax (707) 963-8129; www.beringervineyards.com.*
*Tasting & tour daily 10-4, on the hr.*

Established in 1876, this winery's Visitor Center is inside a beautiful oak-paneled, stained-glass-laden reproduction of a 19th-century German Tudor mansion known as the Rhine House. It is Napa Valley's oldest continuously operating winery, and its tour is considered one of the most historically informative. The winery is noted for its Chardonnays and Cabernet Sauvignons. Unfortunately, picnicking is not permitted on the beautifully landscaped grounds.

## Charbay Winery & Distillery

*4001 Spring Mountain Rd., (800) M-DISTIL, (707) 963-9327, fax (707) 963-3343; www.charbay.com. No tasting; tour by appt.*

Located off a remote scenic road, at almost 2,300 feet, this "still on the hill," as it is fondly nicknamed, is totally family-run and -operated. Co-owner Miles Karakasevic, who hails from Yugoslavia, is a 12th-generation wine maker and master distiller. Spirits are double-distilled by hand in classic Alambic pot stills. The winery is known for exceptional—and pricey—ports, brandies, and liqueurs. Among them is a grappa, a black walnut liqueur, and California's first pastis. Law prohibits tasting, but the $50 tour fee applies to a purchase.

## Charles Krug Winery

*2800 Main St., 1.5 mi. N of town, (800) 682-KRUG, (707) 963-5057; www.charleskrug.com. Tasting daily 10:30-5; no tour.*

In 1858, using a small cider press borrowed from Agoston Haraszthy at the Buena Vista Winery in Sonoma, this winery made the first commercial wines in the Napa Valley. They also were the very first to stop stomping grapes with human feet and start pressing them with machines. Now producing 16 different wines, the winery is noted most for its Cabernet Sauvignons and Chenin Blancs.

## Folie à Deux Winery

*3070 St. Helena Hwy. N., 2 mi. N of town, (800) 473-4454, (707) 963-1160, fax (707) 963-9223; www.folieadeux.com. Tasting daily 10-5; tour by appt.*

Aptly named for a psychiatric term defined as the mutual sharing of fantasies by two close friends, this winery was the dream come true of two psychiatric professionals. Unfortunately, they eventually divorced and sold the winery. Fortunately, the winery continues on. The tasting room is in a century-old yellow farmhouse originally owned by a Spanish prizefighter who retired to raise sheep and make wine as a part-time business. The stone shed he stored wine in still is used today. The winery is known for its peppery old-vine Zinfandels, and most of the wines are available only at the winery. Scenic picnic grounds overlook the vineyards, and cave tours and barrel tastings are given by appointment.

## Freemark Abbey Winery

*3022 St. Helena Hwy. N., 2 mi. N of town, (800) 963-9698, (707) 963-9694, fax (707) 963-0554; www.freemarkabbey.com. Tasting daily 10-5; no tour.*

The large, lodge-like tasting room here has oriental carpets covering its hardwood floor. Comfortable furniture arranged around a fireplace invites leisurely sampling, and a picnic area is available for purchasers of wine. The winery is noted for its Chardonnays and Cabernet Sauvignons.

## Prager Winery and Port Works

*1281 Lewelling Ln., (800) 969-PORT, (707) 963-PORT, fax (707) 963-7679; www.pragerport.com. Tasting daily 10:30-4:30; no tour.*

Located down a country lane and behind Sutter Home Winery, the valley's premier port purveyor offers a rustic, informal tasting room for sampling the wares. **B&B lodging** is available.

## Sutter Home Winery

*277 St. Helena Hwy. S., (707) 963-3104; www.sutterhome.com. Tasting daily 10-5; self-guided garden tour.*

Bob Trinchero, son of Mario who bought the winery in 1947, introduced a fruity, pink-colored White Zinfandel in 1971. It took the country by storm. That inexpensive signature version is still available, but the winery now also produces some premium Chardonnays and Cabernets. The tasting room is inside a barn that housed the original winery, and the winery's showcase 1884 Victorian home is used now for private lodging. Highlights of the surrounding garden—inspired by the renowned Butchart Gardens in Victoria, B.C.—include a rose garden with over 150 varieties and a garden of dwarf Japanese maples.

## V. Sattui Winery

*1111 White Ln., (800) 799-2337, (707) 963-7774, fax (707) 963-4324; www.vsattui.com. Tasting & self-guided tour daily 9-5; in summer 9-6.*

Established in San Francisco's North Beach in 1885, this winery was shut down during Prohibition then re-established in St. Helena in 1976. Family-owned for four generations, the current winemaker is the great-grandson of founder Vittorio Sattui. V. Sattui wines are sold only at the winery. Favorites include the Johannisberg Rieslings and Cabernet

Sauvignons for which they are best known, as well as the nation's oldest port-style Madera and a Gamay Rouge that was once voted the best hot tub wine. All can be tasted in the stone winery building featuring 3-foot-thick walls and chiseled archways. The goal here is to take wine off the pedestal and make it user-friendly. A deli stocks housemade salads and pâtés along with what is claimed to be the largest selection of international cheeses on the West Coast. Plenty of oak-shaded tables are provided on a 2-acre picnic grounds.

## — WHERE TO STAY —

### Ambrose Bierce House
*1515 Main St., downtown, (707) 963-3003, fax (707) 963-9367; www.ambrosebiercehouse.com. 3 rooms; $$-$$$. Unsuitable for children under 12. No TVs. Hot tub. Evening snack, continental breakfast. No smoking; no pets.*

Named for the witty author who wrote *The Devil's Dictionary* (said to be Rolling Stone Keith Richards' all-time favorite book) and who was portrayed by Gregory Peck in the movie *The Old Gringo*, this 1872 house was once Ambrose Bierce's home. One pleasantly decorated room is named after Eadweard Muybridge, who is known as the "father of the motion picture." It holds two interesting artifacts: an 1897 Eastman Kodak No. 2 Hawk-eye camera and a Smith and Wesson No. 2 that is just like the one Muybridge used in 1874 to shoot his wife's lover. Located at the northern end of town, the inn is within convenient walking distance of shopping and dining.

### El Bonita Motel
*195 Main St., (800) 541-3284, (707) 963-3216, fax (707) 963-8838; www.elbonita.com. 42 rooms; $$-$$$. Heated pool; hot tub; sauna. Pets ok.*

Featuring an art deco decor, this motel has a shaded, grassy pool area and offers an alternative to classy, cutesy, and expensive Wine Country lodgings. Each room is equipped with a microwave, refrigerator, and coffee maker.

### Harvest Inn
*One Main St., (800) 950-8466, (707) 963-WINE, fax (707) 963-4402; www.harvestinn.com. 54 units; $$$-$$$+. Some fireplaces. 2 heated pools (year-round); 2 hot tubs; health spa. Continental breakfast. Small pets ok.*

Situated on a 21-acre working vineyard, this contemporary English Tudor-style inn has beautifully landscaped grounds. Room and cottage furnishings include antiques, and some units have private terrace hot tubs. Bicycles are available to rent.

### La Fleur
*1475 Inglewood Ave., (707) 963-0233, same fax; www.lafleurinn.com. 7 rooms; $$. Unsuitable for children under 12. No TVs; some wood-burning fireplaces. Full breakfast. No smoking.*

Set back from the main highway, this charming 1882 Queen Anne Victorian B&B is *real quiet*. A large rose garden invites relaxing, and some of the spacious rooms feature clawfoot tubs. Breakfast is served in a cheery solarium with vineyard views that sometimes include hot air balloons floating above the vines.

It's just a short stroll through the flower garden to the tiny **Villa Helena Winery** (*1455 Inglewood Ave., (707) 963-4334, fax (707) 963-4748; www.wineweb.com/villahelena.html. Tasting & tour by appt.*) located next door. Call ahead to alert the owner, a former metallurgical engineer from Los Angeles, so that he can be in his office to assist with tasting his Charbono, dessert wines, and unusual white Viognier. He also provides what he calls "the shortest tour in the Napa Valley."

### The Wine Country Inn
*1152 Lodi Ln., (888) 465-4608, (707) 963-7077, fax (707) 963-9018; www.winecountryinn.com. 24 rooms, 5 cottages; $$-$$$+. Unsuitable for children under 13. No TVs; some wood-burning fireplaces. Heated pool (year-round); hot tub. Afternoon snack, full breakfast. No smoking.*

Built in the style of a New England inn, without a lot of fuss and frill, this attractive, quiet lodging is located back from the main highway on top of a small country hill. Rooms are decorated with floral wallpapers and tasteful antiques. Many have views of the surrounding vineyards and hills, and a few have private outdoor hot tubs. The filling breakfast, served on attractive handmade crockery, includes housemade granola and breads.

## — WHERE TO EAT —

### The Culinary Institute of America at Greystone

*2555 Main St., (707) 967-1010; www.ciachef.edu.*

Formerly home to The Christian Brothers winery, this magnificent 1889 landmark building was constructed of locally quarried volcanic tufa stone and is the largest stone building west of the Mississippi. It now houses the Culinary Institute—the only center in the world dedicated exclusively to continuing education and career development for professionals in the food, wine, and hospitality fields. Out front, the Cannard Herb Garden consists of seven terraces and features both an edible flower garden and an herbal tea garden. Across the street, the Organic Garden grows vegetables, fruits, and flowers—many from rare and heirloom seeds. Inside, Brother Timothy's 1,800-strong corkscrew collection is displayed, and the well-stocked **Spice Islands Marketplace** gift shop *((707) 967-2309. Daily 10-6.)* sells cooking accoutrements. Cooking demonstrations are scheduled. Asking questions, sampling the finished product, and taking home a recipe are all part of the package.

The atmospheric, stone-walled **Wine Spectator Greystone Restaurant** *(L-D daily. Free valet parking.)* affords the opportunity to see toqued chefs scurrying about an open kitchen. Though the menu has more substantial entrees, the way to go here is to order up a selection of appetizers called Today's Temptations. Served on a tiered lazy susan, they might include a tiny, tiny bowl of butternut squash soup or a perfect grilled shrimp with green sauce. Order the dessert sampling—The Last Temptation—and get a tiered tea-tray trolley of tidbits: a passion fruit tartlet, a Valrhona chocolate cake hill, a silky pannecotta with fresh pomegranate seeds.

### Gillwoods

*1313 Main St., downtown, (707) 963-1788, fax (707) 226-5003. B-L daily; $. Highchairs, boosters, child menu.*

Known for its breakfasts, this comfortable cafe has all kinds of egg dishes on the menu along with preservative-free Mother Lode bacon and toasted house-baked bread. Not to mention corned-beef hash, buttermilk pancakes, French toast, hot cereals, and granola. Salads and sandwiches are added at 11 a.m.

### Martini House

*1245 Spring St./Oak St., downtown, (707) 963-2233, fax (707) 967-9237; www.martinihouse.com. L-D daily; $$$. Reservations advised.*

Decorated in a sort of contemporary hunting lodge-style by Pat Kuleto, restaurant decorator extraordinaire and local resident, this converted 1920s bungalow is a satisfying venue. On a nice day, diners can opt to sit at cherry-red enamel tables on the arbor-sheltered patio or in the front yard under mature trees. A large 75-year-old fountain populated with koi acts as a soothing kid-magnet. The wine list is excellent, and celebrity chef Todd Humphries' daily-changing menu always is interesting. A delicious fixed-price lunch might include creamy mushroom soup, a shrimp salad, and fabulous crème fraîche ice cream with berries and wildflower-honey cake. An a la carte lunch might consist of tempura-fried soft shell crab, a tender navarin of lamb, and an almond-rhubarb tart. Surprise touches included warm steamed milk in the cream pitcher and coffee served in a French presse pot. The low-ceilinged downstairs bar is worth a look-see, if only to view the acorn mimicking light fixtures.

### Picnic Pick-Ups

• **Dean & Deluca**

*607 S. St. Helena Hwy., (707) 967-9980, fax (707) 967-9983; www.deandeluca.com. M-Sat 7:30-7, Sun 9-6.*

A branch of the fabled Manhattan store in SoHo, this impressively stocked, airy, European-style market hall is a gustatory delight. It is home to the Wine Country's largest cheese-aging room, and truffled butter and Devon cream are stocked along with hand-cut tortilla chips and fresh flowers. Choosing a picnic or take-home dinner from among the fresh breads, expansive array of deli items, and organic produce is a pleasure. Professional quality cookware is also for sale.

• **The Model Bakery**

*1357 Main St., downtown, (707) 963-8192, fax (707) 963-2462. Tu-Sat 7-6, Sun 8-4.*

Among the great hand-formed breads baked in the 1920s-era brick-and-sand ovens here are pain de vin (whole-wheat sourdough made with a starter derived from Napa Valley grape yeasts), sour rye, crusty sourdough, and both sweet baguettes and rounds. Panini, mini-pizzas, and stuffed croissants make quick snacks, and old-fashioned cookies and biscotti are pleasing desserts. Coffee and espresso drinks are also available. Seating is provided for on-the-spot indulgence.

• **Napa Valley Olive Oil Manufacturing Co.**
*835 Charter Oak Ave., (707) 963-4173, fax (707) 963-4301; www.napavalleyoliveoilmfg.com. Daily 8-5.*

Everything needed for a picnic is available inside this 100-year-old barn: cheese, sausage, olives, bread sticks, focaccia, biscotti. This Old World-style Italian deli also offers a variety of pastas, sauces, and dried mushrooms, plus its own cold-pressed olive oil and homemade red wine vinegar—all placed helter-skelter in barrels and on makeshift tables. Tabs are tallied on the shopping bag, and a cigar box holds the receipts. It's really quite unusual. A shaded picnic area is provided outside.

## Pinot Blanc
*641 Main St., (707) 963-6191, fax (707) 963-6192; www.patinagroup.com. L-D Tu-Sun; $$$. Booths, child portions. Reservations advised.*

Owned by super-chef Joachim Splichal, who also owns several acclaimed restaurants in Los Angeles, this impressive venue on the southern edge of town offers indoor seating in a comfortable open room—opt for one of the three-quarter-moon booths—and, in good weather, patio dining. The unusual French-California bistro-style dishes are meant to tantalize: mashed potatoes topped with giant scallops and a truffle vinaigrette; ricotta gnocchi served with long-braised veal cheeks and tiny, tiny baby artichokes; an absolutely superb chocolate croissant pudding. Assistance in picking wines to complement each is a house specialty.

## Terra
*1345 Railroad Ave./Hunt St., downtown, (707) 963-8931; www.terrarestaurant.com. D W-M; $$$; closed first 2 wks. of Jan. Reservations advised.*

Fronted by flower-filled planter boxes, this magical spot has a cave-like stone wall interior and offers a cool respite from the area's often warm weather. Creative menu selections offered by owner-chef Hiro Sone combine the styles of France, northern Italy, and the Pacific Rim. They are unusual and flavorful and change periodically: radicchio salad tossed with a balsamic vinaigrette and plenty of Parmesan; broiled sake-marinated sea bass with shrimp dumplings in shiso broth; grilled salmon with red Thai curry sauce and basmati rice. Desserts can be wicked: rich, moist chocolate bread pudding with sun-dried cherries; chocolate truffle cake with espresso ice cream.

## Tra Vigne
*1050 Charter Oak Ave., (707) 963-4444, fax (707) 963-1233; www.travignerestaurant.com. L-D daily; $$. Highchairs, boosters, booths, child portions. Reservations advised.*

Situated in a rustic stone building, this justly popular northern Italian restaurant features a stunning, wide-open, high-ceilinged room furnished with both comfortable tables and booths. Outside seating on a stone patio is quite desirable on warm days and evenings, when tiny lights twinkle in the mulberry trees. A round of crusty bread and olive oil for dipping are provided to enjoy while perusing the menu. Interesting housemade pastas and pizzas share the bill of fare with fresh fish, meats, and poultry, and it seems that nothing is not delicious. Antipasti items and daily specials are often intriguing, and desserts include such goodies as fresh fruit gelato and biscotti with sweet wine. Wine varietals are available by the glass and include both local and Italian selections.

Take-out sandwiches and salads are available in the adjoining **Cantinetta** *((707) 963-8888.)*, where informal outdoor seating is also an option. The restaurant's own olive oils—infused variously with garlic, rosemary, mint, chives, or porcini mushroom—can be purchased here.

Next door, **Merryvale Vineyards** *(1000 Main St., (800) 326-6069, (707) 963-7777, fax (707) 963-1949; www.merryvale.com. Tasting daily 10-6:30; tour by appt.)* has made its home in the former Sunny St. Helena Winery—the first winery built in the Napa Valley after the repeal of Prohibition. A wine component tasting seminar and winery tour is scheduled every Saturday and Sunday; reservations are necessary.

# Calistoga

## – A LITTLE BACKGROUND –

Calistoga sits on top of a hot underground river. Originally called "Indian Hot Springs," the town's current name is devised from a combination of California and Saratoga—a spa area in New York that was the inspiration for an early 25-cottage spa development by town founder Sam Brannan, California's first millionaire. More of the town's history is waiting to be discovered in Robert Louis Stevenson's *The Silverado Squatters*. But when Stevenson quipped that "sightseeing is the art of disappointment," he couldn't have meant it to apply to this scenic area.

Calistoga is enjoying a renaissance as a popular weekend and summer retreat. Its many unpretentious spas help visitors relax, unwind, and get healthy in pools filled from hot springs. Most offer services such as mud baths, steam baths, and massages, and many make their mineral pools available for day use for a small fee.

While here, don't miss taking a mud bath, one of life's great experiences. The mud is prepared using a mixture of volcanic ash (collected from nearby Mount St. Helena), peat moss, and naturally heated mineral water. After a period of nude immersion, the bather takes a mineral bath and a steam bath, and then, swaddled in dry blankets, rests and cools. Ahhh. (A few notes: Pregnant women, people with high blood pressure or heart conditions, and children under 14 are cautioned against taking mud baths. Technicians are all licensed by the city. It's sanitary; after each use, tubs are flooded with 140-degree mineral water, the mud is turned, and new mud is added. To avoid cramping, don't eat for a while before or after.)

## – VISITOR INFORMATION –

### Calistoga Chamber of Commerce
*1458 Lincoln Ave. #9, (707) 942-6333, fax (707) 942-9287; www.calistogafun.com.*

## – GETTING THERE –

Located approximately 10 miles north of St. Helena, and 25 miles north of Napa, via Highway 29.

## – WHAT TO DO –

### Bothe-Napa Valley State Park
*3801 St. Helena Hwy. N., (707) 942-4575, fax (707) 942-9560; www.parks.ca.gov. Daily 8-sunset. $4/vehicle. Pool: summer only; $2, under 18 free.*

Swimming in the naturally heated pool is a favorite activity at this lovely park, but picnicking and hiking are also popular. Campsites are available.

### Getaway Adventures
*1117 Lincoln Ave., (800) 499-BIKE, (707) 763-3040, fax 707-763-4682; www.getawayadventures.com. $105/1 day.*

Guided bicycle trips visit several small wineries and include a gourmet picnic lunch. Overnight trips, complete with inn stays, are also available, and airport transfer can be arranged.

### Old Faithful Geyser of California
*1299 Tubbs Ln., (707) 942-6463, fax (707) 942-6898; www.oldfaithfulgeyser.com. Daily 9-6. $8, 60+ $7, 6-12 $3.*

Located in the crater of an extinct volcano, this idyllic site is home to one of only three geysers in the world that erupt regularly and merit the name Old Faithful (the other two are in Yellowstone National Park in Wyoming and on North Island in New Zealand). The geyser erupts approximately every 14 minutes, shooting scalding 350-degree water 60 feet into the air. The show lasts from 3 to 4 minutes. Plenty of picnic tables and a snack bar are available.

### The Petrified Forest
*4100 Petrified Forest Rd., 4 mi. W of town, (707) 942-6667, fax (707) 942-0815; www.petrifiedforest.org. Daily 10-5; in summer to 6. $5, 60+ & 12-17 $4, 4-11 $3.*

A self-guided 1/4-mile path leads through this unusual forest holding the world's largest petrified trees. Open to the public since 1870, it contains petrified redwood trees that are over 3 million years old and as long as 126 feet. Facilities include a small museum and picnic tables.

### The Sharpsteen Museum
*1311 Washington St., (707) 942-5911, fax (707) 942-6325; www.sharpsteen-museum.org. Daily 11-4. Free.*

Created by Ben Sharpsteen, a Walt Disney Studio animator and Oscar-winning producer (his Oscar is displayed here), this exceptionally well-designed museum displays an elaborate and extensive diorama of Calistoga as it appeared in 1865 when Sam Brannan opened the town's first spa and began its reputation as a restorative resort area. A working model of the Napa Valley Railroad is also displayed, and an early kitchen, blacksmith shop, and stagecoach round out the exhibits. The adjoining **Sam Brannan Cottage** is beautifully furnished and exemplifies the style in which wealthy San Franciscans lived when they vacationed here in the late 1800s.

## Smith's Mount St. Helena Trout Farm

*18401 Ida Clayton Rd., 14 mi. from town (call for directions), (707) 987-3651, fax (707) 987-0105. Sat-Sun 10-6; Feb-Oct only. $1-$5.*

All ages can enjoy fishing on this lake. Poles and bait are free. Size determines the charge for fish caught, and cleaning and packaging are included.

— WINERIES —

## Château Montelena Winery

*1429 Tubbs Ln., (707) 942-5105, fax (707) 942-4221; www.montelena.com. Tasting daily 9:30-4. Tour daily at 9:30 & 1, Apr-Oct; at 2, Nov.-Mar; reservations required.*

Noted for its Chardonnays and Cabernet Sauvignons, this winery can be difficult to find. Two islets in Jade Lake are reached via footbridge. The lake features a berthed Chinese junk and is populated with ducks, swans, and geese. Picnicking is not permitted.

## Clos Pegase

*1060 Dunaweal Ln., (800) 366-8583, (707) 942-4981, fax (707) 942-4993; www.clospegase.com. Tasting daily 10:30-5; tour at 11, 2.*

This winery opened in 1987 amid much controversy. Even though its post-modern design was the winner in a contest sponsored by the San Francisco Museum of Modern Art, there were those who liked its stark stucco architecture and those who didn't. Surrounded by young vineyards, it has a surreal quality, with tall, thin cypress trees lining an outdoor walkway and modern sculpture dotting the landscape. Named after Pegasus, the winged horse of Greek mythology that gave birth to wine and art, the winery appropriately displays a collec-

tion of fine art within its caves. Among the treasure-trove dating from the 3rd century B.C. to the present are ancient vineyard tools and rare free-blown wine bottles, carafes, and glasses. An elaborate slide presentation that follows wine from the birth of the grape, through its celebration in art, and on into the present is sometimes scheduled. Picnic tables are sheltered by the shady canopy of a 300-year-old oak tree.

## Schramsberg

*1400 Schramsberg Rd., 2 mi. S of town, (800) 877-3623, (707) 942-2414, fax (707) 942-5943; www.schramsberg.com. Tasting & tour by appt.*

Established in 1862, this landmark winery is written about extensively by Robert Louis Stevenson in *The Silverado Squatters*. R.L.S., who called their wine "bottled poetry," was once a guest, as was Ambrose Bierce. Further recognition for its distinctive bottle-fermented sparkling wines made from hand-picked grapes came in 1972 when President Nixon and Premier Chou En-lai poured a bottle of Schramsberg Blanc de Blancs sparkling wine— the country's first commercial sparkling wine using Chardonnay—for the "Toast to Peace" in Beijing. An informative tour goes through portions of the 2 miles of caves, taking in sections draped with ancient cobwebs and sometimes bumping into the famous "riddler" whose job it is to turn approximately 50,000 bottles each day (this is perhaps the *perfect* job for a compulsive-neurotic). Tasting occurs in a private room with participants seated at a glass table supported appropriately by an old riddling rack. It is interesting to note that some of the winery buildings are built from redwoods grown on the property, and the Victorian house was constructed without nails by a shipbuilder.

## Sterling Vineyards

*1111 Dunaweal Ln., (800) 726-6136, (707) 942-3345, fax (707) 942-3445; www.sterlingvineyards.com. Tasting & self-guided tour daily 10:30-4:30.*

Accessible via a 4-minute gondola ride, this winery was built to resemble a Greek monastery. It features stunning and unusual white stucco, cubist-style architecture. Spectacular views of the Napa Valley are provided throughout the self-guided winery tour. For tasting, visitors sit at tables either in a spacious interior room or on an outdoor terrace.

*Sterling Vineyards*

The fee includes the gondola ride and a taste of four wines, and children get a juice drink. A picnic terrace with a magnificent view is available.

## — WHERE TO STAY —

### Brannan Cottage Inn
*109 Wapoo Ave., (707) 942-4200; www.brannan cottageinn.com. 6 rooms; $$. Unsuitable for children under 12. Some TVs. Full breakfast. No smoking.*

Located a pleasant 2-block walk from town, this Greek Revival Victorian cottage was built by Sam Brannan in 1860. It is listed on the National Register of Historic Places. A large palm tree planted by Brannan, and mentioned by Robert Louis Stevenson in *The Silverado Squatters*, still grows in the garden. Rooms are named after flowers and most open onto a quiet courtyard, where breakfast is served in warm weather.

### Calistoga Spa Hot Springs
*1006 Washington St., (707) 942-6269; www.calistoga spa.com. 57 units; $$. Children under 1 free. All kitchens. 4 hot spring pools; fitness room. No smoking; no pets.*

This conveniently located, unpretentious, and particularly family-friendly spa offers motel rooms that open onto the pool area. Four outdoor mineral water pools are available: an 83-degree lap pool, a 90-degree children's wading pool, a 100-degree soaking pool, and a 105 degree covered hot tub. Mud baths, mineral baths, steam baths, and massages are available. Non-guests can also use the facilities (*Daily 8:30am-9pm. $15-$20.*).

### Cottage Grove Inn
*1711 Lincoln Ave., (800) 799-2284, (707) 942-8400, fax (707) 942-2653; www.cottagegrove.com. 16 cabins; $$$-$$$+. Unsuitable for children under 12. All wood-burning fireplaces. Afternoon snack, continental breakfast. No smoking; no pets.*

Nestled here in an historic elm grove, each of these individual cottages is decorated in a different theme. All are equipped with a deep whirlpool soaking tub for two, a stereo system, and a refrigerator.

### Dr. Wilkinson's Hot Springs Resort
*1507 Lincoln Ave., (707) 942-4102, fax (707) 942-4412; www.drwilkinson.com. 42 rooms; $$-$$$+. Children under 2 free. Some kitchens. 1 indoor & 2 outdoor mineral pools; steam room; health spa.*

This long-time spa features a 104-degree indoor mineral pool with a view of the nearby

foothills, a cooler 92-degree outdoor mineral pool, and a refreshing 82-degree outdoor swimming pool. Though the pools are not open to non-guests, the mud baths, mineral baths, steam baths, massage, and separate facial salon are. Lodging is in motel units as well as in the nearby **The Victorian House** and **Hideaway Cottages** *(1412 Fairway Ave., (707) 942-4108; www.hideawaycottages.com. Unsuitable for children under 18.).*

### Indian Springs
*1712 Lincoln Ave., (707) 942-4913, fax (707) 942-4919; www.indianspringscalistoga.com. 17 units; $$-$$$+. Children under 2 free. All kitchens; some gas fireplaces. Mineral pool; health spa; 1 clay tennis court. No pets.*

Dating back to 1910 and built on the site of the town's first spa (which was built in 1860 by Sam Brannan), this resort is where Robert Louis Stevenson vacationed in 1880 and is said to have written part of *The Silverado Squatters.* It is the state's oldest continuously operating thermal pool and spa facility. Its Mission-style, Olympic-size swimming pool is filled with 90- to 102-degree geyser mineral water, and this is the only spa in town offering all ash mud baths. Lodging is in refurbished 1940s housekeeping bungalows, and croquet and other lawn games are available to guests.

### Mountain Home Ranch
*3400 Mountain Home Ranch Rd., 6 mi. from town, (707) 942-6616, fax (707) 942-9091; www.mountain homeranch.com. 23 units; $-$$; closed Dec-Jan. Children under 1 free. No TVs; some kitchens & wood-burning fireplaces & stoves; some shared baths. 1 heated & 1 unheated pool; 1 tennis court. Continental breakfast. No smoking; pets ok.*

Guests at this informal rural spot can stay in modern cabins with a private deck or porch, in lodge rooms, or in rustic cabins (summer only). Summer activities include lake swimming, hiking, and fishing.

### Mount View Hotel & Spa
*1457 Lincoln Ave., (800) 816-6877, (707) 942-6877, fax (707) 942-6904; www.mountviewhotel.com. 32 units; $$-$$$+. Unsuitable for children under 16. Heated pool (year-round); hot tub; health spa. Continental breakfast; restaurant. No smoking; no pets.*

Built in 1918 and furnished with an eclectic mix of contemporary and antique pieces, this beautifully restored grand hotel is a National Historic Landmark. Nine theme suites are furnished with period pieces—two in art deco style—and three private cottages have their own decks and hot tubs. Breakfast is delivered to the room, and an upscale European-style spa offers a variety of treatments.

## The Pink Mansion

*1415 Foothill Blvd., (800) 238-PINK, (707) 942-0558, same fax; www.pinkmansion.com. 6 rooms; $$-$$$. Some fireplaces. Indoor heated pool (year-round) & hot tub. Afternoon snack, full breakfast. Pets ok.*

Nestled against a hillside on the outskirts of town, this restored 1875 Victorian mansion is painted a pleasant shade of pink. A large front porch equipped with a couch swing invites leisurely contemplation of the surroundings, and the indoor pool and hot tub provide a relaxing view of a redwood grove behind the house. Several rooms have clawfoot tubs, and a lavish breakfast is served in the elegant dining room.

### — WHERE TO EAT —

### All Seasons Cafe & Wine Shop

*1400 Lincoln Ave., (707) 942-9111, fax (707) 942-9420. L F-Sun, D Tu-Sun; $$-$$$. Highchairs, boosters. Reservations advised.*

Dress is very casual in this narrow dining room, and children are welcome and accommodated. One dinner enjoyed here began with great housemade bread and a flawless warm spinach salad prepared with pancetta, house-smoked chicken, and Feta cheese. It was followed by a perfectly roasted chicken accompanied by perfectly roasted potatoes, whole cloves of garlic, artichokes, and olives. Dessert was a memorable fresh cherry cobbler with house-made vanilla ice cream arranged artistically on a plate strewn with flower petals.

### Calistoga Inn

*1250 Lincoln Ave., (707) 942-4101, fax (707) 942-4919; www.napabeer.com. L-D daily. Sat-SunBr; $-$$. Highchairs, boosters. Reservations advised.*

Since a delightful collection of turkey platters decorates the walls here, it isn't too much of a surprise that the house specialty is big portions of old-fashioned hardwood-grilled meats and vegetables. Fresh fish and 40-clove garlic chicken are also on the menu, and irresistible down-home desserts include both creamy peanut butter pie and housemade brownies "smushed" with vanilla ice cream and topped with hot fudge. In warm weather, diners are seated outside on a patio overlooking the Napa Valley River.

An informal **brewpub** operating in a cozy old-time bar area offers four house brews—one of them is a Pilsner-style lager (the house specialty)—and inexpensive pub food such as housemade potato chips, a variety of salads, a good hamburger, and jerk chicken.

Modest **lodging** *(18 rooms; $. All shared baths. Continental breakfast.)* is available upstairs in cozy, pleasant rooms equipped with sinks. Several sets of adjoining rooms are suitable for families.

# The Silverado Trail

### — A LITTLE BACKGROUND —

Stretching approximately 30 miles from Napa to Calistoga, this scenic route offers a quieter, less-crowded wine tasting experience.

### — GETTING THERE —

Located 50 miles northeast of San Francisco. Take I-880 north to Highway 29 north to Napa. Turn right on Trancas Street. After about 10 minutes, turn left at the sign onto the Silverado Trail.

### — WHAT TO DO —

### Lake Berryessa

*In Napa take Hwy. 128 E, (707) 966-2111, fax (707) 966-0409; www.recreation.gov. Daily.*

This man-made lake is 26 miles long, 3 miles wide, and has 165 miles of shoreline. Boats and water-skis can be rented, and the swimming and fishing are excellent. Camping and lodging facilities are available.

### — WINERIES —

### Jarvis

*2970 Monticello Rd., 8 mi. E of Silverado Trail, in Napa, (800) 255-5280, (707) 255-5280, fax (707) 255-5282; www.jarviswines.com. Tasting tour daily by appt.*

Located on 1,300 acres in the scenic Mt. George area, this is the only winery in the world entirely inside a cave. The owners, who bought the property on a weekend getaway, didn't want to spoil its beauty and so cleverly hid it away in a 45,000-square-foot cave. Visitors park out in a meadow and walk in. Tour highlights include passing natural springs reformed into gurgling rivers and cascading waterfalls; visiting the Crystal Chamber, a room with a floor of polished Brazilian granite and an impressive collection of huge purple amethysts from Brazil; and viewing the whimsical use of fiber optics throughout. An elegant tasting room with red velvet chairs and a red marble table is entered by crossing the river on stepping stones. There, delicious wines await sampling. Many Jarvis wines are available in half bottles, and good news for those who suffer from wine headaches—the winery uses minimal sulfites.

## Mumm Cuvée Napa

*8445 Silverado Trail, in Rutherford, (707) 967-7700, fax (707) 433-3538; www.mummcuveenapa.com. Tasting daily 10-5; tours 10-3, on the hr.*

In good weather, tasters can sample sparkling wines while sitting under umbrellas on a patio with a magnificent view of the valley's vineyards. The winery's art galleries feature changing exhibits of fine photography.

## Nichelini Winery

*2950 Sage Canyon Rd. (Hwy. 128), 11 mi. E of Silverado Trail, in St. Helena, (800) WE-TASTE, (707) 963-0717, fax (707) 963-3262; www.nichelini winery.com. Tasting & self-guided tour Sat-Sun 10-5; in summer to 6; M-F by appt.*

Established in 1890, this historic, out-of-the-way winery is in a gorgeous location well off the main drag, down a rural side road leading to Lake Berryessa. Pack a picnic to enjoy at tables sheltered by old, old trees, and allow some time for the seasonal bocce ball court. Operated now by four of founder Anton Nichelini's grandchildren, it is the oldest continuously owned family winery in Napa Valley. The winery produces great Zinfandels using vines planted long, long ago by the elder Nichelini.

## Pine Ridge Winery

*5901 Silverado Trail, in Napa, (800) 575-9777, (707) 253-7500, fax (707) 253-1493; www.pineridge winery.com. Tasting daily 10:30-4:30; tour at 10, 12, 2, by appt.*

The tasting room is a pleasant place to sample the premium Cabernets produced by this winery's Stags Leap District grapes. On tours, participants tote along tasting glasses for barrel samplings. Less time is spent among the stainless-steel tanks and barrels in the extensive caves and more time outside in the vineyard (the Demonstration Vineyard is always available for strolling). A picnic area is situated under a young grove of tall pines, and two board swings await the kiddies.

## Rutherford Hill Winery

*200 Rutherford Hill Dr., in Rutherford, (800) MERLOT-1, (707) 963-1871, fax (707) 963-1878; www.rutherford hill.com. Tasting daily 10-5; tour at 11:30, 1:30, 3:30.*

Visitors pass through massive 15-foot-tall doors as they enter the tasting room here. The tour includes viewing the most extensive wine-aging cave system in the U.S. Across the street from the tasting room, a sylvan hillside picnic area beckons with spacious tables sheltered by old oaks and a pleasant view of the valley.

— WHERE TO STAY —

## Auberge du Soleil

*180 Rutherford Hill Rd., in Rutherford, (800) 348-5406, (707) 963-1211, fax (707) 963-8764; www.au bergedusoleil.com. 50 rooms; $$$+. All fireplaces. Heated pool (seasonal); hot tub; steam rooms; health spa; fitness room; 1 tennis court. Unsuitable for children under 16. Restaurant; room service. No pets.*

With a name meaning literally "inn of the sun," this upscale Mediterranean-style bungalow village cascades down a peaceful wooded hillside, spreading over the 33-acre property. Each room in the four-unit cottages has a private deck with panoramic views of the valley, a wood-burning fireplace, and an oversize bathtub big enough for two. They are stocked with a fruit basket and snacks, and beds are made with Frette linens. Paths crisscross the property, passing through a 5-acre **Olive Grove Sculpture Garden** featuring works by California sculptors; all pieces are for sale.

The inn's elegant French **restaurant** *((800) 348-5406. B-L-D daily; $$$. Highchairs, child portions. Reservations required. Free valet parking.)* has plush indoor seating as well as more rustic, and more desirable, outside seating on a heated terrace with sweeping views of the valley. Sumptuous, full-flavored dishes might include: cumin-scented crab cakes; flame-roasted, Spanish-style stuffed peppers; a salad of rosemary-grilled shrimp with haricot verts and shaved fennel; ravioli stuffed with woodland mushrooms and topped with a thyme cream sauce. Desserts are not boring: a Valrhona chocolate soufflé, profiteroles stuffed with cappuccino-chip ice cream, a Meyer lemon-and-white chocolate mousse tart with raspberry sauce.

## Meadowood Resort & Hotel

*900 Meadowood Ln., in St. Helena, (800) 458-8080, (707) 963-3646, fax (707) 963-3532; www.meado wood.com. 85 rooms; $$$+. Children under 12 free. Some kitchens & fireplaces. 2 heated pools (year-round); hot tub; health spa; fitness room; 7 tennis courts; 9-hole golf course. 2 restaurants; room service.*

This luxury resort allows guests an escape from reality. Cabins with skylights and old-fashioned porches dot the secluded property, providing plenty of privacy, and room service will deliver a breakfast basket to the door. Rooms are equipped with heated bathroom floors, terry robes, and down comforters. Facilities on the 250 acres of lush wooded grounds include a children's playground (one of the two pools is also dedicated to children), two regulation English croquet lawns, and 3 miles of hiking trails. Bike rentals are also available. The health spa offers a massage using a unique Chardonnay lotion developed just for the resort, as well as a grape seed mud massage and grape seed body polish.

The **Restaurant at Meadowood** *(D daily, SunBr; $$$.)* complements its refined menu by serving exclusively Napa Valley wines and is said to have the most comprehensive selection in the world. Each can be ordered by the glass. Downstairs, the slightly less formal **Grill** *(B-L-D daily; $$$.)* serves delicious California bistro fare and features a terrace overlooking the green, green golf course.

## Silverado Resort

*1600 Atlas Peak Rd., in Napa, 1 mi. NE of town, (800) 532-0500, (707) 257-0200, fax (707) 257-2867; www.silveradoresort.com. 280 units; $$-$$$+. Children under 14 free. All kitchens & wood-burning fireplaces. 1 heated pool, 8 unheated pools; hot tub; sauna; health spa; fitness room; 17 tennis courts; 2 18-hole golf courses. 2 restaurants; room service.*

Once part of General Vallejo's Rancho Yajome, this 1,200-acre resort has the largest tennis complex in Northern California. Its heart is a gracious 1875 mansion, where guests are greeted and registered and within which are the resort's two restaurants. Accommodations are in individually owned condominiums, and the location, architectural style, and decor of each vary. Some units are available on the grounds adjacent to the mansion, allowing an easy walk to most of the facilities, while larger condos—some opening right onto the golf course—are farther away and require a 1- or 2-mile drive. Facilities include jogging trails, bicycle rentals, and two golf courses designed by Robert Trent Jones, Jr. The 16,000-square-foot spa is fashioned after a classic Roman bath and is the largest private spa facility in the Wine Country. It has a couples massage room with skylight and fireplace, offers a large choice of treatments, and is equipped with saunas, steam baths, whirlpool tubs, a heated pool, a fitness center, and a snack bar.

The **Royal Oak** *(D daily; $$$. Reservations required.)* serves mesquite-grilled steaks and seafood, while the more casual **Silverado Bar & Grill** *(B-L daily; $$.)* serves smaller meals and offers a soothing view of the golf course.

## Silver Rose Inn & Spa

*351 Rosedale Rd., in Calistoga, (800) 995-9381, (707) 942-9581, fax (707) 942-0841; www.silver rose.com. 20 rooms; $$-$$$. No TVs; some fireplaces. 2 hot spring pools (year-round); 2 hot tubs; health spa; fitness room; 2 tennis courts; putting green. Continental breakfast. No smoking; no pets.*

Sitting amid acres of vineyards and mountains, this peaceful enclave provides quiet, serene views. Architecture is contemporary, with huge stone fireplaces and rustic beams in the public rooms. Themed guest rooms—The Porch Room, Cleopatra's Room, Hello Hollywood, The Library—are found in the Inn the Vineyard building, where many rooms feature up-close vineyard-side views and in-room whirlpool tubs for two. However, the property's original building, the Inn on the Knoll, has a more impressive public room and pool area and is just a few steps from the spa. A large pool in the shape of a wine bottle is located between the two buildings. The small spa is available only to guests and offers a variety of water treatments and massage. The pools, hot tubs, and spa tubs are all fed by underground hot springs.

Also on the property, the **Silver Rose Winery** *(Tasting daily 10-5; tour at 11.)* has a daily barrel-tasting tour that begins with koi feeding.

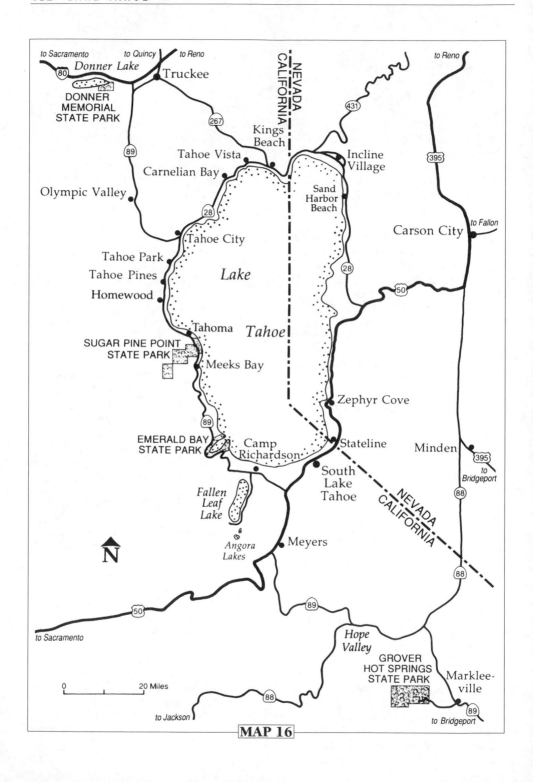

to Sacramento to Quincy to Reno
*Donner Lake* to Reno
80
Truckee
DONNER
MEMORIAL
STATE PARK

NEVADA
CALIFORNIA

267
431

89
Kings
Beach
Tahoe Vista
Carnelian Bay
Incline
Village
395

Olympic Valley
Sand
Harbor
Beach
28
Carson City
to Fallon

Tahoe City
*Lake*

Tahoe Park
Tahoe Pines
28
Homewood

50

Tahoma
*Tahoe*
SUGAR PINE POINT
STATE PARK
Meeks Bay

89
Zephyr Cove
EMERALD BAY
STATE PARK
Camp
Richardson
Stateline
Minden
395
South
Lake
Tahoe
to
Bridgeport

N

*Fallen
Leaf
Lake*
88
NEVADA
CALIFORNIA

*Angora
Lakes*
Meyers
88

50
89

*Hope
Valley*
0      20 Miles
GROVER
HOT SPRINGS
STATE PARK
Marklee-
ville
88
to Sacramento

88
89
to Jackson
to Bridgeport

**MAP 16**

LAKE TAHOE

## South Lake Tahoe

*. . . At last the Lake burst upon us—a noble sheet of blue water lifted six thousand three hundred feet above the level of the sea, and walled in by a rim of snowclad mountain peaks that towered aloft full three thousand feet higher still!*

*It was a vast oval. As it lay there with the shadows of the great mountains brilliantly photographed upon its surface, I thought it must surely be the fairest picture the whole earth affords . . .*

— Mark Twain

Lake Tahoe lies two-thirds in California and one-third in Nevada. It is the largest (192 square miles surface) and deepest (1,645 feet) Alpine lake in North America and the second largest in the world. At 6,227 feet above sea level, its crystal-clear, deep-blue summer waters provide a striking contrast with the extensive green forests and majestic mountains encircling it.

Once a remote area, Tahoe is now a popular and well-equipped vacation destination offering a wide range of recreational activities along with its spectacular scenery. Swimming, hiking, boating, tennis, golf, bicycling, horseback riding, river rafting, camping, fishing, water-skiing, and backpacking are among the summer outdoor activities to be enjoyed. In winter, the skiing is excellent.

On the Nevada side, gambling is another big attraction. A lodging shuttle service provides transportation to the casinos, and some lodgings have discount casino coupons for their guests. In addition, the casinos offer on-demand pick-up shuttle service from most lodgings.

Children may go into a casino with adults but are not allowed to "loiter" (not even babies in backpacks!) or play the slot machines. Fortunately, childcare is relatively easy to find in this area. Many lodgings maintain a list of local sitters, and childcare centers that take drop-ins are listed in the Yellow Pages. Also, the Lake Tahoe Visitors Authority provides a free list of day care providers.

In addition to having more slot machines than any other casino at Lake Tahoe, Harrah's has an unsupervised **Arcade** for children *((800) 648-3773. M-Thur 12-8, F 12-10, Sat 10-10, Sun 10-8. Admission free.)* that is a safe, well-lighted, smoke- and alcohol-free environment and is equipped with the latest video and arcade games as well as some old classics. Sure beats sitting on the curb reading comic books like some people did when they were kids. Harvey's operates **Kid's Camp** for ages 6 through 13 *((866) 454-3386,*

413

*(775) 267-6399; www.harrahs.com/our_
casinos/tah/things_to_do/kids_camp.html.
Daily; 6-10pm, $50; 9-4, summer only, $80.
Reservations required)* and has the largest video
arcade at the lake.

## — VISITOR INFORMATION —

*All addresses in this section are in the city of
South Lake Tahoe unless otherwise noted.*

## Lake Tahoe Visitors Authority
*1156 Ski Run Blvd.; (800) AT-TAHOE (lodging reserva-
tions referral service); (530) 544-5050, fax (530)
544-2386; www.bluelaketahoe.com.*

## — GETTING THERE —

Located approximately 200 miles north of San
Francisco. Take Highway 80 to Highway 50 to
the lake.

## — ANNUAL EVENTS —

## Lights on the Lake
*July 4.*
    This spectacular show is one of the largest
fireworks displays west of the Mississippi. Each
shell is choreographed and computer synchronized to a soundtrack.

## Autumn colors
*October.*
    The area around Kirkwood Mountain
Resort (see page 434) is home to groves of
aspen. Hope Valley, north of Kirkwood on
Highway 89, is particularly colorful.

## — STOPS ALONG THE WAY —

## I-80 North
    See pages 265 through 298.

## Folsom
*Off Hwy. 50, 22 mi. E of Sacramento.*
    This small town is a quick, easy stop.
Restored Gold Rush-era homes and buildings,
many now inhabited by antique shops and
unique boutiques, line historic Sutter Street.
The **Sutter Street Emporium** *(731 Sutter St.,
(800) 255-6243, (916) 985-4647, fax (916) 985-
0379; www.acountrymouse.com/naled/sutter.
Daily 10-5.)* is said to be the largest doll shop in
the state, but also sells contemporary art and
paperweights.

### • Folsom Chamber of Commerce
*200 Wool St., (800) 377-1414, (916) 985-2698,
fax (916) 985-4117; www.folsomchamber.com.*
    Pick up information about the town here.
The chamber's office is located inside the town's
old train depot, which was the terminus of the
first passenger railroad west of the Rockies (it
ran between Sacramento and Folsom).

### • Folsom City Zoo Sanctuary
*403 Stafford St./Natoma St., in Folsom City Park,
(916) 351-3527; www.folsom.ca.us. Tu-Sun 10-4. $3, 5-
12 $2.*
    This tiny zoo exhibits non-releasable
native North American animals, a few exotics,
and the largest captive wolf pack in Northern
California.

### • Folsom Dam
*7794 Folsom Dam Rd., (916) 989-7275, fax (916)
989-7208.*
    Built between 1948 and 1956, this impres-
sive dam measures 340 feet high and 1,400 feet
long. Due to terrorism concerns, tours are can-
celled indefinitely.

### • Folsom History Museum
*823 Sutter St., (916) 985-2707; www.folsomhistory
museum.org. W-Sun 11-4. $2, under 12 free.*
    Exhibits change frequently. Gold-panning
demonstrations occur on Sundays.

### • Folsom Lake State Recreation Area
*7806 Folsom-Auburn Rd., (916) 988-0205;
www.parks.ca.gov. Daily 6am-9pm; mid-Oct-Mar, 7-7.
$6/vehicle.*
    Among the activities to be enjoyed in this
18,000-acre park are hiking, biking, running,
camping, picnicking, horseback riding, water-
skiing, boating, and fishing. Campsites are
available.

### • Folsom Prison Museum
*Prison Rd./Natoma St., in Lincoln, (916) 985-2561
x4589. Daily 10-4. $1, under 12 free.*
    Located just inside the visitor's gate, this
small museum documents the history of this
massive granite structure. Opened in 1880, it is
the state's second-oldest prison and holds about
3,880 prisoners. Johnnie Cash made it famous
with his lyrics, "I'm stuck in Folsom Prison, and
time keeps draggin on."

### • Lake Forest Cafe
*13409 Folsom Blvd., (916) 985-6780. B-L W-Sun; $.
Highchairs, boosters, child portions. No reservations.*

*M.S. Dixie & Tahoe Queen*

Among the breakfast items served in this comfy little house are 43 kinds of omelettes, a variety of Jewish specialties, and freshly-baked giant cinnamon rolls. Some breakfast items are also available at lunch.

### Poor Red's

See page 344.

### Placerville

See pages 344 through 345.

## – WHAT TO DO –

### Amusement centers

These family fun spots are open daily in summer and as the weather permits in winter.

#### • Magic Carpet Golf
*2455 Lake Tahoe Blvd. (Hwy. 50), (530) 541-3787.*

This is the kind of colorful miniature course that has giant plaster dinosaurs and a new theme at each hole. Choose from either 19- or 28-hole rounds.

#### • Tahoe Amusement Park
*2401 Lake Tahoe Blvd. (Hwy. 50), (530) 541-1300. Schedule varies; May-Oct only. Free admission; ride prices vary.*

Facilities include a variety of kiddie rides, a giant slide, and go-carts.

### Angora Lakes Trail
*On Spring Creek Rd., off Hwy. 89.*

Take the road to Fallen Leaf Lake, which passes a waterfall, and then turn left at the sign to Angora Lakes. It is an easy 1/2-mile hike from the end of the road to the lakes, where quiet picnic and swimming spots await.

### Around the lake

#### • By car
A leisurely drive around the 72-mile perimeter of Lake Tahoe takes about 3 hours, but allow all day. Tempting places to stop for picnicking, swimming, and exploring abound.

#### • On foot
*(775) 298-0012, fax (775) 298-0013; www.tahoe rimtrail.org.*

The well-marked 150-mile **Tahoe Rim Trail** circles the lake and passes through part of Desolation Wilderness. It has nine trailheads, is designed for both day trekkers and overnight hikers, and parts are wheelchair accessible.

### Beaches and biking

#### • Pope Beach and Baldwin Beach
*On Hwy. 89, between the Y & Emerald Bay, (530) 544-5994; www.fs.fed.us/r5/ltbmu/recreation. Daily 8-sunset; closed in winter. $5/vehicle.*

These beaches are primo. This same stretch of highway has several bike rental facilities and a nice bike trail.

## Boat rentals

### • Tahoe Sports

*(530) 542-2111; www.tahoesports.com.*

With seven locations, this is the largest rental company in the area. Everything from powerboats and personal watercraft to skis and snowboards are available.

## Boat tours

### • Lake Tahoe Cruises

*(800) 23-TAHOE, (775) 589-4906, fax (775) 589-4915; www.laketahoecruises.com. Basic cruise: $26+, 55+ $23+, 3-11 $9+. Reservations advised.*

### • M.S. Dixie II

*760 Hwy. 50, in Zephyr Cove, Nevada, 4 mi. N of Stateline; www.tahoedixie2.com. Schedule varies; May-Oct only. Parking $6.*

A replica of a cotton barge used on the Mississippi River in the 1920s, this three-deck paddle wheel steamer cruises to Emerald Bay. She is the largest boat on the lake and boasts a glass-bottom viewing window. Dinner cruises with live music for dancing and breakfast/brunch cruises are available at additional charge.

### • Tahoe Queen

*900 Ski Run Blvd.; www.hornblower.com. Schedule varies.*

This slightly smaller paddle wheeler offers 2-hour cruises to Emerald Bay. It also has a large window in its floor for underwater viewing. Family fun cruises, with scavenger hunts for kids, and Tales of Tahoe cruises depart daily, and dinner-dance cruises depart Friday and Saturday evenings.

### • Woodwind II

*760 Hwy. 50, in Zephyr Cove, Nevada, (888) 867-6394, (775) 588-3000; www.sailwoodwind.com. Schedule varies; Apr-Oct only. Basic cruise $28, 60+ $24, 3-12 $12. Reservations advised.*

Only 35 passengers fit on this 55-foot catamaran with two underwater observation windows. A sunset champagne cruise is available at additional charge.

## Camp Richardson Corral and Pack Station

*On Hwy. 89 N., (530) 541-3113. Daily; schedule varies; June-Sept only. Guided rides $30/hr. Must be 6 or older. Reservations required.*

Operated by the same family since 1934, this stable has breakfast rides *($40)*, dinner rides *($60)*, and wagon rides *($20, under 3 free)*. Fishing trips, overnight pack trips, and spot pack trips can be arranged, and sleigh rides are available December through March when there is enough snow.

## Casino showrooms

Big name entertainment is always booked into these showrooms. Call ahead for reservations at the early or late cocktail shows. Seats are assigned. Children 6 and older are usually admitted, but it depends on the show's content.

### • Caesars Circus Maximus

*(800) 648-3353, (775) 586-3515; www.caesarstahoe.com.*

### • Harrah's South Shore Room

*(800) HARRAHS, (800) 648-3773, (775) 588-6611; www.harrahs.com/our_casinos/tah.*

### • Harveys Cabaret

*(800) HARVEYS, (775) 588-2411; www.harrahs.com/our_casinos/hlt. No smoking.*

Holding just 288 seats, this is said to be the only mini-showroom in the world. There are no bad seats.

### • Horizon Golden Cabaret

*(800) 648-3322, (775) 588-6211; www.horizoncasino.com/main.php.*

Another entertainment option here is the **Stadium Cinemas**, where eight screens show first-run movies.

## Gondola at Heavenly

*Hwy. 50/Park Ave., (800) HEAVENLY, (775) 586-7000; www.skiheavenly.com. Schedule varies. $22, 13-19 & seniors $20, 5-12 $14.*

These eight-passenger gondolas take 12 minutes to climb 2.4 miles up Monument Peak to an observation deck that is 3,000 feet above lake level—and more than 9,000 feet above sea level—on the California side. Views are magnificent. The first stop features a viewing deck with telescopes and picnic tables, plus an assortment of dining venues and shops. Farther up, at the second and last stop, is **Adventure Peak Grill**.

## Grover Hot Springs State Park

*3415 Hot Springs Rd., 4 mi. E of Markleeville, 35 mi. SE of town, (530) 694-2248; www.parks.ca.gov. Daily 11-8 in summer; schedule varies rest of year. $5, under 17 $2.*

Beautifully situated in a valley meadow ringed by pine-covered slopes, this hot springs park features a 3-foot deep, 104-degree mineral pool filled by six nonsulfurous springs, and a 70- to 80-degree fresh-water pool. The pools are well maintained, and lifeguards are on duty. The number of bathers permitted is limited so sometimes there is a wait, and swimsuits are always required. Short hiking trails, picnic facilities, and campsites are also available. In winter, this is a popular après-ski destination.

## Lake Tahoe Historical Society Museum

*3058 Lake Tahoe Blvd. (Hwy. 50), (530) 541-5458. Tu-Sat 10-4. $2, 6-18 $1.*

The history of Lake Tahoe's south shore is chronicled here.

## Tahoe Trout Farm

*1023 Blue Lake Ave., off Hwy. 50, (530) 541-1491. Daily 10-7; June-Aug only. Charge determined by size of fish caught.*

Though there is, of course, no challenge to catching trout here, there are some compelling reasons to give it a try: No license in required; bait and tackle are furnished free; and there is no limit. Anglers are almost guaranteed to go home with tasty dinner fare. Even young children, who frustrate easily, will probably succeed in catching a fish. (But do bear in mind that

some children are appalled at just the *idea* of catching a fish—let alone actually *eating* it.)

## Tallac Historic Site

*Off Hwy. 89, 3 mi. W of Hwy. 50, (530) 541-5227, fax (530) 573-2693; www.valhalla-tallac.com. Grounds: Daily dawn-dusk. Museum: Daily 10-4, summer only. Free.*

Composed of three early-20th-century summer estates, this 74-acre site is crisscrossed with fragrant, pine needle-littered paths leading to themed outbuildings—a laundry, a dairy, a boathouse—and to an arboretum. House tours are sometimes available for a fee. Picnic tables and barbecues are provided, and beautiful sandy beaches invite exploration. Cultural and historical programs, including afternoon teas and special children's activities, are sometimes scheduled.

A **Great Gatsby Festival** occurs here each August. Celebrating the area's partying past, this festival brings history to life with era arts and crafts demonstrations, plus some old-fashioned fun and games.

## Taylor Creek Visitor Center

*Off Hwy. 89, 4 mi. W of Hwy. 50, (530) 543-2674. Daily 8-5:30, summer only; closed Nov-May. Free.*

Interpretive programs and guided nature walks are scheduled regularly. Self-guided trails

*Taylor Creek Stream Profile Chamber*

*Tallac Historic Site*

include Smokey's Trail, which teaches kids about campfire safety, and the Lake of the Sky Trail, which leads to the lake's shore. Rainbow Trail winds through a meadow, past Taylor Creek, and on to the Stream Profile Chamber—where the life in a real mountain stream is viewed from underwater. Visit in October to see the annual run of the Kokanee salmon and to take part in the annual **Kokanee Salmon Festival**.

## Vikingsholm
*On Hwy. 89, in Tahoma, (530) 525-7277; www.vikings holm.com. Tours daily 10-4; mid-June-Sept; closed Oct-May. $3, 6-12 $2.*

Butterflies, waterfalls, and wildflowers are encountered on the steep 1-mile trail that descends to this magnificent 39-room, sod-roof Swedish castle home built in 1928. Constructed completely by hand using native materials, it was completed in one summer. Baby strollers are not permitted on the tour. The house is part of **Emerald Bay State Park** *((530) 541-3030; www.parks.ca.gov.).* Picnic tables are available, and swimming is permitted in an area with a sandy beach.

## Winter activities
See pages 434 through 435.

### — WHERE TO STAY -
### LAKEFRONT

## Historic Camp Richardson Resort
*1900 Jameson Beach Rd., off Hwy. 89, 2¹/₂ mi. W of Hwy. 50, (800) 544-1801, (530) 541-1801, fax (530) 541-1802; www.camprichardson.com. 37 rooms, 42 cabins (1-wk. min.); $-$$. Some TVs & kitchens. Continental breakfast; restaurant. Day use $7/vehicle. No pets.*

Spread over 150 lake-side acres leased from the U.S. Forest Service, this complex exudes a nostalgic 1930s Old Tahoe charm. Lodging is in an historic hotel, a beach motel, and rustic cabins spread amid tall pines. An inexpensive Kid's Kamp operates in summer for ages 5 through 15 (children must be accompanied by an adult), and woodsy campsites are also available. It is home to the longest floating pier on the lake, and rents boats, kayaks, and more. The lakeside **Beacon Bar & Grill** is famous for its Rum Runner drink, and in summer, the **Ice Cream Parlor**, which is across the highway, is the place to cool off.

In winter, this is the only place where people can ski along the lake's shoreline on groomed and marked cross-country ski trails. Lessons and rentals are available. A horse-drawn sleigh can be hired to deliver sledders to the resort's hill, and cross-country and snowshoe bonfire parties are held on Friday nights.

## Inn By the Lake

*3300 Lake Tahoe Blvd. (Hwy. 50), (800) 877-1466, (530) 542-0330, fax (530) 541-6596; www.innbythe lake.com. 100 rooms; $-$$$+. Children under 12 free. Some kitchens; 1 wood-burning fireplace. Heated pool; hot tub, sauna. Continental breakfast.*

Located in a grove of pine trees across the street from the lake, this attractive contemporary hotel offers comfortable, quiet accommodations.

## Royal Valhalla Motor Lodge

*4104 Lakeshore Blvd., (800) 999-4104, (530) 544-2233, fax (530) 544-1436; www.tahoeroyal valhalla.com. 80 units; $-$$$. Some kitchens. Heated pool (seasonal); hot tub. Continental breakfast. No pets.*

Pick from one-, two-, or three-bedroom units, many of which have lake views and balconies. Guests have use of a private beach, and the lodge is within walking distance of the casinos.

## Tahoe Beach & Ski Club

*3601 Lake Tahoe Blvd. (Hwy.50), (866)-4MY-VACA TION, (530) 541-6220, fax (530) 541-6187; www.tahoebeachandski.com. 128 rooms; $-$$$+. All kitchens. Heated pool; 2 hot tubs; 2 saunas; fitness room; 1 tennis court. No pets.*

Located 1 mile from the casinos, this lakeside hotel has 400 feet of private beach with volleyball and horseshoe courts. It also offers an on-site activities program for the entire family and a game room with a pool table and Foosball. A **Marie Callenders** restaurant is just next door.

## Tahoe Lakeshore Lodge

*930 Bal Bijou, 1 mi. S of casinos, (800) 448-4577, (530) 541-2180; www.tahoelakeshorelodge.com. 45 rooms, 30 condos; $$-$$$+. Some kitchens; all gas fireplaces. Heated pool (seasonal); hot tub; sauna; health spa. Continental breakfast. No pets.*

This simple, comfortable motel is right on the sand, and every room has a lake view, fireplace, and chunky lodge-pine furnishings. Each room also has a private patio or balcony overlooking the property's 500-foot-long stretch of private beach. Condominiums are adjacent.

## Timber Cove Lodge Marina Resort

*3411 Lake Tahoe Blvd. (Hwy. 50), (800) 972-8558, (530) 541-6722, fax (530) 541-7959; www.timber covetahoe.com. 262 rooms; $-$$$. Children under 12 free. Heated pool (year-round); hot tub; fitness room. Continental breakfast; 2 restaurants; room service. Pets ok in some rooms.*

This well-situated motel has a private beach, full marina, and pier, and many of the rooms have lake views.

## CASINOS

The major casinos offer large numbers of luxury hotel rooms.

- **Caesars Tahoe**
*(800) 648-3353, (775) 586-3515; www.caesars tahoe.com.*

- **Harrah's Lake Tahoe Casino & Hotel**
*(800) 648-3773; www.harrahs.com/our_casinos/tah.*

- **Harveys Lake Tahoe Casino & Resort**
*(800) HARVEYS, (775) 588-2411; www.harrahs.com/ our_casinos/hlt.*

- **Horizon Casino Resort Lake Tahoe**
*(800) 648-3322, (775) 588-6211; www.horizoncasino. com/main.php.*

## CONDOS AND HOMES

## Lakeland Village

*3535 Lake Tahoe Blvd. (Hwy. 50), (800) 822-5969, (800) 646-2779, (530) 544-1685, fax (530) 541-6278; www.lakeland-village.com. 207 units; $-$$$+. Children under 18 free. All kitchens & wood-burning or gas fireplaces. 2 heated pools (1 year-round); children's wading pool (seasonal); 2 hot tubs; sauna; fitness room; 2 tennis courts (fee).*

Though located beside a bustling highway, this condominium complex manages to retain a secluded, restive atmosphere. Some units are lakefront; all are within a short walk. Amenities include a private beach, children's playground, horseshoe pit, watercraft rentals, and free shuttle to the casinos.

## Rental agencies

These services rent privately owned condominiums, cabins, and houses. The rate is determined by the number of bedrooms and type of accommodation.

### • Accommodation Station

*(800) 344-9364, (530) 542-5850, fax (530) 542-4863; www.tahoelodging.com. 85+ units; $-$$$+. All kitchens & fireplaces.*

### • Lake Tahoe Accommodations

*(800) 544-3234, fax (530) 542-1860; www.tahoe accommodations.com. 400+ units; $$-$$$+.*

## OTHER

### Embassy Suites Resort Lake Tahoe

*4130 Lake Tahoe Blvd. (Hwy. 50), (877) 497-8483, (800) EMBASSY, (530) 544-5400, fax (530) 544-7643; www.embassytahoe.com. 9 stories; 400 rooms; $$-$$$+. Children under 12 free. Indoor heated pool; hot tub; sauna; steam room; fitness room. Evening cocktails, full breakfast; 3 restaurants; room service. No pets. Self-parking free, valet $15.*

The first new hotel built in the Tahoe Basin after restrictions were imposed, this link in the popular Embassy Suites chain features a nightclub and a 7-story-tall indoor atrium with waterfalls. Winter amenities include on-site ski rental, repair, and storage, plus next-day lift ticket sales and a complimentary shuttle to the Heavenly Mountain ski area. And, as an ad for the hotel declares, ". . . you don't have to gamble to get a free breakfast and free drinks": An all-you-can-eat breakfast and evening cocktails are complimentary to guests. But for those who *do* want to gamble, Harrah's is right next door.

### Tahoe Seasons Resort

*3901 Saddle Rd., (800) 540-4874, (530) 541-6700, fax (530) 541-7342; www.tahoeseasons.com. 8 stories; 160 units; $$. Children free. Some gas fireplaces. Heated pool; hot tub; 2 tennis courts. Restaurant; room service. No smoking; no pets. Free valet parking.*

Each unit here is a spacious suite equipped with a microwave and refrigerator as well as an oversize whirlpool bathtub big enough for two. And since it is located across the street from the Heavenly Valley ski area, skiers who stay here can just walk there in the morning. No chains. No parking hassles. But if someone in the party doesn't want to ski, it's possible to get a room

with a view of the slopes so they can stay cozy in front of a fireplace and just watch. The resort also provides on-site ski rentals and both chain installation and removal services.

### Motel Row

Highway 50 into town is lined with motels. However, this might be changing. South Lake Tahoe's redevelopment plan, which focuses on upgrading rather than expanding, dictates that for every new hotel room built, 1.31 old rooms must be removed.

## FARTHER AWAY

### Sorensen's Resort

See page 434.

### Zephyr Cove Resort

*760 Hwy. 50, in Zephyr Cove, Nevada, 4 mi. N of Stateline, (775) 589-4907, (775) 588-6644, fax (775) 588-5021; www.tahoedixie2.com. 28 cabins, 4 rooms; $$-$$$+. Some kitchens & wood-burning fireplaces. Restaurant. Pets ok.*

Located in a lovely forested area by the lake, these rustic cabins and lodge rooms provide a convenient, yet out-of-the-way, spot to stay. Facilities include a beach, marina with boat rentals, stable, and arcade. Campsites are also available. Do reserve early; cabins usually book up a year in advance.

## — WHERE TO EAT —

### The Cantina Bar & Grill

*765 Emerald Bay Rd., ¼ mi. W of Hwy. 50, (530) 544-1233, fax (530) 544-0823; www.cantina tahoe.com. L-D daily; $-$$. Highchairs, boosters, booths, child menu. No reservations.*

There is usually a wait to be seated in this festive and popular spot, but that's no reason to stay away. Waiting time can be passed sitting in the bar with a pitcher of margaritas (kids can order tasty niña coladas) and some nachos. Menu standouts include carnitas (roast pork), any of the giant burritos, and fresh fish. Southwestern dishes and wraps are also available.

### Casinos

For some of the best food in this area, try the casino restaurants and buffets. Favorites include:

• **Bill's Lake Tahoe Casino**
*(775) 588-2455; www.harrahs.com/our_casinos/tah/bills_casino.*

Order up a penny-pinching $2 draft and dog at the **bar**. And be sure to take a free pull on **Billy Jean**—the world's largest free-pull slot machine.

• **Caesars**
*(800) 648-3353, (775) 586-3515; www.caesarstahoe.com.*

• **The Broiler Room**
*D daily. Reservations advised.*

This steakhouse has a nice atmosphere and great steaks.

• **Stone Street Bar and Grill**
*L-D daily. Must be 21 or older after 4 p.m.*

This bustling spot is loud and fun, with lots of TVs and pool tables, and the food is good, too.

• **Harrah's**
*(800) 648-3773, (775) 588-6611; www.harrahs.com/our_casinos/tah.*

• **Forest Buffet**
*x2194. B-L M-Sat, D daily, SunBr; $-$$. Highchairs, boosters, child portions. No reservations.*

Located on the 18th floor, this classy restaurant provides spectacular lake and mountain views, plus outstanding food at a reasonable price.

• **North Beach Deli**
*x2148. B-L-D daily; $.*

This is the place to get a picnic lunch packed to go in a Harrah's fanny pack.

• **The Summit**
*x2196. D daily; $$$. Reservations advised.*

Located on the 16th and 17th floors in what was originally the Star Suite, where the rich and famous headliners once were put up, this elegant spot offers heady views and a new menu of refined cuisine every day. Items are beautifully presented, and service is impeccable. One meal enjoyed here began with crispy-crusted mini baguettes and sweet butter shaped like roses. An appetizer of chilled gulf shrimp was arranged in a red seafood sauce swirled with horseradish hearts, and a salad of baby lettuces was arranged in a scooped-out tomato so that it resembled a bouquet. The entree was a perfect rack of lamb with an anise crust and a side of mashed potatoes sprinkled with truffles,

followed by a dessert Frangelico soufflé with a hazelnut-praline crème frâiche.

• **Harveys**
*(800) HARVEYS, (775) 588-2411; www.harrahs.com/our_casinos/hlt.*

• **Cabo Wabo Cantina**
*x2461. L-D daily.*

Menu highlights include tableside made-to-order guacamole, fish tacos, and fajitas. Specialty drinks made with Sammy Hagar's signature tequila and ongoing videos of his band keep things rocking.

• **Carriage House**
*x2252. B-L-D daily; $-$$. Highchairs, boosters, child portions. No reservations.*

Open round-the-clock, this restaurant is known for its delicious fried chicken dinners.

• **Hard Rock Cafe**
*x6597; www.hardrock.com. L-D daily.*

For description, see page 71.

## The Fresh Ketch

*2435 Venice Dr., (530) 541-5683, fax (530) 541-6329; www.thefreshketch.com. L-D daily; $$. Highchairs, boosters, child menu. Reservations advised.*

Located at the Tahoe Keys Marina—the lake's only protected inland marina—this restaurant offers water views and fresh seafood. In addition to a daily special, the menu also has scampi, calamari steak topped with anchovy butter, cioppino, king crab legs, and live Maine lobster. Non-fish items include steaks and hamburgers, and dessert brings on Key lime and hula pies.

## Heidi's

*3485 Lake Tahoe Blvd. (Hwy.50), (530) 544-8113, fax (530) 544-4118. B-L daily; $. Highchairs, boosters, booths, child menu. No reservations.*

Breakfast is served all day in this cozy, casual restaurant. The menu includes pancakes, French toast, crêpes, Belgian waffles, and omelettes—as well as just about any other breakfast item imaginable—and orange juice is fresh-squeezed. At lunch, a variety of sandwiches, hamburgers, and salads are added to the menu.

# North Lake Tahoe

## — VISITOR INFORMATION —

**North Lake Tahoe Resort Association**
*380 North Lake Blvd., in Tahoe City, (800) 824-6348, (530) 581-8795, fax (530) 581-6904; www.mytahoe vacation.*

**Incline Village/Crystal Bay Visitors Bureau**
*969 Tahoe Blvd., in Incline Village, Nevada, (800) GO-TAHOE, (775) 832-1606, fax (775) 832-1605; www.gotahoe.com.*

## — GETTING THERE —

Located approximately 210 miles north of San Francisco. Take Highway 80 to Truckee, then Highway 267 south to the lake.

The Chicago-bound Amtrak train leaves Emeryville daily at 9:35 a.m. and arrives in Truckee at 3:01 p.m. For fare and schedule information and to make reservations, call (800) 872-7245.

## — ANNUAL EVENTS —

**Lake Tahoe Shakespeare Festival**
*July-August. At Sand Harbor State Park, in Nevada; (800) 74-SHOWS, (775) 832-1616; www.laketahoe shakespeare.com. $12-$65.*

"Bard on the Beach," a nickname bestowed by fond locals, is the biggest event of the summer at the lake. Bring a picnic, a blanket, and some low-leg beach chairs.

**Wooden Boat Week**
*August. (530) 581-4700, fax (530) 481-4771; www.tahoeyc.com. $15-$20, under 12 free.*

The Tahoe Yacht Club organizes this annual extravaganza of beautiful boats. Festivities include a Concours d'Elegance. Proceeds support local charitable and cultural organizations, and most events are open to the public.

## — STOPS ALONG THE WAY —

**Along I-80 North**
See pages 265 through 298.

**Auburn**
See pages 346 through 347.

**Grass Valley**
See pages 347 through 349.

**Nevada City**
See pages 349 through 352.

## — WHAT TO DO —

**Best beaches**

**• Sand Harbor State Park**
*In Nevada, 4 mi. S of Incline Village, (775) 831-0494; www.parks.nv.gov/lt.htm. $5/vehicle.*

This is a perfect beach. The sand is clean and fine, lifeguards are usually on duty, and there are plenty of parking spaces and picnic tables.

**• Tahoe City Commons Beach**
*In Tahoe City; stairway across from 510 North Lake Blvd.; parking lot behind Tahoe City Fire Station; (530) 583-3796; www.tahoecitypud.com/parksrec/ parks.shtml#2. Free.*

This family beach boasts a large grassy area and a lakefront playground.

**• William Kent Beach**
*S of Tahoe City. Free.*

Parking is difficult, but this small, rocky beach is worth the hassle.

**Bike trails**
One begins in Tahoe City, following the shoreline and the Truckee River. Bike rentals are

available in Tahoe City and at other locations along the lake.

### Fishing charters

Get a fishing license and the names of captains at one of the local sporting goods shops. The captain usually supplies bait and tackle.

### Gatekeeper's Cabin Museum

*130 West Lake Blvd., in Tahoe City, (530) 583-1762, fax (530) 583-8992; www.tahoecountry.com/nlths. Daily 11-5, mid-June-Sept; closed Oct-May. $2, under 13 free.*

Situated lakeside, this museum is inside a replica 1910 lodge pole-pine log cabin originally inhabited by a succession of keepers whose job it was to raise and lower the gates of the dam. Displays include Native American artifacts and Lake Tahoe memorabilia. An annex holds the **Marion Steinbach Indian Basket Museum**, which displays more than 800 Native American baskets, dolls, and other artifacts that represent the work of more than 50 tribes. The surrounding 3½-acre William B. Layton Park is equipped with picnic tables and barbecue facilities.

### Squaw Valley Stables

*1525 Squaw Valley Rd., in Olympic Valley, (530) 583-RIDE, fax (530) 583-6187. Daily 9-4; summer only. Guided rides $27/hr., must be 7 or older; ponies $6, must be 7 or under.*

The proprietor here says, "We have all kinds of horses . . . gentle horses for gentle people, spirited horses for spirited people, and for those who don't like to ride we have horses that don't like to be ridden." Pony rides occur in a large arena, and an adult must lead the pony.

### Sugar Pine Point State Park

*On west shore, in Tahoma, 9 mi. S of Tahoe City, (530) 525-7232, in summer (530) 525-7982; www.parks.ca.gov. Daily 8-dusk. Mansion: Tours 11-4, on the hr.; July-Aug only. $5/vehicle.*

In this gorgeous, peaceful setting, the 3-story 1902 Queen Anne **Hellman-Ehrman Mansion** has 16 rooms open for public viewing. The General Phipps Cabin, built in 1872 of hand-split logs, is also on the property. A magnificent beach invites swimming and sunning. Picnic tables, hiking trails, and a 1930s tennis court are available, and campsites are open

year-round. In winter, cross-country skiing and ranger-led snowshoe walks join the agenda.

### Thunderbird Lodge

*969 Tahoe Blvd., 2 mi. S of Sand Harbor State Park, (775) 832-8750, fax (775) 832-8798; www.thunder birdlodge.org. Tour schedule varies; May-Oct only. By shuttle bus: (800) 468-2463, (775) 832-1606; W-Sat; $25, students $10, under 5 free. By boat: (800) 553-3288; Sun $65, 5-12 $45, under 5 $20; M & F $80/$55/$20; reservations required.*

Built in 1936 by eccentric original owner George Whittell Jr., this secluded estate sits on 140 forested lakeside acres. It is considered a remarkable example of the Old Tahoe architectural style, and its name means "eternal happiness." Native Americans were taught the various trades and then did most of the stone masonry and hand-wrought ironwork. Unusual features include an Elephant House (for George's pet Indian elephant, Mingo), a 600-foot underground tunnel carved through granite and leading to the mustard-colored boathouse, and a man-made waterfall. Salacious stories tell of showgirls and secret passages. The boat tour sails round-trip from the Hyatt Lake Tahoe aboard the catamaran *Sierra Cloud* and includes muffins and coffee going, beer and soda returning. On Monday and Friday, it includes a barbecue lunch on the beach upon return.

### Truckee River Bridge

*At junction of Hwys. 89 & 28 (the Y), in Tahoe City.*

The only outlet from the lake, the dam below this bridge has gates that control the flow of water into the river. Spectators gather here to view and feed the giant rainbow trout that congregate beneath the bridge. (They favor bread and crackers.) The nickname "**Fanny Bridge**" comes from the sight that develops as people bend over the bridge railing to view the fish.

## Truckin' on the Truckee/river rafting

*Begins at the Y in Tahoe City. Daily 9-3:30; June-Oct only. Rates vary. Must be 4 or older.*

What better way to spend a sunny summer Alpine day than floating down the peaceful Truckee River a la Huckleberry Finn? All that's needed is a swimsuit, water-friendly shoes, and some sun lotion. Packing along a picnic and cold drinks is also a good idea, and a daypack keeps hands free for paddling. White-water enthusiasts—stay away! This trip is so tame that portable toilets are placed strategically along the riverbank. The 4-mile, 3-hour trip ends at **River Ranch Lodge** *(2285 River Rd., off Hwy. 89, (800) 535-9900, (530) 583-4264; www.riverranch lodge.com.)*, where the restaurant prepares an outdoor barbecue lunch on an expansive deck overlooking the river; lodging is also available. Tahoe City concessionaires offer a package that includes raft, life jacket, paddles, and return ride. It is first-come, first-served, so arrive before 11 a.m. to avoid crowds and to get an early-bird discount. A 3½-mile off-road bicycle trail runs along the river here from the River Ranch into Tahoe City.

## Watson Cabin Museum

*560 North Lake Blvd., in Tahoe City, (530) 583-8717, fax (530) 583-8992; www.tahoecountry.com/nlths/ watson.html. Daily 12-4; summer only. Free.*

Built in 1908 and 1909, this log cabin is the oldest building in town still on its original site. Furnished as it was in 1909, it illustrates turn-of-the-century life.

## Winter activities

See pages 432 through 433.

### – WHERE TO STAY –

### CONDOS ON THE LAKE

Rates in condos vary tremendously depending on number of people, length of stay, and time of year. Most units are equipped with kitchens and TVs.

## Brockway Springs

*101 Chipmunk St., in Kings Beach, (530) 546-4201, fax (530) 546-4202; www.brockwaysprings.com. 78 units. Most wood-burning fireplaces. Heated pool; children's wading pool; sauna; 2 tennis courts.*

Most units here have stone fireplaces and balconies overlooking the lake. The resort features ½ mile of private lakefront.

## Chinquapin

*3600 North Lake Blvd., in Tahoe City, (800) 732-6721, (530) 583-6991, fax (530) 583-0937; www.chinqua pin.com. 172 units. All TVs, kitchens, & fireplaces. Heated pool (seasonal); sauna; 7 tennis courts.*

The one- to four-bedroom units here feature vaulted, beamed ceilings, natural rock fireplaces, and lake views. Some of these units also have private saunas, and all are equipped with washers and dryers. Additional resort amenities include three private beaches, boating facilities, a fishing pier, and a 1-mile paved beachfront path.

## Coeur du Lac

*136 Juanita Dr., in Incline Village, Nevada, (800) 869-8308, (775) 831-3318, fax (775) 831-8668. Heated pool (seasonal); indoor hot tub; sauna.*

Located 1 block from the lake, this attractive complex also has a recreation center.

### CONDOS FARTHER OUT

## Carnelian Woods

*5005 North Lake Blvd., in Carnelian Bay, ¼ mi. from lake, (877) NLT-AHOE, (530) 546-5547, fax (530) 546 5448; www.carnelianwoods.com. 30 rental units. Recreation center with heated pool (seasonal); 2 hot tubs; 2 saunas; 3 tennis courts.*

Further amenities here include sports facilities and bicycle rentals. In winter, a 2-mile cross-country ski course and a snow play area are available.

## Granlibakken

*End of Granlibakken Rd., in Tahoe City, 1 mi. from lake, (800) 543-3221, (530) 583-4242, fax (530) 583-7641; www.granlibakken.com. 160 rooms. Children under 2 free. Some kitchens & fireplaces. Heated pool & children's wading pool (seasonal); hot tub; sauna; 6 tennis courts. Full breakfast.*

Situated in a 74-acre forested valley, this resort also has a jogging trail. In winter, it maintains a ski and snow play area (see also page 433).

## Kingswood Village

*1001 Commonwealth Ave., off Hwy. 267, in Kings Beach, 3/4 mi. from lake, (800) 542-2533, (530) 546-2501, fax (530) 546-5448; www.kingswood condos.com. 60 rental units. Heated pool (seasonal); hot tub; sauna; 3 tennis courts.*

Amenities here include access to a private lakefront beach club.

## Northstar-at-Tahoe

*On Northstar Dr., off Hwy. 267, in Truckee, 6 mi. from lake, (800) GO-NORTH, (530) 526-1010, fax (530) 562-2215; www.skinorthstar.com. 260 units. Most kitchens & wood-burning fireplaces. 2 heated pools; 3 hot tubs; 2 saunas; fitness room; 10 clay tennis courts; 18-hole golf course. 5 restaurants.*

In addition to the condos here, hotel rooms and homes can be rented. A complimentary shuttle bus makes it unnecessary to use a car within the complex. Facilities include a teen center and, at an additional fee, horseback riding and a supervised summer children's recreation program for ages 2 through 10. Tahoe's largest mountain bike park is here, with 100 miles of trails. An Adventure Park with rope courses, a climbing wall, and orienteering courses is also available. See also page 433.

## Squaw Valley Lodge

*201 Squaw Peak Rd., in Olympic Valley, 10 mi. from lake, (800) 549-6742, (530) 583-5500, fax (530) 583-0326; www.squawvalleylodge.com. 178 rooms; $$-$$$+. All kitchens, some gas fireplaces. Heated pool (seasonal); 3 indoor & 2 outdoor hot tubs; sauna; steam room; health spa; fitness room; 2 tennis courts. Mostly no smoking; no pets.*

Claiming to be "just 84 steps from the Squaw Valley tram," this resort is convenient for both skiers and non-skiers. Staying here allows skiers to avoid a congested early morning commute to Squaw's parking lot. When ready to ski, it is possible to just walk, or even ski, to the lifts. For non-skiers, a room facing the slopes allows complete warmth and comfort while watching the rest of the group whiz by. The pool here is treated with gentle-on-the-eyes bromine instead of chlorine.

### OTHER

## Cal-Neva Resort

*2 Stateline Rd., in Crystal Bay, Nevada, (800) CAL-NEVA, (775) 832-4000, fax (775) 831-9007; www.calnevaresort.com. 9 stories; 190 rooms, 10 cabins; $-$$. Children under 8 free. Pool (seasonal); indoor hot tub; health spa; 2 tennis courts. Restaurant; room service. Free valet parking.*

This resort straddles California and Nevada. In fact, a line runs right through the pool depicting where the property divides—allowing guests to swim in two states. In its 1940s heyday, it was a popular playground for mobsters and stars, who favored the property's private chalets (Marilyn Monroe stayed in #3, Frank Sinatra in #5). Today, all guests get a lake view. When Sinatra owned 65% of the joint in the 1960s, he had a secret tunnel built so he could get from his cabin to the lodge without any fuss. Today, guests can take a stroll in it as part of a tour that also tells of illicit affairs, money laundering, and much, much more. A drink in the **Circle Bar**, with its lake view and German 7,000-piece stained-glass dome, and a visit to the immense knotty-pine Indian Room, which features a granite boulder fireplace and displays interesting artifacts, are de rigueur. A small **casino** (which is the oldest legal gambling facility in the U.S.) and a large video arcade are on the premises.

## Hyatt Regency Lake Tahoe Resort, Spa and Casino

*111 Country Club Dr./Lakeshore, in Incline Village, Nevada, (800) 233-1234, (775) 832-1234, fax (775) 831-7508; www.laketahoehyatt.com. 12 stories; 424 rooms; $$-$$$+. Children under 18 free. Some fireplaces. Heated pool; 2 hot tubs; health spa; fitness room. 4 restaurants; room service.*

Guests here have a choice between a room in a 12-story high-rise, in a 3-story annex, or in a lakeside cottage, and Lady Luck can be tested 24 hours a day in the 13,000-square-foot casino. Of special note is the resort's magnificent private beach, complete with beach boys who set up lounge chairs and umbrellas wherever desired. In summer, guests can relax with the water lapping at the shore just beneath their toes, causing one to ponder, "Can it get better than this?" The pool is designed like a lagoon, and jet skis and paddleboats can be rented at an adjacent marina. At night, an oceanfront fire pit equipped with comfortable chairs and a hammock invites lingering under the tall pines. During ski season, free shuttle service is provided to nearby ski areas, and both ski rentals and discounted lift tickets can be purchased on the premises. Packages come and go; when making reservations, inquire about current specials. Camp Hyatt, a fee-based program for children ages 3 through 12, operates on weekends year-round and daily during summer and holidays. The inexpensive room service menu for kids offers them applesauce, corn-on-the-cob, gooey chocolate cake, and hot chocolate with marshmallows!

The imposing **Lone Eagle Grille** features an Old Tahoe-style atmosphere, with massive wood-beamed ceilings, gigantic fireplaces made of local rock, and large windows with lake views. Lunch is soups and salads, some pastas and pizzas, and plenty of tempting desserts. The dinner menu offers updated surf-and-turf and a good Caesar salad. **Cutthroat's Saloon** has wooden floors littered with peanut shells. Food is served on camping-style tin plates, and beer comes in big Mason jars. Then there are the drinks—a flaming Toasted Marshmallow (Stoli Vanilla, butterscotch liqueur, Frangelico, and cream), a Girl Scout Cookie (peppermint schnapps, creme de cacao, and cream), or a Beehive (honey liqueur, brandy, and lemon juice). Bottoms up!

## Mourelatos Lakeshore Resort

*6834 North Lake Blvd., in Tahoe Vista, (800) TAHOE-81, (530) 546-9500, fax (530) 546-2744; www.mourelatosresort.com. 33 units; $$-$$$+. Children under 5 free. Some kitchens & fireplaces. No smoking; no pets.*

At this lakefront motel, a small pine forest opens onto a private beach, and a children's playground is available in summer.

## Resort at Squaw Creek

*400 Squaw Creek Rd., Olympic Valley, (800) 3CREEK3, (530) 583-6300, fax (530) 581-5407; www.squawcreek.com. 9 stories; 403 rooms; $$$+. Children under 16 free. Some kitchens & gas fireplaces. 2 heated pools; 1 children's wading pool; 4 hot tubs; sauna; health spa; fitness room; 2 tennis courts (fee); 18-hole golf course. 5 restaurants; room service.*

This sleek, black-toned, high-rise hotel is almost invisible tucked up against a mountain. Two-story windows in the lobby provide a magnificent valley view. The majestic property is impressively landscaped and features a 250-foot man-made waterfall feeding a rushing stream that cascades over boulders. One of the pools has a twisting 120-foot-long waterslide, and the toddler pool includes a large sandy beach for extra diversion. The Mountain Buddies children's program operates year-round for ages 4 through 13; there is an additional fee. Bicycles can be rented and then ridden along a scenic route beside the Truckee River. In winter, ski-in/ski-out access is available to Squaw Valley,

and cross-country skiing, snowshoe tours, an ice-skating pavilion, and horse-drawn sleigh rides are available.

## Motel Row

Last-minute lodging can usually be found among the numerous motels and cabins lining the lake in Kings Beach and Tahoe Vista. Chances are best, of course, on weekdays and in the off-season.

## — WHERE TO EAT —

## Alexander's Bar & Grill

*In Olympic Valley, (530) 581-7278; www.squaw.com/ winter/hicamp_restaurants.html. L-D daily. Boosters, child menu. Reservations advised for D; not accepted for L. Tram: (530) 583-6985; daily 10-9; $19, 65+ & 13-15 $15, under 13 $5; after 5pm, $8, under 13 $5; High Camp facilities additional.*

This restaurant is located on the slopes of the Squaw Valley ski area and is reached via a scenic aerial cable car ride. Call for dining details.

A lovely, though difficult, hike to Shirley Lake begins at the tram building. Hikers pass waterfalls and huge boulders while following Squaw Creek about 2$^1$/2 miles down to the lake. **High Camp Bath & Tennis Club** is at 8,200 feet and is open year-round. Facilities include an Olympic-size outdoor ice-skating rink, six tennis courts, a pool and hot tub, and the **1960 Winter Olympic Museum**.

## Hacienda del Lago

*760 North Lake Blvd., in Boatworks Shopping Center, in Tahoe City, (530) 583-0358. D daily; in summer L-D daily; $. Highchairs, boosters, child portions. No reservations.*

It is definitely worth the wait for seating in the front room, which features a panoramic lake view. Consider passing the time sipping fruit margaritas in the bar—smoothies are popular with children—but beware. Anesthetized by these potent, tangy drinks, it is quite easy to overindulge on the large portions of tasty Mexican food. The menu includes a variety of burritos, chimechangas, and enchiladas. A colossal taco salad consists of a crispy-fried flour tortilla bowl filled to the brim with salad goodies, and make-your-own tacos are available with pork, turkey, or beef stuffing. For those who know when to stop, there are a la carte portions. For those who don't, there is flan topped with whipped cream.

## Lakehouse Pizza

*120 Grove Ct., in Tahoe City, (530) 583-2222. L-D daily; $. Highchairs, boosters. No reservations.*

This casual spot offers lakefront views and a choice of sitting either inside or outside on a deck. Menu choices include pizza, sandwiches, salads, hamburgers, and exceptionally good housemade potato chips. Though the schedule varies, an extensive breakfast menu is served in an area known as the **Eggschange**.

## Sunnyside Restaurant & Lodge

*1850 West Lake Blvd., in Tahoe City, (800) 822-2-SKI, (530) 583-7200, fax (530) 583-7224; www.sunny sideresort.com. L-D daily; also B Sat-Sun in summer; $$-$$$. Highchairs, boosters, child portions. Reservations advised.*

It is hard to beat a summer meal here, especially when eaten outside on the huge deck—the largest on the lake—while watching sailboats or listening to live jazz on Sunday afternoons. Overnight **lodging** is also available.

## Wolfdale's Cuisine Unique

*640 North Lake Blvd., Tahoe City, (530) 583-5700, fax (530) 583-1583; www.wolfdales.com. D W-M; daily July-Aug; $$$. Child portions. Reservations advised.*

The attractive circa 1880 house this restaurant is located within is the town's oldest. It was floated over on a barge from the Nevada side of the lake at the turn of the century and was converted into a restaurant in the 1960s. Colorful art decorates the walls, and a bit of the lake and a lot of trees provide a nice view. Talented owner-chef Douglas Dale combines Asian and European cooking techniques to produce high-flavor, low-fat fresh fish and meat entrees—all artistically arranged and served with yeasty house-baked herb rolls. The appetizers and desserts are also exceptional. Adding to the aesthetics of this dining experience, everything is served on lovely handmade pottery designed especially to enhance the food.

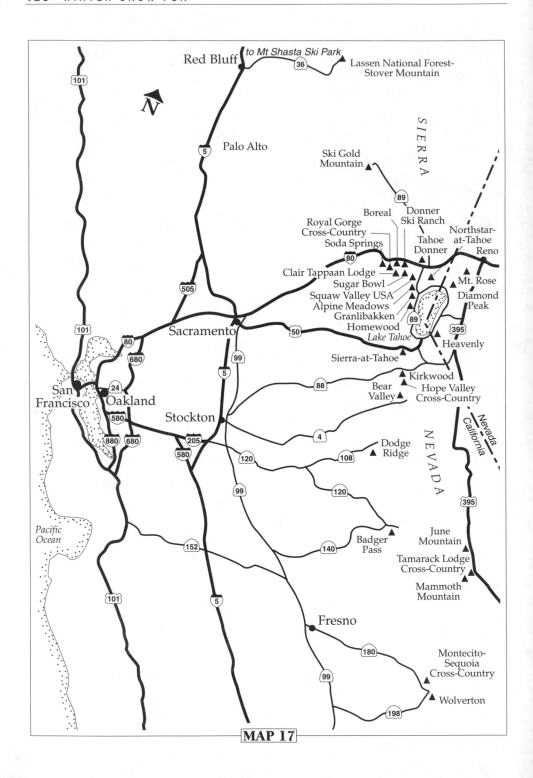

Red Bluff    *to Mt Shasta Ski Park*    ▲ Lassen National Forest-
    36                                        Stover Mountain

*S I E R R A*

Palo Alto

Ski Gold
Mountain ▲

    89

                Boreal    Donner
Royal Gorge     Ski Ranch
Cross-Country              Northstar-
    Soda Springs      Tahoe   at-Tahoe
                      Donner        Reno
Clair Tappaan Lodge                  Mt. Rose
    Sugar Bowl                   Diamond
    Squaw Valley USA             Peak
    Alpine Meadows
    Granlibakken          89
    Homewood    *Lake Tahoe*    395
                              Heavenly
Sacramento        50
                          Sierra-at-Tahoe
                              ▲ Kirkwood
    99                    Bear    Hope Valley
    5                  Valley ▲  Cross-Country

San              88
Francisco   Oakland
    580        Stockton        *N E V A D A*
                              *Nevada*
    880  680      205              *California*
         580      120        ▲ Dodge
                       108      Ridge      395
                  99
                       120
    *Pacific*                         ▲ June
    *Ocean*       152    140   Badger  Mountain
                              Pass    Tamarack Lodge
                                      Cross-Country
    101        5                      Mammoth
                                      Mountain

              Fresno
                   180          Montecito-
                                Sequoia
              99                Cross-Country
                   198          ▲ Wolverton

**MAP 17**

# WINTER SNOW FUN

## Downhill Skiing

Downhill ski areas are plentiful in Northern California. The season runs from the first snow, usually in late November, through the spring thaw in April. Several resorts are known for staying open longer.

Lifts usually operate daily from 9 a.m. to 4 p.m. To avoid parking problems and long lines for lift tickets and rentals, arrive early. On-site equipment rentals are usually available and convenient, and lift tickets are often discounted mid-week. Many resorts now post tickets prices and daily weather reports at their website.

The least crowded times at the resorts are the three weeks after Thanksgiving, the first two weeks in January, and late in the season. The two weeks around Christmas are ridiculous.

Those who know say it is worthwhile to buy ski equipment if someone skis more than 10 days per season. Otherwise, it is financially beneficial to rent. Avoid buying children plastic skis; they break easily.

Most ski areas now have a terrain park, where man-made snow formations—halfpipes, tabletops, etc.—allow snowboarders to practice tricky moves.

## Cross-country Skiing

Cross-country skiing becomes more popular each year. One reason for this surging popularity is the advantages it has over downhill skiing: no lift tickets to purchase; equipment is less expensive; is considered safer; can be enjoyed in groups; allows escape from crowds. However, the sport also has several disadvantages: requires more stamina; is less exhilarating.

Specialized cross-country centers offer equipment rentals, maintained trails with maps, and warming huts. Some centers also offer lodging, guided tours, snowshoeing, and the option of downhill facilities.

Children age 4 and older are usually taught in classes with their parents, but some centers have special children's classes. Parents who have the strength can carry younger children in a backpack or pull them along in a "pulk."

It is a good idea for beginners to rent equipment and take a few lessons to learn safety guidelines and basic skiing techniques. Once the basics are learned, this sport can be practiced just about anywhere there is a foot of snow.

The state **Sno-Park** program *((916) 324-1222; www.ohv.parks.ca.gov. $5/1 day, $25/season pass Nov.1-May30.)* makes it easier to park at popular trail heads. Parking areas are kept cleared of snow, and overnight RV camping is permitted at some locations.

## Snow Play

Toboggans, saucers, inner tubes, and sleds are the equipment for snow play. For safety's sake, take note that sleds are lots of fun to use but extremely dangerous. Truck inner tubes are also dangerous because the rider is high off the ground with nothing to hold on to and no way to steer.

When people do not pay attention to safety rules, snow play can become dangerous. (I once had the wind knocked out of me by an antsy bear of a man who didn't wait for me and my young child to come to a stop before he pushed down the same hill in his saucer. After the collision he said, "Sorry. But you shouldn't have been there." I'm sure worse stories are waiting to be told.)

Some commercial snow play areas allow people to bring their own equipment, but others require that equipment be rented on-site.

Dress for cold, wet weather. Wear wool when possible, and pack a change of clothes. Protect feet with boots. When boots aren't available, an inexpensive improvisation is to wrap feet in newspapers, then in plastic bags, and then put on shoes. Also, cutting a few holes in a large plastic garbage bag lets it serve as a raincoat. Always wear gloves to protect hands from sharp, packed snow.

The high-speed fun of snowmobiling is an exciting adventure. Many snowmobile concessions provide protective clothing and equipment. Though not inexpensive, especially for a family, it is an exhilarating, memorable experience.

*In the following listings, difficulty of terrain at downhill ski resorts is specified in percentages: %B (beginner), %I (intermediate), %A (advanced).*

## Way Up North: Shasta-Cascade

### Coffee Creek Ranch
See page 325.

### Lassen National Forest—Stover Mountain
*On Forest Service Road 316A, at Hwy. 36/Hwy. 89, 3 mi. SW of Chester, (530) 258-3987. Sat-Sun only. Downhill only: 2 surface. 50%B, 50%I. Snow play area. Lodging nearby.*

California's "undiscovered National Park" is an excellent area for families and beginners. The scenery includes hot steam vents and mud pots.

### Mt. Shasta Board & Ski Park
*104 Siskiyou Ave., in Mt. Shasta, 10 mi. E of Mt. Shasta City, (800) SKI-SHASTA, (530) 926-8610, fax (530) 926-8607; www.skipark.com. Downhill: 3 triple, 1 surface. 20%B, 55%I, 25%A. Children's ski school (4-10); snowboard terrain park. Cross-country: 17 mi. groomed trails. Lodging nearby.*

Night skiing is available at this low-key, family-oriented ski area, and all trails are open to snowboarders.

## Donner Summit

### Boreal Mountain Resort
*Castle Peak exit off Hwy. I-80, 10 mi. W of Truckee, (530) 426-3666, fax (530) 426-3173; www.boreal ski.com. Downhill only. 2 quad, 3 triple, 4 double. 30%B, 55%I, 15%A. Children's ski school; (4-10);*

snow play area; snowboard terrain park. Lodging on premises, (530) 426-1012.

Known for being relatively inexpensive and convenient to the Bay Area, this resort has the Sierra's most extensive night skiing facilities. Slopes are especially good for beginners and intermediates, and skiers of all ability levels can ride on the same chairs together. A Shared Pass allows two parents to buy just one ticket if they want to take turns skiing and babysitting their children.

## Clair Tappaan Lodge

In Norden, on Hwy. 40, 3 mi. E of Norden/Soda Springs exit off Hwy. I-80, (530) 426-3632, fax (530) 426-0742; www.sierraclub.com/outings/ lodges/ctl. Cross-country only. 7 mi. groomed trails.

This area is said to be the snowiest in the continental U.S. Both the massive timbered lodge, which was built by volunteers in 1934, and the track system are owned and operated by the Sierra Club. Lodging is dormitory-style with bunk beds, and, as at hostels, guests bring their own bedding and everyone is expected to do a chore. Overnight trips to wilderness areas can be arranged. Special programs and workshops are scheduled throughout the year. Children under 4 are free but are not permitted on winter weekends or on holidays.

## Donner Ski Ranch

19320 Donner Pass Rd., in Norden, off Hwy. 40, 3 mi. from the Norden/Soda Springs exit off Hwy. I-80, (530) 426-3635, fax (530) 426-9350; www.donner skiranch.com. Downhill only. 1 triple, 5 double. 25%B, 50%I, 25%A. Snowboard terrain park. Lodging on premises.

Best for beginners and intermediates, this area offers no frills.

## Royal Gorge Cross Country Ski Resort

9411 Hillside Dr., in Soda Springs, 1 mi. from Soda Springs/Norden exit off Hwy. I-80, near Donner Pass, (800) 666-3871, (530) 426-3871, fax (530) 426-9221; www.royalgorge.com. Cross-country only. 200 mi. groomed trails. Children's ski school (5-12). Lodging on premises.

Modeled after Scandinavian ski resorts, this was the first cross-country ski resort in California. The overnight **Wilderness Lodge** here is not accessible by road. Guests are brought in by snowcat-drawn sleigh (sorry, no

reindeer or horses) and leave by skiing the 2 miles back out. Accommodations are rustic. In the old 1920s hunting lodge, everyone shares the same toilet areas. Bathing facilities—showers, a sauna, and an outdoor hot tub—are located in an adjacent building and reached by a short trek through the snow. Sleeping facilities are tiny roomettes, each with either a double bed or a bunk bed and a cloth-covered doorway, and several three-bed rooms for families. Some private cabins are also available. The food, however, is remarkably civilized. A chef works full-time in the kitchen preparing attractive, tasty, and bountiful French repasts. Oh, yes. The skiing. Guests may cross-country ski whenever they wish, and the capable staff gives lessons each morning and guided tours each afternoon. Guided moonlight ski tours are scheduled after dinner. The nightly fee includes everything except equipment, which can be rented on site.

Royal Gorge also operates a more accessible B&B, **Rainbow Lodge** ((530) 426-3661), nearby.

The cross-country ski center is open to non-guests and features the largest cross-country track system in the U.S. Facilities include ten warming huts, four trail-side cafes, and four surface lifts. The Rainbow Interconnect Trail allows skiers to enjoy 8 miles of scenic downhill cross-country skiing; shuttle buses return skiers to the trailhead. A special program is available for skiers with disabilities.

## Soda Springs Mountain Resort

In Soda Springs, at Soda Springs exit off Hwy. I-80, 4 mi. W of Donner Summit, (530) 426-3901, fax (530) 426-3173; www.skisodasprings.com. Downhill only. 2 chair lifts, 2 tube tows. 30%B, 50%I, 20%A. Children's lessons; snowtubing area; snowboarding permitted.

Built on the former site of one of the first Sierra ski resorts, this relatively new ski area is among the closest to the Bay Area and is particularly well designed for beginners. Boreal ski area owns it and shares some facilities. All or part of the resort can be rented on weekdays.

## Sugar Bowl Ski Resort

629 Sugar Bowl Rd., in Norden, off Hwy. 40, 2 mi. E of Soda Springs exit off Hwy. I-80, (530) 426-9000, fax (530) 426-3723; www.sugarbowl.com. Downhill only.

*1 gondola, 7 quad, 3 double, 2 surface. 17%B, 45%I, 38%A. Childcare (3-6); children's ski school & lessons (4-12); snow play area; snowboard terrain park. Lodging on premises.*

Exuding a 1930s Tyrolean charm, this ski resort is one of the Sierra's oldest and is said to have had the first chairlift in the state. It is known for having short lift lines, good runs at all ability levels, and a lack of hotdoggers. Skiers park their cars carefully (to avoid tickets), and then ride a gondola or chairlift up to the resort.

### Tahoe Donner

*11603 Slalom Way, in Truckee, off Hwy. I-80, fax (530) 587-0685; www.tahoedonner.com. Downhill: (530) 587-9444. 1 quad, 1 double, 1 surface. 40%B, 60%I. Children's ski school (3-6); children's ski lessons (7-12); snow play area; snowboard terrain park. Cross-country: 15275 Alder Creek Rd., (530) 587-9484. 42 mi. groomed trails. Children's ski school (5-9). Lodging on premises, (530) 587-6586 or (530) 587-5411.*

This small resort is especially good for families. The number of lift tickets sold each day is limited, assuring that it never gets too crowded. Snow-biking a la the Beatles in *Help!* was introduced in 1998. The cross-country ski center offers lighted night skiing and schedules special tours: Ski With Santa, Morning Nature Tour, Sauna Tour, Donner Trail Tour.

#### — SNOW PLAY —

### Western Ski Sport Museum

*At Boreal Ridge exit off Hwy. I-80, (530) 426-3313 x113, fax (530) 426-3501. In winter, W-Sun 10-4; in summer, Sat-Sun 10-4. Free.*

See just how cumbersome that charming old-time ski equipment really was. This museum chronicles the history of skis in the West from gold camp days—when skis were used by pioneers to help open this mountain area—to current times. Vintage ski films are shown upon request.

## Nevada

### Diamond Peak Ski Resort

*1210 Ski Way, in Incline Village, off Hwy. 28, (775) 832-1177, fax (775) 832-1281; www.diamondpeak.com. Downhill only. 3 quad, 3 double. 18%B, 46%I, 36%A. Childcare center (2-6); children's ski school (4-7);*

*children's ski lessons (3-12); snowboard terrain park. Lodging nearby.*

This well-sheltered, family-oriented resort is especially good on inclement days. It is the area's first and only ski resort to use the European-style easy-loading "Launch Pad" system—similar to a moving walkway—on both quad chairlifts. The cross-country center also has snowshoe facilities, and complimentary shuttle service is available to Incline Village.

### Mt. Rose-Ski Tahoe

*22222 Mt. Rose Hwy., in Reno, on Hwy. 431, 11 mi. NE of Incline Village, (800) SKI-ROSE, (775) 849-0704, fax (775) 849-9080; www.skirose.com. Downhill only. 1 six, 2 quad, 2 triple, 1 surface. 30%B, 30%I, 40%A. Children's ski school (4-10); 3 snowboard terrain parks.*

At 8,260 feet, this is the highest base elevation at Tahoe.

## North Lake Tahoe

### Alpine Meadows

*2600 Alpine Meadows Rd., in Tahoe City, off Hwy. 89, 6 mi. N of town, (800) 441-4423, (530) 583-4232, fax (530) 583-0963; www.skialpine.com. Downhill only. 1 six, 1 quad, 4 triple, 5 double, 2 surface. 25%B, 40%I, 35%A. Children's snow school (4-6); children's ski lessons (7-12); snowboard terrain park.*

Alpine is usually open through Memorial Day and some years is open into July, giving it the longest ski season at Lake Tahoe. Free 1-hour guided tours that show skiers the main runs and how to avoid crowds are offered daily at 10 a.m. The **Tahoe Adaptive Ski School** *((530) 581-4161)* for people with disabilities operates here, and the **Family Ski Challenge** is scheduled each March.

### Granlibakken
*In Tahoe City, 1 mi. S of town, (800) 543-3221, (530) 581-7333, fax (530) 583-7641; www.granlibakken.com. 2 surface. 50%B, 50%I. Snow play area.*

This small ski area is protected from the wind and caters to beginners and families with small children. It is said to be the oldest ski resort at Tahoe and to have the least expensive lift ticket. Downhill, cross-country, snowboarding, and snowshoeing are all accommodated. See also page 424.

### Homewood Mountain Resort
*5145 West Lake Blvd., in Homewood, off Hwy. 89, 6 mi. S of Tahoe City, (530) 525-2992, fax (530) 525-0417; www.skihomewood.com. Downhill only. 1 quad, 2 triple, 1 double, 4 surface. 15%B, 50%I, 35%A. Childcare center/ski school (4-10); snowboard terrain park.*

The slopes here are ideal for intermediates and provide panoramic views of Lake Tahoe. Ferry service from South Lake Tahoe is provided by the *Tahoe Queen.*

### Northstar-at-Tahoe
*Off Hwy. 267, 6 mi. S of Truckee, (800) GO-NORTH, fax (530) 562-2221,; www.skinorthstar.com. Downhill: (530) 562-1010. 1 gondola, 5 quad, 2 triple, 2 double, 2 Magic Carpets, 3 surface. 25%B, 50%I, 25%A. Childcare center (2-6); children's ski school (5-12); children's ski lessons (3+); snowtubing area; snowboard terrain parks. Cross-country: (530) 562-2475; 40 mi. groomed trails. Lodging on premises.*

This attractive ski area is reputed to be the least windy at Tahoe. Catering to families, it is good for beginners and excellent for intermediates. Lift ticket sales are limited to assure that the slopes don't get overcrowded, so arrive early. Organized activities are scheduled throughout the week, and free 1-hour introductory tours— in which participants are shown the best runs and given a history of the area—are given daily

at 10 a.m. Sleigh rides and snowmobile tours are available, and Polaris Park is open on Friday and Saturday evenings with lighted slopes for tubing, snowshoeing, and other selected snow sports. See also page 425.

### Squaw Valley USA
*1960 Squaw Valley Rd., in Olympic Valley, off Hwy. 89, 5 mi. N of Tahoe City, (888) SNOW-321, (800) 545-4350, (530) 583-6985, fax (530) 581-7106; www.squaw.com. Downhill: 1 tram, 1 Funitel gondela, 1 Pulse, 3 six, 5 quad, 8 triple, 9 doubles, 1 Magic Carpet, 2 surface. 25%B, 45%I, 30%A. Childcare (2-3); children's ski school (4-12); snow play area; 3 snowboard terrain parks. Cross-country: 10 mi. groomed trails. Lodging on premises.*

Squaw Valley made its name in 1960 when it was home to the VIII Winter Olympic Games. Today it is a top ski area known internationally for its open slopes and predictably generous snowfall, which usually allows it to stay open into May. Expert skiers consider it the best ski resort in the state because it has the steepest, most challenging slopes. Indeed, there are good slopes for every ability level. A special area for children ages 2 through 12, is equipped with two rope tows and a Magic Carpet. A snow-tubing area with a dedicated lift and ice-skating are available at High Camp, and night skiing is available mid-December through mid-March.

– SNOW PLAY –

### Carnelian Woods condominiums
See page 424.

### North Tahoe Snow Festival
*(530) 583-7167; www.tahoesnowfestival.com.*

Held for a week each year in March, this is the largest winter carnival in the West. In the past activities have included a fireworks display over the slopes at Squaw Valley followed by the awe-inspiring sight of scores of torch-bearing skiers making a twisting descent down Exhibition Run. Other popular events include The Great Ski Race (a 30-kilometer Nordic ski competition) and the Localman Triathlon (a competition in winter survival skills in which participants must stack firewood, shovel snow, and put on tire chains).

### Sugar Pine Point State Park
See page 423.

# South Lake Tahoe

## Heavenly Mountain Resort
*In South Lake Tahoe, (800) 2-HEAVEN, (775) 586-7000, fax (775) 541-2643; www.skiheavenly.com. Downhill only. 1 gondola, 1 tram, 1 six, 7 quad, 7 triple, 4 double, 10 surface. 20%B, 45%I, 35%A. Childcare (6 wks.-6); children's ski school (4-12); 3 snowboard terrain parks. Lodging nearby.*

Situated in two states, this is the largest, and one of the most scenic, ski areas in the country. Runs on the California side offer breathtaking views of Lake Tahoe. This resort has been rated as having the best intermediate skiing in California. It also has exhilarating expert slopes, offers both night and helicopter skiing, and has the longest descent—5½ miles—in the west.

## Hope Valley Outdoor Center at Sorensen's Resort
*14255 Hwy. 88, in Hope Valley, 16 mi. S of Lake Tahoe, (800) 423-9949, (530) 694-2203; www.sorensens resort.com. Cross-country only; 60 mi. marked trails. Children's ski school (8-12). Lodging on premises.*

Small and informal, this is a great place for families. Lodging is available in 29 housekeeping cabins. Some are newish log cabins equipped with kitchenettes and wood-burning fireplaces. Others are older and smaller. The resort is open year-round and is 100% non-smoking, with a sauna and cafe among its facilities. In the summer it offers a family-oriented fly-fishing school, history tours of the Emigrant Trail and Pony Express Trail, and both kayak and mountain bike rentals.

## Kirkwood Mountain Resort
*1501 Kirkwood Meadows Dr., in Kirkwood, on Hwy. 88, 30 mi. S of South Lake Tahoe, (800) 967-7500, (209) 258-6000, fax (209) 258-8899; www.kirkwood.com. Downhill: 2 quad, 7 triple, 1 double, 2 surface. 15%B, 50%I, 35%A. Childcare center (2-6); children's ski school (4-12); 3 snowboard terrain parks; tubing park. Cross-country: (209) 258-7248; 48 mi. groomed trails. Lodging on premises, (800) 967-7500.*

This very large, uncrowded family resort is reputed to have the deepest snow in North America. It is often snowing here when it is raining at other Tahoe ski areas. Horse-drawn sleigh rides are available, and the cross-country

area offers inexpensive Family Days as well as guided snowshoe adventures and night hikes.

## Sierra-at-Tahoe Snowsport Resort
*1111 Sierra-at-Tahoe Rd., in Twin Bridges, on Hwy. 50, 12 mi. W of South Lake Tahoe, (530) 659-7453, fax (530) 659-7453; www.sierratahoe.com. Downhill only. 3 quad, 1 triple, 5 double, 1 Magic Carpet. 25%B, 50%I, 25%A. Childcare center (18 mo.-5); children's ski school (4-12); snow play area; 5 snowboard terrain parks. Lodging nearby.*

This ski area is reputed to be particularly popular with college students and families with teenagers. Free shuttles are available from South Lake Tahoe.

## — SNOW PLAY —

## Borges Carriage and Sleigh Rides
*On Hwy. 50 next to Caesar's Tahoe casino, in Stateline, (800)726-RIDE, (775) 588-2953, fax (775) 588-7583; www.sleighride.com. Daily 10-sunset, weather permitting. $20, 2-10 $10.*

Take a ride around a meadow in an old-fashioned "one-horse open sleigh." Five hand-made sleighs are used, ranging from a cozy two-seater to a 20-passenger super model. Sleighs are pulled either by a 2,000-pound Blonde Belgian horse or by a rare American-Russian Baskhir Curly.

## Hansen's Resort
*1360 Ski Run Blvd./Needle Peak Rd., 3 blks. from Heavenly ski area, in South Lake Tahoe, (530) 544-3361, fax (530) 541-3824; www.hansensresort.com. Daily 9-5. $6/person/hr.*

Facilities include a saucer hill and a packed toboggan run with banked turns. All equipment is furnished. Lodging in secluded cabins is available.

## Husky Express dog sled tours
*In Hope Valley, 25 mi. S of South Lake Tahoe, (775) 782-3047; www.highsierra.com/sst. $90/1 hr., under 12 $45. Reservations required.*

As the sled swooshes over the scenic trails and through the trees on these enjoyable excursions, the frisky, well-tempered huskies seem to be having as much fun as their passengers. So does the "musher," who never utters the word "mush" but instead hollers "Hike!" or "Let's Go!" Two sleds are available, and each can carry two adults or a combination of kids and adults that doesn't exceed 375 pounds.

## Snow hikes

*Sierra District, P.O. Box 266, Tahoma 96142, (530) 525-7232. Dec-Mar only, depending on snow.*

Request a schedule of free ranger-led snowshoe and cross-country hikes in Lake Tahoe area state parks by sending a stamped, self-addressed, legal size envelope to the above address.

# Central Sierra

## Badger Pass

*In Yosemite National Park, off Hwy. 41 on Glacier Point Rd., 23 mi. from the valley; www.badgerpass. com. Downhill: (209) 372-1000, fax (209) 372-8673. 1 triple, 3 double, 1 surface. 35%B, 50%I, 15%A. Childcare center (3-6); snowboarders welcome; snowtubing area. Cross-country: (209) 372-8444; 21 mi. groomed trails. Lodging nearby.*

Badger Pass opened in 1935, making it California's first, and oldest, organized ski area. A prime spot for beginners and intermediates and especially popular with families, it has a natural bowl with gentle slopes that provide shelter from wind. A free shuttle bus delivers valley guests to the slopes. Ask about the bargain Midweek Ski Package. Free ranger-led snowshoe walks are also available (*$3 snowshoe maintenance fee. Must be 10 or older.*). A good place to snowshoe without a guide is in the Mariposa Grove of Giant Sequoias.

Cross-country skiing is arranged through

**Yosemite Cross-Country School**—the oldest cross-country ski school on the West Coast. Survival courses, snow camping, and overnight tours that include lodging and meals are also available.

## Bear Valley Mountain Resort

*In Bear Valley, on Hwy. 4, 45 mi. E of Angels Camp. Downhill: (209) 753-2301, fax (209) 753-6421; www.bearvalley.com. 2 triple, 7 double, 1 carpet. 30%B, 40%I, 30%A. Childcare center (2-6); children's ski school (4-8); 4 snowboard terrain parks. Lodging 3 mi. from ski area, (209) 753-BEAR; www.bear valleylodge.com.*

Intermediate or better skiers staying in this secluded resort village can ski the 3-mile Home Run trail back to the resort area at the end of the day. A bus takes skiers to and from the village lodgings and the slopes. Bear is one of the biggest ski areas in the state and generally has short lift lines. However, that Ski Bare campaign must have caught people's attention: Now there are lines where once there were none. The resort is popular with families and especially good for beginners and intermediates.

**Bear Valley Cross Country** (*(209) 753-2834, fax (209) 753-2669; www.bearvalleyxc.com; 40 mi. groomed trails. Children's lessons (4-12).*) is not affiliated with the downhill resort. It has snowshoeing and a kid's **sledding hill** for ages 3 through 12 (*Must rent sled, $8; child must be*

*The old days*

*Yosemite's first ski lift (skier's stood skis upright in center of "upski,"*
*then sat down beside them to be pulled up the hill via funicular cable)*

*accompanied by adult.).* Stays at ski-in snow-bound cabins can be arranged.

Inexpensive modern rooms, with bathrooms down the hall, are available at nearby **Base Camp Lodge** *((209) 753-6556; www.base camplodge.com.).*

## Dodge Ridge

*In Pinecrest, off Hwy. 108, 32 mi. E of Sonora, (209) 965-3474, fax (209) 965-4437; www.dodgeridge.com. Downhill only. 1 quad, 2 triple, 5 double, 1 conveyer, 2 surface. 20%B, 40%I, 40%A. Children's ski school (4-12); 5 snowboard terrain parks. Lodging nearby.*

This low-key, family-oriented ski area is known for short lift lines. It is also the ski resort nearest to the Bay Area.

## Montecito-Sequoia Winter Sports & Cross Country Ski Resort

*8000 Generals Hwy., in Giant Sequoia National Monument, betw. Kings Canyon & Sequoia National Parks, (800) 227-9900, (650) 967-8612, fax (650) 967-0540; www.mslodge.com. Cross-country only. 37 mi. groomed trails. Babysitting (4-11); children's lessons (5-11). Lodging on premises.*

Skiers here enjoy breathtaking ski tours and snowshoe walks through groves of giant sequoias. The children's program is included, and parents can rent "pulkas" to pull younger children with them. Because of its high-altitude location at 7,500 feet, this resort usually retains its snow and stays open for skiing through spring.

Lodge guests have plenty to do besides skiing. In the lodge they feast on "California fresh" cuisine and have access to snacks around the clock. There are board games, Ping-Pong, and plenty of movies for the VCR. Outside activities include snow sculpture, igloo building, and ski football. A session on the naturally frozen **Miracle Ice Rink** *((559) 565-3388. Daily. $8, children $5, includes skates.)* is also a possibility, as is a soak in the outdoor hot tub overlooking the Great Western Divide or a romp on the snowboard area or a run down the chute on the tubing and sledding hills—complete with tow. But just resting in front of the massive stone fireplaces is also an option. See also page 441.

## Wolverton Ski Area

*Sequoia National Park; www.visitsequoia.com. Giant Forest, (559) 565-3435; Grant Grove, (559) 335-2314. Cross-country only. 45 mi. marked trails. Children's lessons.*

The big attraction here is the scenic national park ski trails leading through groves of cinnamon-colored giant sequoias. Free hot drinks are provided, and moonlight and overnight tours are available. Snow play areas are located at Azalea campground and Big Stump picnic areas.

## — SNOW PLAY —

### Bear River Lake Resort
*40800 Hwy. 88, on Bear River Reservoir, in Pioneer, 3 mi. off Hwy. 88., 42 mi. E of Jackson, (209) 295-4868, fax (209) 295-4585; www.bearriverlake.com. F-Sun 7-7. Free; parking $5/vehicle. Lodging on premises.*

Visitors may use their own equipment in this groomed snow play area. Backcountry cross-country trips can be arranged.

### Long Barn Lodge Ice Rink
*In Long Barn, off Hwy. 108, 23 mi. E of Sonora, (800) 310-3533, (209) 586-3533; www.longbarn.com. $4, skates $2.*

Located behind a bar and restaurant built in 1925, this rink is covered but has two sides open to the outdoors.

### Yosemite National Park ice-skating rink
*In Curry Village, (209) 372-8319; www.yosemite park.com. $6.50, under 12 $5, skates $3.25.*

Ice skate in the shadow of Glacier Point and enjoy a spectacular view of Half Dome at the same time at this scenic outdoor rink.

# Way Down South: Mammoth Lakes

## June Mountain
*In June Lake, 4 mi. S of Hwy. 395, 58 mi. N of Bishop, (888) JUNE MTN, (760) 648-7733, fax (760) 648-7367; www.junemountain.com. Downhill only. 2 quad, 4 double, 1 surface. 35%B, 45%I, 20%A. Childcare center (newborn-6); children's ski school (3-12); snow play area; 5 snowboard terrrain parks. Lodging nearby.*

This compact, uncrowded area has an Old World-village atmosphere. It is excellent for beginners and popular with families.

## Mammoth Mountain
*1 Minaret Rd., in Mammoth Lakes, 50 mi. N of Bishop, (800) MAMMOTH, (760) 934-2571, fax (760) 934-0603; www.mammothmountain.com. Downhill only. 3 gondolas, 3 six, 9 quad, 7 triple, 5 double, 2 surface. 30%B, 40%I, 30%A. Childcare center (newborn-12); children's ski school (4-12); 3 snowboard terrain parks. Lodging on premises, (800) 367-6572, (760) 934-2581.*

One of the three largest ski areas in the country, Mammoth is located on a dormant volcano and has the highest elevation of any California ski area. It also is said to have some of the longest lift lines and one of the longest seasons—usually staying open through June and sometimes into July. A 7-hour drive from the Bay Area, it is understandably more popular with Southern Californians.

## Tamarack Lodge & Resort and Cross-Country Ski Center
*In Mammoth Lakes, on Twin Lakes, 2.5 mi. from Mammoth Lakes Village, (800) MAMMOTH, (760) 934-2442, fax (760) 934-2281; www.tamarack lodge.com. Cross-country only. 30 mi. groomed trails. Children's ski lessons (6-11). Lodging on premises.*

Lodging is a choice of either rooms in a rustic 1923 Alpine lodge or housekeeping cabins, some of which have fireplaces or wood-burning stoves.

# MISCELLANEOUS ADVENTURES

## Family Camps

Most adults remember the good old days when they were kids and got to go away to summer camp, and most adults think those days are gone for good. Well, they're not. A vacation at a family camp can bring it all back!

Family camps provide a reasonably priced, organized vacation experience. They are sponsored by city recreation departments, university alumni organizations, and private enterprise. The city and private camps are open to anyone, but some university camps require a campus affiliation.

And it isn't necessary to have children to attend. One year at one camp, a couple was actually *honeymooning*! Elderly couples whose children are grown occasionally attend alone, and family reunions sometimes are held at a camp. Whole clubs and groups of friends often book in at the same time.

Housing varies from primitive platform tents and cabins without electricity, plumbing, or bedding to comfortable campus dormitory apartments with daily maid service. Locations vary from the mountains to the sea. Predictably, costs also vary with the type of accommodations and facilities. Some camps allow stays of less than a week, but most require a weeklong commitment. Children usually are charged at a lower rate according to age.

Most family camps operate during the summer months only. Fees usually include meal preparation and clean up, special programs for children, and recreation programs for everyone. Activities can include river or pool swimming, hikes, fishing, volleyball, table tennis, badminton, hayrides, tournaments, campfires, crafts programs, songfests, tennis, and horseback riding.

Each camp has its own special appeal, but all offer an informal atmosphere where guests can really unwind. Often more than half the guests return the following year. Repeat guests and their camp friends tend to choose the same week each year.

For detailed rate information, itemization of facilities, session dates, and route directions, contact the camp reservation offices directly and request a descriptive brochure. Reserve early to avoid disappointment.

### CITY/GROUP CAMPS

**Berkeley Tuolumne Camp**
*Berkeley Camps Office, Berkeley, (510) 981-5140, fax (510) 883-6519; www.berkeleycamps.com. Located*

on the south fork of the Tuolumne River, near Yosemite National Park. Daily rates. Platform tents without electricity; provide own bedding; community bathrooms; family-style meals. Programs for toddlers-6, 6-12, & teens. Swimming in river; evening programs; breakfast hikes.

## Camp Concord

Concord Leisure Services, Concord, (925) 671-3273, fax (925) 671-3449; www.ci.concord.ca.us/recreation/camp. Located near Camp Richardson at South Lake Tahoe. Daily rates. Cabins with electricity; provide own bedding; community bathrooms; cafeteria-style meals. Special program for ages 3-6 & 7-16. Horseback riding & river rafting at additional fee.

## Camp Mather

San Francisco Rec. and Park Dept., San Francisco, (415) 831-2715, fax (415) 668-3330; http://parks.sfgov.org. Located on the rim of the Tuolumne River gorge near Yosemite National Park. Daily rates. Cabins with electricity; provide own bedding; community bathrooms; cafeteria-style meals. Playground area; program for age 6+. Pool; lake swimming; tennis courts; horseback riding (fee).

## Camp Sacramento

Dept. of Parks and Rec., Sacramento, (916) 277-6098, fax (916) 277-6180; www.cityofsacramento.org/parksandrecreation/campsac. Located in the El Dorado National Forest, 17 mi. S of Lake Tahoe. Daily & weekly rates. Cabins with electricity; provide own

bedding; community bathrooms; cafeteria-style meals. Programs for all ages.

## Co-op Camp Sierra

Berkeley, (888) 708-CAMP, (510) 595-0873; www.coopcamp.com. Located in a pine forest between Huntington & Shaver Lakes, 65 mi. NE of Fresno. Daily & weekly rates. Cabins with electricity, lodge rooms, or bring own tent; provide own bedding; community bathrooms; family-style meals. Special activities for teens; playground & crafts program for younger children. Discussion groups and workshops for adults.

## Feather River Camp

Office of Parks & Rec., Oakland, (510) 336-CAMP, fax (510) 336-0362; www.featherrivercamp.com. Located in the Plumas National Forest, N of Lake Tahoe near Quincy. Daily rates. Cabins & platform tents with electricity; provide own bedding; community bathrooms; family-style meals. Play area & activities for ages 2-5; program for age 6+. Theme weeks.

## San Jose Family Camp

Dept. of Parks, Rec. & Neighborhood Services, San Jose, (408) 277-2757; www.ci.san-jose.ca.us/prns/familycamp.htm. Located in Stanislaus National Forest, 30 mi. from Yosemite National Park. Daily rates; tent cabins without electricity (electricity avail. at additional fee); provide own bedding; community bathrooms. Cafeteria-style (B-L) & family-style (D) meals. Play area; program for age 3+. Dammed-off river pool.

## Silver Lake Camp

Dept. of Parks and Rec., Stockton, (209) 937-8293, fax (209) 937-8260; www.stocktongov.com/parks/silverlake/silverlake.htm. Located 40 mi. S of Lake Tahoe. Daily rates. Platform tents & cabins with electric lights; provide own bedding; community bathrooms; cafeteria-style meals. Program for toddlers & older children. Swimming in lake; horseback riding nearby.

### PRIVATE ENTERPRISE CAMPS

## Coffee Creek Ranch

See page 325.

## Emandal Farm

See page 249.

## Feather River Inn

See page 297.

### Montecito-Sequoia High Sierra Family Vacation Camp

*(800) 227-9900, (650) 967-8612, fax (650) 967-0540; www.mslodge.com. Located in Giant Sequoia National Monument, betw. Kings Canyon & Sequoia national parks. Weekly rates. Lodge rooms with private bathrooms; rustic cabins with community bathrooms; bedding provided. Buffet meals. Parent-child program for babies 6mo.-23mo.; programs for age 2+. Tennis courts; lake swimming; pool; hot tub; sailing; canoeing; boating; archery; fishing; riflery; mountain biking; golf cage; extra fee for water-skiing & horseback riding. See also page 436.*

---

### UNIVERSITY CAMPS

---

### Lair of the Golden Bear

*Sponsored by Calif. Alumni Assoc. at U.C. Berkeley, (888) CAL-ALUM, (510) 642-0221, fax (510) 642-6252; www.alumni.berkeley.edu/lair. Located in Stanislaus National Forest near Pinecrest. Weekly/weekend rates. Tent cabins with electricity; provide own bedding; community bathrooms; family-style meals. Organized activities for ages 2+. Heated pools; tennis courts; softball; hiking; art activities.*

This is actually three separate camps—**Camp Blue, Camp Gold,** and **Camp Oski**—that operate side by side. Each has its own staff and facilities.

---

# Houseboats

---

Living in a houseboat for a few days is an unusual way to get away from it all. It is possible to dive off the boat for a refreshing swim, fish for dinner while sunbathing, and dock in a sheltered, quiet cove for the night.

Houseboats are equipped with kitchens and flush toilets. Most rental agencies require that renters bring their own bedding, linens, and groceries, but almost everything else is provided on the floating hotel, including life jackets.

Rates vary quite dramatically depending on the time of year, the size and quality of the boat, and how many people are in the party. Summer rentals are most expensive, and a group of six to ten people gets the best rates. Weekly rates range from $895 to $4,895. Fuel is additional. Most facilities offer midweek specials and 3-day weekends; some offer a Thanksgiving

special tha... pie. During... approximat... rent their b... facilities dir...

442   MISCELLANEO... LAK... • Bridge Bay... (800) 752-9... 10300 B... fax (

---

### • Herman & ...
15135 W. Eight...
(209) 951-463...
helens.com.

### • Paradise Point Marina
*8095 Rio Blanco Rd., in Stockton, (800) 752-9669, (209) 952-1000, fax (209) 952-7974; www.seven crown.com.*

---

### LAKE OROVILLE

---

### • Bidwell Canyon Marina
*801 Bidwell Canyon Rd., in Oroville, (800) 637-1767, (530) 589-3165, fax (530) 589-4873; www.gobidwell.com.*

### • Lake Oroville Marina
*(800) 834-7517, (530) 877-2414, fax (530) 877-6552; www.foreverresorts.com.*

### • Lake Oroville State Recreation Area
*(800) 444-7275, (530) 538-2200; www.parks.ca.gov. $67-$100/night.*

Floating campsites have fully equipped kitchens, bathrooms, and sleeping space for up to 15 people.

For more information on this area contact:
**Oroville Area Chamber of Commerce**
*1789 Montgomery St., (800) 655-GOLD, (530) 538-2542, fax (530) 538-2546; www.oroville-city.com.*

...esort and **Digger Bay Marina**
...69; www.sevencrown.com. Bridge Bay:
...dge Bay Rd., in Redding, (530) 275-3021,
...30) 275-8365. Digger Bay: End of Digger Bay
...d., in Central Valley, (530) 275-3072.

- **Holiday Harbor**
20061 Shasta Caverns Rd., in O'Brien, (800) 776-
BOAT, (530) 238-2383, fax (530) 238-2102;
www.lakeshasta.com.

- **Packers Bay Marina**
16814 Packers Bay Rd., in Lakehead, (800) 331-3137,
(530) 275-5570, same fax; www.packersbay.com.

## TRINITY LAKE

- **Trinity Lake Resorts & Marinas**
See page 325.

# River Trips

The adventure of rafting down an unpredictable
river offers a real escape for the harried, city-
weary participant. But don't expect it to be
relaxing. Participants are expected to help with
setting up and breaking camp, and sometimes
they are exposed mercilessly to the elements.
While usually not dangerous when done with
experienced guides, an element of risk is
involved. Still, most participants walk away
ecstatic and addicted to the experience.

The outfitter provides shelter, food, and
equipment for the trip. Participants need only
bring sleeping gear and personal items. Costs
range from $185 to $590 per person for an
overnight run. Some day trips are available.
Seasons and rivers vary with each company.

Most outfitters offer special trips for families with young children. The minimum age
requirement for children ranges from 4 to 8.
For details, contact the tour operators directly.

- **The American River Touring Association**
In Groveland, (800) 323-ARTA, (209) 962-7873,
fax (209) 962-4819; www.arta.org.

- **ECHO: The Wilderness Company**
In Oakland, (800) 652-ECHO, (510) 652-1600,
fax (510) 652-3987; www.echotrips.com.

- **Kern River Outfitters**
In Wofford Heights (in Southern California), (800)
323-4234, (760) 376-3370, fax (760) 376-8830;
www.kernrafting.com.

This company caters to families with
campfire games and songs and other activities.

- **Mariah Wilderness Expeditions**
In Lotus, (800) 4-MARIAH, (530) 626-6049,
fax (530) 626-4305; www.mariahwe.com.

This is California's only woman-owned
and- operated white water raft and wilderness
company. Family trips are accompanied by a
professional storyteller and include both female
and male guides.

- **O.A.R.S.**
In Angels Camp, (800) 3-GO-OARS, (209) 736-4677,
fax (209) 736-2902; www.oars.com.

- **Turtle River Rafting Company**
In Mt. Shasta, (800) 726-3223, (530) 926-3223,
fax (530) 926-3443; www.turtleriver.com.

Among the special trips are personal
growth workshops and family river trips.

- **Whitewater Connection**
In Coloma, (800) 336-7238, (530) 622-6446, fax
(530) 622-7192; www.whitewaterconnection.com.

- **Whitewater Voyages**
In El Sobrante, (800) 488-RAFT, (510) 222-5994,
fax (510) 758-7238; www.whitewatervoyages.com.

If that guide looks familiar, she might be
Kelly Wiglesworth of *Survivor* TV fame, who
works as a guide for this outfitter. Several discounted Clean-Up Trips are scheduled each
year. Participants get the same amenities as on
any other trip but are expected to pick up any
debris they encounter.

For information on more California river outfitters, contact **California Outdoors** *((800) 552-3625; www.caloutdoors.org.).*

# Pack Trips

Packing equipment onto horses or mules allows for a much easier and more comfortable trek into the wilderness than does backpacking.

Campers need simply choose the type of pack trip desired. On a spot pack trip, the packers will load the animals with gear, take them to a prearranged campsite, unload the gear, and return to the pack station with the pack animals. They return to repack the gear on the day campers are scheduled to leave. Campers can either hike or ride on horses to the campsite. If riding, campers usually have a choice of keeping the horses at the campsite or of having the packers take them back out. If keeping the horses, campers should be experienced with horses and need to arrange in advance for a corral and feed. Children who haven't had at least basic riding instruction should not be included on such a trip.

A more rugged trip (where the campsite is moved each day) or an easier trip (with all expenses and a guide included) can also usually be arranged with the packer.

This is not an inexpensive vacation. Prices will vary according to which options are selected. Often there are special rates for children, who must be at least 5 years old to participate. Trips are usually available only in the summer.

One of the biggest and most organized packers is **Red's Meadow Pack Station** *(Mammoth Lakes, (800) 292-7758, (760) 934-2345, fax (760) 872-4940; http://reds-meadow. com.).* Trips include horses, saddles, and meals. Day rides can be arranged, and special family trips, horse drives, and wagon rides are scheduled.

For general information and a list of packers, contact the **Eastern High Sierra Packers Association** *(c/o Bishop Area Chamber of Commerce & Visitors Bureau, 690 N. Main St., Bishop 93514, (760) 873-8405, fax (760) 873-6999; www.bishopvisitor.com.).*

# Camping

Because there are excellent resources available on campgrounds, this book mentions only briefly those that fit into the text. For convenience, they are also included in the index under "campsites."

## Making reservations

• **State Park campgrounds**
*(800) 444-7275; www.parks.ca.gov. Reservations advised. Fee.*

Reservations can be made by phone from 2 days to 7 months in advance.

• **California National Parks**
*(800) 365-2267; http://reservations.nps.gov. Yosemite: (800) 436-7275. Fee.*

• **KOA Kampgrounds**
*www.koa.com.*

In this book, these sites are listed in each section under "Where to Stay." An inexpensive Kamping Kabin is a great option for those who don't own a tent yet long for an outdoors camping vacation. These rustic one-room cabins provide all the fun and excitement of camping out with all the security and comfort of sleeping in. Each sleeps four and is equipped with a double bed plus kid-pleasing bunk beds. A two-room cabin sleeps six. Campers need bring only sleeping bags and cooking gear. Some locations also have Kamping Kottages, complete with fully equipped kitchenette and bathroom. Tents and RVs are also welcome here. Most of the campgrounds in the KOA chain have swimming pools, and some offer additional recreational facilities. To get a free KOA Directory, stop in at any KOA Kamp-

ground, visit the website, or send $3 to: KOA Directory, P.O. Box 30558, Billings, MT 59114-0558.

## Camping references

### • *CampBook* for California-Nevada

This book and its companion maps list camping facilities and fees. They are available free to California State Automobile Association members.

### • California State Parks Camping Reservation Guide

This informative brochure provides campground details on all state parks, reserves, recreation areas, and historic parks. It is available free by calling (800) 777-0369.

# Miscellany

## American Hiking Society

*Washington, D.C., (301) 565-6704, fax (301) 565-6714; www.americanhiking.org.*

This group organizes vacations using teams of volunteers for work trips in remote backcountry areas. Their annual directory, *Helping Out in the Outdoors*, tells how to get a job as a state park or forest volunteer—hosting a campground, helping improve trails, collecting data on wildlife, or explaining an area's history to visitors. Very few of these jobs reimburse travel and food costs or provide accommodations. Opportunities are available in all 50 states; most are not suitable for children. For a copy of the directory, send $7 to: American Hiking Society, P.O. Box 20160, Washington, D.C. 20041-2160.

## Bike Trek for Life and Breath

*Oakland, (510) 638-LUNG, fax (510) 638-8984; www.californialung.org. $50.*

Sponsored by the American Lung Association of California, these bicycle trips are fully supported and are led by an experienced staff. Vans carry gear, and mechanics are available for repairs. Camping accommodations and both breakfast and dinner are provided. Though prices are reasonable, if participants raise pledges for the organization, they can go along for even less.

## Cal Adventures

*Dept. of Recreational Sports, University of California, Berkeley, (510) 642-4000, fax (510) 642-8343; www.oski.org.*

Adventure trips include backpacking, rafting, rock climbing, sailing, sculling, sea kayaking, windsurfing and more. Day classes and a special program for children in grades 3 through 12 are also available.

## California Academy of Sciences

*San Francisco, (415) 321-8000, fax (415) 321-8601; www.calacademy.org.*

These nature study trips are led by members of the academy staff and by outside instructors. Destinations include Point Reyes National Seashore, Santa Cruz Island, and other Bay Area locations.

## Coastwalk

*Sebastopol, (800) 550-6854, (707) 829-6689, fax (707) 829-0326; www.coastwalk.org. $50+/day.*

Organized summer hikes in California's coastal counties range from 3 to 9 days, with camping gear shuttled by vehicle. The goals of this non-profit organization are to nurture an awareness of the coastal environment and to promote development of a continuous California Coastal Trail.

## Green Tortoise

*San Francisco, (800) TORTOISE, (415) 956-7500, fax (415) 956-4900; www.greentortoise.com.*

Travel on this groovy, laid-back, alternative bus line is enjoyed at bargain rates. The clientele tends to be the under-30s crowd, but all ages are welcome. Trips are available to almost anywhere on this continent. There are river rafting trips to Baja and cross-country trips with stops at national parks. Usually the scenic route, which is not necessarily the most direct route, is followed. Overnight accommodations are often arranged in hostels, but sometimes riders must bring their own bedding and sleep onboard on padded platforms. The jack-of-all-trades bus drivers often organize cookouts, and they get out and fix breakdowns themselves. Passengers have also been known to get out and push when necessary. All in all, a trip on this bus line is really a *trip*.

## Hostelling International—USA (American Youth Hostels), Golden Gate Council

*San Francisco, (415) 863-1444, fax (415) 863-3865; www.norcalhostels.org.*

The idea behind hostelling is to save money, so accommodations are simple. Traditionally women bunk in one dormitory-style room, men in another, but nowadays many hostels also have separate rooms for couples and families. Guests provide their own bedding and linens (sleepsheets can be rented), and bathrooms and kitchens are shared. Guests are expected to contribute about 10 minutes to a chore, except in urban hostels. Fees are low, ranging from $11 to $20 per person per night, and children under 18 with a parent are half of that; fees for separate rooms are slightly more. Note that some hostels close during the day, usually from 10 to 4:30. Call for a free brochure detailing the hostels in Northern California. (In this book, hostels are included in the "Where to Stay" section.) For toll-free reservations using a credit card as a deposit, call (800) 909-4776. After prompting, enter the first three letters of the hostel's city. Members get a discount at most hostels and receive a newsletter and hand-book describing U.S. hostels.

## Junior Ranger Program

*At California State and National Parks, (916) 653-8959; www.parks.ca.gov.*

Designed for children ages 7 through 12, but sometimes including children who are younger or older, the Junior Ranger program operates usually just in summer. It includes nature walks and activities related to learning more about the particular park and helps kids discover the rich natural and cultural heritage of California's parks. Sessions last about an hour each day for several days, and awards are presented as the kids progress. A child can begin the program at one park and continue at a later date in another location. To join, kids promise, "I pledge to do what I can to protect and preserve the plants, animals, and history of our National Parks." Why, some Junior Rangers have even grown up and become *real* park rangers.

## Sierra Club Outings

*San Francisco, (415) 977-5522, fax (415) 977-5795; www.sierraclub.org/outings/national.*

Of the more than 370 global outdoor adventures scheduled each year, close to 20% are in California. Trips last from 4 to 8 days and typically include lodging and meals. Shorter day and overnight trips are organized by local Sierra Club chapters *(www.sierraclub.org/ outings/chapter)*.

## University Extension and research programs

Many state colleges and universities have travel/ study programs.

### • San Jose State University

*(408) 924-2670, fax (408) 924-2616; http://galaxy. sjsu.edu.*

On-location natural history programs are offered through the Extension Division. Special programs that include children 6 through 16 are scheduled in summer.

### • University of California

*(530) 752-8811, fax (530) 752-8596; www.extension. ucdavis.edu/urep.*

The University Research Expeditions Program trips are not suitable for children under 16.

# INDEXES

## Annual Events Index

# Alphabetical Index

# MORE GREAT BOOKS FROM CAROUSEL PRESS

## MILES OF SMILES:
## 101 Great Car Games & Activities

Anyone who has ever been trapped in a hot car with bored kids is well aware that the world needs a sure-fire way of easing the resulting tensions. This clever book fills that need. In fact, according to one enthusiastic user it just "may be the ultimate solution for back seat squabbling." The book is filled with games and activities that have travel-related themes. Ninety-seven require just your minds and mouths to play, and the other four need only simple props: a penny, a pencil, and some crayons. A helpful index categorizes each game and activity according to age appropriateness, and humorous illustrations that kids can color add to everyone's enjoyment. *128 pages. $8.95.*

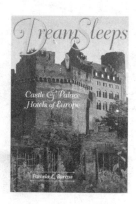

## DREAM SLEEPS:
## Castle & Palace Hotels Of Europe

Designed to make fairy tales come true, this book details the exciting castles and palaces in Europe that are open to the public for lodging and dining. Using the positioning maps included for each country, readers can easily determine which hotels potentially fit their itinerary. All information needed to make an informed decision (driving instructions, rates, food services, family amenities, on-site recreation, nearby diversions) is included along with the basic phone and fax numbers and U.S. booking representatives. The author, who has personally visited each hotel, includes a fascinating history for each and an enticing description of the present day facilities.
*304 pages. $17.95.*

## TO ORDER DIRECT CALL
Carousel Press at (510) 527-5849

## WEEKEND ADVENTURES UPDATE: The E-Letter

Updates to this 8th edition of *Weekend Adventures in San Francisco & Northern California,* as well as some completely new adventures, are periodically posted at our website. To be notified of new postings, sign up for the free *"Weekend Adventures E-Letter Update"* at our website: **www.carousel-press.com.**